BOOKMARK

Living Liturgy™

Using this book for small group sharing

Groups using *Living Liturgy*™ for prayer and faith-sharing might begin with the following general format and then adjust it to fit different needs.

OPENING PRAYER
- Begin with a hymn
- Pray the opening prayer for the Sunday or solemnity

GOD'S WORD
- Proclaim the gospel
- Observe a brief period of silence

INDIVIDUAL STUDY, REFLECTION, PRAYER
- Read and consider one or more of the following: "Reflecting on the Gospel," "Living the Paschal Mystery," and/or "Understanding Scripture"
- Spend some time in reflection and prayer

FAITH-SHARING
- Use the "Assembly & Faith-sharing Groups" spirituality statements (and the specific liturgical ministry statements if they apply)
- Consider what ways the gospel is challenging you to *live* the liturgy you will celebrate on Sunday

CONCLUDING PRAYER
- Pray the "Model General Intercessions"
- Pray the Our Father at the end of the intercessions
- Conclude with a hymn

Using this book for personal prayer

The best preparation for Sunday celebration of Eucharist is prayer. Here are two suggested approaches for an individual to use this book for personal prayer.

• Daily Prayer

MONDAY
- Read the gospel prayerfully

TUESDAY
- Read and study "Understanding Scripture"
- Reflect on the statements from "Assembly and Faith-sharing Groups" and let your reflection lead you to prayer

WEDNESDAY
- Read again the gospel
- Read "Reflecting on the Gospel" and let it lead you to prayer

THURSDAY
- Read and study "Living the Paschal Mystery"
- Pray the "Model General Intercessions"

FRIDAY
- Pray the responsorial psalm
- Read "Appreciating the Responsorial Psalm"

SATURDAY
- Read the gospel and first reading
- Read and study "Focusing the Gospel"
- Reflect on how you have been able to live this gospel during the week

SUNDAY
- Enter fully into the celebration of Eucharist
- Enjoy a day of rest

• Prayer as Time and Opportunity Permit

A daily routine of study and prayer is not always possible. As time and opportunity permit:
- Read the gospel prayerfully
- Reflect on "Living the Paschal Mystery"
- Pray the "Model General Intercessions"

Living Liturgy™

Living Liturgy™

Spirituality, Celebration, and Catechesis for Sundays and Solemnities

Year C • 2007

Joyce Ann Zimmerman, C.PP.S.
Thomas A. Greisen
Kathleen Harmon, S.N.D. de N.
Thomas L. Leclerc, M.S.

LITURGICAL PRESS
Collegeville, Minnesota

www.litpress.org

Design by Ann Blattner. Art by Julie Lonneman.

Excerpts from the *Lectionary for Mass for use in the Dioceses of the United States* Copyright © 2001, 1998, 1997 and 1970 Confraternity of Christian Doctrine, Inc., Washington, D.C. Used with permission. All rights reserved. No portion of this text may be reproduced without permission in writing from the copyright holder.

The English translation of the Psalm Responses and the Introduction to the Lectionary for Mass from the *Lectionary for Mass* © 1969, 1981, 1997, International Committee on English in the Liturgy, Inc. (ICEL); the Alternative Opening Prayers and the English translation of the Opening Prayers from *The Roman Missal* © 1973, ICEL; excerpts from the English translation of *Book of Blessings* © 1987, ICEL; excerpts from the English translation of the *General Instruction of the Roman Missal* © 2002, ICEL. All rights reserved.

The poetic English translations of the sequences of the Roman Missal are taken from the *Roman Missal* approved by the National Conference of Catholic Bishops of the United States © 1964 by the National Catholic Welfare Conference, Inc. All rights reserved.

© 2006 by Order of Saint Benedict, Collegeville, Minnesota. All rights reserved. No part of this book may be reproduced in any form, by print, microfilm, microfiche, mechanical recording, photocopying, translation, or by any other means, known or yet unknown, for any purpose except brief quotations in reviews, without the previous written permission of Liturgical Press, Saint John's Abbey, P.O. Box 7500, Collegeville, Minnesota 56321-7500. Printed in the United States of America.

ISSN 1547-089X

ISBN 13: 978-0-8146-2744-0
ISBN 10: 0-8146-2744-7

CONTENTS

CONTRIBUTORS

Joyce Ann Zimmerman, C.PP.S. is the director of the Institute for Liturgical Ministry in Dayton, Ohio, and is the founding editor and columnist for *Liturgical Ministry*. She is also an adjunct professor of liturgy, liturgical consultant, and frequent facilitator of workshops on liturgy. She has published numerous scholarly and pastoral liturgical works. She holds civil and pontifical doctorates of theology.

Thomas A. Greisen is a priest of the Archdiocese of Omaha, Nebraska, who is presently the director of the Lay Ministry Formation Office for the Archdiocese of Omaha and a spiritual director. He has been the director of spiritual formation for college seminarians and a professor of spirituality. He holds graduate degrees in both theology and spirituality.

Kathleen Harmon, S.N.D. de N. is the music director for programs of the Institute for Liturgical Ministry in Dayton, Ohio, and is the author of the *Music Notes* column for *Liturgical Ministry*. An educator and musician, she facilitates liturgical music workshops and cantor formation programs, teaches private voice lessons, and has been a parish liturgical music director. She holds a graduate degree in music and a doctorate in liturgy.

Thomas L. Leclerc, M.S. is a priest of the Missionaries of La Salette (North American Province) who teaches at Emmanuel College in Boston. He has been director of theology for his congregation, an associate pastor in parishes in Georgia and Connecticut, and has been involved with adult education in the Archdioceses of Atlanta and Boston. He holds a doctorate of theology in Hebrew Bible/Old Testament.

✚ USING THIS RESOURCE

An article was featured for appraisal on the TV show *Antiques Roadshow*. It was very old, and consisted of nothing but a round rock which was flat on two sides—looking something like a donut. The hole couldn't have been more than about five inches in diameter. The appraiser explained that it was a game; the players would take turns throwing stones at the hole. That was all there was to the game. This didn't sound very interesting until the appraiser went on to say that if the player missed, he was killed right there on the spot. The appraiser facetiously said, "This gives new meaning to 'three strikes and you are out.'"

LITURGY HAS MUCH AT STAKE!

Liturgy has much more at stake than even that ancient game of stone-throwing! At stake is not only our natural life, but our eternal life. It is wonderful, though, that liturgy gives us more than one or three chances to win our life; in fact, we celebrate at least weekly. But perhaps because we do this regularly, liturgy can easily become just one more thing on our schedule, something rote which we hardly think about. *Living Liturgy*™ is an antidote for routine. It is intended to be a liturgy preparation guide which takes us to the heart of the matter: the paschal mystery. By careful preparation, our lives and attention are more easily focused on this very significant "game" of eternal Life: our weekly celebration of the Lord's resurrection. At liturgy we have an opportunity to appraise our own Christian living and grow in it! We gain life, not lose it!

LITURGICAL SPIRITUALITY: PASCHAL MYSTERY LIVING

Living Liturgy™: *Spirituality, Celebration, and Catechesis for Sundays and Solemnities* is, therefore, designed to help people prepare for liturgy and live a liturgical spirituality (that is, a way of living that is rooted in liturgy) which opens their vision to their baptismal identity as the Body of Christ and shapes their living according to the rhythm of paschal mystery dying and rising. The paschal mystery is the entire saving mystery of Jesus Christ—that is, his life, mission, passion, death, resurrection, ascension, sending of the Spirit, and promised second coming—and *our* participation in this mystery. Liturgy both *enacts* in the here and now Christ's mystery as well as sends each one of us forth to *live* this mystery.

WHAT'S NEW IN THIS VOLUME

This volume is entirely new in content, with but two changes to its overall plan: we have simplified the layout and added a leading quotation for Christmas and the Triduum; in this way these two major festivals have the same architecture in this book, helping us catch that they are two sides of the one event of salvation which we celebrate during the entire liturgical year. We have again included with this volume a separate, more lengthy article at the beginning of the book to offer readers a more substantial introduction to Luke's gospel and its use in the Lectionary. As with the last several volumes, we've also included a pronunciation guide to aid lectors in proclaiming the Scriptures with greater ease. We have also continued to include liturgical and biblical indices.

Clearly, anyone involved directly with liturgical planning and preparation would benefit from using this resource, including **clergy, pastoral ministers, liturgy directors, musicians,** and **liturgy committee members**. *Living Liturgy*™ also assists those who serve the community in the **visible liturgical ministries** (presiders, deacons, music ministers, hospitality ministers, altar ministers, lectors, Eucharistic ministers) because it clearly shows that each ministry deserves not only practical preparation but (even more importantly) spiritual preparation, suggestions for which are a key component of *Living Liturgy*™. Further, **catechumens, candidates,** and **sponsors** could use *Living Liturgy*™ to support and deepen their liturgical journey within the R.C.I.A. and **members of faith-sharing groups** could use this resource as the focus of weekly prayer and reflection together. **Parents** and **teachers** could improve their ministry by simplifying its content and sharing it with younger members of the liturgical community.

A threefold dynamic of daily living, prayer, and study determines the basic structure of *Living Liturgy*™. The content under the heading "Spirituality" helps us grasp that our living the paschal mystery is shaped by focusing the word which leads to prayerful reflection on the gospel. The content under "Celebration" suggests models for introductory rites and general intercessions which are derived from the readings and/or liturgical season; also on this page is content which enables the assembly to understand better the responsorial psalm and its relationship to the readings. The content under "Catechesis" (omitted in the shorter, two-page format for solemnities and other days) leads to a better grasp of elements of liturgy and liturgical music. Rather than a systematic approach to liturgical catechesis, these catechetical points flow from aspects of the readings or the liturgical season and are not intended to be comprehensive; in time, however, much is covered!

Certain unique features mark this resource. First, *Living Liturgy*™ clearly identifies the paschal mystery as the core of liturgy and our everyday living. Second, *Living Liturgy*™ takes the gospel as the starting point of liturgical preparation, for there we learn about Jesus' identity and mission and are challenged to take these up as our own. Third, *Living Liturgy*™ integrates spirituality, celebration, and catechesis. Fourth, it was written by a pastorally-experienced team with expertise in each area. Fifth, *Living Liturgy*™ includes solemnities (and a few other important days), since these festivals are so intimately connected to our annual unfolding of the paschal mystery; for those unable to participate in Mass on these days, the material here can still be used for personal prayer and reflection. Sixth, *Living Liturgy*™ has a simple and consistent format with short and to-the-point sections which aid using only snatches at a time for reflection. And finally, seventh, *Living Liturgy*™ suggests methods (printed on a handy bookmark card) for how both individuals and groups might use this resource.

During this year when we draw so heavily on Luke's Gospel, we are challenged to walk with Jesus toward Jerusalem, embracing daily dying so that we might continually rise to new life in him. Liturgy strengthens us and nourishes us for our journey.

INTRODUCTION to the Lectionary's Proclamation of the Gospel according to Luke

This liturgical year our Scriptural guide to living the paschal mystery is Saint Luke. From the First Sunday of Advent to the Last Sunday of the year (the solemnity of Our Lord Jesus Christ the King), the universal Church will walk in the company of Saint Luke whose lively narratives, vivid characters, and poignant scenes unfold the mission, message, and meaning of Jesus, the Savior.

Yet our journey with Luke is not a mini-course in Luke's Gospel, that is, the liturgy is not a classroom in which we will study the theology and themes of this year's Gospel. To approach the Gospel in this way would be a serious misunderstanding of liturgy. The liturgy is not a forum in which to present the Gospel; instead, the Gospel is placed at the service of the liturgy where we encounter the living Lord Jesus and, through word, ritual, and sacrament, enter more deeply into the pattern of his dying and rising. This introduction will describe, first, some of the characteristics of the Gospel so that our proclamation of individual passages will benefit from the context of Luke's work and, second, how the Lectionary (the assigned readings) makes use of the Gospel according to Luke, drawing the worshiping community into deeper union with Jesus.

Luke and his Gospel. Luke was an extraordinary writer whose monumental two-volume work (the Gospel and the Acts of the Apostles) fills almost one-quarter of the New Testament. It seems likely that Luke was a Gentile (perhaps a convert to Judaism) who wrote in the mid-eighties. It is possible, though not certain, that he was a companion of St. Paul (see Phlm 24; Col 4:14). Luke himself acknowledges that he is not an eyewitness to the ministry of Jesus but he assures readers that he has spoken to eyewitnesses and has carefully examined other written accounts of Jesus' life (Luke 1:1-4).

While we may not know a lot about Luke, most people know a good deal about his Gospel. Some of the most cherished stories about Jesus are reported by Luke: the annunciation to Mary, the birth in a manger, the disciples on the road to Emmaus. Some of the New Testament's most memorable characters are found in Luke: the diminutive but resourceful Zacchaeus, the aged and as-

tonished Elizabeth and Zechariah, the hospitable Martha and the attentive Mary. Some of Jesus' most beloved parables—brimming with poignancy and compassion, and universal in their broad religious and humanitarian appeal—are jewels of Luke's Gospel: the Good Samaritan, the Prodigal Son, the rich man and poor Lazarus, the Pharisee and the tax collector. The backbone of the Church's daily prayer comes from Luke's Gospel: Zechariah's canticle at morning prayer, Mary's *Magnificat* at evening prayer, and Simeon's canticle at night prayer.

His Gospel is such a treasure trove of themes that it has invited numerous nicknames, such as "The Gospel of Joy," "The Gospel of the Holy Spirit . . . of Prayer . . . of the Poor," among others. Other obvious themes include warnings against wealth; frequent meals with sinners; the inclusion of women; and concern for tax collectors, lepers, and outcasts. Luke's portrait of Jesus is perhaps the most beloved and easily approachable of all the Gospels: Luke's Jesus is the embodiment of divine compassion. Indeed, Luke's portrayal of Jesus is at the heart of his proclamation of the Good News.

Luke advances his understanding of Jesus in two noteworthy ways. One way is in the titles he uses of Jesus. While Luke follows other Gospel writers in calling Jesus "Son of God," "Son of Man," and "Messiah," Luke is distinctive among the Synoptic Gospels in calling Jesus the "Savior" (2:11). Jesus' work as Savior is anticipated in many healing stories in which one is "saved" (7:50/Sunday 11C; 8:36, 48, 50; 17:19/Sunday 28C; 18:42). Discussion about Jesus as Savior appropriately dominates the crucifixion (23:35, 37, 39). Another favorite title Luke uses of Jesus is "Lord." In the New Testament "Lord" is typically a post-Easter title; its occurrence throughout the Gospel, especially its use by the narrator, serves to present the entire Gospel as an Easter proclamation of faith in Jesus.

A second distinctive feature of Luke's portrayal of Jesus is his presentation of Jesus as compassionate and merciful. Early in the Gospel the Canticle of Mary (the *Magnificat*) indicates that God is acting now because "he has remembered his promise of mercy . . .

to Abraham and his descendants for ever" (1:54-55). As the Canticle of Zechariah makes clear, the "tender mercy" of God "promised through the holy prophets of old" and sworn "to our father Abraham" is a promise of "redemption" and a "horn of salvation" (1:68-79). For Luke "mercy" means "salvation." Jesus, born "within the house of David," is the fulfillment of that ancient promise.

This theme of divine mercy/compassion is evident throughout the Gospel, from beginning to end. At the outset angels announce to shepherds the Savior's birth; at the close of the Gospel Jesus assures the thief who was crucified with him, "today you will be with me in Paradise" (23:43). In between these enactments of salvation, Jesus uses the image of a father welcoming the return of the Prodigal Son to describe the compassion of God (15:11-32/ Sunday 24C and Lent 4C); in the parable of the Good Samaritan (10:25-37/Sunday 15C), Jesus urges his disciples to extend to others a similar compassion and mercy. The astounding and confounding compassion of God is announced programmatically by Mary who declares that God "has thrown down the rulers from their thrones but lifted up the lowly; the hungry he has filled with good things; the rich he has sent away empty" (Luke 1:52-53). The ministry of Jesus is the realization of this compassion for the lowly and the poor, the outcast and the sinner.

Jesus' ability to embody such a tender divine compassion is rooted in his profound prayer, an aspect of Jesus' personal life which Luke develops more completely than any another evangelist. Not surprisingly, then, this prayerful Jesus devotes particular attention to instructing his disciples in prayer (the friend at night, 11:5-8/Sunday 17C; the persistent widow, 18:1-8/Sunday 29C; the Pharisee and the tax collector, 18:9-14/Sunday 30C). The inner strength which comes from prayer is showcased in the Passion narrative which describes Jesus at prayer no fewer than six times. Luke further shows Jesus ending his life by praying from the cross that his executioners be forgiven—the consummate extension of mercy. Finally, Jesus serenely commends his life into God's hands. Jesus' ministry of mercy and compassion, grounded in his prayer, is the basis of the "good news" that God, in Christ, is fulfilling the ancient promise of mercy to Jews and Gentiles alike.

Luke in the Lectionary. The primary purpose of the Lectionary is to draw people into the liturgical experience of the paschal mystery celebrated in both word and sacrament. Our focus in these brief comments is on the word. As indicated above, Mary's *Magnificat* and the Canticle of Zechariah set out some of the major themes Luke develops throughout his Gospel: the Canticle of Zechariah highlights the themes of mercy and salvation so central to the Gospel, while the *Magnificat* announces the pattern of reversal which illuminates both Jesus' teaching and

ministry to outcasts. As central as these are to the themes and theology of Luke, neither is included in the Sunday readings. Instead, the Lectionary develops these aspects in the ministry of Jesus as aspects of the paschal mystery to be lived, rather than as literary themes to be understood and appreciated.

Another example of the Lectionary's distinctive approach is found in the infancy stories. Luke presents the annunciation and birth of Jesus alongside the annunciation and birth of John the Baptist: the two annunciations and two births are presented back to back, John's stories first, then those of Jesus. Luke goes to great lengths to show how extraordinary John is and then he shows how Jesus is even greater. This is key to Luke's understanding of Jesus in the history of salvation. Yet the Sunday Lectionary includes none of the stories about John, for the paschal mystery is embodied in Jesus, not in his esteemed forerunner. In Jesus the compassion and mercy of God find their fullest expression.

Though the Lectionary's selection of readings is chosen to unfold the paschal mystery, it does not disregard all the special features of Luke. On the one hand, it is selective in developing some of his favorite themes (mercy, compassion, salvation, prayer) but not others (the Passion predictions, the centrality of the Temple). It is careful to include all fourteen parables that only Luke recounts, as well as events unique to Luke, for example, the stories of Martha and Mary (Sunday 16C), Zacchaeus (Sunday 31C), and the disciples on the road to Emmaus (Easter Sunday). With only one exception, the Lectionary for year C does not repeat any parable which is proclaimed in year A (Matthew) or year B (Mark); and with so many parables found only in Luke, the Lectionary only once gives Luke's version of a parable which is also found in one of the other Gospels. All of this is to point out that the Lectionary is conscious of the three-year cycle of gospels, carefully avoiding undue repetition and taking advantage of the distinctive material in each of the three Synoptic Gospels. Because of the three-year architecture of the Lectionary, repeated events or stories can be omitted even if they are central to an individual Gospel's structure or theme. On the other hand, by repeating certain stories in each of the three years (e.g., Peter's profession of faith: Sundays 21A, 24B, 12C; the feeding of the five-thousand: Sundays 18A, 17B, Body and Blood of Christ, C), the Lectionary draws attention to those passages which are of particular significance to the Church. Which brings us back to an important point: the Gospel serves the liturgy, and the liturgy does not serve the Gospel. What is paramount is the paschal mystery. Though there may be a variety of ways to approach it, there is only one paschal mystery. The Gospel according to Luke is this year's guide to our entering more deeply into the dying and rising of Jesus.

ABBREVIATIONS

LITURGICAL RESOURCES

BofB   *Book of Blessings*. International Commission on English in the Liturgy. Collegeville: Liturgical Press, 1989.

BLS   *Built of Living Stones: Art, Architecture, and Worship.* Guidelines of the National Conference of Catholic Bishops, 2000.

GIRM   *General Instruction of the Roman Missal* (2002).

GNLYC   General Norms for the Liturgical Year and the Calendar

ILM   Introduction to the Lectionary for Mass

L   *Lectionary*

NT   New Testament

OT   Old Testament

SC   *Sacrosanctum Concilium*. The Constitution on the Sacred Liturgy. Vatican II.

MUSICAL RESOURCES

BB   *Breaking Bread*. Portland, OR: Oregon Catholic Press, annual.

CBW3   *Catholic Book of Worship III*. Ottawa, Ontario: Canadian Conference of Catholic Bishops, 1994.

CH   *The Collegeville Hymnal*. Collegeville: Liturgical Press, 1990.

G2   *Gather*. 2nd edition. Chicago: GIA Publications, Inc., 1994.

GC   *Gather Comprehensive*. Chicago: GIA Publications, Inc., 1994.

GC2   *Gather Comprehensive*. 2nd edition. Chicago: GIA Publications, Inc., 2004.

HG   *Hymns for the Gospels*. Chicago: GIA Publications, Inc., 2001.

JS2   *Journeysongs*. 2nd edition. Portland, OR: Oregon Catholic Press, 2003.

LMGM   *Lead Me, Guide Me*. Chicago: GIA Publications, Inc., 1987.

PMB   *People's Mass Book*. Schiller Park, IL: World Library Publications, 2003.

RS   *Ritual Song*. Chicago: GIA Publications, Inc., 1996.

SS   *Sacred Song*. Collegeville: Liturgical Press, annual.

W3   *Worship*. 3rd edition. Chicago: GIA Publications, Inc., 1986.

WC   *We Celebrate*. Schiller Park, IL: World Library Publications, 2004.

WS   *Word and Song*. Schiller Park, IL: World Library Publications, 2005.

GIA   GIA Publications, Inc.

OCP   Oregon Catholic Press

WLP   World Library Publications

Season of Advent

SPIRITUALITY

Gospel

Luke 21:25-28, 34-36; L3C

Jesus said to his disciples:
"There will be signs in the sun, the
   moon, and the stars,
   and on earth nations will be in
      dismay,
   perplexed by the roaring of the sea
      and the waves.
People will die of fright
   in anticipation of what is coming
      upon the world,
   for the powers of the heavens will
      be shaken.
And then they will see the Son of Man
   coming in a cloud with power and
      great glory.
But when these signs begin to happen,
   stand erect and raise your heads
   because your redemption is at hand.

"Beware that your hearts do not
   become drowsy
   from carousing and drunkenness
   and the anxieties of daily life,
   and that day catch you by surprise
      like a trap.
For that day will assault everyone
   who lives on the face of the earth.
Be vigilant at all times
   and pray that you have the strength
   to escape the tribulations that are
      imminent
   and to stand before the Son of Man."

Reflecting on the Gospel

Sometimes we humans have great difficulty being faithful in our commitments to each other and to God. Broken contracts are but one example of failed fidelity to another; sin is the product of failed fidelity to God. Both the first reading and gospel of this Sunday present us with a contrast between lives lived in faithful commitment to God's covenant and lives which have strayed from that covenant.

In the first reading the prophet Jeremiah is preaching to a people in exile. Israel's infidelity and injustice have brought them to a day of captivity and ensuing longing for their homeland. Jeremiah assures Israel of God's utter fidelity (in spite of Israel's infidelity) and a day of security and justice. For us, Jeremiah's future is already fulfilled in Christ. We get a glimpse of redemption which fortifies us for right living.

The gospel presents a similar contrast, but in the context of a choice to be made. If the followers of Christ allow themselves to get caught up in "carousing and drunkenness and the anxieties of daily life" (gospel), they will become "drowsy" and complacent with Christ's coming and be caught "by surprise like a trap." On the other hand, if the followers of Christ are vigilant and have lives "blameless in holiness," then when Christ comes they can "stand erect" without fear but with joyful anticipation of their redemption.

Fidelity breeds confidence ("stand erect and raise your heads") and hope ("your redemption is at hand"); straying breeds "dismay" and "anxieties." God is faithful: the promise made through Jeremiah is fulfilled in Jesus, the "just shoot" from the stump of David. Jesus, the embodiment of God's fidelity, also makes a promise: he will return in glory with redemption. Such divine fidelity calls us to similar fidelity: we are to "conduct [our]selves to please God" (second reading). We can be faithful because God is faithful.

Living the Paschal Mystery

We tend to think that *if* we are faithful, *then* God will be faithful to us. In fact, the opposite is true: *because* God is faithful, we *can* be faithful. God is the One who is just and always faithful. "Justice" here means "righteousness," that is, being in right relationship. We are in right relationship with God and each other when we align ourselves (by right living) with the "Son of Man" (Christ). Faithful living, then, presupposes right relationship with God expressed by patterning our life after that of the divine Son.

The way we live our faithfulness *now* is shaped by this particular time of the liturgical year, Advent. During Advent we Christians wait for more than a *day* (Christmas); we await a *Person*—Jesus Christ who now reigns in glory. The paradox here is that we await the One who has already come! This paradox is played out in our everyday living as irreconcilable opposites: sometimes we live like Christ did and make his presence felt in our world; at other times we live as though our hearts have become drowsy and give in to the temptations to commit selfish acts. Then Christ seems far away and our relationship with God and each other is weakened.

Christ's coming becomes a time of judgment of our relationship with him and, thus, of our fidelity. The way we live now makes all the difference in the world.

Focusing the Gospel

Key words and phrases: There will be, Son of Man coming in . . . great glory, your redemption, Beware, have the strength

To the point: God is faithful: the promise made through Jeremiah is fulfilled in Jesus, the "just shoot" from the stump of David. Jesus, the embodiment of God's fidelity, also makes a promise: he will return in glory with redemption. Such divine fidelity calls us to similar fidelity: we are to "conduct [our]selves to please God" (second reading). We can be faithful because God is faithful.

Connecting the Gospel

to the first reading: The first reading is from a part of the Book of Jeremiah known as "The Book of Consolation." Jeremiah has witnessed the destruction of Jerusalem and consoles his people with the promise of redemption—they "shall be safe" and "shall dwell secure."

to religious experience: We tend to think that *if* we are faithful, *then* God will be faithful to us. In fact, the opposite is true: *because* God is faithful, we *can* be faithful.

Understanding Scripture

God's fidelity: The first reading is taken from Jeremiah's "Book of Consolation" (chs. 30–33). The city of Jerusalem with its magnificent Temple had been destroyed and the survivors carried to exile in Babylonia. In a grim way, this sad catastrophe was an instance of God's fidelity. In the covenant God had established with Israel, God had promised blessing to the people if they remained faithful and warned of punishment if they sinned. Sin they did—and greatly so. God, true to the promises made, sent punishment upon them. Oddly, this devastating punishment now affords hope. After all, if God were true to the promise of punishment, God would also be true to the promise of blessing if the people turned to God and remained faithful to God's covenant.

This is the confidence which underlies the reading from Jeremiah: "I will fulfill the promise I made to the house of Israel and Judah." God had promised that the House of David would have an everlasting kingship. Now, at its darkest hour when the heir to David's throne was in Babylonian captivity and all hope seemed dim, Jeremiah reminds the people of God's promise and assures them, "I will raise up for David a just shoot"; the result will be that Judah and Jerusalem would dwell in safety and security. Hope is found in God's fidelity in fulfilling promises.

The gospel continues this theme in two significant ways. First, as the Introduction to the Lectionary for Mass instructs us (see no. 93), all prophetic readings for Advent are prophecies of Christ. In this sense, the promise of eternal kingship made to the House of David is fulfilled in Christ, the eternal Son of God. Thus it is that the gospel foresees "the Son of man coming in a cloud with power and great glory." The second way in which the gospel continues the theme of fidelity is this: Jesus, too, makes a promise, namely, that he will return. Just as the restoration of the House of David will mean security, the return of the Son of Man will mean redemption.

**ASSEMBLY &
FAITH-SHARING GROUPS**

- My response to how these readings connect Advent preparations to growing in fidelity to God and others is . . .
- God has demonstrated being faithful by . . .
- God's fidelity empowers me to be faithful to my commitments in that. . . .

PRESIDERS
Some examples of people being faithful to their commitments which have inspired my ministry are . . .

DEACONS
God's promise of righteousness is being fulfilled through my ministry in that . . .

HOSPITALITY MINISTERS
Attentiveness to the *whoms* over the *whats* of hospitality models to the assembly the focus of this season in that . . .

MUSIC MINISTERS
Jesus calls me to remain faithful to him until the day of his final coming. One way participating in music ministry helps me remain faithful is . . .

ALTAR MINISTERS
Genuine service of others requires me to grow in fidelity both to God and to others in that . . .

LECTORS
My preparations with the word keep me vigilant to Christ's coming in that . . . My proclamation shares this by . . .

**EXTRAORDINARY MINISTERS
OF HOLY COMMUNION**
My visits with the elderly and infirmed embody God's faithfulness to his promises made to his people in that . . .

3

Model Act of Penitence

Presider: As we begin this season of Advent, Christ, who promised to return in glory, is present as we gather in his name. Standing in his holy presence, let us ask for his mercy . . . [pause]

> Lord Jesus, you will come in great glory: Lord . . .
> Christ Jesus, you will come to bring redemption: Christ . . .
> Lord Jesus, you strengthen us on our journey toward everlasting life: Lord . . .

Appreciating the Responsorial Psalm

The words of Psalm 25 remind us that God is constant, steadfast, and merciful. Psalm 25 voices our prayer on this the first day of a new liturgical year. As we set our sights on the final coming of Christ, we know how easy it is for us to abandon vigilance and wander from the path of righteousness (gospel). And so we ask God to point our lives in the right direction. We ask God to teach us to do what is "right and just" (first reading), conducting ourselves as Christ has instructed (second reading). We ask God to keep us faithful when catastrophes come, or when "anxieties of daily life" overwhelm us, or when our own human weakness tempts us to abandon fidelity (gospel). We raise our prayer to the One whose eternal faithfulness will keep us faithful.

Model General Intercessions

Presider: Christ will come "with power and great glory." Let us pray for what we need to be ready for that day.

Response:

Lord, hear our prayer.

Cantor:

we pray to the Lord,

That the Church may be faithful at all times and assist others to stand confidently before God . . . [pause]

That the people of the world may always conduct themselves so as to please God . . . [pause]

That those who experience anxiety over the things of daily life may find comfort in the God who is always faithful . . . [pause]

That we here gathered may be vigilant and ready when Christ comes . . . [pause]

Presider: All-powerful God, your Son will come with great glory and power to gather us into your loving embrace: hear these our prayers that we may be ready for his coming. We ask this through that same Christ our Lord. **Amen.**

OPENING PRAYER

Let us pray

Pause for silent prayer

All-powerful God,
increase our strength of will for doing
    good
that Christ may find an eager welcome at
    his coming
and call us to his side in the kingdom of
    heaven,
where he lives and reigns with you and the
    Holy Spirit,
one God, for ever and ever. **Amen.**

FIRST READING
Jer 33:14-16

The days are coming, says the LORD,
    when I will fulfill the promise
    I made to the house of Israel and Judah.
In those days, in that time,
    I will raise up for David a just shoot;
    he shall do what is right and just in the
      land.
In those days Judah shall be safe
    and Jerusalem shall dwell secure;
    this is what they shall call her:
    "The LORD our justice."

CATECHESIS

RESPONSORIAL PSALM
Ps 25:4-5, 8-9, 10, 14

R⁷. (1b) To you, O Lord, I lift my soul.

Your ways, O LORD, make known to me;
    teach me your paths,
guide me in your truth and teach me,
    for you are God my savior,
    and for you I wait all the day.

R⁷. To you, O Lord, I lift my soul.

Good and upright is the LORD;
    thus he shows sinners the way.
He guides the humble to justice,
    and teaches the humble his way.

R⁷. To you, O Lord, I lift my soul.

All the paths of the LORD are kindness and
        constancy
    toward those who keep his covenant
        and his decrees.
The friendship of the LORD is with those
        who fear him,
    and his covenant, for their instruction.

R⁷. To you, O Lord, I lift my soul.

SECOND READING
1 Thess 3:12–4:2

Brothers and sisters:
May the Lord make you increase and
        abound in love
    for one another and for all,
    just as we have for you,
    so as to strengthen your hearts,
    to be blameless in holiness before our
        God and Father
    at the coming of our Lord Jesus with all
        his holy ones. Amen.

Finally, brothers and sisters,
    we earnestly ask and exhort you in the
        Lord Jesus that,
    as you received from us
    how you should conduct yourselves to
        please God
    —and as you are conducting
        yourselves—
    you do so even more.
For you know what instructions we gave
        you through the Lord Jesus.

About Liturgy

Advent waiting and fidelity: Most Catholics understand Advent as a time of waiting and anticipation. However, we await not just the celebration of Christmas, that festival commemorating Christ's coming into the world incarnated in the flesh of an infant, but also the celebration of Christ's Second Coming at the end of the world. We begin Advent with looking forward to Christ's Second Coming.

Accompanying Christ's Second Coming will be the general judgment and resurrection. It is in this context that we especially connect waiting and fidelity. As we await the Second Coming, we know that we will face this cosmic event either with calmness and joyful anticipation begotten by lives lived in fidelity to the gospel or we will face this cosmic event with dread because we know we have been unfaithful to our relationship with God. Thus Advent calls us to fidelity—lives patterned after Christ—so that we will be ready for the end times.

Each liturgy we celebrate helps strengthen our relationship with God and each other. In a real way, then, each liturgy prepares us for Christ's Second Coming and helps us overcome any fear of the judgment which will accompany Christ's coming. This is one sense of how we call all liturgy "eschatological," that is, having to do with the end times.

About Liturgical Music

Cantor preparation: In this psalm you ask God to teach you a way which is far more than a set of rules. You ask to be formed in "ways" of goodness, uprightness, constancy, and fidelity. In other words, you ask that your behavior become like God's. How might this prayer deepen your humility? How might it shape your living of Advent?

Appropriate music for Advent: An important principle guiding the type of music to be sung during the season of Advent is found in GIRM no. 313: "In Advent the organ and other musical instruments should be used with a moderation that is consistent with the season's character and does not anticipate the full joy of the Nativity of the Lord." In other words, a certain restraint should mark the music during this season. However, this restraint does not have the penitential character of Lent. Instead, its intent is to express a kind of "fasting" before the "feasting" which will enable us to enter more consciously into the waiting which marks Advent. We may certainly sing songs which express joy and expectation (many of the Advent readings do this very thing), but the music overall should be characterized by a sense of holding back until the time for full celebration arrives.

DECEMBER 3, 2006
FIRST SUNDAY OF ADVENT

SPIRITUALITY

Gospel

Luke 1:26-38; L689

**The angel Gabriel was sent from God
to a town of Galilee called Nazareth,
to a virgin betrothed to a man named
Joseph,
of the house of David,
and the virgin's name was
Mary.
And coming to her, he said,
"Hail, full of grace! The
Lord is with you."
But she was greatly troubled
at what was said
and pondered what sort of
greeting this might be.
Then the angel said to her,
"Do not be afraid, Mary,
for you have found favor with God.
Behold, you will conceive in your womb
and bear a son,
and you shall name him Jesus.
He will be great and will be called Son of
the Most High,
and the Lord God will give him the
throne of David his father,
and he will rule over the house of
Jacob forever,
and of his Kingdom there will be no end."
But Mary said to the angel,
"How can this be,
since I have no relations with a man?"
And the angel said to her in reply,
"The Holy Spirit will come upon you,
and the power of the Most High will
overshadow you.
Therefore the child to be born
will be called holy, the Son of God.
And behold, Elizabeth, your relative,
has also conceived a son in her old age,
and this is the sixth month for her who
was called barren;
for nothing will be impossible for God."
Mary said, "Behold, I am the handmaid of
the Lord.
May it be done to me according to your
word."
Then the angel departed from her.**

See Appendix A, p. 261, for the other readings.

Reflecting on the Gospel

The word "innocent" usually conjures up for us courtroom scenes. When "not guilty" is pronounced there is a huge sigh of relief. At the same time we humans react differently to another kind of innocence, often without thinking of it in those terms. When family members and friends go to visit the parents of a newborn baby, everyone usually wants her or his turn to hold the baby (even the smaller children beg for their turn). It's impossible not to plant a warm kiss on the tiny one's little head. We cradle and caress, coo and sing lullabies. Without needing to think or speak, we respond to the baby as one who is innocent, free from guile and wrongdoing. We also know that this child will hit the terrible twos, the peer pressure of adolescence, the challenge of adulthood. We seek innocence but we often choose another path. This is the human condition. Only two human beings have not shared in human sinfulness—Jesus and his mother Mary.

This festival in honor of Mary celebrates her innocence from the very moment of her conception in her mother's womb. She is the new Eve and, through her, God reverses the shame brought forth by the first mother of the living. Mary's innocence gained her a singular intimacy with God, for it was she who conceived by the Holy Spirit (gospel) and carried within her womb for nine months the very Son of God. Her body—conceived in innocence and kept free from the stain of sin throughout her life—was a fitting temple to nurture the human life of the divine Son.

The second reading for this solemnity also speaks of initial innocence "granted to us in the beloved" (God "chose us in him, before the foundation of the world, to be holy and without blemish before him"). In baptism we are grafted onto Christ and so we, too, enjoy intimacy with God, we who "exist for the praise of his glory."

Like Mary, we must respond to God's offer of graceful innocence with our "Behold, I am the handmaid [servant] of the Lord." Then, like Mary, we, too, bear the Son of God within us. She is the model for God-like innocence. She is our Mother and helps us attain for ourselves the fruits of her great privilege—Emmanuel, God is with us!

Living the Paschal Mystery

This is a feast of grace. The sin of Adam and Eve is met by God's promise that the ancient enemy will be crushed. Mary is chosen to be "holy and without blemish" (second reading) and is, indeed, "full of grace" (gospel). The grace which preserved Mary free from all sin is the same grace by which "we were also chosen" and are "blessed . . . with every spiritual blessing" (second reading).

Thus, God chose us, too! This is the Good News! Our baptism is our "conception" into new, innocent life. We plunge into the waters whereby our old selves die and we are raised as new selves who are now members of the Body of Christ. The intimacy of innocence we share with God is "adoption" whereby we are God's own sons and daughters. Before God we gain an innocence which is befitting those chosen by God. Mary is the model for a lifelong yes to fidelity to God's will which upholds our innocence before God.

Rather than a distant model, Mary is one who is close to us because she was close to her divine Son. Mary is a model for us of grace-filled living; all we need do is say yes!

Focusing the Gospel

Key words and phrases: full of grace, you have found favor with God

To the point: This is a feast of grace. The sin of Adam and Eve is met by God's promise that the ancient enemy will be crushed. Mary is chosen to be "holy and without blemish" (second reading) and is, indeed, "full of grace" (gospel). The grace which preserved Mary free from all sin is the same grace by which "we were also chosen" and are "blessed . . . with every spiritual blessing" (second reading).

Model Act of Penitence

Presider: God kept Mary free from sin from the very moment of her conception. Let us pause and reflect on how we, too, have been blessed by God . . . [pause]

   Lord Jesus, you are the Son of God and son of Mary: Lord . . .
   Christ Jesus, you have given us every spiritual blessing: Christ . . .
   Lord Jesus, your kingdom will have no end: Lord . . .

Model General Intercessions

Presider: Standing in God's grace, let us turn with confidence to God with our needs.

Response:

Lord, hear our prayer.

Cantor:

we pray to the Lord,

That members of the Church, with Mary, might always be faithful servants of the Lord . . . [pause]

That all world leaders might mediate God's blessings by working for peace and justice . . . [pause]

That those in grief and hopelessness remember that nothing will be impossible with God . . . [pause]

That we here gathered may be preserved from sin and grow in holiness . . . [pause]

Presider: O God, you preserved Mary from all sin: hear our prayers that we, with Mary, might one day enjoy everlasting life with you. We pray through Christ our Lord. **Amen.**

SPIRITUALITY

Gospel

Luke 3:1-6; L6C

In the fifteenth year of the reign of
    Tiberius Caesar,
  when Pontius Pilate was governor of
    Judea,
  and Herod was tetrarch of Galilee,
  and his brother Philip tetrarch
    of the region of Ituraea and
    Trachonitis,
  and Lysanias was tetrarch of Abilene,
  during the high priesthood of Annas
    and Caiaphas,
  the word of God came to John the
    son of Zechariah in the desert.
John went throughout the whole region
    of the Jordan,
  proclaiming a baptism of repentance
    for the forgiveness of sins,
  as it is written in the book of the
    words of the prophet Isaiah:
  *A voice of one crying out in the
    desert:*
  "Prepare the way of the Lord,
    make straight his paths.
  Every valley shall be filled
    and every mountain and hill
      shall be made low.
  The winding roads shall be made
    straight,
    and the rough ways made smooth,
  and all flesh shall see the salvation
    of God."

Reflecting on the Gospel

The beginning of this Sunday's gospel is a fine example of how Luke uses historical detail to ground us in real events. By mentioning in such detail these Roman rulers (and those appointed by them), Luke sets up a contrast between this world's ways and the "straight" and "smooth" way of the One who is to come. It was to none of the powerful (Caesar, Pilate, etc.) that God's word came; it was not in the centers of power that God's word was announced. God's word came to John and was announced in the desert. So it is with us: God's word comes to us in the desert places of our lives as we struggle to "[p]repare the way of the Lord." One way we prepare for the coming of the Word is by *listening* to God's word. Indeed, already in the listening is God present to us!

The prophet Baruch (first reading) invites his audience to "look to the east," the direction of the rising sun, of a new day, the direction from which the remnant returns to the land of promise. Baruch's is a message of hope, for the exiles are "remembered by God" and "advance secure in the glory of God." Finally, Israel returns home! What Isaiah (in the gospel) only yearns to be fulfilled, Baruch announces as already happening. Paul also brings a word of hope when he speaks of the "glory and praise of God" which is given when the faithful disciples of Jesus are "pure and blameless" on the "day of Christ." In the hope is God present; we only need listen to the word and be attentive to that presence.

These readings nudge us to a deeper appreciation of what Advent is really about. Rather than prolonged *waiting,* Advent brings us to active *listening.* We prepare for Christ's coming (in glory at the end of time and as an infant in a manger) by opening ourselves to the expansiveness of God's word of salvation. This word is expressed in divine mercy, justice, hope, and forgiveness. But most of all, it is expressed in the Word made flesh. Jesus brings what no ruler can bring: salvation. We only need to listen for his word.

Living the Paschal Mystery

In an age when we are inundated with sounds, words, music, etc., it can be difficult to hear God's word. We need a place of quiet—our own desert—to listen for and hear God's word to us. But although we hear God's word in the desert, the desert is not our home. The "word of the Holy One" calls us out of the desert and leads us to the new Jerusalem.

The Liturgy of the Word challenges us to take the real events of our everyday lives—all the suffering and pain, all the anxiety and hopelessness, all the joy and peace—and see them as means to recognize the presence of Christ to us. These events in their own way are God's word coming to us. Words then are not merely spoken; they are deeds enacted in love increased, knowledge shared, discernment embraced, righteousness integrated into the very fabric of our being (see second reading).

In this way we make our Advent something more than the preparation for a single-day feast of a birth. This is what Advent is all about—recognizing the presence of Christ in our lives as salvation already come because God's Word has already been spoken to us. Christian living challenges us to stop our busyness long enough to hear that Word, to be overshadowed by the Word, to allow the Word to make straight our paths.

Focusing the Gospel

Key words and phrases: Caesar, Pilate, the word of God came to John . . . in the desert, Prepare the way of the Lord

To the point: It was to none of the powerful (Caesar, Pilate, etc.) that God's word came; it was not in the centers of power that God's word was announced. God's word came to John and was announced in the desert. So it is with us: God's word comes to us in the desert places of our lives as we struggle to "[p]repare the way of the Lord."

Connecting the Gospel

to the first reading: Although we hear God's word in the desert, the desert is not our home. The "word of the Holy One" calls us out of the desert and leads us to the new Jerusalem.

to our culture: In an age when we are inundated with sounds, words, music, etc., it can be difficult to hear God's word. We need a place of quiet—our own desert—to listen for and hear God's word to us.

Understanding Scripture

The word of the Lord: "The word of the Lord came to X" occurs more than seventy times in the Bible as a standard formula introducing a prophet (e.g., Ezek 1:3; Jonah 3:1; Hag 2:10; Zech 1:1). Luke uses this expression of John the Baptist (Luke 3:2) to alert readers that John is like a prophet of old. John is not only a prophet, he is also the fulfillment of the prophecy Luke quotes from Isaiah 40:3-5. These images found in Isaiah, describing the mountains and valleys being made level for the return of God's people from exile, were widely known in post-exilic Judah (the period after 538 B.C.), as we see in the first reading from Baruch which makes use of these same images (Bar 5:7).

While Baruch is identified as Jeremiah's scribe (Jer 36; 43), the book which bears his name is widely considered to be an anonymous collection of individual compositions attributed to Baruch. The context for this Sunday's passage is the return of the people of Jerusalem from the Babylonian Exile. Baruch envisions Jerusalem as both priest and mother. As priest, Jerusalem is crowned with the miter of Aaron, inscribed with "the glory of the eternal name" of Yahweh (5:2; see Exod 28:36-37). Jerusalem, vested in glory, peace, and justice, manifests these same attributes of God. Then the metaphor switches and Jerusalem is presented as a mother gathering her returning children (5:5), whose journey from captivity has been made smooth by God. Their return comes about "at the word of the Holy One."

Jerusalem—priest and mother—is the setting in which God's salvation is accomplished and revealed, for it is there that "your children [are] gathered from the east and the west at the word of the Holy One." That word of the Lord, which brings salvation and restoration, justice and mercy, is what John announces and which Jesus will reveal and accomplish. The historical redemption of Jerusalem and her people is the pledge and foretaste of the final completion of salvation which will come with Christ's return in glory.

ASSEMBLY & FAITH-SHARING GROUPS

- My "desert" where I hear God's word is . . .
- The struggle to "prepare the way of the Lord" necessitates from me . . .
- My daily living announces to others the importance of "preparing the way of the Lord" whenever I . . .

PRESIDERS

While I minister I "prepare the way of the Lord" and "see the salvation of God" in that . . .

DEACONS

People whom I am accompanying from desert (gospel) to new Jerusalem (first reading) are . . .

HOSPITALITY MINISTERS

Ways that my hospitality aids others to experience "see[ing] the salvation of God" are . . .

MUSIC MINISTERS

Participating in music ministry helps me listen better by . . . One way I am able to hear God's word more clearly because of this listening is . . .

ALTAR MINISTERS

Serving others is a way of preparing for the Lord in that . . .

LECTORS

I shall consider how my lector preparations require me to *hear* first God's word in my own desert *before* I can truly proclaim it to others . . .

EXTRAORDINARY MINISTERS OF HOLY COMMUNION

Like the Eucharist, I am food for others as they struggle to prepare the way of the Lord in that . . .

Model Act of Penitence

Presider: John the Baptist heard God's word in the desert and announced it. We have come today to hear God's word; let us prepare ourselves . . . [pause]

Lord Jesus, you are the Word which John announced: Lord . . .

Christ Jesus, in you we see the salvation of God: Christ . . .

Lord Jesus, you lead us to everlasting life: Lord . . .

Appreciating the Responsorial Psalm

When God delivered Israel from their captivity in Babylon, they responded by creating Psalm 126. Over time they came to use this psalm as a song of confidence any time they were in danger of destruction. The text moves from memorial of past deliverance (stanzas 1 and 2) to petition for new deliverance (stanzas 3 and 4). Israel's confidence was based on real historical event, not dreamed imaginings. Of this they were certain: the God who *had* saved them *would* save them again.

This, too, is our confidence as we journey through the season of Advent. We hear of restoration to come (first reading) and of salvation to be completed (second reading). With the Israelites we know our hope is not an empty dream but a realistic vision of what God will accomplish when Christ comes at last. We stand in the desert of Advent, but we dance with hope and joy.

Model General Intercessions

Presider: Let us place our needs before God so that we are strengthened for our mission to prepare the way of the Lord.

Response:

Lord, hear our prayer.

Cantor:

we pray to the Lord,

That all members of the Church may hear God's word and live it . . . [pause]

That all peoples of the world come to salvation . . . [pause]

That those who have lost their way may find guidance in God's word . . . [pause]

That each of us enter the desert journey of Advent to hear the word of God . . . [pause]

Presider: O God, you come to save the world: hear these our prayers that one day we might live with you forever. We pray through Christ our Lord. **Amen.**

ALTERNATIVE OPENING PRAYER

Let us pray

Pause for silent prayer

Father in heaven,
the day draws near when the glory of
    your Son
will make radiant the night of the waiting
    world.
May the lure of greed not impede us from
    the joy
which moves the hearts of those who seek
    him.
May the darkness not blind us
to the vision of wisdom
which fills the minds of those who find
    him.

We ask this in the name of Jesus the Lord.
    Amen.

FIRST READING

Bar 5:1-9

Jerusalem, take off your robe of mourning
        and misery;
    put on the splendor of glory from God
        forever:
wrapped in the cloak of justice from God,
    bear on your head the mitre
    that displays the glory of the eternal
        name.
For God will show all the earth your
        splendor:
    you will be named by God forever
    the peace of justice, the glory of God's
        worship.

Up, Jerusalem! stand upon the heights;
    look to the east and see your children
gathered from the east and the west
    at the word of the Holy One,
    rejoicing that they are remembered by
        God.
Led away on foot by their enemies they
        left you:
    but God will bring them back to you
    borne aloft in glory as on royal thrones.
For God has commanded
    that every lofty mountain be made low,
and that the age-old depths and gorges
    be filled to level ground,
    that Israel may advance secure in the
        glory of God.
The forests and every fragrant kind of
        tree
    have overshadowed Israel at God's
        command;
for God is leading Israel in joy
    by the light of his glory,
    with his mercy and justice for company.

RESPONSORIAL PSALM
Ps 126:1-2, 2-3, 4-5, 6

R⃫. (3) The Lord has done great things for us; we are filled with joy.

When the LORD brought back the captives
of Zion,
we were like men dreaming.
Then our mouth was filled with laughter,
and our tongue with rejoicing.

R⃫. The Lord has done great things for us; we are filled with joy.

Then they said among the nations,
"The LORD has done great things for
them."
The LORD has done great things for us;
we are glad indeed.

R⃫. The Lord has done great things for us; we are filled with joy.

Restore our fortunes, O LORD,
like the torrents in the southern desert.
Those who sow in tears
shall reap rejoicing.

R⃫. The Lord has done great things for us; we are filled with joy.

Although they go forth weeping,
carrying the seed to be sown,
they shall come back rejoicing,
carrying their sheaves.

R⃫. The Lord has done great things for us; we are filled with joy.

SECOND READING
Phil 1:4-6, 8-11

Brothers and sisters:
I pray always with joy in my every prayer
for all of you,
because of your partnership for the
gospel
from the first day until now.
I am confident of this,
that the one who began a good work
in you
will continue to complete it
until the day of Christ Jesus.
God is my witness,
how I long for all of you with the
affection of Christ Jesus.
And this is my prayer:
that your love may increase ever more
and more
in knowledge and every kind of
perception,
to discern what is of value,
so that you may be pure and blameless
for the day of Christ,
filled with the fruit of righteousness
that comes through Jesus Christ
for the glory and praise of God.

About Liturgy

Advent and Morning Prayer. Two cautions may be in order as we celebrate this Second Sunday of Advent. (1) We might move too quickly to thinking about Christmas; the readings for this Sunday still orient us toward Christ's Second Coming. (2) In spite of the opening lines of this Sunday's gospel, we want to be careful about "historicizing" these feasts. We are celebrating a mystery which both opens up God's saving event and also eludes us.

Advent is the time par excellence for preparation for Christ's comings. But it is not the only time when the Church opens and prepares us for Christ's comings. Each morning, if we join ourselves to the whole Church in praying Morning Prayer from the Liturgy of the Hours, we are preparing for the way of the Lord. Part of the intent of the Church's Morning Prayer is to open the mystery of Christ as it comes to us during the day. Liturgy is not something which merely happens in church or during formal times of prayer. Liturgy is an immersion in Christ's paschal mystery and unfolds in each and every event of our lives. We need simply look for Christ all around us. Looking is a kind of preparing!

Morning Prayer, too, always includes Scripture, and so this prayer affords us an opportunity at the beginning of our day to open ourselves to God's word. Thus fortified, we are more equipped then to recognize in the many deeds of the day our own faithful living of this word.

About Liturgical Music

Cantor preparation: In this responsorial psalm you call the community to dream about the future by remembering what God has done in the past. You remind them that the God who *has* saved *will* save again. What past experiences help you maintain this hope? When for you has God transformed "weeping" into "rejoicing"?

Music suggestions: The readings this second Sunday call to mind that our hope for future salvation is based on experience of God's past interventions. Examples of songs which communicate this hope include "The King Shall Come" (found in most hymnals) and "City of God, Jerusalem" [RS, W3]. The text of "City of God, Jerusalem" is based on the first reading from Baruch. The hymn would make a strong processional song. "The King Shall Come" would be appropriate for either the entrance procession or the presentation of the gifts. G2, RS, WC, and W3 give five verses which nicely round out the "King shall come" imagery of the text.

DECEMBER 10, 2006
SECOND SUNDAY OF ADVENT

SPIRITUALITY

Gospel

Luke 3:10-18; L9C

The crowds asked John the
　　Baptist,
　　"What should we do?"
He said to them in reply,
　　"Whoever has two cloaks
　　should share with the
　　　　person who has none.
And whoever has food
　　should do likewise."
Even tax collectors came to
　　be baptized and they
　　said to him,
"Teacher, what should we do?"
He answered them,
　　"Stop collecting more than what is
　　　　prescribed."
Soldiers also asked him,
　　"And what is it that we should do?"
He told them,
　　"Do not practice extortion,
　　do not falsely accuse anyone,
　　and be satisfied with your wages."

Now the people were filled with
　　expectation,
　　and all were asking in their hearts
　　whether John might be the Christ.
John answered them all, saying,
　　"I am baptizing you with water,
　　but one mightier than I is coming.
I am not worthy to loosen the thongs of
　　his sandals.
He will baptize you with the Holy Spirit
　　and fire.
His winnowing fan is in his hand to
　　clear his threshing floor
　　and to gather the wheat into his barn,
　　but the chaff he will burn with
　　　　unquenchable fire."
Exhorting them in many other ways,
　　he preached good news to the people.

Reflecting on the Gospel

This Sunday's gospel showcases the teaching of John and turns us toward the Jesus who is near, the One who teaches us the Good News of our salvation. This is the longest passage we have concerning what John taught. He taught hard things! How strange that, after John's announcement that the mighty One will "gather the wheat" and burn the chaff in "unquenchable fire," the gospel would describe his message as "good news"! Such news is good, however, because the just judgment it announces also proclaims the advent of the One who is to come. The Good News is not a message but a person—Jesus.

The "good news" is announced to all those who would hear. John baptizes and preaches to "crowds" (presumably, the "common folk") and to tax collectors and soldiers (marginalized people because of what they did). When the crowd asks, "What should we do?" John answers to the effect, "more than what you would expect or wish—share what you have with those who have not." When the tax collectors and soldiers ask, "What should we do?" John answers to the effect, "do your job justly and exact no more." John tells us that preparing for the Lord means caring for the needy and acting with justice.

The question "What should we do?" which occurs three times in this Sunday's gospel, occurs two other times in Luke's Gospel (Luke 10:25; 18:18). In both these latter incidents, the question is put to Jesus and concerns what the individual must do to inherit eternal life. Jesus' response to the question is invariable: reach out to the marginalized with whatever one has and they need. Clearly the good news preached by John is identical to the Good News preached by Jesus. In this teaching John directs our attention to Jesus and to the ministry to the marginalized and needy he will inaugurate.

Traditionally, this is "Gaudete," "rejoice" Sunday, named after the Introit antiphon in the Roman Missal. The second reading also refers to rejoicing and suggests to us that the cause of our joy is Christ and Christ alone ("The Lord is near"). When we say "The Lord is near," we mean not that Christmas is almost here, but that Christ is always being enfleshed in our midst. "What should we do?" to celebrate this Presence already and always so near to us? John tells us, and so does Jesus.

Living the Paschal Mystery

The gospel imagery of chaff and wheat captures well the dying and rising mystery. Those who refuse to die to themselves and be transformed into those over whom God rejoices (see first reading) will "burn with unquenchable fire." "What should we do" to avoid this judgment? The gospel is clear: live as green wheat rising to new life. The second reading is specific: "Your kindness should be known to all." Only by dying to self now do we avoid the everlasting judgment to "burn with unquenchable fire."

Here is the key to gospel living: when we live as wheat risen to new life in Christ, when we make our kindness known to all, we preach the Good News by our very lives. We announce with John that the Lord is near and that we have discovered anew what we should do.

Focusing the Gospel

Key words and phrases: What should we do?, one . . . is coming, gather the wheat, unquenchable fire, good news

To the point: How strange that, after John's announcement that the mighty One will "gather the wheat" and burn the chaff in "unquenchable fire," the gospel describes John's message as "good news." Such news is "good" not only because of the just judgment it announces, but because of the One who is coming. The Good News is not a message but a person—Jesus.

Connecting the Gospel

to the second reading and Church tradition: Traditionally, this is "Gaudete," "rejoice" Sunday, named after the Introit antiphon in the Roman Missal. The second reading also refers to rejoicing and suggests to us that the cause of our joy is Christ and Christ alone ("The Lord is near"). When we say "The Lord is near," we mean not that Christmas is almost here, but that Christ is always being enfleshed in our midst.

to our culture: Christmas is coming very quickly, and so we may be caught up in what we still need to do—complete shopping, Christmas cards, etc. John tells us that preparing for the Lord means caring for the needy and acting with justice.

Understanding Scripture

Good news! The traditional theme of the Third Sunday of Advent is "Gaudete! Rejoice!" (second reading). One reason for joy is all the good news announced by Zephaniah in the first reading. While Zion/Jerusalem is exhorted to shout for joy, the one who actually does the rejoicing in this passage is the Lord who rejoices over Zion/Jerusalem with gladness (3:17). What is the cause of this divine joy? Jerusalem is about to be restored: her enemies will be turned back and the city will once again be established in security. Why? Because the Lord "is in your midst" (3:15, 17); with the Lord, a "mighty savior," in the midst of Jerusalem, the city need not "fear," nor be "discouraged." The safety, security, peace, and joy of the city find their source in the divine presence taking up residence once more in Zion. Divine presence brings concrete transformations: judgment, enemies, misfortune, and discouragement are all banished; in their place the King of Israel, the mighty savior, brings joy, exultation, and love. This good news is cause for rejoicing!

As John the Baptist announces the "good news," he encourages people to prepare for the coming of the Christ by making concrete changes in their lives. The materially fortunate, soldiers, and tax collectors are all exhorted to act with generosity and justice. Such transformation of their lives will serve them well on the coming day of Christ's purifying judgment. The theme of judgment, especially with its image of burning "with unquenchable fire" is rather scary and difficult to appreciate as an announcement of "good news." Yet Luke specifically tells us that John "preached good news to the people" (3:18). Why is this good news? Because, in part, the harvest imagery—separating wheat from chaff; storing wheat, burning chaff—is all prelude to the coming day of salvation. These are the necessary actions which take place in preparation for the "one mightier . . . [who] is coming." From John's perspective, and that of all who look forward in hope, the coming of Jesus is good news and the cause for our rejoicing.

ASSEMBLY & FAITH-SHARING GROUPS

- I believe John the Baptist would tell me to do . . . in order to prepare for the Lord's coming.
- Heeding John's call to act generously and justly towards others means to me . . .
- Christ's "winnowing fan" is "good news" in that . . .

PRESIDERS

Like John, my preaching is explicit, challenging, and "good news" in that . . .

DEACONS

The marginalized experience the nearness of the Lord (see second reading) through my outreach whenever I . . .

HOSPITALITY MINISTERS

I experience that the "Lord is near" (second reading) in my ministry of hospitality whenever . . .

MUSIC MINISTERS

If I were to ask John the Baptist "What should I do?" as a music minister to prepare for the coming of the Lord, he would answer . . .

ALTAR MINISTERS

I am a servant of generosity and justice (the call of John in the gospel) whenever I . . .

LECTORS

God's word is like a "winnowing fan" in that . . .

EXTRAORDINARY MINISTERS OF HOLY COMMUNION

Receiving the Eucharist nourishes my efforts toward caring for the needy and acting for justice in that . . .

CELEBRATION

Model Act of Penitence

Presider: We gather to hear the good news of Christ's coming. Let us quiet our hearts that we may hear this good news . . . [pause]

Lord Jesus, you are the Christ who brings salvation to all: Lord . . .

Christ Jesus, you baptize with the Holy Spirit and fire: Christ . . .

Lord Jesus, you are the good news preached by John: Lord . . .

Appreciating the Responsorial Psalm

Instead of psalm verses this Sunday, we have a text taken from the prophet Isaiah who reminds us the Holy One we await is already in our midst. To the question asked three times of John the Baptist in the gospel—"What should we do"?—Isaiah answers: cry out with joy, sing praise, give thanks, shout with exultation. We are also to make God's deeds known to all nations. We do this by putting into practice the good news the Holy One in our midst has come to proclaim. We are to care for the needy and to act with justice (gospel); we are to show kindness to all (second reading). Then will we hear the Lord rejoicing and singing because of us (first reading). What a chorus that will be!

Model General Intercessions

Presider: John the Baptist announced to his listeners that One who is mightier than he is coming. With confidence we lift our needs to this mighty One.

Response:

Lord, hear our prayer.

Cantor:

we pray to the Lord,

That the Church may be faithful to her mission to preach the Good News to all people . . . [pause]

That those in official government positions heed the Baptist's instructions to act with justice . . . [pause]

That those who desire a closer relationship with God encounter the Christ who is near . . . [pause]

That we here gathered may hear the Good News and rejoice in Christ's nearness . . . [pause]

Presider: O saving God, you hear those who cry to you: answer our prayers and help us to ready ourselves for the coming of your Son, Jesus Christ our Lord. **Amen.**

ALTERNATIVE OPENING PRAYER
Let us pray

Pause for silent prayer

Father of our Lord Jesus Christ,
ever faithful to your promises
and ever close to your Church:
the earth rejoices in hope of the Savior's
     coming
and looks forward with longing
to his return at the end of time.
Prepare our hearts and remove the
     sadness
that hinders us from feeling the joy and
     hope
which his presence will bestow,
for he is Lord for ever and ever. **Amen.**

FIRST READING
Zeph 3:14-18a

Shout for joy, O daughter Zion!
    Sing joyfully, O Israel!
Be glad and exult with all your heart,
    O daughter Jerusalem!
The LORD has removed the judgment
    against you,
    he has turned away your enemies;
the King of Israel, the LORD, is in your
    midst,
    you have no further misfortune to fear.
On that day, it shall be said to Jerusalem:
    Fear not, O Zion, be not discouraged!
The LORD, your God, is in your midst,
    a mighty savior;
he will rejoice over you with gladness,
    and renew you in his love,
he will sing joyfully because of you,
    as one sings at festivals.

RESPONSORIAL PSALM
Isa 12:2-3, 4, 5-6

R̸. (6) Cry out with joy and gladness: for among you is the great and Holy One of Israel.

God indeed is my savior;
    I am confident and unafraid.
My strength and my courage is the LORD,
    and he has been my savior.
With joy you will draw water
    at the fountain of salvation.

R̸. Cry out with joy and gladness: for among you is the great and Holy One of Israel.

Give thanks to the LORD, acclaim his name;
    among the nations make known his
        deeds,
    proclaim how exalted is his name.

R̸. Cry out with joy and gladness: for among you is the great and Holy One of Israel.

Sing praise to the LORD for his glorious
        achievement;
    let this be known throughout all the
        earth.
Shout with exultation, O city of Zion,
    for great in your midst
    is the Holy One of Israel!

R̸. Cry out with joy and gladness: for among you is the great and Holy One of Israel.

SECOND READING
Phil 4:4-7

Brothers and sisters:
Rejoice in the Lord always.
I shall say it again: rejoice!
Your kindness should be known to all.
The Lord is near.
Have no anxiety at all, but in everything,
    by prayer and petition, with
        thanksgiving,
    make your requests known to God.
Then the peace of God that surpasses all
        understanding
    will guard your hearts and minds in
        Christ Jesus.

About Liturgy

Advent's uniqueness. This is the last full week of Advent, and this year Advent is the shortest time it possibly can be. Next Sunday, the Fourth Sunday of Advent, coincides with Christmas Eve so the fourth week of Advent lasts only one day! This deftly underscores that Advent is a season of four Sundays rather than one of four weeks.

Monday, December 18, begins the time for Advent weekday propers, including the great "O" antiphons. The liturgies for these final weekdays before Christmas specifically focus our attention on the coming feast. Prior to December 17, the weekdays of Advent have a one-week series of propers which are repeated. Now, with only one week to go, there are propers for every day. The "O" antiphons, dating from about the seventh century, are magnificent poetic compositions extolling name-imagery for the Savior combined with a petition; they are used as gospel acclamations and as antiphons for the *Magnificat* from December 17 to 23 (see the weekday Lectionary, L201). The name-imagery extols Christ as Wisdom (omitted this year since December 17 falls on the Third Sunday of Advent), Leader, Root of Jesse, Key of David, Emmanuel, King (on both December 22 and 23), and Radiant Dawn.

About Liturgical Music

Cantor preparation: In these verses you are the prophet Isaiah announcing God's saving presence in the midst of the people. Even more, you are the Church proclaiming the Holy One in her midst to be Jesus who saves through the paschal mystery of his death and resurrection. How can you lead the assembly to see and encounter this Presence?

Music suggestions: This Sunday the focus of Advent turns from looking toward the final coming of Christ at the end of time to remembering his coming in incarnation 2,000 years ago. Hymns expressing this focus and available in most hymnals include "O Come, O Come, Emmanuel"; "On Jordan's Bank"; "Savior of the Nations, Come"; "O Come, Divine Messiah"; "Come, O Long Expected Jesus"; "People, Look East"; "Creator of the Stars of Night" (also titled "O Lord who Made the Stars of Night"); "Awake! Awake, and Greet the New Morn" (some hymnals categorize this as a Christmas song because of a variation of one word in the first verse, but the text as a whole better serves the final weeks of Advent). Less widely available but also appropriate songs include "Emmanuel" [PMB, WC, WS], "See How the Virgin Waits" [BB, JS2], and "Each Winter as You Grow Older" [G2, GC, GC2, RS].

SPIRITUALITY

Gospel

Luke 1:39-45; L12C

Mary set out
  and traveled to the hill country in
    haste
  to a town of Judah,
  where she entered the house of
    Zechariah
  and greeted Elizabeth.
When Elizabeth heard Mary's greeting,
  the infant leaped in her womb,
  and Elizabeth, filled with the Holy
    Spirit,
  cried out in a loud voice and said,
  "Blessed are you among women,
  and blessed is the fruit of your
    womb."
And how does this happen to me,
  that the mother of my Lord should
    come to me?
For at the moment the sound of your
    greeting reached my ears,
  the infant in my womb leaped for joy.
Blessed are you who believed
  that what was spoken to you by the
    Lord
  would be fulfilled."

Reflecting on the Gospel

How astounding and unexpected that the majestic ruler of Israel should come from so small and insignificant a place as Bethlehem (see first reading)! Even more astounding is that the Son of God should come to share our humanity. Elizabeth was astounded when, "filled with the Holy Spirit," she realized that the mother of her Lord came to her. Here is the Christmas mystery: it is entirely astounding that the Lord himself comes to *us* and that we who believe are also blessed.

The gospel portrays two women on the move. Mary "set out" through the "hill country" to visit Elizabeth. Elizabeth receives Mary into her home and reaches out and blesses Mary for her belief expressed in her yes to God's will. We, too, are a people on the move. We must "set out" to encounter our God in the Christmas celebrations. We must express our own belief in God's coming to us by our yes to God's will. Thus, we have just one more day to prepare for the coming of our God. We have just this last day of Advent left to realize the extent of our own blessedness before we begin our Christmas celebration. Our God comes to us, too!

Especially this year when the Fourth Sunday of Advent coincides with Christmas Eve, it is very easy to overlook the real demands of this festal season. It is too easy to sing the uplifting Christmas hymns with their wonderful, familiar melodies. It is too easy to glow in the warmth of the colorful lights and the good cheer and generosity that this time of year tends to bring out in people. It is too easy to focus on the wonderful imagery of the virgin birth and delight in the natural appeal of the newborn. The challenge of this Sunday, however, is to shake us out of our lofty sentiments and help us realize that we must surrender ourselves to God's presence and will. Jesus' body was "prepared" as the fruit of Mary's womb. He came to "do [God's] will." Mary believed and said yes to God's will and it was fulfilled. So must it be with us: our yes also fulfills God's will and makes the Word incarnate.

Living the Paschal Mystery

Christmas and Easter are two cornerstone festivals for us Christians. They are really two sides of the same coin; both celebrations essentially derive their meaning from self-giving. Mary gave her body so that the Son of God could become incarnate. Jesus gave his body so that humanity could become daughters and sons of God. In both cases the giving of their bodies required an act of the will (see second reading), an act conforming their wills to that of God, without counting the cost.

What is Christmas about? Giving! More than gifts which bring temporary joy, Christmas is about self-giving which makes possible everlasting joy. What has Advent really been about? We have been getting ready for our own bodies to be "consecrated" (second reading), like Christ's. Like Mary, we must believe so that what God speaks might be fulfilled in us.

By giving do we receive and convey the blessedness we have received in Christ. During these holidays, with family and friends gathering, there will be many opportunities for self-giving. Perhaps it is a matter of taking a few minutes to be present individually to the elderly. Perhaps it means playing awhile with the little ones. Perhaps it means simply helping to clean up and do dishes. However the opportunity for self-giving presents itself, it always is an opportunity for blessing.

Focusing the Gospel

Key words and phrases: Elizabeth, filled with the Holy Spirit, mother of my Lord should come to me, Blessed are you who believed

To the point: Elizabeth was astounded when, "filled with the Holy Spirit," she realized that the mother of her Lord came to her. Here is the Christmas mystery: it is entirely astounding that the Lord himself comes to *us* and that we who believe are also blessed.

Connecting the Gospel

to the first reading: How astounding and unexpected that the majestic ruler of Israel should come from so small and insignificant a place as Bethlehem. Even more astounding is that the Son of God should come to share our humanity.

to our culture: There is an aspect of Christmas that we take for granted—it is a civil holiday and a religious observance. But the astounding good news is that the Son of God comes to us.

Understanding Scripture

The unexpected ways of God: There was more than one town in Israel named Bethlehem. The one the prophet Micah has in mind in the first reading had an older name, Ephrath (Gen 35:19) which is used to distinguish it from the Bethlehem in the tribe of Zebulun.

The oldest history of Bethlehem-Ephrathah is uncertain. When Joshua apportioned the promised land to the twelve tribes, the towns belonging to each territory were listed (for the towns of Judah, see Josh 15:1-63). Bethlehem is not mentioned in that list; hence does Micah say "too small to be among the clans of Judah" (5:1). It was to this small and insignificant town that the prophet Samuel set out to find a replacement for Saul, Israel's first king whom the Lord had rejected. Samuel came to the home of Jesse (1 Sam 16:1-13). Surveying the first seven of Jesse's sons—tall, handsome, and strapping fellows—Samuel fails to find a suitable king and asks if there is another son. The youngest, the boy David, is in the field tending the sheep. It is from this insignificant village, from an otherwise undistinguished family, that the least of the sons is chosen to become one whose "greatness shall reach to the ends of the earth" (Mic 5:3). Who would have thought it?

This seems typical of God—to work in unexpected ways through unexpected people. The pattern continues in the gospel. God chose a young maiden of Nazareth and a barren, elderly woman from the hill country of Judah. Through the one would come the Son of God and Savior of all people; through the other, a great prophet and herald of the Messiah. To look upon these villages, clans, and peasants, one would never expect the world to be radically changed, the kingdom of darkness overthrown, and salvation to come to all people. Most unexpected of all is that these people and places were in the service of God's wondrous plan: to come to us personally in the birth of Jesus. The Word becomes flesh and dwells among us—how unexpected!

**ASSEMBLY &
FAITH-SHARING GROUPS**

- Like Elizabeth, where I have been astounded to find the Lord's presence is . . .

- Like Mary, my believing is a blessing (for me and others) because . . .

- Like Mary, I am giving birth to the Christ for others whenever I . . .

PRESIDERS

My ministry goes beyond sacrifice (as enacting a ritual) to an offering of my will and body to God and God's people (see second reading) whenever I . . .

DEACONS

Others' belief in the Lord's word spoken to them blesses me by . . .

HOSPITALITY MINISTERS

I recognize the presence of the Lord during my visitations with others whenever I . . .

MUSIC MINISTERS

Mary gave her body that Jesus might be born (gospel). Jesus gave his body that all might be saved (second reading). Through my participation in music ministry I give my body for others when . . .

ALTAR MINISTERS

Service teaches me to offer my body and will for the sake of others by . . .

LECTORS

Where God's word is being fulfilled in my daily living is . . .

**EXTRAORDINARY MINISTERS
OF HOLY COMMUNION**

My visiting of the elderly and infirmed focuses on the blessedness that the Lord is near whenever I . . .

Model Act of Penitence

Presider: Elizabeth recognized the infant in Mary's womb as her Lord. Let us reflect on how we recognize the Lord and prepare for his coming . . . [pause]

Lord Jesus, your coming brings us joy: Lord . . .

Christ Jesus, your coming brings us blessing: Christ . . .

Lord Jesus, your coming brings us life: Lord . . .

Appreciating the Responsorial Psalm

Psalm 80, from which these verses are taken, laments the destruction by enemies of the community of Israel. Israel reminds God that they were a vine transplanted by him from Egypt, tended, and protected. Now they are trampled by wild beasts, plucked bare by strangers, burnt down by enemies (see vv. 13-17). They call upon God to "rouse your power and come to save us." If only you will "let us see your face," they beg, we will be saved.

On this Fourth Sunday of Advent we, too, beg to see the face of God. Beyond all expectation, God responds to our request by showing us this face in human flesh. God uses the body of Mary (see gospel) to prepare a body for his Son (second reading). God then uses our bodies, consecrated through the self-offering of the Son (second reading), to continue showing this divine face on earth until all humankind is saved. Beyond all expectation, God has heard our plea; beyond all expectation, God has made us blessed.

Model General Intercessions

Presider: Our God comes to our aid and so we pray in confidence.

Response:

Lord, hear our prayer.

Cantor:

we pray to the Lord,

That all members of the Church might faithfully proclaim Christ's saving presence . . . [pause]

That all people of the world might share more fully in Christ's joy and peace . . . [pause]

That expectant mothers be preserved in health and joy . . . [pause]

That we who believe might live our faith more perfectly . . . [pause]

Presider: O God, you sent your Son into the world that we might have life: bless us now and grant what we ask through Christ our Lord. **Amen.**

ALTERNATIVE OPENING PRAYER
Let us pray

Pause for silent prayer

Father, all-powerful God,
your eternal Word took flesh on our earth
when the Virgin Mary placed her life
at the service of your plan.
Lift our minds in watchful hope
to hear the voice which announces his
    glory
and open our minds to receive the Spirit
who prepares us for his coming.

We ask this through Christ our Lord.
    Amen.

FIRST READING
Mic 5:1-4a

Thus says the LORD:
You, Bethlehem-Ephrathah
    too small to be among the clans of
        Judah,
from you shall come forth for me
    one who is to be ruler in Israel;
whose origin is from of old,
    from ancient times.
Therefore the Lord will give them up, until
        the time
    when she who is to give birth has borne,
and the rest of his kindred shall return
    to the children of Israel.
He shall stand firm and shepherd his flock
    by the strength of the LORD,
    in the majestic name of the LORD, his
        God;
and they shall remain, for now his
        greatness
    shall reach to the ends of the earth;
    he shall be peace.

RESPONSORIAL PSALM
Ps 80:2-3, 15-16, 18-19

R⁷. (4) Lord, make us turn to you; let us see your face and we shall be saved.

O shepherd of Israel, hearken,
　from your throne upon the cherubim,
　　shine forth.
Rouse your power,
　and come to save us.

R⁷. Lord, make us turn to you; let us see your face and we shall be saved.

Once again, O LORD of hosts,
　look down from heaven, and see;
take care of this vine,
　and protect what your right hand has
　　planted,
　the son of man whom you yourself
　　made strong.

R⁷. Lord, make us turn to you; let us see your face and we shall be saved.

May your help be with the man of your
　　right hand,
　with the son of man whom you yourself
　　made strong.
Then we will no more withdraw from you;
　give us new life, and we will call upon
　　your name.

R⁷. Lord, make us turn to you; let us see your face and we shall be saved.

SECOND READING
Heb 10:5-10

Brothers and sisters:
When Christ came into the world, he said:
　"Sacrifice and offering you did not
　　desire,
　but a body you prepared for me;
　in holocausts and sin offerings you took
　　no delight.
　Then I said, 'As is written of me in the
　　scroll,
　behold, I come to do your will, O God.'"

First he says, "Sacrifices and offerings,
　holocausts and sin offerings,
　you neither desired nor delighted in."
These are offered according to the law.
Then he says, "Behold, I come to do your
　　will."
He takes away the first to establish the
　　second.
By this "will," we have been consecrated
　through the offering of the body of
　　Jesus Christ once for all.

About Liturgy

Annunciation and visitation. In years A and B the Lectionary selection assigned for the gospel of the Fourth Sunday of Advent is the annunciation account. The gospel acclamation assigned to year C is also from the annunciation account. It is easy to relate this familiar gospel story to the coming Christmas celebration; after all, physiologically, conception precedes birth. However, in year C the gospel is the visitation story. Putting aside our logic of how things happen naturally, this account can also bring us to the Christmas mystery as does the annunciation. The visitation is another *annunciation*—Elizabeth recognizes and "cri[es] out in a loud voice" that her Lord is near, indeed, the fruit of Mary's womb.

Every liturgy is both an annunciation and a visitation. During each Liturgy of the Word Christ's presence is uniquely announced in the proclamation of the gospel. Even more: in the very proclamation, the person of Jesus comes to dwell within the liturgical assembly. Each Liturgy of the Eucharist is also a kind of visitation when *we ourselves* take into our very own bodies the Body and Blood of our Lord Jesus Christ and are *transformed* into being more perfect members of the Body. Each liturgy, then, is Christmas. The Word is made flesh and dwells among us!

About Liturgical Music

Cantor preparation: In this responsorial psalm you express the community's desire to turn more fully toward God. You lead them in begging to see God's face. How might you turn more toward God? Where might you look to see God's face?

Music suggestions: This Sunday brings the challenge of celebrating the final day of Advent while people are immersed in preparing to celebrate the first liturgies of Christmas which will begin in the late afternoon or evening. It is very important to maintain the sense of Advent in the Sunday liturgy. Songs which express the mystery of Mary's involvement in the incarnation include "See How the Virgin Waits" [BB, JS2] and "Emmanuel" [PMB, WC, WS]. "When to Mary, the Word" [HG] tells the story of Mary's visitation to Elizabeth and calls us to reach out to our neighbor as did Mary, and to see the Christ hidden within the other as did the infant John in Elizabeth's womb.

Finally, even though we have only a day rather than a week to finish Advent, John A. Dalles' thought-provoking hymn "We Blew No Trumpet Blasts to Sound" [found in the collection *Swift Currents and Still Waters,* © 2000 GIA] would be an excellent text to sing either as a post-Communion song or a recessional. In it we sing: "We blew no trumpet blasts . . . . We built no bonfire . . . . We spread no welc'ming canopy . . . . [instead] We hurried through another week, unheeding, and unmoved . . . . Dear God, how unprepared we were to welcome Jesus, then. We pray you, help us not to miss your priceless gift again."

Season of Christmas

He put on a created body,

that in our custom He might capture us.

Lo! in this *our* form,

He that formed us healed us;

and in this created shape, our Creator gave us life.

He drew us not by force:

blessed be He Who came in ours,

and joined us in His.

—St. Ephraim the Syrian
Nineteen Hymns on the Nativity of Christ in the Flesh
Hymn XIV (12)

SPIRITUALITY

The Vigil Mass

Gospel

Matt 1:1-25; L13 ABC

The book of the
   genealogy of Jesus
   Christ,
   the son of David, the
      son of Abraham.

Abraham became the
   father of Isaac,
   Isaac the father of
      Jacob,
   Jacob the father of
      Judah and his
      brothers.
Judah became the father
   of Perez and Zerah,
   whose mother was Tamar.
Perez became the father of Hezron,
   Hezron the father of Ram,
   Ram the father of Amminadab.
Amminadab became the father of
      Nahshon,
   Nahshon the father of Salmon,
   Salmon the father of Boaz,
   whose mother was Rahab.
Boaz became the father of Obed,
   whose mother was Ruth.
Obed became the father of Jesse,
   Jesse the father of David the king.

Continued in Appendix A, p. 262

or Matt 1:18-25 in Appendix A, p. 262.

See Appendix A, p. 263, for these readings:

FIRST READING
Isa 62:1-5

RESPONSORIAL PSALM
Ps 89:4-5, 16-17, 27, 29

SECOND READING
Acts 13:16-17, 22-25

Reflecting on the Gospel and Living the Paschal Mystery

"Merry Christmas!" How many times will this greeting be given and received over the next few days? Yet, Christmas is a time for more than merriment. It is a time to be aware of how blessed we are by God's saving presence. The birth of this Baby ushers in for us a new indwelling of God among humanity and within us. Never before had God been so close; now, the divine Son takes on human flesh and becomes one with us in all things except sin. God's plan over many generations has been to enter into an intimate relationship with people. Isaiah describes this with the image of marital union (see first reading). In Christ, the divine-human union is as intimate as possible: in Jesus, "God is with us."

The gospel relates truly extraordinary events—Mary conceives by the Holy Spirit and Joseph is apprised in a dream not to fear taking Mary into his home. We might surmise that Mary and Joseph could say yes, could cooperate so willingly with God's plan of salvation, because they were holy and prepared for their respective roles. The amazing mystery of Christmas is that, because of God's dwelling with us and within us, we, too, have been raised to a new holiness and a share in God's life. Even the espousal imagery of Isaiah does not come close to what God is offering us in Christ. Bound as one with Christ, we are also bound as one with each other. God's intimacy shared with us becomes our intimacy shared with each other.

The harsh reality of our society is that Christmas is anything but merry for all too many citizens. For some, poverty keeps them from providing for their loved ones in the way they would like; for others, alienation and loneliness divide and separate what this season is meant to unite; for still others selfishness and greed and self-centeredness keep family or friends at bay and result in emptiness and isolation. All too many signs are all around us of weakened or broken relationships, yearned-for intimacy, misplaced ambitions.

This blessed season is an opportunity in that at this time when it is natural to reach out to the less fortunate, rather than simply donating money or gifts or even time, we might put these wonderful charitable acts into the larger picture of the Incarnation's reminder of the closeness of all humanity in Christ. In reaching out to others we ourselves are making present a kind of "incarnation"—we are enfleshing the intimacy we share with our God through care and mercy and compassion for others.

Yes, incarnation is more than the birth of a Baby. What we celebrate at Christmas is the incarnation of God among us which transforms us into God's very presence for others. In this we are all most blessed.

Key words and phrases from the gospel: generations, Jesus, God is with us

To the point: God's plan over many generations has been to enter into an intimate relationship with people. Isaiah describes this with the image of marital union (see first reading). In Christ, the divine-human union is as intimate as possible: in Jesus, "God is with us."

SPIRITUALITY

Mass at Midnight

Gospel

Luke 2:1-14; L14ABC

In those days a decree went out from
    Caesar Augustus
  that the whole world should be
    enrolled.
This was the first enrollment,
  when Quirinius was governor of
    Syria.
So all went to be enrolled, each to
    his own town.
And Joseph too went up from
    Galilee from the town of
    Nazareth
  to Judea, to the city of David that
    is called Bethlehem,
  because he was of the house and
    family of David,
  to be enrolled with Mary, his
    betrothed, who was with
    child.
While they were there,
  the time came for her to have her
    child,
  and she gave birth to her firstborn son.
She wrapped him in swaddling clothes
    and laid him in a manger,
  because there was no room for them
    in the inn.

Now there were shepherds in that region
    living in the fields
  and keeping the night watch over their
    flock.
The angel of the Lord appeared to them
  and the glory of the Lord shone
    around them,
  and they were struck with great fear.

Continued in Appendix A, p. 263.

See Appendix A, p. 264, for these readings:

FIRST READING
Isa 9:1-6

RESPONSORIAL PSALM
Ps 96:1-2, 2-3, 11-12, 13

SECOND READING
Titus 2:11-14

Reflecting on the Gospel and Living the Paschal Mystery

This Christmas gospel from Luke for the Mass at Midnight is the one we all want to hear on Christmas. It is a beautiful, comfortable, familiar story. This gospel is filled with all the imagery which feeds what each of us hopes for out of Christmas: good feelings, warmth and security, nearness of family and friends, a sense that everything in our world is right. Yet, is this really what the gospel is portraying?

Mary and Joseph set out from Galilee to Bethlehem, about ninety miles. Can we really imagine what it was like to ride that donkey that long, while nine months pregnant? (How many pregnant women don't worry about how to get to the hospital for a safe delivery? Or can't afford a hospital? Or anguish over not being able to give the child all he or she needs?) Luke passes rather quickly over the fact that "there was no room for them in the inn" and that Jesus was "laid . . . in a manger." This messiah-king was hardly born in luxury and comfort! (How many people in our world today experience "no room for them" because of their race, nationality, color, religion, gender, sexuality?) Our Christmas creche statues paint the shepherds in nice clothes and beautiful colors, but in reality they were a scruffy bunch assigned to the night watch because they were the "outcasts."

In Luke, Jesus is born among outcasts and dies among outcasts, crucified between two thieves. (Who are the "outcasts" of our society? of our families?) The Savior of the world was born during the night of the year when darkness is the longest. Jesus comes for the people in dark places. The real, lasting, and deep joy of Christmas is that the Light shines there. This is why we can say to each other "Merry Christmas!"

In a manger, in a town far away, among shepherds, and in the dark of night, Jesus is born. Our salvation dawned in the messiness, poverty, and weakness of ordinary human life. This hardly seems like a very auspicious beginning to the dawn of salvation! Yet, we have hope not because we are perfect or because our world is perfect, but because Jesus was born into the house and family of our humanity. This birth by divinity into humanity dispels darkness and raises us up to new heights of a share in God's life. No wonder the shepherds sang "Glory to God in the highest." Indeed, no wonder our daily lives must reflect this same mystery: we ourselves must enter into the dark reaches of people and places and bring light and hope and peace. God's glory is proclaimed not simply by words but by our own mighty deeds of salvation. We only need to reach out and be the presence for others of this firstborn Son.

Key words and phrases from the gospel: house and family of David, manger, shepherds, night, a savior has been born for you

To the point: In a manger, in a town far away, among shepherds, and in the dark of night, Jesus is born. Our salvation dawned in the messiness, poverty, and weakness of ordinary human life. We have hope not because we are perfect, but because Jesus was born into the house and family of our humanity.

SPIRITUALITY

Mass at Dawn

Gospel

Luke 2:15-20; L15ABC

**When the angels went away
from them to heaven,
the shepherds said to one
another,
"Let us go, then, to
Bethlehem
to see this thing that has
taken place,
which the Lord has made
known to us."
So they went in haste and
found Mary and Joseph,
and the infant lying in the
manger.
When they saw this,
they made known the
message
that had been told them
about this child.
All who heard it were amazed
by what had been told them
by the shepherds.
And Mary kept all these things,
reflecting on them in her heart.
Then the shepherds returned,
glorifying and praising God
for all they had heard and seen,
just as it had been told to them.**

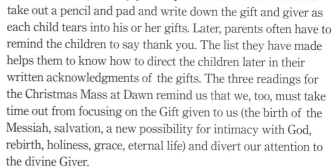

See Appendix A, p. 264, for these readings:

FIRST READING
Isa 62:11-12

RESPONSORIAL PSALM
Ps 97:1, 6, 11-12

SECOND READING
Titus 3:4-7

Reflecting on the Gospel and Living the Paschal Mystery

Sometimes in their excitement, children focus on the gifts given to them and forget just about all else. At large family parties parents have been known to take out a pencil and pad and write down the gift and giver as each child tears into his or her gifts. Later, parents often have to remind the children to say thank you. The list they have made helps them to know how to direct the children later in their written acknowledgments of the gifts. The three readings for the Christmas Mass at Dawn remind us that we, too, must take time out from focusing on the Gift given to us (the birth of the Messiah, salvation, a new possibility for intimacy with God, rebirth, holiness, grace, eternal life) and divert our attention to the divine Giver.

Having heard the angel's message, the shepherds choose to "go . . . and see" for themselves. They search for the Gift revealed to them by the heavenly choir of angels. Finding what they had been told to be true, they glorify and praise God. In this simple act of worship they change the focus of their attention from seeking the Gift to worshiping the divine gift-Giver. Like the shepherds, our hearing and seeing the Christmas mystery is fulfilled when we glorify and praise God. It is not enough simply to focus on the Gift, as wonderful as the incarnated God is. The Gift always leads us to worship. The Gift always returns us to the divine Giver.

The astounding thing about the incarnation mystery is that the Giver and Gift are one and the same God! Encounter with the Gift is encounter with the Giver. This is why we are led to glorifying and praising God—the Divine One has "[f]requented" (first reading) us, is present to us, and out of divine mercy has redeemed us (see second reading). These are the gifts beyond compare which draw us out of ourselves in grateful worship of the divine Giver.

Further, "glorifying and praising God" is more than what we do at liturgy. Like the shepherds, we too must make "known the message" by the very way we live each day, always remembering that any good we do is possible because of God's dwelling *with* us and *within* us. Our own priceless gift to each other this season (and all year long) is to bring Christ's presence to others. This Gift may be as simple as helping to pick up the wrapping paper and clean up after a family party. It may be as demanding as choosing to do with less food and drink this festive season so that others with so much less might have a bit more. Then with the shepherds we, too, are drawn by our encounters with the Gift to sing out "Glory to God in the highest!"

Key words and phrases from the gospel: shepherds, Let us go . . . to see, glorifying and praising God

To the point: Having heard the angel's message, the shepherds choose to "go . . . and see" for themselves. Finding what they had been told to be true, they glorify and praise God. Like the shepherds, our hearing and seeing the Christmas mystery is fulfilled when we glorify and praise God.

SPIRITUALITY

Mass during the Day

Gospel   John 1:1-18; L16ABC

In the beginning was the Word,
   and the Word was with God,
   and the Word was God.
He was in the beginning with
   God.
All things came to be through
   him,
   and without him nothing
      came to be.
What came to be through him
   was life,
   and this life was the light of
      the human race;
the light shines in the
   darkness,
   and the darkness has not
      overcome it.
A man named John was sent from God.
He came for testimony, to testify to the
   light,
   so that all might believe through him.
He was not the light,
   but came to testify to the light.
The true light, which enlightens
   everyone, was coming into the world.
He was in the world,
   and the world came to be through
      him,
   but the world did not know him.
He came to what was his own,
   but his own people did not accept
      him.

Continued in Appendix A, p. 265

or John 1:1-5, 9-14 *in Appendix A, p. 265.*

*See Appendix A, pp. 265–66, for these
readings:*

FIRST READING
Isa 52:7-10

RESPONSORIAL PSALM
Ps 98:1, 2-3, 3-4, 5-6

SECOND READING
Heb 1:1-6

Reflecting on the Gospel and Living the Paschal Mystery
Many of us take time out of our busy Christmas schedules to take a leisurely
ride through the neighborhoods after dark to see the outdoor light displays. We
can travel the same neighborhoods year after year and generally be treated to
something new. Something very interesting has been happening in the last several
years with respect to outdoor Christmas decorations—the multicolor lights have
largely given way to "clear" lights which sparkle with a kind of soft yellow light.
In the darkest night of the year we light the paths to our homes with sparkling
strands of tiny lights; in the darkest night of the year God lights the path to salva-

tion with the mighty and inextin-
guishable Light who is the "glory
. . . of the Father's only Son."
This gospel for the Mass during
the Day reveals for us the lofty
divinity of the humble Baby
born in this darkest of nights, for
the "true light, which enlightens
everyone, was coming into the
world."
   This gospel states the deepest meaning of the Christmas
stories in startling clarity: "And
the Word became flesh and
made his dwelling among us." Because Jesus participates fully in our humanity,
we participate fully in his divinity: "[f]rom his fullness we have all received."
Surely the first and foremost fullness we receive because of the Incarnation
is to have that divine life dwell *within* us and thereby raise humanity up to a
unique share in divinity. That fullness of divine life imparts other gifts: grace,
truth, revelation of God (gospel); peace, salvation, restoration, comfort, redemption (first reading); purification from sins (second reading). All of these gifts
reveal God's desire for us from the very beginning of creation: that we enjoy a
most intimate relationship with God.
   The gifts have their cost, however. In Christ God has spoken to us and "sustains
. . . [us] by his mighty word." God's Word, now the divine Son, came to dwell
among us and live as an example of how we should live. Rather than mere *receivers* of the "fullness we have all received," by Christ's taking on flesh he identified
with us to the extent that we, too, participate in salvation, in restoring all things
to God as it was in the beginning. The mighty act of God's Son taking on flesh
and "dwelling among us" does not diminish the good enfleshed in every small and
seemingly insignificant act we do for the sake of others. In a very real way our
acts of kindness and mercy toward others are incarnations of the "fullness we
have all received." In this way we ourselves become a light for the nations and our
good acts testify to the truth. With such an intimate relationship with God and
with Christ as our Light, we cannot help but sing out God's glory and praise.

Key words and phrases from the gospel: Word was God, Word became
flesh, From his fullness we have all received

To the point: The deepest meaning of the Christmas stories is stated in startling clarity: "And the Word became flesh and made his dwelling among us."
Because Jesus participates fully in our humanity, we participate fully in his
divinity: "[f]rom his fullness we have all received."

CELEBRATION

Model Rite of Penitence

Presider: Today we lift our hearts with joy to praise our God who dwells among us. Let us prepare ourselves to hear the word of salvation and receive the gift of life God offers us . . . [pause]

Lord Jesus, you are the Word made flesh: Lord . . .

Christ Jesus, you make your dwelling among us: Christ . . .

Lord Jesus, you share with us your own divine life: Lord . . .

Model General Intercessions

Presider: On this wondrous day when we celebrate the nearness of our God, let us make our prayers known with confidence in God's care for us.

Response:

Lord, hear our prayer.

Cantor:

we pray to the Lord,

That the Church may grow in the joy of Christ's abiding presence among us . . . [pause]

That all peoples may share in the peace that Christ brings . . . [pause]

That those without joy or family or friends may experience the nearness of God . . . [pause]

That we here gathered may rejoice in the salvation offered us in God's only Son . . . [pause]

Presider: O wondrous God, you give us joy in this celebration of the birth of your Son: hear these our prayers that we may sing with the angels your glory and praise always. We pray through that same Son, Jesus Christ our Lord. **Amen.**

(from the Mass during the Day)

Let us pray
[for the glory promised by the birth of
Christ]

Pause for silent prayer

Lord God,
we praise you for creating man,
and still more for restoring him in Christ.
Your Son shared our weakness:
may we share his glory,
for he lives and reigns with you and the
Holy Spirit,
one God, for ever and ever. **Amen.**

FOR REFLECTION

- I celebrate Christmas as revealing God's plan of intimacy with all humanity by . . .

- Ways I have assisted others to recognize and experience Christ *in the midst of* their darkness, messiness, poverty, and weakness are . . .

- Like the angels and shepherds that first Christmas night, I glorify and praise God by . . .

SPIRITUALITY

Gospel Luke 2:41-52; L17C

Each year Jesus' parents went to
    Jerusalem for the feast of Passover,
  and when he was twelve years
      old,
  they went up according to
      festival custom.
After they had completed its
    days, as they were returning,
  the boy Jesus remained behind
      in Jerusalem,
  but his parents did not know it.
Thinking that he was in the
    caravan,
  they journeyed for a day
  and looked for him among
      their relatives and
      acquaintances,
  but not finding him,
  they returned to Jerusalem to look
      for him.
After three days they found him in the
    temple,
  sitting in the midst of the teachers,
  listening to them and asking them
      questions,
  and all who heard him were astounded
  at his understanding and his answers.
When his parents saw him,
  they were astonished,
  and his mother said to him,
  "Son, why have you done this to us?
Your father and I have been looking for
    you with great anxiety."
And he said to them,
  "Why were you looking for me?
Did you not know that I must be in my
    Father's house?"
But they did not understand what he
    said to them.
He went down with them and came to
    Nazareth,
  and was obedient to them;
  and his mother kept all these things
      in her heart.
And Jesus advanced in wisdom and age
    and favor
  before God and man.

Reflecting on the Gospel

Any parent (or anyone close to them) who has lost a child through an abduction or running away or through divorce would readily relate to the "great anxiety" of Mary and Joseph related in this Sunday's gospel. Child loss is a heartbreaking experience. Family and neighbors—even total strangers—quickly rally around the bereaved to help in any way possible. Most parents love their children dearly, try to be good parents, and protect their children from danger and pain as much as they can. Good parents gladly suffer themselves in trying to protect their children. Mary and Joseph were no different. But their "great anxiety" actually involves more than a lost child. The context of the gospel is key: it is Passover time, a Jewish "identity" festival during which every Jewish household celebrates their "passing over" from slavery to freedom and becoming God's people.

This whole event is a "passing over" for Mary, Joseph, and Jesus, but in a unique way. The Passover journey of the Holy Family involved more than a trip to Jerusalem for a religious festival: they "pass over" to new ways of understanding one another. While Jesus was (and would always be) the son of Mary and his foster father Joseph, he was most profoundly the Son of God who "must be in [his] Father's house." So too, our Christian journey continually invites us to "pass over" to a deeper understanding of who we are: "God's children" (second reading) called to "love one another" (second reading) as members of God's family.

Hannah (see first reading) and Mary both gave their sons back to God, recognizing that all of us come from God and ultimately belong to God. We celebrate this day our primary identity—as the family of God. We belong to God. The loyalty normally ascribed to parents is transferred to God. Often this feast gets us thinking about our own families. The second reading points to our common identity as God's children and implies a much larger understanding of family—all of us together are members of God's family, striving to be continually in our "Father's house." During this season our rich family ties prompt a generous spirit of sharing. How wonderful it would be to have this attitude toward our larger human family!

Living the Paschal Mystery

"Passing over" is a process which is part of all family life. Every good family strives for continued growth in fidelity to God and each other. Just the everyday rubbing off the "sharp edges" taking place by living closely together calls us to enter into one "passing over" after another. Each time we let go of one attitude, habit, annoying behavior (that is, each time we embrace dying to self) we "pass over" into a newer and deeper relationship with those around us. The family is stronger and so are we for it.

A holy family is one in which their relationships include God at the center. Parenting is a great entry into the paschal mystery! Good parents spend their children's growing-up years emptying themselves of their own desires for the sake of the well-being of their children, endlessly and willingly sacrificing for them. Then, when the children are adults, parents must be willing to "cut the apron strings" and let go so the children can be about their own business. Like Hannah and Mary, good parents always nurture and take care of their children but, then, they willingly give back what they have received. Dying and rising. Sacrificing and giving back. Passing over. Such is what holy family living is really all about.

Focusing the Gospel

Key words and phrases: Passover, boy Jesus, his parents did not know, in my Father's house

To the point: The Passover journey of the Holy Family involved more than a trip to Jerusalem for a religious festival: they "pass over" to new ways of understanding one another. While Jesus was (and would always be) the son of Mary and his foster father Joseph, he was most profoundly the Son of God who "must be in [his] Father's house." So too, our Christian journey continually invites us to "pass over" to a deeper understanding of who we are: "God's children" (second reading) called to "love one another" (second reading) as members of God's family.

Connecting the Gospel

to second reading: Often this feast gets us thinking about our own families. The second reading points to our common identity as God's children and implies a much larger understanding of family—all of us together are members of God's family.

to our culture: During this season our rich family ties prompt a generous spirit of sharing. How wonderful it would be to have this attitude toward our larger human family!

Understanding Scripture

A new family: According to Deuteronomy 16:16, every Jewish male was required to appear before the Lord (in Jerusalem) to make an offering three times a year: Passover, which commemorates the deliverance from Egypt; Pentecost, which commemorates the giving of the Law on Sinai; and Booths (or Tabernacles) which recalls the forty-year sojourn in the wilderness. This Sunday's gospel finds the Holy Family in the company of other devout Jews fulfilling the requirement of the Law during the Feast of Passover.

Luke uses this episode to showcase the Holy Family's piety and to highlight their fidelity to the Law. As his parents bring the child Jesus on pilgrimage to the Temple, Jesus finds himself in the great Temple and in the midst of teachers. But for Jesus, this is more than the Temple; it is "my Father's house." Luke uses the physical setting to comment on Jesus' intimacy with God. Jesus is not just another faithful Israelite fulfilling an obligation at the Temple; he is the Son of God in his Father's house. His identity is now revealed in terms of this primary relationship—something Mary and Joseph "did not understand."

The first reading tells the story of another young boy in "the temple of the Lord." Samuel's barren mother, Hannah, had made a vow to God that if she should have a son, she would dedicate him to the Lord's service. It is in fulfillment of this vow that Samuel is brought to the Temple where he will now live and study under the tutelage of the priest, Eli. The parallels to the gospel are clear: in both readings, the male child is brought by his family to the Temple to fulfill religious obligations; both will be dedicated to the Lord's service, even from youth. With respect to this Sunday's feast, both boys come to a new experience of "family": Samuel leaves his natural family behind to serve God; and Jesus reveals to his parents his identity as God's Son. For both Samuel and Jesus, family derives its identity, not from blood relations, but from their primary relationship with God.

ASSEMBLY & FAITH-SHARING GROUPS

- What I have learned from my own family that I need to extend toward the family of God is . . .
- Like Mary and Joseph, I have grown to deeper understandings of Jesus, such as . . .
- Celebrating Christmas and its accompanying feast days is a "pass over" for me in that . . .

PRESIDERS
When I recall that the people I serve are God's family my ministry looks like . . .

DEACONS
My diaconal calling has enriched my family by . . . It has distracted me from my family life when . . .

HOSPITALITY MINISTERS
My hospitality ennobles others so that they might truly hear and believe that they are "God's children now" (second reading) whenever I . . .

MUSIC MINISTERS
As in this Sunday's gospel, being God's holy family does not mean that we never experience conflicts with one another, but that we allow these conflicts to deepen our relationship with God and with one another. One interpersonal conflict I experience in my music ministry is . . . This conflict is calling me to deeper relationship by . . .

ALTAR MINISTERS
I serve the bonds among people so that the family of God may be strengthened whenever I . . .

LECTORS
Where God's word is advancing me "in wisdom and . . . favor before God and [humanity]" is . . .

EXTRAORDINARY MINISTERS OF HOLY COMMUNION
My own family is like Christ's Eucharist and sustains me in that . . .

CELEBRATION

Model Act of Penitence

Presider: We come together as God's family in our Father's house. Let us open our hearts to the gift of God's grace and mercy . . . [pause]

Lord Jesus, you are the son of Mary: Lord . . .

Christ Jesus, you reveal yourself as the Son of God: Christ . . .

Lord Jesus, you make us God's children now: Lord . . .

Appreciating the Responsorial Psalm

For the Israelites, God's dwelling place was the Temple in Jerusalem. There all who could journeyed three times a year to keep festival. These annual pilgrimages were joyous occasions, expressing the community's sense of identity as God's chosen people and their longing to be with God forever. Psalm 84 communicates this joy and this hope.

As Israelites who knew themselves to be God's chosen people, Hannah could give her son to God (first reading) and Jesus could know where his true home was (gospel). On this solemnity of the Holy Family we celebrate who we are ("the children of God") and where we dwell ("in him"; second reading). We celebrate our identity and we call ourselves blessed (psalm refrain).

Model General Intercessions

Presider: As the children of God, we have confidence that God hears and answers our prayers. And so we pray.

Response:

Lord, hear our prayer.

Cantor:

we pray to the Lord,

That all members of the Church model to the world that we are all brothers and sisters . . . [pause]

That all parents may help their children grow in wisdom and love of God . . . [pause]

That those who have lost children may have their anxiety eased and find solace in the Holy Family . . . [pause]

That as Mary and Joseph sought and found Jesus, all of us here gathered may seek and find Jesus in one another . . . [pause]

Presider: God our Father, you call us your children: hear these our prayers that we may grow in your love and attain life everlasting with you. We pray through Christ our Lord. **Amen.**

OPENING PRAYER

Let us pray

Pause for silent prayer

Father,
help us to live as the holy family,
united in respect and love.
Bring us to the joy and peace of your
    eternal home.

Grant this through our Lord Jesus Christ,
    your Son,
who lives and reigns with you and the
    Holy Spirit,
one God, for ever and ever. **Amen.**

FIRST READING

1 Sam 1:20-22, 24-28

In those days Hannah conceived, and at
    the end of her term bore a son
    whom she called Samuel, since she had
        asked the LORD for him.
The next time her husband Elkanah was
    going up
    with the rest of his household
    to offer the customary sacrifice to the
        LORD and to fulfill his vows,
    Hannah did not go, explaining to her
        husband,
    "Once the child is weaned,
    I will take him to appear before the LORD
    and to remain there forever;
    I will offer him as a perpetual nazirite."

Once Samuel was weaned, Hannah
    brought him up with her,
    along with a three-year-old bull,
    an ephah of flour, and a skin of wine,
    and presented him at the temple of the
        LORD in Shiloh.
After the boy's father had sacrificed the
    young bull,
    Hannah, his mother, approached Eli and
        said:
    "Pardon, my lord!
As you live, my lord,
    I am the woman who stood near you
        here, praying to the LORD.
I prayed for this child, and the LORD
    granted my request.
Now I, in turn, give him to the LORD;
    as long as he lives, he shall be dedicated
        to the LORD."
Hannah left Samuel there.

RESPONSORIAL PSALM

Ps 84:2-3, 5-6, 9-10

℟. (cf. 5a) Blessed are they who dwell in
your house, O Lord.

How lovely is your dwelling place, O LORD
    of hosts!

My soul yearns and pines for the courts
of the LORD.
My heart and my flesh cry out for the
living God.

R℣. Blessed are they who dwell in your
house, O Lord.

Happy they who dwell in your house!
Continually they praise you.
Happy the men whose strength you are!
Their hearts are set upon the
pilgrimage.

R℣. Blessed are they who dwell in your
house, O Lord.

O LORD of hosts, hear our prayer;
hearken, O God of Jacob!
O God, behold our shield,
and look upon the face of your
anointed.

R℣. Blessed are they who dwell in your
house, O Lord.

SECOND READING
1 John 3:1-2, 21-24

Beloved:
See what love the Father has bestowed
on us
that we may be called the children of
God.
And so we are.
The reason the world does not know us
is that it did not know him.
Beloved, we are God's children now;
what we shall be has not yet been
revealed.
We do know that when it is revealed we
shall be like him,
for we shall see him as he is.

Beloved, if our hearts do not condemn us,
we have confidence in God and receive
from him whatever we ask,
because we keep his commandments
and do what pleases him.
And his commandment is this:
we should believe in the name of his
Son, Jesus Christ,
and love one another just as he
commanded us.
Those who keep his commandments
remain in him, and he in them,
and the way we know that he remains
in us
is from the Spirit he gave us.

*See Appendix A, p. 266, for optional
readings:*

CATECHESIS

About Liturgy

Children and liturgy: A great deal of the parish catechesis and liturgical energy is directed to the children, as well it should be. We have an important liturgical document (Directory for Masses with Children) as well as a Lectionary for Children to help us draw the younger members of our liturgical communities into the Christian family. These two resources and many others available through various Catholic publishers can help us do well the sometimes daunting task of teaching the children about the deepest meaning of liturgy and helping them be in their "Father's house" fruitfully, leading them to growth. There are some important principles to keep in mind as we help children celebrate liturgy.

1. The children's Lectionary is not a "watered down" set of readings. They are simplified, surely, but the selections remain faithful to Scripture. We always proclaim Scripture at liturgy, never a paraphrase, even with children.

2. It is better not to have the children do something simply to keep them occupied (and, hopefully, quiet). For example, rather than teach gestures which might be peripheral to the liturgical action (such as gesturing during a song), we need to teach and explain well the many postures and gestures which are part of liturgy.

3. We need to teach the children how to pray. This is best supported by family prayer at home, especially family prayer which coincides and is respectful of the liturgical seasons and festivals.

4. Whatever we teach the children, it ought not be in opposition to what takes place at an "adult" liturgy. We are always to help the children grow into full, conscious, and active participation in any parish celebration.

5. If children are to know what to do at Mass (and how to behave), they must be taught that and practice it with "quiet times" at home during which they are helped to pray.

About Liturgical Music

Cantor preparation: In leading this responsorial psalm, you call the assembly to become conscious of who they are—a holy family who dwell in the house of the Lord. What would strengthen your own sense of yourself as a member of God's family? How might you live this week so that this identity be more evident to others?

Music suggestions: On the heels of Christmas, the feast of the Holy Family arrives with its gospel about the disappearance of the twelve-year-old Jesus in Jerusalem and Mary and Joseph's confrontation with who he is and what his life must be about. Most appropriate for this day would be Christmas songs which speak about the revelation of who this Child will become. One good choice, for example, would be "Once in Royal David's City" [found in most hymnals]; its length makes it suitable for the Communion procession. A good choice for presentation of the gifts would be "Within the Father's House" [HC], which retells the story of the gospel and asks God to reveal Jesus' hidden identity to us in "full epiphany." Alan Hommerding's "Come, Sing a Home and Family" [PMB, WC, WS] makes vivid the influence of Mary and Joseph on the adult person Jesus was to become. This hymn would be appropriate either for the entrance procession or during the presentation of the gifts.

SPIRITUALITY

Gospel

Luke 2:16-21; L18ABC

The shepherds went in haste to
    Bethlehem and found Mary and
    Joseph,
and the infant lying in the manger.
When they saw this,
    they made known the message
    that had been told them about this
        child.
All who heard it were amazed
    by what had been told them by the
        shepherds.
And Mary kept all these things,
    reflecting on them in her heart.
Then the shepherds returned,
    glorifying and praising God
    for all they had heard and seen,
    just as it had been told to them.

When eight days were completed for
    his circumcision,
he was named Jesus, the name given
    him by the angel
before he was conceived in the womb.

See Appendix A, p. 267, for these readings:

FIRST READING
Num 6:22-27

RESPONSORIAL PSALM
Ps 67:2-3, 5, 6, 8

SECOND READING
Gal 4:4-7

Reflecting on the Gospel

It is quite fitting that one of our Christmas season festivals focuses on Mary's motherhood. For who ever conceived by the Holy Spirit? Who ever gave birth to God's very Son? Jesus' birth is like no other birth! The greatest blessing for Mary and for us is that Jesus is born for us and *within* us. Mary is not the only "Christ-bearer." As we are reminded in the second reading, we have been adopted by God and are heirs to God's blessings.

Both the first reading and the responsorial psalm speak of God's blessings. How "blessed among women" is Mary! What were God's blessings to her? What things did she "keep" and "reflect on . . . in her heart"? Moreover, her blessings spill over into blessings for ourselves. What happens when we consider the motherhood of Mary under the banner of blessing?

➤ Because of Mary's motherhood, we are no longer slaves, but children and heirs of almighty God.

➤ Because of Mary's motherhood, we see and hear a new presence of God and are drawn, like the shepherds in the gospel, to give glory and praise to God.

➤ Because of Mary's motherhood, we enjoy an incarnated, "earthy" presence of God among us; God's Son takes on humanity and becomes one of us.

➤ Because of Mary's motherhood, the light of God's face shines on all people in and through the presence of Jesus.

➤ Because of Mary's motherhood, the lowly (the shepherds in the gospel, but anyone who is displaced, untitled, outranked, unknown, etc.) hear and see first.

➤ Because of Mary's motherhood, we have a powerful, loving, and solicitous intercessor before God.

➤ Because of Mary's motherhood, her privilege of an immaculate conception and glorious assumption into heaven beckon us home.

These blessings are the Good News! To realize them in our lives, we need to reflect on them in our own hearts and say the same yes to God as Mary. What Mary treasured in her heart was the wonder of Jesus' birth. How blessed she was! How blessed we are that Jesus was born *for us*! So much to ponder! So much for which to praise and give glory to God!

Living the Paschal Mystery

"Don't get in my face!" It's an expression we all understand readily: "leave me alone; don't bug me!" On the contrary, the readings for this festival remind us that God has shown us the divine countenance, invites us into divine presence, and thus offers us salvation. Mary is the model for our response to these blessings of God in our daily lives.

This gospel prompts us to Gospel living in some surprising ways. First of all, simply taking quality time to reflect on God's mysteries and blessings is its own kind of dying and rising. Gospel living also entails an abiding habit of giving God praise and glory. Finally, Gospel living prompts us to listen for God's word in many different kinds of circumstances. Thus do God's many blessings become for us an invitation to a holy way of life.

Focusing the Gospel

Key words and phrases: kept all these things, reflecting on them in her heart, glorifying and praising God

To the point: What Mary treasured in her heart was the wonder of Jesus' birth. How blessed she was! How blessed we are that Jesus was born *for us*! So much to ponder! So much for which to praise God!

Model Act of Penitence

Presider: Mary was blessed in becoming the mother of the divine Son. At the beginning of this New Year, we pause to reflect on God's blessings to us in Christ . . . [pause]

Lord Jesus, you were born of Mary: Lord . . .

Christ Jesus, you are the Savior of all nations: Christ . . .

Lord Jesus, you are God's blessing to us: Lord . . .

Model General Intercessions

Presider: We have a powerful intercessor before God in our Mother Mary. Let us offer our prayers with confidence.

Response:

Lord, hear our prayer.

Cantor:

we pray to the Lord,

That all members of the Church, like Mary, treasure God's blessings and share them with others . . . [pause]

That the leaders of all nations, like Aaron, be instruments of God's blessings for their people . . . [pause]

That the poor of this world, like the shepherds, find blessing in glorifying and praising God . . . [pause]

That we, like the newborn Savior, be faithful to our mission to make present God's eternal kingdom . . . [pause]

Presider: Good and gracious God, Father of us all, you shower your blessings with love upon your faithful people: hear these our prayers that we might one day live with you forever and ever. **Amen.**

ALTERNATIVE OPENING PRAYER

Let us pray

Pause for silent prayer

Father,
source of light in every age,
the virgin conceived and bore your Son
who is called Wonderful God, Prince of
    Peace.
May her prayer, the gift of a mother's love,
be your people's joy through all ages.
May her response, borne of a humble heart,
draw your Spirit to rest on your people.

Grant this through Christ our Lord. **Amen.**

FOR REFLECTION

* Some of the fruit I have gained by reflecting in my heart (like Mary did) is . . .

* The purpose and value of "glorifying and praising God" like the shepherds is . . .

* I am enslaved by . . . (see second reading); what helps me to realize my true dignity as child and heir of God is . . .

SPIRITUALITY

Gospel   Matt 2:1-12; L20ABC

When Jesus was born in Bethlehem of
   Judea,
   in the days of King Herod,
   behold, magi from the east arrived
      in Jerusalem, saying,
   "Where is the newborn king of
      the Jews?
We saw his star at its rising
   and have come to do him homage."
When King Herod heard this,
   he was greatly troubled,
   and all Jerusalem with him.
Assembling all the chief priests and
      the scribes of the people,
   he inquired of them where the
      Christ was to be born.
They said to him, "In Bethlehem of Judea,
   for thus it has been written through
      the prophet:
   And you, Bethlehem, land of Judah,
      are by no means least among the
         rulers of Judah;
   since from you shall come a ruler,
      who is to shepherd my people Israel."
Then Herod called the magi secretly
   and ascertained from them the time of
      the star's appearance.
He sent them to Bethlehem and said,
   "Go and search diligently for the child.
When you have found him, bring me word,
   that I too may go and do him homage."
After their audience with the king they
      set out.
And behold, the star that they had seen
      at its rising preceded them,
   until it came and stopped over the
      place where the child was.
They were overjoyed at seeing the star,
   and on entering the house
   they saw the child with Mary his
      mother.
They prostrated themselves and did him
      homage.
Then they opened their treasures
   and offered him gifts of gold,
      frankincense, and myrrh.
And having been warned in a dream not
      to return to Herod,
   they departed for their country by
      another way.

Reflecting on the Gospel

We generally think of the young as those who are most willing to set off on a journey with little more than a bit of money in their pocket. As we get older and wiser, we tend to plan more, take plenty of clean clothes, make reservations ahead of time for overnights, take credit or debit cards to augment the cash we might have. We probably go to one of the many map-generating sites on the World Wide Web and get detailed directions to our destination. Few of us would start off without a destination. Some of us might even pay a professional travel agent to help us plan our trip and make sure everything is in place. If this kind of planning is true for most of us humans, then the Magi in this Sunday's gospel are strikingly different from us! They begin a long journey with no more map than a star, with no clear idea of a destination except Jerusalem (a pretty big city to find such a tiny Baby!), and only a vague idea of whom they are looking for ("newborn king of the Jews"). Moreover, there isn't much in the trip for them, for they bring this "newborn king" gifts and make the trip "to do him homage." How strange! How wonderful! What faith and trust the Magi possessed to be willing to be guided by an unknown light!

Of course, the light of the guiding star is not simply light. For Isaiah, the "light [which] has come" to Jerusalem is God's glory. For us the light is Christ himself. In Christ God's light and glory have taken flesh. Moreover, this light is not something possessed by a single people or nation, but it shines so that "all might gather and come to" (first reading) Christ. The Light of Christ shines beyond the boundaries of Israel, extending the gift of salvation to Gentiles. Ironically, it is not the king nor the chief priests and scribes, but Magi-foreigners who model both a driving desire to find the Christ and, when they find him, to offer homage. What leads us and prompts us to seek the divine is more than simple light; it is always God's power acting in Christ to lead us to encounter the divine. The Light brings us to God and elicits from us the homage we instinctually know we must render God.

The Magi's epiphany journey is the pattern of our Christian living: we follow God's promptings, seek God diligently, overcome many obstacles, and finally, finding God, we offer homage. Rather than gifts of things, we offer God the greatest gift we can—our very selves.

Living the Paschal Mystery

God leads us just as surely as the star led the Magi to Bethlehem. We are not in control but must trust in God's loving presence and sure guidance. There will be setbacks and challenges before we attain that for which we look: our everyday lives are filled with obstacles and contradictions which can get us off track. We must "search diligently": God and God's will can be found in many circumstances of our family life, work, and leisure times. Sometimes we must change course and take "another way": conversion is an ongoing milestone in Christian living.

This feastday of the Lord's epiphany reminds us that the Light of Christ is a diffuse one; it permeates all the world, and diffuses salvation everywhere. Our response: do God homage.

Focusing the Gospel

Key words and phrases: magi from the east, saw his star, searched diligently, found him, did him homage

To the point: The Light of Christ shines beyond the boundaries of Israel, extending the gift of salvation to Gentiles. Ironically, it is not the king nor the chief priests and scribes, but foreigners who model both a driving desire to find the Christ and, when they find him, to offer homage. Their epiphany journey is the pattern of our Christian living.

Connecting the Gospel

to the first reading: For Isaiah, the "light [which] has come" to Jerusalem is God's glory. For us the light is Christ himself. In Christ God's light and glory have taken flesh.

to our culture: As a culture, we don't any have problem with doing homage—we offer virtual worship to sports, rock, and movie stars; political figures; and celebrities. The real issue here is discerning what is worthy of our instinct to offer homage.

Understanding Scripture

Light and salvation: The theological meaning of this solemnity is declared matter-of-factly in the second reading: God's plan, a mystery for so long, has been revealed in Christ, namely, "that the Gentiles are coheirs, members of the same body, and copartners in the promise in Christ Jesus through the gospel." In other words, the salvation which had been the birthright of the Jews is now made a universal gift.

What Paul describes theologically, Matthew tells in story form. The first people who come to recognize and worship Jesus are not his own people—not the Jewish King, Herod; not the learned chief priests and scribes who can accurately quote the Scriptures and have all the requisite knowledge but none of the necessary faith. No, it is outsiders, foreigners, Gentiles who by the guidance of a star come from afar to prostrate themselves before the "newborn king of the Jews," who is in fact the Messiah ("the Christ").

Isaiah describes all this poetically. This exuberant passage illuminates two aspects of this solemnity. First, and obviously, it serves as a prophecy which the Magi fulfill: "Caravans of camels shall fill you. . . . All from Sheba shall come bearing gold and frankincense, and proclaiming the praises of the LORD." Secondly, it highlights the universal nature of God's gift of salvation which embraces "nations" and "kings." The metaphor for salvation is "light." This is a theme Isaiah sounds repeatedly: "Your light has come"; "the Lord shines upon you" (twice); "your light"; "shining radiance"; "be radiant." To say that "the Lord shine upon you" is the prophet's poetic way of announcing that salvation or deliverance is dawning. The people in exile will be saved from their banishment and be brought back to their own homes in Jerusalem. As the prophet says, "they all gather and come to you: your sons come from afar, and your daughters in the arms of their nurses." The same theme is taken up in the responsorial psalm, "Lord, every nation on earth will adore you." God's salvation—as radiant as light—is a gift that shines upon all people.

Model Act of Penitence

Presider: The Magi were guided by the light of God's star to the newborn king and offered him homage and gifts. As we've come to offer worship, let us open our hearts to God's gifts of light and mercy . . . [pause]

    Lord Jesus, you are the light of all peoples: Lord . . .

    Christ Jesus, you are the revelation of God's love: Christ . . .

    Lord Jesus, you are the Savior of the world: Lord . . .

Appreciating the Responsorial Psalm

The Israelite community understood their king to be the agent of God on earth. He was the intermediary of God's saving action among the people. Psalm 72 was an intercessory prayer on the king's behalf. The Israelites prayed that God would grant him divine judgment and a reign marked by justice and peace. They prayed that he would act to rescue the poor and uplift the lowly and that, seeing this behavior, other nations would offer him homage.

On this solemnity of the Epiphany we use verses from Psalm 72 to acknowledge the Infant born in Bethlehem to be the definitive intermediary of God on earth for the salvation of humanity. This Child is *the* King who will govern with justice and save the lives of the poor. With the Magi from the East we join the line of all nations who come to adore him.

Model General Intercessions

Presider: Just as surely as God's star led the Magi to find the infant Jesus and pay him homage, so will God guide us in all we do. Let us pray for this guidance.

Response:

Lord, hear our prayer.

Cantor:

we pray to the Lord,

That the Church may be a star guiding all people to salvation . . . [pause]

That all people of the world may be awakened to God's guiding presence . . . [pause]

That those who search may find God patiently and lovingly waiting for them . . . [pause]

That all of us here gathered may recognize the Light of Christ guiding us to salvation . . . [pause]

Presider: O God, you are worthy of all homage: hear these prayers we offer you as a fitting expression of our dependence upon you for guidance. We pray through Christ our Lord. **Amen.**

ALTERNATIVE OPENING PRAYER
Let us pray

Pause for silent prayer

Father of light, unchanging God,
today you reveal to men of faith
the resplendent fact of the Word made
    flesh.
Your light is strong,
your love is near;
draw us beyond the limits which this
    world imposes,
to the life where your Spirit makes all life
    complete.

We ask this through Christ our Lord.
    Amen.

FIRST READING
Isa 60:1-6

Rise up in splendor, Jerusalem! Your light
    has come,
    the glory of the Lord shines upon you.
See, darkness covers the earth,
    and thick clouds cover the peoples;
but upon you the LORD shines,
    and over you appears his glory.
Nations shall walk by your light,
    and kings by your shining radiance.
Raise your eyes and look about;
    they all gather and come to you:
your sons come from afar,
    and your daughters in the arms of their
        nurses.

Then you shall be radiant at what you see,
    your heart shall throb and overflow,
for the riches of the sea shall be emptied
    out before you,
    the wealth of nations shall be brought
        to you.
Caravans of camels shall fill you,
    dromedaries from Midian and Ephah;
all from Sheba shall come
    bearing gold and frankincense,
    and proclaiming the praises of the LORD.

RESPONSORIAL PSALM
Ps 72:1-2, 7-8, 10-11, 12-13

R⎓. (cf. 11) Lord, every nation on earth will adore you.

O God, with your judgment endow the king,
   and with your justice, the king's son;
he shall govern your people with justice
   and your afflicted ones with judgment.

R⎓. Lord, every nation on earth will adore you.

Justice shall flower in his days,
   and profound peace, till the moon be no more.
May he rule from sea to sea,
   and from the River to the ends of the earth.

R⎓. Lord, every nation on earth will adore you.

The kings of Tarshish and the Isles shall offer gifts;
   the kings of Arabia and Seba shall bring tribute.
All kings shall pay him homage,
   all nations shall serve him.

R⎓. Lord, every nation on earth will adore you.

For he shall rescue the poor when he cries out,
   and the afflicted when he has no one to help him.
He shall have pity for the lowly and the poor;
   the lives of the poor he shall save.

R⎓. Lord, every nation on earth will adore you.

SECOND READING
Eph 3:2-3a, 5-6

Brothers and sisters:
You have heard of the stewardship of God's grace
   that was given to me for your benefit,
namely, that the mystery was made known to me by revelation.
It was not made known to people in other generations
as it has now been revealed
to his holy apostles and prophets by the Spirit:
that the Gentiles are coheirs, members of the same body,
and copartners in the promise in Christ Jesus through the gospel.

About Liturgy

Connecting the two great festal seasons: There are hints in this Sunday's gospel which help us connect the two great festal seasons (Advent-Christmas-Epiphany and Lent-Triduum-Easter) as two sides of salvation. (1) The Magi saw the "star at its rising"; that is, in the East. This is the direction from which Israel expected the Messiah to come and the direction from which the early Church expected Christ to come at the parousia. (2) King Herod has an exchange with the Jewish leaders, as happened at the trial of Jesus. (3) Jesus manifested himself to Gentiles as an infant, as it was a Gentile (the centurion) who recognized Jesus on the cross as the Son of God. (4) There is fear and a power struggle among the leadership at Jesus' birth as there was at his trial, suffering, and death.

Baptism of the Lord: Usually, the feast of the Baptism of the Lord is celebrated on the Sunday after January 6 (see GNLYC no. 38). But whenever Epiphany falls on January 7 or 8 (as it does this year), the feast of the Baptism of the Lord occurs on the following Monday (this year, on January 8); hence, this is the first week of Ordinary Time. This transference of the feast of the Baptism of the Lord to Monday is unfortunate, since many parishioners miss this important celebration. Celebrating the Lord's baptism at the beginning of Ordinary Time reminds us that our Christian journey is begun at our own baptism; baptism is both a commitment to and the inauguration of a mission.

About Liturgical Music

Cantor preparation: In the liturgy for Epiphany, Psalm 72 is not an intercessory prayer that the Israelite king fulfill the role given him by God, but a description of Christ who completely fulfills that role. In singing it you proclaim who Christ is and why every nation on earth will adore him. As part of your preparation to sing this psalm, take some time each day to offer Christ your personal adoration.

Music suggestions: "Hail to the Lord's Anointed" [PMB, WC] identifies Christ as "David's greater Son" come to fulfill God's saving plan for all the earth. Its text is based on Psalm 72 (the responsorial psalm for this day). Its majestic tune would work well for the entrance procession. Another hymn suitable for the entrance procession would be "What Star Is This" [BB, CBW3, GC, GC2, JS2, PMB, RS, WC, W3]. The song has been widely used since the early 18th century as a hymn for vespers on Epiphany. Its delightful dance-like quality expresses well the festive mood of this day. "How Brightly Shines the Morning Star" [WC] speaks of Christ as the Morning Star and calls all earth and heaven to give praise. The tune's broad pace makes this hymn suitable for the presentation of the gifts.

Ordinary Time I

SPIRITUALITY

Gospel

John 2:1-11; L66C

There was a wedding at Cana
   in Galilee,
   and the mother of Jesus
      was there.
Jesus and his disciples
   were also invited to the
   wedding.
When the wine ran short,
   the mother of Jesus said to
      him,
   "They have no wine."
And Jesus said to her,
   "Woman, how does your
      concern affect me?
My hour has not yet come."
His mother said to the servers,
   "Do whatever he tells you."
Now there were six stone water jars
   there for Jewish ceremonial
      washings,
   each holding twenty to thirty gallons.
Jesus told them,
   "Fill the jars with water."
So they filled them to the brim.
Then he told them,
   "Draw some out now and take it to
      the headwaiter."
So they took it.
And when the headwaiter tasted the
      water that had become wine,
   without knowing where it came from
   —although the servers who had
      drawn the water knew—,
   the headwaiter called the bridegroom
      and said to him,
   "Everyone serves good wine first,
   and then when people have drunk
      freely, an inferior one;
   but you have kept the good wine until
      now."
Jesus did this as the beginning of his
   signs at Cana in Galilee
   and so revealed his glory,
   and his disciples began to believe in
      him.

Reflecting on the Gospel

With the espousal language of the first reading and the wedding feast context of the gospel, one is tempted to think these readings focus us on marriage. But the critical line in the gospel comes in the very last sentence: "Jesus did this as the beginning of his signs at Cana in Galilee and so revealed his glory, and his disciples began to believe in him." Thus does John's Gospel mark the beginning of Jesus' public ministry. But as beginning, it also contains a preview of the

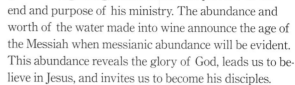

end and purpose of his ministry. The abundance and worth of the water made into wine announce the age of the Messiah when messianic abundance will be evident. This abundance reveals the glory of God, leads us to believe in Jesus, and invites us to become his disciples.

Yes, this sign Jesus performed at the wedding feast at Cana inaugurates Jesus' public ministry, but not the life the miracle might lead us to expect. With so much power at hand we might expect Jesus to take advantage of the best and finest life can offer. Instead Jesus shows us another way, and this other way is also the way of those who believe in him.

Jesus' life was an entire life spent meeting the needs of other people. This is his true glory and his whole ministry: not only turning water into wine but giving himself for others. His total attentiveness and response to others is the model for our own self-giving and is the promise of our own glory. As Isaiah could not keep silent but announced the glory of Israel, so Jesus could not keep silent but "revealed his glory." Yet we hardly think of glory in terms of self-emptying! But this is the way Jesus shows us. This is the way of his disciples.

It's telling that at the very beginning of his public ministry, Jesus manifests his glory in terms of response to his mother and concern for others. Here is the Good News: giving oneself for the sake of another is how we achieve salvation, how we march steadily toward messianic abundance, how we share in Jesus' glory. Glory doesn't simply mean high renown or honor won by notable achievements. In this sense it means self-giving. By thus emptying ourselves do we achieve the fullness of abundance Jesus promises in the age to come.

Living the Paschal Mystery

The messianic age announced in the gospel is given a different concrete description in the first reading from Isaiah. There God is the Spouse and rejoices in us who are God's beloved. Like the disciples in the gospel, we are to "believe in him."

This lays out for us a lifelong task of accepting all the signs of Jesus' presence and messianic abundance among us. It means that we are to make a lifelong covenant with God. Traditionally, this is how we understand our baptism. It is our initial celebration of a relationship with God that is intimate, loving, lasting. Our fidelity during this life assures us that death is not a separation but an entrance into eternal life where the wine never runs out, the rejoicing never ceases, and the depths of love are never exhausted.

During Ordinary Time we journey with Jesus through a Gospel (this year, Luke's Gospel) toward our fulfillment at the messianic banquet. Let us taste the wine, and know that the good only gets better!

Focusing the Gospel

Key words and phrases: kept the good wine until now, beginning of his signs, revealed his glory

To the point: This sign Jesus performed at the wedding feast at Cana inaugurates Jesus' public ministry—an entire life spent meeting the needs of people. This is his true glory and his whole ministry: not only turning water into wine but giving himself for others. His total attentiveness and response to others is the model for our own self-giving and is the promise of our own glory.

Connecting the Gospel

to the first reading: As Isaiah could not keep silent but announced the glory of Israel, so Jesus could not keep silent but "revealed his glory."

to our culture: We hardly think of glory in terms of self-emptying. But this is the way Jesus shows us.

Understanding Scripture

Glory: The "miracle" at the wedding feast at Cana, the first of Jesus' seven great signs in the Gospel of John, does two things: it reveals his glory and moves his disciples to believe in him. The two are obviously related. Seeing a sign is an invitation to believe. While signs do not compel belief—some people see signs and conspire against Jesus—they provide an opportunity for people to see behind the sign the identity of the one who performs it. Indeed, this is why John records them: "these [signs] are written that you may believe that Jesus is the Messiah, the Son of God" (20:31).

The sign at Cana discloses the glory of Jesus. Throughout the Gospel Jesus frequently speaks of his Father's glory and of sharing that same glory; he speaks, too, of being glorified. The moment of his glorification on earth happens, paradoxically, when he is lifted up on the cross to die. In chapter 12, Jesus says, "The hour has come for the Son of Man to be glorified. Amen, amen, I say to you, unless a grain of wheat falls to the ground and dies, it remains just a grain of wheat; but if it dies, it produces much fruit" (12:23-24). He says that the purpose of his coming was just this: to die on the cross and bear the fruit of eternal life for all who believe in him: "When I am lifted up from the earth [on the cross], I will draw everyone to myself" (12:32). Then, at the Last Supper, just as Judas leaves to set in motion the final plans which will lead Jesus to his death, Jesus announces to his disciples, "Now is the Son of Man glorified, and God is glorified in him" (13:31). His death discloses his glory.

At the wedding feast in Cana, Jesus lays aside his own needs (his hour had not yet come) to meet the needs of the couple. This is typical of his entire ministry of self-giving which leads through death to life. Rightly, then, does John say that Jesus revealed his glory.

ASSEMBLY & FAITH-SHARING GROUPS

- Jesus' glory was shown in meeting the needs of the couple. Jesus' glory is shown through me whenever I . . .
- Mary's concern became Jesus'. My concerns for our Church and world that I bring to Jesus are . . .
- Giving myself to others glorifies me in Christ in that . . .

PRESIDERS

Leading others for their benefit demands greater self-giving on my part because . . .

DEACONS

My ministry manifests God's glory to others by . . .

HOSPITALITY MINISTERS

My hospitality is about self-giving rather than self-grandiosement when . . .

MUSIC MINISTERS

There is a great deal in this Sunday's readings about transformation: desolate Jerusalem becomes God's delight; water becomes wine; disciples become believers. My participation in music ministry transforms me by . . .

ALTAR MINISTERS

Serving others has taught me that God's glory is like . . .

LECTORS

When it comes to God's word I cannot be "silent" or "quiet" (first reading) when . . .

EXTRAORDINARY MINISTERS OF HOLY COMMUNION

The abundance of wine Christ offered at the wedding inspires my own self-giving for others when . . .

Model Act of Penitence

Presider: Today's gospel is about the wedding feast at Cana at which Jesus reveals his glory. As we stand before the glory of God, let us prepare ourselves to celebrate this liturgy . . . [pause]

Lord Jesus, you reveal your glory to us: Lord . . .

Christ Jesus, you are attentive to the needs of others: Christ . . .

Lord Jesus, you are the One in whom we believe: Lord . . .

Appreciating the Responsorial Psalm

The verses from Psalm 96 used for this Sunday divide thematically. The first two strophes command us to sing to God, bless God's name, announce God's wondrous deeds to all the world. In the last two strophes we command all nations to join us in our praise and worship of God.

The first reading and gospel give the reasons for our praise. Isaiah promises that God's actions on our behalf will far surpass our wants and dreams (first reading). The gospel shows us Jesus acting in a way which far surpasses the expectations of his disciples. We sing this psalm because we have "marvelous deeds" to proclaim and we know the best is yet to come.

Model General Intercessions

Presider: Let us pray for our needs, confident that our generous God hears our prayers.

Response:

Lord, hear our prayer.

Cantor:

we pray to the Lord,

May the Church through her service of others always reveal the glory of God . . . [pause]

May all peoples of the world come to believe in the salvation offered by a loving God . . . [pause]

May those who lack basic necessities have their needs met . . . [pause]

May we here gathered find our glory in serving others . . . [pause]

Presider: O God of abundance, you fulfill the needs of those who come to you: hear these our prayers that we might one day enjoy life eternal with you. We pray through Christ our Lord. **Amen.**

ALTERNATIVE OPENING PRAYER

Let us pray

Pause for silent prayer

Almighty and ever-present Father,
your watchful care reaches from end to
    end
and orders all things in such power
that even the tensions and the tragedies
    of sin
cannot frustrate your loving plans.
Help us to embrace your will,
give us the strength to follow your call,
so that your truth may live in our hearts
and reflect peace to those who believe in
    your love.

We ask this in the name of Jesus the Lord.
    Amen.

FIRST READING

Isa 62:1-5

For Zion's sake I will not be silent,
    for Jerusalem's sake I will not be quiet,
until her vindication shines forth like the
    dawn
    and her victory like a burning torch.

Nations shall behold your vindication,
    and all the kings your glory;
you shall be called by a new name
    pronounced by the mouth of the LORD.
You shall be a glorious crown in the hand
    of the LORD,
    a royal diadem held by your God.
No more shall people call you "Forsaken,"
    or your land "Desolate,"
but you shall be called "My Delight,"
    and your land "Espoused."
For the LORD delights in you
    and makes your land his spouse.
As a young man marries a virgin,
    your Builder shall marry you;
and as a bridegroom rejoices in his bride
    so shall your God rejoice in you.

RESPONSORIAL PSALM

Ps 96:1-2, 2-3, 7-8, 9-10

R̂. (3) Proclaim his marvelous deeds to all the nations.

Sing to the LORD a new song;
    sing to the LORD, all you lands.
Sing to the LORD; bless his name.

R̂. Proclaim his marvelous deeds to all the nations.

Announce his salvation, day after day.
Tell his glory among the nations;
    among all peoples, his wondrous deeds.

R̂. Proclaim his marvelous deeds to all the nations.

Give to the LORD, you families of nations,
    give to the LORD glory and praise;
    give to the LORD the glory due his name!

R̂. Proclaim his marvelous deeds to all the nations.

Worship the LORD in holy attire.
    Tremble before him, all the earth;
say among the nations: The LORD is king.
    He governs the peoples with equity.

R̂. Proclaim his marvelous deeds to all the nations.

SECOND READING

1 Cor 12:4-11

Brothers and sisters:
There are different kinds of spiritual gifts
        but the same Spirit;
    there are different forms of service but
        the same Lord;
    there are different workings but the
        same God
    who produces all of them in everyone.
To each individual the manifestation of
        the Spirit
    is given for some benefit.
To one is given through the Spirit the
        expression of wisdom;
    to another, the expression of knowledge
        according to the same Spirit;
    to another, faith by the same Spirit;
    to another, gifts of healing by the one
        Spirit;
    to another, mighty deeds;
    to another, prophecy;
    to another, discernment of spirits;
    to another, varieties of tongues;
    to another, interpretation of tongues.
But one and the same Spirit produces all
        of these,
    distributing them individually to each
        person as he wishes.

About Liturgy

Ordinary Time: After weeks of celebrating, it seems as though the Church knows and expresses in the rhythm of her liturgical year that we are ready to get on with our journey toward salvation. We are ready to let go of the exuberance of festivity and begin to follow through with the demands of the festal season: living as Jesus did. Ordinary Time leads us through a Gospel journey with Jesus (during this year C we read from Luke's Gospel), through his public ministry to his death and resurrection. This liturgical journey symbolizes our life journey as Christians.

This gospel of the wedding feast at Cana is associated with the celebration of Epiphany in the Eastern Church and has strong baptismal overtones. Even at this placement in the Western Lectionary (separate from Epiphany and the Baptism of the Lord), the feast can still speak to us about our baptism. In the gospel selection for this Sunday Jesus inaugurates his public ministry. Baptism is our own "inauguration" of our public ministry and an ongoing expression of our belief in and commitment to Jesus. It is our public avowal to make Jesus the very center of our lives. Baptism leads us into the task of Ordinary Time: to walk with Jesus through death to resurrection.

About Liturgical Music

Cantor preparation: You can only sing about the saving acts of God if you recognize them. Sometimes these saving acts come in extraordinary ways, but most often they come in the quiet events of ordinary, everyday living. The trick is to see them so that you can believe. Be on the lookout this week for how Christ will turn the ordinary water of your life into the wine of salvation.

Service music for Ordinary Time: The purpose of liturgical music is not to entertain us but to help us surrender to the transforming action of the liturgy. During Ordinary Time the liturgy pulls us into the paschal mystery journey of ongoing Christian living. The liturgical music we sing during this period is meant to help us deepen our understanding of and participation in that journey. For this we need music which is ritually consistent rather than constantly changing. We need, for example, to sing the same service music—from the gospel acclamation to the *Lamb of God*—throughout these weeks between the end of the Christmas season and the beginning of Lent. Only then will we find ourselves singing this music with increasing intentionality and deepening intensity.

SPIRITUALITY

Gospel   Luke 1:1-4; 4:14-21; L69C

Since many have undertaken to compile
a narrative of the events
that have been fulfilled among us,
just as those who were eyewitnesses
from the beginning
and ministers of the word have
handed them down to us,
I too have decided,
after investigating everything
accurately anew,
to write it down in an orderly
sequence for you,
most excellent Theophilus,
so that you may realize the
certainty of the teachings
you have received.

Jesus returned to Galilee in the
power of the Spirit,
and news of him spread
throughout the whole region.
He taught in their synagogues and
was praised by all.

He came to Nazareth, where he had
grown up,
and went according to his custom
into the synagogue on the sabbath day.
He stood up to read and was handed a
scroll of the prophet Isaiah.
He unrolled the scroll and found the
passage where it was written:
The Spirit of the Lord is upon me,
because he has anointed me
to bring glad tidings to the poor.
He has sent me to proclaim liberty to
captives
and recovery of sight to the blind,
to let the oppressed go free,
and to proclaim a year acceptable
to the Lord.
Rolling up the scroll, he handed it back
to the attendant and sat down,
and the eyes of all in the synagogue
looked intently at him.
He said to them,
"Today this Scripture passage is
fulfilled in your hearing."

Reflecting on the Gospel

"Sticks and stones may break my bones, but words will never hurt me." Really? Experience tells us that words have incredible power, and they can hurt—deeply and lastingly. Children can sometimes taunt or make fun of the playmate who doesn't quite fit in or measure up, often ostracizing him or her. The words of breaking up with a steady girl or boyfriend can sear deeply and throw the adolescent tender about relationships into a tailspin of moodiness. Negative gossip can cost adults their good reputation. Angry words can irreparably damage relationships. Cutting, sarcastic, smug words can demean another. Words can and do hurt.

Words can also bring comfort and joy. They can heal and nourish spiritually and emotionally. Encouraging words can bring success to those faltering in a task. Words of praise lift the self-esteem of not just children but adults as well. Words of beauty couched in poetry or sublime prose immortalize our deepest sense of worth and reality, heroes, or heroic actions. Words can provide moral guidance as well as a challenge to mend one's ways. Words can bring laughter and joy, lightness and humor, meaning and understanding. But for all our experience with our own words, we are not prepared for the Good News announced by Jesus' word.

The public proclamation of God's word described in the first reading is a tradition which sustained Israel's life and identity. Jesus stands in that tradition by turning to Scripture to inaugurate his ministry and announce his identity. This word prepares us for something entirely new happening: "Today . . . Scripture . . . is fulfilled in [our] hearing."

Jesus is in the synagogue in his hometown of Nazareth. Here is his place of origin. Here is the place where he first learned his Scriptures. Here is where he first lived out the will of God. Here is where he turns to Scripture to describe his identity. Here is where he rehearses his mission. The Isaian prophecy read by Jesus proclaims a vision of a world God has long desired—a world of freedom and wholeness. The Good News ("glad tidings") is that God's desire is being fulfilled *now* in Jesus. We, too, are called to bring God's vision to fulfillment in our service of the poor, the oppressed, and those in need. The Word of God is given for the life of the community.

Jesus' ministry is shaped by God's word. And it is a ministry which turns his society upside down. The poor become rich in God's word and delight in it. The confined and oppressed go free. The sightless see. This is resurrection. This is salvation. This is the fruit of God's word.

Living the Paschal Mystery

We are all familiar with the power of words to shape our identity and way of life. Society offers conflicting messages which often pull us in many directions. In the midst of all these competing words, God's word is the true source of our identity as Christian people.

As the Lukan community received Jesus' teachings, so have we. Our ministry? Transpose Jesus' teachings from words on a page to a way of living. Who are the poor, the captives, the sightless in our midst? How is our word Jesus' word that "is fulfilled in [our] hearing"? Do our lives bear out our own certainty about the "teachings [we] have received"? Christian living is none other than taking God's word and making it concrete by the very way we live.

Focusing the Gospel

Key words and phrases: glad tidings, liberty, recovery, fulfilled

To the point: The Isaian prophecy read by Jesus proclaims a vision of a world God has long desired—a world of freedom and wholeness. The good news ("glad tidings") is that God's desire is being fulfilled *now* in Jesus. We, too, bring God's vision to fulfillment in our service of the poor, the oppressed, and those in need.

Connecting the Gospel

to the first reading: The public proclamation of God's word described in the first reading is a tradition which sustained Israel's life and identity. Jesus stands in that tradition by turning to Scripture to inaugurate his ministry and announce his identity.

to our culture: We are all familiar with the power of words to shape our identity and way of life. Society offers conflicting messages that often pull us in many directions. In the midst of all these competing words, God's word is the true source of our identity as Christian people.

Understanding Scripture

God's word: When the Israelites returned to Judah after exile, they found their Temple and their land in ruins. After almost three generations in a foreign land, their religious, national, and ethnic identity had been weakened. To meet the challenge of reconstituting the people, Ezra the priest initiated a reform. He recognized that the destruction of Jerusalem and the exile of the people were the deserved punishment for infidelity. To avoid such punishment in the future, it was essential that "all the people" hear, understand, and observe the Law. And so it is that the refounding of the nation begins in earnest when Ezra, in this Sunday's first reading, assembles the community and reads to all the people the Law "from daybreak till midday." The Law which God had given Moses henceforth becomes the defining feature of Judaism, the cornerstone of their national and religious identity, the center of their individual and corporate lives.

This Sunday's gospel recounts the first event of Jesus' public ministry that Luke records in detail. Jesus begins by teaching in the synagogue on a Sabbath, tacitly affirming three basic institutions of Judaism: Sabbath, Scripture, and synagogue worship. The community had gathered to hear God's word recorded in the Law and the Prophets and Jesus chooses a passage from Isaiah 61:1-2. Jesus thus stays the course set out earlier by Ezra. As Ezra had read from God's word in his own day, Jesus also reads from the sacred texts and announces that the ancient prophecy is fulfilled "today . . . in your hearing." Thus, the prophet whom Isaiah described as the "anointed" (which in Greek is *Christos*) is now present in Jesus who brings "glad tidings to the poor," "liberty to captives," "sight to the blind," "and freedom to the oppressed." The word of God, whether expressed in the Law proclaimed by Ezra or the prophecies fulfilled by Jesus, is a sign of God's active and redeeming presence in the life of God's people. God's word, described as good news and glad tidings, is the basis of the life of Israel and the starting point of the ministry of Jesus.

ASSEMBLY & FAITH-SHARING GROUPS

- Biblical stories or passages which best describe my Christian living are . . .
- The Isaian prophecy read by Jesus is being fulfilled through me whenever I . . .
- Where my faith community needs to improve in order to advance the Isaian prophecy selected by Jesus is . . .

PRESIDERS

Like Jesus, I find and nurture my identity and mission in God's word by . . .

DEACONS

I embody Jesus' "glad tidings" for the disadvantaged by . . .

HOSPITALITY MINISTERS

Ways I assist the assembly to hear the proclaimed Scriptures are . . .

MUSIC MINISTERS

In this gospel we encounter a Jesus deeply formed by the word of God: he knew who he was because he studied, prayed, and lived the Scriptures. My study of the word of God helps me know who I am as a music minister by . . .

ALTAR MINISTERS

My serving at the altar-table places a demand upon me to serve the needy of the world because . . .

LECTORS

My daily living is a genuine interpretation of God's word for others (see first reading) whenever I . . .

EXTRAORDINARY MINISTERS OF HOLY COMMUNION

Eating and drinking the Food of Christ *drives* me to serve the needy because . . .

Model Act of Penitence

Presider: Jesus inaugurates his public ministry by announcing liberty and wholeness for all. Let us prepare ourselves to hear this good news . . . [pause]

> Lord Jesus, you heal the sick: Lord . . .
>
> Christ Jesus, you free the oppressed: Christ . . .
>
> Lord Jesus, you are glad tidings to the poor: Lord . . .

Appreciating the Responsorial Psalm

The whole of Psalm 19 is a prayer in which the psalmist declares the beauty and trustworthiness of God's Law, then prays that "the words of my mouth and the thought of my heart" find favor with God. The psalmist is asking God to keep him faithful to the Law.

In other words, the psalmist prays that what he thinks and speaks be as trustworthy as God's own word. The gospel gives us an example *par excellence* of One whose word is true and whose actions match his speech. What Jesus proclaims before the community, he has come to do. Truly in him the word of God is made flesh. May we who hear this Word weep and rejoice (first reading).

Model General Intercessions

Presider: God desires our freedom and wholeness. In Jesus let us make known our needs.

Response:

Lord,—— hear our prayer.

Cantor:

we pray to the Lord,

That the Church faithfully proclaim the good news of Jesus . . . [pause]

That leaders of the world work tirelessly to establish justice for the poor and oppressed . . . [pause]

That those unjustly bound be freed . . . [pause]

That each of us listen attentively to God's word and live it . . . [pause]

Presider: O saving God, your word is Spirit and life: hear these our prayers that your desire for our salvation may be fulfilled. We ask this through that same Christ our Lord. **Amen.**

ALTERNATIVE OPENING PRAYER

Let us pray

Pause for silent prayer

Almighty Father,
the love you offer
always exceeds the furthest expression of
    our human longing,
for you are greater than the human heart.
Direct each thought, each effort of our life,
so that the limits of our faults and
    weaknesses
may not obscure the vision of your glory
or keep us from the peace you have
    promised.
We ask this through Christ our Lord.
    Amen.

FIRST READING
Neh 8:2-4a, 5-6, 8-10

Ezra the priest brought the law before the
    assembly,
    which consisted of men, women,
    and those children old enough to
        understand.
Standing at one end of the open place that
        was before the Water Gate,
    he read out of the book from daybreak
        till midday,
    in the presence of the men, the women,
    and those children old enough to
        understand;
    and all the people listened attentively to
        the book of the law.
Ezra the scribe stood on a wooden
        platform
    that had been made for the occasion.
He opened the scroll
    so that all the people might see it
    —for he was standing higher up than
        any of the people—;
    and, as he opened it, all the people rose.
Ezra blessed the LORD, the great God,
    and all the people, their hands raised
        high, answered,
    "Amen, amen!"
Then they bowed down and prostrated
        themselves before the LORD,
    their faces to the ground.
Ezra read plainly from the book of the law
        of God,
    interpreting it so that all could
        understand what was read.
Then Nehemiah, that is, His Excellency,
        and Ezra the priest-scribe
    and the Levites who were instructing
        the people
    said to all the people:
    "Today is holy to the LORD your God.

Do not be sad, and do not weep"—
for all the people were weeping as they
heard the words of the law.
He said further: "Go, eat rich foods and
drink sweet drinks,
and allot portions to those who had
nothing prepared;
for today is holy to our LORD.
Do not be saddened this day,
for rejoicing in the LORD must be your
strength!"

RESPONSORIAL PSALM

Ps 19:8, 9, 10, 15

R̸. (cf. John 6:63c) Your words, Lord, are
Spirit and life.

The law of the LORD is perfect,
refreshing the soul;
the decree of the LORD is trustworthy,
giving wisdom to the simple.

R̸. Your words, Lord, are Spirit and life.

The precepts of the LORD are right,
rejoicing the heart;
the command of the LORD is clear,
enlightening the eye.

R̸. Your words, Lord, are Spirit and life.

The fear of the LORD is pure,
enduring forever;
the ordinances of the LORD are true,
all of them just.

R̸. Your words, Lord, are Spirit and life.

Let the words of my mouth and the
thought of my heart
find favor before you,
O LORD, my rock and my redeemer.

R̸. Your words, Lord, are Spirit and life.

SECOND READING

1 Cor 12:12-30

Brothers and sisters:
As a body is one though it has many parts,
and all the parts of the body, though
many, are one body,
so also Christ.
For in one Spirit we were all baptized into
one body,
whether Jews or Greeks, slaves or free
persons,
and we were all given to drink of one
Spirit.

Continued in Appendix A, p. 267.

About Liturgy

Importance of the Liturgy of the Word: One of the most significant liturgical reforms since Vatican II has been to restore a Liturgy of the Word to every celebration of a sacrament (see SC no. 24). This underscores the relationship of word to sacrament. It also says that the context for God's work of salvation in and among the people is always the efficacious word of God proclaimed. The Liturgy of the Word, then, at Sunday Mass is hardly a preamble so that the assembly can get to the "good part," Communion. The word is the context and Communion is the response. Further, Christ is present in the word proclaimed (see SC no. 7). In the Liturgy of the Word, then, we celebrate a presence of Christ just as we do in the Liturgy of the Eucharist.

Just as this Sunday's gospel passage quoting the prophet Isaiah is challenging to us—we, too, are sent to "proclaim liberty to captives and recovery of sight to the blind, and let the oppressed go free"—so is this true for every proclamation of the word. There is always challenge there to hear God in a new way, to discern afresh how we are to respond in our daily living, and to examine the fruitfulness of our responses. For us God's word must become as "rich foods and . . . sweet drinks"; thus we already share in an abundance of ways in the Lord's table.

About Liturgical Music

Cantor preparation: Only one who lives according to the Law of God can sing about the joy and wisdom that Law brings. How does God's Law shape your everyday attitudes and actions—toward family members? others at work? neighbors? strangers on the street?

The gospel acclamation: Both the first reading and the gospel this Sunday present occasions when the word of God is being proclaimed in the midst of the community. This makes a good opportunity to examine the meaning and importance of the gospel acclamation.

Whereas we remain seated during the proclamation of the first and second readings, we stand for the proclamation of the gospel and we greet this proclamation by singing the acclamation. By singing this acclamation we greet the person of Christ made present among us in the proclamation of the gospel. We acclaim our belief that he is the One who is addressing us. The accompanying verse sung by cantor or choir is usually taken from the gospel text and acts as an invitation that we open our hearts truly to hear what will be proclaimed and let ourselves be transformed by it (like a "liturgical *hors d'oeuvre*" offered to whet our appetites for the meat to come). The most suitable gesture during the acclamation is to turn the body toward the Book of the Gospels as it is carried to the ambo.

SPIRITUALITY

Gospel Luke 4:21-30; L72C

Jesus began speaking in the
  synagogue, saying:
  "Today this Scripture
    passage is fulfilled in
    your hearing."
And all spoke highly of him
  and were amazed at the
    gracious words that
    came from his mouth.
They also asked, "Isn't this
  the son of Joseph?"
He said to them, "Surely you will quote
  me this proverb,
  'Physician, cure yourself,' and say,
  'Do here in your native place
  the things that we heard were done
    in Capernaum.'"
And he said, "Amen, I say to you,
  no prophet is accepted in his own
    native place.
Indeed, I tell you,
  there were many widows in Israel in
    the days of Elijah
  when the sky was closed for three
    and a half years
  and a severe famine spread over the
    entire land.
It was to none of these that Elijah was
    sent,
  but only to a widow in Zarephath in
    the land of Sidon.
Again, there were many lepers in Israel
  during the time of Elisha the
    prophet;
  yet not one of them was cleansed, but
    only Naaman the Syrian."
When the people in the synagogue
    heard this,
  they were all filled with fury.
They rose up, drove him out of the
    town,
  and led him to the brow of the hill
  on which their town had been built,
  to hurl him down headlong.
But Jesus passed through the midst of
  them and went away.

Reflecting on the Gospel

Hitler was said to have mesmerized people with his compelling words. He was a charismatic leader who rallied a whole nation around him. And he killed six million Jews. Martin Luther King, Jr. also mesmerized people with his visionary words. He was a charismatic speaker who rallied a subjected race to claim their

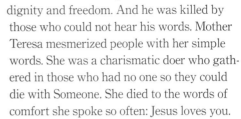

dignity and freedom. And he was killed by those who could not hear his words. Mother Teresa mesmerized people with her simple words. She was a charismatic doer who gathered in those who had no one so they could die with Someone. She died to the words of comfort she spoke so often: Jesus loves you.

The power of words to move people can hardly be disputed. We know they can stir up hate and violence as well as love and gentleness. Truly the word of God is a two-edged sword. Those who proclaim it (Jeremiah and Jesus in this Sunday's readings) must remain steadfast even when resisted and rejected. Those who hear it must be open to a new understanding of God who works for the salvation of all ("the nations," "Sidon," Syria). We are both proclaimers and hearers and the sword cuts us both ways.

In the prophetic tradition Jeremiah is the classic example of the rejected prophet. Jeremiah contrasts the tenderness and protection of God toward those who faithfully hear God's word and the inevitable resistance that God's word wells up in those who cannot or will not hear its message of challenge and salvation. God's word inevitably stirs up conflict. Just as inevitably, it is a word of deliverance.

Jesus understood his own prophetic role as one which would lead to rejection and, ultimately, death. When he spoke "gracious words" his message "amazed" his hearers and his message was accepted. But when he spoke challenging words, his hearers were "filled with fury." Ultimately, God's words not only lead to a new understanding of God and God's ways of bringing salvation to all, but they also lead to a new understanding of ourselves and where we are on our saving journey. When God's words satisfy us, we are faced with the goodness in ourselves and how we are already responding to God. When God's words make demands on us, we are faced with new ways we must die to ourselves in order to become better disciples. Truly the word of God is a two-edged sword, always leading us to salvation.

Living the Paschal Mystery

All of us struggle to hear and respond to God's word in our lives. This Sunday we are confronted with the reality that we are not always going to like what we hear in God's word. God's word always takes us beyond where we are (or where we want to go). It is the very word which questions our status quo and asks us to give up our own wills and embrace God's will. It is the very word which nudges us to surrender ourselves and our own small world to encompass the larger vision of a world in which God assures that all are met with love and dignity.

In our desire to be accepted, how readily we adjust what we say to what our audience will accept! Announcing the message of the gospel is not undertaken for the sake of being accepted but in order to be faithful to God's word. And, as those baptized into Christ's death and resurrection, being faithful to God's word always means dying to self for the sake of others.

Focusing the Gospel

Key words and phrases: Jesus, saying, gracious words, no prophet is accepted, widow in . . . Sidon, Naaman the Syrian, heard this, filled with fury, drove him out

To the point: Truly the word of God is a two-edged sword. Those who proclaim it (Jeremiah and Jesus) must remain steadfast even when resisted and rejected. Those who hear it must be open to a new understanding of God who works for the salvation of all ("the nations," "Sidon," Syria). We are both proclaimers and hearers and the sword cuts us both ways.

Connecting the Gospel

to the first reading: In the prophetic tradition Jeremiah is the classic example of the rejected prophet. Jesus understood his prophetic role as one which would lead to rejection and, ultimately, death.

to our culture: In our desire to be accepted, how readily we adjust what we say to what our audience will accept. Announcing the message of the gospel is not undertaken for the sake of being accepted but in order to be faithful to God's word.

Understanding Scripture

Persecuted preachers of the word: The "gracious words" of Jesus find a chilly reception in his hometown. Apparently, the people have heard that Jesus had done great things in Capernaum, a town with a large non-Jewish population. It is for this reason that Jesus defends his actions there with references to Elijah and Elisha, both of whom had ministered to non-Jews, namely to the Sidonian widow of Zarephath (1 Kings 17:8-14) and Naaman the Syrian (2 Kings 5:1-19). These references to Israel's own history imply that the Jews should have been able to recognize in the ministry of Jesus the continuation of God's favor for all people, evidenced earlier in the covenant with Noah (Gen 9), and the election of Abraham as a mediator of blessing for all peoples (Gen 12:1-3).

The outreach to Gentiles first by Jesus, and later by the Church, results in conflicts with the authorities. In the gospel, this conflict will escalate to the crucifixion; in Acts of the Apostles, the Church will make a definitive break with the Jews because of its mission to the Gentiles. Luke anticipates these developments in a solemn saying of Jesus, "no prophet is accepted in his native place." To find a hearing, Jesus and the Church will have to move beyond their "hometown crowd."

This theme of the rejected prophet is found fully developed in Nehemiah 9:26-31. Basically, God sends a prophet; the people reject or kill the prophet; God punishes the people but shows mercy in sending another prophet whom the people again reject. Appropriately, the first reading is the call of Jeremiah—himself a much rejected prophet—which includes divine provision for strength against rejection: Jeremiah will be like a fortified city, an iron pillar, a brass wall able to stand against the whole land. God's final words to Jeremiah ("They will fight against you, but not prevail over you, for I am with you to deliver you") apply perfectly to Jesus. Indeed, this Sunday's gospel ends in just this way, with the townsfolk ready to hurl Jesus over the hill, but he manages to escape.

ASSEMBLY & FAITH-SHARING GROUPS
- The prophetic words of Jesus which amaze me and which I embrace wholeheartedly are . . .
- The prophetic words of Jesus which are upsetting and which I am resisting are . . .
- I am sustained in living Jesus' words, especially when they are countercultural, by . . .

PRESIDERS
Times when I have preached "less than" the gospel are . . . because . . .

DEACONS
Where Jesus' prophetic word is challenging how I minister is . . .

HOSPITALITY MINISTERS
Ways I might assist the assembly to ready themselves for a challenging word of God are . . .

MUSIC MINISTERS
This gospel reading reveals that God's word is a two-edged sword. As a music minister, I am comforted by God's word when . . . God's word challenges me as a music minister when . . .

ALTAR MINISTERS
I serve the prophetic word by . . .

LECTORS
Some ways I reconcile within myself proclaiming a word which demands more of me than I am willing to live are . . .

EXTRAORDINARY MINISTERS OF HOLY COMMUNION
The Eucharistic banquet is a prophetic challenge in that . . .

Model Act of Penitence

Presider: God speaks a challenging word to us. Let us reflect on when and how God speaks to us in our lives and our response to God's word . . . [pause]

Lord Jesus, you are the prophet to the nations: Lord . . .

Christ Jesus, you are the divine physician who heals us: Christ . . .

Lord Jesus, you grant us salvation: Lord . . .

Appreciating the Responsorial Psalm

Like Jesus (gospel) and Jeremiah (first reading), we are sent to proclaim salvation to the world. Like Jesus and Jeremiah, we will meet opposition, persecution, even death as we fulfill this mission. But the psalm promises we shall be protected even as we are persecuted, for the one who has loved us since before our birth will be our salvation. The psalm invites us to fulfill our mission, fully conscious of the suffering it will bring, but equally conscious of the salvation which has been promised beyond that suffering. This is not a psalm which we sing naively, but with hope-filled realism. And Jesus sings with us.

Model General Intercessions

Presider: God is our rock of refuge, our stronghold. In confidence we bring our needs to him.

Response:

Lord,—— hear our prayer.

Cantor:

we pray to the Lord,

That all members of the Church boldly speak God's word . . . [pause]

That all world leaders be guided by God's word to truth and justice . . . [pause]

That those persecuted for announcing God's word may be upheld and delivered . . . [pause]

That we here gathered may boldly speak and live God's word . . . [pause]

Presider: Almighty God, your word brings life: hear these our prayers and lead us to everlasting life. We ask this through Christ our Lord. **Amen.**

OPENING PRAYER

Let us pray

Pause for silent prayer

Lord our God,
help us to love you with all our hearts
and to love all men as you love them.

Grant this through our Lord Jesus Christ,
    your Son,
who lives and reigns with you and the
    Holy Spirit,
one God, for ever and ever. **Amen.**

FIRST READING

Jer 1:4-5, 17-19

The word of the LORD came to me, saying:
    Before I formed you in the womb I knew
        you,
    before you were born I dedicated you,
    a prophet to the nations I appointed you.

    But do you gird your loins;
        stand up and tell them
        all that I command you.
    Be not crushed on their account,
        as though I would leave you crushed
            before them;
    for it is I this day
        who have made you a fortified city,
    a pillar of iron, a wall of brass,
        against the whole land:
    against Judah's kings and princes,
        against its priests and people.
    They will fight against you but not
        prevail over you,
        for I am with you to deliver you, says
            the LORD.

RESPONSORIAL PSALM

Ps 71:1-2, 3-4, 5-6, 15, 17

R̷. (cf. 15ab) I will sing of your salvation.

In you, O LORD, I take refuge;
    let me never be put to shame.
In your justice rescue me, and deliver me;
    incline your ear to me, and save me.

R̷. I will sing of your salvation.

Be my rock of refuge,
    a stronghold to give me safety,
        for you are my rock and my fortress.
O my God, rescue me from the hand of the
        wicked.

R̷. I will sing of your salvation.

For you are my hope, O LORD;
   my trust, O God, from my youth.
On you I depend from birth;
   from my mother's womb you are my
      strength.

℞. I will sing of your salvation.

My mouth shall declare your justice,
   day by day your salvation.
O God, you have taught me from my
      youth,
   and till the present I proclaim your
      wondrous deeds.

℞. I will sing of your salvation.

SECOND READING
1 Cor 12:31–13:13

Brothers and sisters:
Strive eagerly for the greatest spiritual
      gifts.
But I shall show you a still more excellent
      way.

If I speak in human and angelic tongues,
   but do not have love,
   I am a resounding gong or a clashing
      cymbal.
And if I have the gift of prophecy,
   and comprehend all mysteries and all
      knowledge;
   if I have all faith so as to move
      mountains,
   but do not have love, I am nothing.
If I give away everything I own,
   and if I hand my body over so that I
      may boast,
   but do not have love, I gain nothing.

Love is patient, love is kind.
It is not jealous, it is not pompous,
   it is not inflated, it is not rude,
   it does not seek its own interests,
   it is not quick-tempered, it does not
      brood over injury,
   it does not rejoice over wrongdoing
   but rejoices with the truth.
It bears all things, believes all things,
      hopes all things, endures all things.
Love never fails.
If there are prophecies, they will be
      brought to nothing;
   if tongues, they will cease;
   if knowledge, it will be brought to
      nothing.

Continued in Appendix A, p. 268.

About Liturgy

Liturgy and words: There is always a danger that we speak so many words at liturgies, they fall on unhearing ears. There must be a right balance between the words, gestures, and symbols of the liturgy. For this reason, great care must be taken that we don't add many extra words, even in those places where they are permitted. For example, introductions are best kept short and simple. Further, although brief descriptions of the readings are permitted to be given before the proclamation in order to help people listen better (see GIRM no. 31), this practice runs a high risk of constraining God's word. Finally, God's word spoken in liturgy is proclamation, not didactic teaching; it is encounter rather than explanation.

Another problematic area concerns announcements. Although announcements are permitted "if they are necessary" (see GIRM no. 90), too many parishes still read most of the upcoming week's events already listed on the parish bulletin. Examples of "necessary" announcements would include mentioning approaching funerals which were scheduled after the bulletin was printed (but not other pertinent information such as visitation times; that can be handled on a parish bulletin board), or anything else for the coming week which didn't get printed in the bulletin.

The placement of announcements is also critical. Structurally, the announcements belong to the concluding rites. They are made after the Communion prayer but before the presider's greeting and blessing. The place for the announcements is not the ambo but some other place, for example, the cantor stand.

About Liturgical Music

Cantor preparation: The confidence of this psalm is perfect counterbalance to the reality of persecution spoken of in both first reading and gospel. If you choose to be faithful to the mission you share with Christ, you will know rejection. But you will also know in an ever-deepening way the intimate presence of the God who guides and protects you. Are you willing to take the risk?

Music suggestions: A number of songs capture the struggle with God's word which this Sunday's gospel exemplifies. "Good News" [LMGM, G2, GC, GC2, RS] is based on the gospel and speaks of Jesus as the fulfillment of Isaiah's prophecy of good news for the needy, of the opposition Jesus met, and of his refusal to flee his mission no matter what the cost. Its dancing and joyful Ethiopian melody would work well at the presentation of the gifts, or as a hymn of praise after Communion. "Praise to You, O Christ, Our Savior" [CBW3, G2, GC, GC2, JS2, RS] is a hymn of praise to Christ the Word who calls, leads, and teaches us. It would work well as an entrance hymn, and can be sung either responsorially between cantor/choir and assembly, or in direct fashion by everyone. The text of "God Has Spoken by His Prophets" [HG, JS2, PMB, RS, WC, W3] progresses from "God has spoken by his prophets . . ." to "God has spoken by Christ Jesus . . ." to "God is speaking by his Spirit . . ." This strong text and tune would suit the entrance procession.

SPIRITUALITY

Gospel

Luke 5:1-11; L75C

While the crowd was pressing in on Jesus
and listening to the word of God,
he was standing by the Lake of
Gennesaret.
He saw two boats there alongside the
lake;
the fishermen had disembarked and
were washing their nets.
Getting into one of the boats, the one
belonging to Simon,
he asked him to put out a short
distance from the shore.
Then he sat down and taught the
crowds from the boat.
After he had finished speaking, he said
to Simon,
"Put out into deep water and lower
your nets for a catch."
Simon said in reply,
"Master, we have worked hard all
night and have caught nothing,
but at your command I will lower the
nets."
When they had done this, they caught a
great number of fish
and their nets were tearing.
They signaled to their partners in the
other boat
to come to help them.
They came and filled both boats
so that the boats were in danger of
sinking.
When Simon Peter saw this, he fell at
the knees of Jesus and said,
"Depart from me, Lord, for I am a
sinful man."
For astonishment at the catch of fish
they had made seized him
and all those with him,
and likewise James and John, the sons
of Zebedee,
who were partners of Simon.
Jesus said to Simon, "Do not be afraid;
from now on you will be catching men."
When they brought their boats to the
shore,
they left everything and followed him.

Reflecting on the Gospel

We might surmise that Simon Peter in this Sunday's gospel is an experienced fisherman. He's been at this awhile. He knows his business. And this particular night wasn't a good night for fishing! All night at work, no results. The first part of Simon Peter's response to Jesus' imperative to go back out and lower the nets is, therefore, quite understandable to us. We might paraphrase Peter's response as something like "been there, done that; it's a bad night for fishing; it would be a waste of time." It's the second part of the response that's surprising: "but at your command I will lower the nets."

At the ensuing great catch, Peter declares himself for what he is: "a sinful man," one who has less than pure motives, one who has doubts and misgivings. Jesus assures him ("Do not be afraid") and calls him to discipleship. Peter's response? He left everything. Immediately. This gospel account aptly illustrates that Jesus' self-revelation takes place through the ordinary circumstances of life, is a personal encounter, and helps us overcome our fears and respond in hope.

The first reading captures a common expectation that God appears to religious people (the prophet Isaiah) in holy places (a temple). But the gospel assures us that the call of God also comes to sinful people (Peter) and in unexpected places (boats). The call depends not on the individual or the place, but on the graciousness of God. God initiates the call. In both calls Isaiah's and Peter's responses came as a consequence of a theophany—God makes divine presence known (in the vision of the heavenly hosts praising God, in the large catch of fish). Hearing and answering God's call is a matter of encountering and responding to God's divine presence to us.

Both the first reading and gospel also make clear that while God is present to us and calls us, our freedom is respected—God truly does give us a choice about answering the call. In the first reading God asks, "Whom shall I send?" In the gospel Jesus merely announces, "from now on you will be catching men." In both cases Isaiah and Peter were free to respond or not. Such is divine graciousness—God calls, but in the divine encounter gives us the strength and grace to respond. How can we not answer, "send me!"

Living the Paschal Mystery

If we pay attention to details in this gospel beyond the immediate call and response events, we might be caught by surprise. Too often we feel the burden of discipleship is solely on our own shoulders. The gospel depicts Jesus initiating the call—he comes to Peter at his boat; he invites Peter to follow. Our discipleship rests upon Jesus long before we begin to follow. The surprise of the gospel is that we are never alone when we hear and follow God's call; divine Presence always abides within us and enables us both to answer the call and remain faithful to it.

God meets people where they are. Sinfulness isn't a stumbling block to following God's call. We simply go deeper, beyond our sinfulness, to hear God call each of us (because of our baptism) to discipleship. In spite of our objections, God gently and persistently says to each of us, "You're still the one I want." Like Isaiah and Peter, we are invited to be overwhelmed by God's graciousness and self-revelation and answer, "send me!"

Focusing the Gospel

Key words and phrases: Jesus, boats, sinful man, from now on you will be, left everything and followed him

To the point: The first reading captures a common expectation that God appears to religious people (a prophet) in holy places (a temple). But the call of God also comes to sinful people (Peter) and in unexpected places (boats). The call depends not on the individual or the place, but on the graciousness of God. And this is truly good news for us.

Connecting the Gospel

to the last two Sundays: In the gospels of the last two Sundays, Jesus is sent to bring "glad tidings to the poor" (third Sunday), both to Jews and Gentiles (fourth Sunday). Disciples are called by Jesus for the same mission.

to religious experience: Too often we feel the burden of discipleship is solely on our own shoulders. The gospel depicts Jesus initiating the call—he comes to Peter at his boat; he invites Peter to follow. Our discipleship rests upon Jesus long before we begin to follow.

Understanding Scripture

Divine call, human response: The Lectionary omits Luke's accounts of an exorcism, the healing of Peter's mother-in-law, and the evening-time healings. In Mark's gospel, all these things happened after Jesus had called his first disciples. But Luke places these events *before* the call of the first disciples (this Sunday's gospel); in this way, the disciples have some evidence on which they can decide whether or not to follow Jesus. The call of the first disciples, which takes place as they are at work, is paired with the call of Isaiah.

Isaiah's vision in the first reading is a classic Old Testament theophany, or appearance of God. One of the most dramatic accounts of God's appearance is to the prophet Moses on Mount Sinai. God's appearance is accompanied by an earthquake, lightning, and smoke (Exod 19:16-19). The prophet Isaiah is in the Temple in Jerusalem. In his vision of the heavenly throne room, these elements are represented by shaking doorposts, fire ("seraphim" literally means "burning ones"), and smoke. While Isaiah cannot see God directly, he does see a lofty throne and the train of God's garment. Isaiah's response characterizes a human encounter with the divine: he is filled with fear—"I am doomed"—and with an overwhelming recognition of his sinfulness in the presence of the all-holy God. One of the seraphim purges Isaiah of his sin and then Isaiah is sent as a prophet to the people.

The gospel episode is presented as an encounter between the human and the divine. Although the setting is not the Temple or the mountain of God, and although Peter is a fisherman, not a prophet, this human encounter with the divine has some of the same key elements found in Isaiah's call story: Peter is overcome with fear ("Do not be afraid"), and overwhelmed by his own sinfulness ("depart from me, Lord, for I am a sinful man"). Despite human sinfulness, Jesus calls Peter to discipleship and sends him to be a fisher of people. Being a disciple depends not on personal worthiness or qualifications, but solely on the call of God.

ASSEMBLY & FAITH-SHARING GROUPS

- What is most unexpected about God's calling me is . . .
- What God's call of me reveals about God's Self is . . .
- Some of my excuses for not accepting God's call are . . .

PRESIDERS

Some ways I help others to cast their reflection into the deep waters of daily living so as to hear God's call are . . .

DEACONS

My daily living announces God's call to others whenever I . . .

HOSPITALITY MINISTERS

When I see my welcoming care as a ministry rather than as a job, then my hospitality is like . . .

MUSIC MINISTERS

I am most aware of God's having called me to the ministry of music when . . . When I am aware of my inadequacies, I feel God strengthening me by . . .

ALTAR MINISTERS

Serving at the altar demands that I also serve God's call in the lives of others because . . .

LECTORS

Whenever I "press in on Jesus" in order to "listen to the word of God," my proclamation is like . . .

EXTRAORDINARY MINISTERS OF HOLY COMMUNION

The privilege of distributing Holy Communion calls me to . . . in my daily living.

Model Act of Penitence

Presider: God calls each of us in the ordinary circumstances of our everyday lives. Let us reflect on our response to God's call and our willingness to be disciples of Jesus . . . [pause]

> Lord Jesus, you call us to follow you: Lord . . .
>
> Christ Jesus, you replace our fears with hope: Christ . . .
>
> Lord Jesus, you command us to spread the good news of God's reign: Lord . . .

Appreciating the Responsorial Psalm

Encounter with the Holy One, be it the Lord of hosts in heaven (first reading) or Jesus in an ordinary life situation (gospel), is a wake-up call. Individuals are shaken out of their complacency and change the direction of their lives. Both Isaiah and Peter acknowledge their own unholiness, and then find themselves sent on mission. The responsorial psalm reveals more beneath the surface, however. God heard the "words of my mouth" uttered by each individual. God perceived the weakness each felt and replaced it with strength. Supported by such divine initiative, these two readily accept their mission, for they are confident that God "will complete what he has" begun in them.

The Holy One comes to us, too, sometimes in extraordinary ways, most times in the ordinary circumstances of our daily lives. Each time, the Holy One shows us ourselves as we really are, strengthens us, then sends us to continue our baptismal mission. Like Isaiah and Peter, we can give a ready "Send me!" for we know, as does the psalmist, who has begun and who will complete this work in us.

Model General Intercessions

Presider: Jesus says, "Do not be afraid." And so we are encouraged to make our needs known to God.

Response:

Cantor:

That the Church may respond courageously to God's call to preach the good news to all people . . . [pause]

That all people of the world may hear God's call to salvation . . . [pause]

That those who are overcome by a sense of unworthiness may know God's love . . . [pause]

That all of us here may find God and heed God's call in our everyday lives . . . [pause]

Presider: Good and gracious God, you call us before you this day: hear our prayers for we ask this through Christ our Lord. **Amen.**

OPENING PRAYER

Let us pray

Pause for silent prayer

Father,
watch over your family
and keep us safe in your care,
for all our hope is in you.

Grant this through our Lord Jesus Christ,
  your Son,
who lives and reigns with you and the
  Holy Spirit,
one God, for ever and ever. **Amen.**

FIRST READING
Isa 6:1-2a, 3-8

In the year King Uzziah died,
  I saw the Lord seated on a high and
    lofty throne,
  with the train of his garment filling the
    temple.
Seraphim were stationed above.

They cried one to the other,
  "Holy, holy, holy is the LORD of hosts!
All the earth is filled with his glory!"
At the sound of that cry, the frame of the
    door shook
  and the house was filled with smoke.

Then I said, "Woe is me, I am doomed!
For I am a man of unclean lips,
  living among a people of unclean lips;
    yet my eyes have seen the King, the
    LORD of hosts!"
Then one of the seraphim flew to me,
  holding an ember that he had taken
    with tongs from the altar.

He touched my mouth with it, and said,
  "See, now that this has touched your
    lips,
  your wickedness is removed, your sin
    purged."

Then I heard the voice of the Lord saying,
  "Whom shall I send? Who will go for
    us?"
"Here I am," I said; "send me!"

RESPONSORIAL PSALM
Ps 138:1-2, 2-3, 4-5, 7-8

℟. (1c) In the sight of the angels I will sing
your praises, Lord.

I will give thanks to you, O LORD, with all
   my heart,
   for you have heard the words of my
      mouth;
   in the presence of the angels I will sing
      your praise;
I will worship at your holy temple
   and give thanks to your name.

℟. In the sight of the angels I will sing
your praises, Lord.

Because of your kindness and your truth;
   for you have made great above all things
   your name and your promise.
When I called, you answered me;
   you built up strength within me.

℟. In the sight of the angels I will sing
your praises, Lord.

All the kings of the earth shall give
    thanks to you, O LORD,
   when they hear the words of your mouth;
and they shall sing of the ways of the LORD:
   "Great is the glory of the LORD."

℟. In the sight of the angels I will sing
your praises, Lord.

Your right hand saves me.
   The LORD will complete what he has
      done for me;
your kindness, O LORD, endures forever;
   forsake not the work of your hands.

℟. In the sight of the angels I will sing
your praises, Lord.

SECOND READING
1 Cor 15:1-11

I am reminding you, brothers and sisters,
   of the gospel I preached to you,
   which you indeed received and in which
      you also stand.
Through it you are also being saved,
   if you hold fast to the word I preached
      to you,
   unless you believed in vain.
For I handed on to you as of first
    importance what I also received:
   that Christ died for our sins
    in accordance with the Scriptures;
   that he was buried;
   that he was raised on the third day
    in accordance with the Scriptures;
   that he appeared to Cephas, then to the
      Twelve.

Continued in Appendix A, p. 268.

About Liturgy

Parish call and response: The average Catholic parish in North America has fewer than ten percent of its registered members involved in various parish activities. This raises an important question: Do we understand part of the response to our baptismal call is to help build up the Body of Christ? We cannot simply *belong* to a parish; we must be *involved* in its life and ministry. In a general way, Christian discipleship means spreading the good news of Jesus Christ to all those one meets, living an upright life, doing as Jesus would have done. More specifically, each baptized person, as a member of a parish, is called to be involved actively in the affairs of the parish, thus building up the Body of Christ.

Generally, the activity involving the largest number of parishioners is some form of liturgical ministry. In order to keep these ministries from mere "doing" and clearly understanding the liturgical ministries as our response to God's presence and call, we must include a spiritual component in our preparation for the ministry (which is much more than simply practicing "how to"). That is, we must ensure that our liturgical ministers understand that ours is a ministry, not a "job," and that we are called to live the deep meaning of the ministry. For example, lectors must live the word of God (as a two-edged sword) throughout the week before they proclaim the word. Hospitality ministers must practice hospitality in their own homes and inclusivity at church in welcoming others into the community. Extraordinary ministers of Holy Communion must treat all those they meet each day as members of the Body of Christ. By growing in this spiritual dimension of the liturgical ministry we both grow in our awareness of God's abiding presence and in our awareness that our call to serve reaches way beyond the hour or so we spend weekly in church.

About Liturgical Music

Cantor preparation: Your role as cantor is an awesome one. You are not only singing before a large crowd of people, you are leading them in prayer. Such a ministry requires humility and vulnerability. But this Sunday's psalm reminds you that God will accomplish in you what needs to be done. You have only to sing God's praises.

Suggestion for the music director: This Sunday's gospel shows how Jesus meets people where they are and as they are, and then calls them to "put out into deep water." Part of your ministry is to help cantors and choir members go deeper than the surface level of the music to see that they are doing far more than singing acclamations and hymns at Mass; they are enacting the paschal mystery. One way to help them go deeper is to incorporate liturgical pedagogy into your rehearsals. For example, when teaching or reviewing a set of Eucharistic acclamations, pause to point out that the acclamations are exclamations of creed and commitment. Ask them where the acclamations occur in the Mass, and help them explore the meaning of each. Then encourage them to sing these acclamations with the energy of faith.

SPIRITUALITY

Gospel

Luke 6:17, 20-26; L78C

Jesus came down with the Twelve
and stood on a stretch of level ground
with a great crowd of his
disciples
and a large number of
the people
from all Judea and
Jerusalem
and the coastal region of
Tyre and Sidon.
And raising his eyes toward
his disciples he said:
"Blessed are you who are
poor,
for the kingdom of God
is yours.
Blessed are you who are now hungry,
for you will be satisfied.
Blessed are you who are now
weeping,
for you will laugh.
Blessed are you when people hate you,
and when they exclude and insult
you,
and denounce your name as evil
on account of the Son of Man.
Rejoice and leap for joy on that day!
Behold, your reward will be great in
heaven.
For their ancestors treated the
prophets in the same way.
But woe to you who are rich,
for you have received your
consolation.
Woe to you who are filled now,
for you will be hungry.
Woe to you who laugh now,
for you will grieve and weep.
Woe to you when all speak well of
you,
for their ancestors treated the false
prophets in this way."

Reflecting on the Gospel

Among some of Luke's contemporaries there was a presumption that the poor, hungry, and weeping (the oppressed) were outside the venue of God's blessings and graciousness. At the same time, it was believed that those who were wealthy and powerful had been blessed by God. Jesus' sermon corrects these presumptions by teaching that God's blessings are not conditioned by economic or social status but are the free gift of God's graciousness. The only condition for God's blessings is clearly spelled out in the first reading: "trust in the LORD." Similarly, woes are the consequence of those who turn to themselves, "whose heart[s] turn[ ] away from the LORD."

Jesus, following a long biblical tradition, sets up a sharp contrast delineating two ways of life. The first is the "way of the just" (responsorial psalm) which is to "trust in the Lord" (first reading). Those who follow this path are blessed (gospel). The second path in life is the "way of the wicked" (responsorial psalm) which is to "trust in human beings" (first reading). Those who follow this path are cursed (gospel: "woe"). In other words, blessings are "available" according to whether we trust in the Lord and follow God's way.

In the real world of the Good News, blessings are signs that we have recognized that the source of everything is God. We are blessed when we surrender to God, and God alone. The Good News in this gospel is that whether we are rich or poor, oppressed or secure, if we trust in God we are blessed. Blessings are dependent simply upon our trusting in God, our placing ourselves in God's hands. Thus, walking in God's way is a blessed life even if one is poor, hungry, or sorrowful; not walking in God's way is a life of woe even if one is rich, full, or content. There is only one way in which a disciple can walk, and that way is to walk in God's way.

Living the Paschal Mystery

In Luke's community, the radicalness of this Sunday's gospel was to realize that being poor (weeping, hungry) didn't exclude one from God's blessing. Perhaps for us the radicalness of this gospel involves more the question of whether our lives are oriented to God. Luke's audience was concerned with what they thought were the signs of God's blessings. Jesus challenges them and us to be rooted in the source of blessing: God who blesses all those who trust. In this sense, then, this gospel isn't simply about moral imperatives and behaviors (as important as those are). Instead the gospel challenges us to trust in God, keep God at the center of our lives, and recognize that all blessings come from God.

Trusting in God isn't some naive platitude. Nor is trusting in God something we pay lip service to and then go on with our daily living. The reversals in this gospel are startling reminders that what is of this life isn't lasting nor what we ought to be concerned about. Trusting in God is a permeating religious stance ("on account of the Son of Man") such that all the decisions about the kind of living we do emanate from God who is the center of our life. As such, God blesses our life as it is. In whatever circumstances. In whatever happens to us. Then every day we can "rejoice and leap for joy!"

Focusing the Gospel

Key words and phrases: he said, Blessed are, But woe to

To the point: Jesus, following a long biblical tradition, sets up a sharp contrast delineating two ways of life. Walking in God's way is a blessed life even if one is poor, hungry, or sorrowful; not walking in God's way is a life of woe even if one is rich, full, or content. There is only one way in which a disciple can walk.

Connecting the Gospel

to biblical culture: Among some of Luke's contemporaries there was a presumption that the poor, hungry, and weeping were outside the venue of God's blessings and graciousness. Jesus' sermon corrects this presumption by teaching that God's blessings are not conditioned by economic or social status but are the free gift of God's graciousness.

to our culture: In a desire to be inclusive and accepting, we tend to endorse all ways of life as equally valid. Jesus tells us otherwise.

Understanding Scripture

Two paths: This Sunday's passage from Luke is the first of three consecutive Sunday gospels which present the "Sermon on the Plain" (Luke's equivalent to Matthew's more famous "Sermon on the Mount"). It begins with a series of four blessings followed by four corresponding "woes": poor-rich, hungry-filled, weeping-laughing, despised-esteemed. This unexpected reversal of fortune is a favorite Lukan theme already encountered in Mary's *Magnificat:* "He has thrown down the rulers from their thrones but lifted up the lowly. The hungry he has filled with good things; the rich he has sent away empty" (1:52-53). Luke's attention to the "poor" and "hungry" rather than Matthew's "poor in spirit" and "hunger for holiness" cautions us against "spiritualizing" the message.

Luke's Beatitudes evoke Old Testament themes found in two different but related traditions: wisdom's two paths (the way of the wise which is righteousness, and the way of the foolish which is wickedness) and Deuteronomy's retributive justice (the righteous are blessed, the wicked are cursed). Elements from both come together in the first reading from Jeremiah. The prophet presents two paths in life: trust in God which leads to blessing, or trust in humans which leads to curse. Jeremiah's image of the barren and fruitful trees appears in this Sunday's responsorial psalm: the wise find fruitfulness and life in God's Law but the foolish perish.

This is spelled out in Deuteronomy's teaching about "retributive justice." At the risk of oversimplifying, this view held that righteousness brought blessing, wickedness brought woe; the converse could be inferred: a cursed life was due to one's sin while a blessed life was evidence of a righteous life. The conclusion is obvious: the poor are cursed, the wealthy are blessed. Similar notions were also found in Hellenistic religious thought in which "poor" described this wretched earthly life, and "rich" referred to eternal life with God (see also Col 8:9). Thus, Jesus' words, which turned the expected order upside down, must have been shocking. The kingdom which Jesus was inaugurating reversed all common expectations, setting the stage for the greatest reversal of all—death leads to life.

ASSEMBLY & FAITH-SHARING GROUPS

- Walking in God's way means to me . . .
- For me the blessedness of walking in God's way is . . .
- For me the woe of not walking in God's way is . . .

PRESIDERS

God's word is both blessing and woe for me in that . . .

DEACONS

My ministry embodies God's blessings and graciousness to the poor, hungry, and weeping whenever I . . .

HOSPITALITY MINISTERS

I look beyond appearances and reputations and recognize the Source of all blessings in each person I meet and greet by . . .

MUSIC MINISTERS

One way participating in music ministry helps me stay faithful to the way of God is . . . One "blessedness" I experience because of my music ministry is . . .

ALTAR MINISTERS

The blessedness I have found in the poverty of serving others is . . .

LECTORS

I shall reflect upon the difference in my life when I trust in human beings and when I trust in the Lord (see first reading).

EXTRAORDINARY MINISTERS OF HOLY COMMUNION

What helps me stay focused on the *Source* of blessing rather than the *signs* of blessing is . . .

CELEBRATION

Model Act of Penitence

Presider: God meets us with graciousness and blessing. Let us open our hearts to the gift of God's mercy . . . [pause]

Lord Jesus, you bless the poor: Lord . . .

Christ Jesus, you fill the hungry: Christ . . .

Lord Jesus, you comfort those who weep: Lord . . .

Appreciating the Responsorial Psalm

In Jewish Wisdom literature, there are two ways to live: faithful to the Law of God, or unfaithful. The first way brings blessings and fruitfulness, the second waste and destruction. Psalm 1 introduces the entire collection of psalms by deliberately laying before the Israelites the call to be faithful to the way of God in the midst of all the ups and downs, the losses and deliverances, the laments and thanksgivings which will characterize their history (as the ensuing psalms reveal). The readings for this Sunday remind us that we are called to the same choice, that we will face the same struggles, and that—if faithful—we will know the same blessedness. By singing Psalm 1 we indicate our choice, and our trust, in the One in whom we hope.

Model General Intercessions

Presider: Let us place ourselves in God's hands, trusting that God hears our prayers.

Response:

Lord, hear our prayer.

Cantor:

we pray to the Lord,

That the Church may generously minister God's blessings . . . [pause]

That all nations walk in God's way . . . [pause]

That the poor, the hungry, and the sorrowful be lifted up . . . [pause]

That each of us be a source of blessing for others by the way we live . . . [pause]

Presider: O God, you bless those who walk in your way: hear these our prayers that we might have an everlasting reward in heaven. We pray through Christ our Lord. **Amen.**

OPENING PRAYER

Let us pray

Pause for silent prayer

God our Father,
you have promised to remain for ever
with those who do what is just and right.
Help us to live in your presence.

We ask this through our Lord Jesus Christ,
    your Son,
who lives and reigns with you and the
    Holy Spirit,
one God, for ever and ever. **Amen.**

FIRST READING

Jer 17:5-8

Thus says the LORD:
    Cursed is the one who trusts in human
        beings,
        who seeks his strength in flesh,
        whose heart turns away from the
            LORD.
    He is like a barren bush in the desert
        that enjoys no change of season,
        but stands in a lava waste, a salt and
            empty earth.
    Blessed is the one who trusts in the
        LORD,
        whose hope is the LORD.
    He is like a tree planted beside the
        waters
        that stretches out its roots to the
            stream:
    it fears not the heat when it comes;
        its leaves stay green;
    in the year of drought it shows no
        distress,
        but still bears fruit.

RESPONSORIAL PSALM

Ps 1:1-2, 3, 4, 6

R⃫. (40:5a) Blessed are they who hope in the Lord.

Blessed the man who follows not
   the counsel of the wicked,
nor walks in the way of sinners,
   nor sits in the company of the insolent,
but delights in the law of the LORD
   and meditates on his law day and night.

R⃫. Blessed are they who hope in the Lord.

He is like a tree
   planted near running water,
that yields its fruit in due season,
   and whose leaves never fade.
Whatever he does, prospers.

R⃫. Blessed are they who hope in the Lord.

Not so the wicked, not so;
   they are like chaff which the wind
      drives away.
For the LORD watches over the way of the
   just,
   but the way of the wicked vanishes.

R⃫. Blessed are they who hope in the Lord.

SECOND READING

1 Cor 15:12, 16-20

Brothers and sisters:
If Christ is preached as raised from the
   dead,
   how can some among you say there is no
      resurrection of the dead?
If the dead are not raised, neither has
     Christ been raised,
   and if Christ has not been raised, your
     faith is vain;
   you are still in your sins.
Then those who have fallen asleep in
     Christ have perished.
If for this life only we have hoped in
     Christ,
   we are the most pitiable people of all.

But now Christ has been raised from the
   dead,
   the firstfruits of those who have fallen
     asleep.

About Liturgy

Two ways to approach Sunday: This Sunday's gospel and the selections for the Seventh and Eighth Sundays in Ordinary Time (the Eighth Sunday drops out this year because of when Easter falls) are presented in Luke as a single sermon. This reminds us that the Sunday celebrations can never be taken in isolation but always as one part of a seamless whole: the liturgical year which unfolds the paschal mystery. It is ever a danger that each Sunday Mass be perceived as a single entity. We are always challenged to see the Sundays—and the entire liturgical year—as a fluidity or connectedness unfolding the paschal journey. Thus the pastoral issue of whether we prepare for liturgy the week *before* or live the liturgy the week *after* really is a wrong question. In fact, we do both if our celebrations are truly to be fruitful; these two ways to approach Sunday are really one way.

Preparing ahead of time for the next Sunday does not mean that we forget about last Sunday. In fact, last Sunday gives us something of a lens for this Sunday. There is always growth forward. In other words, the readings are a progression into which we immerse ourselves. Preparing ahead of time is really one way to live last Sunday and helps us see the connection of the readings from Sunday to Sunday. Always it is the same mystery we are delving into, reflecting upon, and living.

Another consideration is that preparing the readings ahead of time is less an intellectual exercise than it is a living response. Here is where we locate the hope which is part of the Liturgy of the Word: we hear the readings and know they can be lived because we have already done it (imperfectly as that may be). Without that experience, the readings too often can be discouraging or even so difficult that they fall on deaf ears.

It is also helpful to think of Sunday as the "Eighth Day" . . . neither the beginning nor end of a week but a resurrection day celebrated out of our ordinary human experience of time. Thus, preparing the readings ahead of time and living them the following week really meld into one, always with new layers of meaning.

Finally, of course we are dismissed from liturgy to live what we have celebrated. This is the whole point of the transformation which occurs during the celebration of liturgy. But this living does not isolate Sundays; rather, living liturgy actively works to keep the Sundays connected.

About Liturgical Music

Cantor preparation: This Sunday's psalm and readings promise blessing to those who trust in God and live according to God's ways. Who, "like a tree planted near running water," helps you trust in God?

Suggestion for the music director: Since the gospel readings for this and next Sunday are part of a single unit (see *Two ways to approach Sunday,* above), it would be good to sing a relevant hymn or choral piece both weeks. For example, "Choose Life" [WC; choral octavo WLP #7936] reiterates the content of these readings: "I have set before you life and death, the blessing and the curse. Choose life . . . that you may live" (Deut 30:15-20). Since the text is direct address to the people, the piece needs to be sung by cantor or choir rather than by the assembly themselves. You might use it as a choral prelude this Sunday and as a choir-only piece during the presentation of the gifts next Sunday.

SPIRITUALITY

Gospel Luke 6:27-38; L81C

Jesus said to his disciples:
"To you who hear I say,
    love your enemies, do good to those
        who hate you,
    bless those who curse you, pray
        for those who mistreat you.
To the person who strikes you on
    one cheek,
    offer the other one as well,
    and from the person who takes
        your cloak,
    do not withhold even your tunic.
Give to everyone who asks of you,
    and from the one who takes
        what is yours do not
            demand it back.
Do to others as you would have
    them do to you.
For if you love those who love you,
    what credit is that to you?
Even sinners love those who love them.
And if you do good to those who do good
    to you,
    what credit is that to you?
Even sinners do the same.
If you lend money to those from whom
    you expect repayment,
    what credit is that to you?
Even sinners lend to sinners,
    and get back the same amount.
But rather, love your enemies and do
    good to them,
    and lend expecting nothing back;
    then your reward will be great
    and you will be children of the Most
        High,
    for he himself is kind to the
        ungrateful and the wicked.
Be merciful, just as your Father is
    merciful.

"Stop judging and you will not be judged.
Stop condemning and you will not be
    condemned.
Forgive and you will be forgiven.
Give, and gifts will be given to you;
    a good measure, packed together,
        shaken down, and overflowing,
    will be poured into your lap.
For the measure with which you measure
    will in return be measured out to you."

Reflecting on the Gospel

This Sunday's gospel is a continuation of Luke's Sermon on the Plain begun last Sunday with the Beatitudes. The blessings mentioned last week lay out the ideals by which Jesus' followers are to live; in this next part, Jesus concretizes these ideals in a series of moral imperatives.

There is so much here, but some of these imperatives have become so familiar to us (if someone strikes you on the cheek, turn your other cheek; do unto others as you would have them do unto you; judge not lest ye be judged) that they may have largely lost their "punch." We take these ideals as ways to live and, indeed, they are. In a society where the standard for many is "dog eat dog" and getting ahead at any cost, Jesus' moral imperatives at the beginning of the gospel set a high standard, indeed. What a challenge the gospel poses! Jesus nudges us one step beyond already exemplary behavior and challenges us with even loftier ideals. Jesus invites us to live as "children of the Most High."

The norms of behavior Jesus lays down move us from the already high standard "do to others as you would have them do to you" to the even higher standard "Be merciful, just as your Father is merciful." We are empowered to act in this divine way because of the extravagant "good measure" with which God continually acts toward us. The first reading is another concrete example of what happens when one acts according to the blessings already bestowed by God.

It was perfectly permissible and encoded in the Law to exact an "eye for an eye and a tooth for a tooth." Saul's attempts on David's life justify Abishai's desire to kill Saul whom, after all, "the Lord delivered" into David's hands. David's sparing Saul's life was a gesture of mercy which superseded the Law. David was already anointed as Israel's future king; his generous mercy toward Saul (also the Lord's anointed) exemplifies God's extravagant "good measure" toward David. The gospel challenges us to the same measure of mercy.

Living the Paschal Mystery

The gospel today offers something of a blueprint for dying to self so that we might rise to new life in Christ. Just as Saul was God's anointed, so are we. In baptism we, too, were anointed as God's own and became "priests," "prophets," and "kings." Baptism confers on us this identity which makes its demands on us. We are to live with the same self-sacrificing attitude as Christ: love our enemies, go beyond the expected or needed. To what extent? Jesus tells us that we are to "be merciful, just as [our] Father is merciful." How much is that? God sent the only Son to teach, suffer, and die for us. Christ's living example is the measure of our own self-sacrificing for others.

We might become overwhelmed by the demands of this divine self-sacrificing if we would not remember that God is always present to us, measuring out our blessings long before we choose to give to others. The self-sacrificing becomes easier when we have identified ourselves with Christ, work to develop a personal relationship with him, keep his name on our lips in all we do. In other words, the first step in self-sacrificing is giving ourselves over to an intimate relationship with God. With that relationship fortifying us, the challenge of the gospel to be "merciful, just as [our] Father is merciful" can be undertaken with faith and trust.

Focusing the Gospel

Key words and phrases: Do to others; children of the Most High; Be merciful, just as your Father is merciful; good measure

To the point: Jesus makes our call to live as "children of the Most High" concrete and practical. The norms of behavior he lays down move us from the already high standard "do to others as you would have them do to you" to the even higher standard "Be merciful, just as your Father is merciful." We are empowered to act in this way because of the extravagant "good measure" with which God continually acts toward us.

Connecting the Gospel

to the first reading: It was perfectly permissible and encoded in the Law to exact an "eye for an eye and a tooth for a tooth." Saul's attempts on David's life justify Abishai's desire to kill Saul whom, after all, "the Lord delivered" into David's hands. David's sparing Saul's life was a gesture of mercy which superseded the Law. The gospel challenges us to the same measure of mercy.

to our culture: In a society where the standard for many is "dog eat dog" and getting ahead at any cost, the golden rule "do unto others as you would have them do unto you" is a high standard, indeed. What a challenge the gospel poses!

Understanding Scripture

The measure of mercy: Lest the words of Jesus to "love your enemies" and "do good to them" be taken as merely ideals or his examples taken as hypothetical, the Lectionary pairs the gospel with a reading from 1 Samuel which shows these principles in action.

Saul, fearing David's designs on the kingship (1 Sam 18:8; 28:31), sets out to kill David. David would certainly have been justified to protect his life by taking the life of Saul. The Law of Retaliation ("eye for eye"; cf. Exod 21:24; Lev 24:20; Deut 19:21), though designed to set a limit to damages which can be exacted for harm, also establishes the right to seek damages in kind, even "a life for a life." And so when both Abishai and David acknowledge that the Lord had delivered Saul, "your enemy," into David's grasp, it could be assumed that God has indeed sanctioned the taking of Saul's life. David's restraint, however, is motivated by reverence for the "anointed of the Lord," that is, one chosen by God. As David explains in verses omitted from the reading, "it must be the LORD himself who will strike him, whether the time comes for him to die, or he goes out and perishes in battle" (26:10). David considers this restraint, for which he hopes to be rewarded, a measure of his "justice and faithfulness," not an act of mercy.

For Jesus, the actions of disciples are modeled on the actions of God. Neither the evil that enemies do (vv. 27-29) nor the good that friends do (vv. 32-34) sets the standards for "children of the Most High." Just as God is "kind to the ungrateful and the wicked," disciples are called to be kind, generous, and forgiving. These norms for disciples address both their material response to others (giving, lending), and their estimation of others (loving, forgiving). The closing line, "the measure with which you measure will in return be measured out to you," finds its more familiar expression in the Lord's prayer, "forgive us our trespasses as we forgive those who trespass against us."

ASSEMBLY & FAITH-SHARING GROUPS
- Some examples of God's "good measure" toward me and my family are . . .
- I share that "good measure" with others by . . .
- What it means to me to be as merciful as the Father is merciful to us is . . .

PRESIDERS
My ministry leads others to the high dignity (and standard) of "children of the Most High" by . . .

DEACONS
I shall consider to what extent the measure by which I have received from God is the measure by which I am serving others.

HOSPITALITY MINISTERS
If I saw each member of the assembly as "the Lord's anointed" (first reading) my care and concern would look like . . .

MUSIC MINISTERS
Jesus tells his disciples that they will receive what they give, and that their giving is to be as boundless as God's (gospel). I find myself giving wholeheartedly to others through my music ministry when . . . What I receive in return is . . .

ALTAR MINISTERS
For my reward to be great the measure of my service to others needs to be . . .

LECTORS
Where I am being invited in my relationships with others to supersede the requirements of the Law (see first reading) is . . .

EXTRAORDINARY MINISTERS OF HOLY COMMUNION
Since the Eucharist is *the* expression of God's mercy, some ways I *distribute* that mercy to others are . . .

CELEBRATION

Model Act of Penitence

Presider: Today's gospel invites us to love our enemies, do good to those who hurt us, forgive one another. Let us prepare ourselves to hear this gospel and to be nourished at the Table . . . [pause]

Lord Jesus, you are the Son of the Most High: Lord . . .

Christ Jesus, you are kind and merciful: Christ . . .

Lord Jesus, you are the full measure of the Father's love: Lord . . .

Appreciating the Responsorial Psalm

These verses chosen from Psalm 103 pursue a clear progression of thought. The psalm begins by calling us to bless God with all our being because of the blessings God bestows upon us. The psalm then identifies one of these divine blessings as pardon and redemption (second strophe). In the face of our sins, God chooses mercy over justice (third strophe). But there is even more—God not only forgives our sins but removes them far from us (fourth strophe). God's mercy and compassion know no limits.

Jesus calls us in the gospel to be like this God whose children we are: we are to show the same compassion to one another. We are to move beyond judgment and condemnation to mercy. As with God, our mercy is to know no limits, but is to be full-measured, overflowing, freely poured out. Then our greatest blessing to one another will become the greatest blessing we receive.

Model General Intercessions

Presider: Our God is gracious and gives us "good measure." We are confident that our prayers will be heard.

Response:

Lord,—— hear our prayer.

Cantor:

we pray to the Lord,

That all members of the Church embrace those seeking mercy, forgiveness, or solace . . . [pause]

That all leaders of the world enact policies which bring a full measure of life and security to their people . . . [pause]

That those in need of God's forgiveness have confidence in God's mercy . . . [pause]

That all of us here live as "children of the Most High" . . . [pause]

Presider: Gracious and merciful God, you hear those who call out to you in need: hear our prayers that all may enjoy life with you for ever and ever. **Amen.**

ALTERNATIVE OPENING PRAYER

Let us pray

Pause for silent prayer

Almighty God,
Father of our Lord Jesus Christ,
faith in your word is the way to wisdom,
and to ponder your divine plan is to grow
    in the truth.
Open our eyes to your deeds,
our ears to the sound of your call,
so that our every act may increase our
    sharing
in the life you have offered us.
Grant this through Christ our Lord.
    Amen.

FIRST READING
1 Sam 26:2, 7-9, 12-13, 22-23

In those days, Saul went down to the
    desert of Ziph
    with three thousand picked men of Israel,
    to search for David in the desert of Ziph.
So David and Abishai went among Saul's
    soldiers by night
    and found Saul lying asleep within the
        barricade,
    with his spear thrust into the ground at
        his head
    and Abner and his men sleeping around
        him.

Abishai whispered to David:
    "God has delivered your enemy into
        your grasp this day.
Let me nail him to the ground with one
        thrust of the spear;
    I will not need a second thrust!"
But David said to Abishai, "Do not harm
        him,
    for who can lay hands on the LORD's
        anointed and remain unpunished?"
So David took the spear and the water jug
        from their place at Saul's head,
    and they got away without anyone's
        seeing or knowing or awakening.
All remained asleep,
    because the LORD had put them into a
        deep slumber.

Going across to an opposite slope,
    David stood on a remote hilltop
    at a great distance from Abner, son of
        Ner, and the troops.
He said: "Here is the king's spear.
Let an attendant come over to get it.
The LORD will reward each man for his
        justice and faithfulness.
Today, though the LORD delivered you into
        my grasp,
    I would not harm the LORD's anointed."

RESPONSORIAL PSALM

Ps 103:1-2, 3-4, 8, 10, 12-13

℟. (8a) The Lord is kind and merciful.

Bless the LORD, O my soul;
    and all my being, bless his holy name.
Bless the LORD, O my soul,
    and forget not all his benefits.

℟. The Lord is kind and merciful.

He pardons all your iniquities,
    heals all your ills.
He redeems your life from destruction,
    crowns you with kindness and
        compassion.

℟. The Lord is kind and merciful.

Merciful and gracious is the LORD,
    slow to anger and abounding in
        kindness.
Not according to our sins does he deal
    with us,
    nor does he requite us according to our
        crimes.

℟. The Lord is kind and merciful.

As far as the east is from the west,
    so far has he put our transgressions
        from us.
As a father has compassion on his
    children,
    so the LORD has compassion on those
        who fear him.

℟. The Lord is kind and merciful.

SECOND READING

1 Cor 15:45-49

Brothers and sisters:
It is written, *The first man, Adam, became
    a living being,*
    the last Adam a life-giving spirit.
But the spiritual was not first;
    rather the natural and then the spiritual.
The first man was from the earth, earthly;
    the second man, from heaven.
As was the earthly one, so also are the
        earthly,
    and as is the heavenly one, so also are
        the heavenly.
Just as we have borne the image of the
        earthly one,
    we shall also bear the image of the
        heavenly one.

About Liturgy

Mercy and the introductory rites: Whenever a form of the act of penitence is used for the introductory rites of Mass, liturgy gives us an opportunity to remember God's mercy toward us. The introduction by the presider using various words invites us to recall our sinfulness, and then we ask for God's mercy. Although we ask for-giveness, something more is going on here. An examination especially of the tropes (attributes of Christ) and our response "Lord [Christ], have mercy" is as much an accla-mation of praise as it is petition. The rite enables us to offer God praise for the mercy already bestowed upon us. As this gospel reminds us, then, our response is also to live lives whereby we are merciful toward others.

If the introductory rites are directed entirely toward the forgiveness of sins, we run a high risk of losing an opportunity to be reminded of God's mercy. Further, God's mercy can never be separated from God's love for us. Our merciful God is a loving God who has blessed us beyond measure. We begin Mass in this context, which encourages us to surrender to God's transforming action during Mass.

About Liturgical Music

Cantor preparation: Walking the way of forgiveness is not easy. Nonetheless, you are called to be as merciful to others as God is to you (gospel). In what ways do you ex-perience God's mercy? What would help you grow in your capacity to show this same mercy to others?

Importance of the responsorial psalm text: Although the Lectionary gives a number of common seasonal responsorial psalms (see nos. 173–174) and GIRM al-lows for an alternative to the psalm for the day given in the Lectionary, GIRM itself directs that "the responsorial Psalm should correspond to each reading and should, as a rule, be taken from the Lectionary" (no. 61). The more we understand the connection between the psalm and the readings of the day (this is the purpose of "Appreciating the Responsorial Psalm" on the opposite page), the more we understand the reasoning behind this directive.

In the design of the Lectionary, the psalm acts as a lens which helps us bring the readings into clearer focus. Its purpose is to "foster meditation on the word of God" (GIRM no. 61). We sing the psalm, then, in order to enter more deeply into and respond to what God is saying to us in the readings. Singing the psalm of the day is important because it pulls us into the Liturgy of the Word and prepares us for encounter with Christ in the gospel.

Season of Lent

SPIRITUALITY

Gospel   Matt 6:1-6, 16-18; L219

Jesus said to his disciples:
  "Take care not to perform righteous
      deeds
  in order that people may see them;
  otherwise, you will have no
      recompense from your
      heavenly Father.
When you give alms,
  do not blow a trumpet before you,
  as the hypocrites do in the
      synagogues and in the streets
  to win the praise of others.
Amen, I say to you,
  they have received their reward.
But when you give alms,
  do not let your left hand know what
      your right is doing,
  so that your almsgiving may be
      secret.
And your Father who sees in secret will
  repay you.

"When you pray,
  do not be like the hypocrites,
  who love to stand and pray in the
      synagogues and on street corners
  so that others may see them.
Amen, I say to you,
  they have received their reward.
But when you pray, go to your inner room,
  close the door, and pray to your Father
      in secret.
And your Father who sees in secret will
  repay you.

"When you fast,
  do not look gloomy like the hypocrites.
They neglect their appearance,
  so that they may appear to others to be
      fasting.
Amen, I say to you, they have received
      their reward.
But when you fast,
  anoint your head and wash your face,
  so that you may not appear to be
      fasting,
  except to your Father who is hidden.
And your Father who sees what is hidden
  will repay you."

See Appendix A, p. 269, for other readings.

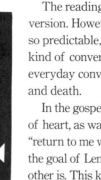

Reflecting on the Gospel

Usually without giving it much thought, we are doing conversions all the time. For example, we might double (convert) a favorite casserole recipe if we expect guests for dinner. All of our auto speedometers have miles per hour as well as kilometers per hour. We might convert liters to quarts or currency at the going foreign exchange rate. We do this pretty automatically (sometimes with the help of a calculator). And, generally, these conversions are predictable, measurable, and accurate.

The readings for Ash Wednesday also speak about conversion. However, this kind of conversion isn't so easy, nor so predictable, measurable, and accurate. The Scriptures' kind of conversion is far more critical than our convenient everyday conversions. Scriptures' conversions deal with life and death.

In the gospel Jesus points beyond *behaviors* to a *conversion* of heart, as was also commanded by Joel in the first reading: "return to me with your whole heart." Mere self-denial is not the goal of Lent; renewed relationships with God and each other is. This kind of conversion demands of us a unique self-giving—a forgetting about ourselves which places God at the very center of our lives. Behaviors are important, to be sure; changed behaviors and habits are also a goal of Lent and often witness to a conversion of heart. But changed behaviors are worthless if they don't lead to and express something deeper: that conversion of heart which brings us closer to God and each other. A comparison of the first reading and gospel offers us insight into how our conversion of heart takes place.

In the first reading the prophet Joel commands Israel to "call an assembly . . . let the priests . . . say, 'Spare, O LORD, your people.'" Clearly the context for conversion is the community. Presumably not only the priests (who, as mediators between God and people would naturally pray for the assembly), but the whole assembly raised their prayers to God. In this context conversion of heart and restored relationships are directly brought about from the *communal* experience of prayer. In the gospel the context is private prayer and works of penance. In this context conversion of heart and restored relationships are brought about directly from an *individual's* self-emptying and reliance upon God.

Public/communal conversion and private/individual conversion are but two necessary aspects of what is common to both: surrendering self to something beyond self for the good of both self and community. If we share a solidarity of identity (as God's chosen people, as the Body of Christ), then all we do affects all our relationships—to God, others, self. Sometimes it is the challenge of rubbing shoulders with others which brings about conversion. At other times it is the solace of being alone and wrestling with our own demons which brings conversion. Lent is an opportunity to change behaviors and come to conversion in both communal and individual ways. In either case, we surrender ourselves to God and seek mercy and forgiveness.

Living the Paschal Mystery

The size or difficulty or quantity of our penance during Lent isn't the measure of a successful Lent; conversion of heart is. During Lent we practice dying to self in new ways which bring us to a true celebration of Easter life. It's better to accomplish something small which makes a difference in our relationships with God and others than to tackle something large which may bring failure. The choice is ours.

Focusing the Gospel
Key words and phrases: give alms, do not, pray, do not, fast, do not

To the point: Jesus points beyond *behaviors* to a *conversion* of heart, as was also commanded by Joel in the first reading: "return to me with your whole heart." Mere self-denial is not the goal of Lent; renewed relationship with God and each other is.

Model General Intercessions
Presider: God who is merciful hears our prayers. With confidence we pray.

Response:

Lord, hear our prayer.

Cantor:

we pray to the Lord,

That all the members of the Church take to heart the work of conversion during these Lenten days . . . [pause]

That all peoples live so as to receive the salvation offered by God . . . [pause]

That those burdened with poverty and need may be lifted up by acts of charity and justice . . . [pause]

That all gathered here grow in love of God and neighbor . . . [pause]

Presider: God of mercy, you know our needs: hear the prayers of those who cry out to you and grant them through Christ our Lord. **Amen.**

OPENING PRAYER
Let us pray

Pause for silent prayer

Lord,
protect us in our struggle against evil.
As we begin the discipline of Lent,
make this day holy by our self-denial.

Grant this through our Lord Jesus Christ,
     your Son,
who lives and reigns with you and the Holy
     Spirit,
one God, for ever and ever. **Amen.**

FOR REFLECTION
- The conversion of heart that I seek for myself this Lent is . . .
- My Lenten practices go beyond mere self-denial to renewing my relationships with God and others by . . .
- The conversion of heart that I seek for our world and for our Church this Lent is . . .

SPIRITUALITY

Gospel Luke 4:1-13; L24C

Filled with the Holy Spirit, Jesus
 returned from the Jordan
and was led by the Spirit into the
 desert for forty days,
to be tempted by the devil.
He ate nothing during those days,
 and when they were over he was
 hungry.
The devil said to him,
 "If you are the Son of God,
 command this stone to become
 bread."
Jesus answered him,
 "It is written, *One does not live on
 bread alone.*"
Then he took him up and showed him
 all the kingdoms of the world in a
 single instant.
The devil said to him,
 "I shall give to you all this power and
 glory;
 for it has been handed over to me,
 and I may give it to whomever I wish.
All this will be yours, if you worship
 me."
Jesus said to him in reply,
 "It is written:
 *You shall worship the Lord, your God,
 and him alone shall you serve.*"
Then he led him to Jerusalem,
 made him stand on the parapet of the
 temple, and said to him,
 "If you are the Son of God,
 throw yourself down from here, for it
 is written:
  *He will command his angels
   concerning you, to guard you,*
and:
  *With their hands they will support
  you,
  lest you dash your foot against a
  stone.*"
Jesus said to him in reply,
 "It also says,
 *You shall not put the Lord, your God,
 to the test.*"
When the devil had finished every
 temptation,
 he departed from him for a time.

Reflecting on the Gospel

"Don't tempt me!" Without thinking, these words pop out of the mouths of dieters who are offered a hot fudge sundae or someone who is trying to quit smoking when offered a cigarette. While these may be serious enough temptations for the dieter or would-be nonsmoker, the temptations put to Jesus in this Sunday's readings are far more invasive, for they cut to the quick of Jesus' identity (gospel), that of Israel (first reading), and of us (second reading).

Jesus' identity as the Son of God was revealed at his baptism (see Luke 3:22). Following this, Jesus was led into the desert "by the Spirit" and there confronted evil. Twice the devil taunts Jesus, "If you are the Son of God." Jesus is being tested about *how* he will be the Son of God—whether or not he will use his power for his own advantage. His choices—both in the desert and throughout his ministry— reveal who he really is. Every choice ultimately is about identity. While he is God, he humbles himself to be fully human. In the desert, by resisting the devil's temptations, Jesus embraces humanity's finiteness, needs, and simplicity—these characterize who Jesus is rather than a raw use of power.

"If you are the Son of God" . . . ironically, doing what the devil offers (turn stone into bread, seeking power, testing God) seems at first sight to be proper actions for the Son of God. Yet, by resisting the devil's temptations does Jesus truly act as who he is: bread does not fill (see Deut 8:3), but the Spirit does; worshiping false gods does not give power, but serving (worshiping) the true God does (see Deut 6:13); testing God in false ways does not bring salvation, but relying on God's care does (see Deut 6:16). The true identity of the Son of God is revealed not by using his power selfishly but by preparing himself for his mission of bringing salvation to others.

Living the Paschal Mystery

Whatever Lenten practices we undertake, it is important to remember their purpose. Lenten practices are not about losing weight or finally stopping smoking, but they are about deepening our baptismal identity as children of God and members of the Body of Christ. "If you are [children] of God" . . . this is the identity conferred upon us at baptism. This is the identity out of which we enter into our own Lenten desert. This is the identity out of which we face our own worst temptations. By remaining faithful to who we are—God's children, members of the Body of Christ—we can resist temptations and grow in our relationships with God, self, and others.

Traditionally, Christian penance has always included three prongs: fasting, prayer, and almsgiving (charity). This suggests to us that penance isn't a matter of "giving up" something, nor is it a single act—even if performed faithfully over a long period like forty days. Christian penance has as its purpose genuine conversion of life, so that at the end of Lent when we renew our baptismal promises we are able to do so with full throat, well aware of our own wonderful identity as sons and daughters of God. The new life we celebrate at Easter cannot happen without our dying to ourselves, without our going to Jerusalem with Jesus and willingly embracing whatever death is in store for us. For that is the road to new life. That is the road we travel during Lent.

Focusing the Gospel

Key words and phrases: tempted by the devil, If you are the Son of God

To the point: Twice the devil taunts Jesus, "If you are the Son of God." Jesus is being tested about *how* he will be the Son of God—whether or not he will use his power for his own advantage. His choices—both in the desert and throughout his ministry—reveal who he really is. Every choice ultimately is about identity.

Connecting the Gospel

to baptism: In his baptism Jesus was revealed as the beloved Son of God. At the temptations Jesus acted in accord with that identity. Baptism gives us our identity as children of God. Our Christian life is about making choices in accord with our baptismal identity.

to Catholic culture: Whatever Lenten practices we undertake, it is important to remember their purpose. Lenten practices are not about losing weight or finally stopping smoking, but they are about deepening our baptismal identity as children of God and members of the Body of Christ.

Understanding Scripture

Temptation, choice, and identity: Immediately preceding this Sunday's story of the temptation is Luke's genealogy of Jesus. Luke works backwards from Jesus all the way to Adam, ultimately identifying Jesus as "the son of God"—an identity revealed in the baptism: "you are my beloved Son" (3:22). Jesus' identity is the starting point for the tempter whose first words are, "If you are the Son of God . . ." At stake in the temptations is the identity of Jesus and whether the choices he makes confirm or deny his identity.

Jesus' temptations in the desert recall various experiences of Israel in the wilderness. Luke takes all three of Jesus' quotes from the book of Deuteronomy. The first quote, "not by bread alone," is from Deuteronomy 8:3. In that story, Moses informs the people that their forty-year wilderness experience was "to test you by affliction and find out whether or not it was your intention to keep his commandments" (8:2). Specifically, the "testing" by manna was to learn that they would live by obedience to God's word. Jesus, the obedient son of God, will use his power, not to feed himself, but to provide bread for the 5,000 in a "deserted place" (Luke 9:12).

The second quote about serving God alone (Deut 6:13) alludes to the episode of the golden calf (see Exod 32): the issue for Israel and for Jesus is, whom will you serve? The final quote about not testing God (Deut 6:16) refers to Israel's having tested God by demanding water and God providing it from the rock. In all three instances, Israel was "tested" and failed. By contrast, Jesus is victorious in these encounters with the devil, but it is not yet a definitive victory. The story ends with the ominous verse, "the devil left him for a time." Indeed, at the outset of the passion, Luke tells us that the devil entered Judas (22:3) and this sets the stage for the final test on the cross where Jesus' identity as the compassionate savior is confirmed as he refuses to save himself but brings the repentant thief to salvation.

ASSEMBLY & FAITH-SHARING GROUPS

- The significance to me that Jesus was tempted by the devil is . . .
- The common temptations posed to me by the culture today are . . .
- When I am hungry, tempted, and testy, what helps me to *remember* and *trust* in my true identity as a child of God is . . .

PRESIDERS

I am leading others to a conversion of heart by . . .

DEACONS

I assist others to remain faithful to their true dignity by . . .

HOSPITALITY MINISTERS

My care and concern remind those gathering of their true dignity whenever I . . .

MUSIC MINISTERS

In my music ministry, I find myself tempted to seek my own power and glory whenever . . . What helps me keep God as the focus is . . .

ALTAR MINISTERS

Serving at liturgy reminds me of my true identity because . . .

LECTORS

My daily living is a proclamation of what it means to be a child of God in that . . .

EXTRAORDINARY MINISTERS OF HOLY COMMUNION

Some ways I serve and strengthen those enduring temptations are . . .

Model Act of Penitence

Presider: As we come together on this First Sunday of Lent, let us ask for the grace of conversion and seek forgiveness for the times we have given in to temptation . . . [pause]

　　Confiteor: I confess . . .

Appreciating the Responsorial Psalm

As the psalm refrain indicates, Jesus is in "trouble." Hungry after forty days of fasting, he is accosted by Satan with every possible temptation. Yet he steadfastly "clings" to God (psalm). He chooses to "bow down" (first reading) only before God; he chooses to live not by bread, but by the word of God; he refuses to test God, but chooses to trust instead in a guarantee already given (psalm). Jesus' mission will lead to his death, but he knows God will "deliver and glorify him" nonetheless because this is what God has promised to do. Jesus remains true to who he is because he knows he can count on God remaining true to who God is. As we enter this new season of Lent, our forty-day testing period, let us sing this psalm with Jesus; let us stand with Jesus on this promise.

Model General Intercessions

Presider: God sustains us in life's struggles and temptations. Let us ask God's help.

Response:

Lord, hear our prayer.

Cantor:

we pray to the Lord,

That the Church may always remain faithful to her identity as the Body of Christ . . . [pause]

That all people of the world may recognize and overcome every form of evil . . . [pause]

That those who are hungry and in need be delivered through the generous charity of others . . . [pause]

That our identity as sons and daughters of God may be strengthened through our Lenten penance . . . [pause]

Presider: Ever-faithful God, you hear the prayers of those who turn to you in faith and trust: hear our prayers that our Lenten journey may bring us closer to you and each other. We ask this through Christ our Lord. **Amen.**

OPENING PRAYER

Let us pray

Pause for silent prayer

Father,
through our observance of Lent,
help us to understand the meaning
of your Son's death and resurrection,
and teach us to reflect it in our lives.

Grant this through our Lord Jesus Christ,
　　your Son,
who lives and reigns with you and the
　　Holy Spirit,
one God, for ever and ever. **Amen.**

FIRST READING

Deut 26:4-10

Moses spoke to the people, saying:
　　"The priest shall receive the basket from
　　　　you
　　and shall set it in front of the altar of
　　　　the LORD, your God.
Then you shall declare before the LORD,
　　　　your God,
　　'My father was a wandering Aramean
　　who went down to Egypt with a small
　　　　household
　　and lived there as an alien.
But there he became a nation
　　great, strong, and numerous.
When the Egyptians maltreated and
　　　　oppressed us,
　　imposing hard labor upon us,
　　we cried to the LORD, the God of our
　　　　fathers,
　　and he heard our cry
　　and saw our affliction, our toil, and our
　　　　oppression.
He brought us out of Egypt
　　with his strong hand and outstretched
　　　　arm,
　　with terrifying power, with signs and
　　　　wonders;
　　and bringing us into this country,
　　he gave us this land flowing with milk
　　　　and honey.
Therefore, I have now brought you the
　　　　firstfruits
　　of the products of the soil
　　which you, O LORD, have given me.'
And having set them before the LORD, your
　　　　God,
　　you shall bow down in his presence."

RESPONSORIAL PSALM

Ps 91:1-2, 10-11, 12-13, 14-15

℟. (cf. 15b) Be with me, Lord, when I am
in trouble.

You who dwell in the shelter of the Most
    High,
    who abide in the shadow of the
        Almighty,
say to the LORD, "My refuge and fortress,
    my God in whom I trust."

℟. Be with me, Lord, when I am in trouble.

No evil shall befall you,
    nor shall affliction come near your tent,
for to his angels he has given command
        about you,
    that they guard you in all your ways.

℟. Be with me, Lord, when I am in trouble.

Upon their hands they shall bear you up,
    lest you dash your foot against a stone.
You shall tread upon the asp and the viper;
    you shall trample down the lion and the
        dragon.

℟. Be with me, Lord, when I am in trouble.

Because he clings to me, I will deliver him;
    I will set him on high because he
        acknowledges my name.
He shall call upon me, and I will answer
    him;
    I will be with him in distress;
I will deliver him and glorify him.

℟. Be with me, Lord, when I am in trouble.

SECOND READING

Rom 10:8-13

See Appendix A, p. 269.

About Liturgy

Lent, forty days, and fasting: "Forty" is a number which comes up often in Scripture (see, for example, Gen 7:4; Exod 16:35; 24:18; Num 14:33; Judg 3:11; 1 Kgs 2:11; Jon 3:4; Acts 1:3) and it means "for a sufficient time." When Lent began to be a more extended period of time, it first lasted forty days. But since Sundays have always been excluded as fast days (because that is the day of the Lord, the day of resurrection, the day when we celebrate the Bridegroom's presence), that meant Lent consisted of fewer than forty fast days. During a time when the Church emphasized the sinfulness and unworthiness of the baptized rather than their blessedness, Lent was extended back to the Wednesday before the First Sunday of Lent in order to have forty fast days (hence, the origin of Ash Wednesday, in place by the eighth–ninth century). The reform of the liturgical year in the wake of Vatican II kept intact the period of Lent with forty fast days. This being said, we cannot understand Lent properly only in terms of fasting. Lent is, essentially, a period of conversion. Lenten penance always has as its goal turning away from evil and turning toward Christ. This conversion culminates in the renewal of baptismal promises at the Easter Vigil or Easter Sunday Mass.

About Liturgical Music

Cantor preparation: It would be good to read and pray with the whole of Psalm 91 as you prepare to sing some of its verses this Sunday. Notice that in verses 1-13 it is the psalmist who is speaking, but in verses 14-16 it is God who speaks. With intimate words God promises to be with and deliver whoever calls for help. Can you speak these words to the assembly? Do you hear God speaking them to you?

Service music for Lent: The penitential character of Lent makes quieter, more reflective, musically more "sparse" service music in order. Good examples include David Hurd's "New Plainsong Mass," Vermulst's "People's Mass," Kraehenbuehl's "Danish Amen Mass," Edward Connor's "Mass in Honor of Pope Paul VI," and the simple Gregorian chant setting in either Latin or English.

Music suggestions: The hymn "Jesus, Tempted in the Desert" [RS] fits both this Sunday's gospel and the beginning of Lent. By barely moving outside the tonic triad, the melody conveys a sense of being in place, of being grounded in faith. At the same time its triplet figures and dotted rhythms propel one into the challenges of Lent. The text reassures that faithful disciples do not face temptation alone: "When we face temptation's power, Lonely, struggling, filled with dread, Christ, who knew the tempter's hour, Come and be our living bread" (v. 4). The hymn would work well during the presentation of the gifts, after the gospel has been proclaimed.

SPIRITUALITY

Gospel

Luke 9:28b-36; L27C

Jesus took Peter, John, and
  James
  and went up the mountain to
  pray.
While he was praying his face
  changed in appearance
  and his clothing became
  dazzling white.
And behold, two men were
  conversing with him,
  Moses and Elijah,
who appeared in glory and
  spoke of his exodus
that he was going to accomplish in
  Jerusalem.
Peter and his companions had been
  overcome by sleep,
  but becoming fully awake,
they saw his glory and the two men
  standing with him.
As they were about to part from him,
  Peter said to Jesus,
  "Master, it is good that we are here;
  let us make three tents,
  one for you, one for Moses, and one
  for Elijah."
But he did not know what he was
  saying.
While he was still speaking,
  a cloud came and cast a shadow over
  them,
  and they became frightened when
  they entered the cloud.
Then from the cloud came a voice that
  said,
  "This is my chosen Son; listen to
  him."
After the voice had spoken, Jesus was
  found alone.
They fell silent and did not at that time
  tell anyone what they had seen.

Reflecting on the Gospel

We have all seen little children's faces light up when offered something they want. Or the glow on the faces of a bride and groom. Or the utter wonder written on the faces of new parents. We've seen contentment on the faces of a retired, long-loving couple. Or the elation written on the face of a youngster who just landed her or his first job. Or the excitement of a tee-baller who just made his or her very first hit. All of these are familiar human experiences which warm our own hearts as we behold the jubilation of others. These many splendid human experiences, however, are nothing compared to what Peter, John, and James beheld in their Master.

"Jesus . . . went up the mountain to pray." Like us, Jesus sought communion with his God and Father. He most likely didn't go up the mountain expecting to be transfigured, but his prayerful union with his Father manifested his identity as One who shares in the Father's glory. Luke explicitly relates the glory of the transfiguration to the glory of the new life that Jesus shares after his resurrection. Luke is the only synoptic evangelist who gives us a hint about the conversation among Jesus, Moses, and Elijah—they talked about Jesus' "exodus," that is, his "passover" which would be "accomplished in Jerusalem."

In this transfiguration account, Luke relates divine affirmation of Jesus' radical new teaching—consider the demanding Sermon on the Plain that we heard on the two Sundays prior to the beginning of Lent—and that all his suffering would end in glory. This divine affirmation of Jesus and his mission at the same time includes a divine imperative for us: "listen to him." On the mountain of transfiguration the disciples witnessed the glory of Jesus' identity as the "chosen Son." We, too, are destined for glory when Christ will "change our lowly body to conform with his glorified body" (second reading). On that day our identity as God's sons and daughters will be fully revealed.

Living the Paschal Mystery

At the beginning of Lent, the goal is laid out for us. Jesus went up the mountain to pray and was transformed. Lent is not only a desert (as in last Sunday) but is also our "mountain" that we go up to pray in order to be transformed. Jesus talks about his exodus, his passing through suffering and death to the glory of resurrected life. Our salvation is to follow Jesus into his passion and death so that we, too, might attain the glory of new life.

Our following Jesus is spelled out in the ordinary "dyings" of our everyday living: reaching out to visit a lonely elderly person, listening to a troubled adolescent, biting our tongue instead of saying sharp words, still having patience when we've been pushed too far. The utterly amazing thing about our embracing these little, everyday "dyings" is that we ourselves experience a kind of transfiguration. As we learn to say yes to God and others, we grow deeper into our own identity as the chosen ones of God. We become more perfectly members of Christ's Body when we act like Jesus did—when we reach out to others who are in need, when we bring a comforting touch, when we forgive. God's command to "listen to" Jesus isn't a passive hearing words; we listen by *doing* as Jesus did. Our whole life, then, is a transfiguration, a passing over from our old sinful ways to the ways of light and grace offered by God.

Focusing the Gospel

Key words and phrases: mountain, saw his glory, this is my chosen Son

To the point: On the mountain of transfiguration the disciples witnessed the glory of Jesus' identity as the "chosen Son." We, too, are destined for glory when Christ will "change our lowly body to conform with his glorified body" (second reading). On that day our identity as God's sons and daughters will be fully revealed.

Connecting the Gospel

to last Sunday: The devil's stark challenge in the desert to Jesus' identity as "Son of God" (last Sunday) gives way to the glorious affirmation of Jesus as the "chosen Son" on the mountain of transfiguration.

to our culture: As a society we tend to plan carefully for the future: college bank accounts begun in infancy, corporate long-range planning, IRAs, social security, etc. As Christians, our future orientation is even more farsighted, for our "citizenship is in heaven" (second reading).

Understanding Scripture

Glory and identity: In Luke's gospel and in the Acts of the Apostles, there are several manifestations of Jesus' glory: the transfiguration, baptism, resurrection, and ascension. This Sunday's gospel of the transfiguration shares many common elements with the account of the baptism: in both Jesus is in prayer, a voice comes from heaven/the cloud, and there is an announcement of Jesus as "my beloved [chosen] Son." There may be a link between the transfiguration and the resurrection suggested by Luke's indicating that the transfiguration took place "on the eighth day," an early Christian name for the resurrection; finally, the transfiguration is linked to both the resurrection and the ascension by the expression, "behold, two men" (Luke 9:30; 24:4; Acts 1:10). All these events reveal the glory of Jesus (see OT 2).

The cloud which overshadows the mountain of transfiguration is an important image of the divine presence found throughout the Old Testament and in this Sunday's first reading. The cloud and/or smoke is a symbol of God's presence in Exodus 16:10; 19:9; 20:21, and elsewhere; the cloud, along with a pillar of fire, also figures prominently in the Exodus from Egypt, guiding the Hebrews on their way through the wilderness (Exod 13:21; Num 14:14). It is from the cloud of divine presence that the voice comes, confirming Jesus' glory as God's "chosen Son."

The changed appearance of Jesus' face and his "dazzling white" clothes is a sneak preview of what Paul refers to in the second reading as Christ's "glorified body." Moreover, Paul indicates that what is true for Jesus will be true for us: our "lowly body" will be transformed so as to "conform with his glorified body." This is in keeping with our true status for, as followers of Jesus, "our citizenship is in heaven." The first part of the longer version of this second reading fittingly urges Christians to "conduct themselves" in a way which befits their citizenship and will merit their glorification. Paul concludes by urging people to "stand firm in the Lord." Those who do will share Jesus' glory and be acknowledged as God's own chosen children.

ASSEMBLY & FAITH-SHARING GROUPS
- Where I have witnessed the glory of Jesus is . . .
- What it means to me that I am destined to share in Jesus' glory is . . .
- My Lenten practices direct me toward glory in that . . .

PRESIDERS
I keep the Lenten grace and work of transformation before the assembly by . . .

DEACONS
The glory of Jesus revealed in serving others is . . .

HOSPITALITY MINISTERS
My ministry points to the glory of Christ and his Body when I . . .

MUSIC MINISTERS
In the gospel God proclaims, "This is my chosen Son; listen to him." As a music minister, I find it easy to listen to Jesus when . . . I find it difficult when . . .

ALTAR MINISTERS
My serving at liturgy manifests the glory of God to the assembly in that . . .

LECTORS
I proclaim to the assembly that our "citizenship is in heaven" (second reading) by . . .

EXTRAORDINARY MINISTERS OF HOLY COMMUNION
I nurture others to be transformed more perfectly into the Body of Christ by . . .

Model Act of Penitence

Presider: Peter, John, and James went up the mountain with Jesus and saw his glory. Let us repent of our sins which mar God's glory in us . . . [pause]

Confiteor: I confess . . .

Appreciating the Responsorial Psalm

These verses from Psalm 27 move from confidence to lament, then back to confidence. In the context of Lent, the psalm indicates that the fearlessness which comes from knowing God is our salvation will not spare us from the reality of suffering and death. Yet we are emboldened to face the dying which discipleship brings because we believe that we shall see "the bounty of the Lord in the land of the living."

Praying this psalm unites our experience with that of Christ. He glowed with divine light (gospel) because he saw God as his "light and [his] salvation." He faced the "terrifying darkness" of his passion and death because he knew that he could count on the covenant relationship God had established (first reading). With Christ we make God the center and focus of our lives. With Christ we choose to undergo the "exodus" (gospel) required of us. And with Christ we, too, shall be transformed into glory by the light of God (second reading).

Model General Intercessions

Presider: The God who chooses us to be sons and daughters will give us all we need. So we pray.

Response:

Lord, hear our prayer.

Cantor:

we pray to the Lord,

That all members of the Church may listen to Jesus and be transformed by his words . . . [pause]

That all leaders of the world respect and safeguard the dignity of their people . . . [pause]

That those overwhelmed by worthlessness and shame may recover their dignity as God's children . . . [pause]

That all of us use these Lenten days as a time of transformation . . . [pause]

Presider: Gracious God, you hear the prayers of those who turn to you: may we be transformed by your grace and enjoy everlasting glory with you. We ask this through Christ your transfigured Son. **Amen.**

OPENING PRAYER

Let us pray

Pause for silent prayer

God our Father,
help us to hear your Son.
Enlighten us with your word,
that we may find the way to your glory.

We ask this through our Lord Jesus Christ,
    your Son,
who lives and reigns with you and the
    Holy Spirit,
one God, for ever and ever. **Amen.**

FIRST READING

Gen 15:5-12, 17-18

The Lord God took Abram outside and
    said,
    "Look up at the sky and count the stars,
        if you can.
Just so," he added, "shall your descendants
    be."
Abram put his faith in the LORD,
    who credited it to him as an act of
        righteousness.

He then said to him,
    "I am the LORD who brought you from
        Ur of the Chaldeans
    to give you this land as a possession."
"O Lord GOD," he asked,
    "how am I to know that I shall possess
        it?"
He answered him,
    "Bring me a three-year-old heifer, a
        three-year-old she-goat,
    a three-year-old ram, a turtledove, and a
        young pigeon."
Abram brought him all these, split them
    in two,
    and placed each half opposite the other;
    but the birds he did not cut up.
Birds of prey swooped down on the
    carcasses,
    but Abram stayed with them.
As the sun was about to set, a trance fell
    upon Abram,
    and a deep, terrifying darkness
        enveloped him.

When the sun had set and it was dark,
    there appeared a smoking fire pot and a
        flaming torch,
    which passed between those pieces.
It was on that occasion that the LORD made
    a covenant with Abram,
    saying: "To your descendants I give this
        land,
    from the Wadi of Egypt to the Great
        River, the Euphrates."

CATECHESIS

RESPONSORIAL PSALM
Ps 27:1, 7-8, 8-9, 13-14

R̶j̶. (1a) The Lord is my light and my salvation.

The LORD is my light and my salvation;
    whom should I fear?
The LORD is my life's refuge;
    of whom should I be afraid?

R̶j̶. The Lord is my light and my salvation.

Hear, O LORD, the sound of my call;
    have pity on me, and answer me.
Of you my heart speaks; you my glance
    seeks.

R̶j̶. The Lord is my light and my salvation.

Your presence, O LORD, I seek.
    Hide not your face from me;
do not in anger repel your servant.
    You are my helper: cast me not off.

R̶j̶. The Lord is my light and my salvation.

I believe that I shall see the bounty of the
    LORD
    in the land of the living.
Wait for the LORD with courage;
    be stouthearted, and wait for the LORD.

R̶j̶. The Lord is my light and my salvation.

SECOND READING
Phil 3:17–4:1

Join with others in being imitators of me,
    brothers and sisters,
    and observe those who thus conduct
        themselves
    according to the model you have in us.
For many, as I have often told you
    and now tell you even in tears,
    conduct themselves as enemies of the
        cross of Christ.
Their end is destruction.
Their God is their stomach;
    their glory is in their "shame."
Their minds are occupied with earthly
    things.
But our citizenship is in heaven,
    and from it we also await a savior, the
        Lord Jesus Christ.
He will change our lowly body
    to conform with his glorified body
    by the power that enables him also
    to bring all things into subjection to
        himself.

Therefore, my brothers and sisters,
    whom I love and long for, my joy and
        crown,
    in this way stand firm in the Lord.

or Phil 3:20–4:1, *see p. 269.*

About Liturgy

Lent, first reading, and gospel: For most of the liturgical year the Roman Catholic Lectionary's first reading for Sundays relates well to the gospel. The first reading relates to the gospel thematically (sometimes with a parallel incident from the Old Testament) or it may include a promise/fulfillment relationship. However, during Lent the first reading and gospel are not harmonized, but the first reading runs its own course with its own purpose.

Always during Lent the first reading gives us a glimpse of major salvation events. For example, in this year C, the Old Testament reading from Deuteronomy for the First Sunday of Lent rehearses Israel's passover from slavery to freedom and reminds them of God's mighty deeds in making them God's own chosen people, eliciting from them a profession of faith. On the Second Sunday of Lent we hear about God's covenant with Abraham; Third Sunday: Moses' encounter with God in the burning bush; Fourth Sunday: Israel celebrates the Passover in the Promised Land; Fifth Sunday: prophecy about God's doing something new for the people; and Palm Sunday: the opening verses of the Third Song of the Suffering Servant.

None of these readings are repeated on Holy Saturday at the Vigil, although there, too, the Old Testament readings recount for us salvation history. It is as though these first readings during Lent prepare us for the Easter Vigil—we've been hearing our salvation history unfolding throughout Lent.

About Liturgical Music

Cantor preparation: As part of your preparation to sing this responsorial psalm, read and pray with the whole of Psalm 27. Filled with images of danger and death, the psalm nonetheless maintains its confidence in God's ultimate promise of life. For you as a baptized Christian, the danger is the struggle with evil and the death is to self. How are you being called this Lent to this death? How are you experiencing God's promise of resurrection?

Music suggestions: One of the finest contemporary hymn texts for this Sunday (and for the feast of the Transfiguration, August 6) is Sylvia Dunstan's "Transform Us" [GC2, HG, RS, SS]. The text is particularly fitting for Lent because it asks Christ to "transform us," to "search us with revealing light," to "lift us from where we have fallen." Set to the tune PICARDY, the hymn would work well during the presentation of the gifts. "'Tis Good, Lord, to Be Here" [BB, CH, GC, GC2, JS2, PMB, RS, W3, WC, WS] would be a good text to sing either for the entrance procession or as a hymn of praise after Communion, for it fits the story of the transfiguration as well as the season of Lent. Another excellent choice for the entrance procession would be "O Sun of Justice" [CBW3, RS, SS, W3]. The text speaks of the light of Christ dispelling darkness and bringing new life. The tune JESU DULCIS MEMORIA (CBW3 uses a different tune and text) can be accompanied by tone chimes or bells playing open chords or chord clusters at the places of primary rhythmic impulse.

SPIRITUALITY

Gospel
Luke 13:1-9; L30C

Some people told Jesus about the
  Galileans
    whose blood Pilate had mingled with
      the blood of their sacrifices.
Jesus said to them in reply,
  "Do you think that because
    these Galileans suffered in
    this way
  they were greater sinners than
    all other Galileans?
By no means!
But I tell you, if you do not
  repent,
  you will all perish as they did!
Or those eighteen people who
    were killed
  when the tower at Siloam fell on
    them—
  do you think they were more guilty
  than everyone else who lived in
    Jerusalem?
By no means!
But I tell you, if you do not repent,
  you will all perish as they did!"

And he told them this parable:
  "There once was a person who had a
    fig tree planted in his orchard,
  and when he came in search of fruit
    on it but found none,
  he said to the gardener,
  'For three years now I have come in
    search of fruit on this fig tree
  but have found none.
So cut it down.
Why should it exhaust the soil?'
He said to him in reply,
  'Sir, leave it for this year also,
  and I shall cultivate the ground
    around it and fertilize it;
  it may bear fruit in the future.
If not you can cut it down.'"

*See Appendix A, pp. 270–72, for optional
readings.*

Reflecting on the Gospel
It shakes us up to see newspaper headlines such as these: "Children Struck Down in School Shooting" or "More than 100,000 Die in Tsunami." Similarly, the incidents recorded in this Sunday's gospel might have come out of a "Galilean Gazette" or "Jerusalem Journal" (we have no other data concerning these events so we know nothing more about them). They must have been on peoples' minds because Jesus uses them to illustrate his point—don't speculate on other peoples' lives and why disaster befell them but look at your own lives and repent.

Jesus offers no explanation for the tragedies mentioned in the gospel. Instead he uses these tragedies to call the people to repent. While the stakes are high (repent or perish, bear fruit or be cut down), the parable offers this hope: that in our work of repentance God shows us patience ("leave it for this year") and assists us ("I shall cultivate . . . and fertilize"). Thus, at the same time that we are jarred into the reality of repentance, we also hear about God's great compassion. We must allow Jesus to "cultivate" and "fertilize" *us* so that we can bear fruit and live.

In our own human experience, change is hard; for example, changing jobs, losing weight, stopping smoking. It is not surprising, then, that repentance as a change of heart is a lifelong task. Also, while Lent is a specific liturgical season given us for repentance and conversion, it is always good to remember that repentance, change, bearing fruit is really the lifelong task of every follower of Jesus. Therefore, repentance is not something we can choose to do over a period of time nor even pretend to accomplish simply by doing specific acts. Repentance is an *attitude* of relationship—we receive God's compassion which strengthens us to change our behaviors and conform more perfectly to Christ. Repentance characterizes Christian living as much as loving and caring for others. In fact, without repentance we cannot bear the fruit of right relationships with God, self, and others. Much is at stake in our choice to repent or perish!

Living the Paschal Mystery
The challenge of Lent is urgent: "repent or perish; bear fruit or be cut down." But what does this urgency mean, for most of us really are scarcely huge sinners! Although murder and adultery and apostasy (giving up the faith) and other public, scandalous, heinous sins are as much a part of our Church now as they were when the early Church practiced public penitence, the vast majority of us are just common sinful folk. Sometimes it's not so obvious to us of what we must repent. We are sort of stuck—like the fig tree; it was still alive, just wasn't doing much.

The challenge of Lent is to allow Jesus to "cultivate" and "fertilize" us so that we know of what we are to repent and can begin bearing even more fruit. The gospels are one way to help us prune out our sins. They are the measure against which we can examine our daily living. Another way is to pay attention to the people around us. They can reflect back to us behaviors which need to change as well as draw us out of ourselves to act in charity and graciousness. Christian living—and repenting—isn't something undertaken in isolation. It always involves other people. They are the "examples" who teach us what needs to change in us so that we can bear fruit—sometimes even a bumper crop!

Focusing the Gospel

Key words and phrases: repent, perish, leave it for this year, I shall culti-vate . . . and fertilize, bear fruit, cut it down

To the point: Jesus offers no explanation for the tragedies mentioned in the gospel. Instead he uses these tragedies to call the people to repent. While the stakes are high (repent or perish, bear fruit or be cut down), the parable offers this hope: that in our work of repentance God shows us patience ("leave it for this year") and assists us ("I shall cultivate . . . and fertilize").

Connecting the Gospel

to the second reading: Paul, like Jesus, offers examples from the people's experience as a "warning to us" (second reading). Moreover, God offered every means of salvation to Israel; so, too, Jesus offers us every means of salvation ("I shall cultivate the ground . . . and fertilize it").

to experience: In our own human experience, change is hard; for example, changing jobs, losing weight, stopping smoking. It is not surprising, then, that repentance as a change of heart is a lifelong task.

Understanding Scripture

Repent now! In the second reading, Paul uses some key events in Israel's history for moral exhortation: the past serves as an example that calls the Corinthians to repentance—precisely the point Jesus makes in reviewing con-temporary events in Galilee. The first incident was apparently an act of politi-cal reprisal. Pilate, known for his brutality, had executed some pilgrims who came to Jerusalem to offer sacrifice; perhaps they had been implicated in some seditious or rebellious act. The second event was an accident at a construction site that took the lives of eighteen workers. Despite the differences in circum-stances, all the victims met with an unexpected and sudden death.

Jesus rejects the current religious explanation for such tragedies, namely, that they are sent by God as punishment for sin. If God punished sin in this way, then all Galileans (indeed all people!) should expect the same inasmuch as all sin. For Jesus, the fate of Pilate's victims and of the workmen in Siloam is not an opportunity to speculate about *their* sins, but an invitation to disciples to put their own lives in order. He warns his hearers that "you will all perish as they did" (13:3, 5)—not necessarily by tragedy, but suddenly and without warn-ing, without the opportunity to repent. One cannot know when or how death will come. The time for repentance is now, while there is time.

The brief parable about the fig tree is a story of God's mercy. The owner of the orchard has already waited patiently three years for the fig tree to produce fruit. Although he decides to cut down the tree, he is dissuaded by the gardener who will redouble his efforts to make the tree fruitful. The orchard owner agrees. But even the gardener acknowledges that the day will come when the unfruitful tree will be cut down. So it is with the ministry of Jesus. His call to repentance is an act of mercy, inviting people to avoid judgment. But there will be a day when time has run out and then it will be too late. Repent now!

ASSEMBLY & FAITH-SHARING GROUPS

- Jesus' call to repent or perish means to me . . .
- The urgency with which I am living this Lent is demonstrated by . . .
- Jesus is patiently "cultivating" and "fertil-izing" my life by . . .

PRESIDERS

My ministry demonstrates the patience of God and, at the same time, the urgency to repent by . . .

DEACONS

My ministry embodies God's plan to rescue the afflicted (see first reading) whenever I . . .

HOSPITALITY MINISTERS

My care and concern for others assists them in bearing the good fruit of discipleship by . . .

MUSIC MINISTERS

God uses my participation in music min-istry to cultivate (see gospel) my conver-sion to fuller life in Christ. One fruit I have already borne because of this cultivation is . . .

ALTAR MINISTERS

I serve the assembly in their work of re-pentance by . . .

LECTORS

My own work of repentance impacts my Sunday proclamation in that . . .

EXTRAORDINARY MINISTERS OF HOLY COMMUNION

As Body of Christ I "cultivate" and "fertil-ize" the discipleship of others by . . .

Model Act of Penitence

Presider: During Lent we are called to repent. Let us reflect on how we have failed to use opportunities this week to repent and bear fruit . . . [pause]

    Confiteor: I confess . . .

Appreciating the Responsorial Psalm

This Sunday's gospel and second reading demand that we repent and do so immediately. The demand is unequivocal: if we do not repent we shall perish. Yet Jesus, in his parable of the fig tree, seems to soften his own demand. God, he says, will always give us one more chance. The psalm reveals why.

With numerous images the psalm tells us how merciful God is, how compassionate, forgiving, and kind. God is not vindictive, but "slow to anger" and quick to "pardon . . . iniquities." The demand that we repent remains, but the way there is to reach out and accept this mercy offered without stint. This is the task of Lent: that we let our hearts be cultivated by a divine mercy which transforms the barren into new life.

Model General Intercessions

Presider: God is kind and merciful and so we are encouraged to make our needs known.

Response:

Lord, hear our prayer.

Cantor:

we pray to the Lord,

That all people of God strive for repentance and bear much fruit . . . [pause]

That all people of the world cultivate justice and peace . . . [pause]

That those who suffer tragedies in their lives find comfort in their faith . . . [pause]

That we ourselves always turn toward Jesus as the one who nourishes and cares for us . . . [pause]

Presider: Kind and merciful God, you hear the prayers of your people who cry out to you: answer our prayers and lead us to life everlasting. Grant this through Christ our Lord. **Amen.**

ALTERNATIVE OPENING PRAYER

Let us pray

Pause for silent prayer

God of all compassion, Father of all
    goodness,
to heal the wounds our sins and
    selfishness bring upon us
you bid us turn to fasting, prayer, and
    sharing with our brothers.
We acknowledge our sinfulness, our guilt
    is ever before us:
when our weakness causes
    discouragement,
let your compassion fill us with hope
and lead us through a Lent of repentance
    to the beauty of Easter joy.
Grant this through Christ our Lord.
    Amen.

FIRST READING
Exod 3:1-8a, 13-15

Moses was tending the flock of his father-
    in-law Jethro,
    the priest of Midian.
Leading the flock across the desert, he
    came to Horeb,
    the mountain of God.
There an angel of the LORD appeared to
    Moses in fire
    flaming out of a bush.
As he looked on, he was surprised to see
    that the bush,
    though on fire, was not consumed.
So Moses decided,
    "I must go over to look at this
        remarkable sight,
    and see why the bush is not burned."

When the LORD saw him coming over to
    look at it more closely,
    God called out to him from the bush,
        "Moses! Moses!"
He answered, "Here I am."
God said, "Come no nearer!
Remove the sandals from your feet,
    for the place where you stand is holy
        ground.
I am the God of your fathers," he
    continued,
    "the God of Abraham, the God of Isaac,
        the God of Jacob."
Moses hid his face, for he was afraid to
    look at God.
But the LORD said,
    "I have witnessed the affliction of my
        people in Egypt
    and have heard their cry of complaint
        against their slave drivers,
    so I know well what they are suffering.
Therefore I have come down to rescue
    them

from the hands of the Egyptians
and lead them out of that land into a good and spacious land,
a land flowing with milk and honey."

Moses said to God, "But when I go to the Israelites
and say to them, 'The God of your fathers has sent me to you,'
if they ask me, 'What is his name?' what am I to tell them?"
God replied, "I am who am."
Then he added, "This is what you shall tell the Israelites:
I AM sent me to you."

God spoke further to Moses, "Thus shall you say to the Israelites:
The Lord, the God of your fathers,
the God of Abraham, the God of Isaac, the God of Jacob,
has sent me to you.

"This is my name forever;
thus am I to be remembered through all generations."

RESPONSORIAL PSALM
Ps 103:1-2, 3-4, 6-7, 8, 11

℟. (8a) The Lord is kind and merciful.

Bless the LORD, O my soul;
and all my being, bless his holy name.
Bless the LORD, O my soul,
and forget not all his benefits.

℟. The Lord is kind and merciful.

He pardons all your iniquities,
heals all your ills.
He redeems your life from destruction,
crowns you with kindness and compassion.

℟. The Lord is kind and merciful.

The LORD secures justice
and the rights of all the oppressed.
He has made known his ways to Moses,
and his deeds to the children of Israel.

℟. The Lord is kind and merciful.

Merciful and gracious is the LORD,
slow to anger and abounding in kindness.
For as the heavens are high above the earth,
so surpassing is his kindness toward those who fear him.

℟. The Lord is kind and merciful.

SECOND READING
1 Cor 10:1-6, 10-12

See Appendix A, p. 270.

CATECHESIS

About Liturgy

Lenten Sundays connect: In our personal and parish preparations for this and the next two Sundays, it is good to keep in mind that these Sundays are linked during all three years. During year A (and at Masses when the Scrutinies are celebrated) a baptismal motif runs through the gospels; during year B, the third to fifth Sundays of Lent have as a motif the dying and rising mystery of Christ; and during this year C, the motif for these three Sundays is repentance. Moreover, not only are the three Sundays during each year linked, but the years are linked together as well. The baptismal motif (year A) reminds us that it is through our baptism that we are plunged into the mystery of Christ (year B), and we remain faithful to that mystery through continuing repentance (year C).

Further, the first two Sundays (temptations and transfiguration) as well as Palm Sunday (hosannah! gospel at the procession with palms and Passion gospel during the Liturgy of the Word) also frame Lent with the paschal mystery rhythm of dying and rising. The more effort we make to connect the Sundays, the more able we are to experience the liturgical year as an unfolding of the paschal mystery, as an invitation to enter more deeply into our Christian identity as disciples, and as an encounter with God who offers us salvation.

About Liturgical Music

Cantor preparation: As during previous weeks, you need to prepare yourself to sing the responsorial psalm by praying the whole of the psalm from which its verses have been taken. Jesus' insistence on repentance (gospel) cannot be understood outside of God's continuing compassion for human weakness (psalm). Do you see the mercy behind the call to repentance? Can you tell the assembly about it?

Communion song during Lent: No. 86 in GIRM states that the purpose of the Communion song is to express unity of spirit through unity of voices, to express joy, and to emphasize the communal nature of the procession. This means that even though it is Lent, the Communion song ought not be primarily penitential. If the Communion song speaks only of our sinfulness and our need for conversion (a valid disposition for Lent), we inadvertently make the Communion procession a penitential rite. This procession is an eschatological moment, however, both a promise and a completion of heaven, a celebration of having arrived at the messianic banquet where we are already transformed more fully into the Body of Christ. The Communion song, then, needs to communicate joy, praise, and thanksgiving. One example of a good Lenten Communion song is "Bless the Lord, My Soul" [BB]. Based on Psalm 103 (the source of this Sunday's responsorial psalm), the text thanks God for the mercy shown us despite our sins. Both tune and text communicate the joy appropriate for the Communion procession.

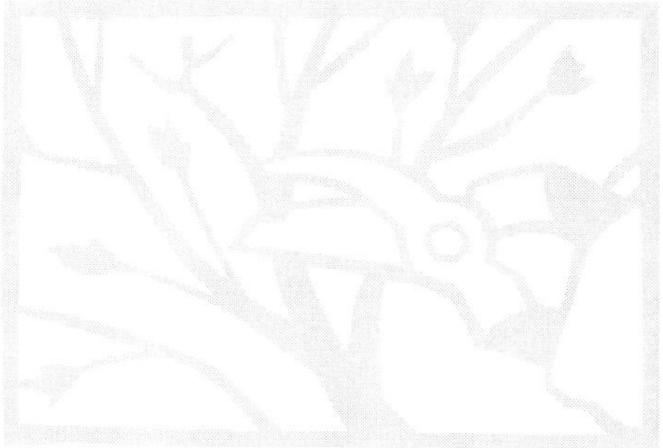

SPIRITUALITY

Gospel

Luke 15:1-3, 11-32; L33C

Tax collectors and sinners were all
    drawing near to listen to Jesus,
  but the Pharisees and scribes began
    to complain, saying,
  "This man welcomes
    sinners and eats with
    them."
So to them Jesus addressed
    this parable:
"A man had two sons, and the
    younger son said to his
    father,
  'Father give me the share of
    your estate that should
    come to me.'
So the father divided the property
    between them.
After a few days, the younger son
    collected all his belongings
  and set off to a distant country
    where he squandered his inheritance
    on a life of dissipation.
When he had freely spent everything,
    a severe famine struck that country,
    and he found himself in dire need.
So he hired himself out to one of the
    local citizens
  who sent him to his farm to tend the
    swine.
And he longed to eat his fill of the pods
    on which the swine fed,
  but nobody gave him any.
Coming to his senses he thought,
  'How many of my father's hired
    workers
  have more than enough food to eat,
  but here am I, dying from hunger.
I shall get up and go to my father and I
    shall say to him,
  "Father, I have sinned against heaven
    and against you.

Continued in Appendix A, p. 272.

See Appendix A, pp. 273–74, for optional readings.

Reflecting on the Gospel

Last week, repent or perish. This week, repent and feast. In this parable of the Prodigal Son we have an example of someone who does repent and enjoys the fruits of repentance: a welcome home, a loving embrace of the father, and a feast. Both sons hurt their father: the younger son takes his inheritance and leaves the family; the elder son refuses to celebrate when his brother returns. Toward each the father shows compassion and solicitude by inviting both to the feast. Neither the self-centeredness of the one nor the self-righteousness of the other diminishes the father's love for them. Entering the feast depends on their choice to repent.

Sometimes an outside catalyst brings us to repentance and conversion. For the younger son, the choice to repent is sparked by necessity (spent money and famine); he is humbled to seek forgiveness and accept a new relationship with his father ("treat me . . . as one of your hired workers"). The father, however, forgives him and restores him to his former relationship as son ("finest robe . . . ring . . . sandals . . ."). The generosity of the father, then, goes well beyond the tangible gifts he bestows upon his son. The surprise of the parable is that the father expresses his forgiveness by restoring the younger son to their former relationship.

The elder son, however, replies to his father's pleas to come to the feast that he has "all these years *served*" him. Here is the problem: the elder son *served* the father; there is no sense in the parable that the elder son ever responded to the father's constant generosity ("everything I have is yours") out of a filial, *loving* relationship. The elder son also needed to heal a relationship with his father that had gone awry, but he remained deaf to his father's compassionate overtures: he clung to his self-righteousness.

This Sunday's gospel is probably one of the most familiar to us; our Lenten challenge is to hear it anew and respond to the parable's call to repent and come to the feast. Reconciliation is, indeed, a "passing over" from famine to feast, from self-indulgence to self-giving. Like the father in the parable, our heavenly Father is loving and compassionate, always inviting us to his feast. This ought to give us courage to undertake our own repenting, no matter what our sinfulness. Let the feast begin!

Living the Paschal Mystery

Our Lenten penance calls us to go beyond where we are (like either the younger son or elder son) to the compassion and generosity of the father. Every day in countless ways we are faced with a choice to repent and make stronger our relationships with others. Only by choosing to repent can we feast. Ultimately, our Lenten (and life) journey is one of reconciliation which brings healing and restored relationship. Reconciliation implies a letting go of whatever binds us or hinders us or turns us in on ourselves and a "passing over" to receiving the compassion and mercy which can only be celebrated in the abundance of a feast.

Lent tends to pass all too quickly. We cannot let it go by and be satisfied only with "giving up" something. Lent also offers us a positive opportunity to reflect on our many relationships, especially with those closest to us (family, parish community, colleagues at work). Repentance challenges us to look deeply into our own selves and root out whatever self-centeredness keeps us from receiving God's mercy and compassion and from offering forgiveness to (or seeking it from) others.

Focusing the Gospel

Key words and phrases: younger son . . . give me the share . . . set off; Father, I have sinned; father . . . embraced him; celebrate with a feast; older son . . . refused; father came out and pleaded with him; celebrate and rejoice

To the point: In the parable both sons hurt their father: the younger son takes his inheritance and leaves the family; the elder son refuses to celebrate when his brother returns. Toward each the father shows compassion and solicitude by inviting both to the feast. Neither the self-centeredness of the one nor the self-righteousness of the other diminishes the father's love for them. Entering the feast depends on their choice to repent.

Connecting the Gospel

to last Sunday's gospel: Last week, repent or perish. This week, repent and feast. In this parable of the Prodigal Son we have an example of someone who does repent and enjoys the fruits of repentance: the embrace of the father and a feast.

to our culture: Societies and families often have a hard time dealing with people who change their point of view or way of life. At the most profound level, Lent calls us both to change ourselves and to accept the changes in others.

Understanding Scripture

Rejoicing in mercy: In his self-centeredness, the Prodigal Son in this Sunday's familiar parable is in no way admirable. He demanded his share of his father's estate even before the father is dead and then "he squandered his inheritance on a life of dissipation." Even his "coming to his senses" is self-centered: it is not because he recognized the error of his ways, nor because he has hurt his father and acted irresponsibly. Rather, it is because of his reduced circumstances and his severe hunger that he decides to return to his father. Nevertheless, though his motives are tainted, he returns.

For his part, the older brother is self-righteous. To his credit, he is altogether admirable in serving his father faithfully and never—not even once—disobeying orders. Although he perhaps imagines himself as the ideal son (someone from whom his brother could learn!), the irony is that he needs to learn from his brother what it means to repent. To start, he reacts peevishly to his brother's return; he thinks his filial duties should have been rewarded with a feast; he cannot recognize or share his father's relief and joy in having his son back; he stands on his hurt pride and refuses to enter the feast; he virtually disowns his brother by referring to him as "your son," not as "my brother." He, though he never wandered far from family or home or entertained a life of sin, has much about which he needs to repent.

The older brother, though obedient and faithful, is called to more. He is called to a compassion which celebrates when mercy is extended even to his undeserving brother. Luke's introduction to the parable tells us that Jesus addresses the parable to the Pharisees and the scribes who complain that Jesus "welcomes sinners and eats with them." Instead of rejoicing that sinners are being welcomed to the Father's feast, they are upset. The Pharisees and scribes—like the older brother—are called to more than personal goodness. Even good and faithful disciples are called to a compassion which rejoices in God's mercy.

ASSEMBLY & FAITH-SHARING GROUPS
- Of the two sons, I am more like . . . because . . .
- The difference in my life when I experience the Father's forgiving embrace and kiss is . . .
- I have been like the extravagant, forgiving father when . . .

PRESIDERS
Of the two sons I am most comfortable serving people like the . . . son because . . .

DEACONS
Where I might serve reconciliation in my faith community is . . .

HOSPITALITY MINISTERS
I am extravagant in hospitality to even the undeserving whenever I . . .

MUSIC MINISTERS
I find myself acting self-righteously in my music ministry when . . . I find myself acting in a self-centered way when . . . What calls me back "home" (gospel) to right relationship with God and others is . . .

ALTAR MINISTERS
Where I need to promote reconciliation in my family is . . .

LECTORS
I invite others, even the most undeserving, to return to the Lord by . . .

EXTRAORDINARY MINISTERS OF HOLY COMMUNION
Others "taste and see" (psalm) in me God's mercy whenever I . . .

Model Act of Penitence

Presider: God invites us to this Eucharistic feast. To celebrate worthily, let us confess our sins and ask for mercy . . . [pause]

   Confiteor: I confess . . .

Appreciating the Responsorial Psalm

The psalmist in Psalm 34 has experienced God's saving intervention in some personal, concrete way and now wants everyone to "taste and see" how good God is. The Israelites experienced this goodness when God acted to save them from Egypt, fed them manna in the desert, then nourished them with the fruits of the Promised Land (first reading). The Prodigal Son met this goodness when he returned to his father's house (gospel). We meet it in Christ who eats with sinners (gospel) and reconciles us to God (second reading). In the context of Lent the goodness of God we taste is forgiveness and reconciliation. These verses from Psalm 34 invite us to come now to the feast which awaits us at the end of our Lenten journey home.

Model General Intercessions

Presider: Surely our merciful and compassionate God hears the prayers of those who cry out. And so we pray.

Response:

Lord, hear our prayer.

Cantor:

we pray to the Lord,

That the Church may faithfully herald God's reconciling love . . . [pause]

That warring nations and peoples may be reconciled . . . [pause]

That those alienated from their families may be reconciled . . . [pause]

That Lent may be a time of true repentance for all of us . . . [pause]

Presider: Merciful and compassionate God, you sent your Son Jesus to reconcile us to you and each other: hear these our prayers that we might come joyfully to your promised feast. We ask this through Christ our Lord. **Amen.**

ALTERNATIVE OPENING PRAYER

Let us pray

Pause for silent prayer

God our Father,
your Word, Jesus Christ, spoke peace to a
    sinful world
and brought mankind the gift of
    reconciliation
by the suffering and death he endured.
Teach us, the people who bear his name,
to follow the example he gave us:
may our faith, hope, and charity
turn hatred to love, conflict to peace, death
    to eternal life.

We ask this through Christ our Lord.
   Amen.

FIRST READING

Josh 5:9a, 10-12

The LORD said to Joshua,
   "Today I have removed the reproach of
      Egypt from you."

While the Israelites were encamped at
      Gilgal on the plains of Jericho,
   they celebrated the Passover
   on the evening of the fourteenth of the
      month.
On the day after the Passover,
   they ate of the produce of the land
   in the form of unleavened cakes and
      parched grain.
On that same day after the Passover,
   on which they ate of the produce of the
      land, the manna ceased.
No longer was there manna for the
      Israelites,
   who that year ate of the yield of the
      land of Canaan.

RESPONSORIAL PSALM

Ps 34:2-3, 4-5, 6-7

R̲. (9a) Taste and see the goodness of the Lord.

I will bless the LORD at all times;
    his praise shall be ever in my mouth.
Let my soul glory in the LORD;
    the lowly will hear me and be glad.

R̲. Taste and see the goodness of the Lord.

Glorify the LORD with me,
    let us together extol his name.
I sought the LORD, and he answered me
    and delivered me from all my fears.

R̲. Taste and see the goodness of the Lord.

Look to him that you may be radiant with
        joy,
    and your faces may not blush with
        shame.
When the poor one called out, the LORD
        heard,
    and from all his distress he saved him.

R̲. Taste and see the goodness of the Lord.

SECOND READING

2 Cor 5:17-21

Brothers and sisters:
Whoever is in Christ is a new creation:
    the old things have passed away;
    behold, new things have come.
And all this is from God,
    who has reconciled us to himself
        through Christ
    and given us the ministry of
        reconciliation,
    namely, God was reconciling the world
        to himself in Christ,
    not counting their trespasses against
        them
    and entrusting to us the message of
        reconciliation.
So we are ambassadors for Christ,
    as if God were appealing through us.
We implore you on behalf of Christ,
    be reconciled to God.
For our sake he made him to be sin who
        did not know sin,
    so that we might become the
        righteousness of God in him.

or, these readings from year A:

1 Sam 16:1b, 6-7, 10-13a
Ps 23:1-3a, 3b-4, 5, 6
Eph 5:8-14
John 9:1-41

See Appendix A, pp. 273–74.

About Liturgy

Eucharist and reconciliation: Eucharist is considered the sacrament of reconciliation *par excellence*. This is so for two reasons. First, Eucharist is a sacrament of reconciliation because Eucharist celebrates and strengthens our unity in the Body of Christ. At Eucharist we are nourished at both the tables of the Word and Sacrament. The word helps us shape our lives after Christ's, a life of compassion and forgiveness. At the table we share in the same Body and Blood of Christ, enabling us to grow together in our common identity. Second, Eucharist is a sacrament of reconciliation because in Eucharist we come to the feast—God's messianic feast whereby we already share in the fullness of life (and relationships) which is to come. There is a price to pay for this reconciliation: both becoming one in Christ and sharing in the feast entails a letting go of whatever behaviors are stumbling blocks to unity and feasting.

The Sacrament of Penance, the Church's specific ritual of reconciliation, is not unrelated to Eucharist's reconciliation. In this sacrament we acknowledge to another our sinfulness and seek the forgiveness and reconciliation of the Church. Having healed broken or weakened relationships (with God, self, others), we come to the Eucharistic feast to celebrate our restored relationships.

About Liturgical Music

Cantor preparation: The verses of this Sunday's responsorial psalm are not sung *to* God, but *about* God. They come out of personal experience of the God who leads from famine to feast (first reading) and from sin to reconciliation (gospel). What experience of God's goodness and mercy can inspire your singing of this psalm? What radiance (see last strophe) will shine on your face?

Music suggestions: Good Lenten hymns and songs abound. A particularly appropriate one for this Sunday is "Our Father, We Have Wandered" [PMB, JS2, WC, WS]. Based on the parable of the Prodigal Son, this hymn is set to the PASSION CHORALE tune so strongly associated with the season of Lent. The hymn could be used for either the entrance procession or the presentation of the gifts. Another excellent choice is "Eternal Lord of Love" [CBW3, G2, GC, JS2, RS]. The image in the first verse of God's watching and leading the Church on its "pilgrim way of Lent" identifies the Church with the Israelites on their journey to the Promised Land, but it is also reminiscent of the journey home of the Prodigal Son, with the father compassionately watching for his return. To all—the Israelites in the desert, the Church on her Lenten journey, the Prodigal Son returning home—the conclusion of the verse beautifully applies, "Moved by your love and toward your presence bent: Far off yet here, the goal of all desire."

SPIRITUALITY

Gospel Luke 2:41-51a; L543

Each year Jesus' parents went to
    Jerusalem for the feast of Passover,
    and when he was twelve years
        old,
    they went up according to
        festival custom.
After they had completed
    its days, as they were
        returning,
    the boy Jesus remained
        behind in Jerusalem,
    but his parents did not know
        it.
Thinking that he was in the
    caravan,
    they journeyed for a day
    and looked for him among their
        relatives and acquaintances,
    but not finding him,
    they returned to Jerusalem to look
        for him.
After three days they found him in the
    temple,
    sitting in the midst of the teachers,
    listening to them and asking them
        questions,
    and all who heard him were astounded
    at his understanding and his answers.
When his parents saw him,
    they were astonished,
    and his mother said to him,
"Son, why have you done this to us?
Your father and I have been looking for
    you with great anxiety."
And he said to them,
"Why were you looking for me?
Did you not know that I must be in my
    Father's house?"
But they did not understand what he
    said to them.
He went down with them and came to
    Nazareth,
    and was obedient to them.

See Appendix A, p. 275, for other readings.

Reflecting on the Gospel

"Each year Jesus' parents went to Jerusalem for the feast of Passover . . ." Thus begins this solemnity's gospel from Luke, noting the great spring festival of Jewish identity. Each year about this time our various "rites of spring" begin. So many of these rites are concerned with "passings." For example, the winter "death" of nature in the northern hemisphere passes over to the budding of new life. The past budding of new love "passes over" for many in the abundance of spring weddings and the new relationships the marriages bring for the couples. First Communions celebrate passing over into fuller initiation in Christ. Junior-senior proms mark the passing of high school days for some and the passing into final year of high school for others. The life around us and our own personal lives are always filled with "passovers."

This gospel suggests to us two "passovers"—one for Jesus and one for Joseph and Mary. Jesus announces that he "must be in [his] Father's house" and indicates that he is "passing over" in his life journey from his hidden childhood toward assuming his public ministry of announcing that God's reign is at hand. Mary and Joseph continue the normal care and concern of parents, but also are challenged to "pass over" into secondary roles as Jesus will soon take up his adult ministry. As head of this Jewish household, we presume Joseph led the way and modeled for his family the virtues necessary for each of them to embrace their own passover events.

In this gospel Joseph models three particular virtues. First, he is obedient to the requirements of Jewish Law ("Each year . . . went to Jerusalem for . . . Passover"). Thus Joseph reminds us that our "passing over" into greater maturity in Christ through our own decisions to live as he taught is in continuity with a whole tradition of holy people who placed their lives at God's disposition. Second, Joseph takes responsibility for his son's whereabouts and welfare ("your father and I have been looking for you with great anxiety"). Joseph challenges us to take responsibility for how we are disciples of Jesus, how we have assumed our own role in the tradition of saving events. Third, Joseph humbly accepts the secondary role assigned to him when Jesus acknowledges God as his Father. We, too, find our deepest identity and ministry not in a holy city or feast or sacred space, but in a person: Jesus Christ. Our whole lives must be lived by keeping our focus on Jesus whom we serve.

Living the Paschal Mystery

This feastday and the virtues Joseph models for us provide an opportunity for us to reflect on our own "passing over" into more perfectly continuing Jesus' saving ministry. So little is known about Joseph; he achieved sainthood not by big, ostentatious saving actions but by simply, obediently following the saving role God asked of him. We, too, are called to simply, obediently follow the saving role God asks of us and we do so most faithfully when we discern the pattern of Jesus' own dying and rising in our lives and continually grow in our ability to give of ourselves for the sake of others. Such is the mystery of Christ into which we are initiated. Such is the mystery Joseph modeled.

Like Joseph, we must continually search for Jesus in our daily lives. We find him not only in invitations to do acts of kindness and compassion, but also when we see his countenance on the face of others. Our role in bringing about salvation is to remain faithful to the presence of Jesus.

Focusing the Gospel

Key words and phrases: parents went to Jerusalem, Passover, temple

To the point: In this gospel Joseph models three virtues. First, he is obedient to the requirements of Jewish Law ("Each year . . . went to Jerusalem for . . . Passover"). Second, he takes responsibility for his son's whereabouts and welfare ("your father and I have been looking for you with great anxiety"). Third, he humbly accepts the secondary role assigned to him when Jesus acknowledges God as his Father.

Model Act of Penitence

Presider: St. Joseph is the patron of the universal Church and model of obedience, responsibility, and humility. Let us pray that we may grow in these virtues . . . [pause]

Lord Jesus, you are the son of David: Lord . . .

Christ Jesus, you dwell in your Father's house: Christ . . .

Lord Jesus, you are the obedient Son of your Father: Lord . . .

Model General Intercessions

Presider: With St. Joseph as our protector and intercessor, we are encouraged to make our needs known to God.

Response:
Lord, hear our prayer.

Cantor:
we pray to the Lord,

That all members of the Church be obedient to our loving God . . . [pause]

That all people of the world live humbly and act responsibly . . . [pause]

That those suffering from the anxiety of lost loved ones may be comforted . . . [pause]

That all of us continually search for Jesus in our daily lives . . . [pause]

Presider: Loving God, you provided a loving family for your Son: show us the same love and grant our prayers through Christ our Lord. **Amen.**

OPENING PRAYER
Let us pray

Pause for silent prayer

Father,
you entrusted our Savior to the care of
      St. Joseph.
By the help of his prayers
may your Church continue to serve its Lord,
      Jesus Christ,
who lives and reigns with you and the Holy
      Spirit,
one God, for ever and ever. **Amen.**

FOR REFLECTION

- St. Joseph's life teaches me that the faith journey is . . .

- I diligently look for Jesus by . . .

- What I have learned about Jesus after finding him in some surprising places is . . .

SPIRITUALITY

Gospel

John 8:1-11; L36C

Jesus went to the Mount of Olives.
But early in the morning he arrived
    again in the temple area,
  and all the people started coming
    to him,
  and he sat down and taught them.
Then the scribes and the Pharisees
    brought a woman
  who had been caught in adultery
  and made her stand in the middle.
They said to him,
  "Teacher, this woman was caught
  in the very act of committing
    adultery.
Now in the law, Moses commanded us
    to stone such women.
So what do you say?"
They said this to test him,
  so that they could have some charge
    to bring against him.
Jesus bent down and began to write on
    the ground with his finger.
But when they continued asking him,
  he straightened up and said to them,
  "Let the one among you who is
    without sin
  be the first to throw a stone at her."
Again he bent down and wrote on the
    ground.
And in response, they went away one
    by one,
  beginning with the elders.
So he was left alone with the woman
    before him.
Then Jesus straightened up and said to
    her,
  "Woman, where are they?
Has no one condemned you?"
She replied, "No one, sir."
Then Jesus said, "Neither do I condemn
    you.
Go, and from now on do not sin any
    more."

See Appendix A, pp. 276–78, for optional readings.

Reflecting on the Gospel

It was at a religious education conference a good number of years ago attended by almost a thousand people. Mother Teresa was the featured afternoon speaker. About a half hour before the event, people began to congregate in the auditorium, milling about meeting colleagues and sharing shop talk. The room was noisy and full of people going this way and that. At about ten minutes before the hour, the chairperson walked out on the stage to adjust the microphone. Unbeknownst to him, Mother Teresa followed him out. Immediately, as if by some unsounded signal, the entire auditorium became totally still and silent. All eyes turned to the stage in one sweeping movement. The air was electric. This tiny woman's presence was so intense that hundreds of people were immediately affected. The encounter was overwhelming. If this tiny woman can effect so much in so many, what would an overwhelming encounter with Jesus effect?

The center of this gospel is not the woman or her sin of adultery, but a personal encounter with Jesus. Encountering Jesus always exposes the truth—both the woman *and* the crowd learn the truth about their own sin. The crowd was led to the truth that they are more like the woman in also being sinners than they would want to admit. The woman is led to the truth of her own sinfulness (Jesus: "sin no more"). They and we are not that different: we are all sinners who need to encounter Jesus, ask the truth about ourselves, and receive Jesus' mercy. Encounter with Christ is the occasion for changing both the condemners and the condemned.

These encounters with Jesus bring about two changes: those who are willing to condemn no longer condemn ("they went away"), and the one condemned is no longer condemned ("neither do I condemn you"). Although at face value this gospel doesn't seem to deal with the repentance motif of the last two Sundays, at closer look it does. For repentance means turning away from sinful behavior because one has encountered the One who is the author of truth and holiness. It is this encounter with Jesus that enables repentance in our lives.

Living the Paschal Mystery

Deep down inside, too many fear their sin is bigger than God's mercy. Jesus, however, responds to profound sin with even more profound mercy. Once we encounter Jesus, we are moved to repent, to change our behaviors. After the encounter, what previously seemed valuable to us (our own way) is seen in truth to be sinful or "rubbish": "I consider everything as loss because of the supreme good of knowing Christ Jesus" (second reading). Consequently, our encounter with Jesus moves us to die to self ("For his sake I have accepted the loss of all things") so that we "gain Christ." Therein lies repentance.

Repentance, then, includes both a dying and a rising. Changing our ways is the dying; a new relationship with Christ is the rising. The deepest truth about ourselves lies not so much in recognizing our sinfulness (as important as that is!) as it lies in deepening our relationship with Christ. Encountering Christ and desiring to be more like him is what calls forth from us a repentant attitude. The closer we become to Christ the more able are we to recognize our own sinfulness (that which weakens our relationship with him) and repent of our ways. Then we hear Christ say to us, "Neither do I condemn you."

Focusing the Gospel
Key words and phrases: Jesus, all the people started coming to him, woman . . . caught in adultery, who is without sin, he was left alone with the woman, Neither do I condemn

To the point: The center of this gospel is not the woman or her sin of adultery, but a personal encounter with Jesus. Encountering Jesus always exposes the truth—both the woman *and* the crowd learn the truth about their own sin. They and we are not that different: we are all sinners who need to encounter Jesus, ask the truth about ourselves, and receive Jesus' mercy.

Connecting the Gospel
to the last two Sundays' motif of repentance: This Sunday we take the act of repentance to its source: encounter with Christ. That encounter is the occasion for changing both the condemners and the condemned.

to our Catholic culture: Deep down inside, too many fear their sin is bigger than God's mercy. Jesus, however, responds to profound sin with even more profound mercy.

Understanding Scripture
Caught in the act of sin: Although the scribes and Pharisees make the woman caught in adultery "stand in the middle" of the crowd, she is not the center of their concern. To them the woman is merely a prop. Although they present a legal case to Jesus, their concern is not the Law of Moses. To them, the law is merely a device to test Jesus.

As often pointed out, although the woman was allegedly "caught in the very act of committing adultery," the man is not present. The law to which the scribes and Pharisees appeal prescribes death for both the man and the woman (Deut 22:22; Lev 20:10). Again, the intent of this banana court is not justice; all that matters is that Jesus be discredited and possibly convicted of violating the law himself.

Interestingly, Jesus does not respond to the legal case presented to him. Rather, he views the entire matter as a moral concern. Whereas the scribes and Pharisees frame the issue in terms of law, Jesus frames it in terms of sin. While it may, perhaps, be possible for people to be always law abiding, sin is something in which all share. But in suggesting that all are sinners, Jesus is not saying that sin should not be condemned; rather each person should look to his or her own sin. This is similar to the Gospel on the Third Sunday of Lent in which Jesus redirected the crowd's curiosity about the sin of the victims of Pilate and the building accident to reflect rather on their own sin.

Jesus, the true center of the story, draws everyone into the charged situation: the spectators, the accusers, and the woman. Standing before Jesus, seeing his response, hearing his words—all learn the truth about themselves: they are sinners. The elders (traditionally honored as the wisest folks in town) are the first to see the wisdom of Jesus and so are the first to leave. The accusers, foiled again, also leave. The woman is given a reprieve from death and is offered a fresh start: "from now on do not sin any more."

ASSEMBLY & FAITH-SHARING GROUPS
- What this gospel teaches me about condemnation is . . .
- What this gospel teaches me about mercy is . . .
- What helps me replace condemning others with mercy for them is . . .

PRESIDERS
The truth about myself that Jesus is exposing is . . . Addressing this honestly impacts my ministry in that . . .

DEACONS
Someone who fears condemnation that I might guide to Jesus' mercy is . . .

HOSPITALITY MINISTERS
In my ministry I share Jesus' mercy towards others whenever I . . .

MUSIC MINISTERS
One way my participation in music ministry has led me to deeper encounter with Jesus is . . . One way it has helped me become more honest about myself is . . . One way it calls me to show greater mercy towards others is . . .

ALTAR MINISTERS
Serving others teaches me to replace condemnation with mercy for them in that . . .

LECTORS
Prayerfully receiving Jesus' mercy for me impacts my Sunday proclamation in that . . .

EXTRAORDINARY MINISTERS OF HOLY COMMUNION
I shall consider how celebrating the truth of my identity as Body of Christ empowers me to be merciful toward the sinner and to go and sin no more . . .

Model Act of Penitence

Presider: Wherever Jesus went he drew crowds to himself and taught them about love, mercy, and compassion. Let us ask God for forgiveness and mercy . . . [pause]

    Confiteor: I confess . . .

Appreciating the Responsorial Psalm

The first reading from Isaiah recounts God's mighty acts in restoring Israel as a nation after the Babylonian captivity. As Isaiah asserts, this restoration will make the Exodus look as if it were nothing ("Remember not the events of the past. . . . I am doing something new!"). The Gospel reading recounts God's acting again to do something new in Jesus. Instead of death, Jesus grants the adulterous woman life; instead of condemnation, he offers her forgiveness; instead of the past, he invites her into a new future.

Psalm 126 was Israel's song of liberation when they returned to their homeland after the Babylonian captivity. It is our song today. God constantly revolutionizes our own expectations by saving us in newer, deeper ways. The readings remind us, however, that the challenge is not just to see God's acting, but to act on what we see. We must let this new righteousness take possession of us (second reading). We must let go of our judgments and change our ways (Gospel). We must "forget what lies behind" and embrace the new future offered us (second reading). Only then can we know the past about which we sing is just the beginning.

Model General Intercessions

Presider: God hears the prayers of those who come in need. And so we pray.

Response:

Lord, hear our prayer.

Cantor:

we pray to the Lord,

That the Church may always nurture personal encounters with Jesus who is merciful, compassionate, and truthful . . . [pause]

That all leaders of nations be slow to condemn and quick to show compassion . . . [pause]

That those who stand condemned receive justice, mercy, and compassion . . . [pause]

That our encounters with Jesus may lead us to repentance . . . [pause]

Presider: God of mercy and compassion, you sent your Son to heal and forgive us: hear our prayers that we might enjoy union with you now and for ever. We ask this through Christ our Lord. **Amen.**

Let us pray

Pause for silent prayer

Father in heaven,
the love of your Son led him to accept the
    suffering of the cross
that his brothers might glory in new life.
Change our selfishness into self-giving.
Help us to embrace the world you have
    given us,
that we may transform the darkness of
    its pain
into the life and joy of Easter.

Grant this through Christ our Lord.
    Amen.

FIRST READING

Isa 43:16-21

Thus says the LORD,
    who opens a way in the sea
    and a path in the mighty waters,
who leads out chariots and horsemen,
    a powerful army,
till they lie prostrate together, never to rise,
    snuffed out and quenched like a wick.
Remember not the events of the past,
    the things of long ago consider not;
see, I am doing something new!
    Now it springs forth, do you not
        perceive it?
In the desert I make a way,
    in the wasteland, rivers.
Wild beasts honor me,
    jackals and ostriches,
for I put water in the desert
    and rivers in the wasteland
    for my chosen people to drink,
the people whom I formed for myself,
    that they might announce my praise.

RESPONSORIAL PSALM

Ps 126:1-2, 2-3, 4-5, 6

R̸. (3) The Lord has done great things for us; we are filled with joy.

When the LORD brought back the captives
    of Zion,
    we were like men dreaming.
Then our mouth was filled with laughter,
    and our tongue with rejoicing.

R̸. The Lord has done great things for us; we are filled with joy.

Then they said among the nations,
    "The LORD has done great things for
        them."
The LORD has done great things for us;
    we are glad indeed.

R̸. The Lord has done great things for us; we are filled with joy.

Restore our fortunes, O LORD,
    like the torrents in the southern desert.
Those that sow in tears
    shall reap rejoicing.

℟. The Lord has done great things for us;
we are filled with joy.

Although they go forth weeping,
    carrying the seed to be sown,
they shall come back rejoicing,
    carrying their sheaves.

℟. The Lord has done great things for us;
we are filled with joy.

SECOND READING
Phil 3:8-14

Brothers and sisters:
I consider everything as a loss
    because of the supreme good of
        knowing Christ Jesus my Lord.
For his sake I have accepted the loss of all
        things
    and I consider them so much rubbish,
    that I may gain Christ and be found in
        him,
    not having any righteousness of my
        own based on the law
    but that which comes through faith in
        Christ,
    the righteousness from God,
    depending on faith to know him and the
        power of his resurrection
    and the sharing of his sufferings by
        being conformed to his death,
    if somehow I may attain the
        resurrection from the dead.

It is not that I have already taken hold of it
    or have already attained perfect maturity,
    but I continue my pursuit in hope that I
        may possess it,
    since I have indeed been taken
        possession of by Christ Jesus.
Brothers and sisters, I for my part
    do not consider myself to have taken
        possession.
Just one thing: forgetting what lies behind
    but straining forward to what lies
        ahead,
    I continue my pursuit toward the goal,
    the prize of God's upward calling, in
        Christ Jesus.

or, these readings from year A:
Ezek 37:12-14
Ps 130:1-2, 3-4, 5-6, 7-8
Rom 8:8-11
John 11:1-45

See Appendix A, pp. 276–78.

CATECHESIS

About Liturgy

Lent and personal relationship with Christ: Sometimes we can get so caught up during Lent with doing "penance" that we forget that Lent is ultimately about encountering Jesus and coming to a deeper union with him. Our Lenten penance is never an end in itself but is always a means to a deeper relationship with Christ. As we discipline ourselves, we gradually learn new priorities and what's most important in our lives and are then better able to keep Christ at the center of our lives.

We are a full four weeks into our Lenten journey. Now is a good time to assess how well our Lenten penance has helped us overcome sin and come closer to Jesus. At liturgy during Lent we particularly focus the act of penitence at the beginning of Mass on begging God's mercy for our sinfulness. We might evaluate whether this act is simply a ritual element that we "go through" or whether it is truly a time for seeking God's mercy and forgiveness.

About Liturgical Music

Cantor preparation: In just six verses, Psalm 126 tells the entire story of salvation—wherever there is suffering and oppression, God acts to save. God always turns today's tears into tomorrow's rejoicing. Do you believe this story? Where do you see it unfolding in your own life? in the lives of others? in the life of the Church? in the world?

Choir preparation: The measure of your encounter with Christ during these weeks of Lent will be that "something new" (first reading) is coming to birth within and among you. Do you relate to one another with more compassion and forgiveness? Do you handle conflicts more justly? Do you witness the unity of the Body of Christ more clearly to the assembly? All of these "conversion points" will be evident in the way you lead the music of the liturgy and will enable you to lead the assembly to deeper encounter with Christ.

Music director preparation: Every Lent is a call to conversion, and the readings of year C focus particularly on the need for repentance. How have you been helping the choir and the other music ministers in the parish enter into this Lenten purpose? Do you incorporate prayer into your rehearsals? Do you model attentive listening during the liturgy? Do you practice compassion and charity in your dealings with those whom you direct and with whom you work? Most importantly, do you make time in your life for personal encounter with Christ so that you can hear his call for your repentance and conversion?

SPIRITUALITY

Gospel   Luke 1:26-38; L545

The angel Gabriel was sent from God
　to a town of Galilee called Nazareth,
　to a virgin betrothed to a man named
　　Joseph,
　of the house of David,
　and the virgin's name was
　　Mary.
And coming to her, he said,
　"Hail, full of grace! The Lord
　　is with you."
But she was greatly troubled at
　what was said
　and pondered what sort of
　　greeting this might be.
Then the angel said to her,
　"Do not be afraid, Mary,
　for you have found favor with God.
Behold, you will conceive in your womb
　and bear a son,
　and you shall name him Jesus.
He will be great and will be called Son
　of the Most High,
　and the Lord God will give him the
　　throne of David his father,
　and he will rule over the house of
　　Jacob forever,
　and of his Kingdom there will be no
　　end."
But Mary said to the angel,
　"How can this be,
　since I have no relations with a man?"
And the angel said to her in reply,
　"The Holy Spirit will come upon you,
　and the power of the Most High will
　　overshadow you.
Therefore the child to be born
　will be called holy, the Son of God.
And behold, Elizabeth, your relative,
　has also conceived a son in her old age,
　and this is the sixth month for her
　　who was called barren;
　for nothing will be impossible for God."
Mary said, "Behold, I am the handmaid
　of the Lord.
May it be done to me according to your
　word."
Then the angel departed from her.

See Appendix A, p. 278, for the other readings.

Reflecting on the Gospel

Those "terrible twos" are no joke! At a very early age we human beings learn to assert our own will, to say "NO!" One of the daunting tasks of parents is to teach their children obedience, "minding them." We do this not so much to make the children cower or mindlessly submissive, but so that the children grow in their ability to make right choices for themselves. Moreover, obedience doesn't just mean doing the will of another. Parents can force their children merely to do what they want. Beyond this, obedience means "hearing" what the parents want (the phrase "ears open to obedience" from the responsorial psalm refers to the ancient practice of a slave having his or her ears pierced to show willing obedience to the master). The readings for this solemnity all speak to obedience as more than saying "yes" ("be it done to me"). It involves being a "handmaid of the Lord," that is, being in relationship to God. Obedience is not an act of subservience but living out a relationship to God.

Obedience involves both a demand that is made—Ahaz to ask God for a sign, Christ to do God's will, Mary to say yes to being the mother of the Savior—and a response that is required. Ahaz didn't follow through on the response; Jesus did, as did Mary. Mary's yes begets Jesus and is a sign that "nothing is impossible with God." Jesus' yes brings salvation and is a sign of God's continuing mercy and love. Jesus' yes is a sign that God wishes to be in a personal relationship with us; our yes is a response to that relationship.

This solemnity of the Annunciation of the Lord is an important salvation feast marking much more than the beginning of Jesus' human life. It inaugurates in a "physical" way a unique relationship to God that humankind can now enjoy. Jesus' body was prepared—first in the womb of Mary through her obedience, then in Jesus' public ministry through his obedience—as a new sacrifice and offering for our sake. Thus it is that we all can find "favor with God." This is, indeed, Good News!

Living the Paschal Mystery

Jesus' willing obedience to his Father "consecrates" us (second reading) to a unique relationship with God. Through obedience to our baptismal commitment to put off the old self—renounce evil—and rise with Christ we do God's will. The "demand" of our baptismal obedience is to renounce evil and do good. The further response required of us is the willingness to see in our obedience a new relationship with God. For in baptism we are anointed ("consecrated") to be members of the Body of Christ. So we enjoy an obedience that involves a unique, new relationship with God. Through the Son we can "know" the Father. This obedience sets us free! This obedience dispels all our fears! This obedience promises life everlasting! Why say "No!" when our yes can bring us so much?

At the same time, our yes does have its cost. The paschal mystery always reminds us that there is no life except through death. As Mary had to die to her own expectations in saying yes to God, so must we. This means, in practical terms, that we allow our yes for the good of others to guide us into new and unexpected paths to grace. Each time we say yes we are placing our own trust in God and placing ourselves at God's disposal for bringing about salvation. Indeed, why say "No!" when our yes can mean so much?

Focusing the Gospel

Key words and phrases: handmaid of the Lord, may it be done to me

To the point: Obedience is more than saying "yes" ("be it done to me"). It involves being a "handmaid of the Lord," that is, being in relationship to God. Obedience is not an act of subservience but living out a relationship to God.

Model Act of Penitence

Presider: Mary was obedient to doing God's will as was Christ, whose obedience won for us salvation. Let us reflect on our own obedience to God's will . . . [pause]

Lord Jesus, you were conceived in the womb of the Virgin Mary: Lord . . .
Christ Jesus, you came to do God's will: Christ . . .
Lord Jesus, you gave yourself for our salvation: Lord . . .

Model General Intercessions

Presider: God showed unbounded love for us when Jesus was conceived by the Holy Spirit. With this same love God hears our prayers.

Response:

Lord, hear our prayer.

Cantor:

we pray to the Lord,

That all members of the Church live as God's obedient servants . . . [pause]

That the leaders of nations be guided by the Spirit in all they do . . . [pause]

That the lonely find relationships of love and support . . . [pause]

That we here gathered faithfully imitate Mary in our response, "I come to do your will" . . . [pause]

Presider: Loving God, you hear the prayers of your obedient children: may we always be faithful to doing your will so that one day we may enjoy life with you for ever. We ask this through Christ our Lord. **Amen.**

OPENING PRAYER

Let us pray

Pause for silent prayer

God our Father,
your Word became man and was born of
    the Virgin Mary.
May we become more like Jesus Christ
whom we acknowledge as our redeemer,
    God and man.

We ask this through our Lord Jesus Christ,
    your Son,
who lives and reigns with you and the Holy
    Spirit,
one God, for ever and ever. **Amen.**

FOR REFLECTION

- What it means to me to be a "handmaid of the Lord" is . . .
- What helps me go beyond *doing* acts of service for the Lord to *becoming* the Lord's servant is . . .
- Some ways I encourage and assist others to say "yes" like Mary to God's will are . . .

SPIRITUALITY

Gospel at the Procession with Palms

Luke 19:28-40; L37C

Jesus proceeded on his journey up to
    Jerusalem.
As he drew near to Bethphage
    and Bethany
    at the place called the Mount
    of Olives,
    he sent two of his disciples.
He said, "Go into the village
    opposite you,
    and as you enter it you will
    find a colt tethered
    on which no one has ever sat.
Untie it and bring it here.
And if anyone should ask you,
    'Why are you untying it?'
    you will answer,
    'The Master has need of it.'"
So those who had been sent went off
    and found everything just as he had
    told them.
And as they were untying the colt, its
    owners said to them,
    "Why are you untying this colt?"
They answered,
    "The Master has need of it."
So they brought it to Jesus,
    threw their cloaks over the colt,
    and helped Jesus to mount.
As he rode along,
    the people were spreading their cloaks
    on the road;
    and now as he was approaching the
    slope of the Mount of Olives,
    the whole multitude of his disciples
    began to praise God aloud with joy
    for all the mighty deeds they had seen.
They proclaimed:
    "Blessed is the king who comes
    in the name of the Lord.
    Peace in heaven
    and glory in the highest."
Some of the Pharisees in the crowd said
    to him,
    "Teacher, rebuke your disciples."
He said in reply,
    "I tell you, if they keep silent,
    the stones will cry out!"

*See Appendix A, pp. 279–81, for
the Gospel at Mass.*

Reflecting on the Gospel

This Sunday is the sixth and last Sunday of Lent, and it begins the most solemn of all weeks in the entire liturgical year. We begin this week with a proclamation of the Passion. When we hear this gospel proclamation, we tend to be most mindful of all the suffering Jesus endured. Our human experience of suffering is that we become (usually necessarily and rightly) more focused on ourselves: how to relieve or minimize the pain or difficult situation. Our own needs come first because they are of immediate concern. This is not necessarily a selfish response, but a natural one. Jesus, on the other hand, even in his hour of greatest need and suffering still reaches out to those in need around him. Even at this time he still musters the strength and love and compassion to care for others. Even in this hour of need he shows us how our Lenten penance must be undertaken and where it leads—beyond penance to reaching out to others.

Luke's Passion (whose account we read this year) thus reminds us that the Passion also proclaims Jesus' ultimate self-giving ministry for others. Though Jesus is facing his own death, his gaze and concern are always directed to those around him: affirming his disciples, healing the man with the severed ear, comforting the women of Jerusalem, forgiving his executioners, saving the repentant thief. In his darkest hour, Jesus' identity as compassionate Savior shines most brightly. Already in his suffering and death Jesus is showing us that the very dying includes life-giving to others.

The first reading illustrates this point most profoundly, for Isaiah's prophecy finds its fulfillment in Jesus: it not only describes his suffering but also his concern for others, "speak[ing] to the weary a word" of comfort. Jesus' concern for others in the midst of suffering speaks not only of his own startling self-giving, but also of the startling *value of the needy person.* Even when suffering Jesus loves the other so much! Such is the care modeled by our Savior. Such is the life of his disciples.

Living the Paschal Mystery

In spite of the fact that we have two distinct gospels with two distinct "feelings" at Mass this Sunday (quite unusual in itself), the purpose of the first gospel and procession is to ready us in a most profound way to hear the proclamation of the Passion and to celebrate well the Triduum. Our procession with the palms is a way to engage our whole selves—including the actual bodily movement from one place to another—in symbolizing our own paschal journey with Christ. This procession with palms brings us, literally, to the doorstep of the Passion and in this way it prepares and readies us for the proclamation of the Passion.

This suggests two ways to live Holy Week. First, to see all our actions this week as a continuation of the procession with palms, joining ourselves with Jesus on his journey to the cross. Rather than a somber, morbid week we live in anticipation of embracing the cross so that we might experience new life on Easter.

Second, knowing full well that the journey this week (and of our whole Christian life) leads to the cross, to commit ourselves to be especially aware of those around us in need, as Jesus was always compassionate toward those in need. No matter how busy we are preparing for a holiday weekend, we want to redouble our efforts to be mindful of the countless ways each day we are called to die to self for the sake of others.

Focusing the Gospel

Key words and phrases: the hour came; you . . . have stood by me; healed him; do not weep; Father, forgive them; you will be with me in Paradise

To the point: Though Jesus is facing his own death, his gaze and concern are always directed to those around him: affirming his disciples, healing the man with the severed ear, comforting the women of Jerusalem, forgiving his executioners, saving the repentant thief. In his darkest hour, Jesus' identity as compassionate savior shines most brightly.

Connecting the Gospel

to the first reading: Isaiah's prophecy finds its fulfillment in Jesus: it not only describes his suffering but also his concern for others, "speak[ing] to the weary a word" of comfort.

to Catholic culture: When we hear the proclamation of the Passion, we are most mindful of all the suffering Jesus endured. Luke reminds us that the Passion also proclaims Jesus' ultimate self-giving ministry for others.

Understanding Scripture

The servant who suffers, trusts, encourages: Although Palm Sunday's first reading from Isaiah is the same in all three years of the Lectionary, it is particularly well suited to this year's Passion according to Luke. Isaiah 50:4-7 is the third of four passages that describes the ministry of an unnamed "servant of the Lord." (The fourth passage will be read as the first reading on Good Friday.) It is easy to see how Jesus' suffering fulfills Isaiah's prophecy: "I gave my back to those who beat me, my cheeks to those who plucked my beard; my face I did not shield from buffets and spitting" (50:6). In the house of the high priest, Jesus was ridiculed, beaten, and reviled (Luke 22:63-65); Herod and his men "treated him contemptuously and mocked him" (23:11); Pilate offered to have him flogged (23:22). In all this, Jesus fulfills Isaiah's prophecy of a suffering servant of the Lord.

At the same time the passage from Isaiah makes two other points. First, the servant encourages and rouses the weary (Isa 50:4). And so it is that Jesus encourages the disciples (Luke 22:28-30), comforts the women of Jerusalem (23:27-31), forgives his executioners (23:34), and brings the repentant thief to Paradise (23:42-43). Although Jesus is undergoing the greatest trial of his life and is suffering at the hands of those who hate him, he is still reaching out with care and concern to others. Second, Isaiah's mysterious servant, even under duress and great threat, trusts in God to deliver him: "GOD is my help . . . I am not disgraced . . . I shall not be put to shame" (Isa 50:7). And so it is that Jesus, with sublime trust rather than with Mark's agonizing doubt (see Mark 15:34), commends his spirit into the hands of God (Luke 23:46). It is confidence in God which steels his nerves or, in the words of Isaiah, allows him to "set [his] face like flint" (Isa 50:7).

**ASSEMBLY &
FAITH-SHARING GROUPS**

- As I watch that Jesus in his suffering (Passion) is still concerned for others, I realize . . .
- What helps me remain other-centered when I am suffering is . . .
- What my suffering has taught me about being compassionate toward others is . . .

PRESIDERS

Where I am challenged to be compassionate in the midst of my suffering is . . .

DEACONS

My service not only comforts others in their suffering, but also assists their growth in compassion in that . . .

HOSPITALITY MINISTERS

My hospitality includes a spirit of compassion toward others in that . . .

MUSIC MINISTERS

Music ministry during Holy Week will demand much more of me than usual. In the midst of these demands, one way I can focus not on myself but on the needs of others is . . .

ALTAR MINISTERS

My service to others embodies the suffering Jesus' compassion toward others in that . . .

LECTORS

As part of my preparation, I shall identify someone who is "weary" and consider how I might "rouse" or comfort him or her (see first reading)—in word or deed—in Christ . . .

**EXTRAORDINARY MINISTERS
OF HOLY COMMUNION**

Ways that I am Christ's living bread for those carrying the cross are . . .

Model Act of Penitence *(only at Masses with the simple entrance)*

Presider: Today we begin the most solemn week of the year. To prepare ourselves to enter into these sacred mysteries, let us empty our heart of all that keeps us from God.

    Confiteor: I confess . . .

Appreciating the Responsorial Psalm

The whole of Psalm 22 is a masterpiece of poetry and theology. The psalmist struggles with an increasing sense of being abandoned (from "My God, my God, why have you abandoned me," to "all who see me scoff at me," to violent imagery of destruction and death) while also experiencing deepening intimacy with God (the One who is far away and does not answer is also the One who has been present "from my mother's womb"). The psalmist begs to be saved from suffering and violence, then offers God lengthy praise. Most lament psalms end with one or two short verses of praise but here the praise continues for nearly one-third of the text. Furthermore, the psalmist invites an ever-widening circle to join in the praise: first the psalmist's immediate family, then all of Israel, then all nations, then generations yet unborn, and, finally, even the dead.

Psalm 22 helps us understand the Passion—both Christ's and ours. God is not distant from the suffering, but very near. And the depth of the suffering can be the wellspring of the most profound praise. May our singing of these verses from Psalm 22 give us the courage we need to enter Holy Week aware of both the sorrow and the praise to which it will lead.

Model General Intercessions

Presider: As Jesus was concerned for others, we now bring our concerns for others to God.

Response:

Lord, hear our prayer.

Cantor:

we pray to the Lord,

That all members of the Church may manifest Christ's compassion by lives of generous service . . . [pause]

That all people may extend to one another the mercy God has shown the whole world . . . [pause]

That those who are sick, suffering, or dying may find comfort in Christ's compassionate embrace . . . [pause]

That all of us here may walk with Jesus through death to new life . . . [pause]

Presider: Redeeming God, you sent your Son to save us from sin: hear these our prayers that we might unite ourselves with the passion of Jesus Christ and so rise with him to new life. We pray through that same Jesus Christ our Lord. **Amen.**

OPENING PRAYER

Let us pray

Pause for silent prayer

Almighty, ever-living God,
you have given the human race Jesus
    Christ our Savior
as a model of humility.
He fulfilled your will by becoming man
and giving his life on the cross.
Help us to bear witness to you
by following his example of suffering
and make us worthy to share in his
    resurrection.

We ask this through our Lord Jesus Christ,
    your Son,
who lives and reigns with you and the
    Holy Spirit,
one God, for ever and ever. **Amen.**

FIRST READING

Isa 50:4-7

The Lord GOD has given me
    a well-trained tongue,
that I might know how to speak to the
    weary
    a word that will rouse them.
Morning after morning
    he opens my ear that I may hear;
and I have not rebelled,
    have not turned back.
I gave my back to those who beat me,
    my cheeks to those who plucked my
        beard;
my face I did not shield
    from buffets and spitting.

The Lord GOD is my help,
    therefore I am not disgraced;
I have set my face like flint,
    knowing that I shall not be put to
        shame.

RESPONSORIAL PSALM

Ps 22:8-9, 17-18, 19-20, 23-24

℟. (2a) My God, my God, why have you abandoned me?

All who see me scoff at me;
    they mock me with parted lips, they
        wag their heads:
"He relied on the LORD; let him deliver him,
    let him rescue him, if he loves him."

℟. My God, my God, why have you abandoned me?

Indeed, many dogs surround me,
    a pack of evildoers closes in upon me;
they have pierced my hands and my feet;
    I can count all my bones.

R7. My God, my God, why have you abandoned me?

They divide my garments among them,
    and for my vesture they cast lots.
But you, O LORD, be not far from me;
    O my help, hasten to aid me.

R7. My God, my God, why have you abandoned me?

I will proclaim your name to my brethren;
    in the midst of the assembly I will
        praise you:
"You who fear the LORD, praise him;
    all you descendants of Jacob, give glory
        to him;
    revere him, all you descendants of
        Israel!"

R7. My God, my God, why have you abandoned me?

SECOND READING
Phil 2:6-11

Christ Jesus, though he was in the form
    of God,
    did not regard equality with God
        something to be grasped.
Rather, he emptied himself,
    taking the form of a slave,
    coming in human likeness;
    and found human in appearance,
    he humbled himself,
    becoming obedient to the point of
        death,
    even death on a cross.
Because of this, God greatly exalted him
    and bestowed on him the name
    which is above every name,
    that at the name of Jesus
    every knee should bend,
    of those in heaven and on earth and
        under the earth,
    and every tongue confess that
    Jesus Christ is Lord,
    to the glory of God the Father.

About Liturgy

Palm Sunday entrances: The Sacramentary provides three forms of entrance. The *procession* includes the ministers and assembly processing together from a building or place at a distance from or separate from the worship space. The *procession* may take place only once, at the principal Mass. The *solemn entrance* includes the ministers and assembly, who process into the worship space either from in front of the church doors or from just inside the building. This may take place at any Mass. Therefore, the difference between the procession and solemn entrance is a matter of starting point—a place separate and at some distance from the worship space or near the entrance. Both of these forms replace the penitential rite.

The *simple entrance* including only the priest would not be the usual form for a parish liturgy. If this is used (for example, in a nursing home), then the act of penitence is used.

With both the procession and solemn entrance, the intention is to underscore the expansiveness of liturgical gesture and movement and the involvement of the whole self in celebrating the paschal mystery. Indeed, historically, liturgical processions were sometimes choreographed to the point where they were almost liturgical dance.

Name for Palm Sunday: The name assigned to this Sunday in the Lectionary—Palm Sunday of the Lord's Passion—already indicates something of a contrast between triumph and dying, between the gospel proclaimed before the procession with palms begins and the proclamation of the Passion gospel during the Liturgy of the Word. In the popular mind, the core of this Sunday's liturgy is the blessing of palms and taking them home. In fact, the core of this liturgy is the proclamation of the Passion.

About Liturgical Music

Cantor preparation: To sing this psalm well, you must take some time to pray the full text of Psalm 22. You sing not only about Christ's suffering, but also about his transformation into new life through his suffering and death. You sing about your own transformation as well, for through baptism you have been incorporated into Jesus' death and resurrection. How willing are you to undergo this transformation? How willing are you to invite the assembly to do so?

Music and the procession: Because the procession or the solemn entrance which opens this Sunday's liturgy is meant to symbolize the assembly's willingness to enter into the mystery of the cross and resurrection, it needs to be done with as many assembly members as possible participating. Singing whatever music is involved always takes logistical planning, especially when the procession begins in a place other than the church. One way to support the singing is to have the choir flank the procession on either side. Another way is to divide the choir into small groups interspersed throughout the procession. A third option is to have the assembly sing a well-known Christ the King hymn while standing in place, then process in silence to the door of the church (or in the case of the solemn entrance, into the body of the church). With this option it is important to encourage the assembly to process slowly and reflectively, letting each step truly be a choice to move closer to the cross. Processing in silence may take some catechizing of the assembly, but doing it can move participants from historical reenactment of Jesus' entry into Jerusalem to actual enactment of their here-and-now choice to walk with Jesus to the cross.

Easter Triduum

Christ Jesus, though he was in the form of God,
did not regard equality with God
something to be grasped.
Rather, he emptied himself,
taking the form of a slave,
coming in human likeness;
and found human in appearance,
he humbled himself,
becoming obedient to the point of death,
even death on a cross.
Because of this, God greatly exalted him . . .

—Phil 2:6-9a

Reflecting on the Triduum

The magnificent hymn from the Letter to the Philippians (Phil 2:6-11; proclaimed as the second reading on Palm Sunday) opens for us the meaning of the entire paschal Triduum. Jesus—empty, humble, obedient—modeled for us the way to exaltation. To share in risen life we must walk the way of the cross with the Humble One.

Jesus' entire life was spent in humble obedience to his Father—becoming incarnate, being in his Father's house, proclaiming the kingdom, walking a steadfast journey to Jerusalem—knowing full well that suffering and death awaited him. By his humility and obedience Jesus remained absolutely true to who he was—fully divine and fully human. Moreover, in the humble Jesus the full potential of our own humanity is realized—to be raised up to share in divine life itself.

"Humility" is an English word which derives from the Latin *humus* meaning ground, soil, earth. Through humility we recover the identity conferred on us at creation when God took the soil of the earth and fashioned the first humans, breathing into them the divine breath of life (Gen 2:7). Thus humility has to do with our basic humanness and our relationship with God the Creator. In face of God's perfection, we recognize ourselves to be finite and mortal; in face of God's holiness, we recognize ourselves to be weak and sinful.

Self-emptying is the key to embracing humility. The paradox is that self-emptying doesn't lead to nothingness but to fullness. Through the surrender of self-emptying we give ourselves over to the divine Mystery which beckons us to become fully who we are; we choose to be what God wants of us and what Christ modeled for us—dying to self which leads to the exaltation of new life.

We spend our lives stretched between the two greatest events of our lives—birth and death. In a real sense we are born to die and spend our whole lives dying. However, more is happening in this dying process than the gradual diminishment of life. The movement from birth to death captures the very rhythm which defines us in relation to God. Dying and rising are but two poles of the same mystery of coming into our own humanity in such a way that we grow to realize that our truest selves are found in surrendering into divinity.

These Triduum days call us to empty ourselves and become humble like Jesus. Only in humility do we realize the full potential of who we can become; only in humility can we grow into the divine life which is offered us. Just as Christ was raised up, so does God raise us up. This is the mystery we celebrate these days: obedience brings victory and humility brings exaltation.

Living the Paschal Mystery

In everyday terms, self-emptying demands of us that we let go of all that distracts us from fully embracing our *humus,* our humanity. In an age of abundant goods, perhaps this means that we buy less. At a time of ravishing our good earth, perhaps it means that we pay more attention to how we use our natural resources. In societies which depreciate the value of lasting human relationships, perhaps self-emptying means that we let go of our own expectations of others so that they can be who they were created to be. An attitude of self-emptying helps us look afresh at all our relationships—to God, self, others—and reevaluate what is truly important to us. Humility calls us to set right priorities—that entering into Jesus' dying and rising is why we were created in God's image.

TRIDUUM

"Triduum" comes from two Latin words (*tres* and *dies*) which mean "a space of three days." But since we have four days with special names—Holy Thursday, Good Friday, Holy Saturday, and Easter Sunday—the "three" may be confusing to some.

The confusion is cleared up when we understand how the days are reckoned. On all high festival days the Church counts a day in the same way as Jews count days and festivals; that is, from sundown to sundown. Thus, the Triduum consists of *three* twenty-four-hour periods that stretch over four calendar days.

Therefore, the Easter Triduum begins at sundown on Holy Thursday with the Mass of the Lord's Supper and concludes with Easter evening prayer at sundown on Easter Sunday; its high point is the celebration of the Easter Vigil (GNLYC no. 19).

SOLEMN PASCHAL FAST

According to the above calculation, Lent ends at sundown on Holy Thursday; thus, Holy Thursday itself is the last day of Lent. This doesn't mean that our fasting concludes on Holy Thursday, however; the Church has traditionally kept a solemn forty-hour fast from the beginning of the Triduum until the fast is broken at Communion during the Easter Vigil.

SPIRITUALITY

Gospel   John 13:1-15; L39ABC

Before the feast of Passover, Jesus knew
   that his hour had come
   to pass from this world to the
      Father.
He loved his own in the world and
   he loved them to the end.
The devil had already induced
   Judas, son of Simon the
   Iscariot, to hand him over.
So, during supper,
   fully aware that the Father had
      put everything into his
      power
   and that he had come from God
      and was returning to God,
   he rose from supper and took
      off his outer garments.
He took a towel and tied it around
   his waist.

Then he poured water into a basin
   and began to wash the disciples' feet
   and dry them with the towel around his
      waist.
He came to Simon Peter, who said to him,
   "Master, are you going to wash my
      feet?"
Jesus answered and said to him,
   "What I am doing, you do not
      understand now,
   but you will understand later."
Peter said to him, "You will never wash
   my feet."
Jesus answered him,
   "Unless I wash you, you will have no
      inheritance with me."
Simon Peter said to him,
   "Master, then not only my feet, but my
      hands and head as well."
Jesus said to him,
   "Whoever has bathed has no need
      except to have his feet washed,
      for he is clean all over;
   so you are clean, but not all."
For he knew who would betray him;
   for this reason, he said, "Not all of you
      are clean."

Continued in Appendix A, p. 282.
See Appendix A, p. 282, for the other readings.

Reflecting on the Gospel and Living the Paschal Mystery

Most of us could probably come up with quite a list of things which we think are beneath our dignity to stoop to do. For example, we might not want to pick up another person's trash in the neighborhood. Or we might not want to offer a supporting hand to the homeless person stumbling across the street. Or we might ignore the elderly person with dementia who seems to be all alone but is so very difficult to hold a conversation with. Even in societies with no inherited class or caste, there seems to be at least a subtle "pecking order": adults/children, teacher/student, employer/employee, white collar/blue collar.

In the gospel for Holy Thursday Jesus gives us an example of the deepest kind of humility—he stoops to wash the disciples' feet. His purpose wasn't to clean feet; his purpose was to give us an example of relationships based on a pattern of divine humility. If the divine Son so humbled himself, how much more ought we! The most profound humility is identifying with another in such a way that he or she is lifted up to new dignity, new life.

On this night before he died, Jesus emptied himself in two most unfathomable ways. First, he gave us Food for our journey. But this Food isn't the making of human industry; it is the very bread of his Body and the wine of his Blood. In giving us the Eucharist Jesus verified his humble life—he so emptied himself that he gave his very Body and Blood as a new covenant for our salvation. Giving oneself for the sake of another is taken to unprecedented heights; we commune with the divine by eating and drinking the very Body and Blood of the divine Son.

Second, Jesus (teacher and master) did what only a slave would do. In this act of foot-washing, Jesus identified not only with humanity, but abandoned his divinity ("come from God") in an unprecedented way. He did not cling to power, wealth, or divine attributes. He did not cling to the leadership status of being teacher and master. He let go of even this to enter into a whole new relationship with his disciples—he became one with them in their weak, impoverished humanity. No other humble act could have so profoundly exemplified for us the extent to which Jesus became one like us.

This night Jesus showed the depths of his love for humanity: he gave us heavenly Food by being earthly humble. This night calls us: this so "should [we] also do." We become truly human by partaking in the heavenly Food which transforms us more perfectly into being members of the Body of Christ. We become truly human by becoming the slave to all by our own self-emptying for the sake of others. Of such is true humility. Of such is true humanity.

Key words and phrases from the gospel: Passover, everything into his power, come from God, wash the disciples' feet, you should also do

To the point: In the gospel for Holy Thursday Jesus gives us an example of the deepest kind of humility—he stoops to wash the disciples' feet. His purpose wasn't to clean feet; his purpose was to give us an example of relationships based on a pattern of divine humility. If the divine Son so humbled himself, how much more ought we!

About Liturgy: Special Features of the Ritual

Two special ritual features mark this night as different from any other. Both features draw us to a self-emptying posture before God and each other and help us realize the demands of Jesus' command, "you should also do."

First, after the homily a foot-washing ceremony may take place. More than simply copying the actions of Jesus at the Last Supper with his disciples, this ritual gesture reminds us of our posture toward God and each other: one of humility and service. It is surely not necessary that everyone actually have their feet washed in order to capture the ritual impact of this gesture. The ritual gesture provides a model for how we are to live our lives. It helps us remember that serving others is how we serve God.

Second, the liturgy concludes with a procession of the Blessed Sacrament to the place of reservation and provides for adoration by the assembly. Our adoration of the Blessed Sacrament includes gratitude for this great gift of Christ's Body and Blood given for our nourishment. At the same time it allows us to express in another gesture our profound attitude toward God—adoration of the almighty expressed in praise and thanksgiving.

Model Act of Penitence

Presider: On this night we remember Jesus' humility in washing his disciples' feet and generously giving us his very Self. Let us begin our celebration by standing humbly before him . . . [pause]

    Lord Jesus, you love your own in the world: Lord . . .

    Christ Jesus, you came from God and returned to God: Christ . . .

    Lord Jesus, you give us yourself in humble service: Lord . . .

Model General Intercessions

Presider: Having observed, prayed about, and reflected on Jesus' example of humble service, let us pray that we might also do likewise.

Response:

Lord, hear our prayer.

Cantor:

we pray to the Lord,

That the Church be a model of humility and service for all people . . . [pause]

That all leaders uplift the dignity of those they govern by deeds of humble service . . . [pause]

That the lowly be raised up, the poor be enriched by God's blessings, and the sorrowful be joyful in God's care . . . [pause]

That each of us here empty ourselves for the good of others . . . [pause]

Presider: Gracious God, you raised us up in Christ: hear our prayers that we might follow him in laying down our lives. We ask this through Christ our Lord. **Amen.**

OPENING PRAYER

Let us pray

Pause for silent prayer

God our Father,
we are gathered here to share in the supper
which your only Son left to his Church to
    reveal his love.
He gave it to us when he was about to die
and commanded us to celebrate it as the
    new and eternal sacrifice.
We pray that in this Eucharist
we may find the fullness of love and life.

Grant this through our Lord Jesus Christ,
    your Son,
who lives and reigns with you and the Holy
    Spirit,
one God, for ever and ever. **Amen.**

FOR REFLECTION

- Jesus' call to be humble means to me . . .
- Jesus' challenge to be servant means to me . . .
- Humble service leads to Easter in that . . .

SPIRITUALITY

Gospel

John 18:1–19:42; L40ABC

Jesus went out with his disciples
  across the Kidron valley
  to where there was a garden,
  into which he and his disciples
    entered.
Judas his betrayer also knew the
    place,
  because Jesus had often met
    there with his disciples.
So Judas got a band of soldiers
    and guards
  from the chief priests and the
    Pharisees
  and went there with lanterns,
    torches, and weapons.
Jesus, knowing everything that
    was going to happen to him,
  went out and said to them,
    "Whom are you looking for?"
They answered him, "Jesus the
    Nazorean."
He said to them, "I AM."
Judas his betrayer was also with them.
When he said to them, "I AM,"
  they turned away and fell to the
    ground.
So he again asked them,
  "Whom are you looking for?"
They said, "Jesus the Nazorean."
Jesus answered,
  "I told you that I AM.
So if you are looking for me, let these
    men go."
This was to fulfill what he had said,
  "I have not lost any of those you gave
    me."
Then Simon Peter, who had a sword,
    drew it,
  struck the high priest's slave, and cut
    off his right ear.
The slave's name was Malchus.
Jesus said to Peter,
  "Put your sword into its scabbard.
Shall I not drink the cup that the Father
    gave me?"

Continued in Appendix A, pp. 283–84.
See Appendix A, p. 285, for the other readings.

Reflecting on the Gospel and Living the Paschal Mystery

Clearly Jesus had the power to escape ignominious betrayal by a disciple, the painful scourging at the command of a weak and fearful leader, the mockery of his kingship by the soldiers' placing upon him a crown of thorns and purple cloak, the criminal's lot of crucifixion. No one had power over Jesus; he was the Son of God whose "kingdom does not belong to this world."

Jesus is the divine I AM, the name revealed to Moses and which identified him as the Son of God. He is the I AM who was with God from the beginning of creation. He was with God when life was breathed into the *humus*-clay forming the first humans. Yet it was this humble Son of God who also "handed over the spirit" and breathed out his mortality, expiring the very breath of life.

Clearly Jesus chose to die, for by dying Jesus bore witness to the extent to which he embraced humanity. He relinquished all vestiges of divinity and emptied himself to the extent that he was "spurned and avoided by people" (first reading).

By his humble obedience (see the gospel acclamation), Jesus drank the cup of suffering and passed over from death to life. His Passover opened the gates for us to pass over from mortal humanity to a share in divine life. Jesus' embrace of death is the ultimate act of throwing his lot in with us humans—he embraced *mortality,* one trait which distinguishes us clearly from God. At the same time that he embraced death he conquered death. Good Friday is not so much a somber recollection of suffering and death by one Man, as it is the sober remembering that this humble servant of all clearly answered Pilate's question, "What is truth?," by his ultimate human act of surrender to death. Amazingly, even in the very hour of his passing over from death to life he still identifies with humanity through concern and care for his mother. This divine Son passes over from death to risen life, yet never forsakes us, never concedes his humanity, and always remains one like us in all things except sin.

Each time we sign ourselves with the cross or look upon a cross we've hung upon a wall in our home, we embrace our own humanity as well as surrender ourselves to the Mystery which enables us to pass over from death to new life. To live this Mystery to the fullest we must humble ourselves to become the servant of all as Jesus did. This is really more than a matter of saying yes to the obvious ways to die to self which come our way each day—getting to work on time so the family has the sustenance they need; spending a few minutes of our coffee break to listen to someone; being patient with the children when they need our attention. To live this Mystery well means that we surrender to the very truth of our own identity and do as Jesus did—humbly die to self for the sake of others. We actually *look for* ways to embrace death. For this is how we live.

Key words and phrases from the gospel: for this I came into the world, What is truth?, he handed over the spirit

To the point: In the gospel text Jesus does not answer Pilate's probing question, "What is truth?" Yet this humble servant of all does clearly answer Pilate's question, not in words but by freely and humbly surrendering to death.

About Liturgy: Special Features of the Ritual

Perhaps no other liturgy throughout the entire liturgical year draws us to humble ourselves before our God as does this Good Friday Liturgy of the Lord's Passion. Three acts of humility are rather obvious in the rite. First, the presider and deacon enter in silence and then prostrate themselves before the altar. They stretch themselves out on the *ground* and thus lower themselves to become one with the *humus*-clay out of which we are created. Second, at the veneration of the cross all are invited to come forward to make some act of humble reverence toward this sign of our salvation.

Third, and perhaps a less obvious invitation to humility, the solemn prayers which follow the proclamation of the Passion according to St. John invite us to unite ourselves with all of humanity. We hear proclaimed Jesus' acts of generosity toward us humans for our salvation. Our response is to pray in a more extended way than usual for the needs of the Church, ourselves, and all people. Today especially these prayers must take place with sufficient time so that we can truly pour out our hearts to God. This act on behalf of humanity is also a pledge that our own response to Jesus' generosity toward us is to be generous to those for whom we pray. In an extended way, then, John's Passion account and the solemn prayers call us to be the humble servants of all.

Suggestions for Music

Singing the general intercessions:

Just as the Easter Vigil is the mother of all vigils, so the Good Friday intercessions are the mother and model of all general intercessions. Because of their solemnity they are meant to be sung, using the simple chant given in the Sacramentary, and to include short periods of silent prayer after each statement of intention. If it is not possible that these intercessions be sung, they should be spoken with solemnity, with time allowed for the appropriate silent pauses.

Music during the veneration of the cross:

As the title—"Veneration of the Cross"—of this part of the Good Friday liturgy indicates, what we honor in this procession is not the One crucified but the *cross* which embodies the mystery of his—and our—redemptive triumph over sin and death. Because we are not *historicizing* nor *reenacting* a past event, but *ritualizing* the meaning of this event for our lives here and now, this procession is not one of sorrow or expiation but of gratitude, of triumph, and of quiet and confident acceptance (the very sentiments expressed in the responsorial psalm).

The music during this procession needs, then, to sing about the mystery and triumph of the cross rather than about the details of Jesus' suffering and death. Examples of appropriate music include "We Acclaim the Cross of Jesus" [PMB, WC, WS]; "O Cross of Christ, Immortal Tree" [CBW3, PMB, WC, SS]; "Behold, Before Our Wond'ring Eyes" [BB, JS2]; Ricky Manalo's "We Should Glory in the Cross" [JS2; choir octavo OCP #11355CC]; and Francis Patrick O'Brien's "Tree of Life and Glory" [GIA G-5452]. Gerard Chiusano's choral setting of the entrance antiphon for Holy Thursday, "We Should Glory In the Cross" (OCP octavo #10884) would be an excellent piece for the choir to sing. If already sung as part of the Holy Thursday liturgy, repeating it would emphasize the unity of these celebrations.

OPENING PRAYER

Let us pray

Pause for silent prayer

Lord,
by shedding his blood for us,
your Son, Jesus Christ,
established the paschal mystery.
In your goodness, make us holy
and watch over us always.

We ask this through Christ our Lord.
 Amen.

FOR REFLECTION

- The truth about Christ that I speak and live is . . .
- The cross in my life empties and humbles me in that . . .
- Humility gives rise to Easter joy because . . .

SPIRITUALITY

Gospel

Luke 24:1-12; L41ABC

At daybreak on the first day of the week
  the women who had come from
    Galilee with Jesus
  took the spices they had prepared
  and went to the tomb.
They found the stone rolled away
  from the tomb;
  but when they entered,
  they did not find the body of the
    Lord Jesus.
While they were puzzling over this,
  behold,
  two men in dazzling garments
    appeared to them.
They were terrified and bowed their
  faces to the ground.
They said to them,
  "Why do you seek the living one
    among the dead?
He is not here, but he has been raised.
Remember what he said to you while he
  was still in Galilee,
  that the Son of Man must be handed
    over to sinners
  and be crucified, and rise on the third
    day."
And they remembered his words.
Then they returned from the tomb
  and announced all these things to the
    eleven
  and to all the others.
The women were Mary Magdalene,
  Joanna, and Mary the mother of
    James;
  the others who accompanied them
    also told this to the apostles,
  but their story seemed like nonsense
  and they did not believe them.
But Peter got up and ran to the tomb,
  bent down, and saw the burial cloths
    alone;
  then he went home amazed at what
    had happened.

Readings in Appendix A, pp. 286–91.

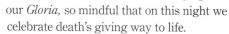

Reflecting on the Gospel and Living the Paschal Mystery

This is the night when we see the full flowering of our Lenten penance and conversion. Humbled by darkness, we welcome awe-inspiring Light. Humbled by the telling of the story of our salvation, we renew with full throat our baptismal commitment. Humbled by a Lent of restrained refrains, we sing out with full voice our Easter alleluias. Yes, this is the night when we come to the deepest conviction about who we are: those united with their risen Lord, ringing out our *Gloria,* so mindful that on this night we celebrate death's giving way to life.

As we listen to an Easter gospel proclamation for the first time this year, we might remember Jesus' words, too, and be "amazed at what had happened" (gospel). We have heard over and over that dying is the way to life. Now, on this night, we remember how true this is. Yes, we are humbled by the utter truth of Jesus' words: he will die and in three days rise. We are even more humbled to celebrate our own risen life in Christ. We are humbled as we celebrate during this night the consummate identity of who Jesus is: the man who died and was raised up three days later. We are humbled as we celebrate our own identity: the baptized ones who have been plunged into Christ's death so that we might share in his resurrection.

We sing our alleluias during this night with joy in our hearts because Christ is risen from the dead. But no small part of our alleluias comes from the joy we receive by sharing in Christ's life. As members of his Body, we share in his identity, his life. This is a night of deepest humility for we come face to face with who Christ is and a challenge to become more perfectly that risen life for others.

As the women in the gospel were terrified and questioned and remembered and announced, we find ourselves struggling with the same sentiments. Even as we celebrate Easter the immensity of the mystery is not easy to grasp. We, too, struggle with "seek[ing] the living one among the dead." Perhaps part of our struggle comes because risen life is outside of our ordinary human experience. But perhaps part of our struggle and surely our amazement comes because to believe that Jesus—who identified with our humanity even to the point of embracing death—is risen from the dead is to believe that we, too, who have been identified with Christ will also rise from the dead. But even more: as faithful disciples, we *already* share in that risen life.

As we sing alleluia during this night and throughout our Easter celebration, we remember that our alleluia can be true only if we conform our life to Christ's. To do so means that even in this season of celebrating resurrection, we also remember that our share in risen life only comes by dying to self. The living comes from the dying. Alleluia!

Key words and phrases from the gospel: did not find the body, he is raised, they remembered his words, amazed

To the point: Christ is risen! No small part of our joy comes from sharing in Christ's life because we are members of his Body. This is a night of our deepest humility: we come face to face with who Christ is as our risen, glorified Savior and who we are as the presence of the living Christ in the world.

About Liturgy: Special Features of the Ritual

The Easter Vigil begins in darkness. The new fire is blessed. The new paschal candle is prepared. And then lit. If the new fire is a healthy one, the lighting of the paschal candle is probably eclipsed by it. Only when the candle is carried in procession to the door of the darkened church can the one light clearly be seen to glow in the darkness and dispel it. But at the church door, with the second proclamation of "Light of Christ," the fire is taken from the paschal candle and passed throughout the assembly—the Body of Christ—and all have their candles lit. Now there is enough light to see our way; there is enough light to follow the service; there is enough light to light our faces with the countenance of Christ.

We focus on the paschal candle during this night and throughout the Easter season, and rightly so. It is also wise to consider the individual candles we light and hold. They are lit twice. They are lit the first time after the second procla- mation of light and held during the *Exsultet,* that great hymn of praise to the Light. Then they are extinguished, to be lit again when we renew our baptismal promises. In both cases—during the thanksgiving for Light and during our baptismal renewal—our lit candles remind us of our intensified identity with Christ. Those individual lit candles remind us that this is *our night,* too; a night when we recommit ourselves to become more fully like Christ so that by dying with him we might also rise with him.

Model General Intercessions

Presider: On this night when we celebrate the risen life of our Savior, Jesus Christ, we pray for our Church and world that all might share in the gift of new life.

Response:

Lord, hear our prayer.

Cantor:

we pray to the Lord,

That the Church might always light the way to new life for all who come seek- ing the risen Christ . . . [pause]

That all peoples of the world strive ever more diligently to live lives worthy of the salvation offered by God . . . [pause]

That all those whose lives are darkened by poverty, sickness, anxiety, or uncer- tainty might find solace and light in the risen Christ . . . [pause]

That all of us here celebrate our Easter joy by being the light of Christ for all we meet . . . [pause]

Presider: God of light and salvation, you raised your divine Son to new life: hear our prayers that we might share forever that same risen life. We pray through the risen Son, Jesus Christ our Lord. **Amen.**

OPENING PRAYER

Let us pray

Pause for silent prayer

Lord God,
you have brightened this night
with the radiance of the risen Christ.
Quicken the spirit of sonship in your
    Church;
renew us in mind and body
to give you wholehearted service.

Grant this through our Lord Jesus Christ,
    your Son,
who lives and reigns with you and the Holy
    Spirit,
one God, for ever and ever. **Amen.**

FOR REFLECTION

• My Lenten dying to self prepared me for Easter joy in that . . .

• The darkness in my life that Christ's Light dispels is . . .

• What it means to me to become the living presence of the risen Christ in the world is . . .

SPIRITUALITY

Gospel

John 20:1-9; L42ABC

On the first day of the week,
  Mary of Magdala came to the
    tomb early in the morning,
  while it was still dark,
  and saw the stone removed from
    the tomb.
So she ran and went to Simon
  Peter
  and to the other disciple whom
    Jesus loved, and told them,
  "They have taken the Lord from
    the tomb,
  and we don't know where they
    put him."
So Peter and the other disciple
  went out and came to the tomb.
They both ran, but the other
  disciple ran faster than Peter
  and arrived at the tomb first;
  he bent down and saw the burial
    cloths
    there, but did not go in.
When Simon Peter arrived after him,
  he went into the tomb and saw the
    burial cloths there,
  and the cloth that had covered his
    head,
  not with the burial cloths but rolled
    up
    in a separate place.
Then the other disciple also went in,
  the one who had arrived at the tomb
    first,
  and he saw and believed.
For they did not yet understand the
  Scripture
  that he had to rise from the dead.

or

Luke 24:1-12; L41C *in Appendix A, p. 292.*

or, at an afternoon or evening Mass

Luke 24:13-35; L46 *in Appendix A, p. 292.*

See Appendix A, p. 293 for the other readings.

Reflecting on the Gospel and Living the Paschal Mystery

Many of us in our families have a sense of a "pecking order." Parents have the authority and final say. Older children have more privileges than younger children. Younger children tend to get excused and get away with more than the older children. Usually this pecking order is simply a matter of where one finds oneself chronologically in the family. The gospel for this Easter morning also exhibits a pecking order among Mary of Magdala, Simon Peter, and the Beloved Disciple. Mary arrives at the tomb very early and finds "the stone removed from the tomb." She runs to Peter and the Beloved Disciple. The two of them run to the tomb but the Beloved Disciple defers to Peter who enters first.

In this resurrection account the pecking order really didn't make much difference; all of them "did not yet understand." Herein is the paradox of the resurrection: we believe but do not understand. We believe because we encounter the risen Lord, because we still experience him through "sincerity and truth" (second reading from 1 Corinthians), because not to believe means that we can never rise above being *humus*, the clay of the earth. This gospel shows the extent to which Jesus' resurrection calls all of us to examine the deepest truth about ourselves, our most intensified act of humbling ourselves: Jesus' resurrection calls us to surrender misunderstanding to belief, to surrender our humanity to be raised up to share in divine life, to surrender any resemblance of pecking order among us to focus on Christ as the One who makes us who we are.

In Christ we are all members of his Body, we all share in his risen life. Although from a human point of view there may still remain a pecking order among us, after the resurrection the one thing that matters is that we surrender our all (even as Christ surrendered his all) to the Father and Christ, who clothe us with an identity beyond our just deserts.

The resurrection is a mystery which we can never understand but only believe. This mystery takes us beyond all which is familiar to us—the very *humus* of our selves—to a realm where God's glory and majesty and power lift us up to a share in the new dignity of risen life. Easter is a celebration of Jesus' taking his rightful place in the divine kingdom of his Father where the truth of his divine being is known. Easter is also a celebration whereby we ourselves acknowledge who Christ really is—the one who shared in our humanity even to the point of accepting death, but who conquered death to raise us up to a share in his life. This new life and dignity isn't something which can be measured or calculated or grasped. It is a freely given gift by the Divine One who has loved us from the beginning of creation, who breathed life into us, and who continues to beckon us to grow in the truth of who we are.

Key words and phrases from the gospel: Mary of Magdala, she ran, Simon Peter, disciple whom Jesus loved, both ran, did not go in, saw and believed, did not yet understand

To the point: Like the first disciples, who "did not yet understand," for us the resurrection is a mystery which we can never understand but only believe. This mystery takes us beyond all which is familiar to us to a realm where God's glory and majesty and power lift us up to a share in the new dignity of risen life.

About Liturgy: Special Features of the Ritual

During all the Masses on Easter the assembly is invited to renew their baptismal promises after the proclamation of the Easter gospel and the homily. We might take note that these promises unfold in two distinct parts. First, we renounce evil and its hold on us; we are acknowledging how our sinful humanity still has a hold on us and takes us away from the loving relationship we wish to have with God. Then in the next part of the promises we express our belief in our triune God and all God has done for us, especially by giving us the new life of faith. We have in these two parts of the baptismal renewal a reminder of the dying and rising of the paschal mystery into which we are plunged at baptism. We are also reminded of the truth of our selves: we are sinners while we are at the same time graced beloved of God who are saved. Our renewal of these promises reminds us that we, too, share in Christ's humanity and divinity, in his suffering and death as well as his resurrection. May we renew our commitment with truth and fervor.

Model Penitential Rite

Presider: Today is the day for which we've been preparing; today is the day we celebrate Jesus' risen life. Let us pause to acknowledge God's gracious mercy to us and open ourselves to God's offer of new life . . . [pause]

Lord Jesus, you were raised from the dead: Lord . . .

Christ Jesus, you conquered sin and death: Christ . . .

Lord Jesus, you share your new life with us at this banquet: Lord . . .

Model General Intercessions

Presider: On this joyous day of celebrating risen life, we pray to the Lord of life for our needs.

Response:

Lord, hear our prayer.

Cantor:

we pray to the Lord,

That all members of the Church might witness through word and deed to the new life God offers us in the risen Christ . . . [pause]

That all people of the world share in the joy of new life . . . [pause]

That those whose lives are diminished by poverty and oppression might come to the fullness of life . . . [pause]

That all of us here encounter the risen Christ in the joy and goodness of others . . . [pause]

Presider: God of creation and life, you raised up your divine Son: hear these our prayers that our Easter joy might be complete in one day sharing in your everlasting life. We ask this through the risen Son, Jesus Christ our Lord. **Amen.**

OPENING PRAYER

Let us pray

Pause for silent prayer

God our Father,
by raising Christ your Son
you conquered the power of death
and opened for us the way to eternal life.
Let our celebration today
raise us up and renew our lives
by the Spirit that is within us.

Grant this through our Lord Jesus Christ,
    your Son,
who lives and reigns with you and the Holy
    Spirit,
one God, for ever and ever. **Amen.**

FOR REFLECTION

• What helps me believe in Jesus' resurrection is . . .

• Some ways I assist others to believe in Jesus' resurrection are . . .

• The good news of the resurrection impacts my daily living in that . . .

Season of Easter

SPIRITUALITY

Gospel

John 20:19-31; L44B

On the evening of that first day of
    the week,
  when the doors were locked,
      where the disciples were,
  for fear of the Jews,
  Jesus came and stood in their
      midst
  and said to them, "Peace be
      with you."
When he had said this, he showed
    them his hands and his side.
The disciples rejoiced when they
    saw the Lord.
Jesus said to them again, "Peace
    be with you.
As the Father has sent me, so I
    send you."
And when he had said this, he breathed
    on them and said to them,
  "Receive the Holy Spirit.
Whose sins you forgive are forgiven
    them,
  and whose sins you retain are
      retained."

Thomas, called Didymus, one of the
    Twelve,
  was not with them when Jesus came.
So the other disciples said to him, "We
    have seen the Lord."
But he said to them,
  "Unless I see the mark of the nails in
      his hands
  and put my finger into the nailmarks
  and put my hand into his side, I will
      not believe."

Now a week later his disciples were
    again inside
  and Thomas was with them.
Jesus came, although the doors were
    locked,
  and stood in their midst and said,
      "Peace be with you."

Continued in Appendix A, p. 293.

Reflecting on the Gospel

Much goodness can come out of many years of persistent efforts and hard work. The Wright brothers' first flying machine didn't fly—it crashed. But they kept trying until they finally triumphed that day over a century ago at Kitty Hawk. One may begin work after college at the bottom of the corporate rung, but through persistence gradually work up to a high executive position. Someone may be introduced to another, fall in love, and through persistence become engaged, marry, have children, celebrate happily a golden wedding anniversary. In the gospel this Sunday we see the persistence of the risen Jesus in being present to his disciples. His presence brings the goodness of peace, forgiveness, and risen life.

Through locked doors, despite the disciples' fear, beyond their doubting and disbelief, the risen Jesus came and "stood in their midst"—not just once, but twice. Nothing deters Jesus from sharing his Spirit and new life with his disciples. He persists until he brings *all*—not just the early disciples and Thomas but also all of us today—to peace, forgiveness, and new life. Even in the glory of his resurrection, Jesus is caring for his disciples and calling them to a belief in him which brings new life and presence.

The disciples believed because they saw the Lord. The early converts believed because they saw "signs and wonders" (first reading). We believe because we, too, see the signs and wonders of God's presence. But now the risen Jesus continues to stand in the midst of the world through the "signs and wonders" worked by us who are his disciples.

Our Easter alleluia isn't simply a song on our lips during these weeks of Easter. It is a song in our hearts which spills out in the way we relate to others in being the risen Christ for them. Alleluia is the song of our lives which, like Jesus, brings new life to others. Alleluia is the song of our belief which calls others to utter "My Lord and my God!"

Living the Paschal Mystery

Everything Jesus did the apostles did—forgave, preached, taught, healed, added numbers to the follower-believers. Today the Church brings the presence of the risen Jesus to others, and we are the Church. Perhaps not in stupendous ways, but in our own simple, everyday acts we, too, do what Jesus did. Faithful disciples are Jesus' persistent presence in today's world.

We forgive when we see and treat someone who has hurt us as the risen Christ. We preach when we share with our young ones the gospels and the Christian way to live what they announce. We teach when we live in ways which clearly put the other ahead of ourselves, ways which speak of self-sacrificing for the good of others. We heal when we touch others physically or emotionally or psychologically, helping them realize that they are not alone but have a community to support and encourage them. We add to our numbers when our lives witness the love and care that Jesus had in real, concrete, tangible ways. It's in the moment-by-moment everyday things—even changing a diaper with a caress or being more patient with the inevitable endless bother of everyday nitty-gritty living—that we witness that we are "believers in the Lord" (first reading).

God doesn't ask us to be heroes in our witnessing to resurrection faith and bringing Jesus' presence to others. God only asks that we be as alive to new, Easter life as was the Jesus who showed the disciples his hands and side.

Focusing the Gospel

Key words and phrases: locked, fear, Jesus came, stood in their midst, receive the Holy Spirit, I will not believe, Jesus came, stood in their midst

To the point: Through locked doors, despite the disciples' fear, beyond their doubting and disbelief, the risen Jesus came and "stood in their midst"—not just once, but twice. Nothing deters Jesus from sharing his Spirit with his disciples. He persists until he brings *all*—including us—to new life.

Connecting the Gospel

to the first reading: The risen Jesus continues to stand in the midst of the world through the "signs and wonders" worked by those who are his disciples.

to our religious culture: As a religious culture we often emphasize our need to persist in devotional practices and spiritual exercises. The gospel redirects our attention to a far greater persistence—Christ's continually coming and standing with us.

Understanding Scripture

Believing leads to life: John explains explicitly why this resurrection story is told: "that you may come to believe . . . and that through this belief you may have life." The Greek actually says, "so that believing you may have life," the difference being that John uses a verbal form (believing) where our translation uses a noun (belief). This is not an insignificant point. In the Gospel, John never uses the noun "faith" or "belief," although he uses the verb "to believe" ninety-eight times. For John, it is not so much a matter of having faith, as it is a matter of believing; more than an inward attitude or system of thoughts, believing is an active commitment to trust in Jesus and in his word. Believing in this sense is what it means to be a disciple. This active commitment to the person of Jesus is what gives disciples life.

Coming to life through believing is more than the point of the story in this Sunday's gospel. It was the very reason the Father sent Jesus and why Jesus came: "that everyone who believes in him may have eternal life" (John 3:15). His whole life, ministry, death, and resurrection are oriented to this one outcome. It is why Jesus persisted in performing signs and teaching even when some conspired to kill him (5:18; 7:1, 19, 25; 8:22, 37, 40; 11:53; 12:10); it is why Jesus persisted even when some rejected and abandoned him (6:66); it is why Jesus appeared to the disciples after his resurrection: to bring them to believe in him. He appeared not just once, but several times. In this Sunday's gospel, he appears twice to the disciples, apparently making the extra effort to bring Thomas to believe in him.

Through the work of the disciples—their preaching, ministry, and their forgiving sins—it is possible for others to encounter the same risen Lord. Although we may not "see" Jesus as those first disciples did, we can nonetheless believe in him and through believing in him come to share eternal life.

**ASSEMBLY &
FAITH-SHARING GROUPS**

- I can identify with Thomas in that . . .
- Some ways I have witnessed Jesus' persistence in bringing me to faith are . . .
- If I wrote an Easter gospel, signs of Christ's resurrection I would highlight are . . .

PRESIDERS
Christ's resurrection shines through my ministry whenever I . . .

DEACONS
I bear Christ's risen peace to those locked in fear whenever I . . .

HOSPITALITY MINISTERS
The peace of Christ is part of my hospitality in that . . .

MUSIC MINISTERS
Sometimes the "locked doors" (gospel) Jesus must pass through are our attitudes and expectations. One door I know I keep locked in terms of my music ministry is . . . I experience Jesus walking through this locked door when . . .

ALTAR MINISTERS
I am a servant of peace and forgiveness within the community by . . .

LECTORS
The "signs and wonders" (first reading) of Christ's resurrection which are manifested in my daily living are . . .

**EXTRAORDINARY MINISTERS
OF HOLY COMMUNION**
My ministry is expanding beyond distributing the Body and Blood of Christ to living as the risen Christ in that . . .

CELEBRATION

Model Rite of Blessing and Sprinkling Holy Water

Presider: We are a people baptized into Christ's death and resurrection. As we ask God to bless this water, let it remind us of our baptism and of the presence of the risen Christ within us and among us.

[Continue with Form C of the blessing of water]

Appreciating the Responsorial Psalm

The psalmist in Psalm 118 invites an ever-widening circle to join in praising God for mercy and deliverance. This is our mission as the risen Body of Christ, to "write down what [we] have seen, and what is happening, and what will happen afterwards" (second reading). What has happened and will continue to happen is God's victory over death (second reading), disease (first reading), and sin (gospel). God takes what is flawed, useless, and inconsequential—the rejected stone (psalm), our failing lives (psalm), our diseased bodies (first reading), our doubting hearts (gospel)—and makes them the corner-stone of faith and forgiveness. This is resurrection, done "by the Lord" and "wonderful in our eyes." And it happens every day in "signs and wonders" (first reading) both great and small. For this, let us "give thanks to the Lord" (psalm refrain).

Model General Intercessions

Presider: The God who raised Jesus from the dead is the same God who will hear our prayer and answer our needs.

Response:

Lord, hear our prayer.

Cantor:

we pray to the Lord,

That all members of the Church be an effective sign of Christ's presence in the midst of the world . . . [pause]

That leaders of the world may work to establish Christ's gift of peace . . . [pause]

That those who struggle to believe may experience the persistence of the risen Christ to bring them peace and new life . . . [pause]

That we here assembled may be signs to others that Jesus is risen and among us . . . [pause]

Presider: Ever-present God, you raised your Son to new life: hear these our prayers that we may be filled with the breath of your Spirit. We ask this through your risen Son, Jesus Christ our Lord. **Amen.**

ALTERNATIVE OPENING PRAYER

Let us pray

Pause for silent prayer

Heavenly Father and God of mercy,
we no longer look for Jesus among the dead,
for he is alive and has become the Lord of life.
From the waters of death you raise us with him
and renew your gift of life within us.
Increase in our minds and hearts
the risen life we share with Christ
and help us to grow as your people
toward the fullness of eternal life with you.

We ask this through Christ our Lord.
Amen.

FIRST READING

Acts 5:12-16

Many signs and wonders were done among the people
  at the hands of the apostles.
They were all together in Solomon's portico.
None of the others dared to join them, but the people esteemed them.
Yet more than ever, believers in the Lord,
  great numbers of men and women, were added to them.
Thus they even carried the sick out into the streets
  and laid them on cots and mats
  so that when Peter came by,
  at least his shadow might fall on one or another of them.
A large number of people from the towns in the vicinity of Jerusalem also gathered,
  bringing the sick and those disturbed by unclean spirits,
  and they were all cured.

RESPONSORIAL PSALM

Ps 118:2-4, 13-15, 22-24

R. (1) Give thanks to the Lord for he is good, his love is everlasting.
  or:
R. Alleluia.

Let the house of Israel say,
  "His mercy endures forever."
Let the house of Aaron say,
  "His mercy endures forever."
Let those who fear the LORD say,
  "His mercy endures forever."

R. Give thanks to the Lord for he is good, his love is everlasting.
  or:
R. Alleluia.

112

I was hard pressed and was falling,
  but the LORD helped me.
My strength and my courage is the LORD,
  and he has been my savior.
The joyful shout of victory
  in the tents of the just.

R⁊. Give thanks to the Lord for he is good,
his love is everlasting.
    or:
R⁊. Alleluia.

The stone which the builders rejected
  has become the cornerstone.
By the LORD has this been done;
  it is wonderful in our eyes.
This is the day the LORD has made;
  let us be glad and rejoice in it.

R⁊. Give thanks to the Lord for he is good,
his love is everlasting.
    or:
R⁊. Alleluia.

SECOND READING
Rev 1:9-11a, 12-13, 17-19

I, John, your brother, who share with you
  the distress, the kingdom, and the
    endurance we have in Jesus,
  found myself on the island called
    Patmos
  because I proclaimed God's word and
    gave testimony to Jesus.
I was caught up in spirit on the Lord's day
  and heard behind me a voice as loud as
    a trumpet, which said,
  "Write on a scroll what you see."
Then I turned to see whose voice it was
    that spoke to me,
  and when I turned, I saw seven gold
    lampstands
  and in the midst of the lampstands one
    like a son of man,
  wearing an ankle-length robe, with a
    gold sash around his chest.

When I caught sight of him, I fell down at
    his feet as though dead.
He touched me with his right hand and
    said, "Do not be afraid.
I am the first and the last, the one who
    lives.
Once I was dead, but now I am alive
    forever and ever.
I hold the keys to death and the
    netherworld.
Write down, therefore, what you have
    seen,
  and what is happening, and what will
    happen afterwards."

About Liturgy

Easter octaves: In a sense Easter has two octaves. One is the eight-day octave that this second Sunday of Easter concludes, a solemn and sustained celebration of Jesus' resurrection. The other is the fifty-day octave (seven weeks of seven days plus one; 7 x 7 + 1 = 50) which is sometimes called "the great octave." Even the eight days of solemnities just concluded are not sufficient to plumb the depths of the Easter mystery. And so the Church gives an even longer period of time to celebrate—this great octave.

Each day of the first week of Easter has the rank of solemnity. Beyond that week, however, even though the Church celebrates all these fifty days as the Easter season, the weekdays no longer have the rank of solemnity. We must be careful, however, that these days don't just become like other days in the liturgical year. They are still days in the Easter season. The joyous festivity, the beautiful sacred space, the ringing alleluias must continue all the way to Pentecost.

We are given these two octaves so that we might truly embrace the Easter mystery: Christ is alive and shares that risen life with each of us. Now is our time to encounter the risen Jesus in new ways so that we can continue throughout the year to be that risen presence for the good of others.

About Liturgical Music

Cantor preparation: In singing Psalm 118 you call the Church to recognize and give thanks for the enduring mercy of God. You can only give a "joyful shout" because you have had personal experience of God's saving intervention, because you have been "hard pressed and falling" and known God's help. What story will you be telling when you sing?

Music suggestions: In all three Lectionary years the gospel readings for the weeks of Easter carry the same progression. The first three weeks relate appearance stories—Christ truly has risen from the dead; the fourth Sunday presents Christ as the Good Shepherd; and the last weeks, including Pentecost, deal with our call to participate in the mission of the risen Christ.

The texts of the songs we sing during these weeks can help us experience this progression. Hymns for the first three weeks can simply exult over Christ's resurrection (most Easter hymns fit this category). Songs for the fourth Sunday can speak of Christ's ongoing presence, of his tender nurturance, of his active support as we live out our discipleship (for example, "Sing of One Who Walks Beside Us" [CBW3]). For the final weeks we need to sing texts which challenge us to participate actively in bringing risen life to all people (for example, "We Know That Christ Is Raised," "Christ Is Alive!," "Go to the World," "Now We Remain").

APRIL 15, 2007
SECOND SUNDAY OF EASTER
or DIVINE MERCY SUNDAY

SPIRITUALITY

Gospel

John 21:1-19; L48C

At that time, Jesus revealed himself
   again to his disciples at the Sea of
   Tiberias.
He revealed himself in this
   way.
Together were Simon Peter,
   Thomas called Didymus,
Nathanael from Cana in
   Galilee,
Zebedee's sons, and two
   others of his disciples.
Simon Peter said to them, "I
   am going fishing."
They said to him, "We also
   will come with you."
So they went out and got into the boat,
   but that night they caught nothing.
When it was already dawn, Jesus was
   standing on the shore;
   but the disciples did not realize that
   it was Jesus.
Jesus said to them, "Children, have you
   caught anything to eat?"
They answered him, "No."
So he said to them, "Cast the net over
   the right side of the boat
   and you will find something."
So they cast it, and were not able to
   pull it in
   because of the number of fish.
So the disciple whom Jesus loved said
   to Peter, "It is the Lord."
When Simon Peter heard that it was
   the Lord,
   he tucked in his garment, for he was
   lightly clad,
   and jumped into the sea.
The other disciples came in the boat,
   for they were not far from shore, only
   about a hundred yards,
   dragging the net with the fish.
When they climbed out on shore,
   they saw a charcoal fire with fish on
   it and bread.

Continued in Appendix A, p. 294.

Reflecting on the Gospel

The risen Jesus revealed himself to his disciples—again, and again. As in other appearances, Jesus is attentive to their needs, bringing their futile fishing expedition to a wildly successful conclusion and providing breakfast for the weary fishermen. These are tangible manifestations of his love and lordship. The Jesus we follow is both Lover of humanity and Lord of humanity.

While it is always nice to hear *words* of love, far more powerful are *deeds* which demonstrate tangibly another's love for us. Jesus most profoundly demonstrates his love for us in his death and resurrection. Then, to make that mystery concrete for us, he demonstrates his love in the simple deed of cooking breakfast for the disciples. We demonstrate our love for him and each other by faithfully loving him, following him, and feeding and tending his lambs and sheep. Love is not simply good feelings but the tangible caring for others.

In the gospel the beloved disciple announces "It is the Lord." The second reading gives us a vision of Jesus' lordship over "everything in the universe." Jesus is not only Lover, but also Lord and, as such, this Jesus is worthy of "honor and glory and blessing." Jesus' lordship is not exercised in having power over others, but in loving them and inviting them to follow him. Jesus' lordship is expressed in persistent presence and love for others, now carried on by his disciples.

With such wonderful detail and storytelling the Evangelist brings together recognition of the presence of the risen Lord, being nourished by him in a meal, and the mission to continue his ministry. Jesus' risen presence is always a harbinger of abundance, whether of a great catch of fish or of the call to follow him. Peter and the early disciples were persistent in their discipleship of following Jesus and making known his Good News. The first reading relates how they did not "stop teaching in that name." Peter is affirming before the Sanhedrin what he had previously denied. The love of Peter is manifest in the concreteness of continuing Jesus' mission, even in the face of adversaries.

This great Lover of humanity and Lord of humanity is gracious in calling us to be his risen presence for others. Of such is the Easter mystery: that we love and care as Jesus did.

Living the Paschal Mystery

Just as Jesus' presence is persistent, so is the call. So, then, must our response to follow him be persistent. Like Peter and the early disciples, our love is to be incarnated in continuing Jesus' mission—preaching, teaching, forgiving, etc. Jesus laid down his life for us—"you had killed him by hanging him on a tree" (first reading)—and so we lay down ours for others.

Taking up Jesus' mission, however, is more than simply *doing*. We cannot forget that to *do* Jesus' mission is to bring his risen presence to others by tangible manifestations. We might not provide an abundance of fish to weary fishermen, but we can provide an abundance of nourishment, love, and care to anyone we meet.

This means that we begin to see the risen Jesus in the "everydayness" of our lives. This means that we allow ourselves to be fully nourished by Jesus (on his very Body and Blood; through his word) and gradually be transformed more and more into his risen presence for others. Thus is Easter every day!

Focusing the Gospel

Key words and phrases: Jesus revealed himself; "It is the Lord"; dragged the net ashore full; "Come, have breakfast"

To the point: The risen Jesus revealed himself to his disciples—again, and again. As in other appearances, Jesus is attentive to their needs: bringing their futile fishing expedition to a wildly successful conclusion and providing breakfast for the weary fishermen. These are tangible manifestations of his love and lordship.

Connecting the Gospel

to the second reading: In the gospel the beloved disciple announces, "It is the Lord." The second reading gives us a vision of Jesus' lordship over "everything in the universe." This risen Jesus is worthy of "honor and glory and blessing."

to our culture: While it is always nice to hear *words* of love, far more powerful are *deeds* which demonstrate tangibly another's love for us. Jesus demonstrates his love for us in his death and resurrection.

Understanding Scripture

The solicitude of Jesus: The reflections for Palm Sunday highlighted Jesus' concern for others even in the midst of his own passion. The same solicitude of Jesus is revealed in this Sunday's gospel in four ways.

First, seeing the futile efforts of his hardworking disciples, Jesus tells them where to cast their nets. When they follow his instruction, their fishing expedition is spectacularly successful. This suggests the nature of ministry in the Church: ministry will be successful if the ministers follow the commands of Jesus.

Second, knowing that after working all night the disciples would be hungry, Jesus has breakfast prepared for them. The simple act of preparing a meal expresses his concern for them. The meal of bread and fish recalls the story of the feeding of the 5,000 with five barley loaves and two fish (John 6:8). Jesus, who knows humanity's hunger, feeds his disciples as he fed the crowd.

Third, he rehabilitates Peter. The set of three questions Jesus poses to Peter ("Do you love me?") recalls Peter's threefold denial of Jesus in the high priest's courtyard. In this poignant encounter between friends whose relationship has been strained, Jesus does not scold, rebuke, or chastise Peter; he does not demand an apology or an explanation. Rather, he offers an opportunity for Peter himself to undo his denial and to affirm his love.

Finally, Jesus shows his love and care for succeeding generations of disciples (us!) in providing for their care. He commissions Peter to take up the Lord's own work as one who tends the sheep (see John 10 on the Good Shepherd). Peter, fed by Jesus on the shore, is told to "feed my sheep."

This Sunday's gospel thus serves many purposes. It again affirms that Jesus has risen and appeared to his disciples; it confirms his solicitude for his disciples; it rehabilitates Peter; the meal of bread and fish also recalls the Eucharistic discourse of John 6. Moreover, it stresses the ongoing nature of discipleship. Despite denials, despite age, despite position in the community, the persistent call of Jesus is simply, "Follow me."

ASSEMBLY & FAITH-SHARING GROUPS

- The risen Jesus has manifested his love for me by . . .
- For me to "feed" and "tend" Jesus' "sheep" means . . .
- My daily dying to self "glorif[ies] God" in that . . .

PRESIDERS

The abundance the risen Christ has shared through me, despite my weariness, is . . .

DEACONS

My love for the Lord motivates my feeding and tending his flock in that . . .

HOSPITALITY MINISTERS

My greeting and concern for those who are gathering help them become the visible Body of Christ because . . .

MUSIC MINISTERS

Attentive to their needs, the risen Jesus fed the weary disciples after their labors at sea (gospel). One way Jesus feeds me after my labors at music ministry is . . . I find this nourishment to be . . .

ALTAR MINISTERS

Whenever I recall the connection between the earthly sacrament and the heavenly worship (see second reading), my ministry is like . . .

LECTORS

The word of God rouses me to worship God (see second reading) when . . .

EXTRAORDINARY MINISTERS OF HOLY COMMUNION

For "the sake of [Jesus'] name" (first reading), I am willing to . . .

CELEBRATION

Model Rite of Blessing and Sprinkling Holy Water

Presider: The risen Jesus revealed himself to his disciples in tangible ways. We ask God to bless this water and make it a tangible sign of Christ's presence and gift of new life . . . [pause]

[Continue with Form C of the blessing of water]

Appreciating the Responsorial Psalm

From what has God rescued us (psalm refrain)? From death certainly, yet not really from death, for if we follow the Lamb who has been slain (second reading), we shall face suffering and death as surely as he did (first reading). What God rescues us from is our fear of dying for Jesus' sake, our cowardice in face of the very real costs of discipleship, and our shame for the times we have, out of fear and cowardice, abandoned discipleship and run from death (gospel). To Peter who knows he has failed in discipleship, Jesus comes with understanding and forgiveness, and says, "Follow me." Jesus shows Peter that despite all the limitations of his fears and his failures, he will nonetheless catch an abundant harvest for God's kingdom. And so for us. We are rescued from our limited courage and our tenuous fidelity by One who understands our weakness, forgives our failures, and knows our hidden strengths.

Model General Intercessions

Presider: The God who provided the disciples with an abundance of fish provides us with abundance to take care of our needs. And so we pray with confidence.

Response:

Lord, hear our prayer.

Cantor:

we pray to the Lord,

That the Church feed her members richly with word and sacrament as Jesus did . . . [pause]

That all peoples of the world manifest the presence of God through tangible works of care and concern . . . [pause]

That those lacking in the necessities of life share in the abundance God offers . . . [pause]

That all of us here may live so as to exalt the lordship of Jesus . . . [pause]

Presider: God of abundance, you nourish your people with love and care: hear these our prayers and help us to follow your Son faithfully, who lives and reigns with you and the Holy Spirit, one God, for ever and ever. **Amen.**

ALTERNATIVE OPENING PRAYER
Let us pray

Pause for silent prayer

Father in heaven, author of all truth,
a people once in darkness has listened to
    your Word
and followed your Son as he rose from the
    tomb.
Hear the prayer of this newborn people
and strengthen your Church to answer
    your call.
May we rise and come forth into the light
    of day
to stand in your presence until eternity
    dawns.

We ask this through Christ our Lord.
    Amen.

FIRST READING
Acts 5:27-32, 40b-41

When the captain and the court officers
        had brought the apostles in
    and made them stand before the
        Sanhedrin,
    the high priest questioned them,
    "We gave you strict orders, did we not,
        to stop teaching in that name?
Yet you have filled Jerusalem with your
        teaching
    and want to bring this man's blood
        upon us."
But Peter and the apostles said in reply,
    "We must obey God rather than men.
The God of our ancestors raised Jesus,
    though you had him killed by hanging
        him on a tree.
God exalted him at his right hand as
        leader and savior
    to grant Israel repentance and
        forgiveness of sins.
We are witnesses of these things,
    as is the Holy Spirit whom God has given
        to those who obey him."

The Sanhedrin ordered the apostles
    to stop speaking in the name of Jesus,
        and dismissed them.
So they left the presence of the Sanhedrin,
    rejoicing that they had been found
        worthy
    to suffer dishonor for the sake of the
        name.

RESPONSORIAL PSALM
Ps 30:2, 4, 5-6, 11-12, 13

℟. (2a) I will praise you, Lord, for you have
rescued me.
    or:
℟. Alleluia.

I will extol you, O Lord, for you drew me
    clear
    and did not let my enemies rejoice over
        me.
O Lord, you brought me up from the
        netherworld;
    you preserved me from among those
        going down into the pit.

Ry. I will praise you, Lord, for you have
rescued me.
    or:
Ry. Alleluia.

Sing praise to the Lord, you his faithful
        ones,
    and give thanks to his holy name.
For his anger lasts but a moment;
    a lifetime, his good will.
At nightfall, weeping enters in,
    but with the dawn, rejoicing.

Ry. I will praise you, Lord, for you have
rescued me.
    or:
Ry. Alleluia.

Hear, O Lord, and have pity on me;
    O Lord, be my helper.
You changed my mourning into dancing;
    O Lord, my God, forever will I give you
        thanks.

Ry. I will praise you, Lord, for you have
rescued me.
    or:
Ry. Alleluia.

SECOND READING
Rev 5:11-14

I, John, looked and heard the voices of
        many angels
    who surrounded the throne
    and the living creatures and the elders.
They were countless in number, and they
        cried out in a loud voice:
    "Worthy is the Lamb that was slain
        to receive power and riches, wisdom
            and strength,
        honor and glory and blessing."
Then I heard every creature in heaven and
        on earth
    and under the earth and in the sea,
    everything in the universe, cry out:
    "To the one who sits on the throne
        and to the Lamb
        be blessing and honor, glory and
            might,
        forever and ever."
The four living creatures answered,
        "Amen,"
    and the elders fell down and worshiped.

About Liturgy

Appearance accounts and hospitality ministry: The Easter Lectionary includes a number of "appearance accounts," gospel recordings of Jesus' appearance to his disciples after the resurrection. This is the third and final Sunday of Easter for which appearance accounts are the gospel selection. These accounts not only proclaim Jesus' resurrection—he is alive!—but they also remind us of the many ways Jesus is present to us. For the early disciples, he was present in encounters, seeing and believing, eating, and in calling his disciples to follow him. Today, too, Jesus is present to us in abundant ways.

The Constitution on the Sacred Liturgy explicitly mentions four liturgical ways Jesus is present (no. 7): in the presiding priest, the proclamation of the word, in the Eucharistic bread and wine, in the assembly. One of the roles of the hospitality ministers and their important ministry to the assembly is to help those gathering become aware of the many presences of the risen Christ to us, but especially to help the assembly become more aware that their very coming together is already a manifestation of the presence of Christ among us. The hospitality ministers' greeting and welcome help those who come to Mass become the visible Body of Christ, to be the risen presence of Jesus. It is a challenge for hospitality ministers to help people understand themselves as the presence of the risen Christ for each other, and also to help the assembly understand how is this carried out in everyday, simple ways.

About Liturgical Music

Cantor preparation: The readings this Sunday indicate that one sign of resurrection is movement from fear of the cost of discipleship to willing embrace of its cost. Lack of confidence and commitment is a kind of death from which God's life-giving power frees you, just as it freed Peter and the apostles. In singing Psalm 30 you celebrate not a private resurrection but a very public call to mission. Can you, like Peter, rejoice in it?

Music suggestions: Bob Hurd's "Two Were Bound for Emmaus" [BB, JS] retells the stories of both the Emmaus journey and this Sunday's gospel. Verse 4 is particularly expressive of the weariness and weakness we often feel in discipleship and the need to keep our attention turned toward the risen Jesus who will support us: "When the road makes us weary, when our labor seems but loss, when the fire of faith weakens and too high seems the cost, let the Church turn to its risen Lord, who for us bore the cross, and we'll find our hearts burning at the sound of his voice." This hymn would work well during the presentation of the gifts. A good choice for Communion would be "Behold the Lamb" [BB, JS2; choral arrangement can be found in OCP's *Choral Praise Comprehensive,* 2nd ed.] which integrates our sharing in the glory of the Lamb (see second reading) with our participation in eating and drinking his Body and Blood.

SPIRITUALITY

Gospel

John 10:27-30; L51C

Jesus said:
"My sheep hear my voice;
   I know them, and they follow me.
I give them eternal life, and they shall
      never perish.
No one can take them out of my hand.
My Father, who has given them to me,
      is greater than all,
   and no one can take them out of the
      Father's hand.
The Father and I are one."

Reflecting on the Gospel

We've all seen them—those saccharine statues and pictures of the Good Shepherd with a cute little lamb draped over his shoulders. These images may mislead us, steering us toward thinking that following Jesus is a sweet, pious, easy venture. But Jesus is both the Good Shepherd and the Lamb who was slain. As Shepherd, Jesus is the one who cares for us and leads us. As Lamb, Jesus is the one who lays down his life in sacrifice for us. Jesus is both Shepherd and Lamb.

Encountering Jesus as the Good Shepherd opens us to his care and love for us. The Risen One remains with us, and no one can take us "out of [his] hand" (gospel). The joy and delight of the Good Shepherd is a foretaste of the eternal life which is given to Jesus' faithful followers.

Encountering Jesus as the Lamb who was slain opens us to the cost of following Jesus. Yes, the voice of Jesus calls us to "follow me" (gospel). While following the Good Shepherd truly leads to "eternal life," the way of discipleship is not easy. Discipleship always takes us through suffering, rejection, and persecution (first reading). However, no matter what the cost of following Jesus, we are not alone nor are we abandoned to our own resources. The risen Jesus is always present within us. This is the good news of these Easter gospels.

Hearing Jesus' voice and fidelity to its call involves us in the harsh realities of the world in which we live. As the first reading reminds us, we will meet with jealousy and persecution. Not everyone wants to hear a message of forgiveness and repentance, of self-sacrificing and surrender, even when there is assurance that this is the only way to life. Yet, the tumult of the world is not a sign that God has abandoned us. Jealousy, violent abuse, persecution, expulsions, etc. have always been part of our human condition. In all of this, Jesus is at "the center," will shepherd us, lead us to "springs of life-giving water," and "wipe away every tear" (second reading). No matter what we encounter in following Jesus, nothing or no one can take us out of his care. This is, indeed, Easter Good News.

Living the Paschal Mystery

Longing for wholeness and goodness is at the very center of who we are. The ways for achieving them are up for grabs. Some people choose to focus on themselves, amassing as much money or wealth as they can since these seem to promise them security and pleasure. Some people control other people, thinking power can make them whole. Others try to be "goody, goody two-shoes," attracting others to a false image of themselves that cannot last. Still others withdraw within themselves, trying to shut out the evil and sadness and loss of hope which surround us.

And some get it right: the only true way to wholeness and goodness is to follow Jesus along the path of self-sacrifice, willingly, to be a lamb for the sake of others. We hardly need to look for opportunities to give ourselves over for the sake of others; they abound in our daily living. Easter further reminds us that when we sacrifice ourselves for others, we are never alone; the Good Shepherd is always with us.

This is what Good Shepherd Sunday is all about: not about some too-good statues and pictures; it's all about a God who so deeply cares for us that the only Son became the Lamb who was slain. This is why whatever we may endure in following Jesus as faithful disciples is worth the cost—because God cares for us as our Good Shepherd and "lead[s] [us] to springs of life-giving water" (second reading).

Focusing the Gospel

Key words and phrases: hear my voice, follow me, eternal life, No one can take them

To the point: The voice of Jesus calls his disciples to "follow me" (gospel). While following the Good Shepherd truly leads to "eternal life," the way of discipleship is not easy. Discipleship always takes us through suffering, rejection, and persecution (first reading). However, no matter what the cost of following Jesus, we are not alone nor are we abandoned to our own resources. Nothing or no one can take us out of Jesus' care.

Connecting the Gospel

to the second reading: Jesus is both the Good Shepherd and the Lamb who was slain. As Shepherd, Jesus is the one who cares for us and leads us. As Lamb, Jesus is the one who lays down his life in sacrifice for us.

to our culture: The tumult of the world is not a sign that God has abandoned us. Jealousy, violent abuse, persecution, expulsions, etc. have always been part of our human condition. In all of this, Jesus is at "the center," will shepherd us, lead us to "springs of life-giving water," and "wipe away every tear" (second reading).

Understanding Scripture

The Shepherd gives life: This Sunday's passage unfolds during the Jewish Feast of Dedication (10:22) which is more commonly called *Hanukkah*. It commemorates the victory of the Jews, led by the Maccabees, over Antiochus Epiphanes in 164 B.C. That evil ruler had made the practice of Judaism illegal and punishable by death. The unspeakable suffering devout Jews endured is described in the First and Second Books of Maccabees. Antiochus Epiphanes inflamed Jews when he set up a pagan altar in the Holy of Holies of the Temple to offer sacrifice to the Greek god, Zeus. This was an outrage because, for Jews, the Temple is the visible sign of the presence of God in their midst. There is no holier place. The worship of God alone is the greatest commandment, and idolatry is the worst sin. Thus, the desecration of the Temple was a grievous offense. The Jews rebelled, defeated their enemies, and purified the Temple. The rededication of the Temple on the 25th of Chislev, 164 B.C., was a cause of great joy. God could dwell among the people again.

Against this background, Jesus in this Sunday's gospel claims, "I and the Father are one" (10:30). According to John, the Temple's function as a visible sign of God's presence is taken over by Jesus. To see God, one need not go to the Temple; as Jesus tells Philip, "Whoever has seen me has seen the Father" (14:9).

This identity between Jesus and the Father is suggested in another way in this gospel. The protection Jesus provides for his sheep means that "no one can take [the sheep] out of my hand" and "no one can take them out of the Father's hand" (10:28-29).

It is as Shepherd that Jesus cares for the sheep his Father has entrusted to him. Jesus instructs the sheep to "hear my voice" and "follow me." "Hearing and following" in this passage have the same meaning as "seeing and believing" in John 20:19-31 (Second Sunday of Easter). The outcome of both sets of activities is the same: "eternal life" / "life in his name" (10:28/20:31).

ASSEMBLY & FAITH-SHARING GROUPS

- I hear the voice of the Good Shepherd calling me to . . .
- Hearing Jesus announce that "no one can take [me] out of the Father's hand" means to me . . .
- Imitating Christ, I am like a good shepherd to others when I . . . ; I am like a lamb slain for others when I . . .

PRESIDERS

I model how to hear and follow the Shepherd's voice whenever I . . .

DEACONS

Sharing the voice of the Shepherd with others sometimes brings strife (see first reading). I am sustained to remain faithful by . . .

HOSPITALITY MINISTERS

My hospitality "urge[s] [others] to remain faithful to the grace of God" (first reading) whenever I . . .

MUSIC MINISTERS

In my music ministry right now I hear the voice of the Good Shepherd calling me to . . .

ALTAR MINISTERS

When I keep the Lamb at the center of my ministry (see second reading), my service is like . . . ; when I keep myself at the center, my service is like . . .

LECTORS

Whenever I recall that the word I proclaim is the voice of the Good Shepherd to the assembly, my proclamation is like . . .

EXTRAORDINARY MINISTERS OF HOLY COMMUNION

I "distribute" and "nurture" the security we have in Christ ("No one can take them out of the Father's hand") by . . .

Model Rite of Blessing and Sprinkling Holy Water

Presider: Jesus is the Lamb who was slain and the Good Shepherd whose voice calls us. As we ask God to bless this water, may it remind us of our baptism and help us to hear more clearly the Good Shepherd's voice.

[Continue with Form C of the blessing of water]

Appreciating the Responsorial Psalm

Psalm 100 is one of a set of psalms (93, 95–100) which celebrate God's sovereignty over all things. Peoples of the ancient Near East acclaimed a god powerful because of specific acts, the greatest of which was creation. The Israelites believed that God acted not only to create the world but also to create them as a people. All forces inimical to Israel as a community—from natural disasters to human enemies—quelled before the power of God, who arranged all events in the cosmos to support their coming together as a people.

In Christ God showed the ultimate creative power by overcoming death with resurrection. Out of this act God formed a new people beyond the boundaries of the community of Israel (first reading), a people "which no one could count, from every nation, race, people, and tongue" (second reading). No powers of hell or destruction will prevail against this people for it is God who leads and shepherds them (second reading, gospel). In singing Psalm 100 we proclaim who we are because of Christ's death and resurrection: a people created by God, protected by God, and called by God to eternal life.

Model General Intercessions

Presider: God will never let anything or anyone take us out of God's hands. This encourages us to lift our prayers to the God who loves us and cares for us.

Response:

Lord, hear our prayer.

Cantor:

we pray to the Lord,

That the Church always hear the voice of the Good Shepherd and follow him faithfully to eternal life . . . [pause]

That world leaders hear the voice of the Good Shepherd and strive only for the care of their people . . . [pause]

That those who struggle to follow the voice of the Good Shepherd for fear of persecution or rejection find courage and strength . . . [pause]

That all of us here gathered rejoice in being known by the Good Shepherd and come to love him more deeply . . . [pause]

Presider: Good and gracious God, you care for us with mercy and compassion: hear these our prayers that we might one day enjoy eternal life with you and your Son, Jesus Christ, who lives and reigns with you and the Holy Spirit, one God, for ever and ever. **Amen.**

ALTERNATIVE OPENING PRAYER

Let us pray

Pause for silent prayer

God and Father of our Lord Jesus Christ,
though your people walk in the valley of
  darkness,
no evil should they fear;
for they follow in faith the call of the
  shepherd
whom you have sent for their hope and
  strength.
Attune our minds to the sound of his
  voice,
lead our steps in the path he has shown,
that we may know the strength of his
  outstretched arm
and enjoy the light of your presence for
  ever.

We ask this in the name of Jesus the Lord.
  Amen.

FIRST READING

Acts 13:14, 43-52

Paul and Barnabas continued on from
  Perga
  and reached Antioch in Pisidia.
On the sabbath they entered the
  synagogue and took their seats.
Many Jews and worshipers who were
  converts to Judaism
  followed Paul and Barnabas, who spoke
    to them
  and urged them to remain faithful to the
    grace of God.

On the following sabbath almost the whole
  city gathered
  to hear the word of the Lord.
When the Jews saw the crowds, they were
  filled with jealousy
  and with violent abuse contradicted
    what Paul said.
Both Paul and Barnabas spoke out boldly
  and said,
  "It was necessary that the word of God
    be spoken to you first,
  but since you reject it
  and condemn yourselves as unworthy
    of eternal life,
  we now turn to the Gentiles.
For so the Lord has commanded us,
  I have made you a light to the Gentiles,
  that you may be an instrument of
    salvation
  to the ends of the earth."

The Gentiles were delighted when they
heard this
and glorified the word of the Lord.
All who were destined for eternal life came
to believe,
and the word of the Lord continued to
spread
through the whole region.

The Jews, however, incited the women of
prominence who were worshipers
and the leading men of the city,
stirred up a persecution against Paul
and Barnabas,
and expelled them from their territory.
So they shook the dust from their feet in
protest against them,
and went to Iconium.
The disciples were filled with joy and the
Holy Spirit.

RESPONSORIAL PSALM
Ps 100:1-2, 3, 5

R∕. (3c) We are his people, the sheep of his
flock.
or:
R∕. Alleluia.

Sing joyfully to the LORD, all you lands;
serve the LORD with gladness;
come before him with joyful song.
R∕. We are his people, the sheep of his
flock.
or:
R∕. Alleluia.

Know that the LORD is God;
he made us, his we are;
his people, the flock he tends.
R∕. We are his people, the sheep of his
flock.
or:
R∕. Alleluia.

The LORD is good:
his kindness endures forever,
and his faithfulness, to all generations.
R∕. We are his people, the sheep of his
flock.
or:
R∕. Alleluia.

SECOND READING
Rev 7:9, 14b-17

See Appendix A, p. 294.

About Liturgy

The Easter Lectionary and serving others: This Fourth Sunday of Easter,
Good Shepherd Sunday, is at the center of our fifty-day celebration of Easter. The appearances of the risen Lord proclaimed in the gospels of the first three Sundays open
onto this Sunday where the focus is on God's continued love and care for us. In turn,
this Sunday opens onto the next Sundays which begin to prepare the Church to receive
the Holy Spirit and take up the mission of Christ—what hearing his voice and following him entails.

During this joyous time of celebrating Easter's new life, we might be fooled into
thinking that discipleship is easy since the risen Jesus is always with us. Even during
our Easter celebration, however, the Lectionary begins to move us toward the cost of
discipleship which we can take up only because we have received the Holy Spirit to
strengthen and enlighten us.

Serving others, then, is hardly something we do only during Lent (as part of our
penance) or at other specific times. Jesus has modeled for us that serving others is
what he came to teach us. Liturgical ministers model for us serving others so that we
can be dismissed from Mass to go and do likewise. Of such is Easter life: dying to self
in order to serve others.

About Liturgical Music

Cantor preparation: The Israelites understood that God created them as a people
and continually shepherded them. So, too, does the Church recognize that she is created
and shepherded by God. How have you experienced God's shepherding love for the
Church? How has God shepherded you as an individual disciple? In what way(s) does
the Church particularly need God's shepherding care today? In what way(s) do you?

Music suggestions: With last Sunday's gospel Jesus already began calling the
Church to ministry ("Feed my lambs"). In the coming weeks the challenge to take on
Jesus' mission will become even more intense. This week's readings couch the hardships of discipleship within the Shepherd's promise of continual care and of eternal
life. Good Shepherd songs abound (for example, "My Shepherd Will supply My Need";
"Shepherd of Souls, Refresh and Bless"; "The King of Love My Shepherd Is"; "Shepherd Me, O God"). Most would be suitable for either the presentation of the gifts or
Communion. With so much repertoire available, however, there is the danger that we
can overload the liturgy with too many Good Shepherd songs. One is sufficient; two
would be appropriate only if their texts complement rather than repeat one another.

SPIRITUALITY

Gospel

John 13:31-33a, 34-35; L54C

When Judas had left them, Jesus said,
    "Now is the Son of Man glorified, and
        God is glorified in him.
If God is glorified in him,
    God will also glorify him in himself,
    and God will glorify him at once.
My children, I will be with you only a
    little while longer.
I give you a new commandment: love
    one another.
As I have loved you, so you also should
    love one another.
This is how all will know that you are
    my disciples,
    if you have love for one another."

Reflecting on the Gospel

Most of us get a pile of junk mail every week. Included among these glossy lures is usually a peck of catalogues. Open them up, and frequently sprawled across a product will be the letters NEW!—often printed in bright red, very large letters. The advertising ploy is that by simply being new, customers will be enticed to buy. Some people have a drive to "keep up with the Joneses." Whatever the newest gimmick is, they have to have it. The computer industry is fond of telling us that our brand new computer is really obsolete by the time we get it home and set up. So how long does "new" really last? This Sunday's gospel tells us that some new things last forever!

The "new" commandment Jesus gives will last as long as Jesus himself loves. Last Sunday's Good Shepherd gospel assures us his love will last through eternity. In this Sunday's gospel Jesus speaks of his impending departure ("I will be with you only a little while longer"), but his love for us and his command that we love one another in the same way remain forever.

There is another aspect of the "new" commandment besides its eternal endurance, however. This love has a cost. The commandment given in Leviticus 19:18 was "love your neighbor as yourself." Jesus commands us, however, to love one another as he has loved us. This is a "new love" because it calls for the self-emptying of the slain Lamb. Our paschal transformation challenges us to make the norm of our love not self-love but the self-sacrificing love of Jesus. This is a demanding love because it will require that we die to self.

But this dying to self transforms the world! The divine love to which Jesus calls us produces dramatic results: "a new heaven and a new earth," a "new Jerusalem," indeed the making of "all things new" (second reading). This love wipes away every tear and lasts forever. Our Easter joy is not found in avoiding its costs, but in embracing its price for the sake of the new heaven and earth it promises.

Living the Paschal Mystery

We are able to love as Jesus did only because of the power and grace which come from our first being loved by God. God's dwelling is now "with the human race" (second reading). God transforms us into those who love as the divine Son loved.

Our "paschal transformation" is our passing from keeping the old commandment to keeping the new, from loving as ourselves to loving as Jesus did, from dying to the old self-centered, sinful self to rising to a new life in Christ. What is "new" in our paschal love is that now our love is like divine love. What is "new" in our paschal living is that now our very identity is that of the risen Christ. The "new" measure of love is Jesus. He has been raised to glory and lives forever. So will we by loving!

By our own self-sacrificing love, we are the presence of the risen Christ for others. Christian living is, bottom line, to love as Jesus loved, to be the risen Christ for others. By loving as Jesus did, we are transformed, and so is all the world: "Behold, I make all things new" (second reading). And this newness will last forever.

Focusing the Gospel

Key words and phrases: new commandment, As I have loved you . . . love one another

To the point: The commandment given in Leviticus 19:18 was "love your neighbor as yourself." Jesus' new commandment is "As I have loved you, so you also should love one another." The norm of our love is not to be self-love, but the self-sacrificing love of Jesus. It is this kind of love which makes "all things new" (second reading).

Connecting the Gospel

to the second reading: When we live Jesus' new commandment of love, the results are dramatic: "a new heaven and a new earth," "new Jerusalem," indeed, "all things new" (second reading).

to our religious experience: We are keen on underscoring obligation—we must "love one another." This is only possible because of the power and grace which come from our first being loved by God.

Understanding Scripture

As I have loved you: This Sunday's gospel passage begins the very lengthy "Last Discourse" or "Farewell Speech" (13:31–17:26) which Jesus addresses to the disciples at the Last Supper. The first part of chapter 13, from which this Sunday's gospel passage is taken, begins with Jesus' washing the feet of his disciples. After performing that profound act, Jesus informs his disciples, "I have given you a model to follow, so that as I have done for you, you should also do" (13:15). It is with this dramatic and unexpected act in mind that the disciples now hear Jesus command them, "I give you a new commandment: love one another. As I have loved you, so you also should love one another" (13:34). The parallel wording links the two acts: "as I have done/loved . . . you also should . . ."

There are two characteristics to the love with which disciples are to love one another. First, the standard and model of love is Jesus himself: "As I have loved you . . ." Again, chapter 13 begins with this notice: Jesus "loved his own in the world and he loved them to the end" (13:1): "the end," of course, is his death. Thus, the love demonstrated in the foot washing anticipates Jesus' ultimate act of love on the cross. This is what is "new" about the command: it is Jesus himself, in his life, service, and self-giving unto death, who models what it means to love one another. Second, on a practical level, disciples express love in service to one another. This is different from the once-for-all love of Jesus on the cross and, in a sense, is harder because such service requires a daily laying down of one's wishes, needs, and desires for the sake of the other.

There is one final aspect of this love. It is not exclusively for the mutual benefit of disciples. Rather, "This is how all will know that you are my disciples, if you have love for one another" (13:35). In other words, love is a vehicle for evangelization, announcing to all people a new way of life characterized by love.

ASSEMBLY & FAITH-SHARING GROUPS

- As I understand it, that which is "new" in Jesus' commandment to love is . . .
- The extent to which Jesus is my norm for loving others is . . .
- The difference in my relationships when I love as Jesus loves is . . .

PRESIDERS

The "new" which is occurring in and through me this Easter (see second reading) is . . .

DEACONS

My ministry is conforming me more and more into the risen Christ in that . . .

HOSPITALITY MINISTERS

My hospitality calls attention to God's dwelling with the human race (see second reading) whenever I . . .

MUSIC MINISTERS

My participation in music ministry challenges me to love as Jesus does when . . . It helps me love as Jesus does by . . .

ALTAR MINISTERS

When I minister to others according to the norm of Jesus' commandment, my service is like . . .

LECTORS

The way I love others is the most important way of proclaiming the risen Christ because . . .

EXTRAORDINARY MINISTERS OF HOLY COMMUNION

My ministry signifies the "new heaven and new earth" (second reading) whenever I . . .

Model Rite of Blessing and Sprinkling Holy Water

Presider: Jesus gives us a new commandment to love as he loves us. We now ask God to bless this water as a reminder of our baptism through which we have been made a new creation.

[Continue with Form C of the blessing of water]

Appreciating the Responsorial Psalm

Paul and Barnabas are highly energetic and immensely successful in their mission to the Gentiles. All this they credit to God working in them (first reading). John relays his vision of a new heaven and new earth, God working to "make all things new" (second reading). Jesus speaks of his glorification, God's final work to complete the mission for which he was sent (gospel). In the responsorial psalm we command these works and more to give God thanks and to proclaim the power of God's might and the splendor of God's kingdom to all peoples. One work yet remains: that we who are God's people choose to love one another as Jesus has loved us (gospel). This, too, will be God's work and the one which will most definitively declare who God is and who we are because of God. May our surrender to this new and final commandment be the praise we sing, and may our praise last forever.

Model General Intercessions

Presider: The God who first loves us will hear our prayers and grant our needs. And so we pray.

Response:

Lord, hear our prayer.

Cantor:

we pray to the Lord,

That all members of the Church be known as disciples of Jesus by their self-sacrificing love . . . [pause]

That all world leaders promote justice and peace through self-sacrificing love . . . [pause]

That the homeless and lonely find a haven of love . . . [pause]

That our parish be known for our love that bears much fruit . . . [pause]

Presider: Generous God, you revealed your love for us in Christ your risen Son: hear these our prayers that we might love one another as you have loved us. We ask this through Christ our Lord. **Amen.**

OPENING PRAYER

Let us pray

Pause for silent prayer

God our Father,
look upon us with love.
You redeem us and make us your children
    in Christ.
Give us true freedom
and bring us to the inheritance you
    promised.

We ask this through our Lord Jesus Christ,
    your Son,
who lives and reigns with you and the
    Holy Spirit,
one God, for ever and ever. **Amen.**

FIRST READING
Acts 14:21-27

After Paul and Barnabas had proclaimed
    the good news to that city
    and made a considerable number of
        disciples,
    they returned to Lystra and to Iconium
        and to Antioch.
They strengthened the spirits of the
    disciples
    and exhorted them to persevere in the
        faith, saying,
    "It is necessary for us to undergo many
        hardships
    to enter the kingdom of God."
They appointed elders for them in each
    church and,
    with prayer and fasting, commended
        them to the Lord
    in whom they had put their faith.
Then they traveled through Pisidia and
    reached Pamphylia.
After proclaiming the word at Perga they
    went down to Attalia.
From there they sailed to Antioch,
    where they had been commended to the
        grace of God
    for the work they had now
        accomplished.
And when they arrived, they called the
    church together
    and reported what God had done with
        them
    and how he had opened the door of
        faith to the Gentiles.

RESPONSORIAL PSALM
Ps 145:8-9, 10-11, 12-13

R℟. (cf. 1) I will praise your name forever,
my king and my God.
    or:
R℟. Alleluia.

The LORD is gracious and merciful,
    slow to anger and of great kindness.
The LORD is good to all
    and compassionate toward all his
        works.

R̷. I will praise your name forever, my
king and my God.
    or:
R̷. Alleluia.

Let all your works give you thanks, O
    LORD,
    and let your faithful ones bless you.
Let them discourse of the glory of your
        kingdom
    and speak of your might.

R̷. I will praise your name forever, my
king and my God.
    or:
R̷. Alleluia.

Let them make known your might to the
        children of Adam,
    and the glorious splendor of your
        kingdom.
Your kingdom is a kingdom for all ages,
    and your dominion endures through all
        generations.

R̷. I will praise your name forever, my
king and my God.
    or:
R̷. Alleluia.

SECOND READING
Rev 21:1-5a

Then I, John, saw a new heaven and a new
        earth.
The former heaven and the former earth
        had passed away,
    and the sea was no more.
I also saw the holy city, a new Jerusalem,
    coming down out of heaven from God,
    prepared as a bride adorned for her
        husband.
I heard a loud voice from the throne
        saying,
    "Behold, God's dwelling is with the
        human race.
He will dwell with them and they will be
        his people
    and God himself will always be with
        them as their God.
He will wipe every tear from their eyes,
    and there shall be no more death or
        mourning, wailing or pain,
    for the old order has passed away."

The One who sat on the throne said,
    "Behold, I make all things new."

About Liturgy

Eucharistic praying and love: Since the "new" commandment to love one another as Jesus has loved us is so essential in the life of his disciples, we would naturally expect that our Eucharistic prayers reflect this same commandment of love. And, indeed, they do in at least two ways.

First, excluding the prefaces, the word "love" appears in all ten Eucharistic prayers except the first two. The Eucharistic Prayer for Masses with Children II includes a paraphrase of the commandment of this Sunday's gospel: "He [Jesus] came to show us how we can love you, Father, by loving one another." The Eucharistic Prayer for Masses of Reconciliation II continues after the institution narrative with "Lord our God, your Son has entrusted to us this pledge of his love." What is the antecedent of "this"? What is the "pledge of . . . love"? It would seem to be not only the institution narrative itself and the command to "Do this in memory of me," but also the Eucharistic acclamation where we proclaim our faith in terms of Jesus' dying and rising. This leads to the second way the Eucharistic prayers reflect the commandment of love.

All the Eucharistic prayers clearly narrate for us Jesus' self-giving—both in terms of his sacrifice on the cross as well as his sacrifice on this altar which becomes his Body and Blood given as our heavenly Food. Thus the Eucharistic prayers not only *narrate* Jesus' love, but they model again and again within the whole Eucharistic action the *meaning* and *demands* of this love—giving oneself over for the good of others.

About Liturgical Music

Cantor preparation: In singing this psalm you announce to the world a kingdom which is a new order of creation (second reading). Old ways of relating have been replaced by Jesus' manner of loving (gospel). Where do you see this new creation already present? Where is it most lacking? How can you contribute to its completion?

Music suggestions: An excellent hymn for the entrance procession (or for the sprinkling rite) this Sunday would be "We Know That Christ Is Raised and Dies No More" [CBW3, CH, RS, SS, WC, W3]. The text speaks of sharing by water in Jesus' death and new life. Especially apropos is verse 4, "A new creation comes to life and grows As Christ's new body takes on flesh and blood. The universe restored and whole will sing." Another hymn which speaks of the new creation ushered in by Christ's resurrection is "Christ Is Risen! Shout Hosanna!" [G2, GC, GC2, PMB, SS, WC, WS]. The text is full of the Scriptural allusions and poetic imagery which mark Brian Wren's work. The catchy and upbeat tune would make the hymn work well either for the entrance procession or as a song of praise after Communion. A setting of *Ubi Caritas* would be most appropriate for Communion, as would James Chepponis' "Love One Another" [CG, RS] or Bob Dufford's song of the same name [BB, JS2].

SPIRITUALITY

Gospel

John 14:23-29; L57C

Jesus said to his disciples:
"Whoever loves me will keep
my word,
and my Father will love him,
and we will come to him and
make our dwelling with
him.
Whoever does not love me does
not keep my words;
yet the word you hear is not
mine
but that of the Father who
sent me.

"I have told you this while I am
with you.
The Advocate, the Holy Spirit,
whom the Father will send in my
name,
will teach you everything
and remind you of all that I told you.
Peace I leave with you; my peace I give
to you.
Not as the world gives do I give it to
you.
Do not let your hearts be troubled or
afraid.
You heard me tell you,
'I am going away and I will come
back to you.'
If you loved me,
you would rejoice that I am going to
the Father;
for the Father is greater than I.
And now I have told you this before it
happens,
so that when it happens you may
believe."

Reflecting on the Gospel

At one time words were laboriously and beautifully hand copied. Manuscripts and books were rare and treasured items. This art was largely lost after Gutenberg's invention of the printing press in the fifteenth century. Tradition holds that the first book printed by Gutenberg was a Bible. Today the art of fine calligraphy and illumination has been recovered in the creation of a very different Bible, the Saint John's Bible, commissioned by Saint John's University in Collegeville, Minnesota. In contrast to today's mass-produced books, every page of this Bible is hand lettered and illuminated. The Saint John's Bible is a project of beautiful words, an expensive work undertaken out of love for aesthetics of the word and love for the word of God itself.

This Sunday's gospel makes an important correlation between loving and living God's word. The connection is a simple one: "Whoever loves me will keep my word," Jesus says. For us today, however, it can be a real challenge to hear the gospel as more than simply words, but as words we come to love, and love so much that they become a way of life for us—a way of life, moreover, which will make demands on us. Jesus is telling us that his words cannot be simply skimmed and then discarded. They invite a commitment of self which is no less than the giving of self which Jesus modeled. These, indeed, are "expensive" words!

"Keep my word," Jesus commands. By this do disciples prove their love for Jesus. Lest the disciples feel disheartened or afraid, Jesus gives his Spirit to guide them and his peace to reassure them. The risen Jesus gives us the same command and the same gifts. Like the disciples, we are to make keeping Jesus' word our way of life; like the disciples, we have been given the power to do so. Jesus' words usher in new life and a new way of being, one where the risen Christ dwells within us: "I will come back to you."

Jesus' resurrection redefines everything. Words are no longer jots on a page, no matter how beautifully or lovingly done, but a command to a new way of living the intimate indwelling of Father, Son, and Spirit. Here is what is wholly new: God dwells within us! This intimate union between God and humanity is made possible by Jesus' farewell gift, the Holy Spirit. Indeed, in the Spirit all things are new!

Living the Paschal Mystery

The new creation and new life effected by Christ's resurrection resulted in an entirely new self-understanding by the first Christian communities (as reported in Acts) and a new religious order (as described in Revelation). Because we Christians today are so inundated with words and pay little attention to most of them, it is possible that any newness of the Resurrection escapes us or else the newness has become so commonplace that it has lost its power. Even "love" and "God's word" are so overloaded with variant meanings that they have largely lost their power to stir us.

Each year our Easter celebration challenges us to assess our treasure trove: God's dwelling among us, the relationship of hearing (living) God's word and loving as Jesus did, being taught by the Holy Spirit. These cannot be discarded like cheap paperbacks. They are our life!

Focusing the Gospel

Key words and phrases: word, Holy Spirit, peace, Do not . . . be . . . afraid, rejoice

To the point: "Keep my word," Jesus commands. By this do disciples prove their love for Jesus. Lest the disciples feel disheartened or afraid, Jesus gives his Spirit to guide them and his peace to reassure them. The risen Jesus gives us the same command and the same gifts. Like the disciples, we are to make keeping Jesus' word our way of life; like the disciples, we have been given the power to do so.

Connecting the Gospel

to the second reading: In the gospel God dwells with those who keep Jesus' words. In the second reading God lives directly in the midst of the people. This intimate union between God and humanity is made possible by Jesus' farewell gift, the Holy Spirit.

to culture: In our experience gifts are tangible and the most prized ones satisfy our wants and desires. Jesus offers us a gift beyond what we can imagine or desire—his very self.

Understanding Scripture

Farewell gifts: Jesus' promise in the gospel that the Holy Spirit "will teach you everything" is dramatized in this Sunday's first reading. This is the issue: do Gentiles who want to become Christians have to be circumcised and observe the Law of Moses? The first reading begins with Paul and Barnabas deciding to get a ruling from the "apostles and elders" in Jerusalem. The startling decision "of the Holy Spirit and of us" is "no" to circumcision and the Law. The community in Jerusalem, guided by the Spirit, obviously recognized the radical newness of the Christian life and made a decisive break with Judaism.

Some of that "newness" was described in last Sunday's gospel in which Jesus gave a "new commandment": disciples are to love one another as Jesus loved them. In this Sunday's gospel, Jesus describes what it means for disciples to love Jesus himself: they must keep his word. This is of paramount importance for the words Jesus speaks are really God's own words. When disciples keep the word, both Jesus and God will dwell in them.

To help disciples keep his words, Jesus will send the Holy Spirit to "teach you everything" and to "remind you of all that I told you." The Holy Spirit will not only enable the disciples to recall what Jesus taught, but will also teach them how to live those words in every age. This is certainly the function of the Holy Spirit in the first reading as the Spirit guides the fledgling Church in matters unaddressed by Jesus in his earthly teachings.

Jesus not only gives the disciples his word and Spirit, he gives them his peace. Peace is not freedom from conflict, strife, or hostility. Indeed, Jesus is about to enter the greatest conflict of his life. Rather, it is the confidence that disciples will never be abandoned. Jesus will always be present to them through his word; the Father will dwell in them; the Holy Spirit will guide them. As Jesus is about to take his leave of the disciples, he gives them his word, the Holy Spirit, and his peace.

ASSEMBLY & FAITH-SHARING GROUPS

- Keeping Jesus' word as a sign of love means to me . . .
- Whenever I keep Jesus' word, God makes a "dwelling" with me. I understand this to mean . . .
- Jesus' "peace" is different from the world's in that . . .

PRESIDERS

An example of when I have sensed that the word I preach is not mine but the Father's was . . .

DEACONS

I have glimpsed the "splendor of God" (second reading) while ministering to God's people when . . .

HOSPITALITY MINISTERS

I am sharing with others Jesus' peace whenever I . . .

MUSIC MINISTERS

One sign of keeping Jesus' word (gospel) is that a person becomes less rigid toward others (first reading). My participation in music ministry has helped me become less rigid toward others by . . . What/who has helped me grow in this way is . . .

ALTAR MINISTERS

My service includes assisting others in their keeping of Jesus' word whenever I . . .

LECTORS

I shall consider to what extent keeping and loving Jesus' word are parts of my proclamation preparation . . .

EXTRAORDINARY MINISTERS OF HOLY COMMUNION

My desire for Christ to dwell with me in the Eucharist also cultivates my hearing and keeping of Christ's word in that . . .

Model Rite of Blessing and Sprinkling Holy Water

Presider: Water is a gift which sustains life. Let us ask God to bless this water and sustain us in Christ's risen life.

[Continue with Form C of the blessing of water]

Appreciating the Responsorial Psalm

Psalm 67 was a hymn of thanksgiving for a fruitful harvest. The Israelites prayed that God would extend these abundant blessings to all the earth. In this way all nations would know God's saving care and offer joyful praise. In the context of this Sunday's readings, Psalm 67 invites us to make our very way of living the abundant harvest God offers the world. When we love Jesus and keep his word we move beyond the temptation to limit God's presence and power to specific practices (first reading) and places (second reading). We become the very dwelling place of God on earth (gospel). Let us pray together that our manner of living and relating will make God's way "known upon earth" (psalm) and that through us all nations will come to know salvation.

Model General Intercessions

Presider: The God who dwells among us gives all we need to live Christ's risen life. So we are encouraged to bring our needs to God.

Response:

Lord, hear our prayer.

Cantor:

we pray to the Lord,

For the Church, the manifestation of Christ's love and word . . . [pause]

For the world, raised to a new order by the resurrection . . . [pause]

For the troubled and afraid, in whom God dwells . . . [pause]

For ourselves here gathered, loved by the Father, raised to new life by Jesus, taught by the Holy Spirit . . . [pause]

Presider: Loving God, the resurrection of your Son brings joy and peace: hear these our prayers that we may one day enjoy eternal life. We ask this through Christ our Lord. **Amen.**

OPENING PRAYER

Let us pray

Pause for silent prayer

Ever-living God,
help us to celebrate our joy
in the resurrection of the Lord
and to express in our lives
the love we celebrate.

Grant this through our Lord Jesus Christ,
    your Son,
who lives and reigns with you and the
    Holy Spirit,
one God, for ever and ever. **Amen.**

FIRST READING
Acts 15:1-2, 22-29

Some who had come down from Judea were
    instructing the brothers,
    "Unless you are circumcised according
        to the Mosaic practice,
    you cannot be saved."
Because there arose no little dissension
    and debate
    by Paul and Barnabas with them,
    it was decided that Paul, Barnabas, and
        some of the others
    should go up to Jerusalem to the
        apostles and elders
    about this question.

The apostles and elders, in agreement
    with the whole church,
    decided to choose representatives
    and to send them to Antioch with Paul
        and Barnabas.
The ones chosen were Judas, who was
        called Barsabbas,
    and Silas, leaders among the brothers.
This is the letter delivered by them:

"The apostles and the elders, your brothers,
    to the brothers in Antioch, Syria, and
        Cilicia
    of Gentile origin: greetings.
Since we have heard that some of our
        number
    who went out without any mandate
        from us
    have upset you with their teachings
    and disturbed your peace of mind,
    we have with one accord decided to
        choose representatives
    and to send them to you along with our
        beloved Barnabas and Paul,
    who have dedicated their lives to the
        name of our Lord Jesus Christ.

So we are sending Judas and Silas
    who will also convey this same message
        by word of mouth:
    'It is the decision of the Holy Spirit and
        of us
    not to place on you any burden beyond
        these necessities,
    namely, to abstain from meat sacrificed
        to idols,
    from blood, from meats of strangled
        animals,
    and from unlawful marriage.
If you keep free of these,
    you will be doing what is right. Farewell.'"

RESPONSORIAL PSALM
Ps 67:2-3, 5, 6, 8

R℣. (4) O God, let all the nations praise you!
    or:
R℣. Alleluia.

May God have pity on us and bless us;
    may he let his face shine upon us.
So may your way be known upon earth;
    among all nations, your salvation.

R℣. O God, let all the nations praise you!
    or:
R℣. Alleluia.

May the nations be glad and exult
    because you rule the peoples in equity;
    the nations on the earth you guide.

R℣. O God, let all the nations praise you!
    or:
R℣. Alleluia.

May the peoples praise you, O God;
    may all the peoples praise you!
May God bless us,
    and may all the ends of the earth fear
        him!

R℣. O God, let all the nations praise you!
    or:
R℣. Alleluia.

SECOND READING
Rev 21:10-14, 22-23

See Appendix A, p. 294.

CATECHESIS

About Liturgy

Lectors and God's word: More than readers, lectors are those who *proclaim* God's word. One difference between reading and proclaiming lies in lectors' "owning" the word before they approach the ambo. This means that, first, they must prayerfully read over their selection (this has traditionally been called "divine reading" or *lectio divina*) and learn to love God's word. Only then will the lectors be able to live the word during the week preceding their ministry. Only then will the lectors truly *proclaim* the word. Proclamation, then, involves prayer, making the word one's own, living it, and loving it. This is no small task, but lectors must always remember that Jesus sends his Spirit to be with them.

Mother's Day and Mary: This Sunday is Mother's Day; it is also the month of May. There may be a tendency here to focus on mothers and Mary, but that runs the risk of overshadowing the Easter season. Perhaps the hospitality ministers could wish the mothers well on their special day, but it is best to let the liturgy reflect the Easter season.

It is always appropriate, however, to include another intention at the general intercessions on days like this. Here is a model: For all mothers, models of self-giving and love . . . [pause]

The *Book of Blessings* includes an Order for the Blessing of Mothers on Mother's Day (Chapter 55) and gives sample intercessions which may be added to those of the day as well as a Prayer over the People used at the end of Mass in the place of the usual blessing before dismissal.

About Liturgical Music

Cantor preparation: The harvest for which you praise God in this responsorial psalm is the salvation wrought through the death and resurrection of Christ. You pray that all nations will come to know this salvation. Who has helped you come to know and believe in it? To whom are you making it known?

Music suggestions: "For Your Gift of God the Spirit" [HG] combines thanksgiving for the gift of the Spirit with proclamation about what this Spirit does within us—stirs life, interprets Scripture, gives strength to conquer evil, etc. Verse 3 is particularly relevant to this Sunday's gospel: "He, himself the living Author, Wakes to life the sacred Word, Reads with us its holy pages And reveals our risen Lord. . . ." The final verse is a petition that God give this Spirit full sway in our hearts. HG suggests HYMN TO JOY as the tune, making this a strong processional hymn which would work well for the entrance. The hymn could also be used during the presentation of the gifts provided this be long enough to accommodate all the verses. Two Easter hymns from Africa which fit this Sunday's readings are found in LMGM. "Christ Has Risen" uses a verse-refrain format with a soloist singing the verses. The song would be wonderful during the Communion procession. "Jesus Has Conquered Death" uses call-response style, and would work well either for the entrance procession or the presentation of the gifts. Both songs would sound best with simple percussion accompaniment (see *Leading the Church's Song,* Augsburg Fortress #3-402, for coaching on African rhythmic patterns).

SPIRITUALITY

Gospel

Luke 24:46-53; L58C

Jesus said to his disciples:
"Thus it is written that the Christ
would suffer
and rise from the dead on the third
day
and that repentance, for the
forgiveness of sins,
would be preached in his name
to all the nations, beginning from
Jerusalem.
You are witnesses of these things.
And behold I am sending the promise
of my Father upon you;
but stay in the city
until you are clothed with power from
on high."

Then he led them out as far as Bethany,
raised his hands, and blessed them.
As he blessed them he parted from
them
and was taken up to heaven.
They did him homage
and then returned to Jerusalem with
great joy,
and they were continually in the
temple praising God.

Reflecting on the Gospel

Some reports claim that fully one third of North Americans move each year. Truly, we are "displaced persons." More and more, it is difficult to claim roots. Extended family is rarely a reality. Being "at home" has taken on new and sometimes discomforting meaning—becoming more enclosed and self-reliant. In the midst of "displacement" the readings for this solemnity offer some security and grounding, some connectedness and hope.

We can imagine that the disciples felt something like our modern "displaced persons." Only they weren't the ones who moved, Jesus did! And there they were . . . left gawking! The one whom they thought would restore Israel ("Lord, are you at this time going to restore the kingdom to Israel?") was gone! Now what?

The "Now what?" is simple—although Jesus "was taken up to heaven," the ascension does not end Jesus' work but inaugurates a new way of carrying it out: Jesus passes the mission on to his disciples ("you are witnesses of these things") and promises them the power to fulfill it ("clothed with power from on high"). The mission and the power are now theirs. With Jesus' ascension, the necessity of discipleship is clear. The ascension of Jesus prepares the way for the powerful and enduring presence of the Spirit in the disciples who continue his ministry.

True, the one in whom the disciples had placed their hope had ascended to the right hand of God. Interestingly enough, rather than leaving the disciples "homeless," Jesus' ascension leads them to grasp what being "at home" really means. They witness, pay homage, and are "continually in the temple praising God." With Jesus' ascension and blessing, after the coming of the Spirit, we are the new temples. We are the ones in whom the Holy Spirit dwells. We are the ones in whom others can be "at home." We are the living presence of the risen Christ in our world today!

Living the Paschal Mystery

In this solemnity absence and presence become yet another metaphor for the not yet/already of the paschal mystery. By our faithful witnessing we are the present day disciples who make Jesus' presence and salvation known in the world. At the same time, we are reminded that there is more to our Christian life than what we are living now.

The "two men dressed in white garments" told the disciples that Jesus would "return in the same way as you have seen him going into heaven." The ascension challenges us to look beyond this time to the Christ of glory. Resurrection is fulfilled only on the last day. Thus, absence and presence refer to even more than Jesus' ascension and sending of the Spirit to dwell within us. They also remind us that our suffering and rising, repenting and forgiving, preaching, witnessing, and blessing all carry us forward to that final day of hope when we, too, share in Jesus' glory. Hope itself is an act of discipleship!

The challenge which remains is to make all this practical in our daily living. Perhaps we could begin the habit of thinking about those we are with every day in terms of "Body of Christ." Perhaps we could make it a point to say an encouraging word to someone each week. Perhaps we could encourage others who have been absent to come to church to worship on Sunday. In all these ways we are disciples, making Jesus' risen life present to others.

Focusing the Gospel

Key words and phrases: witnesses of these things, clothed with power from on high, was taken up to heaven

To the point: Although Jesus "was taken up to heaven," the ascension does not end Jesus' work but inaugurates a new way of carrying it out: Jesus passes the mission on to his disciples ("you are witnesses of these things") and promises them the power to fulfill it ("clothed with power from on high"). The mission and the power are now ours.

Connecting the Gospel

to the second reading from Hebrews: Jesus' ministry on our behalf does not end with resurrection and his return to the Father for "he . . . now appear[s] before God on our behalf" as "a great priest over the house of God."

to our culture: When a strong cultic leader is present, a cult survives. In the absence of such a leader, a cult often disperses. This is not so with Christianity. The ascension of Jesus prepares the way for the powerful and enduring presence of the Spirit in the disciples who continue his ministry.

Understanding Scripture

Salvation history in Luke's Gospel: Luke tends to "dramatize" his theology: people and details of geography and time are all used to describe his understanding of the work of God in Jesus. Over the course of the Gospel and Acts, Luke divides salvation history into three periods: the time of Israel (represented by the various characters in the infancy narratives who recall figures from the Old Testament), the time of Jesus (Gospel), and the time of the Church (Acts). In this way, Luke unfolds the continuity of God's saving plan and sees the divine work begun in Israel consummated in the Church. For this reason, Luke reinterprets some key Jewish feasts, as he is about to give a new significance to Pentecost. When we compare Luke's report of Easter, Ascension, and Pentecost to John's Gospel, in which the Ascension and the giving of the Spirit occur on Easter Sunday, we see that Luke is more concerned with theology than with history.

For Luke, the "forty days" between Resurrection and Ascension are presented as a time in which Jesus prepares the disciples to undertake their preaching (see also 13:31) by "speaking [to them] about the kingdom of God." This time recalls the forty days Moses (Exod 24:18; 34:28) and Elijah (1 Kgs 19:8) spent before their new commission from God. Further, the forty days between the Resurrection and Ascension might also allude to the forty days Jesus himself spent in the wilderness before he began his preaching (Luke 4:2-15). In this way, Luke establishes the early Church's continuity both with the time of Israel and the time of Jesus.

The Jewish feast of Pentecost was observed fifty days after Passover. Originally an agricultural feast celebrating the grain harvest (Lev 23:15-22; Deut 16:9-12), Pentecost later came to commemorate the giving of the land (Deut 26:1-11) and later still with the giving of the Law on Sinai. But in Acts, what is given now is neither the land nor the Law, but the Spirit. In Luke, Ascension and Pentecost are key moments which continue to unfold Luke's theology of salvation history.

ASSEMBLY & FAITH-SHARING GROUPS

- The Ascension is important to me because . . .
- When it comes to extending Jesus' mission, I am a witness in my daily living to . . .
- Where I have learned my dependence upon being "clothed [by the Father] with power from on high" is . . .

PRESIDERS

Jesus' priestly intercession "on our behalf" (second reading) is embodied in my ministerial care whenever I . . .

DEACONS

My ministry puts me in the posture of waiting for "the promise of [the] Father" because . . .

HOSPITALITY MINISTERS

The very gathering of the assembly moves me to praise God and offer God homage because . . .

MUSIC MINISTERS

Jesus' last gesture over the disciples was a blessing (gospel). I feel Jesus blessing me in my music ministry when . . . I feel myself blessing the Church through my music ministry when . . .

ALTAR MINISTERS

Serving others is an act of homage to the risen Lord whenever I . . .

LECTORS

Ways I share with others the forgiveness of sins given all in Christ are . . .

EXTRAORDINARY MINISTERS OF HOLY COMMUNION

I shall consider how my *Amen* at Eucharist announces my promise to witness to Christ in my daily living . . .

Model Rite of Blessing and Sprinkling Holy Water

Presider: Today we celebrate the risen Christ's return to glory at the right hand of God. With the disciples we await the coming of the Spirit to strengthen and enlighten us. And so we ask God to bless this water over which the Spirit moves . . . [pause]

[Continue with Form C of the blessing of water]

Appreciating the Responsorial Psalm

Psalm 47 was an enthronement psalm used when the Ark of the Covenant was carried in procession into the Temple. It celebrated God's sovereignty over all heaven and earth. The song contains verses (omitted from this responsorial psalm) which express Israel's belief that God chose them to play a special role in establishing God's kingship over all nations.

Knowing the full text of this psalm brings its use on this solemnity into fuller perspective. The psalm is not just about the ascension of Jesus to the throne of God, but includes our ascension with him. We, too, "have confidence of entrance into the sanctuary" (second reading). Although we do not know the time of the kingdom's coming, we nonetheless witness to its presence (first reading). We have been blessed and sent by Christ to tell of it (gospel). Through Jesus' ascension all humanity is raised to the glory of God. This is what we celebrate and proclaim in our singing of Psalm 47.

Model General Intercessions

Presider: Just as Jesus blessed his disciples before ascending into heaven, so will God bless us with whatever we need. So we pray with confidence.

Response:

Lord, hear our prayer.

Cantor:

we pray to the Lord,

That the Church may always be a faithful witness to Jesus' dying and rising . . . [pause]

That all people of the world may be blessed with peace and joy . . . [pause]

That those seeking repentance and forgiveness may be embraced by the mercy of God . . . [pause]

That we disciples gathered here rejoice in our mission and continually praise God in our lives . . . [pause]

Presider: O God, you are faithful to your promises: hear these our prayers and lead us to share in glory with you and the Son, in the unity of the Holy Spirit, for ever and ever. **Amen.**

Let us pray

Pause for silent prayer

Father in heaven,
our minds were prepared for the coming
    of your kingdom
when you took Christ beyond our sight
so that we might seek him in his glory.

May we follow where he has led
and find our hope in his glory,
for he is Lord for ever. **Amen.**

FIRST READING

Acts 1:1-11

In the first book, Theophilus,
    I dealt with all that Jesus did and taught
    until the day he was taken up,
    after giving instructions through the
        Holy Spirit
    to the apostles whom he had chosen.
He presented himself alive to them
    by many proofs after he had suffered,
    appearing to them during forty days
    and speaking about the kingdom of
        God.
While meeting with them,
    he enjoined them not to depart from
        Jerusalem,
    but to wait for "the promise of the
        Father
    about which you have heard me speak;
    for John baptized with water,
    but in a few days you will be baptized
        with the Holy Spirit."

When they had gathered together they
        asked him,
    "Lord, are you at this time going to
        restore the kingdom to Israel?"
He answered them, "It is not for you to
        know the times or seasons
    that the Father has established by his
        own authority.
But you will receive power when the Holy
        Spirit comes upon you,
    and you will be my witnesses in
        Jerusalem,
    throughout Judea and Samaria,
    and to the ends of the earth."
When he had said this, as they were
        looking on,
    he was lifted up, and a cloud took him
        from their sight.

While they were looking intently at the
    sky as he was going,
    suddenly two men dressed in white
        garments stood beside them.
They said, "Men of Galilee,
    why are you standing there looking at
        the sky?
This Jesus who has been taken up from
    you into heaven
    will return in the same way as you have
        seen him going into heaven."

RESPONSORIAL PSALM

Ps 47:2-3, 6-7, 8-9

R︎. (6) God mounts his throne to shouts of
joy: a blare of trumpets for the Lord.
    or:
R︎. Alleluia.

All you peoples, clap your hands,
    shout to God with cries of gladness,
for the LORD, the Most High, the awesome,
    is the great king over all the earth.

R︎. God mounts his throne to shouts of joy:
a blare of trumpets for the Lord.
    or:
R︎. Alleluia.

God mounts his throne amid shouts of joy;
    the LORD, amid trumpet blasts.
Sing praise to God, sing praise;
    sing praise to our king, sing praise.

R︎. God mounts his throne to shouts of joy:
a blare of trumpets for the Lord.
    or:
R︎. Alleluia.

For king of all the earth is God;
    sing hymns of praise.
God reigns over the nations,
    God sits upon his holy throne.

R︎. God mounts his throne to shouts of joy:
a blare of trumpets for the Lord.
    or:
R︎. Alleluia.

SECOND READING

Eph 1:17-23

or

Heb 9:24-28; 10:19-23

See Appendix A, p. 295.

About Liturgy

Ascension and forty days: Luke's time frame for these events is different from that recorded in John's Gospel. In John, Jesus ascends to the Father and sends the Spirit on resurrection day itself. In Luke, Jesus ascends to the Father forty days after the Resurrection and sends the Spirit after fifty days, on Pentecost. While we have two different gospel traditions concerning Ascension and Pentecost, we must always be careful not to "historicize" these events. The timing does not matter; what does matter is that Jesus rose into heaven to take his place of glory at the right hand of his Father and sent the Spirit to dwell within us.

There are a number of uses of the number "forty" in Scripture, but perhaps the one most important for this solemnity is Jesus' forty-day sojourn in the desert prior to the inauguration of his public ministry. We might interpret, intimated by Luke, that during the forty days after his resurrection, Jesus was preparing the disciples for their ministry of witnessing to all nations. The number is symbolic: their preparation was adequate or complete, surely brought to a climax on Pentecost with the sending of the Spirit.

In our language about the Ascension, we need to monitor our "literal" expressions and be leery about spacial images (up, up, and away!) which convey only absence or any disruption in the unity and integrity of our fifty-day celebration of Easter.

About Liturgical Music

Cantor preparation: On the surface you can interpret this psalm as a celebration of the historical event of Jesus' ascension. But it is about far more than that. The psalm is about the complete victory of the whole Body of Christ over the forces of sin and death. Who sits on the "holy throne"? You do. The assembly does. The Church does. As you prepare to sing this psalm, you need to reflect on this fuller understanding so that you can move the assembly, and yourself, beyond historicizing over Jesus' life and mission to participation in it.

Music suggestions: Hymns celebrating the ascension of Jesus into heaven are readily marked in every hymnal. Look for ones which connect Jesus' ascension and the elevation of all humanity. Some Easter hymns do this, for example, "Up from the Earth" [G2, GC, RS]. Its style and energy suit it best either for the entrance procession or for a song of praise after Communion. Other possible choices are hymns for Christ the King, such as "To Jesus Christ Our Sovereign King" and "Rejoice, the Lord Is King." Sylvia Dunstan's Ascension hymn "Lift Up Your Hearts, Believers" [HG] would make an excellent recessional hymn.

SPIRITUALITY

Gospel

John 17:20-26; L61C

Lifting up his eyes to heaven,
Jesus prayed, saying:
"Holy Father, I pray not only
for them,
but also for those who will
believe in me through
their word,
so that they may all be one,
as you, Father, are in me and I
in you,
that they also may be in us,
that the world may believe
that you sent me.
And I have given them the glory
you gave me,
so that they may be one, as we
are one,
I in them and you in me,
that they may be brought to
perfection as one,
that the world may know that you
sent me,
and that you loved them even as you
loved me.
Father, they are your gift to me.
I wish that where I am they also may
be with me,
that they may see my glory that you
gave me,
because you loved me before the
foundation of the world.
Righteous Father, the world also does
not know you,
but I know you, and they know that
you sent me.
I made known to them your name and I
will make it known,
that the love with which you loved me
may be in them and I in them."

Reflecting on the Gospel

One of the best compliments children can pay their parents is to mimic them. Small children seem to do it naturally. We've all seen the little guy take large steps and put a swagger in his walk, imitating his father. Or we've seen the little gal wait for the right moment to get at her mother's makeup and apply it—usually with rather garish results! When the relationship between children and parents is healthy and strong, the children grow up to imitate their parents in much more consequential ways; for example, in continuing family values, upright living, or rearing their own children through loving relationships. Jesus' prayer in this Sunday's gospel is essentially a prayer that we imitate Jesus.

This Sunday's gospel—just a week before Pentecost—situates us with Jesus at the Supper with his disciples the night before he died. Jesus, always the loving one, naturally turns to prayer for his disciples: Jesus prays that the intimate love and union he shares with his Father may take root in his disciples. Experiencing such divine love and intimate union enables and sustains the disciples' mission to the world. In fact, love and unity among believers is the first form of their witness to the world. Our love for each other is God's love in us spilling over. Our unity as the Body of Christ is God's life abounding in us in word and truth. This love and unity is a sign to the world about who Jesus is: the risen One united perfectly with his Father and with us.

The first reading illustrates for us a disciple's love and intimate union with Jesus. Stephen's vision of the "glory of God" was possible because the love of God had taken such deep root in him. This love sustained him and kept him focused on God even at the moment of his martyrdom. In his very moment of martyrdom Stephen repeats the words of Jesus from the cross: "receive my spirit" and "do not hold this sin against them." He witnesses union with Jesus, the Father, and the human community, the very things for which Jesus prays in the gospel. He witnesses how faithful disciples imitate the risen One. He witnesses where faithful and deep love take us: to eternal glory.

This is the greatest compliment we can pay to Jesus: imitate him. Ultimately, this is what discipleship means: imitate him. This is how we are to live as disciples: imitate him. This is the call of the new life of resurrection: imitate him. This is the challenge of Pentecost: imitate him.

Living the Paschal Mystery

Paschal transformation is allowing ourselves to be made into a gift—wrapped in love, tied by unity, and delivered by the word. The first reading is a concrete example of a disciple who is a gift to Jesus. Stephen puts the paschal mystery into action, where the gospel always takes us. He preaches the good news, accepts the fatal consequences, and forgives those who love not. Stephen willingly embraces his death because he knows this is the way to eternal glory and life.

We have been given the glory (presence) of Jesus so that others may see the glory. How do others see the glory? Through our love, unity, and forgiveness which reflect the glory of God. Thus paschal mystery living is more than a "not yet" ideal for which we strive and one day at the end of our human lives will be brought to perfection. It is at the same time the "already" of the glory of God revealed first through Jesus and now through us, his disciples.

Focusing the Gospel

Key words and phrases: Jesus prayed; may be one, as we are one; that the world may know; the love with which you loved me may be in them

To the point: Jesus prays that the intimate love and union he shares with his Father may take root in his disciples. Experiencing such divine love and intimate union enables and sustains the disciples' mission to the world. In fact, love and unity among believers is the first form of their witness to the world.

Connecting the Gospel

to the first reading: In his moment of martyrdom Stephen repeats the words of Jesus from the cross: "receive my spirit" and "do not hold this sin against them." He witnesses union with Jesus, the Father, and the human community, the very things for which Jesus prays in the gospel.

to the Church: The mission of the Church—to witness to God's love and unity—is impeded by persistent division among the churches. Christian unity is not just desirable, it is necessary in order to fulfill effectively Christ's prayer for the world.

Understanding Scripture

Unity and witness: The Fifth Sunday of Easter gave us the opening of Jesus' "Farewell Discourse." That discourse concludes with a formal prayer by Jesus for his disciples; this is called the High Priestly Prayer (ch. 17), a title which highlights Jesus' role as an intercessor. We read from this prayer each year on the Seventh Sunday of Easter. Over the three-year Lectionary cycle, we read the entire prayer.

In the course of this prayer, Jesus asks God for eight specific things, indicated by the language, "so that . . ." or simply "that . . ." (vv. 21a, 21b, 22b [3 times], 23a, 23b, 24a, 24b). Three times, Jesus prays that the disciples may "be one" and twice he prays either that the disciples "may be in us" or "may be with me." Why this focus on intimate union with God/Jesus and on the unity of disciples? The community's unity shows forth the unity of the Father and the Son ("I am in the Father and the Father is in me," 14:10; also 10:38; 14:20). The quality of the community's life together is an act of witness, a proclamation to the world of the very nature of God and the intimacy that Jesus uniquely shares with God. What is implied is that division in the community distorts the community's witness to God and impedes the world's believing in Jesus.

The community's oneness is not its own work: it comes from its union with God and Jesus. The oneness of the community does more than witness to the nature of God. Through the witness and preaching of the disciples, the world will come to "believe" (v. 21) and to "know" (vv. 23, 25) "that you sent me" (vv. 21, 23, 25). Thus Christian unity testifies both to God's love in sending Jesus and to Jesus' divine origin in being sent from the Father.

Jesus, priest and intercessor, prays for his disciples—us. He prays that we may be as deeply united in him as he is in his Father. This is the source of unity and the content of Christian witness.

**ASSEMBLY &
FAITH-SHARING GROUPS**

- Jesus sees me (and all his disciples) as the Father's gift to him. What that means to me is . . .
- Some ways I am a living answer to Jesus' prayer for unity are . . .
- Where I need to grow in imitating Jesus is . . .

PRESIDERS
Ways I assist the community's diversity and differences to be united in Christ are . . .

DEACONS
I am like Stephen and a mediator of forgiveness for the guilty (see first reading) whenever I . . .

HOSPITALITY MINISTERS
My hospitality promotes unity among the assembly whenever I . . .

MUSIC MINISTERS
I easily see my music ministry as a gift of myself to God and to the Church. But Jesus tells the disciples they are God's gift to him (gospel). Music ministry helps me become God's gift to Jesus by . . .

ALTAR MINISTERS
The humility of serving others prepares me to "enter the city" of God (second reading) in that . . .

LECTORS
Jesus' prayer for unity challenges me to work on forgiveness and reconciliation with . . .

**EXTRAORDINARY MINISTERS
OF HOLY COMMUNION**
Communion entails unity with the Lord *and* with each other. I foster communion with each other in our parish by . . .

Model Rite of Blessing and Sprinkling Holy Water

Presider: Jesus prays that we be one as he and the Father are one. We ask God to bless this water from which our baptismal unity flows . . . [pause]

[Continue with Form C of the blessing of water]

Appreciating the Responsorial Psalm

Psalm 97 is a hymn celebrating God's sovereignty over all that exists. The verses used here retell the vision which strengthens Stephen to remain steadfast in discipleship to the point of death (first reading). Stephen sees the glory of God in heaven and Jesus standing at God's right hand and proclaims what he sees to the people surrounding him. Even more, he dies as Jesus did, giving himself over to God and forgiving those who have murdered him. In return he is raised to the glory of eternal life (second reading). We sing these psalm verses because we have been granted the same vision as Stephen and we have been called to the same discipleship. In singing this psalm we acclaim that we, too, have seen the glory of Jesus and that we, too, will stake our lives on it.

Model General Intercessions

Presider: We are united with Jesus and the Father through love. Let us express this love by praying for our own needs and those of the Church and world.

Response:

Lord, hear our prayer.

Cantor:

we pray to the Lord,

That the Church may grow in love and unity so that others may come to believe . . . [pause]

That all peoples of the world, divided by war and violence, may be united in peace and justice . . . [pause]

That fractured relationships may be healed in love . . . [pause]

That we here gathered may be a gift to each other as we are a gift to Jesus . . . [pause]

Presider: Loving God, you call us to unity with you through Christ in the Spirit: hear these our prayers that we may grow in our love for you and one another and come to share in your eternal glory. We ask this through Christ our Lord. **Amen.**

OPENING PRAYER

Let us pray

Pause for silent prayer

Father,
help us keep in mind that Christ our
    Savior
lives with you in glory
and promised to remain with us until the
    end of time.

We ask this through our Lord Jesus Christ,
    your Son,
who lives and reigns with you and the
    Holy Spirit,
one God, for ever and ever. **Amen.**

FIRST READING

Acts 7:55-60

Stephen, filled with the Holy Spirit,
    looked up intently to heaven and saw
        the glory of God
    and Jesus standing at the right hand of
        God,
    and Stephen said, "Behold, I see the
        heavens opened
    and the Son of Man standing at the
        right hand of God."
But they cried out in a loud voice,
    covered their ears, and rushed upon him
        together.
They threw him out of the city, and began
    to stone him.
The witnesses laid down their cloaks
    at the feet of a young man named Saul.
As they were stoning Stephen, he called
    out,
    "Lord Jesus, receive my spirit."
Then he fell to his knees and cried out in a
    loud voice,
    "Lord, do not hold this sin against
        them";
    and when he said this, he fell asleep.

RESPONSORIAL PSALM

Ps 97:1-2, 6-7, 9

℟. (1a and 9a) The Lord is king, the most high over all the earth.
or:
℟. Alleluia.

The LORD is king; let the earth rejoice;
let the many islands be glad.
Justice and judgment are the foundation of
his throne.

℟. The Lord is king, the most high over all the earth.
or:
℟. Alleluia.

The heavens proclaim his justice,
and all peoples see his glory.
All gods are prostrate before him.

℟. The Lord is king, the most high over all the earth.
or:
℟. Alleluia.

You, O LORD, are the Most High over all
the earth,
exalted far above all gods.

℟. The Lord is king, the most high over all the earth.
or:
℟. Alleluia.

SECOND READING

Rev 22:12-14, 16-17, 20

I, John, heard a voice saying to me:
"Behold, I am coming soon.
I bring with me the recompense I will give
to each
according to his deeds.
I am the Alpha and the Omega, the first
and the last,
the beginning and the end."

Blessed are they who wash their robes
so as to have the right to the tree of life
and enter the city through its gates.

"I, Jesus, sent my angel to give you this
testimony for the churches.
I am the root and offspring of David,
the bright morning star."

The Spirit and the bride say, "Come."
Let the hearer say, "Come."
Let the one who thirsts come forward,
and the one who wants it receive the gift
of life-giving water.

The one who gives this testimony says,
"Yes, I am coming soon."
Amen! Come, Lord Jesus!

About Liturgy

Seventh Sunday of Easter readings: In all of Canada and most U.S. dioceses, Ascension Thursday is transferred to the following Sunday, so this Sunday's proper readings (for the Seventh Sunday of Easter) are not proclaimed. On the one hand, this is unfortunate since these readings are so important: they clearly bring home the mission to bring others to believe in Jesus the Messiah and the inevitable consequences disciples of Jesus must bear because of their commitment. This Sunday—surely preparing for the celebration of the coming of the Spirit on Pentecost—reminds us that the paschal mystery is not only Jesus' way of living, dying, and rising but also our own.

On the other hand, the Ascension can bring home this same important point: Jesus accomplished his work of salvation, and then returned to his rightful place at God's right hand and shares in God's glory given him from the beginning. Our mission is to be the presence of Jesus in the world today, reflect the glory already given us, and make salvation known. Although ascended, Jesus is still present—in us and through us.

Supporting the importance of the readings for the Seventh Sunday of Easter, the Lectionary note before the Sixth Sunday of Easter says that "[w]hen the Ascension of the Lord is celebrated the following Sunday, the second reading and Gospel from the Seventh Sunday of Easter [see nos. 59–61] may be read on the Sixth Sunday of Easter."

About Liturgical Music

Cantor preparation: Because Psalm 97 is a generic text about the glory of God, it would be easy to sing it in a perfunctory way. But the context of Stephen's martyrdom (first reading) and Jesus' prayer that his disciples be one with him and the Father (gospel) invite a much deeper interpretation. To see the glory of God means to discover the mystery of your own glory. To become one with Christ means to accept that such glorification can come only through death. To sing these verses means to lay down your life in surrender and belief as did Stephen. This, then, is no simple song. Are you ready to sing it?

Music suggestions: Owen Alstott's "We Have No Glory" [JS2; OCP octavo 8971] is particularly fitting for this Sunday's readings. The refrain reads, "We have no glory, we have no name. We are as grains of sand upon the shore. Our only glory, our only name, is Jesus Christ." The verses speak of Christ as the source of all our life and being, and of our mission to "become the name of Christ upon the earth." The piece would work well as a choral prelude or as a Communion hymn with choir singing the verses and the assembly the refrain. Both refrain and verses are written SATB, and a part for solo instrument is included. If used for Communion its length will need to be extended (for example, by interludes of the instrumental part played against melody only on piano or organ or against the choir humming a verse *a cappella*). Another good choice for Communion would be "Draw Near" [PMB, WC, WS], the text of which correlates well with the second reading.

SPIRITUALITY

Gospel John 14:15-16, 23b-26; L63C

Jesus said to his disciples:
"If you love me, you will keep my
    commandments.
And I will ask the Father,
    and he will give you
        another Advocate to
        be with you always.

"Whoever loves me will
        keep my word,
    and my Father will love
        him,
    and we will come to him
        and make our dwelling
        with him.
Those who do not love me
    do not keep my words;
    yet the word you hear is not mine
    but that of the Father who sent me.

"I have told you this while I am with you.
The Advocate, the Holy Spirit whom
        the Father will send in my name,
    will teach you everything
    and remind you of all that I told you."

or John 20:19-23

On the evening of that first day of the
        week,
    when the doors were locked, where
        the disciples were,
    for fear of the Jews,
    Jesus came and stood in their midst
    and said to them, "Peace be with you."
When he had said this, he showed them
        his hands and his side.
The disciples rejoiced when they saw
        the Lord.
Jesus said to them again, "Peace be
        with you.
As the Father has sent me, so I send
        you."
And when he had said this, he breathed
        on them and said to them,
    "Receive the Holy Spirit.
Whose sins you forgive are forgiven
        them,
    and whose sins you retain are
        retained."

Reflecting on the Gospel

Pentecost culminates our fifty-day celebration of the Easter mystery. The first Sundays of the Easter season focused on the risen Jesus as the embodiment of the paschal mystery. These last Sundays transfer the focus from Jesus to ourselves as his disciples. All that Jesus was and did, the Spirit empowers us to become and do.

The first reading from Acts narrates the Lukan Pentecost account in *powerful* terms: "strong driving wind," "tongues of fire," "speak in different tongues." These are God's actions undertaken on our behalf. The Johannine gospel, on the other hand, promises the coming of the Spirit in gentler, *relational* terms: as a teacher and One who comes to remind us of what Jesus has taught. In the gospel the emphasis is not so much on God's power as on our receptivity to God's indwelling presence, word, and commandment which enable us to be faithful disciples. Both power and gentle relationship characterize the disciple who has received the Spirit. God's power in the Spirit gives birth to a new relationship of love and divine indwelling.

In this Pentecost gospel Jesus speaks to his disciples about the relationship of love and commandment (word). In fact, we are able to love and keep commandment or word *because* we have been given the Spirit. The Spirit's dwelling within us *is* the Father's and Jesus' love and the precondition for why we can continue Jesus' mission. The Spirit is our "soul's most welcome guest," our "strength," (sequence). The Spirit is the source of the disciple's life and mission. Filled with this Spirit, the disciples are able to love as Jesus loves and to keep his commandments and word as he desires. The Spirit is the power planted within us to remember ("remind you of all that I told you"), to understand ("teach you everything"), and ultimately to fulfill the mission Jesus entrusted to us.

The Father's love for disciples and Jesus' abiding presence with and in them *is* the Holy Spirit. Here is the import of Pentecost: divine indwelling ("make our dwelling"), outfitting for mission ("teach you everything and remind you of all that I told you"), and way of life ("love me . . . keep my commandments . . . keep my word"). Easter culminates in Pentecost when Jesus' risen life is shared with us in a most profound way through the coming of the Spirit. We ourselves now go forth to carry on Jesus' mission, equipped with divine indwelling. We are never alone in our demanding discipleship; the Spirit is always with us.

Living the Paschal Mystery

The Spirit is not a gift like other gifts we might receive—open them, appreciate and use them, wear them out or discard them. The Spirit is received in baptism and the Spirit's presence is strengthened in confirmation so that we might carry on Jesus' saving mission.

Sometimes in our lives we might witness to a *powerful* presence of the Spirit. Perhaps we must confront another who has done wrong and refuses to change, stand up to injustice, or challenge another to more ethical and generous living. Sometimes in our lives we might witness to a gentler, *relational* Spirit. Perhaps we spend extra quality time with the children, or visit an elderly relative and bring them some cheer, or help someone pick up the pile of oranges in the grocery which has come tumbling down. In these great and simple acts the Spirit works through us and makes Jesus' saving mission present.

Focusing the Gospel (John 14:15-16, 23b-26)

Key words and phrases: love me, keep my commandments, keep my word, Father will love, make our dwelling, Holy Spirit, teach you, remind you

To the point: The Father's love for disciples and Jesus' abiding presence with and in them *is* the Holy Spirit. Filled with this Spirit, the disciples are able to love as Jesus loves and to keep his commandments and word as he desires. The Spirit is the power planted within us to remember ("remind you of all that I told you"), to understand ("teach you everything"), and ultimately to fulfill the mission Jesus entrusted to us.

Connecting the Gospel

to the Easter season: Pentecost culminates our fifty-day celebration of the Easter mystery. The first Sundays of the season focused on the risen Jesus as the embodiment of the paschal mystery. These last Sundays transfer the focus from Jesus to ourselves as his disciples. All that Jesus was and did, the Spirit empowers us to become and do.

to our culture: Keeping laws is something we tend to do because we must or because we fear the consequences of not keeping them. This gospel highlights a different motivation: we keep commandments out of love.

Understanding Scripture

Gift of the Spirit: Pentecost is a fitting conclusion to the fifty-day celebration of Easter. Throughout this festive time, we have reflected on the extraordinary gift that God has given us: eternal life through the death, resurrection, and ascension of Jesus. Like a commercial on TV which is too good to be true: "Wait! There's more!"

This Sunday's gospel, taken from John's account of Jesus' Last Supper Discourse, highlights the gifts already given and those yet to come. Jesus urges the disciples to pray for "another Advocate to be with you always" (14:16). This means that God has already sent one Advocate—Jesus (1 John 2:1). Like a true advocate (this term refers to a legal defender) who helps, defends, and pleads a cause, Jesus has interceded for his disciples (see Easter 7). Reading this gospel from an Easter perspective, we know that this first Advocate held nothing back, not even his life. But now that he has ascended, God will send yet another Advocate and this time the Advocate will remain for ever. "The Father who sent me" (14:24) will also "send [the Holy Spirit] in my name" (14:26).

Jesus assures his disciples that, far from leaving them, the Father and he will come to loving disciples and make their dwelling with them. John began his Gospel with this assertion: "The Word became flesh and dwelt among us" (1:14). Although the time of that historical dwelling among us has come to an end, in a more wondrous way Jesus and the Father—through the gift of the Spirit—will dwell with disciples "always."

The Spirit is a truly extraordinary gift. Already John has told us that the Spirit will be our Advocate; the Spirit will also bring the presence of the Father and the Son to abide with disciples always. The Spirit does more. In the absence of the great Teacher/Rabbi (a frequent title of Jesus in John's Gospel), the Spirit will continue to teach disciples by reminding them of the words and teachings of Jesus. The Spirit continues the presence and the work of Jesus.

**ASSEMBLY &
FAITH-SHARING GROUPS**

- I look to the Spirit to assist me with loving God and keeping God's word by . . .
- I experience the Spirit's empowering me when . . .
- Gifts of the Spirit that I have received are . . . ; I am sharing these gifts with others by . . .

PRESIDERS
Some ways that I affirm and nurture the gifts of the Spirit within the community are . . .

DEACONS
How/where I witness the Spirit's power among those I serve is . . .

HOSPITALITY MINISTERS
"Melt the frozen, warm the chill" (Sequence). These two gifts of the Spirit are balanced in my hospitality whenever I . . .

MUSIC MINISTERS
Sunday after Sunday music ministers witness the power of many parts acting as one Body. I am most aware of this unity in the Spirit when . . . What I contribute to this unity in the Spirit is . . .

ALTAR MINISTERS
The gifts of the Spirit I am developing in order to be a genuine servant are . . .

LECTORS
When I intentionally open myself to the Spirit's power, my proclamation of the word is like . . .

**EXTRAORDINARY MINISTERS
OF HOLY COMMUNION**
The Spirit uses me to build up the community as one Body with many parts (see second reading from 1 Cor) whenever I . . .

Model Rite of Blessing and Sprinkling Holy Water

Presider: The Spirit which was given at Pentecost is the Spirit whom we receive through the waters of baptism. We ask God to bless this water and to renew us in this Spirit . . . [pause]

[Continue with Form C of the blessing of water]

Appreciating the Responsorial Psalm

Psalm 104 is a masterful hymn praising God for the creation of the cosmos. It unfolds in a seven-part structure which parallels the creation account of Genesis 1. In Hebrew thought, the cause of creation was God's breath or spirit *(ruach)*. Take breath away and creatures die; give them divine breath/spirit and they live (vv. 29-30).

The second reading from 1 Corinthians reveals that this Breath binds us into one Body. This Breath gives each of us a unique gift meant for the service of this Body and its mission of salvation. This Breath schools us in all that Jesus taught and enables us to be faithful to it (gospel). Our singing of Psalm 104 is more than praise, then. It is also petition that God send this Breath to renew our identity and transform our living.

Model General Intercessions

Presider: Let us ask our loving God to strengthen us in the Spirit, so that we might keep Christ's commandments.

Response:

Lord, hear our prayer.

Cantor:

we pray to the Lord,

That Christian churches throughout the world may grow in that unity which Christ desires for us in the Spirit . . . [pause]

That the people of the world, through the Holy Spirit, may grow in love for one another . . . [pause]

That all those who yearn for a fuller and happier life might be renewed in the Spirit . . . [pause]

That all of us here be faithful to Jesus' words and obedient to his commands . . . [pause]

Presider: O God, you send the Spirit and fill us with your life: hear our prayers that we may grow in love and one day be united with you forever. We ask this through Christ our Lord. **Amen.**

Let us pray

Pause for silent prayer

Father of light, from whom every good
        gift comes,
send your Spirit into our lives with the
        power of a mighty wind,
and by the flame of your wisdom
open the horizons of our minds.
Loosen our tongues to sing your praise
in words beyond the power of speech,
for without your Spirit
man could never raise his voice in words
        of peace
or announce the truth that Jesus is Lord,
who lives and reigns with you and the
        Holy Spirit,
one God for ever and ever. **Amen.**

FIRST READING

Acts 2:1-11

When the time for Pentecost was fulfilled,
        they were all in one place together.
And suddenly there came from the sky
        a noise like a strong driving wind,
        and it filled the entire house in which
                they were.
Then there appeared to them tongues as
        of fire,
        which parted and came to rest on each
                one of them.
And they were all filled with the Holy
        Spirit
        and began to speak in different tongues,
        as the Spirit enabled them to proclaim.
Now there were devout Jews from every
        nation under heaven staying in
        Jerusalem.
At this sound, they gathered in a large
        crowd,
        but they were confused
        because each one heard them speaking
                in his own language.
They were astounded, and in amazement
        they asked,
        "Are not all these people who are
                speaking Galileans?
Then how does each of us hear them in
        his native language?
We are Parthians, Medes, and Elamites,
        inhabitants of Mesopotamia, Judea and
                Cappadocia,
        Pontus and Asia, Phrygia and
                Pamphylia,
        Egypt and the districts of Libya near
                Cyrene,
        as well as travelers from Rome,
        both Jews and converts to Judaism,
                Cretans and Arabs,
        yet we hear them speaking in our own
                tongues
        of the mighty acts of God."

RESPONSORIAL PSALM
Ps 104:1, 24, 29-30, 31, 34

R℟. (cf. 30) Lord, send out your Spirit, and renew the face of the earth.
or:
R℟. Alleluia.

Bless the LORD, O my soul!
O LORD, my God, you are great indeed!
How manifold are your works, O LORD!
The earth is full of your creatures.

R℟. Lord, send out your Spirit, and renew the face of the earth.
or:
R℟. Alleluia.

If you take away their breath, they perish
and return to their dust.
When you send forth your spirit, they are created,
and you renew the face of the earth.

R℟. Lord, send out your Spirit, and renew the face of the earth.
or:
R℟. Alleluia.

May the glory of the LORD endure forever;
may the LORD be glad in his works!
Pleasing to him be my theme;
I will be glad in the LORD.

R℟. Lord, send out your Spirit, and renew the face of the earth.
or:
R℟. Alleluia.

SECOND READING 1 Cor 12:3b-7, 12-13

Brothers and sisters:
No one can say, "Jesus is Lord," except by
the Holy Spirit.
There are different kinds of spiritual gifts
but the same Spirit;
there are different forms of service but
the same Lord;
there are different workings but the
same God
who produces all of them in everyone.
To each individual the manifestation of
the Spirit
is given for some benefit.

As a body is one though it has many parts,
and all the parts of the body, though
many, are one body,
so also Christ.
For in one Spirit we were all baptized into
one body,
whether Jews or Greeks, slaves or free
persons,
and we were all given to drink of one
Spirit.

OR

SECOND READING Rom 8:8-17

See Appendix A, p. 295.

SEQUENCE

See Appendix A, p. 295.

About Liturgy

Pentecost sequence: This is one of only two Sundays of the year (Easter is the other one) when a sequence is obligatory. Sung as an extension of the gospel acclamation, a sequence can be an occasion for a more lengthy gospel procession which clearly draws attention to the gospel as central to the Liturgy of the Word and central in Christians' lives. On this day, Pentecost, when the Church celebrates the coming of the Spirit and the sending of the disciples to be bearers of peace and forgiveness, it is especially fitting to draw attention to the gospel as we sing our request for the Spirit to come and dwell within us. If the worship space permits it, the gospel proclaimer might process throughout the church and hold the gospel book so people can reach out and reverence it.

Neither the Lectionary (no. 63) nor the GIRM (no. 64) mention a rubric for posture during the sequence, but since it is really a hymn it would seem that the assembly ought at least to be standing. This is a festive hymn to the Holy Spirit and the music setting needs to reflect this joyous occasion.

About Liturgical Music

Cantor preparation: You pray in this responsorial psalm for the renewal of the Church—the renewal of her knowledge of Christ (gospel), the renewal of her sense of identity as one Body (second reading), and the renewal of her commitment to mission (first reading). How have these weeks of Easter celebration renewed you as a member of the Church? How has your parish community become renewed?

Music suggestions: Hymns to the Holy Spirit abound, so the task is to be judicious in our choices. For example, "O Holy Spirit, Come to Bless" [CBW3] would be suitable for the presentation of the gifts but not for the entrance procession because the tune to which it is set (ST. COLUMBA) is too gentle. Sung to the metrically stronger tune MORNING HYMN, however, it makes a very fitting entrance hymn. For another example, even though the refrain of David Haas' "Send us Your Spirit" is almost identical to the refrain of the responsorial psalm, it would not make a good substitution for the psalm because its verses are not the psalm text. This piece would be better used as a prayerful prelude with assembly joining in on the canonic refrain. Finally, it is important not to overuse Holy Spirit hymns on this day. Singing one for the entrance procession and another for the presentation of the gifts is sufficient. Some excellent examples of hymns appropriate for this day though not directed to the Holy Spirit are "We Know That Christ Is Raised" [CH, CBW3, SS, WC, W3]; "The Church of Christ in Every Age" [CH, GC2, JS2, RS, SS, WC, W3]; and "As a Fire Is Meant for Burning" [G2, GC, GC2, RS].

Ordinary Time II

SPIRITUALITY

Gospel

John 16:12-15; L166C

Jesus said to his disciples:
  "I have much more to tell you, but
      you cannot bear it now.
But when he comes, the Spirit
    of truth,
  he will guide you to all truth.
He will not speak on his own,
    but he will speak what he hears,
    and will declare to you the things that
        are coming.
He will glorify me,
    because he will take from what is
        mine and declare it to you.
Everything that the Father has is mine;
    for this reason I told you that he will
        take from what is mine
    and declare it to you."

Reflecting on the Gospel

In an Aesop's fable about a stubborn mule, a farmer was driving his mule along a country lane on the way to town to get supplies. Because there was no burden on the mule's back going into town, the beast was allowed to move along as it wished. The mule wandered farther and farther away from the path until, finally, the farmer noticed that the mule was headed for a high cliff. He ran to the mule, grabbed him by the tail, and tried to hold him back. But the mule willfully resisted and continued toward the cliff's edge. Not wanting to be hurled down the steep incline himself, the farmer let go of the mule's tail. As the mule went hurtling over the cliff, the farmer called after him: "Well, if you will be the master, you will have to continue on alone."

If we were to be masters alone of continuing Jesus' mission, we would, indeed, be hurtling over a high cliff. Jesus' mission is a lofty one—no less than bringing salvation to the world, making known the presence of our triune God among us. But Jesus does not leave us alone—he sends the Spirit to be with us and through the Spirit God's very triune Life dwells within us.

The Spirit not only guides us to truth (see gospel), but bears what we cannot bear on our own. Jesus' mission, then, is not entirely on our shoulders. Jesus, through his Spirit, is still present to us; it is always Jesus' mission. We are disciples doing what he commanded—teaching others what he declares to us by the Holy Spirit.

Moreover, the indwelling of the Spirit assures us of the *triune* God's working within and through us: the Father's love, the Son's mission, the Spirit's truth. We need not fear that we have plunged off a high cliff to take up the Son's mission; the gospel assures us we are not alone. Thus, the gospel illuminates two aspects of the Trinity. First, that everything the Father has belongs also to the Son and Spirit. Second, all that God has is given to us through Jesus who sends us the Spirit. Here is the great mystery and grace of Trinity: the riches of God's own life are given to us, empowering us to take up the divine saving mission.

This life "poured . . . into our hearts" empowers us to "boast . . . in the glory of God" and even to "boast of our afflictions" (second reading). Because of the Trinity's divine life within us, even our afflictions become gift, strengthening us for the mission entrusted to us. Because of the Trinity's divine life within us, we weak human beings can be disciples who fruitfully carry on the very work of God.

The Trinity is, indeed, a lofty mystery. In one sense, though, the Trinity's dwelling within us and entrusting us with continuing Jesus' mission of saving the world is an even loftier mystery! We have been raised to the dignity of sharing in triune Life and continuing the divine saving mission!

Living the Paschal Mystery

The Trinity is, indeed, a lofty mystery which comes down from the "heights" when we ourselves make God's presence known by the way we live. The triune mystery is revealed in our own loving others, in our doing good for others, in our being persons of integrity and truth. The mystery of the Trinity is concrete when we act out of the dignity which has been bestowed upon us—those who carry divine Life within them.

Focusing the Gospel

Key words and phrases: the Spirit, everything the Father has is mine, take from what is mine and declare it to you

To the point: The gospel illuminates two aspects of the Trinity. First, that everything the Father has belongs also to the Son and Spirit. Second, all that God has is given to us through Jesus who sends us the Spirit. Here is the great mystery and grace of the Trinity: the riches of God's own life are given to us.

Connecting the Gospel

to the second reading: Since we have received everything that is of God, the Trinity's divine life is within us (see gospel). This life "poured . . . into our hearts" empowers us to be justified and even to "boast of our afflictions" (second reading).

to our culture: Our age has an inherent optimism about unraveling the mysteries of life, whether it be the origins of the universe or the genetic makeup of a person. If there's a mystery, "we'll solve it." This solemnity presents the Trinity as a mystery not to be "solved" or "explained," but as a Trinity of Persons to be encountered.

Understanding Scripture

Jesus, the Wisdom of God: In the first reading, the speaker is the personified figure of Lady Wisdom. She is a personal expression of God's creative power. The feminine aspect of Wisdom is due in part to the grammatical form of the Hebrew word, which is feminine. Whatever the origin of this conceptualization of Wisdom, Lady Wisdom is present to God and with God before creation—as this Sunday's reading affirms: "I was brought forth" before the depths, fountains, and springs, before the mountains, hills, and fields. Thus, Wisdom witnesses God's creative activity: "I was there" when the Lord established the heavens, made the skies, fixed the earth's foundations, etc. But even more, Wisdom is God's "craftsman." The term suggests that Wisdom played a role in the creation of things, but the text does not elaborate. God delights in Wisdom, and Wisdom delights in the human race. In this sense, Wisdom stands between God and humanity. This mediating aspect was suggested earlier in Proverbs when Lady Wisdom was presented in a prophetic role (1:20-33) chiding and confronting the people. This Sunday's text is more tantalizing than it is explicit. The precise nature and identification of Lady Wisdom remains shrouded in mystery.

Later biblical tradition identified God's Wisdom with the Torah (Sir 24:23). New Testament sources moved in a different direction. Colossians 1:14-16 affirms that Christ "is the image of the invisible God, the firstborn of all creation . . . all things have been created through him and for him." Just as Jewish tradition had identified Wisdom with Torah, Christian reflection saw Christ filling that role before creation, or, in the words of St. John, "He was in the beginning with God. All things came to be through him, and without him nothing came to be" (John 1:2-3).

The way we know that Jesus possesses the wisdom and creative power of God is because the Spirit has declared it to us, as the gospel affirms. All that the Father has, the Son possesses; and what the Son possesses is revealed to us by the Spirit whom Jesus sends.

ASSEMBLY & FAITH-SHARING GROUPS
- The Church's profession of God as triune means to me . . .
- Believing that God's divine life is within me influences my daily living in that . . .
- I believe that the "Spirit of truth" is guiding me to . . .

PRESIDERS
My ministry is Trinitarian in that . . .

DEACONS
My diaconal service communicates the mystery and grandeur of God by . . .

HOSPITALITY MINISTERS
My care and concern to others manifests the "love of God" being "poured" into their hearts (see second reading) whenever I . . .

MUSIC MINISTERS
The Spirit does not speak "on his own" but speaks in the name of Christ. What helps me remember that it is not my "own" word I am to communicate through music, but the word of Christ is . . .

ALTAR MINISTERS
The busy details demanded of my ministry become my act of worshiping God when I . . .

LECTORS
Contemplating the mystery and majesty of the triune God impacts how I proclaim the word in that . . .

EXTRAORDINARY MINISTERS OF HOLY COMMUNION
Some ways I acknowledge, affirm, and build up the divine indwelling in members of the Body of Christ are . . .

Model Act of Penitence

Presider: On this, Trinity Sunday, we reflect on the three Persons in our one God. Let us examine our own living this past week, and ask our triune God to bind us into one . . . [pause]

> Lord Jesus, you are glorified by your Father: Lord . . .
>
> Christ Jesus, you taught all things well: Christ . . .
>
> Lord Jesus, you send the Spirit of truth to guide us in all things: Lord . . .

Appreciating the Responsorial Psalm

The responsorial psalm for this solemnity of the Most Holy Trinity asks who we are in the eyes of God. The readings for this Sunday reveal the high value God places on us human beings. In the first reading the wisdom of God "[plays] on the surface of the earth" and "[finds] delight in the human race." In the second reading God pours God's own love into our hearts through the gift of the Holy Spirit. In the gospel Jesus promises that the Spirit will give to us everything that belongs to him and the Father. Truly God has made us "little less than the angels" and has "crowned [us] with glory and honor" (psalm). In singing this psalm we acknowledge the greatness of the Trinity who give all so that we might become more.

Model General Intercessions

Presider: Let us pray that God strengthen us to bring integrity and truth to our Church, our world, our families, and our parish.

Response:

Lord, hear our prayer.

Cantor:

we pray to the Lord,

That the Church, guided by the Spirit of truth, may glorify God by living faithfully all that Christ has taught . . . [pause]

That the people of the world, guided by the Spirit of truth, may live in the peace and love of God . . . [pause]

That families torn by strife, guided by the Spirit of truth, may be reconciled with one another . . . [pause]

That all of us here, guided by the Spirit of truth, may share in the glory of our triune God . . . [pause]

Presider: O God, you will that all people share in the perfection of your triune Persons: hear these our prayers that we might one day enjoy everlasting life with you. We ask this through Jesus Christ our Lord, who lives and reigns with you and the Holy Spirit, one God, for ever and ever. **Amen.**

OPENING PRAYER

Let us pray

Pause for silent prayer

Father,
you sent your Word to bring us truth
and your Spirit to make us holy.
Through them we come to know the
mystery of your life.
Help us to worship you, one God in three
persons,
by proclaiming and living our faith in you.

Grant this through our Lord Jesus Christ,
your Son,
who lives and reigns with you and the
Holy Spirit,
one God, for ever and ever. **Amen.**

FIRST READING

Prov 8:22-31

Thus says the wisdom of God:
"The LORD possessed me, the beginning of
his ways,
the forerunner of his prodigies of long
ago;
from of old I was poured forth,
at the first, before the earth.
When there were no depths I was brought
forth,
when there were no fountains or springs
of water;
before the mountains were settled into
place,
before the hills, I was brought forth;
while as yet the earth and fields were not
made,
nor the first clods of the world.

"When the Lord established the heavens
I was there,
when he marked out the vault over the
face of the deep;
when he made firm the skies above,
when he fixed fast the foundations of
the earth;
when he set for the sea its limit,
so that the waters should not transgress
his command;
then was I beside him as his craftsman,
and I was his delight day by day,
playing before him all the while,
playing on the surface of his earth;
and I found delight in the human race."

CATECHESIS

RESPONSORIAL PSALM
Ps 8:4-5, 6-7, 8-9

R/. (2a) O Lord, our God, how wonderful your name in all the earth!

When I behold your heavens, the work of your fingers,
the moon and the stars which you set in place—
what is man that you should be mindful of him,
or the son of man that you should care for him?

R/. O Lord, our God, how wonderful your name in all the earth!

You have made him little less than the angels,
and crowned him with glory and honor.
You have given him rule over the works of your hands,
putting all things under his feet:

R/. O Lord, our God, how wonderful your name in all the earth!

All sheep and oxen,
yes, and the beasts of the field,
the birds of the air, the fishes of the sea,
and whatever swims the paths of the seas.

R/. O Lord, our God, how wonderful your name in all the earth!

SECOND READING
Rom 5:1-5

Brothers and sisters:
Therefore, since we have been justified by faith,
we have peace with God through our Lord Jesus Christ,
through whom we have gained access by faith
to this grace in which we stand,
and we boast in hope of the glory of God.
Not only that, but we even boast of our afflictions,
knowing that affliction produces endurance,
and endurance, proven character,
and proven character, hope,
and hope does not disappoint,
because the love of God has been poured out into our hearts
through the Holy Spirit that has been given to us.

About Liturgy

Grace as God's indwelling: Many Catholics have grown up thinking about grace as a *quantity,* something they can "get." Liturgy is where we "get more graces." While there is some truth to this understanding, we have come to a deeper appreciation for understanding grace in terms of God's indwelling life. Rather than a quantity to be had, grace is God's life within us which brings us to a unique relationship with God—as beloved daughters and sons (see CCC no. 1997). Basic to any notion of grace is that it is a gracious gift of God, a bestowal of God's favor on us.

It is not insignificant that the Latin word for grace, *gratia,* has as one of its meanings "thanksgiving." This is, of course, the same word which is the meaning of the Greek *eucharistia.* Grace, then, is God's life within us which first and foremost evokes in us an attitude and relationship of thanksgiving. We might speak of the "grace" of the Mass in terms of our making visible our thankful posture toward God, and in that very posture our relationship with God is deepened and strengthened. In this vein, it is clear that any good we do is because of God's grace—because of God's indwelling life, strength, and power.

Any consideration of our continuing Jesus' mission as his faithful disciples must be made within the context of this grace which has been given us. It is not primarily our doing (although we surely do cooperate with God and make a conscious choice to live the Gospel and continue as Jesus did), but God's grace which enables us to be disciples.

About Liturgical Music

Cantor preparation: In singing the responsorial psalm for this solemnity, you lead the assembly in celebrating the wondrousness of God who chooses to raise human beings to a height only a "little less than the angels." Do you believe in this God? Do you believe in who you are? Do you believe in who the assembly is?

A trinitarian spirituality for music ministers: At first look, the responsorial psalm for this solemnity appears to be about the greatness of human beings. But the refrain keeps God as the object of praise. This makes an apt paradigm for your ministry. How easily people can praise the music and the musician for a good experience of liturgy. But your gift of musicianship comes from God who created not only you, but music itself. Even more, your gift of leading the assembly in liturgical prayer comes from God. Everything comes from that Trinity of divine Persons who, in their desire that all people find salvation, hold back nothing of themselves. Give thanks to the Trinity this week, and pray that their gifts to you lead the assembly to them.

Hymn suggestion: Many hymns to the Trinity exist, but most fitting would be ones which connect to this year's readings. An example is Brian Wren's text, "How Wonderful the Three-in-One" [G2, GC, GC2, JS2, PMB, RS, SS, WC]. The first two verses capture especially well the content of the first reading, "How wonderful the Three-in-One, Whose energies of dancing light Are undivided, pure and good, Communing love in shared delight. Before the flow of dawn and dark, Creation's lover dreamed of earth, And with a caring deep and wise, All things conceived and brought to birth." Since the tune will most likely be unfamiliar to your assembly, you might have the choir sing the hymn during the presentation of the gifts with the assembly joining in on the last verse.

SPIRITUALITY

Gospel   Luke 9:11b-17; L169C

Jesus spoke to the crowds about the
kingdom of God,
  and he healed those who needed to
  be cured.
As the day was drawing to a close,
  the Twelve approached him and said,
  "Dismiss the crowd
  so that they can go to the
    surrounding villages and farms
  and find lodging and provisions;
  for we are in a deserted place here."
He said to them, "Give them some food
  yourselves."
They replied, "Five loaves and two fish
  are all we have,
  unless we ourselves go and buy food
  for all these people."
Now the men there numbered about
  five thousand.
Then he said to his disciples,
  "Have them sit down in groups of
  about fifty."
They did so and made them all sit down.
Then taking the five loaves and the two
  fish,
  and looking up to heaven,
  he said the blessing over them, broke
  them,
  and gave them to the disciples to set
  before the crowd.
They all ate and were satisfied.
And when the leftover fragments were
  picked up,
  they filled twelve wicker baskets.

Reflecting on the Gospel

For many reasons, the fish became a much-beloved symbol in early Christianity. The gospels make allusions to fish a number of times: some of the disciples were fishermen; Jesus commands them to put out their nets and they catch an abundance of fish; Jesus is cooking fish on the seashore for the disciples' breakfast; the risen Jesus eats a piece of fish in the upper room. Later, the letters of the Greek word for fish, *ichthus,* became an acronym for "Jesus, Christ, God, Son, Savior."

The gospel for this solemnity mentions two fish. But they were seemingly insufficient for the task at hand: feed a large, hungry crowd. At Jesus' blessing, the fish are sufficient and satisfying. Herein is a lesson: the fish is a symbol for self-giving. Jesus is the one who gave himself totally and continues to give himself to us in the Eucharist. In this Sunday's gospel Jesus not only fills the hungry with good things, he fills them to overflowing. This solemnity reminds us that Jesus' generous extravagance is not measured only by the amount of food but by the kind of Food he offers—his very self in his Body and Blood.

The food the Twelve offered in response to Jesus' command "Give them some food yourselves" was a few loaves and a couple fish, insufficient for so large a crowd. The food Jesus offered was abundant—foreshadowing his own ultimate and abundant self-giving. Human food leaves us hungry and desiring more. Jesus' food leaves us satisfied. But the satisfaction comes not simply from eating and drinking the Food Jesus offers. The real satisfaction comes from what the eating and drinking lead us to do: give ourselves over to others in self-surrender as Jesus did. The focus of this solemnity, therefore, is not limited to the Eucharistic elements, but leads to our eating and drinking as a proclamation of living the paschal mystery: "For as often as you eat this bread and drink the cup, you proclaim the death of the Lord until he comes" (second reading). Our eating and drinking is our own pledge of self-giving.

Living the Paschal Mystery

Our sharing in the Body and Blood of Christ isn't just for ourselves; St. Paul in his First Letter to the Corinthians makes it clear that we eat and drink ourselves into the paschal mystery. That is, when our eating and drinking truly "proclaim the death of the Lord until he comes," we ourselves "hand over" our bodies—our lives—for the salvation of others. What the Twelve were not able to do for the crowd—provide food for so many—we can do if we do as Jesus did: hand ourselves over.

Discipleship is both accepting the abundance of what God gives us and living out the responsibility having that abundance implies. When we eat and drink the Body and Blood of Christ, we ourselves are transformed more perfectly into the presence of that risen Christ for others. This transformation is both gift and challenge. It is the gift and pledge that what we have now—Jesus' Body and Blood—we will also have even more fully at the messianic banquet. It is the challenge to spend ourselves for others, to give of ourselves. Herein is the mystery!

The deepest mystery this solemnity celebrates is not only that Jesus gives us his own Body and Blood as nourishment which satisfies us fully. It is also that we, too, must give our very own body and blood to others so that they might be satisfied. And when the "leftover fragments" of ourselves are gathered up, we will find ourselves sharing in the everlasting abundance of the messianic banquet. Such a mystery!

Focusing the Gospel

Key words and phrases: crowd, they all ate and were satisfied, leftover fragments . . . filled twelve wicker baskets

To the point: In this Sunday's gospel Jesus not only fills the hungry with good things, he fills them to overflowing. This solemnity reminds us that Jesus' generous extravagance is not measured only by the amount of food but by the kind of Food he offers—his very self in his Body and Blood.

Connecting the Gospel

to the second reading: The focus of this solemnity is not limited to the Eucharistic elements, but leads to our eating and drinking as a proclamation of living the paschal mystery: "For as often as you eat this bread and drink the cup, you proclaim the death of the Lord until he comes."

to Catholic culture: We tend to limit our understanding of the Body and Blood of Christ to the Eucharistic elements. This gospel expands our perception to include the whole event of gathering, blessing, breaking, giving, eating, being satisfied.

Understanding Scripture

The kingdom and feeding the 5,000: To understand better the miraculous feeding of the 5,000, it is helpful to look at the larger context in this section of Luke's Gospel.

Chapter 9 begins when Jesus gives the Twelve authority "to proclaim the kingdom of God" and to heal the sick (9:1-2). After they go out, Luke reports Herod's curiosity about Jesus: "who is this about whom I hear such things?" (9:9). Then the Twelve return and Jesus once again "spoke to the crowds about the kingdom of God" (9:11). This is where this Sunday's gospel begins. The feeding of the 5,000, then, is both a partial answer to Herod's question about the identity of Jesus, and is another way in which Jesus, the Teacher, explains the kingdom.

The ministry of the Twelve—to heal and to preach the kingdom (9:1-2)—is an extension of Jesus' own ministry who preaches the kingdom and heals the sick (9:11). Healing is an enactment of the teaching; the visible sign that the kingdom is, indeed, being established is that demons are cast out (9:1) and illness is cured. The two aspects go together: evil diminishes life and enslaves people; God's reign restore life and liberates them from evil. Healing is the wholeness and liberation *(shalom)* that God's merciful rule brings.

The context of the kingdom heightens the significance of the miraculous feeding. In the Beatitudes, Jesus had promised the poor, "the kingdom of God is yours," and said to the hungry, "you will be satisfied" (6:21-22; at the end of the feeding, "they were satisfied," 9:17). In the kingdom, the poor are gathered in and hunger is satisfied. Moreover, there is a super-abundance of food, a sign of the heavenly banquet (see 13:23-30).

While the gospel and this feast clearly point to the Eucharistic aspects of the miracle (he took, blessed, broke, and gave the bread; 9:16; compare Jesus' actions at the Last Supper, 22:19), the context (preaching, healing, feeding, abundance) indicates that in Jesus' ministry, the kingdom of God is being established and identifies the Eucharist with the banquet in God's kingdom.

ASSEMBLY & FAITH-SHARING GROUPS

- Some examples of Jesus' using my few gifts (only "five loaves and two fish") to minister to others abundantly are . . .
- I experience God's lavish generosity to me in my need when . . .
- My faith in the Body and Blood of Christ affects how I live in that . . .

PRESIDERS

"This is my body that is for you" (second reading). I not only pray these words but live them when I . . .

DEACONS

I assist others to share the abundance they have been given by God by . . .

HOSPITALITY MINISTERS

I "dismiss" the needs of others when . . . I am generous in responding to the needs of others when . . .

MUSIC MINISTERS

It is not how big a choir is, or how loud, or how many musical resources they have which makes them effective, but how readily they give whatever they have over to Christ (see gospel). What helps me give whatever I have to Christ is . . . What sometimes gets in the way of my giving is . . .

ALTAR MINISTERS

Serving others is an occasion to learn and practice dying to self in that . . .

LECTORS

My time with God's word helps me live the Eucharistic mystery—giving self for others—because . . .

EXTRAORDINARY MINISTERS OF HOLY COMMUNION

My ministry goes beyond formality to genuine self-giving—imitating Christ's own self-giving in the Eucharist—when I . . .

Model Act of Penitence

Presider: The Body and Blood of Christ sustains our daily Christian living. Let us open ourselves to God's great gift of love . . . [pause]

> Lord Jesus, you fill the hungry with good things: Lord . . .
>
> Christ Jesus, you give yourself to us: Christ . . .
>
> Lord Jesus, your Body and Blood are the pledge of eternal life: Lord . . .

Appreciating the Responsorial Psalm

Psalm 110 was a royal psalm used at the coronation ceremony of a king descended from the line of David. The text promised the king a place of honor next to God, victory over enemies, and a priestly role before the people. In the first reading Melchizedek gives food, drink, and blessing to Abram because he is "a priest of God Most High." In the gospel Jesus heals those in need and feeds the starving crowd, creating an amazing abundance out of a meager supply. In the second reading Paul reminds us that the food and drink Jesus gives is his very Body and Blood. In singing this psalm we recognize what Jesus does and who Jesus is. He is the one victorious over all that impedes fullness of life. He is the one who feeds us with his very self. He is the completion of the Davidic line and a "priest forever, in the line of Melchizedek."

Model General Intercessions

Presider: The God who nourishes us abundantly surely hears our prayers. And so we lift them to God with confidence.

Response:

Lord, hear our prayer.

Cantor:

we pray to the Lord,

May all members of the Body of Christ imitate Jesus in self-giving for the sake of others . . . [pause]

May all people of the world share in the abundant gifts of God's creation . . . [pause]

May all those who hunger and thirst for food, justice, mercy, forgiveness, and peace be satisfied . . . [pause]

May all of us here grow into being more perfectly the Body of Christ . . . [pause]

Presider: Generous God, you give us the Body and Blood of your Son as food for our journey: hear our prayers that one day we may come to the eternal banquet you have prepared for us. We ask this through Christ our Lord. **Amen.**

ALTERNATIVE OPENING PRAYER
Let us pray

Pause for silent prayer

Lord Jesus Christ,
we worship you living among us
in the sacrament of your body and blood.
May we offer to our Father in heaven
a solemn pledge of undivided love.
May we offer to our brothers and sisters
a life poured out in loving service of that
    kingdom
where you live with the Father and the
    Holy Spirit,
one God, for ever and ever. **Amen.**

FIRST READING
Gen 14:18-20

In those days, Melchizedek, king of Salem,
    brought out bread and wine,
    and being a priest of God Most High,
    he blessed Abram with these words:
    "Blessed be Abram by God Most High,
        the creator of heaven and earth;
    and blessed be God Most High,
        who delivered your foes into your
            hand."
Then Abram gave him a tenth of
    everything.

RESPONSORIAL PSALM

Ps 110:1, 2, 3, 4

R̸. (4b) You are a priest forever, in the line of Melchizedek.

The LORD said to my Lord: "Sit at my right
    hand
    till I make your enemies your footstool."

R̸. You are a priest forever, in the line of Melchizedek.

The scepter of your power the LORD will
    stretch forth from Zion:
    "Rule in the midst of your enemies."

R̸. You are a priest forever, in the line of Melchizedek.

"Yours is princely power in the day of
    your birth, in holy splendor;
    before the daystar, like the dew, I have
        begotten you."

R̸. You are a priest forever, in the line of Melchizedek.

The LORD has sworn, and he will not
    repent:
    "You are a priest forever, according to
        the order of Melchizedek."

R̸. You are a priest forever, in the line of Melchizedek.

SECOND READING

1 Cor 11:23-26

Brothers and sisters:
I received from the Lord what I also
    handed on to you,
    that the Lord Jesus, on the night he was
        handed over,
    took bread, and, after he had given
        thanks,
    broke it and said, "This is my body that
        is for you.
Do this in remembrance of me."
In the same way also the cup, after supper,
    saying,
    "This cup is the new covenant in my
        blood.
Do this, as often as you drink it, in
    remembrance of me."
For as often as you eat this bread and
    drink the cup,
    you proclaim the death of the Lord until
        he comes.

OPTIONAL SEQUENCE

See Appendix A, p. 296.

About Liturgy

This solemnity and Ordinary Time: At first look, it may be tempting to see this solemnity simply as a "devotional" feast. In fact, it developed at a time in the Church's Eucharistic spirituality when people rarely actually received the Eucharist, but gazed on the exposed Host and adored it. Many in the Church today can still recall the lavish *Corpus Christi* processions from their youth. On Holy Thursday the Church celebrates Jesus' giving his Body and Blood, in the context of service. Since so much during the Triduum directs our attention elsewhere, this solemnity allows further reflection on that great mystery inaugurated at the Lord's Supper.

Now, however, the context is Ordinary Time. This is the time when we might reflect on Jesus' gift of his very own Body and Blood in the context of our developing notion of discipleship.

Optional sequence: The sequence for this day is optional, but it ought not be dismissed too lightly. There is a profound theology contained therein, especially with the last five verses (the shorter form). If a parish liturgy preparation team does not use the sequence as part of an extended gospel procession, it might at least be used at a liturgy committee meeting for deeper reflection on the mystery of Eucharist. It would be time well spent!

About Liturgical Music

Cantor preparation: The psalm you sing this Sunday is an acclamation of the priesthood of Christ. Do you recognize the blessing Christ offers you in the gift of his Body and Blood? in the gift of his healing touch?

Music suggestions: Steven Janco's "Draw Near" [PMB, WC, WS] is a lovely verse-refrain setting of the seventh-century hymn *Sancti, venite, Christi corpus sumite.* The song invites us to draw near and receive Christ's gift of himself to us in the Eucharist. Also appropriate for Communion on this solemnity would be songs which express our participation in Christ's feeding of the hungry. "Now We Remain," found in most hymnals, comes to mind not only because of its refrain but also because of its final verse, "We are the presence of God; this is our call. Now to become bread and wine: food for the hungry, life for the weary, for to live with the Lord, we must die with the Lord." Another appropriate song would be "Let Us Be Bread" [G2, GC, GC2, RS] with its refrain, "Let us be bread, blessed by the Lord, broken and shared, life for the world. Let us be wine, love freely poured. Let us be one in the Lord."

SPIRITUALITY

Gospel

Luke 15:3-7; L172C

Jesus addressed this
    parable to the
    Pharisees and scribes:
"What man among you
    having a hundred
    sheep and losing one
    of them
would not leave the
    ninety-nine in the
    desert
and go after the lost one
    until
    he finds it?
And when he does find it,
    he sets it on his
        shoulders with great joy
and, upon his arrival home,
he calls together his friends and
    neighbors and says to them,
'Rejoice with me because I have
    found my lost sheep.'
I tell you, in just the same way
    there will be more joy in heaven over
        one sinner who repents
    than over ninety-nine righteous
        people
who have no need of repentance."

See Appendix A, p. 297, for these readings:

FIRST READING
Ezek 34:11-16

RESPONSORIAL PSALM
Ps 23:1-3a, 3b-4, 5, 6

SECOND READING
Rom 5:5b-11

Reflecting on the Gospel

Peruse any card shop—even outside of Valentine's Day—and we would find oodles of cards bearing red hearts. It is always stylized, like so: ♥. Now, we all know that this is not what a human heart looks like. But for all of us this red symbol does immediately bring to mind intimacy, care, love, friendship. This solemnity in honor of the Sacred Heart of Jesus is a day on which we not only rejoice in Jesus' intimate relationship with us and his care, love, and friendship, but also in his incredible sacrificial love.

The gospel, first reading, and responsorial psalm use the image of the good shepherd to define the mystery of the Sacred Heart. Such is the love which seeks the lost, heals the wounded, protects from death, and gives its own life. In this, "God proves his love for us" (second reading). Jesus' sacrificial love is to be the way we love. He gave his life for us sinners (second reading). We are to give our lives for others.

The second reading gives us a hint as to why so many people can take up the sacrificial and life-giving love of Christ: "The love of God has been poured out into [their] hearts through the Holy Spirit that has been given to [them]." This is why this solemnity is cause for rejoicing and not cringing: sacrifice is nothing to shrink from, but something to embrace. Because that is where Life is. That is where Love is. That is where Heart is.

The gospel uses the word "joy" twice and "rejoice" once. Although we know that the Sacred Heart is a symbol of self-giving sacrificial love, the Sacred Heart is also a symbol of great happiness. Jesus rejoices in his work of redemption, when the lost are found (saved). We rejoice because we have such a Good Shepherd to care for us.

Living the Paschal Mystery

This solemnity might hold challenges for two different groups of people. First, those who have yet to develop a life patterned after Jesus' sacrificial love must take it up, since "we are now justified by [Christ's] blood" (second reading). This solemnity, coming early in our resumption of Ordinary Time, encourages us to travel the paschal journey with Christ in which we take up our own cross for the sake of sinners. This solemnity urges us to have the heart of Christ: one which gives all for even one out of love and compassion.

Second, many among us already live sacrificial—indeed, even heroic—lives. Many parents are as caring towards their children as the shepherd in the gospel: guiding them, finding them when they stray, caring for them so they grow into mature Christian adults. And just when the children seem to be "out of the nest," many of those same parents take up the sacrificial love required to care for their own aging and ailing parents. How many "retired" people don't spend their waning energy caring for others? Our nation virtually saves billions of dollars each year because of the millions of volunteers who do everything from taking meals to homebound people to calling the sick and elderly and making sure they are okay, to serving meals to the homeless. How many people give of their holiday time so that the hungry can be fed? For these already very generous people, the challenge of this feast is to couch their generosity and self-sacrificing love within the context of the redeeming love of Christ. The challenge is to see those they serve as Christ himself and to realize that their sacrificial love is Christ's Sacred Heart in them. And it is Christ's Sacred Heart being made present to others.

Focusing the Gospel

Key words and phrases: go after the lost one, finds it, sets it on his shoulders with great joy

To the point: The gospel, first reading, and responsorial psalm use the image of the good shepherd to define the mystery of the Sacred Heart. Such is the love which seeks the lost, heals the wounded, protects from death, and gives its own life. In this, "God proves his love for us" (second reading).

Model Act of Penitence

Presider: On this Friday we celebrate the solemnity of the Most Sacred Heart of Jesus. Let us open ourselves to the Good Shepherd's sacrificial love and ask to be truly faithful in following him . . . [pause]

Lord Jesus, you seek out the lost: Lord . . .

Christ Jesus, you lay down your life for your sheep: Christ . . .

Lord Jesus, you shepherd us on the path to life: Lord . . .

Model General Intercessions

Presider: The God whose own Son is our Good Shepherd hears our prayers and answers our needs. And so we pray.

Response:

Cantor:

That the Church may always faithfully follow the Good Shepherd . . . [pause]

That world leaders always shepherd their people with care and justice . . . [pause]

That the lost be found, the unloved be loved, sinners be reconciled . . . [pause]

That the love of the Sacred Heart be poured forth into our hearts in good measure . . . [pause]

Presider: O God of boundless love, you faithfully hear the prayers of those who cry out to you: may we imitate the Sacred Heart of Jesus by growing in our love for others. We ask this through Christ our Lord. **Amen.**

ALTERNATIVE OPENING PRAYER

Let us pray

Pause for silent prayer

Father,
we honor the heart of your Son
broken by man's cruelty,
yet symbol of love's triumph,
pledge of all that man is called to be.

Teach us to see Christ in the lives we touch,
to offer him loving worship
by love-filled service to our brothers and
    sisters.
We ask this through Christ our Lord.
    Amen.

FOR REFLECTION

- I experience Jesus' Heart as a good shepherd when . . .
- In my opinion, those most in need of the love of the Sacred Heart are . . .
- I imitate the Sacred Heart of Jesus in my care of others when I . . .

SPIRITUALITY

Gospel

Luke 7:36–8:3; L93C

A Pharisee invited Jesus to dine
        with him,
    and he entered the Pharisee's
            house and reclined at table.
Now there was a sinful woman in
        the city
    who learned that he was at
            table in the house of the
            Pharisee.
Bringing an alabaster flask of
        ointment,
    she stood behind him at his feet
            weeping
    and began to bathe his feet with
            her tears.
Then she wiped them with her hair,
    kissed them, and anointed them with
            the ointment.
When the Pharisee who had invited
        him saw this he said to
            himself,
    "If this man were a prophet,
    he would know who and what sort of
            woman this is who is touching
            him,
    that she is a sinner."
Jesus said to him in reply,
    "Simon, I have something to say to
            you."
"Tell me, teacher," he said.
"Two people were in debt to a certain
        creditor;
    one owed five hundred days' wages
            and the other owed fifty.
Since they were unable to repay the
        debt, he forgave it for both.
Which of them will love him more?"
Simon said in reply,
    "The one, I suppose, whose larger
            debt was forgiven."
He said to him, "You have judged rightly."

Continued in Appendix A, p. 298.

Reflecting on the Gospel

A mother might tell two squabbling siblings to "kiss and make up." A father might pick up the little one who has fallen off the bike and kiss the sore spot to make the hurt go away. A fiancée might blow a kiss to her future husband as he leaves to go on a business trip. In these and many other instances, a kiss is used to heal a relationship, hurt, or separation. Without thinking about it, we use a kiss to express love. Kissing another without any regard for another just does not work for us; we are appalled when a kiss is insincere or a betrayal, and then it is one of the most devastating acts we can experience. Kissing and loving just go together.

In this gospel a sinful woman "has not ceased kissing" Jesus' feet while Simon, Jesus' host at the dinner, "did not give [Jesus] a kiss." The woman's encounter with Jesus not only brought her forgiveness, but also was an occasion for her to show her "great love." Of such is the "good news of the kingdom of God."

The gospel and first reading manifest one of the most significant aspects of the relationship between God and human beings: God is the one who forgives sins; human beings are those who sin. The issue is not whether we sin (we do and will!), but whether we will open ourselves to the judgment and mercy of God. This woman does; David does (first reading); Simon, however, resists. Simon himself sits in judgment; the woman kneels in repentance. The gospel concludes with Simon being rebuked and the woman being forgiven. Both Simon and the woman are debtors—they both have much to be forgiven. Love brings the forgiveness.

Simon thought that Jesus was unaware of the "sort of woman" who was lovingly "touching him." In response to Simon's judgment about the woman, Jesus constructed his parable to open Simon's eyes to see both the great love within the heart of this sinful woman and the debt within his own heart. The woman, who knows only too well how great is her debt, throws herself on Jesus' mercy and receives forgiveness. We do not know Simon's response. But we do know what *we* need to do.

Living the Paschal Mystery

Most of us are more like Simon than like the woman. It's far easier to see what is wrong in another than it is to see what is wrong in ourselves. Nathan's work as a prophet was to help David see his sinfulness. Because David acknowledges his sin, he is met with forgiveness. Like David, sometimes we need a "prophet" to help us look deeply into our own hearts and see what needs healing and forgiving.

One way that we might more easily come to acknowledge our own debt is, as Nathan reminded David, to recall all the good God has done for us. David had been anointed king, rescued from Saul, given possessions and family, and even more. In forgetting all this good, he lusted after what he did not have and sinned grievously. If we keep our eyes turned toward all the good God has given us, we ourselves might more easily overcome whatever temptations to sin come our way.

Perhaps one way to live this gospel would be to sit down and make a list of all the good God has given us. This is something we probably have never done. We are good at enumerating our debts; perhaps the challenge of these readings is to enumerate all the good in our lives. And then take some time to utter a prayer of loving thanks to this God who is so merciful and gracious to us.

Focusing the Gospel

Key words and phrases: what sort of woman, she is a sinner, Two people were in debt, her many sins have been forgiven

To the point: Simon thought that Jesus was unaware of the "sort of woman" who was lovingly "touching him." In response to Simon's judgment about the woman, Jesus constructed his parable to open Simon's eyes to see both the great love within the heart of this sinful woman and the debt within his own heart. The woman, who knows only too well how great is her debt, throws herself on Jesus' mercy and receives forgiveness. We do not know Simon's response. But we do know what *we* need to do.

Connecting the Gospel

to the first reading: Nathan's work as a prophet was to help David see his sinfulness. Because David acknowledges his sin, he is met with forgiveness.

to human experience: Most of us are more like Simon than like the woman. It's far easier to see what is wrong in another than it is to see what is wrong in ourselves.

Understanding Scripture

Love and forgiveness: While both the first reading and the gospel celebrate the generosity of divine forgiveness (God forgives David, and Jesus forgives the woman), the two main characters (David and Simon the Pharisee) stand in sharp contrast to one another.

David had sinned grievously: he committed adultery with Bathsheba and then orchestrated the murder of her husband, Uriah. Simon the Pharisee, we may assume, was outwardly pious and law-observant: these are the hallmarks of the Pharisaic way of life. His sin or debt was little in comparison both to the woman and to David. Indeed, his wrongdoing is more a breach of etiquette and hospitality: not washing the guest's feet, kissing the guest in greeting, anointing the guest. But, as Jesus offers the example of the two debtors, it becomes clear that Simon's real fault was in loving little.

David, when confronted by the accusation of Nathan the prophet, immediately acknowledges his sin. There is no making excuses, no rationalization; he knows and confesses immediately the nature of his wrongdoing and the one who was wronged: "I have sinned against the Lord." As serious as his offenses were against both Bathsheba and Uriah, sin is always ultimately an act of rebellion against God. Simon does not respond to the judgment Jesus makes against him: "you did not . . ." (three times). Moreover, we are not told whether he apologized or corrected his sins of omission. But the judgment Jesus makes apparently stands: he is miserly in love. It is because of his small heart that he is unable to see the woman as Jesus sees her. Simon sees only "what sort of woman this is . . . a sinner." To him, she is a class of person and, based on her classification, she is someone with whom he would not associate. Thus Jesus rightly challenges him: Simon, "Do you see *this* woman?" Love would allow him to see this unique person, this individual with her own story, her own life and dignity. It is smallness of love which reduces people to caricatures. It is smallness of love which shuts out others and makes forgiveness impossible.

**ASSEMBLY &
FAITH-SHARING GROUPS**

- Like Simon, I am quick to note the sin (debt) of another when . . .
- Jesus' parable to Simon opens my eyes to . . .
- What I need to learn from the woman is . . .

PRESIDERS

When I am like Simon my priesthood looks like . . . ; when I am like the woman my priesthood looks like . . .

DEACONS

Both Nathan (to David) and Jesus (to Simon) spoke in a way to open another's heart to sin and God's forgiveness. Those who speak this way to me are . . .

HOSPITALITY MINISTERS

My care and concern encourages "great love" for those gathered so they can receive even greater "forgive[ness]" from God when . . .

MUSIC MINISTERS

One thing for which I need forgiveness is . . . I have already received God's overwhelming forgiveness in these ways . . .

ALTAR MINISTERS

I shall consider how the generosity of my service is related to the knowledge of my sin (debt) and God's gracious mercy . . .

LECTORS

My prayer with the word helps me recognize God's word in those who lovingly correct me because . . .

**EXTRAORDINARY MINISTERS
OF HOLY COMMUNION**

I shall consider how I might approach Christ in the Eucharist with the same heart as the woman in the gospel approached Jesus . . .

Model Act of Penitence

Presider: Each Sunday we gather together seeking God's great mercy and forgiveness. Let us open ourselves to God's gift . . . [pause]

Lord Jesus, you are filled with mercy: Lord . . .

Christ Jesus, you forgive the repentant sinner: Christ . . .

Lord Jesus, you bring salvation and peace: Lord . . .

Appreciating the Responsorial Psalm

In this responsorial psalm, the psalmist calls those who have experienced God's forgiveness "blessed" and relates a personal experience of having confessed sin and received divine mercy. The Lectionary omits the verses of Psalm 32 where the psalmist admits to having initially refused to name his guilt (vv. 3-4). For some time the psalmist resists self-examination and honest confession. When the psalmist finally relents and confesses, the forgiveness God grants is overwhelming. God replaces guilt (v. 5) with freedom (v. 7). The Lectionary did not need to include these verses because their story is dramatically told in both the first reading and the gospel. Moreover, how often is it told dramatically in our own lives! This Sunday's first reading, psalm, and gospel urge us to confess our sinfulness that we might receive the forgiveness of God. Like the psalmist, we will find that the latter far surpasses the former.

Model General Intercessions

Presider: Our God is merciful and forgiving; we make our needs known to such a good God.

Response:

Lord, hear our prayer.

Cantor:

we pray to the Lord,

That the Church may always be a sign and instrument of God's mercy . . . [pause]

That leaders of nations may always judge rightly . . . [pause]

That those wronged or misjudged by others may find peace . . . [pause]

That each of us reach out to others with loving mercy and forgiveness . . . [pause]

Presider: Gracious God, you forgive those who come to you for mercy: hear our prayers that one day we might enjoy everlasting life with you. We ask this through Christ our Lord. **Amen.**

OPENING PRAYER

Let us pray

Pause for silent prayer

Almighty God,
our hope and our strength,
without you we falter.
Help us to follow Christ
and to live according to your will.

We ask this through our Lord Jesus Christ,
    your Son,
who lives and reigns with you and the
    Holy Spirit,
one God, for ever and ever. **Amen.**

FIRST READING
2 Sam 12:7-10, 13

Nathan said to David:
"Thus says the LORD God of Israel:
    'I anointed you king of Israel.
I rescued you from the hand of Saul.
I gave you your lord's house and your
    lord's wives for your own.
I gave you the house of Israel and of
    Judah.
And if this were not enough, I could count
    up for you still more.
Why have you spurned the Lord and done
    evil in his sight?
You have cut down Uriah the Hittite with
    the sword;
    you took his wife as your own,
    and him you killed with the sword of
        the Ammonites.
Now, therefore, the sword shall never
    depart from your house,
    because you have despised me
    and have taken the wife of Uriah to be
        your wife.'"
Then David said to Nathan,
    "I have sinned against the LORD."
Nathan answered David:
    "The LORD on his part has forgiven your
        sin:
    you shall not die."

RESPONSORIAL PSALM
Ps 32:1-2, 5, 7, 11

R℣. (cf. 5c) Lord, forgive the wrong I have done.

Blessed is the one whose fault is taken
    away,
    whose sin is covered.
Blessed the man to whom the LORD
    imputes not guilt,
    in whose spirit there is no guile.

R℣. Lord, forgive the wrong I have done.

I acknowledged my sin to you,
    my guilt I covered not.
I said, "I confess my faults to the LORD,"
    and you took away the guilt of my sin.

R℣. Lord, forgive the wrong I have done.

You are my shelter; from distress you will
    preserve me;
    with glad cries of freedom you will ring
    me round.

R℣. Lord, forgive the wrong I have done.

Be glad in the LORD and rejoice, you just;
    exult, all you upright of heart.

R℣. Lord, forgive the wrong I have done.

SECOND READING
Gal 2:16, 19-21

Brothers and sisters:
  We who know that a person is not
    justified by works of the law
    but through faith in Jesus Christ,
    even we have believed in Christ Jesus
    that we may be justified by faith in
      Christ
    and not by works of the law,
    because by works of the law no one will
      be justified.
For through the law I died to the law,
    that I might live for God.
I have been crucified with Christ;
    yet I live, no longer I, but Christ lives
      in me;
    insofar as I now live in the flesh,
    I live by faith in the Son of God
    who has loved me and given himself up
      for me.
I do not nullify the grace of God;
    for if justification comes through the
      law,
    then Christ died for nothing.

About Liturgy

Sign of peace: In the early Church the "sign of peace" was, literally, a "kiss of peace." To kiss another in public was far more common than it is today, so this gesture would not have caused any consternation or question. Today we might still see family members kiss each other at the sign of peace (entirely appropriate!), but rarely anyone else. Whatever the gesture which is extended, it is good to remind ourselves that the gesture is a sign of peace when it is accompanied by genuine Christian love.

Father's Day: A model fifth general intercession for this Sunday might be "That all fathers may be models of self-giving love, generous forgiveness, and merciful compassion in their families . . ." (BofB no. 1730 allows for an extra intention to be added to the general intercessions on Father's Day and allows for adaptions; no. 1732 provides other models). Chapter 56 of the *Book of Blessings* provides a special Prayer over the People for the blessing at the end of Mass on this day.

About Liturgical Music

Cantor preparation: Spend some time this week reflecting on the overwhelming mercy of God who longs to forgive no matter what the sin. What moves you to ask for this forgiveness? What moves you to resist it?

A word to the music director: The return to Ordinary Time raises the temptation to "give the choir a rest." The problem is that they do, in fact, need a break (as do you!). But giving the choir the summer off compromises the importance of *every* Sunday as celebration of the fullness of resurrection. How can you maintain the celebratory character of Ordinary Time Sundays and allow the choir some respite from the intense demands of their ministry?

One way is to establish settings of service music for Ordinary Time which choir and assembly know so well that extra effort is not needed to sing them. Since Ordinary Time is lengthy, it is good to have two settings in place, one for the first two months or so, and the other for the period from early or mid-September to the end of the liturgical year. Another way is to have in place a repertoire of pieces which the choir can sing with just a quick review and with the reduced numbers vacation absences cause. Select and teach these pieces throughout the course of the year so that they can be readily prepared during the summer months. Having the choir sing every Sunday will communicate the importance of Ordinary Time, and stockpiling an easier repertoire will give the choir the "break" they need.

SPIRITUALITY

Gospel
Luke 1:57-66, 80; L587

When the time arrived
for Elizabeth to
have her child
she gave birth to a
son.
Her neighbors and rela-
tives heard
that the Lord had
shown his great
mercy toward her,
and they rejoiced with
her.
When they came on the
eighth day to cir-
cumcise the child,
they were going to call him Zechariah
after his father,
but his mother said in reply,
"No. He will be called John."
But they answered her,
"There is no one among your
relatives who has this name."
So they made signs, asking his father
what he wished him to be called.
He asked for a tablet and wrote, "John
is his name,"
and all were amazed.
Immediately his mouth was opened, his
tongue freed,
and he spoke blessing God.
Then fear came upon all their neighbors,
and all these matters were discussed
throughout the hill country of Judea.
All who heard these things took them
to heart, saying,
"What, then, will this child be?"
For surely the hand of the Lord was
with him.

The child grew and became strong in
spirit,
and he was in the desert until the day
of his manifestation to Israel.

Reflecting on the Gospel

Of all the stories and Scripture references about John the Baptist, probably the one most impressed on our minds is that of his beheading and the daughter of Herodias presenting the head of John the Baptist on a platter to Herod (see Mark 6:17-28; Matt 14:3-11). One would expect, since John was and is a much-revered martyr, that the color for this solemnity would be red. Instead it is white, marking not the martyrdom but the birth of John. (The liturgical calendar does remember the beheading of John the Baptist on August 29 as an obligatory memorial with the color red.) Thus our attention for this solemnity is turned away from John's martyrdom to his role in the history of salvation and relationship to Jesus as precursor. This is the direction the readings take us.

Many remarkable circumstances surrounded the conception and birth of John the Baptist! But the centerpiece of the gospel for this solemnity is the naming of John, the name given to Zechariah by Gabriel. "John" means "the Lord is gracious." The Lord is gracious, certainly, in granting Zechariah and Elizabeth a son; gracious, certainly, in sending John to herald the coming of Jesus (see second reading); but most gracious in sending the Son to bring "salvation . . . to the ends of the earth" (first reading). In celebrating the birth of John the Baptist we are, indeed, celebrating the manifold graciousness of God in granting us salvation.

Our celebration of this solemnity is about a marked man! John was chosen, conceived, born, named, missioned, preached, died—all pointing to Christ. "What, then, will this child be?" John was the precursor. He pointed the way to Jesus and to salvation. He may have been only the precursor, but now he shares in the glory of the One whose sandal he was too humble to stoop to unfasten.

God's manifold graciousness continues into our own graced lives. With us, however, God's interventions might not be so dramatic. But God still acts on behalf of each of us. If we are faithful as John, we too will share in God's abundant graciousness and blessing. We, too, will share in the glory of the One whom we serve.

Living the Paschal Mystery

John was the precursor who preceded Jesus; we are the disciples who follow Jesus. Our own bold announcing of the Messiah's presence and good news does not flow from miraculous conception and naming. This, however, hardly makes us any less precious in God's graciousness. We, too, are "precursors" of the Lord's coming. By our own faithfulness to who we are we witness to the presence of the risen Christ among us.

We must be as faithful to our identity and mission as was John. We often think of God's graciousness in terms of receiving graces, getting what we pray for, good things in life which come our way, etc. Each of these is a manifestation of God's ultimate graciousness in bringing us to salvation. Less often, probably, do we think of ourselves as manifestations of God's graciousness, but we are!

We do not need to look to big things to witness to Jesus' presence and God's graciousness; we must do the simple, everyday things well, in Jesus' name. Thus our smiling at someone who is obviously weary, taking a few extra minutes to put someone at ease, or eating a bit less and less well to give some money or food to a soup kitchen are all gracious behaviors which model to those around us the presence of Jesus. We truly are precursors, too!

Focusing the Gospel
Key words and phrases: gave birth to a son, "John is his name," blessing God

To the point: The centerpiece of this gospel is the naming of John. "John" means "the Lord is gracious." The Lord is gracious, certainly, in granting Zechariah and Elizabeth a son; gracious, certainly, in sending John to herald the coming of Jesus (see second reading); but most gracious in sending the Son to bring "salvation . . . to the ends of the earth" (first reading). In celebrating the birth of John the Baptist we are, indeed, celebrating the manifold graciousness of God.

Connecting the Gospel
to the second reading: Paul's summary of salvation history is yet another reflection on God's graciousness which comes to a climax in the saving work of Jesus.

to religious experience: We often think of God's graciousness in terms of receiving graces, getting what we pray for, good things in life which come our way, etc. Each of these is a manifestation of God's ultimate graciousness in bringing us to salvation.

Understanding Scripture
Naming: Naming is central to this Sunday's gospel and the first reading. So, to borrow a line, "What's in a name?"

In the Bible, naming is part of the creating process. In Genesis 1, as God creates each element, God gives it its name: "God called the light 'day,' and the darkness he called 'night'" (1:4; also 1:8, 10). In Genesis 3, "Adam" shares in the creating process by giving names "to all the cattle, all the birds . . . , and all the wild animals" (2:20). The notice, "whatever the man called each of them would be its name" (2:19), suggests that the name discloses the reality of things. Thus, changed realities require changed names (Isa 62:4), and new realities require new names (Isa 62:2).

Naming establishes a relationship and makes possible communication and communion. To know a name makes it possible to address and call upon another in a personal way. The Bible rightly notes the significance of that moment when humanity "began to invoke the LORD by name" (Gen 4:26). In two different traditions, biblical authors reveal the divine name, Yahweh, at the call of Moses (Exod 3 and 6). In revealing the divine name, God also reveals the divine intent to redeem the people and to establish a covenant with them. Name and mission are linked.

God calls people to mission by giving a new name, for example, Abraham (Gen 17:5) and Jacob (Gen 32:29; 35:10), or by calling them by name, for example, Samuel (1 Sam 3) and the people, Israel (Isa 43:1). In the first reading, the servant is given a name in the womb. But precisely because the name is not known, the identity of the servant also remains a mystery. His mission, however, is clear: to be a light for the nations and to reveal God's salvation. In the gospel, the name given at the annunciation of the Baptist's birth is confirmed by his father at the circumcision: "John," which means "the Lord is gracious." And, indeed, John's mission is to prepare for the coming of the Messiah, the ultimate expression of God's gracious plan for humanity.

ASSEMBLY & FAITH-SHARING GROUPS
- Where I witness the Lord's graciousness (which "John" means) is . . .
- Salvation is God's ultimate act of graciousness. The significance of this gift for me is . . .
- Like John, I herald Jesus' coming whenever I . . .

PRESIDERS
While I sometimes feel as if I were "toil[ing] in vain" (first reading), what helps me remain confident that God is with me is . . .

DEACONS
Like John, I prepare the way of the Lord for others whenever I . . .

HOSPITALITY MINISTERS
My hospitality manifests the graciousness of God whenever I . . .

MUSIC MINISTERS
My role as a music minister is like that of John the Baptist: I am to pave the way for the assembly to encounter Christ in the liturgy. I find myself rejoicing in this role when . . . I find myself struggling with this role when . . .

ALTAR MINISTERS
Serving others is like "a light to the nations" (first reading), drawing others to Christ, in that . . .

LECTORS
My daily living announces God's graciousness whenever I . . .

EXTRAORDINARY MINISTERS OF HOLY COMMUNION
I shall consider how receiving Eucharist makes me God's graciousness (like John) for others . . .

Model Act of Penitence

Presider: This solemnity celebrating the birth of John the Baptist is a festival of salvation. God is gracious to us. Let us reflect on our response to that graciousness . . . [pause]

> Lord Jesus, you were heralded by John the Baptist: Lord . . .
> Christ Jesus, you are a Light to the nations: Christ . . .
> Lord Jesus, you are the Savior of the world: Lord . . .

Appreciating the Responsorial Psalm

Psalm 139 is a moving statement of God's all-encompassing and intimate knowledge of us. God is familiar "with all [our] ways," both the directions we travel and the habits of our heart (vv. 1-3). God knows us because God formed us before our birth (vv. 13-14). God knows our very essence, our "soul" (vv. 14-15). This solemnity applies the words of Psalm 139 to John the Baptist. God "called [him] from birth" to be "a light to the nations" (first reading). At birth he was given a name which revealed he was no ordinary child, but a significant part of God's plan of salvation (gospel). Paul spells out John's role in redemption and indicates that John knew who he was and who he was not (second reading). As we sing Psalm 139 on this day we, too, acknowledge who John was created to be, and with John we offer God praise.

Model General Intercessions

Presider: God is gracious and gives us all the gifts we need to come to salvation. Let us offer our prayers to such a good God.

Response:

Lord, hear our prayer.

Cantor:

we pray to the Lord,

That the Church may always herald the Good News of salvation . . . [pause]

That the hand of the Lord be upon leaders of the world, strengthening them to bring peace and justice to all . . . [pause]

That God's graciousness deliver the poor and needy . . . [pause]

That all of us faithfully announce the goodness of the Lord to all those we meet . . . [pause]

Presider: Gracious God, you faithfully respond to the needs of your people: hear these our prayers that one day we might join John the Baptist in eternal glory and praise you forever and ever. **Amen.**

OPENING PRAYER

Let us pray

Pause for silent prayer

God our Father,
you raised up John the Baptist
to prepare a perfect people for Christ the
    Lord.
Give your Church joy in spirit
and guide those who believe in you
into the way of salvation and peace.

We ask this through our Lord Jesus Christ,
    your Son,
who lives and reigns with you and the
    Holy Spirit,
one God, for ever and ever. **Amen.**

FIRST READING
Isa 49:1-6

Hear me, O coastlands
    listen, O distant peoples.
The LORD called me from birth,
    from my mother's womb he gave me my
        name.
He made of me a sharp-edged sword
    and concealed me in the shadow of his
        arm.
He made me a polished arrow,
    in his quiver he hid me.
You are my servant, he said to me,
    Israel, through whom I show my glory.

Though I thought I had toiled in vain,
    and for nothing, uselessly, spent my
        strength,
yet my reward is with the LORD,
    my recompense is with my God.
For now the LORD has spoken
    who formed me as his servant from the
        womb,
that Jacob may be brought back to him
    and Israel gathered to him;
and I am made glorious in the sight of the
    LORD,
    and my God is now my strength!
It is too little, he says, for you to be my
    servant,
    to raise up the tribes of Jacob,
    and restore the survivors of Israel;
I will make you a light to the nations,
    that my salvation may reach to the ends
        of the earth.

RESPONSORIAL PSALM
Ps 139:1-3, 13-14, 14-15

R℣. (14a) I praise you for I am wonderfully made.

O LORD you have probed me and you know
    me;
    you know when I sit and when I stand;
    you understand my thoughts from afar.
My journeys and my rest you scrutinize,
    with all my ways you are familiar.

R℣. I praise you for I am wonderfully made.

Truly you have formed my inmost being;
    you knit me in my mother's womb.
I give you thanks that I am fearfully,
    wonderfully made;
    wonderful are your works.

R℣. I praise you for I am wonderfully made.

My soul also you knew full well;
    nor was my frame unknown to you
when I was made in secret,
    when I was fashioned in the depths of
        the earth.

R℣. I praise you for I am wonderfully made.

SECOND READING
Acts 13:22-26

In those days, Paul said:
    "God raised up David as their king;
    of him he testified,
    I have found David, son of Jesse, a man
        after my own heart;
    he will carry out my every wish.
From this man's descendants God,
    according to his promise,
    has brought to Israel a savior, Jesus.
John heralded his coming by proclaiming a
    baptism of repentance
    to all the people of Israel;
    and as John was completing his course,
        he would say,
    'What do you suppose that I am? I am
        not he.
Behold, one is coming after me;
    I am not worthy to unfasten the sandals
        of his feet.'

"My brothers, children of the family of
    Abraham,
    and those others among you who are
        God-fearing,
    to us this word of salvation has been
        sent."

About Liturgy

Conceptions and births on the General Roman Calendar: On the present liturgical calendar two festivals nine months apart celebrate the conception and birth of Jesus (March 25, Annunciation of the Lord; December 25, the Nativity of the Lord). This solemnity is a celebration of the nativity of John the Baptist, but the current General Roman Calendar has no conception festival in honor of John; however, from early times the Byzantine Church has retained September 24 as a festival honoring John's miraculous conception. At the "four corners" of the year (spring and fall equinoxes, winter and summer solstices) the Church celebrates respectively the conceptions and births of John the precursor and of Jesus the Messiah. It is as though the Church wishes to remember clearly that the entire year—Christians' entire lives—is framed by saving events and, indeed, the liturgical year is about unfolding those saving events.

Two festivals nine months apart also celebrate the conception (December 8) and nativity (September 8) of Mary. As we celebrate salvation each year, we cannot forget Mary who gave birth to the Messiah, nurtured him, and stood by him through his ministry, death, and resurrection.

About Liturgical Music

Cantor preparation: In this responsorial psalm you sing not only about John the Baptist but also about yourself. You are created by God and loved by God from before your birth. You might spend some time this week thanking God for having created and called you, and asking for the grace to be as faithful to who you are as John the Baptist was.

Music suggestions: Part of what the Church celebrates on this solemnity is the unfolding of God's plan of salvation. An excellent hymn to use would be "God Is Working His Purpose Out" [CH, RS, W3]. This text puts God's saving work in forward drive and shows it is inevitable and nearing completion: "Nearer and nearer draws the time, The time that shall surely be, When the earth shall be filled with the glory of God As the waters cover the sea." God's voice goes forth "by the mouth of many messengers," and we, too, are called to join the movement: "March we forth in the strength of God, with the banner of Christ unfurled. . . ." The hymn is an excellent example of unification between text and music—the tune PURPOSE marches forward melodically, harmonically, and rhythmically. If the hymn is too long for the entrance procession or presentation of the gifts, it could be used as a hymn of praise after Communion.

Another appropriate hymn of praise after Communion on this day would be the *Benedictus,* or the Canticle of Zechariah (sometimes titled "Blest Be the God of Israel"). This is the prayer spoken by Zechariah when his speech was restored at the birth of John (Luke 1:68-79).

SPIRITUALITY

Gospel
Matt 16:13-19; L591

When Jesus went into
    the region of Cae-
    sarea Philippi
he asked his disciples,
    "Who do people say
        that the Son of
        Man is?"
They replied, "Some say
    John the Baptist,
    others Elijah,
    still others Jeremiah
        or one of the
        prophets."
He said to them, "But
    who do you say that I am?"
Simon Peter said in reply,
    "You are the Christ, the Son of the
        living God."
Jesus said to him in reply, "Blessed are
    you, Simon son of Jonah.
For flesh and blood has not revealed
    this to you, but my heavenly
    Father.
And so I say to you, you are Peter,
    and upon this rock I will build my
        Church,
    and the gates of the netherworld
        shall not prevail against it.
I will give you the keys to the Kingdom
    of heaven.
Whatever you bind on earth shall be
    bound in heaven;
    and whatever you loose on earth shall
        be loosed in heaven."

See Appendix A, p. 299, for the other readings.

FIRST READING
Acts 12:1-11

RESPONSORIAL PSALM
Ps 34:2-3, 4-5, 6-7, 8-9

SECOND READING
2 Tim 4:6-8, 17-18

Reflecting on the Gospel
This solemnity of Peter (Apostle to the Jews) and Paul (Apostle to the Gentiles) celebrates both the historical figures and their symbolic roles as representatives of the Church. If we would perceive this solemnity as about individuals, we might think that Paul comes up short, since two readings (the first reading and the gospel) focus on Peter and only the second reading tells of Paul. However, this festival is really one celebrating the Church rather than two individuals as such. These two great apostles represent for us a Church in communion with Christ continuing his saving work.

In response to Jesus' question about who he is (the gospel), Peter names him as "the Christ, the Son of the living God." In turn, Jesus names Peter as the "rock" upon which the Church will be built. Like Peter, we must come to know who Jesus is and who we are in relation to him if, like Paul, we are to finish the race, keep the faith, and receive the crown of life (see second reading). Thus, we can only carry forth Jesus' saving mission if we know who Jesus is. Also, only by knowing who Jesus is can we come to salvation. Peter and Paul both model for us followers of Jesus who knew intimately their Lord and Master.

Neither Peter nor Paul lived for themselves once they encountered Jesus and knew who he was: the Savior of the world. The grace to identify Christ always circles back and creates our own identity in relation to Christ. Now we spend our lives learning about who Christ is and how to find Christ in all the circumstances of our lives. We come to know Christ and realize that we are his presence in our world. This is what it means to be Church! Church is neither building nor empty space; Church is Christ's body carrying on his saving work.

Living the Paschal Mystery
Paul's words in the second reading spell out concretely how our Christian identity plunges us into living the paschal mystery. It means dying: "poured out like a libation," "compet[ing] well," "finish[ing] the race," "[keeping] the faith," completing the proclamation, finding ourselves in "the lion's mouth," having "evil threat[s]." It also means rising: "crown of righteousness await[ing]," "award . . . me . . . his appearance," "gave me strength," "rescued," "bring me safe to his heavenly kingdom." The challenge of this solemnity is to take this dying and rising message of Paul (and Peter) and translate it into our everyday lives.

Our dying may be staying up all night with a sick child, being willing to go the extra step for someone, being satisfied with less, having God as a priority in our lives, or not putting material gains ahead of spiritual gains. Our rising may be in recognizing the risen Jesus in the grateful smile of another, the satisfaction of a job well done even if no one else recognizes it, the inner peace that comes from knowing our life is on course. Peter and Paul were called upon to be leaders in the early Church and they responded with heroic actions. Our heroic actions are the simple, everyday things we do to make Christ no less present in our own day.

Living the dying and rising of Jesus won't keep us from facing difficulties and hardships, pain and disappointment. This kind of living does enable us to see through life's ups and downs to a share in the glory of God. This is who we are. This is who Church is.

Focusing the Gospel

Key words and phrases: You are the Christ, you are Peter, rock

To the point: In response to Jesus' question about who he is, Peter names him as "the Christ, the Son of the living God." In turn, Jesus names Peter as the "rock" upon which the Church will be built. Like Peter, we must come to know who Jesus is and who we are in relation to him if, like Paul, we are to finish the race, keep the faith, and receive the crown of life (see second reading).

Model Act of Penitence

Presider: Today we honor Ss. Peter and Paul who were chosen by Christ to be leaders of the Church and who remained faithful to their Savior even unto death. Let us reflect on our own calling and our dedication to Christ . . . [pause]

> Lord Jesus, you are the Christ, the Son of the living God: Lord . . .
>
> Christ Jesus, you stand by us and give us strength: Christ . . .
>
> Lord Jesus, you are revealed to us by the Father: Lord . . .

Model General Intercessions

Presider: Through the saving work of Jesus God established the Church. Let us make our needs known so the Church can grow in strength and grace.

Response:

Lord, hear our prayer.

Cantor:

we pray to the Lord,

That each member of the Church may always proclaim faithfully that Christ is the Son of the living God . . . [pause]

That leaders of nations may govern with righteousness and peace . . . [pause]

That those imprisoned unjustly may be released and give glory to God . . . [pause]

That each of us may finish the race, keep the faith, and gain the crown of righteousness . . . [pause]

Presider: O God, you love and protect your Church: hear these our prayers that we may one day join with Peter and Paul in proclaiming forever your praises. We ask this through Jesus Christ our Lord. **Amen.**

FOR REFLECTION

- My response to Jesus' question "Who do you say that I am?" would be . . . ; I *live* that answer by . . .

- Like Peter, my naming who Jesus is has redefined who I am in that . . .

- Where I need to improve in order to say like Paul, "I have competed well" (second reading), is . . .

SPIRITUALITY

Gospel

Luke 9:51-62; L99C

When the days for Jesus' being taken
up were fulfilled,
  he resolutely determined to
    journey to Jerusalem,
  and he sent messengers ahead
    of him.
On the way they entered a
    Samaritan village
  to prepare for his reception
    there,
  but they would not welcome him
because the destination of his
    journey was Jerusalem.
When the disciples James and
    John saw this they asked,
  "Lord, do you want us to call
    down fire from heaven
  to consume them?"
Jesus turned and rebuked them,
  and they journeyed to another
    village.

As they were proceeding on their
    journey someone said to him,
  "I will follow you wherever you go."
Jesus answered him,
  "Foxes have dens and birds of the
    sky have nests,
  but the Son of Man has nowhere to
    rest his head."

And to another he said, "Follow me."
But he replied, "Lord, let me go first
    and bury my father."
But he answered him, "Let the dead
    bury their dead.
But you, go and proclaim the kingdom
    of God."
And another said, "I will follow you,
    Lord,
  but first let me say farewell to my
    family at home."
To him Jesus said, "No one who sets a
    hand to the plow
  and looks to what was left behind is
    fit for the kingdom of God."

Reflecting on the Gospel

This Lectionary gospel begins with "When the days for Jesus' being taken up were fulfilled . . ." This indicates to us a radical shift in Luke's Gospel account: the Galilean portion of Jesus' ministry is completed; now, Jesus is off to Jerusalem. The rest of Luke's Gospel unfolds as Jesus' journey to Jerusalem, symbolic of his accepting his destiny to be nailed to a cross and coming closer to fulfilling it. Moreover, this gospel reminds us that Jesus' journey to Jerusalem is not only *his* journey—faithful followers also journey to dying and rising.

The word "journey" appears four times in this Sunday's gospel, and the word "follow," three times. It's pretty hard not to get the message that we are going somewhere, following someone! To those who enthusiastically volunteer to follow him, Jesus issues a word of caution: there will be no comfort or security nor can there be any halfhearted following. Indeed, the following of Jesus must take precedence even over family obligations. Jesus is demanding because the road is demanding: this journey will lead to his death in Jerusalem. Such a journey requires a full and undivided commitment.

The three would-be followers mentioned in the gospel are in contrast with Elisha in the first reading. True, Elisha does not follow the prophet Elijah's call immediately, either. But what does he do? He takes his twelve yoke of oxen—he is apparently a man of means—and destroys them, burns the plows to cook the oxen, and feeds his dependents. Elisha destroys everything—there is nothing to look back for—and he left all to follow Elijah! There is an immediacy in responding to Jesus' call to follow him and a price to pay for those who do follow. As with Elisha in the first reading and those in the gospel, Jesus' call requires a lifelong response and commitment—no wonder they are concerned about putting their affairs in order! Jesus asks no less of us.

Such single-minded following of Jesus would seem like an ideal; yet that is exactly what Jesus asks. We must put Jesus and his mission ahead of everything—even more than the Law, even to the point of putting into a different perspective our relationship to family. We must put our hand to the plow and not look back. Is this possible? Not alone. But if we remember that we follow Jesus to Jerusalem, that he is ahead of us leading the way, then it is possible—not easy, but possible. We only need say, "I will follow you wherever you go."

Living the Paschal Mystery

Jesus' invitation to "Follow me" is not addressed only to those with a vocation to priesthood and religious life. It is addressed to everyone. Our baptism begins our paschal journey with Jesus and initiates our response to follow Jesus "to Jerusalem." We spend our whole lives working out what began at baptism: following Jesus through death into life.

Jesus invites us to follow him in the ordinary circumstances of our lives. This is where the going gets tough: not in the extraordinary, but in the ordinary things do we witness to our faithful following. Sometimes when we read the Scriptures we might be discouraged by the leadership of the prophets or early disciples. We always need extraordinary leaders to help us know where we are going in following Jesus. But the Church is mostly made up of ordinary people whose very faithfulness to the gospel is an extraordinary way to follow Jesus.

Focusing the Gospel

Key words and phrases: journey to Jerusalem, I will follow you, nowhere to rest, No one who . . . looks . . . behind is fit

To the point: To those who enthusiastically volunteer to follow him, Jesus issues a word of caution: there will be no comfort or security, there can be no halfhearted following. Indeed, the following of Jesus must take precedence even over family obligations. Jesus is demanding because the road is demanding: this journey will lead to his death in Jerusalem. Such a journey requires a full and undivided commitment.

Connecting the Gospel

to the first reading: Jesus' call of disciples is even more demanding than the call of an Old Testament prophet. Elisha could put his affairs in order before following Elijah; Jesus would not allow any time for turning back.

to Catholic culture: Jesus' invitation to "Follow me" is not addressed only to those with a vocation to priesthood and religious life. It is addressed to everyone; our baptism is our response to follow Jesus "to Jerusalem."

Understanding Scripture

Following Jesus: In both the first reading and the gospel, family obligations are offered as excuses for not taking up the call to discipleship. Elisha and the third of the three men in the gospel ask for a delay in following until they have the opportunity to say goodbye. Even in the very act of being called, their attention is not on the One calling and they are distracted by other things. The example Jesus uses—the plower who keeps looking back—is an apt description of such distraction. A plower must keep his attention on the oxen, using his goad to keep them in line. Turning aside, or back, or losing attention will result in the oxen going astray and plowing crooked furrows. If there is lack of attention and focus at the moment of the call, what can be expected later?

The second man in the gospel wants to wait until his parents die and he buries them, then he will follow Jesus. Burying one's kin was a pious religious, social, and familial duty. The story of Abraham includes a lengthy description of the trouble he went to in burying his wife, Sarah (Gen 23:1-15). The dying Jacob commands his sons to bury him with his ancestors in the land (Gen 49:29). The importance of this obligation is poignantly and dramatically told in the story of Tobit who lost his property and position, and was sentenced to death, for burying his fellow countrymen against the orders of the king (Tob 1:19-20). Despite his suffering, Tobit instructs Tobiah: "My son, when I die, give me a decent burial. Honor your mother . . . Remember, my son, that she went through many trials for your sake while you were in her womb. And when she dies, bury her in the same grave with me" (4:3-4; cf. also 14:10). Burying the dead is an expression of devotion and piety.

Jesus' call to discipleship takes precedence over all other commitments—not just frivolous or unworthy commitments, but even over family responsibilities and obligations. Family is not an absolute value; following Jesus is.

ASSEMBLY & FAITH-SHARING GROUPS

- Jesus invites me to follow him; my usual excuses to delay are about . . .
- What I need to amend in order to follow Jesus more "resolutely" is . . .
- In following Jesus, my "Jerusalem" looks like . . .

PRESIDERS

Ways I support others to follow Jesus "resolutely" and without excuse are . . .

DEACONS

I balance the calls of marriage, family, and ministry on my way to Jerusalem by . . .

HOSPITALITY MINISTERS

My hospitality fortifies others on their paschal journey to Jerusalem whenever I . . .

MUSIC MINISTERS

Jesus cautions persons in the gospel not to say "yes" to discipleship before they have counted its cost. The demands of music ministry which I find unexpected are . . . I feel overwhelmed by these demands when . . . What helps me stay faithful whenever I am feeling this way is . . .

ALTAR MINISTERS

In order to become more single-minded in my service of others for Christ, I need to . . .

LECTORS

I shall honestly name and pray about my own excuses to avoid God's radical call so that I may proclaim the word without timidity . . .

EXTRAORDINARY MINISTERS OF HOLY COMMUNION

How I might become more like God's Food for those on the journey to Jerusalem is by . . .

Model Act of Penitence

Presider: Jesus calls us in our ordinary circumstances of life. Let us reflect on how faithful we have been in following him . . . [pause]

    Lord Jesus, your journey took you to Jerusalem and the cross: Lord . . .

    Christ Jesus, you call us to follow you on your journey: Christ . . .

    Lord Jesus, you show us the path to life: Lord . . .

Appreciating the Responsorial Psalm

Both the first reading and the gospel this Sunday remind us that discipleship demands giving up everything. The first reading sets an example of instant and complete response. The gospel advises caution about the radical cost. The responsorial psalm invites us to look beyond the price of discipleship to the relationship with God which is its reward. The inheritance of those who give up all for God is the gift of the very presence of God. The inheritance of those who choose discipleship is fullness of life, and the guidance of God along its path. While the readings ask us if we are aware of the costs of discipleship, the psalm asks if we are cognizant of the rewards. Full of divine promise and presence, the psalm gives us the courage to answer the call. May we sing it with confidence and joy.

Model General Intercessions

Presider: God faithfully strengthens those who follow Jesus, the divine Son. Let us confidently lift our prayers to God.

Response:

Lord, hear our prayer.

Cantor:

we pray to the Lord,

That all members of the Church may continually respond to Jesus' invitation to follow him . . . [pause]

That all peoples find the path to life and fullness of joy in God's presence . . . [pause]

That those who struggle to follow Jesus' call may find courage and be strengthened . . . [pause]

That all of us here follow Jesus with undivided hearts . . . [pause]

Presider: O God, you call us to follow your Son without counting the cost: hear these our prayers that we might journey with your Son through death to eternal life with you in your kingdom. We ask this through Christ our Lord. **Amen.**

ALTERNATIVE OPENING PRAYER

Let us pray

Pause for silent prayer

Father in heaven,
the light of Jesus
has scattered the darkness of hatred and
    sin.
Called to that light
we ask for your guidance.
Form our lives in your truth, our hearts in
    your love.

We ask this through Christ our Lord.
    Amen.

FIRST READING
1 Kgs 19:16b, 19-21

The LORD said to Elijah:
    "You shall anoint Elisha, son of Shaphat
        of Abel-meholah,
    as prophet to succeed you."

Elijah set out and came upon Elisha, son
    of Shaphat,
    as he was plowing with twelve yoke of
        oxen;
    he was following the twelfth.
Elijah went over to him and threw his
    cloak over him.
Elisha left the oxen, ran after Elijah,
    and said,
    "Please, let me kiss my father and
        mother goodbye,
    and I will follow you."
Elijah answered, "Go back!
Have I done anything to you?"
Elisha left him and, taking the yoke of
    oxen, slaughtered them;
    he used the plowing equipment for fuel
        to boil their flesh,
    and gave it to his people to eat.
Then Elisha left and followed Elijah as his
    attendant.

RESPONSORIAL PSALM

Ps 16:1-2, 5, 7-8, 9-10, 11

R̀. (cf. 5a) You are my inheritance, O Lord.

Keep me, O God, for in you I take refuge;
   I say to the LORD, "My Lord are you.
O LORD, my allotted portion and my cup,
   you it is who hold fast my lot."

R̀. You are my inheritance, O Lord.

I bless the LORD who counsels me;
   even in the night my heart exhorts me.
I set the LORD ever before me;
   with him at my right hand I shall not be
     disturbed.

R̀. You are my inheritance, O Lord.

Therefore my heart is glad and my soul
   rejoices,
   my body, too, abides in confidence
because you will not abandon my soul to
   the netherworld,
   nor will you suffer your faithful one to
     undergo corruption.

R̀. You are my inheritance, O Lord.

You will show me the path to life,
   fullness of joys in your presence,
   the delights at your right hand forever.

SECOND READING

Gal 5:1, 13-18

Brothers and sisters:
For freedom Christ set us free;
   so stand firm and do not submit again
     to the yoke of slavery.

For you were called for freedom, brothers
   and sisters.
But do not use this freedom
   as an opportunity for the flesh;
   rather, serve one another through love.
For the whole law is fulfilled in one
   statement,
   namely, *You shall love your neighbor as
     yourself.*
But if you go on biting and devouring one
   another,
   beware that you are not consumed by
     one another.

I say, then: live by the Spirit
   and you will certainly not gratify the
     desire of the flesh.
For the flesh has desires against the Spirit,
   and the Spirit against the flesh;
   these are opposed to each other,
   so that you may not do what you want.
But if you are guided by the Spirit, you are
   not under the law.

About Liturgy

Ordinary Time journey: Although we have been in Ordinary Time since Pentecost, we've really only celebrated it one Sunday. Where the Lectionary picks up this Sunday (after replacing last Sunday with the Solemnity of the Nativity of John the Baptist) is fortuitous, for it readily captures the intent of Ordinary Time: to walk with Jesus on his paschal journey. It would be good in the liturgy preparations for this Sunday to consider how we might bridge the transition from festal time to Ordinary Time.

The color for Ordinary Time is green, the same as that of nature during a period of life and growth. As we journey deeper into the paschal mystery during these months, it is good for us to keep the life-giving aspect of this time of the year in mind. What Ordinary Time is about is our walking with Jesus to Jerusalem and salvation. It is with the dying and rising mystery that we receive the life of God within us and renew it each time we celebrate liturgy.

July 4: July 4 occurs this week, and it would be pastorally good to celebrate liturgy on that day (there is a votive Mass for celebrating Independence Day in the U.S.: Sacramentary, Appendix X.6). But it would do an injustice to the incredible paschal message of this Sunday if the homily and music were to anticipate July 4.

About Liturgical Music

Cantor preparation: This Sunday's psalm tells of all that you have been given because you have chosen discipleship: counsel, joy, life, refuge. Above all you have been given God's very self as your "portion" and "lot." Your singing this psalm testifies that you know the reward of discipleship is far greater than its cost. How have you come to know this? Who has taught you this? To whom are you teaching it?

Music suggestions: In the song "Come and Journey with a Savior" [CBW3, GC2] we call one another to follow Jesus wherever he leads and whatever the cost, knowing he will always be present with us, leading the way. The song would be an appropriate entrance hymn for this Sunday. Tracing salvation history from Abraham and Sarah, to Joseph and Mary, to Matthew and Martha, John Bell's "God It Was" [G2, GC, RS] describes the practical consequences of God's call with tangible and picturesque imagery. Sung during the presentation of the gifts, the song would be an effective reflection on the gospel. More meditative in tone, "Jesus, Lead the Way" [GC, GC2, RS, W3] asks Jesus to be our light in darkness, our strength in grief, our source of "redeeming graces," even when leading us "through rough places." This, also, would be an effective reflection on the gospel during the presentation of the gifts. Finally, the gospel hymn "A Follower of Christ" [LMGM] would make an excellent recessional song with its repetitions of "What do I have to do? What do I have to say? How do I have to walk each and ev'ry day? Tell me what does it cost if I carry the cross? Just let me be a follower of Christ."

SPIRITUALITY

Gospel Luke 10:1-12, 17-20; L102C

At that time the Lord appointed
    seventy-two others
  whom he sent ahead of him in pairs
  to every town and place he
    intended to visit.
He said to them,
  "The harvest is abundant but
    the laborers are few;
  so ask the master of the
    harvest
  to send out laborers for his
    harvest.
Go on your way;
  behold, I am sending you like
    lambs among wolves.
Carry no money bag, no sack,
  no sandals;
  and greet no one along the
    way.
Into whatever house you enter, first say,
  'Peace to this household.'
If a peaceful person lives there,
  your peace will rest on him;
  but if not, it will return to you.
Stay in the same house and eat and
    drink what is offered to you,
  for the laborer deserves his payment.
Do not move about from one house to
    another.
Whatever town you enter and they
    welcome you,
  eat what is set before you,
  cure the sick in it and say to them,
  'The kingdom of God is at hand for
    you.'
Whatever town you enter and they do
    not receive you,
  go out into the streets and say,
  'The dust of your town that clings to
    our feet,
  even that we shake off against you.'
Yet know this: the kingdom of God is
    at hand.
I tell you,
  it will be more tolerable for Sodom on
    that day than for that town."

Continued in Appendix A, p. 299.

Reflecting on the Gospel

Many hands make light work, one saying goes. If, as another saying goes, two hands are better than one, then surely seventy-two are better than one! Jesus sends his seventy-two disciples out to the towns as if sending laborers to an abundant harvest. Jesus' ministry is now being extended through the disciples whom he sends forth to do his work and thus announce that "the kingdom of God is at hand."

The tremendous work of the too few laborers was to announce the kingdom of God by extending peace, curing the sick, subjecting demons. When the disciples return reporting the successes of their labors, Jesus reveals that the real abundance of the harvest is in having their "names . . . written in heaven." Jesus redirects the focus of the disciples from power over evil to the glory of dwelling in the kingdom. What a surprise for them and for us!

Isaiah's vision in the first reading uses different images to describe the same reality presented in the gospel. The effects of the kingdom (peace, healing, and subjecting demons) described in the gospel are described in Isaiah as comfort, abundance, and prosperity. Both readings envision a future of joy and rejoicing. In Isaiah, however, the future is not yet a reality for Israel; but it is a reality for the disciples. Isaiah's wonderful future is being fulfilled in Christ. Then Jesus takes this even one step further. The disciples rejoice in the extraordinary feats they are able to accomplish. They come back filled with joy and enthusiasm. Yet Jesus admonishes them not to keep their sights on these things they've accomplished, but on a future glory which still awaits them. The harvest is not what they did in accomplishing healing and casting out demons. The harvest Jesus sends his disciples out to bring in is the larger, even more abundant harvest of heaven.

We disciples can never lose sight that we always minister with two hands: one hand is our selves, the other is God! Our ministry is about making present God's reign, and the success is due to God's giving us the power to do a wondrous thing: have our "names . . . written in heaven." What a surprise!

Living the Paschal Mystery

The disciple's journey to Jerusalem includes both dying and rising. When we describe paschal mystery journey and Gospel living as dying and rising, we are using a metaphor which has any number of interpretations and applications. In this Sunday's context of discipleship, we are saying that ministry brings us to a kind of dying (the pain of the disciple when others don't accept the Gospel) as well as rising (the rejoicing that is ours because we are doing the work of God). The end of the journey in Jerusalem brings both dying and rising, too: cross and resurrection. If the journey is undertaken alone, we will fail. We are successful, however, when the journey is faithful to Jesus' ministry and we are open to the power given us.

Any faithful discipleship and Gospel living calls for an openness to God's presence to us. Part of our very ministry, then, and of living the dying and rising mystery is to spend time every day in prayer being attentive to God's presence, the gifts God gives us to be successful, and the power of the Spirit which washes over us. This kind of prayer helps us remember that the ministry is not ours, but Christ's.

Focusing the Gospel
Key words and phrases: he sent, harvest is abundant, laborers are few, kingdom of God is at hand, returned rejoicing, rejoice because your names are written in heaven

To the point: Jesus sends his disciples out to the towns as if sending laborers to an abundant harvest. The tremendous work of the too few laborers was to announce the kingdom of God—extending peace, curing the sick, subjecting demons. When the disciples return reporting the successes of their labors, Jesus reveals that the real abundance of the harvest is in having their "names . . . written in heaven." What a surprise for them and for us!

Connecting the Gospel
to the first reading: Isaiah's vision uses different images to describe the same reality presented in the gospel. The effects of the kingdom (peace, healing, and subjecting demons) are here described as comfort, abundance, and prosperity. Both readings envision a future of joy and rejoicing.

to our culture: Many people live in fear of a future which is bent on destruction and chaos; they have abandoned hope. These readings invite us to envision the future God has in store for us, one of blessing and joy.

Understanding Scripture
Jerusalem and the kingdom: The first reading's poetic description of Jerusalem captures many aspects of the kingdom of God which Jesus sends his disciples to announce. In many ways, the Book of Isaiah is the story of Jerusalem/Zion. On the one hand, Jerusalem is a place of unspeakable sin and injustice (for example, 1:21-26; 3:8-12; 5:7); on the other hand, she is the center of the Lord's glorious sovereignty and divine rule (for example, 2:1-4; 24:23; 27:13; 52:1-2; 60:14). Despite Jerusalem's failure to live up to the grace of divine election, she is nevertheless the place the Lord has chosen for the divine dwelling. Jerusalem's final status as the worldwide capital of divine sovereignty is testimony to the Lord's fidelity and power to transform.

This Sunday's passage is from the last chapter of Isaiah, and in it many themes from earlier in the book are reprised and reworked. Earlier, the "overflowing torrent" referred to the relentless army of Assyria which God summons to punish Israel (8:7-8; 28:2, 15, 18); it also describes the extent of the punishment God unleashes against arrogant Assyria (30:28). Now, however, the "overflowing torrent" refers to the prosperity and wealth which will inundate the restored and redeemed Jerusalem. Earlier, "grass" was an image of what is impermanent and worthless (5:24; 15:6; 30:33; 40:8), but for God's people resettled in Jerusalem, the flourishing of the grass is an image of growth, health, and vitality. These transformations are testimony, not only to the prophet's creative use of themes and images, but to the power of God to recreate, renew, and restore.

As the place where God's exiled and dispirited people find home and comfort, Jerusalem is presented as a mother nursing her children and fondling them in her lap. The Lord, who had earlier been described as the husband of Zion (54:5), is now described as a nursing mother. It is a maternal God who comforts, protects, and nourishes with tenderness, compassion, and solicitude. Jerusalem, the divine capital, is a city which welcomes her returning children. The abundance, comfort, joy, and life of Jerusalem are gifts realized in the kingdom of God.

ASSEMBLY & FAITH-SHARING GROUPS
- Where I realize the abundant harvest of God's kingdom is . . .
- The labor I am contributing to extending God's kingdom is . . .
- Hoping that my name is "written in heaven" affects my daily living in that . . .

PRESIDERS
When I am motivated by rejoicing that my name is "written in heaven," my ministry looks like . . .

DEACONS
God's motherly comfort shapes my service (see first reading) in that . . .

HOSPITALITY MINISTERS
My greeting and assistance is a prayer of peace for those gathering whenever I . . .

MUSIC MINISTERS
In the gospel Jesus sent the disciples out two by two; they were to work in teams. I find the teamwork of music ministry a joy when . . . I find it a challenge when . . .

ALTAR MINISTERS
The payment which inspires me to labor for God's harvest is . . .

LECTORS
My prayerful time with the word challenges me to labor in God's harvest in that . . .

EXTRAORDINARY MINISTERS OF HOLY COMMUNION
The Eucharist is God's prosperity for me (see first reading) in that . . . ; the Eucharist makes me into God's prosperity for others in that . . .

CELEBRATION

Model Act of Penitence

Presider: God sends disciples to bring in the harvest. Let us reflect on how well we have been God's laborers and ask that we may rejoice now in the gifts God gives us in this Eucharist . . . [pause]

Lord Jesus, you announce that the kingdom of God is at hand: Lord . . .

Christ Jesus, you send laborers to reap the harvest of God's kingdom: Christ . . .

Lord Jesus, you bring faithful disciples into the joy of your kingdom: Lord . . .

Appreciating the Responsorial Psalm

The first reading for this Sunday speaks of a future time when God will feed and comfort the people as a mother nurses her child. Then will all mourning become rejoicing. Then will all know that the "hand of the Lord" has been with us. This reading lays out in tender terms the future which God has planned for us. And the gospel shows us Jesus working to bring that future about by sending his disciples out to spread peace, heal illness, announce the kingdom, and prepare people for his coming.

Because of the ongoing activity of Jesus through his disciples, God's plan for the future is coming to fruition. This is why we call all the earth to "Come and see, . . . Come and hear" when we sing the responsorial psalm. Come and rejoice, we cry, for what God has promised, God is doing.

Model General Intercessions

Presider: The God who sends laborers to gather the harvest is with us to help us. So we are encouraged to make our needs known.

Response:
Lord, hear our prayer.

Cantor:
we pray to the Lord,

That the Church may be blessed with an abundance of priests, deacons, religious, and lay ministers . . . [pause]

That all peoples of the world share in the abundance of God's gifts . . . [pause]

That the sick be healed, the sorrowful be comforted, and the distressed find peace . . . [pause]

That all here take up the call to labor on behalf of God's kingdom . . . [pause]

Presider: Bountiful God, you send us as laborers to gather your harvest: be with us, help us to rejoice, and make our labors fruitful. We ask this through Christ our Lord. **Amen.**

ALTERNATIVE OPENING PRAYER

Let us pray

Pause for silent prayer

Father,
in the rising of your Son
death gives birth to new life.
The sufferings he endured restored hope to
    a fallen world.
Let sin never ensnare us
with empty promises of passing joy.
Make us one with you always,
so that our joy may be holy,
and our love may give life.

We ask this through Christ our Lord.
    Amen.

FIRST READING

Isa 66:10-14c

Thus says the LORD:
Rejoice with Jerusalem and be glad
    because of her,
    all you who love her;
exult, exult with her,
    all you who were mourning over her!
Oh, that you may suck fully
    of the milk of her comfort,
that you may nurse with delight
    at her abundant breasts!
    For thus says the LORD:
Lo, I will spread prosperity over Jerusalem
    like a river,
    and the wealth of the nations like an
        overflowing torrent.
As nurslings, you shall be carried in her
    arms,
    and fondled in her lap;
as a mother comforts her child,
    so will I comfort you;
    in Jerusalem you shall find your
        comfort.

When you see this, your heart shall rejoice
    and your bodies flourish like the grass;
the LORD's power shall be known to his
    servants.

RESPONSORIAL PSALM

Ps 66:1-3, 4-5, 6-7, 16, 20

℟. (1) Let all the earth cry out to God with joy.

Shout joyfully to God, all the earth,
   sing praise to the glory of his name;
   proclaim his glorious praise.
Say to God, "How tremendous are your
      deeds!"

℟. Let all the earth cry out to God with joy.

"Let all on earth worship and sing praise
      to you,
   sing praise to your name!"
Come and see the works of God,
   his tremendous deeds among the
         children of Adam.

℟. Let all the earth cry out to God with joy.

He has changed the sea into dry land;
   through the river they passed on foot.
Therefore let us rejoice in him.
   He rules by his might forever.

℟. Let all the earth cry out to God with joy.

Hear now, all you who fear God,
   while I declare what he has done for me.
Blessed be God who refused me not
   my prayer or his kindness!

℟. Let all the earth cry out to God with joy.

SECOND READING

Gal 6:14-18

Brothers and sisters:
May I never boast except in the cross of
      our Lord Jesus Christ,
   through which the world has been
         crucified to me,
   and I to the world.
For neither does circumcision mean
      anything, nor does uncircumcision,
   but only a new creation.
Peace and mercy be to all who follow this
      rule
   and to the Israel of God.

From now on, let no one make troubles
      for me;
   for I bear the marks of Jesus on my
         body.

The grace of our Lord Jesus Christ be
      with your spirit,
   brothers and sisters. Amen.

About Liturgy

Liturgy of the Word and paschal mystery: Both Isaiah (for example, see Isa 63:1-6) and Luke (for example, the woes recorded in the skipped verses from this Sunday's gospel, vv. 13-16) speak harshly of those who do not hear and accept God's word. The Lectionary selections for this Sunday are for the most part only encouraging words (especially the selection from Isaiah). Although the Liturgy of the Word is always a challenging time, we must be careful not to lose sight of the consolation and encouragement that God's word also brings. This is another play of the dying/rising rhythm of the paschal mystery.

A good pastoral practice is to accustom ourselves to hearing both the challenge to die to self as well as the consolation in the Liturgy of the Word. Both may not be present each Sunday, so this is a good way to begin to connect the Sundays so that we recognize the rhythm of dying and rising, challenge and consolation. Connecting the Sundays is also a good way for us to enter more surely into the rhythm of the paschal mystery which is unfolded each liturgical year.

About Liturgical Music

Cantor preparation: In the gospel Jesus sends the disciples on mission to announce his coming. Your singing of the responsorial psalm is part of this mission. In singing it you tell the world of God's saving action. As part of your preparation, spend some time identifying what you have to sing about. What has God done on your behalf?

Singing the acclamations, part 1: We are very familiar with the four principal acclamations used in the Mass: the gospel acclamation; the *Holy, Holy, Holy;* the memorial acclamation; and the great amen. But GIRM identifies several additional acclamations: the "Amen" to the presidential prayers (nos. 54, 89, 146); the response of "Thanks be to God" to the first and second readings (nos. 128, 130); the responses both before and after the gospel (nos. 60, 134); and the doxology which concludes the Our Father (no. 153).

GIRM provides rich insight into what we are doing when we pronounce these acclamations. By saying "Amen" we take ownership of the prayers and give our personal assent to them (nos. 54, 89). Through the acclamations surrounding the gospel, we acknowledge our belief that Christ is truly present in the proclamation (no. 60). Through the acclamations which form part of the Eucharistic prayer, we join in the proclamation of the story of salvation and offer ourselves with Christ to the Father (nos. 78–79). Truly, the acclamations carry great significance in terms of our role as the assembly. They are part of that "active participation that the gathered faithful are to contribute in every form of the Mass, so that the action of the entire community may be clearly expressed and fostered" (no. 35).

SPIRITUALITY

Gospel
Luke 10:25-37; L105C

There was a scholar of the law who stood up to test Jesus and said,
"Teacher, what must I do to inherit eternal life?"

Jesus said to him,
"What is written in the law?
How do you read it?"
He said in reply,
"You shall love the Lord, your God, with all your heart, with all your being, with all your strength, and with all your mind, and your neighbor as yourself. "
He replied to him, "You have answered correctly;
do this and you will live."

But because he wished to justify himself, he said to Jesus,
"And who is my neighbor?"
Jesus replied,
"A man fell victim to robbers as he went down from Jerusalem to Jericho.
They stripped and beat him and went off leaving him half-dead.
A priest happened to be going down that road,
but when he saw him, he passed by on the opposite side.
Likewise a Levite came to the place, and when he saw him, he passed by on the opposite side.
But a Samaritan traveler who came upon him
was moved with compassion at the sight.

Continued in Appendix A, p. 300.

Reflecting on the Gospel

Jewish Law required the love of God (Deut 6:5) and the love of neighbor (Lev 19:18). As described in the first reading, this is no "pie in the sky" Law, but one literally right under our noses—it is written in our hearts. We *know* what is required of us. *Knowing* the Law is not enough; we must then *do* it! But that is easier said than done, as the "scholar of the law" in this Sunday's gospel demonstrates for us.

In the gospel Jesus does not need to answer the first question posed by the "scholar of the law" ("what must I do to inherit eternal life?") since the lawyer knows the answer. The Law is "already in [his] mouth and in [his] heart" (first reading) and so Jesus instructs him: "do this and you will live." The Law is not "mysterious and remote" (first reading); it bears the human face of our neighbor in need. We learn this most effectively by actually *doing* what is needed to help our neighbor.

Thus Jesus responds to the lawyer's second question ("who is my neighbor") with a parable. The priest and Levite pass by the man in need. Note what the parable says: "passed by on the opposite side." This wasn't so much to ignore the injured one's need as it was to put distance between themselves and the bloodied man, because contact would result in ritual impurity and, therefore, exclusion from worship. They put ritual purity (and worship) above social obligation. In other words, the priest and Levite had the "love God" part of the Law mastered. What they had not learned was the "love neighbor" part and its relationship to love of God or the relationship between caring for those in need and worship.

What the priest and Levite missed is that worship of God is empty if it is not consistent with a larger context for life which very much includes loving and caring for each other. Otherwise, worship runs the risk of being "pie in the sky"; it is without love which is proven. This is what is right under our noses: our neighbor in need. The first step toward authentic worship is responding to the legitimate needs of the people around us.

As the lawyer knew the Law, we know this very familiar parable. The issue for us, therefore, is not knowing the parable; rather, the issue is the hard work of extending mercy not just to the neighbor we know but to any person in need. Worship (love of God) cannot be separated from our neighbor. In fact, caring for our neighbor in need is already a kind of worship, for care for others is a recognition that they are God's beloved children and bear the Law and love of God within them.

Living the Paschal Mystery

This is what the First Letter of John reminds us: "for whoever does not love a brother whom he has seen cannot love God whom he has not seen" (1 John 4:20b). We all know what we should do! The issue is, doing it! The bottom line: we know our responsibility before the law, so do it!

The "dying" part of Gospel living can get awfully burdensome if we always think of it in negative terms. Our reflection on this gospel invites us to place our self-sacrificing to meet the needs of others in the larger context of worshiping God. The beginning of worship is our care for others. This is more than just preaching a "social gospel." It is saying that there is an indissoluble link between caring for others and worship, between loving others and loving God. Thus doing for others is more than a nice act; it is a way we make God's kingdom come.

Focusing the Gospel

Key words and phrases: scholar of the law, answered correctly, do this, treated him with mercy, do likewise

To the point: In the gospel Jesus does not need to answer the first question posed by the "scholar of the law" since the lawyer knows the answer. It is "already in [his] mouth and in [his] heart" (first reading). The issue is not knowing but doing, as Jesus instructs him: "do this and you will live." Similarly, as the lawyer knew the Law, we know this very familiar parable. The issue for us is not knowing the parable; rather, it is the hard work of extending mercy not just to the neighbor we know but to any person in need.

Connecting the Gospel

to the first reading: The Law is not "mysterious and remote," it bears the human face of our neighbor in need. We learn this most effectively by *doing* what is needed to help this neighbor.

to culture: We are not hesitant to offer mercy to those we think deserve it. The gospel challenges us to extend mercy to anyone who needs it.

Understanding Scripture

Love your neighbor: "What must I do to inherit eternal life?" The lawyer answers his own question by quoting Deuteronomy 6:5 on the love of God, and Leviticus 19:18b on the love of "neighbor." The lawyer's second question poses the real issue in this Sunday's gospel: "who is my neighbor?" Is it the person next door? Is it fellow Israelites? Does "neighbor" mean "everyone"? The answer to this question defines the limits of one's obligations under the Law, and only a person who fulfills the Law can be righteous and "inherit eternal life." The stakes are high, indeed! Once the "neighbor" is accurately identified, what does it mean to "love" that person? There were a variety of answers to these questions offered by different rabbis, the Dead Sea scrolls, the Book of Jubilees, and other Jewish sources. The debate continued in the Christian community, as passages from the Didache (2:7; 3:1-2) and the Letter of Barnabas (19:5) indicate.

In Leviticus, the word translated as "neighbor" can also mean "friend" or "fellow." In this portion of Leviticus, this word is often used with such expressions as "countryman" or "kin." Indeed, the first half of Leviticus 19:18 (from which the lawyer quotes) says, "Take no revenge and cherish no grudge against your fellow countrymen. You shall love your neighbor as yourself." It would seem reasonable to conclude that "neighbor" means "countryman." The story Jesus tells shatters that interpretation. The beaten man's countrymen—the priest and the Levite—do not treat him with love. No obligation or duty can excuse their neglect.

The Samaritan is the kind of neighbor anyone in the beaten man's situation would be glad to have—even a law-abiding Israelite lawyer. In such need, one would not turn aside the help proffered even by an enemy. By making the "hero" of the story not only someone from far away, but also of a different—and hated!—nationality (a Samaritan), the answer is clear. "Neighbor" is defined not by nationality, ethnicity, religion, or location. Neighbor is the person in need; being a neighbor means helping those in need.

**ASSEMBLY &
FAITH-SHARING GROUPS**

- The way I understand the relationship between love of God and love of neighbor is . . .
- The challenge for me in the parable of the Good Samaritan is . . .
- Some of the obstacles to loving neighbor as this gospel challenges me are . . .

PRESIDERS
I shall consider how leading others in worship (love of God) requires me to lead others in service, too (love of neighbor) . . .

DEACONS
I shall review how well I am balancing the care of my family (love of neighbor) with my altar ministry (love of God) . . .

HOSPITALITY MINISTERS
My care and concern for those gathering enriches my worship of God in that . . .

MUSIC MINISTERS
For me as a music minister, my neighbor is . . . ; one way I love my neighbor as myself is . . .

ALTAR MINISTERS
My serving at the altar is incomplete without serving those in need because . . .

LECTORS
I have come to realize that God's word "is something very near" (first reading), already in my mouth and heart, by . . .

**EXTRAORDINARY MINISTERS
OF HOLY COMMUNION**
Feeding the spiritually hungry with the Body of Christ challenges me also to serve and feed the hungry because . . .

Model Act of Penitence

Presider: Today's gospel is the parable of the Good Samaritan in which Jesus instructs us to treat our neighbor with mercy. Let us ask Jesus to extend his mercy to us . . . [pause]

> Lord Jesus, you teach us how to love God and neighbor: Lord . . .
>
> Christ Jesus, you write your Law in our hearts: Christ . . .
>
> Lord Jesus, you are filled with kindness and mercy: Lord . . .

Appreciating the Responsorial Psalm

At first glance, the verses of Psalm 69 used for this responsorial psalm seem unrelated to either the first reading or the gospel. But further reflection reveals a rich and rewarding connection.

In the first reading Moses counsels the people that the commandments are not beyond them, but within them. In the gospel Jesus teaches that the commandments to love God and neighbor are not hazy, but clear and applicable: to love God means to love the immediate neighbor in need. Psalm 69 reminds us that whenever we have been in need, God has responded without hesitation. We know God's law of love because we have experienced God's loving us—directly and personally. And we know who is the neighbor in need because we have been that neighbor. It is this knowledge which fills our hearts and inspires us to act compassionately towards others. Psalm 69 grounds our ability to love in the One who has first loved us.

Model General Intercessions

Presider: Jesus gives us an example of care for our neighbor. We are confident that God hears our prayers with the same care.

Response:

Lord, hear our prayer.

Cantor:

we pray to the Lord,

That all members of the Church may extend to neighbors in need the mercy God has shown us . . . [pause]

That all leaders of nations may govern with compassion and mercy . . . [pause]

That all those harmed by abuse, violence, or neglect may receive care and compassion . . . [pause]

That all of us here may know and do what is right . . . [pause]

Presider: Merciful God, you hear our prayers: help us grow in your love, reach out to others in need, and show your mercy to all. We ask this through Christ our Lord. **Amen.**

OPENING PRAYER

Let us pray

Pause for silent prayer

God our Father,
your light of truth
guides us to the way of Christ.
May all who follow him
reject what is contrary to the gospel.

We ask this through our Lord Jesus Christ,
    your Son,
who lives and reigns with you and the
    Holy Spirit,
one God, for ever and ever. **Amen.**

FIRST READING
Deut 30:10-14

Moses said to the people:
> "If only you would heed the voice of the
>   LORD, your God,
> and keep his commandments and
>   statutes
> that are written in this book of the law,
> when you return to the LORD, your God,
> with all your heart and all your soul.

> "For this command that I enjoin on you
>   today
> is not too mysterious and remote for
>   you.
> It is not up in the sky, that you should say,
> 'Who will go up in the sky to get it for
>   us
> and tell us of it, that we may carry it
>   out?'
> Nor is it across the sea, that you should
>   say,
> 'Who will cross the sea to get it for us
> and tell us of it, that we may carry it
>   out?'
> No, it is something very near to you,
> already in your mouths and in your
>   hearts;
> you have only to carry it out."

RESPONSORIAL PSALM
Ps 69:14, 17, 30-31, 33-34, 36, 37

℞. (cf. 33) Turn to the Lord in your need,
and you will live.

I pray to you, O LORD,
    for the time of your favor, O God!
In your great kindness answer me
    with your constant help.
Answer me, O LORD, for bounteous is your
    kindness:
    in your great mercy turn toward me.

℞. Turn to the Lord in your need, and you
will live.

I am afflicted and in pain;
    let your saving help, O God, protect me.

I will praise the name of God in song,
   and I will glorify him with
      thanksgiving.

R℣. Turn to the Lord in your need, and you
will live.

"See, you lowly ones, and be glad;
   you who seek God, may your hearts
      revive!
For the LORD hears the poor,
   and his own who are in bonds he spurns
      not."

R℣. Turn to the Lord in your need, and you
will live.

For God will save Zion
   and rebuild the cities of Judah.
The descendants of his servants shall
      inherit it,
   and those who love his name shall
      inhabit it.

R℣. Turn to the Lord in your need, and you
will live.

OR

RESPONSORIAL PSALM
Ps 19:8, 9, 10, 11

See Appendix A, p. 301.

SECOND READING
Col 1:15-20

Christ Jesus is the image of the invisible
   God,
   the firstborn of all creation.
For in him were created all things in
      heaven and on earth,
   the visible and the invisible,
   whether thrones or dominions or
      principalities or powers;
   all things were created through him and
      for him.
He is before all things,
   and in him all things hold together.
He is the head of the body, the church.
He is the beginning, the firstborn from the
      dead,
   that in all things he himself might be
      preeminent.
For in him all the fullness was pleased to
      dwell,
   and through him to reconcile all things
      for him,
   making peace by the blood of his cross
   through him, whether those on earth or
      those in heaven.

About Liturgy

Liturgy and liturgical law: The readings for this Sunday provide an opportunity for a practical reflection on our attitude toward and application of liturgical law. It is too easy to get caught up in the intricacies of "getting liturgy right" (as important as that might be), and lose sight of the larger picture: the Body of Christ at prayer and worship. Liturgical law is for the sake of prayerful worship for all. That is the goal, not keeping the law in itself. At a time when it seems like liturgical rules reign supreme, it is good always to remind ourselves about what we really do when we gather for liturgy: surrender ourselves to God and raise our hearts and voices in thanksgiving and praise.

It is equally easy to disregard the law and do in worship what we like and what makes us feel good. It is helpful when worship is pleasing and affects us personally in positive ways, but this can also run the risk of our worship becoming self-centered. Worship is not ultimately about us (although we are surely central players, in that we are transformed as the gifts of bread and wine are transformed), but about our giving God praise and thanks.

About Liturgical Music

Cantor preparation: To love one's neighbor as oneself is a tall order, and even more so when that neighbor is a stranger or an enemy. But you have only to turn to God for the strength you need to love in this way (see psalm refrain). When has the grace of God helped you love a neighbor in need?

Singing the acclamations, part 2: The acclamations all come as responses to some invitation, prayer, or acclamation by a liturgical minister, be it the presider, the lector, or the deacon. They are directed, however, not to the liturgical minister, but to God.

Through our "Amen" at the conclusion of the collects and the Eucharistic prayer, we participate in addressing these prayers to God. Through our acclamations at the conclusion of the first and second readings, we shout thanksgiving to God for giving us the Word. In our "Glory to you, Lord" and "Praise to you, Lord Jesus Christ" which surround the proclamation of the gospel, we address Christ, actively present among us. In the *Holy, Holy, Holy* and the memorial acclamation (with the exception of Form A, "Christ has died, Christ is risen, Christ will come again," which is a declarative statement), we speak directly to God, either as Father, or as the person of Christ. What makes the acclamations so significant, then, is that through them we address God face to face as the one Body of Christ.

JULY 15, 2007
FIFTEENTH SUNDAY
IN ORDINARY TIME

SPIRITUALITY

Gospel

Luke 10:38-42; L108C

Jesus entered a village
  where a woman whose name was
    Martha welcomed him.
She had a sister named Mary
  who sat beside the Lord at his feet
    listening to him speak.
Martha, burdened with much serving,
  came to him and said,
  "Lord, do you not care
that my sister has left me by myself
  to do the serving?
Tell her to help me."
The Lord said to her in reply,
  "Martha, Martha, you are anxious
    and worried about many things.
There is need of only one thing.
Mary has chosen the better part
  and it will not be taken from her."

Reflecting on the Gospel

On a purely human level, this gospel reads like an ordinary family with two or more children. How many parents haven't heard complaints from siblings about "He won't help me." Jesus responds to Martha's indignant question ("do you not care . . . by myself to do the serving?") with something Martha probably wasn't too happy to hear: "Mary has chosen the better part and it will not be taken from her." What, exactly, is the "better part"?

The first reading sheds a positive light on the actions of Martha, for Abraham and Sarah behave much as she does in receiving their guests. In juxtaposition with the first reading, the gospel is not so much critiquing Martha's busyness as it is calling her to a deeper level of hospitality. Both Martha and Abraham and Sarah go to great, lavish lengths with their hospitality ("much serving," "tender, choice steer"). Why does Martha receive a rebuke and Abraham a son?

The gospel demonstrates many expressions of hospitality: welcoming, listening, serving. While each expression is valuable, none is complete in itself nor an end in itself. There is no one way to be hospitable. Neither are all expressions of hospitality equal, which is the point that Jesus makes in the gospel. Hospitality in its deepest meaning makes possible a personal encounter of the kind that Mary is having with Jesus. This is the "better part" to which Jesus refers.

Hospitality—genuine welcome of the other and surrender to the other—sets up the possibility of hearing the visitor's message and facilitating the encounter; one critical aspect of discipleship is listening. Thus, the "better part" is listening to Jesus, being attentive to Jesus' presence, responding appropriately. Abraham is totally attentive to the three strangers: he greets them and bows down in respect; he extends an invitation to remain a while, and then acts after he has listened to the strangers' reply ("do as you have said"). In contrast, Martha is "anxious and worried." She loses sight of her guest and gets wrapped up in her task, as well-meaning as that may be.

Note that Jesus does not refuse Martha's hospitality; he does not ask her to forget about the serving and come listen to him. The gospel teaches about surrendering to the Lord. Martha surrendered to anxiety and worry rather than to the presence of her Guest. What is the "better part"? As important as certain aspects of hospitality are, the "better part" is to listen and surrender to the presence of the Lord. Faithful discipleship depends upon these surrendering and listening aspects of hospitality. Faithful discipleship depends upon encountering the Lord.

Living the Paschal Mystery

In the "busyness" of the average person's everyday life, we must take time to listen to others so that we truly *encounter* them. This is primary if we disciples are not to lose sight of the One who teaches us—and often teaches us through those to whom we are truly hospitable. Discipleship relativizes our noble and pious instincts to be busy about others and calls us to *listen* and take the other into our heart. It necessarily requires our surrender to the One who speaks, and that surrender looks like "welcome, listen, do." The encounter with Jesus is essential for Christian hospitality. Let us hear that well!

Focusing the Gospel

Key words and phrases: welcomed, listening, serving, better part

To the point: The gospel demonstrates many expressions of hospitality: welcoming, listening, serving. While each expression is valuable, none is complete in itself nor an end in itself. Rather, hospitality in its deepest meaning makes possible a personal encounter of the kind that Mary is having with Jesus. This is the "better part."

Connecting the Gospel

to the first reading: The first reading sheds a positive light on the actions of Martha, for Abraham and Sarah behave much as she does in receiving their guests. In juxtaposition with the first reading, the gospel is not so much critiquing Martha's busyness as it is calling her to a deeper level of hospitality.

to Catholic culture: Whenever we gather for the Eucharistic meal we must attend to many details of the rite. We can become fixated on these details or we can allow them to lead us to the personal encounter with Christ and one another which is their purpose.

Understanding Scripture

Hospitality: Despite Jesus' praise of the attentive Mary, the Lectionary seems to emphasize Martha's hospitality by pairing the gospel with the story of Abraham welcoming his mysterious guests. In both stories, hospitality sets up the possibility of hearing the words of the visitor.

Abraham is busy with all the details of hospitality. His caring for his guests requires much busyness: making rolls, choosing a steer from the field, slaughtering it, butchering it, roasting it, and serving it. And, as Philo makes clear, this is something he does personally: "That [Abraham] had a multitude of servants is clear . . . [Yet] he himself becomes as an attendant and a servant in order to show his hospitality" (*Questions and Answers in Genesis* 4:10).

The lavish hospitality of Abraham is widely celebrated. Both Abraham as an individual, and the act of hospitality, are praised. Hebrews 13:2 makes of this story a moral lesson: "Do not neglect hospitality, for through it some have unknowingly entertained angels." Abraham, as Israel's great patriarch, becomes an exemplar of hospitality: "All the years of his life [Abraham] lived in quietness, gentleness, and righteousness, and the righteous man was very hospitable. For he pitched his tent at the crossroads of Mamre and welcomed everyone—rich and poor, kings and rulers, the cripples and the helpless, friends and strangers, neighbors and passersby—[all] on equal terms did the pious, entirely holy, righteous, and hospitable Abraham welcome" (Testament of Abraham [A] 1:1-2). The virtue of hospitality gets no higher endorsement than this remarkable statement from the Talmud: "Hospitality to wayfarers is greater than welcoming the Divine Presence" (Shabbat 127a).

In a culture which so highly values hospitality, Jesus' words to his disciples (14th Sunday) make sense: "Whatever town . . . [does] not receive you [Greek = "receive hospitably, entertain"] . . . it will be more tolerable for Sodom than for that town" (Luke 10:8, 12). Hospitality leads to divine encounters. Beyond the busyness of doing for guests, the final act of hospitality in both Genesis and Luke is listening attentively. Abraham learns of the coming birth of his long-awaited son; Mary deepens her relationship with Jesus.

ASSEMBLY & FAITH-SHARING GROUPS

- As I watch Martha and Mary, I am more like . . . because . . .
- To be less "anxious and worried" and become more attentive to the needs of those around me, I need to . . .
- What helps me remain aware that I am encountering Jesus when I welcome/receive a guest is . . .

PRESIDERS

In the midst of busy ministry, what helps me remain genuinely present and attentive to others is . . .

DEACONS

In order to safeguard the "one thing" necessary, what I need to revise is . . .

HOSPITALITY MINISTERS

When I recall that welcoming members of the assembly is welcoming Jesus, then my hospitality is like . . .

MUSIC MINISTERS

In the gospel Mary chooses the "better part" by listening to the voice of Christ. My music ministry challenges me to better listening by . . . I encounter Christ in this listening when . . .

ALTAR MINISTERS

As I attend to the "many things" needed for liturgy, I keep focused on the centrality of encountering Jesus by . . .

LECTORS

When I sit listening, attentive to Jesus (like Mary), my proclamation is like . . .

EXTRAORDINARY MINISTERS OF HOLY COMMUNION

The sort of hospitality necessary in my heart in order to hear the Word and distribute the Body of Christ is . . .

Model Act of Penitence

Presider: Jesus invites us to his table where he speaks to us in his word and nourishes us in his Sacrament. Let us prepare to celebrate . . . [pause]

Lord Jesus, you are present to us in this gathering: Lord . . .

Christ Jesus, you teach us to be attentive disciples: Christ . . .

Lord Jesus, you lead us to your heavenly banquet: Lord . . .

Appreciating the Responsorial Psalm

In the first reading Abraham bows before his visitors and begs to be allowed to serve them. In the gospel Mary sits at the feet of Jesus so that she may listen to him. The psalm seems to imply that such attentiveness to the other is an act of justice. The issue is that of being truly present to the other, be that a neighbor in need or the Lord. The relationship between acting with justice and living in God's presence expressed in the psalm refrain parallels the relationship between love of neighbor and worship of God demonstrated in last Sunday's Liturgy of the Word. In both cases, we are invited to grow in our understanding of what it means to sit in the presence of the Lord. We are invited to choose the "better part" and to discover that it does not divide our attention between God and neighbor but more clearly focuses it.

Model General Intercessions

Presider: God graciously receives the prayers of all who call out in need. And so we pray with confidence.

Response:

Lord, hear our prayer.

Cantor:

we pray to the Lord,

That the Church always be hospitable in word and deed . . . [pause]

That world leaders listen to their people with receptive hearts . . . [pause]

That travelers and refugees may always find a welcome haven . . . [pause]

That each of us here listen attentively to the words of Jesus . . . [pause]

Presider: Merciful God, you hear the prayers of those who cry to you: help us to listen to your Son with hospitable and attentive hearts, that we may always be faithful disciples. We ask this through that same Son, Jesus Christ our Lord. **Amen.**

OPENING PRAYER

Let us pray

Pause for silent prayer

Lord,
be merciful to your people.
Fill us with your gifts
and make us always eager to serve
you in faith, hope, and love.

Grant this through our Lord Jesus Christ,
    your Son,
who lives and reigns with you and the
    Holy Spirit,
one God, for ever and ever. **Amen.**

FIRST READING

Gen 18:1-10a

The LORD appeared to Abraham by the
    terebinth of Mamre,
    as he sat in the entrance of his tent,
    while the day was growing hot.
Looking up, Abraham saw three men
    standing nearby.
When he saw them, he ran from the
    entrance of the tent to greet them;
    and bowing to the ground, he said:
    "Sir, if I may ask you this favor,
    please do not go on past your servant.
Let some water be brought, that you may
    bathe your feet,
    and then rest yourselves under the tree.
Now that you have come this close to your
    servant,
    let me bring you a little food, that you
        may refresh yourselves;
    and afterward you may go on your
        way."
The men replied, "Very well, do as you
    have said."

Abraham hastened into the tent and told
    Sarah,
    "Quick, three measures of fine flour!
        Knead it and make rolls."
He ran to the herd, picked out a tender,
    choice steer,
    and gave it to a servant, who quickly
        prepared it.
Then Abraham got some curds and milk,
    as well as the steer that had been
        prepared,
    and set these before the three men;
    and he waited on them under the tree
        while they ate.

They asked Abraham, "Where is your wife
    Sarah?"
He replied, "There in the tent."
One of them said, "I will surely return to
    you about this time next year,
    and Sarah will then have a son."

RESPONSORIAL PSALM
Ps 15:2-3, 3-4, 5

R⁊. (1a) He who does justice will live in the presence of the Lord.

One who walks blamelessly and does
    justice;
  who thinks the truth in his heart
  and slanders not with his tongue.

R⁊. He who does justice will live in the presence of the Lord.

Who harms not his fellow man,
  nor takes up a reproach against his
    neighbor;
by whom the reprobate is despised,
  while he honors those who fear the
    LORD.

R⁊. He who does justice will live in the presence of the Lord.

Who lends not his money at usury
  and accepts no bribe against the
    innocent.
One who does these things
  shall never be disturbed.

R⁊. He who does justice will live in the presence of the Lord.

SECOND READING
Col 1:24-28

Brothers and sisters:
Now I rejoice in my sufferings for your
    sake,
  and in my flesh I am filling up
  what is lacking in the afflictions of
    Christ
  on behalf of his body, which is the
    church,
  of which I am a minister
in accordance with God's stewardship
    given to me
to bring to completion for you the word
    of God,
  the mystery hidden from ages and from
    generations past.
But now it has been manifested to his holy
    ones,
  to whom God chose to make known the
    riches of the glory
  of this mystery among the Gentiles;
  it is Christ in you, the hope for glory.
It is he whom we proclaim,
  admonishing everyone and teaching
    everyone with all wisdom,
  that we may present everyone perfect
    in Christ.

About Liturgy

Hospitality ministers and encountering Christ: Each gospel proclaimed every Sunday always challenges the assembly in some way. This Sunday's gospel has a number of challenges for hospitality ministers in particular.

First, hospitality ministers must make sure their welcome of the members of the gathering assembly is a welcome of Jesus himself. Members of the assembly are members of the Body of Christ. The focus of the hospitality ministers is, therefore, on Christ himself.

Second, hospitality ministers, in their very greeting of those who are gathering, already play an important part in helping the assembly members have a listening attitude toward the God whom they will encounter in the celebration of liturgy. All the warmth and friendliness of the hospitality minister, then, is directed to opening those they greet to listen better.

Third, the hospitality members themselves must practice listening in their daily living if they are to help assembly members listen better. Their ministry is not one of teaching others how to listen, but of modeling for them a listening attitude.

Fourth, this gospel challenges hospitality ministers to focus on their actions as *ministry,* always serving the greater good of gathering those who come to liturgy as the one Body of Christ.

About Liturgical Music

Cantor preparation: As part of your preparation to sing this responsorial psalm, spend some time reflecting on how you choose to live in the presence of God and how that choice shapes your living of justice. When and how do you take time to hear God's teaching? How, concretely, do you let that teaching change your living?

Singing the acclamations, part 3: The acclamations are central to the celebration of the liturgy because through them we, the gathered Body of Christ, address God directly. Sometimes we address God as Father, other times as Christ, but always as the giver of redemption and the initiator of this here-and-now liturgical action. It is through the acclamations that we most clearly speak with one voice and one identity as the Body of Christ. The acclamations are a unique mode of our priestly participation in the Eucharistic celebration. Other ritual elements are also modes of such participation, but the acclamations carry special significance because through them we stand face to face with God in the great act of redemption. In the acclamations we speak directly to God not as slaves or servants, but as friends and collaborators in the ongoing act of mutual self-surrender which is the wellspring, the core, and the energizing heart of redemption.

SPIRITUALITY

Gospel
Luke 11:1-13; L111C

**Jesus was praying in a certain place,
and when he had finished,
one of his disciples said to
him,
"Lord, teach us to pray
just as John taught his
disciples."
He said to them, "When you
pray, say:
Father, hallowed be your
name,
your kingdom come.
Give us each day our daily
bread
and forgive us our sins
for we ourselves forgive
everyone in debt to us,
and do not subject us to the final
test."**

**And he said to them, "Suppose one of
you has a friend
to whom he goes at midnight and
says,
'Friend, lend me three loaves of
bread,
for a friend of mine has arrived at
my house from a journey
and I have nothing to offer him,'
and he says in reply from within,
'Do not bother me; the door has
already been locked
and my children and I are already in
bed.
I cannot get up to give you anything.'
I tell you,
if he does not get up to give the
visitor the loaves
because of their friendship,
he will get up to give him whatever
he needs
because of his persistence.**

Continued in Appendix A, p. 300.

Reflecting on the Gospel

If persistence were all that is needed to get what we want, we would all be million-aires living in some paradise! We are naturally persistent in seeking what we think is good for us. The gospel this Sunday is about persistence and prayer. Prayer is not magic; we cannot expect to receive whatever we want from God just for the persistent asking. The surprise of the gospel is that persistence in prayer does not lie in asking again and again. The persistence essential for fruit-ful prayer is to ask for what the Father intends to give us: the Holy Spirit. Fruitful, persistent prayer is tied to the desire and will of God.

In the examples Jesus proposes in this gospel, people ask for what is immediate and mundane: three loaves of bread, a fish, an egg. These all sustain life on one level. But Jesus instructs us to pray persistently for what sustains the life of disciples and for what God really wants to give: the Holy Spirit. In the first read-ing Abraham is a model of persistence in prayer because he asks for what he knows God wants to give—mercy to sinners. Prayer always includes a discernment of *what God wants for us,* not sim-ply what we want for ourselves.

Jesus did not just teach the disciples simply to say words in prayer. Oh, yes, he gave them the words to what we now know as the "Lord's Prayer." Beyond the words, though, he taught his disciples what persistence in prayer means. Often we think of persistence in negative terms such as nagging or sheer stubbornness. In prayer persistence is meant to lead us to what *God wants for us*. And perhaps this is the most difficult thing about prayer. Instead of always praying for and fulfill-ing our own shortsighted needs (although sometimes this is perfectly legiti-mate, necessary, and good prayer!), persistent praying leads us to know God's will for us, to receive the Holy Spirit, to open us in new ways to God's goodness.

Living the Paschal Mystery

Most of us first learned to pray by saying prayers—meal prayers, bedtime prayer, the Guardian Angel prayer, the Our Father and Hail Mary. This is a good beginning, because it gives us an anchor. It gives us the words to get started. As we grow older and we come to know God better, however, there is always the risk that these "memorized prayers," prayers known by heart and so familiar to us, might become rote. We could end up just "saying prayers." Some people are proud of the fact that they say three rosaries or more a day. That may be good. Or it may not be so good, if all they are doing is rattling through words.

The kind of prayer Jesus taught is prayer from the heart, a prayer of com-munion, a prayer of attentiveness to divine Presence, a prayer seeking God's will. We cannot ask or seek or find if we are not sure of the presence of the Other. Praying—even saying familiar and much-loved memorized prayers—must bring us to divine encounter and to listen to God's will for us. Prayer is the communion of Person with person.

Prayer cannot be limited to set times, although that is necessary, too. The gospel says Jesus was "praying in a certain place." We know that the Mount of Olives was one of his favorite places for prayer. Jesus had set times for prayer: before undertaking a mission, during ministry, early in the morning. Jesus also was constantly in communion with his Father; this is the "always" of prayer. This is what we really wish to emulate: communion with God as abiding pres-ence. Lord, teach us to pray!

Focusing the Gospel

Key words and phrases: teach us to pray, persistence, ask, receive, how much more, the Father . . . [will] give the Holy Spirit

To the point: In the examples Jesus proposes in this gospel, people ask for what is immediate and mundane: three loaves of bread, a fish, an egg. These all sustain life on one level. But Jesus instructs us to pray persistently for what sustains the life of disciples and for what God really wants to give: the Holy Spirit.

Connecting the Gospel

to the first reading: Abraham is a model of persistence in prayer. He asks for what he knows God wants to give—mercy to sinners.

to human experience: Often we think of persistence in negative terms such as nagging or sheer stubbornness. In prayer persistence is meant to lead us to what God wants for us.

Understanding Scripture

Prayer: More than the other evangelists, Luke talks about prayer and shows Jesus in the act of praying. Luke's Gospel begins with people gathered for prayer at the incense hour (1:10), when Zechariah is told that his prayer has been heard (1:13). The first appearance of the adult Jesus shows him praying after his baptism (3:21). The last act of the earthly Jesus is to pray to his Father from the cross (23:46). Clearly, prayer sets the context—beginning and end—for the life and ministry of Jesus. In between, Jesus is shown at prayer habitually (5:16) and at key moments: before choosing the Twelve (6:12), before Peter's confession at Caesarea Philippi (9:18), at his transfiguration (9:28, 29), and during his agony in the garden (22:41, 44) when he twice urges his disciples to pray (22:40, 46). In addition, he teaches his disciples to pray (this Sunday's gospel) and instructs them about prayer in the parables of the unjust judge (18:1-8) and the Pharisee and the tax collector (18:9-14). Prayer is not an occasional event but a regular part of his life. Because disciples are to follow in the ways of the Master, prayer is a distinguishing and indispensable part of Christian life.

When Luke gives the words of Jesus at prayer, Jesus is shown addressing God as "Father": "Father, hallowed be your name . . ." (11:2); "Father, take this cup . . ." (22:42); "Father, forgive them . . ." (23:34); "Father, into your hands . . ."(23:46). This close and personal relationship with God expressed in prayer stands in marked contrast to the prayer uttered by the Pharisee and the tax collector in the parable Jesus tells: both pray, "O God . . ." (18:11, 13). The kind of relationship Jesus wants his disciples to have with God is as with a "Father," as he instructs them in this gospel.

Those who come to that kind of intimate relationship with God will experience God both as a Father and as the friend who responds to them in need. Moreover, knowing God so intimately, they will ask for and seek what God truly desires to give: the Holy Spirit.

ASSEMBLY & FAITH-SHARING GROUPS

- The part of the Lord's Prayer that I need to ponder (and live) more deeply is . . .
- Times when persistence in prayer leads me to desire what God wants for me are . . .
- In my prayer life, the degree to which I ask the Father for the Holy Spirit is . . . because . . .

PRESIDERS

I assist others to desire what the Father wants for them, namely, the Holy Spirit, by . . .

DEACONS

I assist others to remain persistent in prayer by . . .

HOSPITALITY MINISTERS

When my hospitality unfolds from prayer, my care and concern is like . . .

MUSIC MINISTERS

My ministry is that of leading the assembly in sung prayer. What helps me pray through my music-making is . . . What sometimes gets in the way of my praying is . . .

ALTAR MINISTERS

What helps me keep the liturgy as an encounter with the divine Presence instead of rote prayers is . . .

LECTORS

The difference in my proclamation when it comes out of genuine prayer is . . .

EXTRAORDINARY MINISTERS OF HOLY COMMUNION

The Eucharist nurtures my persistence in prayer in that . . . ; I am "living food" for others in their struggle to remain faithful in prayer when I . . .

Model Act of Penitence

Presider: In today's gospel Jesus teaches the disciples the Lord's Prayer. Let us prepare ourselves to pray as Jesus has taught us . . . [pause]

Lord Jesus, teach us to pray as you did: Lord . . .

Christ Jesus, give us this day our daily bread: Christ . . .

Lord Jesus, forgive our sins: Lord . . .

Appreciating the Responsorial Psalm

This responsorial psalm is a statement of absolute confidence in a God who listens to prayer. This confidence stands on past fulfillment (in the first reading God listened to Abraham's plea for Sodom and Gomorrah) and on future assurance (in the gospel Christ promises, "how much more will the Father in heaven give . . . to those who ask"). And it stands on the very nature of God whose "kindness and truth" will complete what has been begun in us (psalm). These readings and psalm teach us not only about prayer, but also about God's response. Let us sing, and pray, with confidence.

Model General Intercessions

Presider: God is generous beyond measure to those who make their needs known. And so we pray.

Response:

Lord, hear our prayer.

Cantor:

we pray to the Lord,

That all members of the Church always be diligent in prayer and seeking God's will . . . [pause]

That leaders in the world may respond to those who call out for justice . . . [pause]

That those who feel their prayer is fruitless find hope in God's fidelity . . . [pause]

That all of us persist in our asking for the Holy Spirit . . . [pause]

Presider: Generous God, you hear the prayers of those who ask, seek, and knock: open the door of your mercy and grant these our prayers which we ask through Christ our Lord. **Amen.**

ALTERNATIVE OPENING PRAYER
Let us pray

Pause for silent prayer

God our Father,
open our eyes to see your hand at work
in the splendor of creation,
in the beauty of human life.
Touched by your hand our world is holy.
Help us to cherish the gifts that surround us,
to share your blessings with our brothers
    and sisters,
and to experience the joy of life in your
    presence.

We ask this through Christ our Lord.
    Amen.

FIRST READING
Gen 18:20-32

In those days, the LORD said: "The outcry
    against Sodom and Gomorrah is so
    great,
    and their sin so grave,
    that I must go down and see whether or
        not their actions
    fully correspond to the cry against them
        that comes to me.
I mean to find out."

While Abraham's visitors walked on
        farther toward Sodom,
    the LORD remained standing before
        Abraham.
Then Abraham drew nearer and said:
    "Will you sweep away the innocent with
        the guilty?
Suppose there were fifty innocent people
    in the city;
    would you wipe out the place, rather
        than spare it
    for the sake of the fifty innocent people
        within it?
Far be it from you to do such a thing,
    to make the innocent die with the guilty
    so that the innocent and the guilty
        would be treated alike!
Should not the judge of all the world act
        with justice?"
The LORD replied,
    "If I find fifty innocent people in the
        city of Sodom,
    I will spare the whole place for their
        sake."
Abraham spoke up again:
    "See how I am presuming to speak to
        my Lord,
    though I am but dust and ashes!
What if there are five less than fifty
        innocent people?
Will you destroy the whole city because of
        those five?"
He answered, "I will not destroy it, if I find
        forty-five there."
But Abraham persisted, saying, "What if
        only forty are found there?"

He replied, "I will forbear doing it for the sake of the forty."

Then Abraham said, "Let not my Lord grow impatient if I go on.

What if only thirty are found there?"

He replied, "I will forbear doing it if I can find but thirty there."

Still Abraham went on,

"Since I have thus dared to speak to my Lord,

what if there are no more than twenty?"

The LORD answered, "I will not destroy it, for the sake of the twenty."

But he still persisted:

"Please, let not my Lord grow angry if I speak up this last time.

What if there are at least ten there?"

He replied, "For the sake of those ten, I will not destroy it."

RESPONSORIAL PSALM

Ps 138:1-2, 2-3, 6-7, 7-8

℞. (3a) Lord, on the day I called for help, you answered me.

I will give thanks to you, O LORD, with all my heart,
  for you have heard the words of my mouth;
  in the presence of the angels I will sing your praise;
I will worship at your holy temple
  and give thanks to your name.

℞. Lord, on the day I called for help, you answered me.

Because of your kindness and your truth;
  for you have made great above all things
  your name and your promise.
When I called you answered me;
  you built up strength within me.

℞. Lord, on the day I called for help, you answered me.

The LORD is exalted, yet the lowly he sees,
  and the proud he knows from afar.
Though I walk amid distress, you preserve me;
  against the anger of my enemies you raise your hand.

℞. Lord, on the day I called for help, you answered me.

Your right hand saves me.
  The LORD will complete what he has done for me;
your kindness, O LORD, endures forever;
  forsake not the work of your hands.

℞. Lord, on the day I called for help, you answered me.

SECOND READING

Col 2:12-14

See Appendix A, p. 300.

About Liturgy

Praying liturgy: Just as personal prayer runs a risk of becoming rote, just saying prayers, so does liturgy. One of the important things an assembly must always keep in mind is to surrender themselves to the ritual action in such a way as to really *pray* at liturgy.

One of the big mistakes we often make in liturgy is to make choices (about music, environment, introductions, etc.) which are directed to catching people's attention. Rather, efforts by all present must constantly be put forth in order to draw each member of the assembly through prayer into the depths of the mystery being celebrated, which ultimately means encounter with the redeeming God.

We sometimes forget how much our own presence and prayer affects those around us at liturgy, and even the entire assembly. If my posture and attitude is lackadaisical, that does affect how the whole Body present is praying. If I am deeply immersed in prayer, that draws those around me into deeper prayer. If I sing wholeheartedly, that adds to the swell of sung prayer of the whole assembly. If I respond well, that adds to the full voice of the prayer. Liturgy is celebrated by a *community* and each member affects the prayer of each other member. It is not good enough just to be there. We must all be persistent in surrendering to God in prayer, listening for God's will, and welcoming the Holy Spirit into our hearts.

About Liturgical Music

Cantor preparation: When you sing the responsorial psalm, what the assembly hears more than the beauty of your voice is the sound of your praying. Ask Christ to teach you how to pray the psalm and how to invite the assembly to join you in that prayer.

Singing the acclamations, part 4: The acclamations enable us to take ownership of our baptismal identity by letting us directly address the One who initiates and desires this identity. To understand this point more clearly consider, for example, the acclamatory "Amen" which concludes the opening prayer. It is not an arbitrary tag-along, but an essential part of the prayer. The opening prayer begins with an invitation and then a moment of silence during which we individually raise our hearts and intentions to God. The presider then "collects" these silent prayers into a communal one which he speaks on our behalf. The "Amen" is our conclusion to this common prayer, our acknowledgment that we are the one Body of Christ gathered in petition before the all-redeeming God, our ownership of our priesthood in Christ and with one another. This "Amen," then, is no merely murmured second thought, no perfunctory period to someone else's prayer. Rather, it is our expression of ownership of the prayer and of the personal identity out of which the prayer arises.

SPIRITUALITY

Gospel

Luke 12:13-21; L114C

Someone in the crowd said to Jesus,
  "Teacher, tell my brother to share the inheritance with me."
He replied to him,
  "Friend, who appointed me as your judge and arbitrator?"
Then he said to the crowd,
  "Take care to guard against all greed,
  for though one may be rich,
  one's life does not consist of possessions."

Then he told them a parable.
"There was a rich man whose land produced a bountiful harvest.
He asked himself, 'What shall I do,
  for I do not have space to store my harvest?'
And he said, 'This is what I shall do:
  I shall tear down my barns and build larger ones.
There I shall store all my grain and other goods
  and I shall say to myself, "Now as for you,
  you have so many good things stored up for many years,
  rest, eat, drink, be merry!"'
But God said to him,
  'You fool, this night your life will be demanded of you;
  and the things you have prepared, to whom will they belong?'
Thus will it be for all who store up treasure for themselves
  but are not rich in what matters to God."

Reflecting on the Gospel

We are a lot more like the farmer who built bigger barns to hold a bumper crop and then didn't live long enough to enjoy it than we would care to think or admit! "Maxed out" credit cards, multiple bridal registries, working to own bigger homes and newer cars, latest computer gadgetry, proliferating use of cell phones, big-screen TVs, home theater, low or nonexistent savings accounts . . . the list goes on and on. We have created a culture which says having things—more and bigger and fancier—makes us happy. Symptoms of our fixation with possessions (such as rising depression and suicide rates) tell us that, like the farmer in the gospel, we haven't really gained the expected happiness.

The gospel is going far beyond "you can't take it with you." In this gospel Jesus challenges the crowd to "guard against all greed." The "rich man" evaluates his life in terms of possessions and believes he is secure. On God's scale of values, this man is foolish (see gospel) because these things are fleeting (see first reading). The first reading describes in even greater detail the misfortune which befalls the rich man in the gospel parable. According to Qoheleth, laboring for wealth and possessions is not only foolish but results in sorrow, grief, and anxiety.

Jesus teaches us that the only wealth worth acquiring is to become "rich in what matters to God." The question the gospel raises, then, is "what matters to God"? Clearly, in things, possessions, there is no lasting profit. There is only lasting profit in that which leads us to "seek that which is above" (second reading) because we recognize that "Christ is all and in all." Thus, what really matters to God is that we learn a new set of priorities. The readings and psalm give us ample suggestions: wisdom of heart, kindness, joy, gladness, gracious care, put to death what is "earthly," put on a new self, living in the image of our Creator, opening ourselves to the "Christ who is all and in all."

No wonder we tend to lose ourselves in possessions—that is much easier than pursuing only what matters to God! When we make the effort, however, to reorganize our priorities and keep our sight on God, then we gain what the man in the gospel never achieved—absolute security in our future. This is a future which is not in barns filled with grain and other earthly goods; this is a future in God!

Living the Paschal Mystery

Discipleship requires self-emptying, and that is ultimately what we can keep. Dying to our own needs and wants and pleasures is what God wants (see second reading). When we so die, there is a sense in which we come to see things as God sees them. And when that happens, even our needs and desires begin to change because gradually our practical, everyday choices begin to square up with "what matters to God."

This is not to say that discipleship means we must give up all possessions. That is neither practical nor necessary. There is nothing wrong with possessions in themselves and there is everything wrong with destitution, no matter what the reason. All of us deserve whatever material things we need—some of us more than others—in order to pursue a wholesome life. A problem arises when concern for our possessions or the drive to have more and more is our highest priority. The issue is valuing things appropriately, and then making choices so that our priorities are clear and uncompromised. Possessions take a second place to self-emptying. Achieving that is much more difficult than building bigger barns—and more lasting. For self-emptying leads to glory with God.

Focusing the Gospel

Key words and phrases: guard against all greed, rich man, you fool, rich in what matters to God

To the point: In this gospel Jesus challenges the crowd to "guard against all greed." The "rich man" evaluates his life in terms of possessions and wealth. On God's scale of values, this man is foolish (see gospel) because these things are fleeting (see first reading). Jesus teaches us that the only wealth worth acquiring is to become "rich in what matters to God."

Connecting the Gospel

to the first reading: The first reading describes in greater detail the misfortune which befalls the rich man in the gospel parable. According to Qoheleth, laboring for wealth and possessions is not only foolish but results in sorrow, grief, and anxiety.

to our culture: Greed is sometimes manifested as the belief that having more things will satisfy us or having more money will make life easier. The gospel tells us that "life does not consist of possessions" but "in what matters to God."

Understanding Scripture

True wealth: This is the only time in the three-year cycle of Sunday readings that we read from the Book of Ecclesiastes. Despite its relative liturgical obscurity, many people are probably familiar with three sayings from Ecclesiastes: "There's nothing new under the sun" (1:9); "For everything there is a season" (3:1); and the opening line from this Sunday's reading, "Vanity of vanities" (1:2). The choice of the reading to correspond with the gospel is inspired: it forms a wonderful companion piece to, and commentary on, one of Luke's favorite themes—the danger of wealth.

The meaning of the term "vanity" is of key importance for understanding the book: it occurs six times in this Sunday's brief passage, and thirty-seven times in the book. "Vanity" does not mean "pride in one's appearance." The Hebrew word means "breath" or "vapor," that which is insubstantial, fleeting, and transitory. Psalm 39:7 expresses admirably the sentiment of the reading from Ecclesiastes: "Mere phantoms, we go our way; mere vapor (= "vanity"), our restless pursuits; we heap up stores without knowing for whom."

The author of Ecclesiastes sets out to discover what is to be gained by various pursuits in life—the pursuit of wealth and possessions, fame and honor, wisdom and knowledge. All of these are vanity—fleeting at best, and not worth the effort one must invest in them. Because all is transitory, the author favors enjoying life—not a luxurious, wanton life, but what can be enjoyed simply. Ironically, he counsels, "Go, eat your bread with joy and drink your wine with a merry heart, because it is now that God favors your works" (9:7)—just what the rich man in the gospel says to himself! Leaving accumulated wealth to another is what God calls foolish and what Ecclesiastes characterizes as vanity. The rich man worked his whole life in order to enjoy life "for many years"; Ecclesiastes counsels enjoying the blessings of life today. True wealth is "what matters to God" which, according to Luke, means sharing what we have with the poor. This point will return on the Twenty-second Sunday in Ordinary Time (Luke 14:1, 7-14).

ASSEMBLY & FAITH-SHARING GROUPS

- Where greed tempts me is . . .
- I have learned the folly of storing up possessions because . . .
- In order to become "rich in what matters to God," I need to . . .

PRESIDERS

My daily living manifests to others what "matters to God" in that . . .

DEACONS

My diaconal ministry challenges me to take "off the old self with its practices" and "put on the new self" (second reading) when . . .

HOSPITALITY MINISTERS

My care and concern can help those gathering to hear the challenge in God's word when I . . .

MUSIC MINISTERS

As a music minister the "possessions" I work for (see gospel) are . . . What sometimes points my heart in the wrong direction is . . . What brings me back to Christ is . . .

ALTAR MINISTERS

Serving others keeps before them how to become "rich in what matters to God" because . . .

LECTORS

The priorities that I need rearranged in my life in order to proclaim the word with integrity are . . .

EXTRAORDINARY MINISTERS OF HOLY COMMUNION

In order to be "rich in what matters to God," I need to empty in me . . . ; this kind of self-emptying makes me more like Christ in that . . .

CELEBRATION

Model Act of Penitence

Presider: In this Sunday's gospel Jesus warns us how foolish it is to place our hopes in earthly possessions. Let us prepare to receive the riches God gives us in this celebration . . . [pause]

Lord Jesus, you teach us where true riches lie: Lord . . .

Christ Jesus, you are gracious and kind: Christ . . .

Lord Jesus, you lead us to our eternal inheritance: Lord . . .

Appreciating the Responsorial Psalm

In this responsorial psalm we sing about things which fade away: time, human life, the grass of the fields. The readings advise us not to put our hope in material possessions or hard work for these, too, fade away. Yet in the psalm we also ask God to "prosper the work of our hands." What is the work which needs to prosper? The psalm tells us: growth in the wisdom to value things rightly; growth in the capacity to see the kindness and care God grants us every day; growth in the courage to hear what God is saying to us and to change our hearts accordingly. In the end it is not labor which misleads us, but what we labor for. May it be that Christ become our "all in all" (see second reading).

Model General Intercessions

Presider: Let us ask God for those gifts which bring true and lasting wealth.

Response:

Lord, hear our prayer.

Cantor:

we pray to the Lord,

May members of the Church faithfully witness to the nature of true wealth . . . [pause]

May the peoples of the world guard against all greed . . . [pause]

May the greedy become generous and the dispossessed receive a wealth of blessings . . . [pause]

May all of us pattern our lives after what matters to God . . . [pause]

Presider: Good and generous God, you know what we need to have in order to possess eternal life: hear these our prayers that we may share in your glory, through Jesus Christ our Lord. **Amen.**

ALTERNATIVE OPENING PRAYER

Let us pray

Pause for silent prayer

God our Father,
gifts without measure flow from your goodness
to bring us your peace.
Our life is your gift.
Guide our life's journey,
for only your love makes us whole.
Keep us strong in your love.

We ask this through Christ our Lord.
Amen.

FIRST READING

Eccl 1:2; 2:21-23

Vanity of vanities, says Qoheleth,
vanity of vanities! All things are vanity!

Here is one who has labored with wisdom
and knowledge and skill,
and yet to another who has not labored over it,
he must leave property.
This also is vanity and a great misfortune.
For what profit comes to man from all the toil and anxiety of heart
with which he has labored under the sun?
All his days sorrow and grief are his occupation;
even at night his mind is not at rest.
This also is vanity.

RESPONSORIAL PSALM

Ps 90:3-4, 5-6, 12-13, 14, 17

R̶. (8) If today you hear his voice, harden not your hearts.

You turn man back to dust,
saying, "Return, O children of men."
For a thousand years in your sight
are as yesterday, now that it is past,
or as a watch of the night.

R̶. If today you hear his voice, harden not your hearts.

You make an end of them in their sleep;
the next morning they are like the changing grass,
which at dawn springs up anew,
but by evening wilts and fades.

R̶. If today you hear his voice, harden not your hearts.

Teach us to number our days aright,
that we may gain wisdom of heart.
Return, O LORD! How long?
Have pity on your servants!

R℣. If today you hear his voice, harden not your hearts.

Fill us at daybreak with your kindness,
    that we may shout for joy and gladness
        all our days.
And may the gracious care of the LORD
    our God be ours;
    prosper the work of our hands for us!
    Prosper the work of our hands!

R℣. If today you hear his voice, harden not your hearts.

SECOND READING
Col 3:1-5, 9-11

Brothers and sisters:
If you were raised with Christ, seek what
    is above,
    where Christ is seated at the right hand
        of God.
Think of what is above, not of what is on
    earth.
For you have died,
    and your life is hidden with Christ in
        God.
When Christ your life appears,
    then you too will appear with him in
        glory.

Put to death, then, the parts of you that
    are earthly:
    immorality, impurity, passion, evil
        desire,
    and the greed that is idolatry.
Stop lying to one another,
    since you have taken off the old self
        with its practices
    and have put on the new self,
    which is being renewed, for knowledge,
    in the image of its creator.
Here there is not Greek and Jew,
    circumcision and uncircumcision,
    barbarian, Scythian, slave, free;
    but Christ is all and in all.

About Liturgy

Second reading during Ordinary Time: Usually during Ordinary Time the second reading is not related to the gospel or first reading. Instead, the second reading is a sequential selection from one of the New Testament letters; that is, one letter is read for a number of Sundays until it is completed, then another letter is begun. Almost always it takes a great deal of "mental gymnastics" to connect the second reading to the first reading or the gospel. Consequently, the second reading is best disregarded when preparing the communal celebration of liturgy and best used for private prayer and preparation for Sunday liturgy.

This Sunday, however, the second reading from Colossians is a happy coincidence. It not only fits nicely with the first reading and gospel, it even adds perspective and depth to the gospel parable. This Sunday it would be advantageous to dwell on the second reading, especially on the phrase "Christ is all and in all" with respect to Christian priorities of discipleship.

About Liturgical Music

Cantor preparation: The refrain for this responsorial psalm is challenging: whenever God's voice confronts, the human heart resists. This is normal and to be expected, for conversion is never easy. When do you find yourself resisting God's voice? Who or what helps you open your heart despite its resistance?

Singing the acclamations, part 5: The "Amens" with which we conclude each of the presidential prayers parallel the great amen with which we conclude the Eucharistic prayer, the high point and climax of the entire rite (see GIRM nos. 30, 78). These "Amens" are, in a sense, a "practice run" for our great amen. As the collects themselves, the Eucharistic prayer is the prayer of the entire assembly who, through the voice of the presider, "join [themselves] to Christ in acknowledging the great things God has done and in offering the sacrifice" (GIRM no. 78). We participate in this great prayer through both silence and acclamation. The silence called for is not inattentive or distracted, but fully engaged. We listen wholeheartedly to the prayer because we are the ones offering and being offered, we are the ones being transformed into the Body of Christ, we are the ones being given with Christ for the life of the world (see GIRM no. 95). And out of this attentive silence we shout "Amen!" to who we are and who we are becoming.

SPIRITUALITY

Gospel
Luke 12:32-48; L117C

Jesus said to his disciples:
"Do not be afraid any longer, little
flock,
for your Father is pleased
to give you the
kingdom.
Sell your belongings and
give alms.
Provide money bags for
yourselves that do not
wear out,
an inexhaustible treasure
in heaven
that no thief can reach
nor moth destroy.
For where your treasure is,
there also will your heart be.

"Gird your loins and light your lamps
and be like servants who await their
master's return from a wedding,
ready to open immediately when he
comes and knocks.
Blessed are those servants
whom the master finds vigilant on his
arrival.
Amen, I say to you, he will gird
himself,
have them recline at table, and
proceed to wait on them.
And should he come in the second or
third watch
and find them prepared in this way,
blessed are those servants.
Be sure of this:
if the master of the house had known
the hour
when the thief was coming,
he would not have let his house be
broken into.
You also must be prepared, for at an
hour you do not expect,
the Son of Man will come."

Continued in Appendix A, p. 301.

Reflecting on the Gospel
We know there is no pot of gold at the end of the rainbow, but we look for it anyway, do we not? Has there not been a great deal of speculation about what sank with the safe on board the Titanic? Are we not in awe about the incredible gold artifacts discovered in King Tut's tomb? In spite of incredible odds against us, does not the sale of lottery tickets rise proportionately to the size of the payoff? We all dream of finding treasures. We somehow never quite lose that dream, even after we are absorbed by the practicalities of adult living and responsibilities.

What happens to the few lucky ones who actually receive a treasure? Statistics tell us that the majority of large lottery winners are broke and in debt within a few years. How interesting! Where's the treasure? How lasting is it? Not very!

And, yet, how many of us don't spend our whole lives going after these and other just as perishable and exhaustible "treasures"? We are easily lured into fooling ourselves about what really are our needs. Jesus redirects our pursuits when he instructs his disciples that their "treasure [is] in heaven." Jesus admonishes his disciples to be vigilant for the "master's return," to be eager to learn and do the "master's will," and to be "faithful" though the master's coming is delayed. Though much is required of them, more will be given to them: "your Father is pleased to give you the kingdom."

In the first reading we read that the Hebrew people were forewarned about the "night of the passover" and, therefore, were able to "have courage." In the gospel Jesus is forewarning his disciples about their ultimate passover to heavenly treasures so that they may be properly prepared. Indeed, we spend our whole lives "passing over" from pursuing earthly treasures to seeking "inexhaustible treasure in heaven." What helps us in our daily passover is vigilance—keeping our lives focused on God who entrusts us with much: preparing ourselves for the coming of "the Son of Man." All inexhaustible treasure depends upon our readiness. Delay does not matter; seeking God does.

Living the Paschal Mystery
There are many treasures found in this life: education, communication, philanthropy, family. These are good but exhaustible. What Jesus offers us is an inexhaustible treasure: the fullness of life in God's kingdom ("your Father is pleased to give you the kingdom").

It is so true that we live according to where our treasure is. This is why the way we live as disciples is so critical. This is why being a disciple is not something we slot into our already too busy schedules: one hour a week for Mass, so much money in the collection basket, another hour a week doing some volunteer work. Being a disciple is just that—*being*. It is much more a matter of the surrender of our whole selves to the "master's will" which means, first, being true to making present the kingdom which has already been given to us. This is the "much" with which we have been entrusted: who we are and how we live makes present God's kingdom.

The way we live, therefore, witnesses to where our treasure is. Our very living challenges others to prioritize their own treasures. Clearly, God must have priority in our lives. We make this apparent when religion is not so much practices we do as it is a loving relationship we develop as we encounter God and then extend that life we are given to others.

Focusing the Gospel

Key words and phrases: give you the kingdom, treasure in heaven, vigilant, faithful, master's will, Much will be required

To the point: Jesus instructs his disciples that their "treasure [is] in heaven." Therefore, he admonishes them to be vigilant for the "master's return," to be eager to learn and do the "master's will," and to be "faithful" though the master's coming is delayed. Though much is required of them, more will be given to them: "your Father is pleased to give you the kingdom."

Connecting the Gospel

to the first reading: The Hebrew people were forewarned about the "night of the passover" and, therefore, were able to "have courage." In the gospel Jesus is forewarning his disciples about their ultimate passover to heavenly treasures so that they may be properly prepared.

to our culture: There are many treasures found in this life: education, communication, philanthropy, family. These are good but exhaustible. What Jesus offers us is an inexhaustible treasure: the fullness of life in God's kingdom ("your Father is pleased to give you the kingdom").

Understanding Scripture

Vigilance and preparedness: After the parable of the rich man last week, the Lectionary skips Jesus' saying about God's care for the flowers of the field and the birds of the sky. The opening verses of this Sunday's gospel continue the theme of divine providence for the disciples of Jesus—his "little flock." They continue, too, the contrast between earthly treasure which will perish and heavenly treasure which is imperishable. These verses really conclude the previous series of sayings and are connected to last Sunday's gospel about true wealth. The saying, "Gird your loins" (v. 35) begins a new section which first talks about vigilance and then fidelity.

This new section begins with two parables addressed to the disciples in general (vv. 35-40). The first parable about the return of the master from a wedding urges vigilance, even into the third and last watch of the night. Apparently, Luke felt the Master (that is, the Lord) was delayed, but the delay was not cause to relax one's expectation and vigilance for his return. The second parable about the thief who breaks in follows up the theme of vigilance with the theme of preparation. One cannot stay awake all the time—at some point, one must sleep. But even if one cannot be vigilant, one can be prepared. In the language of discipleship, preparedness is being faithful to one's duties despite the delay. Faithfulness leads to the sayings addressed to Peter, that is, to the leadership (vv. 41-48).

Like the parable addressed to the disciples in the first section, this parable is about servants awaiting the return of the master. Again, the issue is the delay of the Master and being prepared. Faithful discipleship does not try to guess when the master will return and calculate how long one can be derelict in duty or abusive of the household staff, and then "change" in time for the master's return. Disciples know the "master's will" and are to "make preparations" or risk the consequences. This requirement is even more pressing for those in leadership, as the closing line makes clear.

**ASSEMBLY &
FAITH-SHARING GROUPS**

- My lifestyle tells me that my treasure and my heart is . . .
- When I act as though my treasure is in heaven, my lifestyle looks like . . .
- I remain vigilant about and faithful to my heavenly treasures while my Master is delayed in returning by . . .

PRESIDERS
In my preaching I balance the *promise* ("Do not be afraid . . . for your Father is pleased to give you the kingdom") and the *challenge* ("Much will be required of the person entrusted with much") by . . .

DEACONS
I balance my work for exhaustible treasures to provide for my family with the preparation for the "inexhaustible treasure in heaven" by . . .

HOSPITALITY MINISTERS
Tending to the demands of hospitality forms me into a vigilant servant because . . .

MUSIC MINISTERS
Jesus tells his disciples that those who have been entrusted with much will have much required of them. As a music minister, God has entrusted me with . . . What God expects of me is . . .

ALTAR MINISTERS
I assist others in being ready for the Son of Man's return when I . . .

LECTORS
The kind of treasure my lifestyle proclaims to others is . . .

**EXTRAORDINARY MINISTERS
OF HOLY COMMUNION**
I help the infirmed realize the heavenly treasure promised them by . . . ; I help them remain vigilant until the Lord's return by . . .

Model Act of Penitence

Presider: God promises inexhaustible treasure in heaven for servants who are vigilant and faithful. Let us prepare to celebrate the inexhaustible treasure given to us in this Eucharist . . . [pause]

Lord Jesus, you teach us how to be vigilant and faithful: Lord . . .

Christ Jesus, you are the Son of Man who will return in glory: Christ . . .

Lord Jesus, you lead us to our treasure in heaven: Lord . . .

Appreciating the Responsorial Psalm

Jesus tells us in this Sunday's gospel that where our treasure is there will be our heart. Along this very line, the responsorial psalm says something remarkable about God: we are God's treasure, chosen as "his own inheritance." And where God's treasure is, God's heart will be. We are the treasure whom God will preserve and deliver whatever the cost (psalm). We are the chosen flock to whom God grants the kingdom (gospel). It is no wonder that we can put indomitable hope in this God who is "our help and our shield." In singing this psalm we proclaim the value God places upon us. We also declare the value we place upon God.

Model General Intercessions

Presider: God is the faithful One who makes good on the promise to give us abundant treasure. Let us pray with confidence for our needs.

Response:

Lord, hear our prayer.

Cantor:

we pray to the Lord,

That the Church always remain vigilant and faithful as she awaits the return of the Lord . . . [pause]

That all people of the world may know God's will for them and act accordingly . . . [pause]

That those who lack their proper share in the treasures of this earth receive justice . . . [pause]

That all of us here may serve others with diligence and grace . . . [pause]

Presider: Good and gracious God, you give inexhaustible treasure in heaven to those who serve you faithfully: hear these our prayers that one day we might share fully in your glory. We ask this through Christ our Lord. **Amen.**

ALTERNATIVE OPENING PRAYER

Let us pray

Pause for silent prayer

Father,
we come, reborn in the Spirit,
to celebrate our sonship in the Lord Jesus Christ.
Touch our hearts,
help them grow toward the life you have promised.
Touch our lives,
make them signs of your love for all men.

Grant this through Christ our Lord.
Amen.

FIRST READING

Wis 18:6-9

The night of the passover was known beforehand to our fathers,
that, with sure knowledge of the oaths in which they put their faith,
they might have courage.
Your people awaited the salvation of the just
and the destruction of their foes.
For when you punished our adversaries,
in this you glorified us whom you had summoned.
For in secret the holy children of the good were offering sacrifice
and putting into effect with one accord the divine institution.

RESPONSORIAL PSALM
Ps 33:1, 12, 18-19, 20-22

R℣. (12b) Blessed the people the Lord has chosen to be his own.

Exult, you just, in the LORD;
    praise from the upright is fitting.
Blessed the nation whose God is the LORD,
    the people he has chosen for his own
        inheritance.

R℣. Blessed the people the Lord has chosen to be his own.

See, the eyes of the Lord are upon those
        who fear him,
    upon those who hope for his kindness,
to deliver them from death
    and preserve them in spite of famine.

R℣. Blessed the people the Lord has chosen to be his own.

Our soul waits for the LORD,
    who is our help and our shield.
May your kindness, O LORD, be upon us
    who have put our hope in you.

R℣. Blessed the people the Lord has chosen to be his own.

SECOND READING
Heb 11:1-2, 8-19

Brothers and sisters:
Faith is the realization of what is hoped
        for
    and evidence of things not seen.
Because of it the ancients were well attested.

By faith Abraham obeyed when he was
        called to go out to a place
    that he was to receive as an inheritance;
    he went out, not knowing where he was
        to go.
By faith he sojourned in the promised land
        as in a foreign country,
    dwelling in tents with Isaac and Jacob,
        heirs of the same promise;
    for he was looking forward to the city
        with foundations,
    whose architect and maker is God.
By faith he received power to generate,
    even though he was past the normal age
    —and Sarah herself was sterile—
    for he thought that the one who had
        made the promise was trustworthy.

Continued in Appendix A, p. 301.

About Liturgy

Sunday collection and responsibility as parish community: This Sunday invites us not only to consider where our own treasure lies, but it also invites us to consider where is our treasure as a parish community. Each Sunday a collection is taken up. Most of the money goes to the necessary financial obligations of the parish—salaries, building upkeep, programs and services. It is good to remind ourselves regularly, in addition to these necessary costs, that some of our gifts each Sunday must be set aside so that others less fortunate than we can share more equally in the treasures of this earth. Yes, each parish community has financial obligations; but each parish community also has *people* obligations. We witness to where our treasure really lies when we make some of our resources available to those less fortunate than we.

Most parishes nowadays are pretty strapped financially. In many cases staffs are being cut, programs curtailed, services less apparent. These are the times when it is very tempting to be less resolved about sharing out of our need with those even more needy. Yet this kind of sharing out of need is really what constitutes our "inexhaustible treasure."

About Liturgical Music

Cantor preparation: Jesus calls you as cantor to be a faithful and vigilant servant, ever ready for his coming. How does Jesus come to you in the Liturgy of the Word each week? How does he come to you as you prepare to sing the responsorial psalm? How does he come to the assembly as you lead them in singing the psalm?

Singing the acclamations, part 6: The acclamations we express as part of the liturgy celebrate the full maturity God desires for us as the baptized. The acclamations are our ritual acknowledgment of the dignity and power bestowed upon us by divine plan. In our "Amen" to the collects we make the prayer our own. In our acclamations before and after the readings we make the Word our own. In our acclamations during and concluding the Eucharistic prayer we make the great offering of Christ our own. We lay ourselves upon the altar in the supreme fulfillment of our shared priesthood, offering and being offered, giving and being given, consuming and being consumed. No wonder GIRM mandates us to sing these acclamations in every celebration of the Mass!

SPIRITUALITY

Gospel
Luke 1:39-56; L622

Mary set out
  and traveled to the hill country in
    haste
  to a town of Judah,
  where she entered the house of
    Zechariah
  and greeted Elizabeth.
When Elizabeth heard Mary's greet-
    ing,
  the infant leaped in her womb,
  and Elizabeth, filled with the Holy
    Spirit,
  cried out in a loud voice and said,
  "Blessed are you among women,
  and blessed is the fruit of your
    womb.
And how does this happen to me,
  that the mother of my Lord should
    come to me?
For at the moment the sound of your
    greeting reached my ears,
  the infant in my womb leaped for joy.
Blessed are you who believed
  that what was spoken to you by the
    Lord
  would be fulfilled."

And Mary said:
  "My soul proclaims the greatness of
    the Lord;
    my spirit rejoices in God my Savior
    for he has looked upon his lowly
      servant.
  From this day all generations will call
    me blessed:
    the Almighty has done great things
      for me,
    and holy is his Name.
  He has mercy on those who fear him
    in every generation.
  He has shown the strength of his arm,
    and has scattered the proud in
      their conceit.

Continued in Appendix A, p. 302.
See Appendix A, p. 302, for the other readings.

Reflecting on the Gospel

Mary's assumption of body and soul into heaven is a dogma defined by the Church. It is fitting that we thus honor Mary because it was her body which was the first temple for the Son of God. She conceived, nurtured, allowed to grow, and gave birth to Jesus—all because she willingly gave her body as an instrument for God to work the wonders of salvation. This holy body now enjoys full union with her divine Son in eternal glory.

Besides this singular privilege of Mary, the assumption also celebrates the faithfulness of God who "remembered his promise of mercy." Mary experienced God's mercy as a "lowly servant" whom God has "looked upon" and "lifted up." God's faithfulness brings that mercy to fulfillment in Mary's assumption when the lowly maiden of Nazareth is "clothed with the sun" (first reading). Mary's call, her giving birth, and her being glorified all testify to the God who faithfully and tirelessly works for our salvation. Mary's blessing goes beyond even what we would have thought (the conception and birth of the divine Son): "all generations will call [her] blessed," and "the Almighty has done great things" for her. By her assumption into glory, God has "shown the strength of his arm" and the greatness of his love.

The high favor God has shown Mary goes beyond even her yes to be the Mother of the divine Son. Throughout her life we see Mary doing these things: she went on a mission ("traveled to the hill country in haste") to meet her cousin Elizabeth; she listened to Elizabeth's acknowledgment of God's great deeds being worked through her; she responded with her great prayer of praise, the *Magnificat;* she allowed God's grace within her to form her perspective and priorities; she responded faithfully to whatever God asked of her, even when it brought pain and suffering; she was faithful to her Son, standing by the cross at his death; and she was no doubt among the disciples who witnessed the presence of the risen Christ.

Surely the "Almighty has done great things" for Mary. She responded with her whole being and life, and now "all generations will call [her] blessed." On this festival we honor Mary for her fidelity and we celebrate God's faithfulness in bringing us salvation through the divine Son.

Living the Paschal Mystery

We have many examples from Scripture where God uses mighty things to carry forward God's plan of salvation. We have only to think of the ten plagues, manna in the desert, and overcoming Israel's Canaanite enemies so they could occupy the Promised Land. God also uses colorful and forceful people. We have only to think of the power of Moses' staff, the wisdom of Solomon, the love of David, the moving and poetic prophecies of Isaiah, the fire of Elijah.

God also uses simple things and persons in the plan of salvation. On this solemnity we honor Mary—a simple maiden without title or means. She it was who in her very being bore the Christ. She it was who heard the Word, bore the Word, and then in her very being was a herald of the Word. If this simple maiden girl can change the course of history with her fervent yes, can we not model our own lives after hers? Just as God chose this simple maiden, so does God choose each of us. Like Mary, we only need say yes and be faithful to that commitment. Like Mary, we must hear the Word, bear the Word, and herald the Word.

Focusing the Gospel

Key words and phrases: lowly servant, lifted up, remembered his promise of mercy

To the point: The assumption celebrates the faithfulness of God who "remembered his promise of mercy." Mary experienced God's mercy as a "lowly servant" whom God has "looked upon" and "lifted up." God's faithfulness brings that mercy to fulfillment in Mary's assumption when the lowly maiden of Nazareth is "clothed with the sun" (first reading). Mary's call, her giving birth, and her being glorified all testify to the God who faithfully and tirelessly works for our salvation.

Model Act of Penitence

Presider: Today we honor Mary who was taken body and soul into heaven to share the divine glory of the One to whom she gave birth. Let us reflect on her Son, the source of our salvation . . . [pause]

Lord Jesus, you were born of the virgin Mary: Lord . . .

Christ Jesus, you are the Son of God: Christ . . .

Lord Jesus, you are God's promise of mercy fulfilled: Lord . . .

Model General Intercessions

Presider: God did mighty things for Mary, and will do mighty things for us. And so we are encouraged to lift our needs to God.

Response:

Cantor:

That all members of the Church may faithfully announce God's mercy by the way they live . . . [pause]

That all peoples of the world surrender themselves to God's plan of salvation . . . [pause]

That the poor be lifted up and the hungry be satisfied . . . [pause]

That all of us here be always attentive to the many visitations of God in our lives . . . [pause]

Presider: All powerful God, you accomplish your plan of salvation through the simple and faithful: hear these our prayers that we might one day share in the glory of your eternal life. We ask this through Jesus Christ. **Amen.**

ALTERNATIVE OPENING PRAYER
Let us pray

Pause for silent prayer

Father in heaven,
all creation rightly gives you praise,
for all life and all holiness come from you.
In the plan of your wisdom
she who bore the Christ in her womb
was raised body and soul in glory to be
    with him in heaven.
May we follow her example in reflecting
    your holiness
and join in her hymn of endless life and
    praise.

We ask this through Christ our Lord.
    Amen.

FOR REFLECTION

- The hope I gain by recalling this "great thing" God has done for Mary is . . .

- I imitate Mary and proclaim the "greatness of the Lord" when I . . .

- The next step for me to become more like Mary is . . .

SPIRITUALITY

Gospel

Luke 12:49-53; L120C

Jesus said to his disciples:
"I have come to set the earth on fire,
and how I wish it were already
blazing!
There is a baptism with which I must
be baptized,
and how great is my anguish until it
is accomplished!
Do you think that I have come to
establish peace on the earth?
No, I tell you, but rather division.
From now on a household of five will
be divided,
three against two and two against
three;
a father will be divided against his
son
and a son against his father,
a mother against her daughter
and a daughter against her mother,
a mother-in-law against her daughter-
in-law
and a daughter-in-law against her
mother-in-law."

Reflecting on the Gospel

Some marriage counselors advocate that a good fight every once in a while makes a marriage strong. Obviously, these experts are not proposing that disagreements are desirable in a marriage! They do suggest that differing needs and desires, talking things through, and coming to a good compromise can make a relationship stronger when the couple comes to understand themselves and each other better. While this may be true, none of us really seeks or desires division and strife, especially among those whom we cherish most. In this Sunday's gospel, Jesus is shocking! Did he come to bring division and not peace? This also seems to contradict what we know of Jesus. After the resurrection Jesus appears to the disciples and extends to them his peace (see Luke 24:36 and parallels). What do we make of this gospel?

Jeremiah's preaching (see first reading) divided the city and incited such opposition that people sought his death. Standing in this prophetic tradition, Jesus, too, preaches a word which divides families and leads ultimately to his death. Like the prophets of old, Jesus has a fire for accomplishing his mission and is single-minded in doing so. He is unswerving in the Good News he preaches, but in this Jesus also brings division: some follow him, some oppose him. Both Jeremiah and Jesus meet fierce and life-threatening opposition to their faithful preaching of God's word. People are divided about whether or not God is, in fact, working through these prophets. Making such a decision is exactly what Jesus came to instigate.

The pivotal point is that neither Jesus nor we *choose* division and strife; we choose to speak God's word and preach the values consistent with God's reign. Divisions occur simply by being faithful to God's message. This is the real shock value of the gospel: being a faithful disciple of Jesus will instigate a clash of values, of principles, of priorities.

Jesus' very message is divisive because it calls others to a radical way of living—self-giving for the good of others. We must make a decision to follow him or not, to share his Passion ("baptism") or not, to be self-giving as he is. This choice results in division, even within families, because all of us do not make the same choice to follow Jesus.

Jesus came to preach the good news of radical fidelity to God. Paradoxically, being faithful to Jesus (even when this brings strife and divisions) is how we come to lasting peace. If we compromise our gospel message in order to have peace now, we forfeit the everlasting peace which is promised the faithful disciple. The choice is ours.

Living the Paschal Mystery

Realistically, most of us do not live our discipleship this dramatically nor are we faced with such consequential choices. We are hardly called like Jeremiah to announce to the Israelites that their beloved Jerusalem will fall into the hands of the Babylonians—nor are we thrown into a cistern to die! Nor like Jesus will we be nailed to a cross because of our preaching. Nevertheless, we are called to be faithful to God's word in the small, everyday things as well as at times when the more serious challenges come along. We do not seek division, but we seek consistency in living Gospel values. The very way we live our lives is a way to preach the Gospel. Sometimes strife and division is a sign of our faithful commitment. Gospel living is not always easy!

Focusing the Gospel

Key words and phrases: fire, baptism, peace, division, household

To the point: Jesus is shocking! Did he come to bring division and not peace? Like the prophets of old (see first reading), Jesus has a fire for accomplishing his mission. In pursuing his mission, he brings division: some follow him, some oppose him. We must make a decision to follow him or not, to share his baptism or not. This choice results in division, even within families.

Connecting the Gospel

to the first reading: Jeremiah's preaching divided the city and incited such opposition that people sought his death. Standing in this prophetic tradition, Jesus, too, preaches a word which divides families and leads ultimately to his death.

to our human experience: None of us seeks or desires division and strife, especially among those whom we cherish most. Sometimes, however, the choice is so clear and the values are so important, that we accept division and strife as a consequence of our choice.

Understanding Scripture

Deciding causes division: In the gospel, Jesus uses the image of "fire" to describe his mission. His zeal for his mission and his sense of urgency for his work are evident in his desire: "how I wish it were already blazing!" In the Bible, fire is sometimes an image for purification (for example, Num 31:23; Ezek 22:19-22), but more often for judgment (for example, Judith 16:17; Isa 66:16; Amos 7:4; 2 Pet 3:7). Built into the act of judgment is the process of separating or deciding for some and against others: the wicked are condemned and the righteous are vindicated and saved. We know this in legal disputes: both parties do not win. There is a winner and a loser.

That kind of clear distinction will also be evident in the ministry of Jesus: his words and deeds will cause division as some decide for him and some against him. Indeed, his very person and presence demand such a decision. The close connection between decision and division is spelled out in highly personal terms: households will be divided and family relations will be disrupted by deciding for or against Jesus. While avoiding a decision may maintain a kind of family peace, it is a hollow peace which serves only to maintain the status quo.

From fire, Jesus moves to the image of the "baptism with which I must be baptized," a reference to his Passion (for example, Mark 10:38). The images of fire and baptism refer to his mission, both in terms of the cost that it will exact from him and the decision it will require of people.

Finally, these words are spoken by Jesus on the way to Jerusalem where he will suffer and die. They recall the words of John the Baptist who had earlier spoken of the coming of one mightier than he who would "*baptize* you with the Holy Spirit and with *fire*" (Luke 3:16). As Jesus walks the road to Jerusalem, disciples must decide to go with him or not. To be with or against Jesus is a decision which has the effect of judgment and division.

ASSEMBLY & FAITH-SHARING GROUPS

- Where I experience "great . . . anguish" for Jesus' mission to be "accomplished" is . . .
- Faith has brought divisiveness into my life when . . .
- I understand these moments of divisiveness to be proper to good discipleship (and not unhealthy) because . . .

PRESIDERS

I support and strengthen others who struggle to remain faithful to God's will by . . .

DEACONS

Even when there is painful divisiveness around me, I am able to remain faithful to Jesus' mission because . . .

HOSPITALITY MINISTERS

I assist the assembly to be vulnerable before God's radical call to discipleship whenever I . . .

MUSIC MINISTERS

Jesus promises division to anyone who remains faithful to him. But divisiveness can also be a sign of lack of fidelity to Christ. What helps me discern the difference whenever divisiveness affects my music ministry is . . .

ALTAR MINISTERS

I serve others by helping them to choose Jesus and follow him faithfully by . . .

LECTORS

The word stirs up a fire inside me to accomplish God's will when . . .

EXTRAORDINARY MINISTERS OF HOLY COMMUNION

The Eucharist brings me peace by . . . the Eucharist challenges me by . . .

Model Act of Penitence

Presider: Jesus was always faithful to his mission. In this liturgy let us pray that we may be strengthened to be faithful to him in all things . . . [pause]

Lord Jesus, you accomplish all that you came to do: Lord . . .

Christ Jesus, you come to set the earth on fire: Christ . . .

Lord Jesus, you strengthen us by word and sacrament: Lord . . .

Appreciating the Responsorial Psalm

In the first reading Jeremiah is thrown into a muddy cistern because he challenged the leaders of Israel. Jesus tells us in the gospel that we, too, will face extreme opposition if we follow him. Discipleship demands a willingness to stand alone, to be cut off even from those close to us when the call of Christ requires it. But the responsorial psalm reminds us that we are not, in fact, left alone. When human persons turn away from or against us because of our fidelity to discipleship, God will stoop close. Nothing can erase the cost of discipleship, but neither can anything destroy God's care for and protection of us. Although we may die, as did Jesus, God will not abandon us to death but will raise us to new life. In singing this psalm we express our absolute trust in God who will "hold back" nothing in our support.

Model General Intercessions

Presider: God hears the cry of the faithful. Let us confidently place our needs in God's hands.

Response:

Lord, hear our prayer.

Cantor:

we pray to the Lord,

That all members of the Church may seek Christ above all else . . . [pause]

That all people of the world may strive for peace in the midst of divisions . . . [pause]

That those struggling with the cost of discipleship may have strength and courage . . . [pause]

That each of us here continually renew our commitment to faithful discipleship . . . [pause]

Presider: O God, you inflame our hearts with passion for the mission of your Son: hear these our prayers that we remain faithful. We ask this through Christ our Lord. **Amen.**

ALTERNATIVE OPENING PRAYER

Let us pray

Pause for silent prayer

Almighty God, ever-loving Father,
your care extends beyond the boundaries
    of race and nation
to the hearts of all who live.
May the walls, which prejudice raises
    between us,
crumble beneath the shadow of your
    outstretched arm.

We ask this through Christ our Lord.
    Amen.

FIRST READING
Jer 38:4-6, 8-10

In those days, the princes said to the king:
    "Jeremiah ought to be put to death;
    he is demoralizing the soldiers who are
        left in this city,
    and all the people, by speaking such
        things to them;
    he is not interested in the welfare of our
        people,
    but in their ruin."
King Zedekiah answered: "He is in your
        power";
    for the king could do nothing with them.
And so they took Jeremiah
    and threw him into the cistern of Prince
        Malchiah,
    which was in the quarters of the guard,
    letting him down with ropes.
There was no water in the cistern, only
        mud,
    and Jeremiah sank into the mud.

Ebed-melech, a court official,
    went there from the palace and said to
        him:
    "My lord king,
    these men have been at fault
    in all they have done to the prophet
        Jeremiah,
    casting him into the cistern.
He will die of famine on the spot,
    for there is no more food in the city."
Then the king ordered Ebed-melech the
        Cushite
    to take three men along with him,
    and draw the prophet Jeremiah out of
        the cistern before he should die.

RESPONSORIAL PSALM
Ps 40:2, 3, 4, 18

R̷. (14b) Lord, come to my aid!

I have waited, waited for the LORD,
    and he stooped toward me.

R̷. Lord, come to my aid!

The LORD heard my cry.
He drew me out of the pit of destruction,
    out of the mud of the swamp;
he set my feet upon a crag;
    he made firm my steps.

R̷. Lord, come to my aid!

And he put a new song into my mouth,
    a hymn to our God.
Many shall look on in awe
    and trust in the LORD.

R̷. Lord, come to my aid!

Though I am afflicted and poor,
    yet the LORD thinks of me.
You are my help and my deliverer;
    O my God, hold not back!

R̷. Lord, come to my aid!

SECOND READING
Heb 12:1-4

Brothers and sisters:
Since we are surrounded by so great a
    cloud of witnesses,
    let us rid ourselves of every burden and
        sin that clings to us
    and persevere in running the race that
        lies before us
    while keeping our eyes fixed on Jesus,
    the leader and perfecter of faith.
For the sake of the joy that lay before him
    he endured the cross, despising its
        shame,
    and has taken his seat at the right of
        the throne of God.
Consider how he endured such opposition
    from sinners,
    in order that you may not grow weary
        and lose heart.
In your struggle against sin
    you have not yet resisted to the point of
        shedding blood.

About Liturgy

Liturgy and strife: Strife and divisiveness is not always located within family households; it can also be evidenced on liturgy committees and in parishes! There are probably few things in parish life which cause divisions the way the decisions about the celebration of liturgy can. Is it not ironic that the very celebration whereby we express our unity in the Body of Christ can be the cause for so much anger, anguish, and divisiveness?

Sometimes a parish can be radically split about how to celebrate liturgy because "good" liturgy is judged in terms of what individuals or groups want, desire, or find satisfying. Ideally, everyone would come to Sunday Mass each Sunday and go home satisfied, filled, and spiritually and emotionally fed. In reality, this does not happen to everyone in the same way and at the same time. One way to deal with this issue is to remember that the purpose of liturgy is not primarily our own satisfaction, but the purpose of liturgy is to give God praise and thanksgiving by offering ourselves with Christ on the altar. Only by such self-giving, and by keeping this the focus, can we hope to overcome divisions and improve our celebration of liturgy.

About Liturgical Music

Cantor preparation: In this psalm you call God to "come to my aid." In the context of the readings, this is a cry raised in face of persecution experienced because you are being faithful to discipleship. When have you found yourself meeting such opposition? What helped you remain faithful? How did God come to your aid?

Singing the acclamations, part 7: As acts of direct address to God, the acclamations have formative impact on our self-understanding and our manner of living out our baptismal identity. Voicing the acclamations is a way of taking ownership of ourselves and our relationship with God. The acclamations teach us that beneath all prayer (whether cries for help, or prayers for healing, or confessions of sin, or words of thanksgiving) stands the empowerment of our baptismal right to address God face to face. When we sing the acclamations we dare the one gesture forbidden mere mortals—to look directly upon the face of God—and discover in that act not death but dignity.

Once we understand what we are doing ritually in the acclamations, we can never again look upon self or others in a demeaning way, nor can we ever again approach life's challenges with a sense of disempowerment. Instead we see in self and others the dignity bestowed by God and act toward both with reverence and appreciation. And we interpret events (both personal and social, both close at hand and worldwide) not as interventions or judgments of a distant God, but as invitations to engage our power with God's in the mutual work of redemption. In short, we grow to full stature before God and take on our share of responsibility for the coming of the kingdom. To sing the acclamations, then, is to engage fully, consciously, and actively both in liturgical celebration and in all of Christian living.

SPIRITUALITY

Gospel
Luke 13:22-30; L123C

Jesus passed through towns and
    villages,
  teaching as he went and making
    his way to Jerusalem.
Someone asked him,
  "Lord, will only a few people be
    saved?"
He answered them,
  "Strive to enter through the
    narrow gate,
  for many, I tell you, will attempt
    to enter
  but will not be strong enough.
After the master of the house has
    arisen and locked the door,
  then will you stand outside
    knocking and saying,
  'Lord, open the door for us.'
He will say to you in reply,
  'I do not know where you are from.'
And you will say,
  'We ate and drank in your company
    and you taught in our streets.'
Then he will say to you,
  'I do not know where you are from.
Depart from me, all you evildoers!'
And there will be wailing and grinding
    of teeth
  when you see Abraham, Isaac, and
    Jacob
  and all the prophets in the kingdom
    of God
  and you yourselves cast out.
And people will come from the east and
    the west
  and from the north and the south
  and will recline at table in the
    kingdom of God.
For behold, some are last who will be
    first,
  and some are first who will be last."

Reflecting on the Gospel

Rejection is never easy to accept. This is the basis for why peer group pressure among adolescents is so strong a force in their lives—they want to belong. Being fired from a job is more than losing salary; it is a rejection—that our work is not adequate or our talents are not needed nor appreciated. Broken friendships are painful—especially when one loses interest and simply does not bother to be in touch with the other. It is probably impossible to go through life and not experience some kind of rejection; it seems to be part of how we humans relate. This Sunday's gospel speaks of a much more painful and lasting rejection—those who are not admitted to eternal life.

"I do not know where you are from," Jesus says twice in this gospel. This is another way of saying, "I do not know you." Such rejection! In such a way Jesus point blank reminds us that some are saved, others are not. Jesus does not answer the gospel person's question about *how many* will be saved; instead, he describes *who* will be saved (people from all over the world, those who are last, those who enter the banquet hall while the door is open). While the gate to salvation is narrow and difficult, it is open to all who are known by Jesus.

Being known by Jesus goes beyond merely associating with him ("We ate and drank in your company") to walking with him to Jerusalem. Therefore, the more significant question we must ask is, "Do we know where Jesus is from?" Even more important, do we know where Jesus is going (Jerusalem) and are we willing to go there with him? Thus the real surprise of the gospel is that being saved is not accomplished by mere association with Jesus, but by the *transformation* which comes from sharing in his life, death, and resurrection.

What is required for salvation? We must walk with Jesus to Jerusalem! Like Jesus, we too will meet opposition; we too must die to ourselves in self-giving to others. Alone, this is a daunting task. But we are not alone; Jesus is with us to support us and give us strength. We need only keep close to him. We need only keep our eyes on him rather than count the cost. Then we, too, can "recline at table in the kingdom of God" with him. His table is the banquet of eternal life. This is why the demands of discipleship do not overwhelm us completely. Sure, it costs. Sure, there is dying. At the same time there is also the rising!

Living the Paschal Mystery

Usually parents barely have begun a long trip with the children when they begin the chant, "Are we there yet?" Sometimes this is our chant, too, on our paschal journey. We want the dying to be over. We want the eternal new life which comes from knowing who Jesus is and being faithful to him. In God's good time, that will come. In the meantime, we are to walk with him to Jerusalem.

Part of discipleship is to be faithful to the everyday "plodding" of our paschal journey. If we try and rush it, we will miss opportunities—graced moments which bring us closer to salvation. Discipleship requires consistent and faithful decisions so that Jesus gets to "know us" on the way. Then we are invited to be his guest at his table. Then we find ourselves numbered among the first. More is required for salvation than eating and drinking—ultimately, we must share in Jesus' passion and death by eating and drinking his Body and Blood now.

Focusing the Gospel

Key words and phrases: making his way to Jerusalem, will only a few be saved?, narrow gate, in your company, I do not know where you are from

To the point: Jesus does not answer the question about *how many* will be saved; instead, he describes *who* will be saved (people from all over the world, those who are last, those who enter the banquet hall while the door is open). While the gate to salvation is narrow and difficult, it is open to all who are known by Jesus. Being known by Jesus goes beyond merely associating with him ("We ate and drank in your company") to walking with him to Jerusalem.

Connecting the Gospel

to the first reading: The universal salvation envisioned by Isaiah ("from all the nations") is personalized in the gospel: it is through Jesus that people from "east . . . west . . . north and . . . south" come to the "table in the kingdom of God."

to our culture: We tend to have strong presumptions and expectations about who is first and last. Even in democratic societies, this is evident in divisions along the lines of race, ethnicity, nationality, religion, sexual orientation, social and economic status. Jesus suggests that our presumptions will not necessarily prove to be true; there will be surprises in the kingdom!

Understanding Scripture

The door of salvation: The opening line of the gospel reminds us that Jesus is on his way to Jerusalem. Everything along the way—signs and sayings—is to help the disciples prepare for the coming Passion. This leads to the opening question and the key issue: who will be saved? The somewhat unfocused answer is due in part to Luke's pulling together a number of sayings from different contexts. The parallel sayings in Matthew are found in six different locations.

The image of the door is central (the word translated as "gate" in 13:24 and as "door" in 13:25 is the same Greek word). For a time the door is open. While it is, anyone can enter; but entry requires seriousness of purpose, not a half-hearted interest. The time is coming when the door will be closed: once the end has arrived and the judgment takes place, the opportunity has passed. At that time, those who claim to have rubbed elbows with Jesus ("we ate with you . . . you taught in our streets") but have not followed him are left outside. By their own admission, they had the opportunity but they did not take it. The door is closed.

Those who can enter through the door include both the faithful among God's elect, represented by the patriarchs and prophets, as well as Gentiles from east and west, north and south. What awaits them inside the door is the table of the messianic banquet. Those whom the chosen people had thought would be "last" are reclining at table, while those who should have been "first" but did not follow Jesus are now "last."

Isaiah, too, testifies to this universal offer of salvation: not only the dispersed people of Israel ("your brothers and sisters from all the nations"), but also "nations of every language" come to the Lord's mountain in Jerusalem, the place of God's worldwide sovereignty. This is one of the major developments in "Third Isaiah" (Isa 56–66): Gentiles are saved and included both among the Lord's people and in the Lord's service. The door of salvation is open to all, but not indefinitely.

CELEBRATION

Model Act of Penitence

Presider: In the gospel for today, Jesus encourages us to strive to enter the narrow gate to salvation. Let us open ourselves to receive the strength offered at God's table . . . [pause]

Lord Jesus, you open the door to salvation: Lord . . .

Christ Jesus, you invite all to your heavenly banquet: Christ . . .

Lord Jesus, you strengthen us on our journey: Lord . . .

Appreciating the Responsorial Psalm

In this Sunday's gospel, Jesus presents the harsh reality that not everyone will be admitted to the kingdom of God. His message, however, is for those who have heard the good news of salvation, not for those who have "never heard of [God's] name, or seen [God's] glory" (first reading). To these God will send messengers to tell them the good news and gather them to the holy dwelling, Jerusalem. For those who have already heard, radical demands are in place (Jesus has been spelling these out in the previous Sunday's gospels). And the responsorial psalm gives yet another command: we are to be the messengers who spread the good news of God's salvation to all the world. This psalm reminds us that we are a necessary part of God's plan of salvation for all. It also suggests that we cannot recline at God's table if we have not invited everyone else to be there with us.

Model General Intercessions

Presider: Jesus desires that all will be saved. And so we pray for our needs with confidence.

Response:

Lord, hear our prayer.

Cantor:

we pray to the Lord,

That all members of the Church may courageously announce Christ as the gate to salvation . . . [pause]

That all peoples from east and west and from north and south find a place at God's table . . . [pause]

That those who are poor and needy find a place at the table of the world's abundant resources . . . [pause]

That all of us will be strong enough to enter through the narrow gate of faithful discipleship . . . [pause]

Presider: Generous God, you invite all to come to your table: help us to meet faithfully the demands of discipleship so that one day we might be with you to share your abundant feast. We ask this through Christ our Lord. **Amen.**

RESPONSORIAL PSALM
Ps 117:1, 2

℟. (Mark 16:15) Go out to all the world and tell the Good News.
or:
℟. Alleluia.

Praise the LORD, all you nations;
glorify him, all you peoples!

℟. Go out to all the world and tell the Good News.
or:
℟. Alleluia.

For steadfast is his kindness toward us,
and the fidelity of the LORD endures forever.

℟. Go out to all the world and tell the Good News.
or:
℟. Alleluia.

SECOND READING
Heb 12:5-7, 11-13

Brothers and sisters,
You have forgotten the exhortation addressed to you as children:
"My son, do not disdain the discipline of the Lord
or lose heart when reproved by him;
for whom the Lord loves, he disciplines;
he scourges every son he acknowledges."
Endure your trials as "discipline";
God treats you as sons.
For what "son" is there whom his father does not discipline?
At the time,
all discipline seems a cause not for joy but for pain,
yet later it brings the peaceful fruit of righteousness
to those who are trained by it.
So strengthen your drooping hands and your weak knees.
Make straight paths for your feet,
that what is lame may not be disjointed but healed.

About Liturgy

Eucharist and salvation: Sunday Mass is as much a part of our week as eating and sleeping. This is not to say we take it for granted; most of us take our Sunday celebrations quite seriously and know they nourish and strengthen us for our weekly journey in discipleship. At the same time, few of us probably think of the direct relationship between Sunday Mass and salvation, other than that we receive grace from a worthy celebration. This is very true, but we can say so much more.

The Eucharistic prayers especially talk about how "we offer you [the Father] his body and blood, the acceptable sacrifice which brings salvation to the whole world" (Eucharistic Prayer IV). The prayers also specifically mention the cup of salvation or saving cup. It is too easy to think of this language as only referring to Christ and his sacrifice. At Mass we place ourselves on the altar with Christ in self-sacrifice; thus our own self-giving united with Christ's is part of bringing "salvation to the whole world."

There is another way to look at Eucharist and salvation. When we come to the table and share in the Body and Blood of Christ, we are coming to the "table in the kingdom of God." In other words, our sharing in the Eucharistic Body and Blood of Christ at Mass is already a sharing in the eternal banquet of everlasting salvation. Our eating and drinking at God's table already brings us to the end of our paschal journey to Jerusalem at the same time we are still plodding along our way!

About Liturgical Music

Cantor preparation: What good news do you have to tell the world? Are you conscious of the kindness and fidelity of God? Where have you experienced it in your own life, in the life of your family, in the life of your parish?

Singing the acclamations, part 8: At this point in Luke's Gospel, Jesus is making his way intentionally toward Jerusalem where he will face his death and resurrection. When asked who will be saved, he responds that the gate is narrow and great strength will be required to pass through it. It will not be enough merely to have eaten with him and listened to him speak. To enter into risen life we must journey with him to Jerusalem, we must join him in his self-emptying on the cross. This marks a good Sunday to change the service music sung for Mass (note on this Sunday, for example, the change in music suggested for the general intercessions in this volume). The change is not arbitrary, but liturgy-driven, for the different music is meant to express our willingness to turn with Jesus toward Jerusalem, and would be a concrete way of applying what has been said these past several weeks about the importance and power of the acclamations we sing.

Note to the music director: Some catechesis might be needed to help people realize the reason for changing service music this week. One way to do this would be to run a short blurb in the bulletin explaining why the change has been made. Run the blurb both this week and next to give people time to catch it.

SPIRITUALITY

Gospel   Luke 14:1, 7-14; L126C

On a sabbath Jesus went to dine
   at the home of one of the leading
      Pharisees,
   and the people there were observing
      him carefully.

He told a parable to those who had been
      invited,
   noticing how they were choosing the
      places of honor at the table.
"When you are invited by someone to a
      wedding banquet,
   do not recline at table in the place of
      honor.
A more distinguished guest than you may
      have been invited by him,
   and the host who invited both of you
      may approach you and say,
   'Give your place to this man,'
   and then you would proceed with
      embarrassment
to take the lowest place.
Rather, when you are invited,
   go and take the lowest place
   so that when the host comes to you he
      may say,
   'My friend, move up to a higher
      position.'
Then you will enjoy the esteem of your
      companions at the table.
For everyone who exalts himself will be
      humbled,
   but the one who humbles himself will
      be exalted."
Then he said to the host who invited him,
   "When you hold a lunch or a dinner,
   do not invite your friends or your
      brothers
   or your relatives or your wealthy
      neighbors,
   in case they may invite you back and
      you have repayment.
Rather, when you hold a banquet,
   invite the poor, the crippled, the lame,
      the blind;
   blessed indeed will you be because of
      their inability to repay you.
For you will be repaid at the resurrection
   of the righteous."

Reflecting on the Gospel

All of us have had the experience of being invited to someone else's home for dinner. When the host and hostess are good friends, the evening is one we look forward to and is an enjoyable and energizing time. When the host and hostess are, perhaps, little-known business acquaintances, we might be more apprehensive, be on our "best behavior," and find the evening more energy-draining than enjoyable. This Sunday's gospel recounts a dinner Jesus attends "at the home of one of the leading Pharisees." We might surmise that Jesus arrived there in a frame of mind different from one he might have had when invited to Martha's, Lazarus', and Mary's home. At this dinner "the people were observing him carefully" and Jesus was "noticing how they were choosing the places of honor at the table." This hardly sounds like a relaxed, friendly meal!

As is often the case in Luke's Gospel (which has Jesus sharing meals with others more than any other Gospel), Jesus uses this social occasion to teach something incredibly significant about God's ways. While at table, Jesus' eye is on the "wedding banquet" in God's kingdom where human expectations are reversed: the humble are exalted and the exalted are humbled. At that same heavenly table, service to those who cannot repay ("the poor, the crippled, the lame, the blind") is repaid by God in "the resurrection of the righteous." Acts of earthly humility and generosity are met with heavenly exaltation and God's generosity. Humility is, in part, knowing one's strengths and weaknesses (see first reading) and one's place (gospel). But it is more. Humility is the virtue by which we acknowledge our status before God: we are "the poor, the crippled, the lame, the blind" who come to God's table because of God's invitation and generosity.

Thus Jesus' remarks in this gospel remind us about our truest identity in relation to God. As deeply humble people, we come to God empty and open ourselves to God's filling us with what is lasting. This reward—everlasting life at God's messianic banquet—is ours if we but treat others as God treats us—we ourselves must bestow dignity and generosity on others. It is God who exalts us, not our own choosing or actions. It is God who repays us with the most unimaginable gift of all—everlasting life. Humility helps us refocus our limited vision and relationship to an enduring perspective which keeps our focus on God.

Living the Paschal Mystery

Jesus is calling the disciples back to the authentic Jewish tradition of caring for the "widow, orphan, and sojourner" (see, for example, Exod 22:22 and Zech 7:10). These three groups in Israelite society were symbolic of those who were in a position of needing others to look after their well-being. Israel's care for them concretized God's care for Israel. Jesus is calling us to authentic relationship with God by caring for those who cannot care for themselves. The surprise: total self-giving to the lowly and needy means reward in heaven—eternal glory with God!

The lowly are those who need food, clothing, and shelter; our cities are full of these kinds of dispossessed people. The lowly are also the children in our midst; the physically, emotionally, mentally, or spiritually challenged; the elderly. We do not need to look very far to put Jesus' teaching this week into practice!

Focusing the Gospel

Key words and phrases: Jesus went to dine, wedding banquet, humbled, exalted, inability to repay, repaid, resurrection

To the point: While Jesus is seated at the table of "one of the leading Phari-sees," his eye is on the "wedding banquet" in God's kingdom where human expectations are reversed: the humble are exalted and the exalted are humbled. At that same heavenly table, service to those who cannot repay ("the poor, the crippled, the lame, the blind") is repaid by God in "the resurrection of the righteous." Acts of earthly humility and generosity are met with heavenly exalta-tion and God's generosity.

Connecting the Gospel

to the first reading: Humility is, in part, knowing one's strengths and weak-nesses (see first reading) and one's place (gospel). But it is more. Humility is the virtue by which we acknowledge our status before God: we are "the poor, the crippled, the lame, the blind" who come to God's table because of God's invita-tion and generosity.

to our religious experience: In this gospel, two kinds of observation are taking place: the people are observing Jesus, and he is observing their behavior. What does Jesus observe whenever we gather for the Eucharistic banquet? What do we observe?

Understanding Scripture

Table-fellowship: This Sunday's gospel records two stories: 14:7-11 is a par-able about being a good guest; 14:12-14 is about being a good host. Jesus tells these parables while he is dining at table.

The first parable is not advice on how to get oneself exalted: pretend to be humble so one's host will call attention to the guest. The reading from Sirach shows that the essence of humility is not phony self-abasement, but rather knowing oneself well: "What is too sublime for you, seek not, into things be-yond your strength search not" (13:20). Know one's limits, and one's strengths, and act accordingly.

The second part of the gospel develops an important biblical theme found both in Sirach and in the responsorial psalm. Jesus counsels the well-to-do Pharisee to use his resources, not for dinner parties for the rich and famous, but for "the poor, the crippled, the lame, the blind" who cannot repay. Such generosity is meritorious: "alms atone for sins" (Sir 13:29). The psalm further develops this tradition of care for the needy. First, care of the needy is acting in a Godlike way, for God is known as the "father of orphans and the defender of widows," that is, God cares for the most economically and socially vulnerable members of the community. The last verse of the psalm reminds the people that they themselves were on the receiving end of God's kindness when God provided for them a home, or to use other images from the psalm, when God gave a pasture to his flock and water to a languishing land. All these images speak of human poverty and divine generosity. Even now, we will be guests at the messianic banquet only because of God's generosity. We are the poor guests unable to repay the generous host. The dining image is crucial, for at a banquet, host and guest sit at the same table. Christian hospitality is not condescension towards the "other": it welcomes the other into the community. Sharing a meal, or "breaking bread," creates fellowship and makes us one. Those "needy people" are now our family.

Model Act of Penitence

Presider: God invites us to this Eucharistic banquet. Let us ready ourselves to be gracious and grateful guests . . . [pause]

  Lord Jesus, you are our heavenly Food and Drink: Lord . . .

  Christ Jesus, you lift up the lowly: Christ . . .

  Lord Jesus, you offer us the resurrection of the righteous: Lord . . .

Appreciating the Responsorial Psalm

This Sunday's gospel tells us that the people were "observing [Jesus] carefully." The responsorial psalm invites us to the same observation of God. For the psalm shows us God "[making] a home for the poor." When Jesus in the gospel advises us to invite to our table "the poor, the crippled, the lame, the blind," he is challenging us to model what we see God doing. And when we do so, we experience a remarkable reversal in our own position. Choosing to give up the first place so that room may be made for the poor and needy exalts us. We become like God. Our singing of this psalm is our prayer that we see the goodness of God toward the needy and act likewise.

Model General Intercessions

Presider: God is a lavish God who invites us to a table of abundance. Let us pray to our generous God.

Response:

Lord, hear our prayer.

Cantor:

we pray to the Lord,

That all members of the Church generously reach out to the poor and those in need . . . [pause]

That world leaders invite all to the table of the world's abundance . . . [pause]

That all those made low be lifted up by God . . . [pause]

That all of us be blessed with the resurrection of the righteous . . . [pause]

Presider: O God, you provide for all our needs: hear these our prayers that one day we might feast at your everlasting banquet. We ask this through Christ our Lord. **Amen.**

OPENING PRAYER

Let us pray

Pause for silent prayer

Almighty God,
every good thing comes from you.
Fill our hearts with love for you,
increase our faith,
and by your constant care
protect the good you have given us.

We ask this through our Lord Jesus Christ,
    your Son,
who lives and reigns with you and the
    Holy Spirit,
one God, for ever and ever. **Amen.**

FIRST READING

Sir 3:17-18, 20, 28-29

My child, conduct your affairs with
    humility,
    and you will be loved more than a giver
        of gifts.
Humble yourself the more, the greater
    you are,
    and you will find favor with God.
What is too sublime for you, seek not,
    into things beyond your strength search
        not.
The mind of a sage appreciates proverbs,
    and an attentive ear is the joy of the
        wise.
Water quenches a flaming fire,
    and alms atone for sins.

RESPONSORIAL PSALM
Ps 68:4-5, 6-7, 10-11

R̸. (cf. 11b) God, in your goodness, you have made a home for the poor.

The just rejoice and exult before God;
    they are glad and rejoice.
Sing to God, chant praise to his name;
    whose name is the Lord.

R̸. God, in your goodness, you have made a home for the poor.

The father of orphans and the defender of widows
    is God in his holy dwelling.
God gives a home to the forsaken;
    he leads forth prisoners to prosperity.

R̸. God, in your goodness, you have made a home for the poor.

A bountiful rain you showered down, O God, upon your inheritance;
    you restored the land when it languished;
your flock settled in it;
    in your goodness, O God, you provided it for the needy.

R̸. God, in your goodness, you have made a home for the poor.

SECOND READING
Heb 12:18-19, 22-24a

Brothers and sisters:
You have not approached that which could be touched
    and a blazing fire and gloomy darkness
    and storm and a trumpet blast
    and a voice speaking words such that those who heard
    begged that no message be further addressed to them.
No, you have approached Mount Zion
    and the city of the living God, the heavenly Jerusalem,
    and countless angels in festal gathering,
    and the assembly of the firstborn enrolled in heaven,
    and God the judge of all,
    and the spirits of the just made perfect,
    and Jesus, the mediator of a new covenant,
    and the sprinkled blood that speaks more eloquently than that of Abel.

About Liturgy

"Liturgy"—the meaning of the word: The very word "liturgy" derives from two Greek words meaning "the work (or service) of the people." In ancient Greece "liturgists" were those who performed public works on behalf of society. In the context of Christian worship, the etymology of the word "liturgy" suggests that worship cannot be removed from doing—serving others, especially those in need. Sometimes we understand liturgy in terms of "the work of the people" to mean that we must work hard to make liturgy beautiful and meaningful. That is only partially true. The real work of liturgy actually begins at the dismissal, when we are sent off to do what we have celebrated—to serve others, to spend our lives for the good of others.

All of us must also accept the responsibility for helping our parish communities come to understand and live out the everyday, practical, social demands of true worshipers. The greatest worship we can give to God is to reach out with God's generosity toward those around us in need. Worship does not only happen within church buildings; it characterizes our relationship to God and to each other—a relationship of humility and service.

Labor Day: This is Labor Day weekend, and it would be very appropriate to add a fifth petition at the general intercessions. Here is a model: That all our nation's laborers work with dignity and honor and receive just compensation for their service . . . [pause]

About Liturgical Music

Cantor preparation: This Sunday's psalm praises God for goodness to the poor and needy. It is only when you see your own lowliness that you can see what God is doing to lift you up and offer you praise. How are you poor and needy? How does God exalt you?

Singing the acclamations, part 9: The acclamations are a direct result of Vatican II's recovery of the priesthood of all the baptized and the essential nature of the liturgy as the celebration of all the people. They are *actions* in the form of song. As the ancient adage states, to sing is to pray twice. When we sing we become more present, more attentive, more participative, and more powerful. When we sing, we enfold all the other members of the assembly with our voice, and communicate our choice to participate fully in the liturgical action, and vice versa. We sing the acclamations, then, not only to address God but also to direct personal support to one another in living out our identity and mission as Body of Christ. The singing of the acclamations is neither neutral nor inconsequential, for it expresses in an intense way the triple directedness of the liturgy toward God, toward our fellow members in Christ, and toward the world. Our singing of the acclamations amplifies their energy and intent: their sound moves out from each of us as individual source, encircles all of us in mutual support, and sends us as community on mission. The more we understand their importance and the more intentionally we sing them, the more we will both deepen our participation in liturgy and our living out of the mission of the Church.

SPIRITUALITY

Gospel
Luke 14:25-33; L129C

Great crowds were traveling with Jesus,
  and he turned and addressed them,
  "If anyone comes to me without hating his father and mother,
  wife and children, brothers and sisters,
  and even his own life,
  he cannot be my disciple.
Whoever does not carry his own cross and come after me
cannot be my disciple.
Which of you wishing to construct a tower
  does not first sit down and calculate the cost
  to see if there is enough for its completion?
Otherwise, after laying the foundation and finding himself unable to finish the work
  the onlookers should laugh at him and say,
  'This one began to build but did not have the resources to finish.'
Or what king marching into battle
  would not first sit down
  and decide whether with ten thousand troops
he can successfully oppose another king
  advancing upon him with twenty thousand troops?
But if not, while he is still far away,
  he will send a delegation to ask for peace terms.
In the same way,
  anyone of you who does not renounce all his possessions
  cannot be my disciple."

Reflecting on the Gospel

We take much time and care over major decisions, for example, marrying, buying a house, having children, taking a new job. Nevertheless, each of these actions brings its own surprises, new challenges, and unpredictable costs which were not initially considered. We get married in loving bliss, and then the reality of sacrificing for the good of the other sets in. We buy a house, and then discover that it is a "money pit." We begin a new position, and then discover that the learning

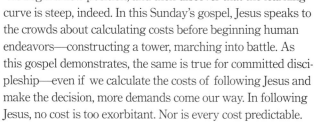

curve is steep, indeed. In this Sunday's gospel, Jesus speaks to the crowds about calculating costs before beginning human endeavors—constructing a tower, marching into battle. As this gospel demonstrates, the same is true for committed discipleship—even if we calculate the costs of following Jesus and make the decision, more demands come our way. In following Jesus, no cost is too exorbitant. Nor is every cost predictable.

In this gospel, Jesus challenges those following him to "calculate the cost" of discipleship. This cost is steep: hate family and one's own life, carry one's cross, and renounce all possessions. Moreover, these costs are not borne only once, when we make our decision to follow Jesus; rather, they are actually the daily demands of discipleship! Jesus teaches the crowds a pretty challenging message about following him: if our absolute priority is not Jesus and his mission, then we "cannot be [his] disciple."

Following Jesus comes ahead of ("hate") family and one's own life, difficulties, and possessions. Jesus is using pretty radical language in order to give us a chance to consider carefully what we do when we say yes to discipleship. Like so many things about life, we might enter into following Jesus with great enthusiasm and energy. But the cost of discipleship is something like inflation—it escalates exponentially! The more faithful we are in following Jesus, the greater the cost.

Being a disciple is not something we can undertake halfheartedly or frivolously. It is a decision to be pondered and weighed. The cost is steep; like Jesus, we give our lives over for the good of others. Are we willing to pay the price? Every day?

Living the Paschal Mystery

The radical cost of discipleship suggests that our yes is one that must be learned; we grow into it. As we make choices to live out our discipleship, we enter more deeply into its meaning and demands. At the same time, as we are faithful disciples, we also continually receive from God the strength to follow Jesus no matter what the cost.

Our yes to being followers of Jesus and taking up his mission is first ritualized at our baptism. Whether babies or adults makes no difference: that yes is always less than perfect. There is always room in our lives to grow deeper into Christ. Our ongoing baptismal yes is our ongoing assessment of the self-emptying stance of discipleship. Jesus is constantly inviting us to listen to him. We spend our whole lives bringing our fullest attention to what he is saying. This gospel gives us no hint about what happens if we cannot follow through on these radical demands of discipleship. From the history of God's dealing with the chosen people, we know God is a God of mercy, compassion, and forgiveness. Jesus lays out the radical demands of discipleship. Our human weakness begs us to call on God's mercy and forgiveness when we cannot quite measure up. In all things, God will sustain us.

Focusing the Gospel

Key words and phrases: come after me, calculate the cost, finish the work

To the point: In this gospel, Jesus challenges those following him to "calculate the cost" of discipleship. This cost is steep: hate family and one's own life, carry one's cross, and renounce all possessions. These costs are not borne only once, however; rather, they are the daily demands of discipleship.

Connecting the Gospel

to the first reading: "What is within our grasp"—calculations about human things such as building a tower or going to war—is difficult enough. Even more difficult is discerning God's will. Knowing this, God has given us the wisdom of Jesus' teachings and the "holy spirit from on high."

to our culture: We take much time and care over major decisions, for example, buying a house, marrying, having children, taking a new job. Nevertheless, each of these brings its own surprises and new challenges, not initially considered. The same is true for committed discipleship—even after we make the decision, there is still much more to be done.

Understanding Scripture

The cost of discipleship: After last Sunday's dinner scene, Jesus is again on the road to Jerusalem, this time with great crowds accompanying him. He knows where the road leads, but apparently the crowd does not. The discourse which follows is a wake-up call challenging them to "calculate the cost" (14:28) of discipleship and to follow him, not blithely, but with awareness and commitment. After all, this road leads to the cross, a cross which all who follow Jesus must carry. Jesus makes demands: failure to meet them means that one "cannot be my disciple" (14:26, 27, 33).

The language is strong: hating one's parents, family, and even one's own life. The sense here is not the chilling, hurtful emotion associated with "hate" groups, or motivated by anger and revenge. Matthew's version of this saying is clearer: "Whoever loves father or mother . . . son or daughter more than me is not worthy of me" (Matt 10:37). It is a question of preference and priority, as we see in Malachi, "Was not Esau Jacob's brother? says the LORD: yet I loved Jacob, but hated Esau" (1:3). God's "love" for Jacob means that God chose Jacob over Esau. Similarly, a disciple must choose Jesus over all else—even family and self. Still strong language and a tough choice!

That no one is exempt from this high cost of discipleship is illustrated by two examples: one involves a laborer about the ordinary business of constructing a tower; perhaps this is a farmer building a watchtower in his field (for example, Matt 21:33; Mark 12:1). The second example is of a king deciding matters of state—war and peace. Whether king or commoner, whether involved with matters lofty or mundane, still everyone must make the ultimate decision: do I have what it takes to follow Jesus?

The Greek in the last line of the gospel literally reads, "anyone of you who does not say good-bye to all he has cannot be my disciple." The issue is not "possessions," per se; it is priorities. Disciples have one priority over all else: following Jesus, cross and all.

**ASSEMBLY &
FAITH-SHARING GROUPS**
- The price I have paid to be a disciple is . . .
- When Jesus says that I need to "renounce all [my] possessions," this means to me . . .
- The next step for me in order to move beyond halfhearted to genuine discipleship is . . .

PRESIDERS
According to my calendar and lifestyle, what is first and primary to me is . . .

DEACONS
I reconcile my vocation to marriage and family with Jesus' demand to put him first by . . .

HOSPITALITY MINISTERS
I help those gathering to be open to Jesus' challenging words whenever I . . .

MUSIC MINISTERS
One of the costs of music ministry which has surprised me is . . . What keeps me faithful despite the cost is . . .

ALTAR MINISTERS
I shall consider to what extent I serve others *as* Jesus' disciple and *in order to be* his disciple . . .

LECTORS
God's wisdom and the Holy Spirit make "straight" my path of discipleship (see first reading) in that . . .

**EXTRAORDINARY MINISTERS
OF HOLY COMMUNION**
At each Eucharist I deepen my baptismal choice to follow Jesus by . . .

CELEBRATION

Model Act of Penitence

Presider: In today's gospel, Jesus challenges us to calculate the cost of discipleship. In this celebration, let us ask for the grace to be faithful disciples . . . [pause]

Lord Jesus, you call us to be your disciples: Lord . . .

Christ Jesus, you enlighten us with the Holy Spirit from on high: Christ . . .

Lord Jesus, you bring to completion the good work you have begun in us: Lord . . .

Appreciating the Responsorial Psalm

"The deliberations of mortals are timid and unsure" (first reading). But Jesus challenges us in this Sunday's gospel to be neither timid nor uncertain when deliberating the cost of discipleship. It is total. Relationships must be abandoned, possessions must be renounced, the cross must be carried. We are not left with only our own meager strength, however. God will "[teach] us to number . . . aright" and will "prosper the work of our hands" (responsorial psalm). God will give us both the wisdom to calculate the cost and the courage to pay it. God knows the all-encompassing cost of discipleship, and will be with us when we need strength, support, encouragement, and mercy. In singing this psalm we profess our confidence that God knows even better than we do what will be exacted of us. But even more: God is promising to see us through.

Model General Intercessions

Presider: God gives us the grace to meet the challenges of discipleship. We now pray for the needs of the Church and world.

Response:

Cantor:

That all members of the Church take up the cross and follow Jesus . . . [pause]

That nations at war may seek the way of peace . . . [pause]

That those struggling with the cost of discipleship be strengthened . . . [pause]

That all of us be directed by the wisdom of Jesus' teaching and the guidance of the Holy Spirit . . . [pause]

Presider: O God, you are with us in our daily following of Jesus: hear these our prayers that we might be faithful disciples. We ask this through Christ our Lord. **Amen.**

Let us pray

Pause for silent prayer

Lord our God,
in you justice and mercy meet.
With unparalleled love you have saved us
    from death
and drawn us into the circle of your life.
Open our eyes to the wonders this life sets
    before us,
that we may serve you free from fear
and address you as God our Father.

We ask this in the name of Jesus the Lord.
    Amen.

FIRST READING
Wis 9:13-18b

Who can know God's counsel,
    or who can conceive what the LORD
        intends?
For the deliberations of mortals are timid,
    and unsure are our plans.
For the corruptible body burdens the soul
    and the earthen shelter weighs down the
        mind that has many concerns.
And scarce do we guess the things on
    earth,
    and what is within our grasp we find
        with difficulty;
    but when things are in heaven, who can
        search them out?
Or who ever knew your counsel, except
    you had given wisdom
    and sent your holy spirit from on high?
And thus were the paths of those on earth
    made straight.

RESPONSORIAL PSALM
Ps 90:3-4, 5-6, 12-13, 14, 17

R̸. (1) In every age, O Lord, you have been
our refuge.

You turn man back to dust,
    saying, "Return, O children of men."
For a thousand years in your sight
    are as yesterday, now that it is past,
    or as a watch of the night.

R̸. In every age, O Lord, you have been
our refuge.

You make an end of them in their sleep;
    the next morning they are like the
        changing grass,
which at dawn springs up anew,
    but by evening wilts and fades.

℟. In every age, O Lord, you have been
our refuge.

Teach us to number our days aright,
    that we may gain wisdom of heart.
Return, O LORD! How long?
    Have pity on your servants!

℟. In every age, O Lord, you have been
our refuge.

Fill us at daybreak with your kindness,
    that we may shout for joy and gladness
        all our days.
And may the gracious care of the LORD
      our God be ours;
    prosper the work of our hands for us!
    Prosper the work of our hands!

℟. In every age, O Lord, you have been
our refuge.

SECOND READING
Phlm 9-10, 12-17

I, Paul, an old man,
    and now also a prisoner for Christ Jesus,
    urge you on behalf of my child
        Onesimus,
    whose father I have become in my
        imprisonment;
    I am sending him, that is, my own heart,
        back to you.
I should have liked to retain him for
      myself,
    so that he might serve me on your
        behalf
    in my imprisonment for the gospel,
    but I did not want to do anything
        without your consent,
    so that the good you do might not be
        forced but voluntary.
Perhaps this is why he was away from you
      for a while,
    that you might have him back forever,
    no longer as a slave
    but more than a slave, a brother,
    beloved especially to me, but even more
        so to you,
    as a man and in the Lord.
So if you regard me as a partner, welcome
      him as you would me.

CATECHESIS

About Liturgy

The challenge of liturgy committees: The task and responsibilities of a liturgy committee may sometimes seem as overwhelming as the cost of discipleship! If committee members were dependent upon their own means to be successful in their ministry, they would surely be crushed by the weight of the cost. What carries them through—enables them to continue to say yes both to this ministry and to their following Jesus every day of their lives—is the strength that God gives to each of them. This is why prayer—both individually and together as a committee—is so important to their liturgical ministry (and, indeed, to all ministry).

It might be encouraging and helpful to committee members if the parish liturgist or liturgy committee coordinator would use the blessing over the oil of catechumens (RCIA no. 207) to begin a meeting when things seem tense and overwhelming. That prayer assures the members of wisdom and strength; through their pre-baptismal anointing they are able to be brought to a "deeper understanding of the Gospel" and able to "accept the challenge of Christian living."

Using this prayer also reminds us that baptism and confirmation are hardly sacraments which happen only in ritual time. They bestow God's graces on us to help us meet whatever challenges of discipleship come our way. So it is good practice regularly to go back to the prayers of our sacraments and implement them in other situations.

About Liturgical Music

Cantor preparation: The cost of following Christ is immense, but this responsorial psalm reminds you that you have more than yourself to depend upon: your faithfulness will prosper because God has underwritten your discipleship. Sing with confidence in God and share this confidence with the assembly!

Music suggestions: A setting of "Take Up Your Cross" would be appropriate for either the entrance song or the song during the presentation of the gifts. "Only This I Want" [CBW3, G2, GC, GC2, BB, JS2] expresses the choice to bear the cross with Christ with full awareness that all other things will seem as loss, that the choice will have its price, but that such a choice brings gladness of heart. The song would be appropriate either as a choir prelude or during the presentation of the gifts. "I Have Decided to Follow Jesus" [LMGM] sings of the choice to follow Jesus with "No turning back, no turning back!" even if "no one join me" and fully aware of "The world behind me, the cross before me." The hymn would make an excellent assembly song during the presentation of the gifts.

SPIRITUALITY

Gospel Luke 15:1-32; L132C

Tax collectors and sinners were all
    drawing near to listen to Jesus,
  but the Pharisees and scribes began
    to complain, saying,
  "This man welcomes sinners
    and eats with them."
So to them he addressed this
  parable.
"What man among you having
    a hundred sheep and
    losing one of them
  would not leave the ninety-
    nine in the desert
  and go after the lost one
    until he finds it?
And when he does find it,
  he sets it on his shoulders
    with great joy
  and, upon his arrival home,
  he calls together his friends and
    neighbors and says to them,
  'Rejoice with me because I have
    found my lost sheep.'
I tell you, in just the same way
  there will be more joy in heaven over
    one sinner who repents
  than over ninety-nine righteous people
  who have no need of repentance.

"Or what woman having ten coins and
    losing one
  would not light a lamp and sweep the
    house,
  searching carefully until she finds it?
And when she does find it,
  she calls together her friends and
    neighbors
  and says to them,
  'Rejoice with me because I have
    found the coin that I lost.'
In just the same way, I tell you,
  there will be rejoicing among the
    angels of God
  over one sinner who repents."

Continued in Appendix A, p. 303.

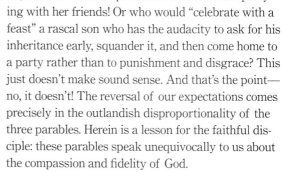

Reflecting on the Gospel

The gospel for this Sunday includes three parables, all of them quite preposterous to a practical-minded, economically sensitive follower of Jesus. Who would go after one stupid, lost sheep and take the chance of losing the other ninety-nine? If "rejoice with me" includes food and drink—and we can hardly imagine that it wouldn't—then the shepherd is still going to lose some of his property! Or who would bother to clean a whole house for one coin? And if "rejoice with me" includes food and drink, then the woman spent more than one coin partying with her friends! Or who would "celebrate with a feast" a rascal son who has the audacity to ask for his inheritance early, squander it, and then come home to a party rather than to punishment and disgrace? This just doesn't make sound sense. And that's the point—no, it doesn't! The reversal of our expectations comes precisely in the outlandish disproportionality of the three parables. Herein is a lesson for the faithful disciple: these parables speak unequivocally to us about the compassion and fidelity of God.

In the first two parables, there is no concern for *how* the sheep and coin are lost: they are not culpable. All that matters is that they are found. By contrast, the prodigal son is culpable: he is "lost" because of his dissolute life. However, the father (unlike the older brother) is not concerned with culpability. His only concern is that he has his son back, as though from death.

The older son, on the other hand, has great concern for *how* the younger son was lost ("swallowed up . . . property with prostitutes") and refuses to come to the feast and rejoice at his return. The bitterness of the older son stands in stark contrast to the mercy and generosity of the father. So, too, with God who is more eager to welcome and receive sinners than to hold them accountable. Such Good News!

Both readings describe the mercy God extends to sinners, whether the sin is idolatry (first reading), dissolute living (younger son), or refusing to forgive (older son). Forgiving an unintended hurt is sometimes difficult for us; forgiving an intended hurt is still more difficult. Yet God's response to sin, which is intentional, is always one of mercy, compassion, and forgiveness. God always seeks the lost (even when it includes an intentional turning from God). Such Good News!

Living the Paschal Mystery

Being a faithful disciple does not mean always doing the logical thing nor the most practical thing. Like God in the first reading—who relented punishing Israel for unfaithfulness because God "brought [them] out of the land of Egypt"—we, too, must put aside our shortsightedness and be merciful and forgiving. If we find this difficult, we only need to remember God's utter fidelity and compassion toward us.

Forgiveness is never easy, and so much more difficult when the hurt is intentional. Perhaps one way to approach this is to consider the good in the other who needs our forgiveness. When we are angry, recite a "litany" of positive virtues. When we want to strike back, think of the dignity of the other because he or she is a baptized son or daughter of God. Maybe we also need to consider our own goodness!

Focusing the Gospel

Key words and phrases: lost, found, I have sinned, filled with compassion, ran to his son, embraced him

To the point: In the first two parables, there is no concern for *how* the sheep and coin are lost: they are not culpable. All that matters is that they are found. By contrast, the prodigal son is culpable: he is "lost" because of his dissolute life. However, the father (unlike the older brother) is not concerned with culpability. His only concern is that he has his son back, as though from death. So, too, with God who is more eager to welcome and receive sinners than to hold them accountable.

Connecting the Gospel

to the first reading: Both readings describe the mercy God extends to sinners, whether the sin is idolatry (first reading), dissolute living (younger son), or refusing to forgive (older son).

to religious experience: Forgiving an unintended hurt is sometimes difficult; forgiving an intended hurt is still more difficult. Yet God's response to sin, which is intentional, is always forgiveness.

Understanding Scripture

God's mercy: In Luke's gospel, the parable of the "Prodigal Son" is the third of three similar parables. There is a standard pattern to stories told in threes. Everyone knows jokes about "the priest, the minister, and the rabbi" (or about people of various nationalities). The first two set up a pattern; the third breaks the pattern and provides the humor of the joke, or the point of the story.

In Luke 15, which includes this Sunday's gospel, three back-to-back parables establish the following pattern. Someone loses something: the man loses a sheep, the woman a coin, the father his son. Each then gets it back. Then each invites neighbors and friends to celebrate. Everyone celebrates with the man who found his lost sheep; everyone celebrates with the woman who found her lost coin. But that pattern is broken in the third story.

The third story has the same structure, though it is greatly elaborated. And there are other differences as well. Unlike the hapless sheep and the coin which are lost through no fault of their own, the younger son chooses a life of dissipation. The younger son, in his self-centeredness, is in no way admirable; however, he comes to his senses and repents—in this he is altogether admirable. When he returns, everyone celebrates with him and his father—everyone, that is, except the older brother! The very structure of the parables tells us that the focus of the parable is the older brother. The older brother, though obedient and faithful to the father, is called to more. He is called to a compassion which celebrates when mercy is extended even to his undeserving brother.

Luke's introduction to the parable tells us that Jesus addresses the parables to the Pharisees and the scribes who complain that Jesus "welcomes sinners and eats with them." Instead of rejoicing that sinners are being welcomed in the Father's embrace, they are upset. The Pharisees and scribes—like the older brother—are called to more than personal goodness. Even good and faithful disciples are called to compassion which rejoices in God's mercy.

ASSEMBLY & FAITH-SHARING GROUPS
- When I consider that God searches for me when I am lost, I think . . .
- As I consider the father and his two sons, I am most like . . . because . . .
- If I am to be as forgiving and merciful as God is, then I must . . .

PRESIDERS
I lead the community to welcome and rejoice at the return of the lost by . . .

DEACONS
I am like the good shepherd and seek the lost in the community by . . .

HOSPITALITY MINISTERS
When I view those gathering as God's lost and found, my ministry is like . . .

MUSIC MINISTERS
As a music minister, I sometimes find myself standing in judgment over . . . What helps me "relent" in my judgment and move toward God's compassion and mercy is . . .

ALTAR MINISTERS
My service includes helping the lost be found when I . . .

LECTORS
I proclaim God's extravagant mercy and forgiveness whenever I . . .

EXTRAORDINARY MINISTERS OF HOLY COMMUNION
Eucharist is a rejoicing with God for the lost having been found in that . . .

CELEBRATION

Model Act of Penitence

Presider: God cares for each one of us and seeks us when we stray. Let us reflect on God's compassion and mercy and open ourselves to God's grace . . . [pause]

Lord Jesus, you are the Good Shepherd who seeks the lost sheep: Lord . . .

Christ Jesus, you rejoice when even one sinner repents: Christ . . .

Lord Jesus, you show us mercy and compassion: Lord . . .

Appreciating the Responsorial Psalm

In the first reading, Moses talks God into relenting of the punishment unfaithful Israel deserves. In the gospel no punishment is meted against sinners; rather it is the Prodigal Son who relents of his sinfulness. The Pharisees and scribes, on the other hand, refuse to relent in their judgment against Jesus for eating with sinners. The responsorial psalm for this Sunday, taken from Psalm 51, is our song of relenting. Through it we align ourselves with the tax collectors and sinners, with the lost sheep, with the Prodigal Son. Such alignment is part of the radical gift of self which discipleship demands, for through it we give up any vestige of false self-image. We can be found because we admit that we are lost. We can receive God's unrestricted and limitless mercy because we confess we are in need of it.

Model General Intercessions

Presider: No one and nothing is too insignificant or too sinful for God's care. This encourages us to offer our prayers for the Church and world.

Response:

Lord, hear our prayer.

Cantor:

we pray to the Lord,

That the Church always welcome sinners with compassion and mercy . . . [pause]

That world leaders generously show compassion and mercy toward the powerless and the poor . . . [pause]

That those struggling to forgive another may be moved by compassion and mercy . . . [pause]

That all of us rejoice because compassion and mercy have been extended to us . . . [pause]

Presider: O God, we praise you for your compassion and mercy: look kindly on our needs and hear our prayers that we may one day rejoice with you in your kingdom of heaven. We ask this through Christ our Lord. **Amen.**

CATECHESIS

RESPONSORIAL PSALM

Ps 51:3-4, 12-13, 17, 19

R⁄. (Luke 15:18) I will rise and go to my father.

Have mercy on me, O God, in your
        goodness;
    in the greatness of your compassion
        wipe out my offense.
Thoroughly wash me from my guilt
    and of my sin cleanse me.

R⁄. I will rise and go to my father.

A clean heart create for me, O God,
    and a steadfast spirit renew within me.
Cast me not out from your presence,
    and your Holy Spirit take not from me.

R⁄. I will rise and go to my father.

O LORD, open my lips,
    and my mouth shall proclaim your
        praise.
My sacrifice, O God, is a contrite spirit;
    a heart contrite and humbled, O God,
        you will not spurn.

R⁄. I will rise and go to my father.

SECOND READING

1 Tim 1:12-17

Beloved:
I am grateful to him who has strengthened
        me, Christ Jesus our Lord,
    because he considered me trustworthy
        in appointing me to the ministry.
I was once a blasphemer and a persecutor
        and arrogant,
    but I have been mercifully treated
    because I acted out of ignorance in my
        unbelief.
Indeed, the grace of our Lord has been
        abundant,
    along with the faith and love that are in
        Christ Jesus.
This saying is trustworthy and deserves
        full acceptance:
    Christ Jesus came into the world to save
        sinners.
Of these I am the foremost.
But for that reason I was mercifully
        treated,
    so that in me, as the foremost,
    Christ Jesus might display all his
        patience as an example
    for those who would come to believe in
        him for everlasting life.
To the king of ages, incorruptible,
        invisible, the only God,
    honor and glory forever and ever. Amen.

About Liturgy

Proclaiming familiar parables: Parables are short stories or sayings which use familiar situations and images. They are metaphorical, that is, they have a hidden meaning which is grasped only through the obvious meaning. The speaker may use a parable in order to grab and hold the hearer's attention; the story is catchy and the hearer wants to know how it ends. The parable is an indirect way for the speaker to get the hearer to apply a message to him- or herself which would otherwise be dismissed. In the classical Greek sense of "rhetoric," they persuade one to a certain viewpoint.

The challenge for the gospel reader (deacon or presider) is how to proclaim the gospel when the assembly already knows the ending of the parables. The surprise, "catchy" element is gone. The reader might think in terms of "pregnant pauses" at unexpected places during the proclamation, or strong emphasis on words that the assembly might not expect. Most important, however, is that the proclaimer cannot read the parable with a tone of voice that really says, "I know this parable and let's just get through it." The reader's voice must say, "This is exciting and there is something new here."

Long or short form of the gospel: The long form of the gospel for this Sunday includes the parable of the Prodigal Son. If only the short form of the gospel is proclaimed (given as an alternative for this Sunday), the impact of the responsorial psalm which obviously leads to the Prodigal Son parable would be curtailed. Moreover, during this year C of the three-year Lectionary cycle, we also heard the Prodigal Son parable on the Fourth Sunday of Lent. The Lenten context invited us to interpret this parable in the direction of mercy, forgiveness, reconciliation, repentance, conversion, etc. The Ordinary Time context along with the other two parables preceding the Prodigal Son story in this Sunday's gospel invites us to interpret the parable along different lines. Different liturgical year contexts suggest different approaches to familiar parables.

About Liturgical Music

Cantor preparation: If you really mean what you are singing, these verses from Psalm 51 will be a kind of public confession. To stand before the assembly and sing them will require vulnerability. But your very vulnerability will invite your heart to the same kind of stance and open it to God's mercy.

Music suggestions: "All Who Hunger Gather Gladly" [G2, GC, GC2, RS, SS] calls all who "once were lost and scattered" to come to the table of the Lord as "welcome guest[s]." The HOLY MANNA setting would work well for the entrance procession. Bob Moore's verse-refrain setting would be excellent at Communion with choir or cantor singing the verses and the assembly the refrain. Another suggestion for Communion would be "Our God Is Rich in Love" [G2, GC, GC2] with cantor or choir singing the verses and assembly the refrain. "Come, You Sinners, Poor and Needy" [RS, W3] would be effective during the presentation of the gifts after the gospel has been proclaimed. Finally, "There's a Wideness in God's Mercy" would be appropriate for either the entrance procession or the presentation of the gifts.

SEPTEMBER 16, 2007
TWENTY-FOURTH SUNDAY IN ORDINARY TIME

SPIRITUALITY

Gospel
Luke 16:1-13; L135C

Jesus said to his disciples,
   "A rich man had a steward
   who was reported to him for
      squandering his property.
He summoned him and said,
   'What is this I hear about
      you?
Prepare a full account of your
   stewardship,
   because you can no longer be
      my steward.'
The steward said to himself,
   'What shall I do,
   now that my master is taking
      the position of steward
      away from me?
I am not strong enough to dig and I am
   ashamed to beg.
I know what I shall do so that,
   when I am removed from the
      stewardship,
   they may welcome me into their
      homes.'
He called in his master's debtors one
   by one.
To the first he said,
   'How much do you owe my master?'
He replied, 'One hundred measures of
   olive oil.'
He said to him, 'Here is your
   promissory note.
Sit down and quickly write one for
   fifty.'
Then to another the steward said, 'And
   you, how much do you owe?'
He replied, 'One hundred kors of
   wheat.'
The steward said to him, 'Here is your
   promissory note;
   write one for eighty.'
And the master commended that
   dishonest steward for acting
   prudently.

Continued in Appendix A, p. 304.

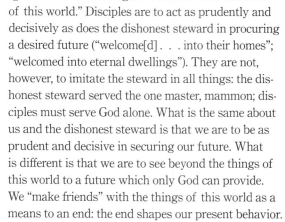

Reflecting on the Gospel

If any of us were to embezzle funds from an employer, we would end up in jail and with a huge civil lawsuit demanding millions! Times have not changed; Jesus is not suggesting that the actions of the steward are morally good. The first reading is a corrective for the gospel and steers us toward realizing that what the steward did was certainly wrong. Jesus is, instead, emphasizing what we must do in order to secure our desired future.

In this parable, Jesus urges the "children of light" to imitate the "children of this world." Disciples are to act as prudently and decisively as does the dishonest steward in procuring a desired future ("welcome[d] . . . into their homes"; "welcomed into eternal dwellings"). They are not, however, to imitate the steward in all things: the dishonest steward served the one master, mammon; disciples must serve God alone. What is the same about us and the dishonest steward is that we are to be as prudent and decisive in securing our future. What is different is that we are to see beyond the things of this world to a future which only God can provide. We "make friends" with the things of this world as a means to an end: the end shapes our present behavior.

The last line of the gospel has become a well-known maxim, usually stated "You cannot serve both God and money." The term "mammon" can mean any wealth or possession. Sometimes it is used as that in which we put our trust, almost in the sense of a god. The maxim really asks, which God do we serve? The answer to that question determines whether or not we share in everlasting life. The context for this gospel, then, is final judgment; the end is near and so we do anything necessary with prudence and decisiveness in order to be saved.

Moreover, prudence and decisiveness about "mammon" is related to which God we serve. The more we keep our eyes focused on God, the easier it is to keep the things of this world in perspective. "Mammon" is a necessary part of this world. The choice is always to use it with a longer view in sight—eternal life. The "full account" of our stewardship will not be a matter of spreadsheets and ledgers. It will be a matter of how well we have been faithful disciples; how well we have consistently kept our life focused on God as the center.

Living the Paschal Mystery

Just as the steward was decisive in how he used his master's possessions to gain his favorable end, so are we to be decisive in our use of possessions and which God we serve in order to gain our eternal end. Eternal life, then, is dependent upon two things: we are to be prudent and decisive in this life, and do all we can to gain eternal life; we are to constantly monitor which God it is we serve.

Most of us do not go through life thinking through each action in terms of eternal life. This would be pretty impossible and probably more than a little distracting! Keeping ourselves focused on God is as simple as doing little acts of kindness each day for the good of others. It may be as demanding as resisting temptation to do something sinful. Keeping ourselves focused on God also means that we do take time each day to pray—to pour out our hearts to God and acknowledge God as the Lord and center of our lives. In these simple, everyday ways we make choices about prudence and decisiveness, mammon or God.

Focusing the Gospel

Key words and phrases: I know what I shall do, acting prudently, dwellings, serve . . . God

To the point: In this parable, Jesus urges the "children of light" to imitate the "children of this world." Disciples are to act as prudently and decisively as does the dishonest steward in procuring a desired future ("welcome[d] . . . into their homes"; "welcomed into eternal dwellings"). They are not, however, to imitate the steward in all things: the dishonest steward served the one master, mammon; disciples must serve God alone.

Connecting the Gospel

to the first reading: Although Jesus uses the dishonest steward to teach a positive lesson, the first reading is a corrective which shows that what the steward did was wrong.

to culture: We invest a great deal of time, money, and energy in acquiring skills, guidance, therapy, and education in order to live better lives. Disciples are called to invest the same time and energy gaining prudence and spiritual insight so to be "welcomed into eternal dwellings."

Understanding Scripture

God or mammon: Jesus continues to instruct his followers about the demands of discipleship. In Luke 16, he addresses the matter of possessions. The parable of the "Prudent Steward" is a minefield of problems. The lesser problems have to do with the sayings of Jesus in verses 10-13: how do these relate to the parable? The greater problems have to do with this dishonest steward being used as a model for faithful discipleship. How can this be?

The issue is the impending fate of the steward. He has been given his notice and will have to render an account of his service. Clearly, the parable is oriented to final judgment and accountability. Knowing what awaits him, he attempts to secure his future by making use of what is in his power. While his falsifying the accounts of his master is hardly admirable or exemplary, he is "prudent" in knowing that the personal stakes are high: nothing less than his survival is at issue. He takes the risks and the necessary steps to insure his survival. In the broadest terms, this is the lesson for disciples. The end is coming, judgment and accountability await: use the present situation to secure one's future.

More narrowly, the issue is the proper use of the goods of this world. Earlier Jesus had indicated the relative worth of earthly possessions and the proper use of them: "Sell your belongings and give alms. Provide money bags for yourselves that do not wear out, an inexhaustible treasure in heaven that no thief can reach nor moth destroy. For where your treasure is, there also will your heart be" (Luke 12:33-34). The things of this world are not of ultimate worth, but they may have ultimate consequences: how one deals with them has a bearing on one's salvation and indicates what one truly values. Jesus, therefore, rightly says that those who are trustworthy in dealing with worldly possessions—"small matters" compared to eternal salvation—will be able to deal with the great matters. It comes down to priorities again: whom will we serve? Where does our treasure lie?

**ASSEMBLY &
FAITH-SHARING GROUPS**

- Jesus uses the dishonest steward to teach me that . . .
- Some examples which show that I am serving God over "mammon" are . . .
- I am using my "mammon" to serve God whenever I . . .

PRESIDERS

I guide the community to prepare for eternal, rather than earthly, dwellings whenever I . . .

DEACONS

As I serve others, I can help them make an honest account of the direction and content of their lives by . . .

HOSPITALITY MINISTERS

The manner of my hospitality points the assembly to "eternal dwellings" whenever I . . .

MUSIC MINISTERS

In my music ministry many masters compete for my allegiance (that is, adulation, praise, dominance, etc.). I know I am following Christ when I . . . I know I am choosing another master when I . . .

ALTAR MINISTERS

How I transform my busy activity into an interior serving of others *for God* is . . .

LECTORS

My life announces a choosing of God over mammon whenever I . . .

**EXTRAORDINARY MINISTERS
OF HOLY COMMUNION**

The Eucharist keeps me focused on "eternal dwellings" in that . . .

CELEBRATION

Model Act of Penitence

Presider: We gather as God's children to celebrate these sacred mysteries. Let us prepare ourselves so that we might be good stewards of these mysteries . . . [pause]

Lord Jesus, you call us to be children of light: Lord . . .

Christ Jesus, you challenge us to serve God alone: Christ . . .

Lord Jesus, you welcome faithful stewards into your eternal dwellings: Lord . . .

Appreciating the Responsorial Psalm

The connection of the responsorial psalm to the first reading is obvious. In the first reading, God swears never to forget an injustice done to the poor. In the psalm, God redresses such wrongs and raises the poor from dust to nobility. The relationship of the psalm to the gospel, however, is not so clear. Both the first reading and the gospel relate incidences of unjust and dishonest behavior pursued for the sake of personal gain. The intimation is that these stories exemplify the choice to serve mammon rather than God. Yet while Jesus condemns dishonest behavior, he commends the dishonest steward for pursuing it.

What Jesus invites, however, is not imitation of the behavior but imitation of the shrewdness which motivates it. We must know what we want and act decisively to obtain it. The psalm offers us a model. We are to desire what is just and true, and act in its service. We are to imitate God who redresses wrongs and raises up the poor. In praying this psalm, we sing the praises of the One whom we wish to be like: we choose our Master.

Model General Intercessions

Presider: Let us ask God for the gifts we need to be able to enter into eternal dwellings.

Response:

Cantor:

That all members of the Church may be faithful stewards of God . . . [pause]

That world leaders may be prudent in their dealings . . . [pause]

That those in need find assistance and support . . . [pause]

That all of us here may serve God in each other all the days of our lives . . . [pause]

Presider: Ever-living God, you call us to serve only you: hear these our prayers that we might enter your eternal dwelling. We ask this through Christ our Lord. **Amen.**

ALTERNATIVE OPENING PRAYER

Let us pray

Pause for silent prayer

Father in heaven,
the perfection of justice is found in your
    love
and all mankind is in need of your law.
Help us to find this love in each other
that justice may be attained
through obedience to your law.

We ask this through Christ our Lord.
    Amen.

FIRST READING

Amos 8:4-7

Hear this, you who trample upon the
    needy
    and destroy the poor of the land!
"When will the new moon be over," you
    ask,
    "that we may sell our grain,
    and the sabbath, that we may display
        the wheat?
We will diminish the ephah,
    add to the shekel,
    and fix our scales for cheating!
We will buy the lowly for silver,
    and the poor for a pair of sandals;
    even the refuse of the wheat we will
        sell!"
The LORD has sworn by the pride of Jacob:
    Never will I forget a thing they have
        done!

RESPONSORIAL PSALM

Ps 113:1-2, 4-6, 7-8

℞. (cf. 1a, 7b) Praise the Lord, who lifts up
the poor.
    or:
℞. Alleluia.

Praise, you servants of the LORD,
    praise the name of the LORD.
Blessed be the name of the LORD
    both now and forever.

℞. Praise the Lord, who lifts up the poor.
    or:
℞. Alleluia.

High above all nations is the LORD;
  above the heavens is his glory.
Who is like the LORD, our God, who is
    enthroned on high
  and looks upon the heavens and the
      earth below?

R⁊. Praise the Lord, who lifts up the poor.
  or:
R⁊. Alleluia.

He raises up the lowly from the dust;
  from the dunghill he lifts up the poor
to seat them with princes,
  with the princes of his own people.

R⁊. Praise the Lord, who lifts up the poor.
  or:
R⁊. Alleluia.

SECOND READING
1 Tim 2:1-8

Beloved:
First of all, I ask that supplications,
    prayers,
  petitions, and thanksgivings be offered
      for everyone,
  for kings and for all in authority,
  that we may lead a quiet and tranquil
      life
  in all devotion and dignity.
This is good and pleasing to God our
    savior,
  who wills everyone to be saved
  and to come to knowledge of the truth.
    For there is one God.
    There is also one mediator between God
        and men,
    the man Christ Jesus,
    who gave himself as ransom for all.
This was the testimony at the proper time.
For this I was appointed preacher and
    apostle
  —I am speaking the truth, I am not
      lying—,
  teacher of the Gentiles in faith and
      truth.

It is my wish, then, that in every place the
    men should pray,
  lifting up holy hands, without anger
      or argument.

About Liturgy

Eucharist and eschatology, part 1: Already by now, nearing the end of September, the Church begins to think about the parousia and eschatological fulfillment, with which the liturgical year ends. Although these motifs are evident in the Liturgy of the Word toward the end of the Lectionary year, eschatology is a motif present in every celebration of Eucharist. Three of the four Eucharistic acclamations explicitly mention the Second Coming of Christ. No. 8 of SC mentions that earthly liturgy is a foretaste of heavenly liturgy, so the assembly already shares to some extent in eschatological glory. Each time we sing the *Holy, Holy, Holy* at the end of the preface, we explicitly join our praise and thanks to the heavenly choir giving worship to God.

Eschatology is a difficult theme. It refers to the end times when all will be brought to fulfillment in Christ. Since most of us are pretty taken up with the present and getting through the demands of each day, our thoughts about the future rarely include more than perhaps looking to the end of the month and bills to pay or perhaps planning a vacation. This time of the year when the Church's liturgy turns us toward the end time is a good time to remind ourselves that the way we live now does make a difference in how we will spend our eternal future! A good weekly practice would be to keep our eternal future and eschatology in mind as we celebrate Eucharist each week, keying into those elements which remind us of what is to come.

About Liturgical Music

Cantor preparation: In singing this psalm, you invite the assembly to praise God for acting on behalf of the poor and oppressed. In the context of the first reading and gospel, you also invite them to imitate God in their own manner of acting. In what ways do you choose God as your Master and guide? In what ways do you struggle with this choice? How might Christ help you?

Music suggestions: Songs which express being decisive and faithful in our choice to serve God above all would connect well with this Sunday's celebration, as would songs which sing of Christ as the center and foundation of our discipleship. Examples include "Rise Up, O Saints of God" [PMB, WC], "Praise to You, O Christ Our Savior" [BB, CBW3, G2, GC, GC2, JS2], "Glorious in Majesty" [G2, GC], and "Be Light for Our Eyes" [CBW3, G2, GC, GC2], all suitable for the entrance procession; "Guide My Feet" [G2, GC, GC2], "I Bind My Heart" [G2, GC], and "Seek Ye First the Kingdom of God" [BB, GC2, JS2, PMB, RS, WC, WS] for the presentation of the gifts; and "The Love of the Lord" [G2, GC, GC2, RS] for Communion.

SPIRITUALITY

Gospel
Luke 16:19-31; L138C

Jesus said to the Pharisees:
  "There was a rich man who dressed
    in purple garments and fine
    linen
and dined sumptuously each day.
And lying at his door was a poor
    man named Lazarus, covered
    with sores,
  who would gladly have eaten his
    fill of the scraps
  that fell from the rich man's
    table.
Dogs even used to come and lick
    his sores.
When the poor man died,
  he was carried away by angels
    to the bosom of Abraham.
The rich man also died and was
    buried,
  and from the netherworld,
    where he was in torment,
  he raised his eyes and saw Abraham
    far off
  and Lazarus at his side.
And he cried out, 'Father Abraham,
    have pity on me.
Send Lazarus to dip the tip of his finger
    in water and cool my tongue,
  for I am suffering torment in these
    flames.'
Abraham replied,
  'My child, remember that you
    received
  what was good during your lifetime
  while Lazarus likewise received what
    was bad;
  but now he is comforted here,
    whereas you are tormented.
Moreover, between us and you a great
    chasm is established
  to prevent anyone from crossing who
    might wish to go
  from our side to yours or from your
    side to ours.'

Continued in Appendix A, p. 304.

Reflecting on the Gospel

Many of us live out of the maxim, "We get what we deserve." We have other ways of saying the same thing: "What goes around comes around"; "As you sow, so shall you reap." Applying these sentiments, we readily know with whom to identify in this Sunday's gospel parable about the rich man and Lazarus.

The opening line presents an attractive figure: a man is rich, wears "purple garments and fine linen," and dines "sumptuously." Who of us would not want to be that person? Yet, none of us who hears this parable identifies with the rich man, but with the poor man Lazarus. Lazarus hardly presents so attractive a personage: he is poor, starving, and covered with sores that dogs lick. How much more uninviting can the description get? Why is it we identify with Lazarus and not with the rich man? This defies common sense! It does make sense to us, however, for we know that this parable is really about eternal life. We know that we get what we deserve.

The rich man's problem is not his wealth. Like the "complacent in Zion" who "are not made ill by the collapse of Joseph" (first reading), the rich man is unconcerned for Lazarus. The chasm which separated the rich man and Lazarus after death is already present while they are living. This chasm—much more than the breach between rich and poor—is a gulf of uncaring. In this life the rich man could have chosen to act differently and the chasm could be bridged. Once we enter the next life, the chasm is unbridgeable.

The gospel uses the metaphor "great chasm" and paints a clear picture of what happens on each side: rich/poor, dined sumptuously/eat scraps, netherworld/bosom of Abraham, received good/received bad, torment/comforted, place of torment/rise from the dead. The metaphor spells out for us the reason why we identify with Lazarus. Although the wealth and comfort of this life are attractive, in face of eternity they are too fleeting to choose. What really counts is living faithfully now so we are on the right side of the chasm in eternity!

The parable of the rich man and Lazarus is blunt: how the rich man spends the afterlife was determined in this life by his lack of concern for the poor man "lying at his door." *Now* is the time to bridge whatever chasms exist between ourselves and those in need. After death the divide is impassable, and our eternity is set. So, *now* is our time: Who is lying at our door?

Living the Paschal Mystery

Although the "great chasm" metaphor in the gospel leads us to compare the two possibilities of the afterlife (heaven or hell), the metaphor also applies to this life and how we are living today, for how we are living now is how we will be living for all eternity. The present moment is amplified in eternity. Ultimately, how we live both now and in eternity is our choice. God makes good (or bad) on our choice!

The problem is not that we do not know how to live our lives. The problem is, we tend to talk about the poor and those in need of our care globally and in abstract terms. In this gospel, the poor and needy one is presented as an individual with a name lying at a doorstep. Besides Moses and the prophets, we also have Jesus to teach us; we, too, only need to listen. Jesus teaches us how to see those in need around us and reach out in concern.

Focusing the Gospel

Key words and phrases: each day, lying at his door, died, during your life-time, great chasm, prevent . . . from crossing

To the point: The parable of the rich man and Lazarus is blunt: how the rich man spends the afterlife was determined in this life by his lack of concern for the poor man "lying at his door." *Now* is the time to bridge whatever chasms exist between ourselves and those in need. After death the divide is impassable, and our eternity is set. So, *now* is our time: Who is lying at our door?

Connecting the Gospel

to the first reading: The rich man's problem is not his wealth. Like the "complacent in Zion" who "are not made ill by the collapse of Joseph," the rich man is unconcerned for Lazarus.

to culture: We tend to talk about the poor globally and in abstract terms. Here the poor is presented as an individual with a name lying at a doorstep.

Understanding Scripture

Blessed are the poor: In last week's gospel, Jesus placed service of God and service of wealth ("mammon") in opposition. The Pharisees, to whom this Sunday's parable is addressed, saw wealth as a sign of God's blessing for a righteous life (for example, Deut 28:3-4; Ps 1:3-4). While this is, indeed, part of the Bible's teaching, the Law equally requires care of the poor and needy (for example, Lev 19:9-10; Deut 14:29; 15:7-11). This disagreement between Jesus and the Pharisees over the interpretation of Scripture leads to this Sunday's parable about "Lazarus and the Rich Man."

The parable is a dramatization of earlier sayings. In the "Sermon on the Plain," Jesus said, "Blessed are you who are poor . . . but woe to you who are rich . . ." (6:20, 24). In the *Magnificat,* Mary praised the God who "has filled the hungry with good things; the rich he has sent away empty" (1:53). All this material about riches and poverty (see also 3:10-14; 12:13-21, 22-31; 14:7-14) demonstrates the importance of this theme to Luke. There are actually two themes in these sayings: God's care for the poor, and the reversal of fortune which characterizes the reign of God.

Luke gives a name to the poor man, "Lazarus," which means "God has helped." This familiar and personal treatment indicates Luke's interest in, and care for, the poor. By contrast, the rich man is unnamed. In the Latin Bible, the word for "rich" or "wealthy" is *"dives,"* which was eventually used as the man's proper name. For all his self-importance, he is still stunningly unimportant, a mere cipher.

The interpretation of "Moses and prophets" returns at the end of the story. "Dives" tacitly admits that, in his lifetime, he had misunderstood the Scriptures; now he wants to warn his brothers. Abraham counters that the Scriptures contain what they need. The issue is not further revelation, but proper understanding. Failure to understand Scripture in such fundamental matters as care of the poor will lead to misunderstanding about the Messiah and his resurrection. After his resurrection, Jesus himself will interpret the Scriptures for his disciples (Luke 24:25-27, 44-47).

ASSEMBLY & FAITH-SHARING GROUPS

- Some "chasms" which exist between people today are . . .
- The poor lying at my door are . . .
- To avoid the mistake of the rich man, I need to examine . . .

PRESIDERS

The "poor" who deserve recognition and assistance through my ministry are . . .

DEACONS

I challenge the community to get beyond "complacency" to compassion for the needy (see first reading) whenever I . . .

HOSPITALITY MINISTERS

My hospitality helps erode the "chasms" which exist in the parish community by . . .

MUSIC MINISTERS

Jesus warns me that how I act now toward those in need will determine my everlasting future (gospel). In my music ministry, the needy person at my doorstep is . . .

ALTAR MINISTERS

Serving others has aligned me with the poor (and with Christ) in that . . .

LECTORS

I encourage the assembly to *listen truly* to the word as God's warning—"they have Moses and the prophets"—by . . .

EXTRAORDINARY MINISTERS OF HOLY COMMUNION

I understand the relationship between distributing Communion and tending to the needy to be . . .

Model Act of Penitence

Presider: Today's gospel is the parable of the rich man and Lazarus. After death, they end up on opposite sides of a great chasm—one side torment and the other comfort. Let us prepare ourselves for this liturgy, so that one day we might join Lazarus in everlasting life with God . . . [pause]

> Lord Jesus, you became poor so that we might be made rich: Lord . . .
>
> Christ Jesus, you raise those who are bowed down: Christ . . .
>
> Lord Jesus, you will come to judge the living and the dead: Lord . . .

Appreciating the Responsorial Psalm

The beloved of God are those who are suffering and in need (gospel, responsorial psalm). If we separate ourselves from the poor and needy, as do the complacent in the first reading and the rich man in the gospel, we separate ourselves from God and from the possibility of blessed life in eternity. As the Body of Christ, we are called to act like God in securing justice for the oppressed, feeding the hungry, freeing captives, protecting strangers, caring for the orphaned and widowed, etc. (responsorial psalm). Psalm 146 praises God for these compassionate and saving deeds. In singing it we express our admiration for the One we are called to imitate.

Model General Intercessions

Presider: God offers us the joy and comfort of everlasting life. Let us pray that we may live today so that we might rise into eternal glory.

Response:

Lord, hear our prayer.

Cantor:

we pray to the Lord,

That the Church always strive to bridge chasms which divide the human community . . . [pause]

That the prosperous of the world generously reach out in concern to the poor and needy . . . [pause]

That those who dedicate their lives to the service of the poor and needy might be strengthened . . . [pause]

That each of us here compassionately assist the needy who lie at our door . . . [pause]

Presider: Just and merciful God, you judge those worthy to enjoy everlasting life with you: hear these our prayers that one day we might be carried by angels to the bosom of Abraham. We ask this through Christ our Lord. **Amen.**

OPENING PRAYER

Let us pray

Pause for silent prayer

Father,
you show your almighty power
in your mercy and forgiveness.
Continue to fill us with your gifts of love.
Help us to hurry toward the eternal life
    you promise
and come to share in the joys of your
    kingdom.

Grant this through our Lord Jesus Christ,
    your Son,
who lives and reigns with you and the
    Holy Spirit,
one God, for ever and ever. **Amen.**

FIRST READING
Amos 6:1a, 4-7

Thus says the LORD, the God of hosts:
Woe to the complacent in Zion!
Lying upon beds of ivory,
    stretched comfortably on their couches,
they eat lambs taken from the flock,
    and calves from the stall!
Improvising to the music of the harp,
    like David, they devise their own
        accompaniment.
They drink wine from bowls
    and anoint themselves with the best oils;
        yet they are not made ill by the collapse
        of Joseph!
Therefore, now they shall be the first to go
    into exile,
    and their wanton revelry shall be done
        away with.

RESPONSORIAL PSALM
Ps 146:7, 8-9, 9-10

℞. (1b) Praise the Lord, my soul!
or:
℞. Alleluia.

Blessed is he who keeps faith forever,
   secures justice for the oppressed,
   gives food to the hungry.
The LORD sets captives free.

℞. Praise the Lord, my soul!
or:
℞. Alleluia.

The LORD gives sight to the blind.
   The LORD raises up those who were
      bowed down.
The LORD loves the just;
   the LORD protects strangers.

℞. Praise the Lord, my soul!
or:
℞. Alleluia.

The fatherless and the widow he sustains,
   but the way of the wicked he thwarts.
The LORD shall reign forever;
   your God, O Zion, through all
      generations. Alleluia.

℞. Praise the Lord, my soul!
or:
℞. Alleluia.

SECOND READING
1 Tim 6:11-16

But you, man of God, pursue righteousness,
   devotion, faith, love, patience, and
      gentleness.
Compete well for the faith.
Lay hold of eternal life, to which you were
      called
   when you made the noble confession in
      the presence of many witnesses.
I charge you before God, who gives life to
   all things,
   and before Christ Jesus,
   who gave testimony under Pontius
      Pilate for the noble confession,
   to keep the commandment without stain
      or reproach
   until the appearance of our Lord Jesus
      Christ
   that the blessed and only ruler
   will make manifest at the proper time,
   the King of kings and Lord of lords,
   who alone has immortality, who dwells
      in unapproachable light,
   and whom no human being has seen or
      can see.
To him be honor and eternal power. Amen.

About Liturgy
Liturgy of the Word and eternal life: Probably most of us would not readily connect our hearing the word proclaimed on Sunday at Mass and eternal life. This Sunday's gospel suggests how we might make this connection.

When the rich man asks Abraham to send someone to warn his brothers about the life they are leading and what eternity will bring them, Abraham replies that they already have more than enough—they need to expect no miraculous revelation because they have always had Moses and the prophets, and now Jesus to teach them to live righteously. We, too, have such a word preached to us each Sunday. This gospel reminds us of the grave importance of attentiveness to the Liturgy of the Word. There is far more at stake than simply listening to the readings and homily. In all we are hearing *God's* word spoken to us, both as a warning and a challenge.

Perhaps one way of "actively listening" to the readings each Sunday is to take some few seconds after each reading and after the homily (hopefully, this silent time is given within the shape of the Liturgy of the Word itself; if not, then the assembly member might take time after leaving church or arriving home) to ask, "How is this calling me to righteous living? How am I called to be sensitive and compassionate to those around me in need?"

About Liturgical Music
Cantor preparation: The content of this Sunday's responsorial psalm is the same as that of last Sunday's psalm: God's compassionate and active care for the poor and suffering. To sing either with conviction you must share this same care. Who are the suffering and needy at your doorstep? How are you reaching out to them?

Music chasms in parishes: The suffering person from whom the rich man in this parable separates himself is not geographically distant, but is right at his doorstep, and the chasm which he allows to divide them is carried into eternity. What chasms—real and potential—challenge music ministry in a parish—ethnic-cultural ones? age-group ones? gender-based ones? The challenge for many parishes today is learning how to bridge these gaps while at the same time honoring the needs and demands of the liturgy.

An excellent resource for understanding and using liturgical music from many different cultures and historical eras is *Leading the Church's Song* (©1998, Augsburg Fortress #33-402). Chapters deal with Asian, African, Latino, African-American, contemporary, North American, Northern European, and chant styles of music. Each section presents historical background on the style, then describes how it is meant to sound and how it needs to be led. Numerous instrumental and vocal examples are given, both printed in musical score in the book and recorded on the accompanying CD.

SEPTEMBER 30, 2007
TWENTY-SIXTH SUNDAY
IN ORDINARY TIME

SPIRITUALITY

Gospel

Luke 17:5-10; L141C

The apostles said to the Lord,
    "Increase our faith."
The Lord replied,
    "If you have faith the size of
        a mustard seed,
    you would say to this
        mulberry tree,
    'Be uprooted and planted in
        the sea,' and it would
        obey you.

"Who among you would say to
    your servant
    who has just come in from
        plowing or tending sheep
        in
        the field,
    'Come here immediately and
        take your place at table'?
Would he not rather say to him,
    'Prepare something for me to eat.
Put on your apron and wait on me while
    I eat and drink.
You may eat and drink when I am
    finished'?
Is he grateful to that servant because
    he did what was commanded?
So should it be with you.
When you have done all you have been
    commanded,
    say, 'We are unprofitable servants;
    we have done what we were obliged
        to do.'"

Reflecting on the Gospel

When the disciples asked Jesus to "increase [their] faith," what exactly were they asking of him? At first glance, it is hard even to see how Jesus granted the apostles' request. He answers them by first saying that quantity is not really the issue (even "faith the size of a mustard seed" is enough) and then goes on to speak about fulfilling everyday obligations. In following Jesus, doing dramatic things is not the issue. After all, the master does not order his servant to move a mulberry tree by faith, but to meet ordinary expectations—serve at table, wait on him, do whatever is commanded. The issue is to be faithful to the master and his commands. It is by such fidelity that faith increases.

In fact, a reflection on faith does not begin with ourselves at all, but with the Master, with God. In the Hebrew Scriptures, Israel has faith because God has unfailingly made good on God's promise to enact mighty deeds of salvation. Israel's faith, then, is a trusting response to a faithful God. Faith is relational—we put our faith not in something but in *Someone*. God is true to who God is when God carries forward the plan for our salvation. We are true to who we are when we obediently cooperate in that plan of salvation. Fulfilling our Christian obligations is more than an exercise of responsibility or obedience. It expresses and reinforces our relationship to Jesus. He is the Master, we are servants.

When we hear the phrase from the gospel "increase our faith," we might look to the first reading where Habakkuk cautions us against a notion of faith as merely giving assent of the mind. Faith is a way of life. Thus, the important thing to remember here is that faith is more a verb than a noun. Faith is expressed in the way we act. Here is the crunch: faith is truly extraordinary, not in the stupendous acts we might do for God and others, but in terms of the consistent and enduring choices we make daily to act righteously, humbly, mercifully, and justly, as well as being forgiving and reconciling—that is, to be obedient to all that Jesus has asked of us. Faith is a way of living, a way of expressing our true selves such that we act toward others like the Divine has acted toward us.

Living the Paschal Mystery

We tend to think of everyday responsibilities as mundane, and they are! But this gospel reveals the hidden dimension of such ordinary actions—they reveal and increase our faith. We Catholics definitely have the idea that if we are good during this life our "reward" is heaven. The second part of this gospel suggests to us that we are to do simply what is obliged of us and expect nothing more. This is what the "unprofitable" in the last line means. We do not do what we are supposed to do in order to be rewarded, but we do it simply because that is what is expected of us.

Thus, one aspect of faith is recognizing that doing what disciples are supposed to do in itself does not earn God's beneficence. Heaven is not a "reward" for being faithful. Heaven is the amplification of the way we live our present life. What we are "obliged to do" is be faithful. What is being faithful? Being servant of all. Habakkuk in the first reading teaches us that faithfulness is trusting while we are waiting for fulfillment of the vision of everlasting goodness and righteousness. Faithfulness is confidence that God will fulfill God's promise to us of salvation and deliverance. Being faithful in this life is already living what heaven will be!

Focusing the Gospel

Key words and phrases: increase our faith, servant, did what was commanded

To the point: In following Jesus, doing dramatic things is not the issue. After all, the master does not order his servant to move a mulberry tree by faith, but to meet ordinary expectations—serve at table, wait on him, do whatever is commanded. The issue is to be faithful to the master and his commands. It is by such fidelity that faith increases.

Connecting the Gospel

to the first reading: When we hear the phrase from the gospel "increase our faith," we might look to the first reading where Habakkuk cautions us against a notion of faith as merely giving assent of the mind. Faith is a way of life.

to culture: We tend to think of everyday responsibilities as mundane, and they are! But this gospel reveals the hidden dimension of such ordinary actions—they reveal and increase our faith.

Understanding Scripture

Faith and faithfulness: The opening line of this Sunday's gospel seems to be a response to the verses omitted by the Lectionary. In Luke 17:1-4, Jesus warns his disciples about sinning against others and requires them to forgive as often as asked. The difficulty of these requirements leads the disciples to ask, "Increase our faith" (17:5). But even with increased faith, the disciples will still be servants required to fulfill their assigned tasks. Faithful service is not something extraordinary which merits praise and recognition; disciples are expected to be faithful in their service of the Master. Further, servants are servants for life. Whether a menial servant or a chief servant, there does not come a time when the master says, "your service and seniority entitles you to be served." All in the Church, even the "apostles" to whom Jesus is speaking, are servants of the Master, and they are servants for life.

This Sunday is the only time in the three-year Sunday cycle that we read from the book of Habakkuk (the first reading). This selection is edited: between 1:2-3 and 2:2-4, it skips 1:4-17, 2:1. It is chosen and edited for the pivotal final verse, "but the just one, because of his faith, shall live." This obviously is a comment on the theme of faith in the gospel. Habakkuk opens with a lament: the prophet complains to God about the "violence . . . destruction . . . strife . . . [and] discord" all around. So insufferable is this condition that it requires God's immediate attention. God answers the prophet's urgent prayer with a vision which will surely come, even if it is delayed. In the meantime, "the just one, because of his faith, will live." The word translated as "faith" usually means "faithfulness." "Faith" in this sense means remaining faithful to God and living according to God's expectations. In short, "faith/ faithfulness" is a way of life more than a commitment of the mind. This is the sense in the gospel and also in Paul for whom trust in God's promises, rather than "works of the Law," leads to salvation (Rom 1:17 and Gal 3:11; see also Heb 10:38).

ASSEMBLY & FAITH-SHARING GROUPS

- I have wanted my faith to be increased when . . .
- My faith has been increased by . . .
- As an "unprofitable servant," what I am "obliged to do" for God is . . .

PRESIDERS

For me, the most difficult part about remaining faithful as God's "unprofitable servant" is . . . ; this reflection helps me support others because . . .

DEACONS

Doing ministry increases my faith because . . .

HOSPITALITY MINISTERS

I encourage others to remain confident in God's vision for us, even if it delays (see first reading), by . . .

MUSIC MINISTERS

What God expects of me as a music minister is . . . I give all that is expected when I . . . In return, God gives me more than I expect by . . .

ALTAR MINISTERS

Serving others increases my faith because . . . ; serving others increases their faith in that . . .

LECTORS

My daily living is a genuine proclamation of the vision God has planned for us (see first reading) when . . .

EXTRAORDINARY MINISTERS OF HOLY COMMUNION

When I witness the assembly receiving Communion, my faith is increased because . . .

CELEBRATION

Model Act of Penitence

Presider: As we prepare for this liturgy, let us open ourselves to God's presence and surrender to God's action within us so that our faith might be increased . . . [pause]

    Lord Jesus, you are God's faithful servant: Lord . . .

    Christ Jesus, you are the One whom we serve: Christ . . .

    Lord Jesus, you give us the strength to be faithful: Lord . . .

Appreciating the Responsorial Psalm

Psalm 95, like other psalms such as Psalm 15, includes a ritual for entrance into the Temple for worship. Before being admitted, the people were asked if they had been faithful to God who created and shepherded them (v. 6). The question was no idle one, for Israel's first ancestors had not been permitted entrance into the Promised Land because of their infidelity. This is the story behind verses 8-9, and the reason for the harsh refrain, "harden not your hearts." Faith means active response to the One who is first and always faithful to us (first reading). Faith means faithful living, doing what God expects of us (gospel). Faith means acting according to who we are, God's chosen people (psalm). Faith means active listening which transforms our hearts and our behavior.

Model General Intercessions

Presider: God is ever faithful and true. Therefore, we are confident when we make our prayers known.

Response:

Cantor:

That all members of the Church express their faith by lives of service . . . [pause]

That all peoples of the world come to true faith in God . . . [pause]

That those who struggle with faith be encouraged by the faith-filled actions of others . . . [pause]

That all of us here grow in faith . . . [pause]

Presider: Ever-faithful God, you keep your promises from all eternity: hear these our prayers that we might serve you in one another and attain our eternal life. We ask this through Christ our Lord. **Amen.**

ALTERNATIVE OPENING PRAYER

Let us pray
[before the face of God in trusting faith]

Pause for silent prayer

Almighty and eternal God,
Father of the world to come,
your goodness is beyond what our spirit
    can touch
and your strength is more than the mind
    can bear.
Lead us to seek beyond our reach
and give us the courage to stand before
    your truth.
We ask this through Christ our Lord.
    Amen.

FIRST READING
Hab 1:2-3; 2:2-4

How long, O LORD? I cry for help
    but you do not listen!
I cry out to you, "Violence!"
    but you do not intervene.
Why do you let me see ruin;
    why must I look at misery?
Destruction and violence are before me;
    there is strife, and clamorous discord.
Then the LORD answered me and said:
    Write down the vision clearly upon the
        tablets,
    so that one can read it readily.
For the vision still has its time,
    presses on to fulfillment, and will not
        disappoint;
if it delays, wait for it,
    it will surely come, it will not be late.
The rash one has no integrity;
    but the just one, because of his faith,
        shall live.

RESPONSORIAL PSALM
Ps 95:1-2, 6-7, 8-9

R̸. (8) If today you hear his voice, harden not your hearts.

Come, let us sing joyfully to the LORD;
  let us acclaim the Rock of our salvation.
Let us come into his presence with
    thanksgiving;
  let us joyfully sing psalms to him.

R̸. If today you hear his voice, harden not your hearts.

Come, let us bow down in worship;
  let us kneel before the LORD who made
    us.
For he is our God,
  and we are the people he shepherds, the
    flock he guides.

R̸. If today you hear his voice, harden not your hearts.

Oh, that today you would hear his voice:
  "Harden not your hearts as at Meribah,
  as in the day of Massah in the desert,
where your fathers tempted me;
  they tested me though they had seen my
    works."

R̸. If today you hear his voice, harden not your hearts.

SECOND READING
2 Tim 1:6-8, 13-14

Beloved:
I remind you to stir into flame
  the gift of God that you have through
    the imposition of my hands.
For God did not give us a spirit of
    cowardice
  but rather of power and love and
    self-control.
So do not be ashamed of your testimony
    to our Lord,
  nor of me, a prisoner for his sake;
  but bear your share of hardship for the
    gospel
  with the strength that comes from God.

Take as your norm the sound words that
    you heard from me,
  in the faith and love that are in Christ
    Jesus.
Guard this rich trust with the help of the
    Holy Spirit
  that dwells within us.

About Liturgy

The structure of collects: The alternative opening prayer for this Sunday is a wonderful example of a collect structure which totally supports and prepares the assembly to surrender to the liturgical action, hear God's word, and be nourished at God's table. Both the opening prayer and alternative opening prayer given in the Sacramentary for each Sunday include an intention after "Let us pray." Sometimes it is helpful, sometimes not. This Sunday it is particularly compelling and helps the assembly focus.

The inclusion of the intention is a reminder that there should be a period of silence after the "Let us pray" so that the assembly can gather their thoughts and intentions and offer them to God (see GIRM no. 54). What happens during this silence is an important structural part of the prayer, not an appendage. What the presider says "collects" the assembly's individual prayers and concludes the opening prayer; it is not the entire prayer. Thus, the structure is (1) invitation to pray with or without the explicit verbalization of an intention by the presider, (2) silent time for the assembly's prayer, (3) the "[Alternative] Opening Prayer" given in the Sacramentary (which functions as a "collect" and the conclusion to the prayer), and (4) the assembly's affirmation of "Amen."

Collects during liturgy (also called the "presidential prayers": the opening prayer, prayer over the gifts, and prayer after Communion) are good examples of liturgy's use of private, personal prayer within communal prayer. There are ample ways to make liturgy very personal; we need only be keyed into these important moments.

About Liturgical Music

Cantor preparation: The harsh shift between the beginning of this responsorial psalm and its conclusion only makes sense when you know the whole story of the psalm (see Appreciating the Responsorial Psalm). The psalm reminds you, and the assembly, that acts of worship must go hand in hand with daily fidelity to God's commands. When do you find such fidelity challenging? When do you find it easy?

Music suggestions: "The Church of Christ in Every Age" [GC2, RS, WC, W3] fits the words of this Sunday's gospel when it reminds us "We have no mission but to serve In full obedience to our Lord . . ." (verse 5). The hymn would be an excellent entrance song. In the refrain of David Haas' "Increase Our Faith" [GC2; GIA octavo #G-4736] we beg God to increase our faith and pray, "With all our heart, may we always follow you." This simple, meditative piece would work well during the presentation of the gifts with cantor or choir singing verses 1-2, and the assembly verse 3.

SPIRITUALITY

Gospel

Luke 17:11-19; L144C

As Jesus continued his journey to
    Jerusalem,
  he traveled through Samaria and
    Galilee.
As he was entering a village, ten
    lepers met him.
They stood at a distance from
    him and raised their voices,
    saying,
  "Jesus, Master! Have pity on
    us!"
And when he saw them, he said,
  "Go show yourselves to the
    priests."
As they were going they were
    cleansed.
And one of them, realizing he had
    been healed,
  returned, glorifying God in a loud
    voice;
  and he fell at the feet of Jesus and
    thanked him.
He was a Samaritan.
Jesus said in reply,
  "Ten were cleansed, were they not?
Where are the other nine?
Has none but this foreigner returned to
    give thanks to God?"
Then he said to him, "Stand up and go;
  your faith has saved you."

Reflecting on the Gospel

How often do we not hear parents remind their children to say thank you when they have received a gift? What does this teach the children? First of all, it helps them understand that gifts are just that—freely given and undeserved. The thank you acknowledges that the giver has gone beyond expectations. Secondly, it helps them understand that giving and receiving a gift establishes a unique relationship between two persons. The thank you acknowledges that the receiver has accepted the gift and by so doing enters into a relationship with the giver.

The gospel this Sunday is the familiar one about ten lepers being healed, but only one returning to give thanks to Jesus. As with any gift, Jesus' healing them went beyond their expectations, was freely given by Jesus, and established a unique relationship between Jesus and the ten lepers. But only one acknowledges that relationship by giving thanks. The parable reminds us that it is not enough to cry to God for help (as did the lepers); it is not even enough to experience God's healing action. We are meant to acknowledge God's gracious activity on our behalf by giving God thanks ("he fell at the feet of Jesus and thanked him") and worship ("returned, glorifying God in a loud voice"). Gratitude was not necessary for the healing (all ten were healed!). God's saving activity does not depend on us. The gratitude was necessary, however, for God's gracious deed to be acknowledged and proclaimed, announcing that God has acted. Gratitude helps make known God's mighty deeds.

Thus the ten lepers exemplify aspects of our relationship with God: acknowledgment of need ("'Have pity on us'"), obedience ("'Go . . .' . . . as they were going"), and reception of divine mercy ("they were cleansed"). The Samaritan leper demonstrates another aspect of this relationship: only when he returns to glorify God and thank Jesus, does Jesus reveal that he has, in fact, been saved. For us, as for the Samaritan leper, salvation is revealed and experienced in worship and thanksgiving.

Salvation, worship, and thanksgiving are closely connected. Both events—God's saving activity and our thankful worship—cement a giver-receiver relationship with God. God freely offers us salvation; worship and thanksgiving manifest within the community our acknowledgment and reception of salvation. Worship and thanksgiving are our *yes* to God's gifts to us.

Living the Paschal Mystery

This is what happens on the journey to Jerusalem: on the way we are all cleansed—saved. This is one reason why all the little things of our everyday lives—those things which happen to us along the journey—are so important. They are manifestations of God's acting on our behalf, healing us and saving us. We want to seize them and give thanks.

One challenge of this Sunday's gospel is to see God's promise of salvation unfolding in these everyday events of our lives. Faithful service, then, is our response to seeing God in these events. Gratitude—acknowledging God's actions on our behalf—is an all-enveloping context for living our lives. When gratitude is put on as a way of living, then worship, too, becomes a way of living. Rather than relegated to an hour on Sunday, worship is part of all the little actions which make up each of our days. For that, let us give thanks!

Focusing the Gospel

Key words and phrases: Have pity on us!, Go, cleansed, glorifying God, thanked him, faith, saved

To the point: The ten lepers exemplify aspects of our relationship with God: acknowledgment of need ("'Have pity on us'"), obedience ("'Go . . .' . . . as they were going"), and reception of divine mercy ("they were cleansed"). The Samaritan leper demonstrates another aspect of this relationship: only when he returns to glorify God and thank Jesus, does Jesus reveal that he has, in fact, been saved. For us, as for the Samaritan leper, salvation is revealed and experienced in worship and thanksgiving.

Connecting the Gospel

to the first reading: The first reading and gospel parallel each other: both present foreigners (Naaman is a Syrian, the grateful leper is a Samaritan) who are healed of leprosy, give thanks, and worship.

to religious experience: We often think of worship as a time to thank and praise God as, indeed, it is. It is, however, also an opportunity to experience God's mercy and salvation.

Understanding Scripture

Faith, thanks, and salvation: The gospel story of Jesus' healing the lepers, including a foreigner, echoes the story of Elisha curing Naaman the Syrian of his leprosy (first reading). Both foreigners seek healing from a holy man; both do as they are instructed to do; both are effusive in their thanks, each according to his means; both worship the God who heals them. But there are some differences in the stories which are instructive.

Although Naaman offers a gift, Elisha will not accept it, perhaps because his piety recognizes that the gift belongs to God who provided the cure. Naaman sees in his cure what the nine lepers in the gospel fail to acknowledge, that the healing is from God. Healing leads to faith, so now this foreigner will worship only the God of Israel. This poses a problem, however. In the ancient world, gods were considered territorial—they were associated with particular places where their power was evident, and were identified with the nations to whom they were patron deities. Beyond their own lands, gods were neither powerful nor present. Thus, in Psalm 137, "by the streams of Babylon," the exiled Judeans cannot sing a song to the Lord in a foreign land. And so it is that Naaman decides to bring the Lord's earth back to Syria. This will allow him to set up an altar to the God of Israel on it and to offer sacrifice to the God who saved him from his leprosy.

The healing of the Samaritan leper adds one more element to the story which is lacking in the first reading. In offering thanks and worship, Jesus has the opportunity to affirm the Samaritan's faith and in so doing he reveals the true nature of the healing. The leper has had an experience of salvation: "your faith has saved you." For both Naaman and the Samaritan, faith expresses itself in worship (Naaman offers sacrifice; the Samaritan glorifies God and falls at the feet of Jesus). But for the Samaritan, faith also reveals the saving power of God made manifest in Jesus.

**ASSEMBLY &
FAITH-SHARING GROUPS**
- Like the ten lepers, I acknowledge before God my need for . . .
- Like the Samaritan leper, I have realized God's goodness to me when . . .
- To be like the Samaritan leper and "give thanks to God" means to me . . .

PRESIDERS
How I keep a *thanksgiving* heart—in the midst of presiding over multiple liturgies—is . . .

DEACONS
I guide others not only to acknowledge their needs before God, but also to return to the Lord with heartfelt gratitude by . . .

HOSPITALITY MINISTERS
Ways that I express my gratitude to those who support me in my ministry are . . .

MUSIC MINISTERS
Through my music ministry, I experience God's gift of salvation when . . . I give God thanks by . . .

ALTAR MINISTERS
When I reflect upon God's goodness to me, my service to others looks like . . .

LECTORS
Gratitude is something I not only express but also *live* when I . . .

**EXTRAORDINARY MINISTERS
OF HOLY COMMUNION**
What brings me back to "the feet of Jesus" in gratitude is . . . ; I shall help others to recall what might bring them back to God in thanksgiving by . . .

Model Act of Penitence

Presider: Just as the ten lepers in today's gospel ask for mercy, we begin this liturgy by acknowledging our needs and praying for mercy . . . [pause]

Lord Jesus, you hear our cries for mercy: Lord . . .

Christ Jesus, you reveal God's saving power: Christ . . .

Lord Jesus, you are worthy of all thanks and praise: Lord . . .

Appreciating the Responsorial Psalm

Psalm 98, from which this Sunday's responsorial psalm is taken, sings about the completion of God's saving plan for Israel. All the forces which threaten God's chosen people—depicted in various psalms as enemy nations, roaring seas, evildoers, famine, disease—have been put to rout by God. God's "wondrous deeds" of salvation have been revealed, and the whole world rejoices. The healing stories in the first reading and gospel are concrete dramatizations of God's saving deeds. By singing Psalm 98 we join Naaman and the grateful leper in offering thanks to God for saving us from disease and death. We express our faith in God and are granted salvation.

Model General Intercessions

Presider: God answers all our needs if we but ask. And so we pray.

Response:

Lord, hear our prayer.

Cantor:

we pray to the Lord,

That the Church always be a font of healing and mercy . . . [pause]

That leaders of nations may respond with compassion to the needs of their people . . . [pause]

That the afflicted be healed and remain steadfast in faith . . . [pause]

That we always and everywhere give God praise and thanksgiving . . . [pause]

Presider: Lord God, you continue to perform mighty deeds on our behalf: may faith and gratitude be ever evident in our world as we strive to reach out to all in need. We ask this through Christ our Lord. **Amen.**

RESPONSORIAL PSALM
Ps 98:1, 2-3, 3-4

R℟. (cf. 2b) The Lord has revealed to the nations his saving power.

Sing to the LORD a new song,
   for he has done wondrous deeds;
his right hand has won victory for him,
   his holy arm.

R℟. The Lord has revealed to the nations his saving power.

The LORD has made his salvation known:
   in the sight of the nations he has
      revealed his justice.
He has remembered his kindness and his
      faithfulness
   toward the house of Israel.

R℟. The Lord has revealed to the nations his saving power.

All the ends of the earth have seen
   the salvation by our God.
Sing joyfully to the LORD, all you lands:
   break into song; sing praise.

R℟. The Lord has revealed to the nations his saving power.

SECOND READING
2 Tim 2:8-13

Beloved:
Remember Jesus Christ, raised from the
      dead, a descendant of David:
   such is my gospel, for which I am
      suffering,
   even to the point of chains, like a
      criminal.
But the word of God is not chained.
Therefore, I bear with everything for the
      sake of those who are chosen,
   so that they too may obtain the
      salvation that is in Christ Jesus,
   together with eternal glory.
This saying is trustworthy:
   If we have died with him
      we shall also live with him;
   if we persevere
      we shall also reign with him.
   But if we deny him
      he will deny us.
   If we are unfaithful
      he remains faithful,
      for he cannot deny himself.

About Liturgy

Eucharist means thanksgiving: Only one leper returned to give thanks to Jesus for having been cleansed. Each Sunday the Christian assembly gathers to celebrate "Eucharist," which in Greek means "thanksgiving." Thus each Sunday the Christian community comes to Jesus to give thanks for the gifts of the week: strength and guidance, healing and cleansing, mercy and forgiveness.

Giving thanks is another reason (to celebrate the resurrection is the primary one) why Christians gather each Sunday for worship. The very nature of what is done together on Sunday is giving thanks. There is a "built-in" guarantee that, like the Samaritan leper in this Sunday's gospel, Christians celebrating Eucharist formalize their thanks at least weekly as they gather. Eucharist is our way of never forgetting to raise grateful hearts to God for all we have. As we come together to remember Jesus' self-giving sacrifice for our salvation, as we place ourselves on the altar in self-giving each week, we are returning to God thanks for all that has been given us.

It is sometimes tempting to phrase a petition at the general intercessions in the form of a thanksgiving; for example, to thank God for good weather for the parish picnic, or for a successful building campaign drive, or for the restoration to health of an ill parishioner. The purpose of the intercessions is not to offer God thanksgiving, however, but to make our needs known to God. It is important to keep the intercessions *petitionary*. The thanksgiving we need to offer God is done through the very doing of the Eucharist.

About Liturgical Music

Cantor preparation: Reflect this week on where you have seen God's salvation unfold—in your own life, in the Church, in the world. Let your singing of this responsorial psalm be both a proclamation of God's deeds and a thanksgiving for them.

Music suggestions: This would be a good Sunday to sing a hymn of praise and thanksgiving after Communion. The assembly could sing a setting of Psalm 136, for example. Marty Haugen's setting in *Psalms for the Church Year, Volume Two* [GIA G-3261] is meant to move at a quick tempo, with the assembly energetically responding to the cantor's litany of God's saving deeds. The choir parts add dimension and use of some percussion (drum, tambourine, triangle) would build intensity. Gelineau's setting of Psalm 136 is reprinted in the Presbyterian collection *The Psalter—Psalms and Canticles for Singing* [Westminster/John Knox Press, Louisville] with an amended, inclusive language refrain. The SATB arrangement is not difficult, but the syncopations which give it life will require attentiveness on the part of the choir.

SPIRITUALITY

Gospel Luke 18:1-8; L147C

Jesus told his disciples a parable
about the necessity for them to pray
always without becoming weary.
He said, "There was a judge in a
certain town
who neither feared God nor respected
any human being.
And a widow in that town used to come
to him and say,
'Render a just decision for me against
my adversary.'
For a long time the judge was unwilling,
but eventually he thought,
'While it is true that I neither fear
God nor respect any human
being,
because this widow keeps bothering
me
I shall deliver a just decision for her
lest she finally come and strike me.'"
The Lord said, "Pay attention to what
the dishonest judge says.
Will not God then secure the rights of
his chosen ones
who call out to him day and night?
Will he be slow to answer them?
I tell you, he will see to it that justice is
done for them speedily.
But when the Son of Man comes, will
he find faith on earth?"

Reflecting on the Gospel

Luke's gospel is beginning to convey more and more urgency. We have a sense that our journey is coming to an end. We must act, and we must act now! This is the liturgical context which shapes our reflection on this gospel. As we approach the end of the liturgical year and the Church's annual remembrance of Christ's Second Coming, it is good for us to recall that God "secure[s] the rights of his chosen ones who call out to him day and night" (gospel). Anticipating Christ's Second Coming, we assume a posture of calling out to God day and night for justice. Only our persistence will secure for us a favorable judgment when Christ comes.

Persistence, at least as presented in the first reading and gospel, is the attitude of one seeking justice. The widow's faith in this Sunday's gospel is a response to a God who delivers the just. By remaining persistent in her petition for justice, the widow exemplifies the steadfast faith sought by "the Son of Man." Both justice and faith have to do with our relationship with God. Justice sets us in right relationship with God and others; faith impels us to do whatever is necessary to establish that right relationship. Moreover, when we are in right relationship with God, we are cooperating with God's plan of salvation. Thus, by impelling us toward justice, faith is ultimately seeking salvation. Persistence in prayer, then, is an expression of our own persistent striving for salvation.

Whether the response to our own prayer is delayed or speedily given, faith and hope uphold our efforts to "pray always." Persistence requires discipline, and it rests on the hope that the desired outcome of our efforts will be achieved. For example, we are persistent in exercise routines, athletic training, musical practice. So it is with prayer: we persist because of our hope that God will hear us. This hope, nonetheless, is not merely future-oriented, concerned only with receiving what we request. This hope rests on the conviction of our steadfast relationship to the God who has always been faithful and who always listens to our prayer. If faith seeks justice and salvation, then hope spawns the confidence that our prayer will be heard and one day we will share in everlasting life.

Living the Paschal Mystery

Will God "find faith on earth?" God does find faith in those who persist in prayer. But what about those of us who feel like we are praying persistently for our needs . . . why is God not answering us?

This raises the important issue about what we pray for. If our prayer is simply about getting what we want, then our focus may only be upon ourselves. If, instead, our focus is on "justice [being] done . . . speedily," then persistence will get us that justice and, ultimately, salvation. The key is to remember that the answer to our prayers is not getting what we want now, but justice, that is, right relationship with God. Ultimately, then, our persistence in prayer leads to receiving more than we could possibly want or imagine. It leads to favorable judgment when Christ comes and our entering into eternal glory with him.

This is not to say that we forgo praying for our own needs; for example, for the good of the family, secure employment, good health, sufficiency in retirement, etc. These needs, however immediate, are always prayed for within the larger picture: what we need to secure right relationship with God and salvation. In this, we are always assured that our prayer will be heard.

Focusing the Gospel

Key words and phrases: pray always, call out . . . day and night, answer, find faith

To the point: By remaining persistent in her petition for justice, the widow exemplifies the steadfast faith sought by "the Son of Man." Whether the response to our own prayer is delayed or speedily given, faith and hope uphold our efforts to "pray always."

Connecting the Gospel

to the first reading: The obvious connection between the first reading and gospel is that both Moses and the widow persist in their petitions. The first reading also suggests that, in order to be persistent, sometimes we need the support of others.

to culture: Persistence requires discipline, and rests on the hope that the desired outcome of our efforts will be achieved. For example, we are persistent in exercise routines, athletic training, musical practice. So it is with prayer: we persist because of our hope that God will hear us.

Understanding Scripture

Persistent prayer: Luke's interest in prayer (see Sunday 17C) is evident in parables this week and next. Both parables have their own introductions in which Luke indicates why the story is being told. This Sunday's parable is "about the necessity . . . to pray always without becoming weary." The first reading admirably exemplifies this theme. But before we comment on the reading from Exodus, a few comments on the gospel are needed.

As was the case in the parable of the "Prudent Steward" (Luke 16:1-13; Sunday 25C), the main character used to illustrate the point is not an admirable person. The "dishonest judge" is not offered as an example of virtue, nor is the relationship of judge-petitioner meant to suggest God-supplicant, with God in the role of the unjust judge. The argument is this: if even a judge who cares nothing for justice responds to his petitioner, we can be certain that God, who "secure[s] the rights of his chosen ones," will "see to it that justice is done for them speedily."

As examples of persistent prayer, Luke offers Jesus, who prayed all night long (6:12) and who, in the Garden, "prayed so fervently that his sweat became like drops of blood" (22:44). The Lectionary gives the example of Moses who grows so tired holding up his arms he has to be supported. Actually, the text does not say that Moses is praying. Ancient interpreters were concerned that this whole episode looked magical and mechanical. They offered various interpretations to clarify the point. One Jewish source suggested that Moses was pointing to heaven to remind the army to trust in God; another specified that Moses was praying. Christian interpreters (Barnabas and Justin Martyr) pictured Moses, on the hilltop, holding his arms out in the form of a cross. Further, the commander of Israel's army in the field is "Joshua," which in Greek is "Jesus." Thus, the entire episode at Rephidim foreshadows Jesus on the cross who wins the victory. Hence, this Sunday's readings show that by prayer the army of Israel is delivered, the widow is vindicated, and God's chosen ones receive justice.

**ASSEMBLY &
FAITH-SHARING GROUPS**

- For me to "pray always" means . . .
- My prayer is faith-filled and justice-centered when . . .
- What helps me persist through weariness and remain faithful in prayer is . . .

PRESIDERS
Like Aaron and Hur (see first reading), I assist fellow pray-ers to persist faithfully by . . .

DEACONS
I help the community to persist for justice by . . .

HOSPITALITY MINISTERS
Some examples of when I have comforted and encouraged others when they were weary in faith are . . .

MUSIC MINISTERS
What helps me persist in music ministry is . . . What I ask God for through this ministry is . . .

ALTAR MINISTERS
My service to others is an expression of persistent faith in God when . . .

LECTORS
I shall consider to what extent I persistently cry out for justice—in prayer, through advocacy, etc.—for those most vulnerable . . .

**EXTRAORDINARY MINISTERS
OF HOLY COMMUNION**
Like God's heavenly food, I aid and nurture those who are weary in faith by . . .

CELEBRATION

Model Act of Penitence

Presider: In today's gospel, Jesus teaches his disciples to pray always. We have come together to pray. Let us prepare to pray well . . . [pause]

Lord Jesus, you teach us how to pray: Lord . . .

Christ Jesus, you hear the prayers of those who call to you: Christ . . .

Lord Jesus, you are our help and our guardian: Lord . . .

Appreciating the Responsorial Psalm

Psalm 121, used in its entirety this Sunday, is a pilgrimage song. Having journeyed to Jerusalem for festival, the Israelites must now travel home. They see the dark mountains which surround them as a threat, the hideout of thieves and enemies, the home of wild animals. The psalm is a prayer of confidence in God's protection, perhaps said in blessing over them by the Temple priest as the pilgrims begin their journey home. What motivates the prayer is surety about God. The Israelites know that God answers the prayer of those who are faithful to the covenant. Moses had such confidence (first reading) as did Jesus (gospel), as do we when we sing this psalm. May our singing reveal the "faith on earth" (gospel) for which Christ longs.

Model General Intercessions

Presider: We are called "to pray always without becoming weary." And so we pray.

 Response:

Lord, hear our prayer.

Cantor:

we pray to the Lord,

That the Church be persistent in prayer and steadfast in faith . . . [pause]

That world leaders be persistent in securing justice for all . . . [pause]

That those without hope find support in the faith and prayer of others . . . [pause]

That all of us here support those who are weary in faith . . . [pause]

Presider: O God, you hear the prayers of those who cry out to you: help us to persevere in prayer, that we might one day live with you forever. We ask this through Christ our Lord. **Amen.**

ALTERNATIVE OPENING PRAYER

Let us pray
[to the Lord who bends close to hear our prayer]

Pause for silent prayer

Lord our God, Father of all,
you guard us under the shadow of your wings
and search into the depth of our hearts.
Remove the blindness that cannot know you
and relieve the fear that would hide us from your sight.
We ask this through Christ our Lord.
Amen.

FIRST READING
Exod 17:8-13

In those days, Amalek came and waged war against Israel.
Moses, therefore, said to Joshua,
"Pick out certain men,
and tomorrow go out and engage Amalek in battle.
I will be standing on top of the hill
with the staff of God in my hand."
So Joshua did as Moses told him:
he engaged Amalek in battle
after Moses had climbed to the top of the hill with Aaron and Hur.
As long as Moses kept his hands raised up,
Israel had the better of the fight,
but when he let his hands rest,
Amalek had the better of the fight.
Moses' hands, however, grew tired;
so they put a rock in place for him to sit on.
Meanwhile Aaron and Hur supported his hands,
one on one side and one on the other,
so that his hands remained steady till sunset.
And Joshua mowed down Amalek and his people
with the edge of the sword.

RESPONSORIAL PSALM
Ps 121:1-2, 3-4, 5-6, 7-8

℟. (cf. 2) Our help is from the Lord, who made heaven and earth.

I lift up my eyes toward the mountains;
whence shall help come to me?
My help is from the LORD,
who made heaven and earth.

℟. Our help is from the Lord, who made heaven and earth.

May he not suffer your foot to slip;
> may he slumber not who guards you:
indeed he neither slumbers nor sleeps,
> the guardian of Israel.

R⁊. Our help is from the Lord, who made heaven and earth.

The LORD is your guardian; the LORD is
> your shade;
> he is beside you at your right hand.
The sun shall not harm you by day,
> nor the moon by night.

R⁊. Our help is from the Lord, who made heaven and earth.

The LORD will guard you from all evil;
> he will guard your life.
The LORD will guard your coming and
> your going,
> both now and forever.

R⁊. Our help is from the Lord, who made heaven and earth.

SECOND READING
2 Tim 3:14—4:2

Beloved:
Remain faithful to what you have learned
> and believed,
> because you know from whom you
> > learned it,
> and that from infancy you have known
> > the sacred Scriptures,
> which are capable of giving you
> > wisdom for salvation
> through faith in Christ Jesus.
All Scripture is inspired by God
> and is useful for teaching, for refutation,
> > for correction,
> and for training in righteousness,
> so that one who belongs to God may be
> > competent,
> equipped for every good work.

I charge you in the presence of God and of
> Christ Jesus,
> who will judge the living and the dead,
> and by his appearing and his kingly
> > power:
> proclaim the word;
> be persistent whether it is convenient or
> > inconvenient;
> convince, reprimand, encourage through
> > all patience and teaching.

CATECHESIS

About Liturgy
Ritual's repetition: Some people see the repetition endemic to ritual as boring—simply doing the same things over and over again. It is always a temptation on the part of liturgy committees and others responsible for preparing and making choices about liturgy to "spice things up."

This Sunday's gospel invites us to resist this temptation. The repetition of liturgy might be seen in the context of the persistent prayer of the gospel: we do the same ritual again and again in order to achieve the higher good—salvation which leads to eternal happiness with God. We must always resist the temptation to try to "make liturgy interesting." This usually serves only to focus the liturgy on ourselves rather than God. Our task as a worshiping community is to help each other prepare and celebrate liturgy in such a way that it leads us into the mystery being celebrated by giving ourselves over to the ritual action. Persistence in this will gain us the goal we desire: faith-filled, transforming worship.

Repetition in ritual has a very specific purpose: to free us from thinking about what we are going to do next (sit, stand, respond, etc.) so that we can focus our minds on the deeper meaning of what we are doing: giving God praise and thanks. If there is too much creativity and novelty in liturgy week after week (and there surely are legitimate choices to be made about liturgy!), the assembly can never "settle in" and just pray.

About Liturgical Music
Cantor preparation: When you sing this responsorial psalm, you are like the Temple priest blessing the people as they begin their journey homeward. The people are the Body of Christ, the journey that of faithful discipleship, the homeland God's kingdom. You are the one assuring the assembly of God's presence and protection on the way.

The value of familiar, repeated music: "About Liturgy" (see above) reminds us that the repetition built into liturgy helps the Church persist in prayer. The same is true for liturgical music. It is not how many new songs or new settings of the Mass the assembly sings which will transform them, but how well they pray liturgically when they sing. For this to happen, the music needs to be familiar. Constantly changing service music and introducing new hymns keeps the assembly on the surface of the liturgy. This may be interesting, stimulating, and entertaining, but it makes liturgy a kind of musical superhighway with so many distracting billboards the assembly soon forgets what road they are on and where they are going. The real role of music, however, is to help the assembly stay focused on where they are going—into the center of the paschal mystery—and help them persist in the prayer needed to go there.

SPIRITUALITY

Gospel

Luke 18:9-14; L150C

Jesus addressed this parable
   to those who were
      convinced of their own
      righteousness
   and despised everyone else.
"Two people went up to the
      temple area to pray;
   one was a Pharisee and
      the other was a tax
      collector.
The Pharisee took up his
   position and spoke this
   prayer to himself,
   'O God, I thank you that I
      am not like the rest of
      humanity—
   greedy, dishonest, adulterous—or
      even like this tax collector.
I fast twice a week, and I pay tithes on
   my whole income.'
But the tax collector stood off at a
   distance
   and would not even raise his eyes to
      heaven
   but beat his breast and prayed,
   'O God, be merciful to me a sinner.'
I tell you, the latter went home
   justified, not the former;
   for whoever exalts himself will be
      humbled,
   and the one who humbles himself
      will be exalted."

Reflecting on the Gospel

This Sunday's gospel contrasts a pious Pharisee and a sinful tax collector. As with the parable of the rich man and Lazarus (see the Twenty-sixth Sunday in Ordinary Time), most of us would immediately identify with the sinful tax collector and his humble prayer. None of us would admit to being like the Pharisee. Yet, some of us really are like the Pharisee in that we put our pious acts above everything else and think this is how we are justified. For example, some people fill their houses with statues and shrines and say prayers constantly, but are anything but charitable and self-giving toward others. Others constantly judge the prayer practice of others (or what they perceive to be inadequate prayer practices), thinking they themselves have the right formula. Truth be told, probably most of us have something of both the Pharisee and tax collector in us. So this Sunday is a wonderful opportunity to assess not only our prayer life, but also our basic stance toward God.

This gospel recounts in a dramatic parable the teaching of Sirach from the first reading: "the prayer of the lowly" is willingly and speedily heard by God. Unexpectedly, it is the sinful tax collector, and not the pious Pharisee, who goes home justified. Although the Pharisee is faithful to pious practices, he is missing the heart of prayer and the core of faith demonstrated by the tax collector: dependence upon God ("be merciful") and humble acknowledgment of one's true identity ("me a sinner"). Such self-abasement would seem to create a greater distance between the holy God and the sinful tax collector, but the opposite is true. The tax collector's humility draws him closer to God and allows him to go home justified. For ourselves to go home justified, we need to imitate the practices of the Pharisee in being faithful to prayer and gospel living. But we must always pray and live in the humble spirit of the tax collector. This is how we are justified.

The Pharisee uses his pious practices to separate himself from "the rest of humanity." Authentic religious practices—for the Pharisee and for us today—ultimately lead us to communion with God and one another and being in right relationship. The Pharisee distances himself from the rest of humanity; the tax collector, in his acknowledgment that he is a sinner, identifies with humanity. The Pharisee focuses on himself; the tax collector focuses on God. The Pharisee is thankful for his own actions; the tax collector simply acknowledges how God acts ("be merciful"). The issue here is not whether one ought to perform pious practices; of course we should! The real issue is whether those practices witness to our true selves before God.

Living the Paschal Mystery

Prayer helps us enter into and maintain an intimate relationship with God. Our final exaltation will flow from our humility, that is, our awareness of being in right relationship with God as creature to Creator. In prayer we not only express this relationship, our prayer actually helps create it. In prayer we acknowledge who we are before our merciful God.

It is difficult to pray like the tax collector! It is difficult to be faithful to prayer! Every day a hundred and one things will tempt us to let it go. Only self-emptying and focusing on God will keep us faithful to prayer. Only fidelity to prayer will bring us the true humility which justifies us—an attitude toward God which acknowledges and begs, "O God, be merciful to me a sinner."

Focusing the Gospel

Key words and phrases: stood off at a distance, be merciful, me a sinner, went home justified

To the point: Although the Pharisee is faithful to pious practices, he is missing the heart of prayer demonstrated by the tax collector: dependence upon God ("be merciful") and humble acknowledgment of one's true identity ("me a sinner"). Such self-abasement would seem to create a greater distance between the holy God and the sinful tax collector, but the opposite is true. The tax collector's humility draws him closer to God and allows him to go home justified.

Connecting the Gospel

to the first reading: The gospel recounts in dramatic form the teaching of Sirach: "the prayer of the lowly" is willingly and speedily heard by God.

to biblical and Catholic culture: The Pharisee uses his pious practices to separate himself from "the rest of humanity." Authentic religious practices—for the Pharisee and for us today—ultimately lead us to communion with God and one another.

Understanding Scripture

The prayer of the humble is heard: This Sunday's parable showcases one of Luke's favorite themes—the reversal of fortunes. The last line generalizes the reversal this way: "everyone who exalts himself will be humbled, and the one who humbles himself will be exalted." More to the point of this parable is the first part of the same verse: "I tell you, [the tax collector] went home justified, not [the Pharisee]."

This reversal is essential to the parable: it fails if we automatically assume that the Pharisee is a "bad guy." In general, the New Testament and subsequent interpretation caricatures the Pharisees as rigid, heartless, and obsessively legalistic. It is important to the parable to see the admirable aspects of the Pharisee's claims. To be sure, he is arrogant—but this is hardly a fatal flaw deserving eternal punishment. In fact, the Pharisee is dedicated to keeping the Law; and while Christians since Paul have tended to evaluate the Law negatively, we must remember that the Law was given by God to Moses and was, therefore, of ultimate importance as the revelation of God's will for people. This Pharisee devoutly exceeds the Law's requirements: while the Law stipulates a fast only on the Day of Atonement, he fasts twice a week; while the Law requires tithes on certain things, he tithes on everything. He is the embodiment of fidelity to the Law.

As for the tax collector: he is not basically a "good guy" in a tough situation. From what we know historically, there is little virtuous—religiously, morally, or socially—about the life of a tax collector in Jesus' day. He is a public sinner. The shock of the parable is lost if we forget that the Pharisee is the very model of a religiously observant person, and the tax collector is a public reprobate. Neither gets what he "deserves"—and that's the point! God's mercy is not "owed" to, or "earned" by, anyone. Its very essence is grace—a gift given by God, in this case, to the one who asks for it, no matter how sinful.

ASSEMBLY & FAITH-SHARING GROUPS

- My spiritual practices tempt me to self-exaltation (like the Pharisee) when . . .
- My spiritual practices lead me to humility and trust in God when . . .
- My spiritual practices have united me more deeply to "the rest of humanity" by . . .

PRESIDERS

I lead others to pray humbly like the tax collector by . . .

DEACONS

My diaconal service for others assists my growth in humility by . . .

HOSPITALITY MINISTERS

My hospitality *signifies* and *effects* the mercy of God and the humility of the tax collector by . . .

MUSIC MINISTERS

Jesus warns his disciples against considering themselves superior to others because of some pious practices. Whenever I catch myself feeling superior to others because of my music ministry, Jesus calls me back to humility by . . .

ALTAR MINISTERS

Serving others sends me home "justified" and "exalted" when . . .

LECTORS

When I imitate the tax collector's reverence and humility, my proclamation is like . . .

EXTRAORDINARY MINISTERS OF HOLY COMMUNION

The privilege of distributing Christ's Body and Blood humbles me and unites me more deeply with "the rest of humanity" in that . . .

Model Act of Penitence

Presider: Let us come before our God in humble prayer, acknowledge our sinfulness, and ask for God's mercy . . . [pause]

Lord Jesus, you hear the cry of the poor: Lord . . .

Christ Jesus, you justify the sinner: Christ . . .

Lord Jesus, you exalt those who humble themselves: Lord . . .

Appreciating the Responsorial Psalm

It is not the self-righteous whom God hears in prayer (gospel), but those "crushed in spirit" (responsorial psalm). God is not close-minded to the rich; indeed, God "knows no favorites" (first reading). Rather, it is that the self-satisfied are closed to God. Only those who recognize their need for mercy can see and receive the action of God on their behalf. In this Sunday's responsorial psalm we identify ourselves with the poor, the broken-hearted, the lowly. We acknowledge our right relationship with God—that of dependency, of humility, and of a need for mercy. Out of this attitude we pray, and God hears us.

Model General Intercessions

Presider: God hears the prayer of those who humbly present their needs. And so we now pray.

Response:

Lord, hear our prayer.

Cantor:

we pray to the Lord,

That all members of the Church may draw near to God in humility . . . [pause]

That all leaders of nations respond to the cry of those in need . . . [pause]

That those who are brokenhearted and crushed in spirit be comforted and healed . . . [pause]

That each of us here may have the humility of the tax collector, praying, "O God, be merciful to me a sinner" . . . [pause]

Presider: O God, you are merciful to sinners who cry out to you: hear these our prayers that we might one day be exalted with you in heaven. We ask this through Christ our Lord. **Amen.**

ALTERNATIVE OPENING PRAYER

Let us pray
[in humble hope for salvation]

Pause for silent prayer

Praised be you, God and Father of our
    Lord Jesus Christ.
There is no power for good
which does not come from your covenant,
and no promise to hope in,
that your love has not offered.
Strengthen our faith to accept your
    covenant
and give us the love to carry out your
    command.

We ask this through Christ our Lord.
    Amen.

FIRST READING
Sir 35:12-14, 16-18

The LORD is a God of justice,
    who knows no favorites.
Though not unduly partial toward the
    weak,
    yet he hears the cry of the oppressed.
The Lord is not deaf to the wail of the
    orphan,
    nor to the widow when she pours out
      her complaint.
The one who serves God willingly is
    heard;
    his petition reaches the heavens.
The prayer of the lowly pierces the clouds;
    it does not rest till it reaches its goal,
nor will it withdraw till the Most High
    responds,
    judges justly and affirms the right,
and the LORD will not delay.

CATECHESIS

RESPONSORIAL PSALM
Ps 34:2-3, 17-18, 19, 23

R̸. (7a) The Lord hears the cry of the poor.

I will bless the LORD at all times;
   his praise shall be ever in my mouth.
Let my soul glory in the LORD;
   the lowly will hear me and be glad.

R̸. The Lord hears the cry of the poor.

The LORD confronts the evildoers,
   to destroy remembrance of them from
      the earth.
When the just cry out, the LORD hears
   them,
   and from all their distress he rescues
      them.

R̸. The Lord hears the cry of the poor.

The LORD is close to the brokenhearted;
   and those who are crushed in spirit he
      saves.
The LORD redeems the lives of his
   servants;
   no one incurs guilt who takes refuge in
      him.

R̸. The Lord hears the cry of the poor.

SECOND READING
2 Tim 4:6-8, 16-18

Beloved:
I am already being poured out like a
   libation,
   and the time of my departure is at
      hand.
I have competed well; I have finished the
   race;
   I have kept the faith.
From now on the crown of righteousness
   awaits me,
   which the Lord, the just judge,
   will award to me on that day, and not
      only to me,
   but to all who have longed for his
      appearance.

At my first defense no one appeared on
   my behalf,
   but everyone deserted me.
May it not be held against them!
But the Lord stood by me and gave me
   strength,
   so that through me the proclamation
      might be completed
   and all the Gentiles might hear it.
And I was rescued from the lion's mouth.
The Lord will rescue me from every evil
   threat
   and will bring me safe to his heavenly
      kingdom.
To him be glory forever and ever. Amen.

About Liturgy

Liturgical and devotional prayer: The Constitution on the Sacred Liturgy expressly supports time for personal prayer along with liturgical prayer (no. 12). The next paragraph endorses popular devotions, provided they "harmonize with the liturgical seasons, accord with the sacred liturgy, are in some way derived from it, and lead the people to it" (no. 13). It concludes this very important section on popular devotions by saying that "liturgy by its very nature far surpasses any" popular devotions.

Parish staff cannot assume responsibility for whether people take time for personal prayer, but part of their concern ought to be to encourage people and help them grow in their personal prayer. Further, the liturgy committee particularly might monitor the overall prayer life of the parish and make sure there is proper balance between liturgical and devotional prayer. Since the liturgical reforms, devotional prayer has been largely abandoned, especially as communal parish prayers. The parish staff or liturgy committee may want to revisit this question and look at the times when appropriate (that is, according to the criteria outlined in SC no. 13) devotional prayer is offered in the parish.

On December 17, 2001, the Congregation for Divine Worship and the Discipline of the Sacraments promulgated the important document, Directory on Popular Piety and the Liturgy: Principles and Guidelines. This document is recommended for parish staff and is filled with solid theology of the relationship of liturgy and devotions as well as an abundance of interesting historical notes regarding the origins and practice of many familiar popular devotions. In 2005 Liturgical Press published a commentary on this document edited by Peter C. Phan (ISBN 8146-2893-1, 5; 180 pp.; $16.95).

About Liturgical Music

Cantor preparation: The words of the responsorial psalm parallel the message of Jesus in this Sunday's gospel. When you sing these words, then, you know what Jesus knew, and you burn to tell it. What was it that Jesus knew?

A word to the music director: One of the biggest tensions in your ministry is that it sets you up for self-exaltation. This is because it requires recognizable talent and a certain degree of ego. It is very important, then, that you make prayer a regular part of your life. Set aside personal time for prayer every day, the same time in the same place. Begin every music planning session, whether alone or with others, with a moment of prayer. Always include prayer as part of choir rehearsal. Before every liturgy sign yourself with the cross as a reminder of who it is who works through you. At the end of every liturgy, take a moment inside yourself to thank God for what God has accomplished in you and others through this liturgy. Your personal prayerfulness will be evident to the assembly who will find more and more that your music-making takes them to God and the Body of Christ rather than to you as a musician.

SPIRITUALITY

Gospel

Matt 5:1-12a; L667

When Jesus saw the crowds, he went
    up the mountain,
  and after he had sat down, his
    disciples came to him.
He began to teach them, saying:
  "Blessed are the poor in spirit,
    for theirs is the Kingdom of
      heaven.
Blessed are they who mourn,
    for they will be comforted.
Blessed are the meek,
    for they will inherit the land.
Blessed are they who
    hunger and thirst for
    righteousness,
    for they will be satisfied.
Blessed are the merciful,
    for they will be shown mercy.
Blessed are the clean of heart,
    for they will see God.
Blessed are the peacemakers,
    for they will be called children of
      God.
Blessed are they who are persecuted
    for the sake of righteousness,
    for theirs is the Kingdom of
      heaven.
Blessed are you when they insult you
    and persecute you
  and utter every kind of evil against
    you falsely because of me.
Rejoice and be glad,
    for your reward will be great in
      heaven."

See Appendix A, p. 305, for the other readings.

FIRST READING
Rev 7:2-4, 9-14

RESPONSORIAL PSALM
Ps 24:1-2, 3-4, 5-6

SECOND READING
1 John 3:1-3

Reflecting on the Gospel

This festival, in addition to having the rank of solemnity (the most solemn festivals on the Church's liturgical calendar have this rank), is also a holy day of obligation (in most dioceses of the United States). This gives us a clue about how the Church perceives the saints: they are so important that we are "obliged" to celebrate Mass on their feastday. This says at least two things to us.

First, "obliged" comes from the Latin *obligare,* from *ligare,* meaning "to bind." We could limit our obligation on this day to being bound by the law to attend Mass. But there is also a richer interpretation: our obligation on this day is to "bind" ourselves to the saints, that is, to unite ourselves with those who have "washed their robes and made them white in the blood of the Lamb" (first reading). These are the ones who have been faithful to following Jesus and they now spend eternity worshiping God in glory. We want to "bind" ourselves to their way of faithful living, to "bind" ourselves to them as models for our own gospel living so that, being faithful ourselves as they, one day we, too, will join with them in heaven giving "Blessing and glory, wisdom and thanksgiving, honor, power, and might . . . to our God forever and ever" (first reading).

Second, these saints of God are forever before the throne of God in worship. Each liturgy, in fact, we join with all the heavenly choir in giving God thanks and praise (see, for example, SC no. 8). Thus, by "binding" ourselves to earthly liturgy, we are also binding ourselves to the heavenly liturgy. Each time we celebrate Mass we are united in a special way with all the praise offered God in heaven and all the saints who have been granted their great reward in heaven. Thus, our celebrations now are a foretaste of the glory which one day we will share with these saints in heaven. Each of the Beatitudes in the gospel promises this same thing: those who are blessed now will share in eternal inheritance, the "kingdom of heaven."

Both the first reading ("salvation comes from our God") and the second reading ("see what love the Father has bestowed on us") underscore that the source of our blessedness is God's acting in us. This is what it means to be a saint: that God's work is manifested in us. Like the saints in heaven who model for us gospel living, we must be "poor in spirit," "meek," "hunger and thirst for righteousness," "merciful," "clean of heart," "peacemakers," accepting of persecution "for the sake of righteousness." All these actual ways of living are manifestations of the blessedness already bestowed on us, who are "called children of God."

This solemnity, then, is not only about the saints in heaven. It is also about ourselves who are blessed, holy ones, saints on this earth.

Living the Paschal Mystery

This solemnity gives us a wonderful opportunity to celebrate our relationship with God and with all the saints who have gone before us. Knowing that we are already "blessed," we are fortified to assume more perfectly the demands of following in the footsteps of the saints in being faithful disciples of Jesus.

Few of us will someday be canonized saints. Nevertheless, we can live now manifesting that blessedness already bestowed on us. May we always be "bound" to the saints, giving God glory and praise!

Focusing the Gospel

Key words and phrases: Blessed, children of God, reward will be great in heaven

To the point: Both the first reading ("salvation comes from our God") and the second reading ("see what love the Father has bestowed on us") underscore that the source of our blessedness is God's acting in us. This is what it means to be a saint: that God's work is manifested in us.

Model Act of Penitence

Presider: The first reading for this wonderful festival honoring all the saints describes how the saints in heaven offer continuous praise to God; let us unite with them as we offer God our praise and thanksgiving . . . [pause]

Lord Jesus, you bestow upon us the love of the Father: Lord . . .

Christ Jesus, you are the Lamb worthy of blessing and glory: Christ . . .

Lord Jesus, you make us God's children now: Lord . . .

Model General Intercessions

Presider: Let us ask God to bring to completion the good work begun in us.

 Response:

Cantor

That all members of the Church grow in holiness so they can one day be with the saints in heaven . . . [pause]

That all peoples of the world strive for peace and harmony . . . [pause]

That those persecuted for the sake of justice may be strengthened by the promise of their reward in heaven . . . [pause]

That all of us live faithfully as children of God . . . [pause]

Presider: O God, you are the joy of the saints: help us to bring justice and peace to all people so that the blessedness of your kingdom may be established on earth. We ask this through Christ our Lord. **Amen.**

Let us pray

Pause for silent prayer

God our Father,
source of all holiness,
the work of your hands is manifest in your saints,
the beauty of your truth is reflected in their faith.
May we who aspire to have part in their joy
be filled with the Spirit that blessed their lives,
so that having shared their faith on earth
we may also know their peace in your kingdom.
Grant this through Christ our Lord. **Amen.**

FOR REFLECTION

- Saintly people have shaped and inspired my faith by . . .
- I live the Beatitudes when I . . .
- I recognize in others that they are God's children now (see second reading) when I . . .

239

SPIRITUALITY

Gospel

John 6:37-40; L668.8

Jesus said to the crowds:
"Everything that the Father gives me
    will come to me,
  and I will not reject anyone who
      comes to me,
  because I came down from heaven
      not to do my own will
  but the will of the one who sent me.
And this is the will of the one who sent
    me,
  that I should not lose anything of
      what he gave me,
  but that I should raise it on the last
      day.
For this is the will of my Father,
  that everyone who sees the Son and
      believes in him
  may have eternal life,
  and I shall raise him up on the last
      day."

See Appendix A, p. 306, for these readings:

FIRST READING
Wis 3:1-9; L668.1

RESPONSORIAL PSALM
Ps 23:1-3a, 3b-4, 5, 6; L668.1

SECOND READING
Rom 6:3-9; L668.3

Reflecting on the Gospel

Other than sex, there are probably no other topics or issues which parents are more uncomfortable discussing with their children than death. But "Mommy, where do babies come from?" is a question which eventually the children will mature into understanding. Parents can begin with simple explanations and, as the children grow older, parents can give them more information. On the other hand, "Daddy, why won't Grandpa wake up?" is a question neither the children nor the adults can ever fully understand. Similar to the sex question, parents begin by giving the children simple explanations, for example, "Grandpa is not sleeping, he's in heaven with God." Yet, even as adults, death is a mystery to us. We understand physiologically what death is; we can even come to deal with it emotionally. If that is all there were to death, it would be fairly simple. However, there is more: we *know* physical death is the end of natural life; we *believe* that there is life eternal. This is why we celebrate this feastday *commemorating* the faithful departed—we believe they live forever. *Believing* and *remembering* are key to this day's celebration.

The gospel is comforting: Jesus "will not reject anyone who comes to me." And for all those who come, Jesus teaches that it is "the will of my Father" that they will "have eternal life." Salvation and eternal life are God's promise to us. God *desires* that we "who have grown into union with [Jesus] through a death like his" (second reading) will live forever. As we unite ourselves with Jesus and pattern our own living after his paschal journey, we do grow into the mystery of everlasting life. Without fully understanding life eternal, we live with the expectation that one day we will be united with Jesus in his resurrection. We respond to the promise and expectation of eternal life by *believing* in Jesus. Believing, in fact, is simply *living* what Jesus taught by our embracing his dying and rising mystery. Believing is *doing* what Jesus did: he gave himself for the good of others. As God raised Jesus up, so does God raise up those who believe.

We also *remember* the faithful departed this day. Remembering here is more than "recalling" our loved ones (although that may well be part of our celebrations this day); our remembering the faithful departed is broader than that. Our remembering on this feastday enables us to enter into the very mystery the faithful departed now live: whatever happens to the faithful who have believed and died, will happen to us. Remembering, then, is a way to express our belief and hope. By uniting ourselves with the faithful departed, we embrace the mystery which we cannot understand: we embrace eternal life.

Living the Paschal Mystery

This is a day to do more than celebrate the faithfulness of those who have died. This is a day to unite ourselves with their goodness in such a way that their faithful lives are mirrored in our own Gospel living.

Perhaps one good family activity might be to recount the virtues and good deeds of the family members we remember and pray for this day. Then choose one good thing to put into practice in daily living. In this way the remembering of our loved ones is translated into our daily living and becomes a permanent, visible memorial of their faithfulness.

Focusing the Gospel

Key words and phrases: will not reject anyone who comes, will of the one who sent me, believes, eternal life

To the point: The gospel is comforting: Jesus "will not reject anyone who comes to me." And for all those who come, Jesus teaches that it is "the will of my Father" that they will "have eternal life." Salvation and eternal life are God's promise to us. We respond to that promise by believing.

Model Act of Penitence

Presider: We gather today to remember our faithful departed. We remember our loved ones as well as all those who have died in Christ. Let us prepare to celebrate this liturgy by asking God to help us to be faithful to the divine will in our own lives . . . [pause]

Lord Jesus, you came down from heaven to do the Father's will: Lord . . .
Christ Jesus, you were raised to new life: Christ . . .
Lord Jesus, you raise us to new life when we believe in you: Lord . . .

Model General Intercessions

Presider: The God who promises not to reject anyone who comes, will surely hear our prayers. And so we are encouraged to make our needs known.

Response:

Cantor:

That the Church may extend strength and hospitality to all those who come seeking faith in Christ . . . [pause]

That all peoples of the world may believe in God and come to eternal life . . . [pause]

That those who feel rejected and alone may be comforted by their faith in Jesus . . . [pause]

That all the faithful departed be granted everlasting peace . . . [pause]

That each of us here learn from the goodness of our departed loved ones how to live the gospel more steadfastly . . . [pause]

Presider: Gracious God, you raised your Son up to new life and promise this life to those who believe in him: hear these our prayers that one day we may come to share in your eternal glory. We pray through that same Son, Jesus Christ our Lord. **Amen.**

OPENING PRAYER (FROM THE FIRST MASS)
Let us pray

Pause for silent prayer

Merciful Father,
hear our prayers and console us.
As we renew our faith in your Son,
whom you raised from the dead,
strengthen our hope that all our departed
          brothers and sisters
will share in his resurrection,
who lives and reigns with you and the Holy
          Spirit,
one God, for ever and ever. **Amen.**

FOR REFLECTION

• As I consider my departed loved ones, my prayer is about . . . because . . .

• My struggle with believing in God's promise of eternal life is . . .

• The Father's will comforts me in that . . .

SPIRITUALITY

Gospel

Luke 19:1-10; L153C

At that time, Jesus came to
    Jericho and intended
    to pass through the
    town.
Now a man there named
    Zacchaeus,
    who was a chief tax
        collector and also a
        wealthy man,
    was seeking to see who
        Jesus was;
    but he could not see him because of
        the crowd,
    for he was short in stature.
So he ran ahead and climbed a
    sycamore tree in order to see
    Jesus,
    who was about to pass that way.
When he reached the place, Jesus
    looked up and said,
    "Zacchaeus, come down quickly,
    for today I must stay at your house."
And he came down quickly and
    received him with joy.
When they all saw this, they began to
    grumble, saying,
    "He has gone to stay at the house of
        a sinner."
But Zacchaeus stood there and said to
    the Lord,
    "Behold, half of my possessions,
        Lord, I shall give to the poor,
    and if I have extorted anything from
        anyone
    I shall repay it four times over."
And Jesus said to him,
    "Today salvation has come to this
        house
    because this man too is a descendant
        of Abraham.
For the Son of Man has come to seek
    and to save what was lost."

Reflecting on the Gospel

In the spring of 2005, Pope John Paul II's funeral drew the largest crowds in human history. When he was alive, he drew large crowds. It mattered little whether one was a Catholic or not, his personage was formidable and someone who was worth the effort to encounter, even if as part of a crowd of millions. We humans seem to have an undying curiosity about people who can draw large crowds. Jesus, as a formidable person of his time, drew large crowds. The gospels frequently attest to this. And, similar to today, not everyone in the crowd was necessarily seeking to follow Jesus. Sometimes they were merely curious. But an encounter with Jesus takes curiosity and turns it into salvation! The gospel account for this Sunday contains an interesting human touch—a curious, short, rich man puts aside his social status and does something not very dignified: he climbs a sycamore tree to see Jesus better!

The tax collector (that is, sinner in the crowd's perception) Zacchaeus, impelled by his desire to see Jesus, makes great effort to seek him out. Jesus responds to Zacchaeus' earnest enthusiasm by doing for him the very thing Jesus came to do: "to seek out and to save what was lost." The dramatic encounter brings to light something about both persons which escapes the grumbling crowd: Zacchaeus is capable of changing, and Jesus is more than an object of curiosity—he is the Savior of sinners.

Because of his encounter with Jesus, Zacchaeus receives Jesus into his own home "with joy." Moreover, this encounter brings a changed behavior in Zacchaeus: he shares his wealth with the poor and mends his sinful ways. Because of this, Jesus says to him, "Today salvation has come to this house." The dignity of means and status is nothing compared to the dignity God bestows on forgiven sinners who are saved.

There is another interesting detail in this gospel. Jesus "intended to pass through the town," but "must stay" after encountering Zacchaeus. Jesus is the Son of Man who has come "to seek and to save what was lost." Jesus' ministry is hindered neither by wealth nor status, but by his passionate desire to bring salvation to anyone who comes seeking. Jesus' very identity and passion for others' salvation compels him to stay. Perhaps it was Jesus' very passion for others' salvation which aroused in Zacchaeus the passion to forget his dignity and climb that tree. This leaves us with an interesting question: Would we go to the same heights as Zacchaeus to encounter Jesus, change, and be saved?

Living the Paschal Mystery

This story of Zacchaeus reminds us that we sinners must come seeking Jesus if we are to have a saving encounter with divine mercy. Sometimes it may seem to many of us that our seeking Jesus is far more difficult than climbing a tree to see and encounter him! Perhaps we are having difficulty with prayer and God seems to have abandoned us. Perhaps we are being tempted in a particular and prolonged way to do something radically against gospel values. Perhaps so much is going wrong in our lives that we are disposed to be bitter or resentful or vindictive. These are times when we can come closest to God by acknowledging our human frailty and giving ourselves over to God's care and mercy. Sometimes just a refocus of our attention away from the difficulty toward Jesus who loves us is enough to remain faithful and encounter Jesus in a new and life-giving way.

Focusing the Gospel

Key words and phrases: seeking, grumble, I shall repay, salvation has come

To the point: Zacchaeus, impelled by his desire to see Jesus, makes great effort to seek him out. Jesus responds to Zacchaeus' earnest enthusiasm by doing for him the very thing Jesus came to do: "to seek out and to save what was lost." The dramatic encounter brings to light something about both persons which escapes the grumbling crowd: Zacchaeus is capable of changing, and Jesus is more than an object of curiosity—he is the Savior of sinners.

Connecting the Gospel

to the first reading: The encounter between Zacchaeus and Jesus exemplifies what Wisdom describes poetically: "you have mercy on all"; "you love all things"; "you spare all things."

to Catholic culture: We tend to think that the order of events is that we repent and then God comes. But the gospel suggests that the opposite is true: Jesus comes to Zacchaeus, who then responds by repenting ("give to the poor," "repay it four times over"). In the language of theology, we do not repent to get grace; God gives us the grace to repent.

Understanding Scripture

Zacchaeus and tax collectors: Tax collectors were hated for two reasons. First, they were collaborators with the occupying Roman Empire, employed to extract taxes from the Jews; these taxes were over and above the tithe (10%) that Jews owed to the Temple. Second, the way the tax system worked lent itself to abuse. Tax collectors were hired by Roman officials; the yearly tax for an area was assessed and the tax collector paid it up front out of his own pocket. The Romans, money in hand, left it to the devices of the tax collector to make back his money with a profit—gained through overcharging, cheating, interest, or other means. Tax collectors, understandably, gained a reputation for dishonesty. Early Rabbinic writings considered tax collecting a despised trade, and associated tax collectors with robbers and murderers; the New Testament also lists them with other "sinners" (Matt 11:19; Mark 2:15-16; Luke 15:1). Zacchaeus, as chief tax collector, had many tax collectors working for him, adding another layer of employees eager to take their cut. Zacchaeus is thus an embodiment of the outcast and the estranged, or, to use the language of this story, "the lost" (19:10).

Jesus' meeting with Zacchaeus, his last encounter with sinners before he enters Jerusalem, summarizes his ministry to this point and replays some earlier themes. Once again, the episode begins by drawing attention to Jesus' journey and it ends with Jesus' announcing salvation (see Luke 17:11-19; Sunday 28C). The metaphor of finding the lost recalls the parable of the Prodigal Son in which the father rejoices that his son who "was lost [ ] has been found" (15:32; Sunday 24C). This episode also recaps the two previous parables. Like the persistent widow, Zacchaeus persists in seeking out Jesus (19:3-4); and like the tax collector in the previous parable, he acknowledges his sin and announces the restitution he repays for extortion committed in the line of business. Such persistence and repentance end with this sinner being saved: this lost child of Abraham has been found—the very reason for which "the Son of Man has come."

ASSEMBLY & FAITH-SHARING GROUPS
- What I have done in order to encounter Jesus is . . .
- How I have experienced Jesus' seeking me in order to save me is . . .
- I permit others to change and have a "second chance" like Zacchaeus when I . . .

PRESIDERS
I help the community realize that "today salvation has come to this house" by . . .

DEACONS
My ministry is like Zacchaeus' sycamore tree, aiding others to encounter Jesus, when I . . .

HOSPITALITY MINISTERS
My ministry embodies the wonderment of God's mercy toward others (see first reading) when I . . .

MUSIC MINISTERS
My participation in music ministry helps me, like Zacchaeus, to see who Jesus is by . . . One change I have made in my life because of this is . . .

ALTAR MINISTERS
What I need to do prior to Jesus' visiting my house is . . .

LECTORS
Like Zacchaeus, I intentionally seek Jesus in the word whenever I . . .

EXTRAORDINARY MINISTERS OF HOLY COMMUNION
As I distribute Communion, I delight in the Son of Man coming "to seek and to save what was lost" when I . . .

Model Act of Penitence

Presider: With great love and mercy God seeks us. Let us prepare to encounter our gracious God in this liturgy . . . [pause]

Lord Jesus, you are gracious and merciful: Lord . . .

Christ Jesus, you are slow to anger and of great kindness: Christ . . .

Lord Jesus, you came to save the lost: Lord . . .

Appreciating the Responsorial Psalm

Psalm 145 is an acrostic hymn, meaning that each verse begins with a successive letter of the Hebrew alphabet. The psalm, consequently, does not develop any theme in depth but simply offers general praise. The verses chosen for this Sunday praise God for showing mercy and compassion rather than anger (v. 8) and for lifting up those who have fallen (v. 14). The reading from Wisdom confirms this attitude of God when it proclaims: "you loathe nothing that you have made . . . you spare all things . . ."

In his encounter with Zacchaeus (gospel), Jesus is the living embodiment of God's orientation toward sinners. He has come "to seek and to save what was lost." In singing this psalm we are the living embodiment of Zacchaeus' response. We recognize ourselves as sinners and shout praise to the One who comes to save us.

Model General Intercessions

Presider: The God who loves all things surely will hear our prayers and grant us our needs.

Response:

Lord, hear our prayer.

Cantor:

we pray to the Lord,

That the Church may always diligently seek the lost . . . [pause]

That all people of the world may encounter the love of God through the mercy and forgiveness of others . . . [pause]

That sinners may repent and the lost may be saved . . . [pause]

That each one of us here go to whatever lengths we must to encounter Jesus and be transformed by his presence . . . [pause]

Presider: Loving and merciful God, you care for each one of us so that no one may be lost: hear these our prayers that we might be saved and enjoy everlasting life with you. We ask this through Christ our Lord. **Amen.**

ALTERNATIVE OPENING PRAYER
Let us pray

Pause for silent prayer

Father in heaven, God of power and Lord
    of mercy,
from whose fullness we have received,
direct our steps in everyday efforts.
May the changing moods of the human
    heart
and the limits which our failings impose
    on hope
never blind us to you, source of every
    good.
Faith gives us the promise of peace
and makes known the demands of love.
Remove the selfishness that blurs the
    vision of faith.

Grant this through Christ our Lord.
    Amen.

FIRST READING
Wis 11:22–12:2

Before the LORD the whole universe is as a
    grain from a balance
    or a drop of morning dew come down
        upon the earth.
But you have mercy on all, because you
    can do all things;
    and you overlook people's sins that they
        may repent.
For you love all things that are
    and loathe nothing that you have made;
    for what you hated, you would not have
        fashioned.
And how could a thing remain, unless you
    willed it;
    or be preserved, had it not been called
        forth by you?
But you spare all things, because they are
    yours,
    O LORD and lover of souls,
    for your imperishable spirit is in all
        things!
Therefore you rebuke offenders little by
    little,
    warn them and remind them of the sins
        they are committing,
    that they may abandon their wickedness
        and believe in you, O LORD!

RESPONSORIAL PSALM
Ps 145:1-2, 8-9, 10-11, 13, 14

℟. (cf. 1) I will praise your name forever,
my king and my God.

I will extol you, O my God and King,
    and I will bless your name forever and
        ever.
Every day will I bless you,
    and I will praise your name forever and
        ever.

R⁊. I will praise your name forever, my
king and my God.

The LORD is gracious and merciful,
    slow to anger and of great kindness.
The LORD is good to all
    and compassionate toward all his
        works.

R⁊. I will praise your name forever, my
king and my God.

Let all your works give you thanks, O
    LORD,
    and let your faithful ones bless you.
Let them discourse of the glory of your
        kingdom
    and speak of your might.

R⁊. I will praise your name forever, my
king and my God.

The LORD is faithful in all his words
    and holy in all his works.
The LORD lifts up all who are falling
    and raises up all who are bowed down.

R⁊. I will praise your name forever, my
king and my God.

SECOND READING
2 Thess 1:11–2:2

Brothers and sisters:
We always pray for you,
    that our God may make you worthy of
        his calling
    and powerfully bring to fulfillment
        every good purpose
    and every effort of faith,
    that the name of our Lord Jesus may be
        glorified in you,
    and you in him,
    in accord with the grace of our God and
        Lord Jesus Christ.

We ask you, brothers and sisters,
    with regard to the coming of our Lord
        Jesus Christ
    and our assembling with him,
    not to be shaken out of your minds
        suddenly, or to be alarmed
    either by a "spirit," or by an oral
        statement,
    or by a letter allegedly from us
    to the effect that the day of the Lord is
        at hand.

About Liturgy

Planning Advent reconciliation service: As we near the end of the Church year and the beginning of Advent, many of us have already planned for this year's Advent Rite of Reconciliation celebrated in common (form B of the Sacrament of Penance). Advent and Lent seem to be the favored times for these celebrations in parishes, and rightly so. The two seasons have a different character, however, and the celebration of this sacrament has a different context, according to the respective season. Jesus' Second Coming with the attendant final judgment suggests the context for such a celebration during Advent. Acknowledging our sinfulness and asking God's sacramental forgiveness is one way we prepare for the Second Coming.

The gospel for this Sunday reminds us that God is merciful and always forgives; we need only seek God. Celebrating communally the Sacrament of Penance is another concrete way to demonstrate that we seek God and have God as a priority in our lives. Taking time out during these busy holiday-preparation weeks to acknowledge our sinfulness and need for God is a way we can help ourselves stay other-centered.

About Liturgical Music

Cantor preparation: Psalm 145 praises God for all God does, but in the context of this Sunday's first reading and gospel, the praise is particularly for God's forgiveness of sin. For what have you been forgiven? In what way have you experienced God's mercy?

Music suggestion: Herman Stuempfle's "When Jesus Passed through Jericho" [HG] turns the story of Zaccheaus into our story: "The friend of sinners Jesus was And is the same today. He never sees a lonely face And looks the other way, And looks the other way. Instead, when bowed by guilt or grief We seek the Lord to see, He sets before us bread and wine And says, 'Come, eat with me.' And says, 'Come, eat with me.'" The text needs to be sung in a light, storytelling fashion. The tune, the American folk melody DOVE OF PEACE, will probably be unfamiliar to most members of the assembly. Let alternating cantors sing verses 1-4, telling the story of Zacchaeus, then have the assembly join in for verses 5-6 when the story becomes theirs. The hymn would be very suitable during the presentation of the gifts.

✠ SPIRITUALITY

Gospel
Luke 20:27-38; L156C

Some Sadducees, those who deny that
there is a resurrection,
came forward and put this
question to Jesus, saying,
"Teacher, Moses wrote for us,
If someone's brother dies
leaving a wife but no
child,
his brother must take the wife
and raise up descendants for
his brother.
Now there were seven brothers;
the first married a woman but
died childless.
Then the second and the third
married her,
and likewise all the seven died
childless.
Finally the woman also died.
Now at the resurrection whose wife will
that woman be?
For all seven had been married to her."
Jesus said to them,
"The children of this age marry and
remarry;
but those who are deemed worthy to
attain to the coming age
and to the resurrection of the dead
neither marry nor are given in
marriage.
They can no longer die,
for they are like angels;
and they are the children of God
because they are the ones who will
rise.
That the dead will rise
even Moses made known in the
passage about the bush,
when he called out 'Lord,'
the God of Abraham, the God of
Isaac, and the God of Jacob;
and he is not God of the dead, but of
the living,
for to him all are alive."

or Luke 20:27, 34-38 in Appendix A, p. 306.

Reflecting on the Gospel
With this Sunday's gospel, we move immediately to the section in Luke's Gospel which addresses the age to come. Next Sunday's gospel describes the events at the end times. Then in two weeks on the solemnity of Our Lord Jesus Christ the King, we celebrate Christ's eternal victory at the end of time. Jesus aligns himself with the later Jewish tradition which categorically affirms the resurrection—there is life after this one.

Belief in the afterlife is as much a struggle for some today as it was for the Sadducees and others in Jesus' time; for example, New Age concepts of cosmic unity and Eastern beliefs in reincarnation witness to our desire for continued life in some form and our struggle with what that might be like. As baptized Christians, we align ourselves with Jesus who teaches resurrection and eternal life shared with him in glory. Nonetheless, our belief in Jesus and the resurrection makes eternal life no less a mystery. We believe, however, because Jesus has died and risen. He has gone before us. He has shown us the way. His victory is our sure hope. Our choices today about whether we follow Jesus faithfully and live gospel values by dying to ourselves reveal the extent of our own hope in sharing in Jesus' risen life.

In the gospel, the Sadducees are putting a question to Jesus in accord with their belief that this life is all there is. In no uncertain terms, Jesus affirms resurrection and eternal life. This "hope God gives of being raised up by him" (first reading) fortifies us to remain faithful to God even when the price in this life is ultimate (an extreme example of which is given in the first reading). We can give our life because God gives us life.

Living the Paschal Mystery
These readings which lead us to reflect on Jesus' Second Coming are not included in the Lectionary and proclaimed at Sunday Mass to scare us, but to prepare us. Yes, Jesus will come to judge the living and the dead. That judgment determines whether we have everlasting glory or everlasting torment. The grace is that we are warned, so we can be prepared. We know that the choices we make now determine the judgment we receive at the Second Coming. What a positive grace—to know what is coming so that we can prepare for it! This is why the Second Coming will not take us by surprise. So let us prepare well!

Few of us will be faced with the extreme choice the brothers in the first reading must make. Nevertheless, we, like the seven brothers, live in a world beset by evil and filled with life-threatening situations (war, poverty, hunger, natural disasters). It is hope in a future that God will provide which upholds and sustains us and guides us in the choices to be faithful to the Gospel, no matter what we face.

We do face "death" every day: dying to self. Gospel living, then, is more than a matter of religious practices. Gospel living means that we align ourselves with Jesus' living and dying. He modeled for us the self-sacrificing giving which leads to eternal life. When we ourselves face conflicts (like in both the gospel and first reading), we can be assured that "the Lord is faithful; he will strengthen [us] and guard [us] from the evil one" (second reading). May we pray with Paul: "May the Lord direct [our] hearts to the love of God and to the endurance of Christ."

Focusing the Gospel

Key words and phrases: deny . . . resurrection, dead will rise, God . . . of the living

To the point: The Sadducees are putting a question to Jesus in accord with their belief that this life is all there is. In no uncertain terms, Jesus affirms resurrection and eternal life. This "hope God gives of being raised up by him" (first reading) fortifies us to remain faithful to God even when the price in this life is ultimate (an extreme example of which is given in the first reading). We can give our life because God gives us life.

Connecting the Gospel

to the end of the liturgical year: With this Sunday's gospel, we move immediately to the section in Luke's Gospel which addresses the age to come. Next Sunday's gospel describes the events at the end times. Then in two weeks on the solemnity of Our Lord Jesus Christ the King, we celebrate Christ's eternal victory at the end of time.

to religious experience: Few of us will be faced with the extreme choice the brothers in the first reading must make. Nevertheless, we, like the seven brothers, live in a world beset by evil and filled with life-threatening situations (war, poverty, hunger, natural disasters). It is hope in a future that God will provide which upholds and sustains us.

Understanding Scripture

Resurrection: Belief in an afterlife arose very late in the Old Testament, and even in New Testament times such a belief was not universal. The Sadducees in this Sunday's gospel reject the notion of survival beyond death. The traditional view maintained that the human person is identified with the physical body which is animated by the breath of God (Gen 2:7; "breath" does not mean "soul"). Death is final: "When you take away their breath, they perish and return to the dust from which they came" (Ps 104:29). The only thing which survives death is a person's name. Thus, one's only shot at "immortality" is a son who bears the father's name. Therefore, Deuteronomy 25:5-6 provided for "levirate marriage": if a man died without a son, the deceased man's brother was required to marry the widow; the first son born of that union was considered the dead man's son who bore his name and inherited his property.

"Resurrection of the body" as the way to survive death is a logical consequence of Jewish belief. For Jews, the human body is identified with the person; if a person were to live beyond death, the body must be restored: hence, resurrection of the body. By contrast, Greeks believed that a person is made of body and soul. The soul was immortal and was trapped in the body until death when it was freed and lived on. Both the Jewish and Greek solutions to the problem of death and immortality are found in the Bible.

The Sadducees propose to Jesus an extreme case: the pattern of childlessness and death is repeated seven times. If there were a resurrection of the dead, would the wife have seven husbands in the afterlife? They thought the very absurdity of the situation proved the foolishness of the belief.

Jesus dismissed the Sadducees' argument. Because resurrection means life, there is no need for sons to carry on the family name. With no need for sons, there was no need for marriage in the Age to Come. The absurdity of multiple marriages does not disprove resurrection; resurrection makes remarriage unnecessary.

**ASSEMBLY &
FAITH-SHARING GROUPS**
- Some beliefs I would question Jesus about are . . .
- I am strengthened to believe in the resurrection by . . .
- My belief in the resurrection impacts my daily living by . . .

PRESIDERS
I build up others' hope in the resurrection by . . .

DEACONS
My ministry embodies the God of the living for those struggling with hardships whenever I . . .

HOSPITALITY MINISTERS
My attentiveness to others is a way of encouraging hope in eternal life when I . . .

MUSIC MINISTERS
Belief in God's promise of resurrection gives disciples the courage to die. One way music ministry leads me to die to myself is . . . I already experience resurrection in this dying in that . . .

ALTAR MINISTERS
I model a dying to self in the hope of being raised up whenever I . . .

LECTORS
My daily living the word proclaims a hope in the resurrection whenever I . . .

**EXTRAORDINARY MINISTERS
OF HOLY COMMUNION**
My receiving Christ's life empowers me to share my life with others in that . . .

CELEBRATION

Model Act of Penitence

Presider: In the Creed we profess that "we look for the resurrection of the dead and the life of the world to come." With this hope in resurrection and everlasting life, let us prepare ourselves to celebrate this liturgy . . . [pause]

Lord Jesus, you are the resurrection and the life: Lord . . .

Christ Jesus, you are Lord of the living and the dead: Christ . . .

Lord Jesus, you raise us to new and everlasting life: Lord . . .

Appreciating the Responsorial Psalm

Psalm 17 is the prayer of an individual who has been unjustly accused by enemies. The psalmist has taken refuge in the Temple and there awaits God's settlement of the case. The psalmist protests innocence (vv. 3-8) and begs God for protection.

On this Sunday when the Church begins to focus on the end times and the Second Coming of Christ, both the first reading and the gospel speak directly of God's promise to raise the just to new life after death. Throughout Ordinary Time, the testing period of Christian life, our steps—like those of the seven brothers—"have been steadfast." Now we look to the glory of Christ to come and know that "in justice" we shall "behold [his] face." In the responsorial psalm we stake our claim to this promised reward.

Model General Intercessions

Presider: The God of the living will hear our prayers and grant our needs. And so we pray with hope.

Response:

Lord, hear our prayer.

Cantor:

we pray to the Lord,

That the Church may proclaim faithfully the gospel of hope and life . . . [pause]

That all people of the world may come to share in everlasting life . . . [pause]

That those who live in the shadow of death may find hope in the resurrection . . . [pause]

That each of us gathered here may live with confident hope in God's promise of life . . . [pause]

Presider: O God, you are the Lord of the living and the dead: guide us to live responsibly each day so that we might come to your glory for ever and ever. **Amen.**

ALTERNATIVE OPENING PRAYER

Let us pray

Pause for silent prayer

Almighty Father,
strong is your justice and great is your mercy.
Protect us in the burdens and challenges of life.
Shield our minds from the distortion of pride
and enfold our desire with the beauty of truth.
Help us to become more aware of your loving design
so that we may more willingly give our lives in service to all.
We ask this through Christ our Lord.
Amen.

FIRST READING 2 Macc 7:1-2, 9-14

It happened that seven brothers with their mother were arrested
and tortured with whips and scourges by the king,
to force them to eat pork in violation of God's law.
One of the brothers, speaking for the others, said:
"What do you expect to achieve by questioning us?
We are ready to die rather than transgress the laws of our ancestors."

At the point of death he said:
"You accursed fiend, you are depriving us of this present life,
but the King of the world will raise us up to live again forever.
It is for his laws that we are dying."

After him the third suffered their cruel sport.
He put out his tongue at once when told to do so,
and bravely held out his hands, as he spoke these noble words:
"It was from Heaven that I received these;
for the sake of his laws I disdain them;
from him I hope to receive them again."
Even the king and his attendants marveled at the young man's courage,
because he regarded his sufferings as nothing.

After he had died,
they tortured and maltreated the fourth brother in the same way.
When he was near death, he said,
"It is my choice to die at the hands of men
with the hope God gives of being raised up by him;
but for you, there will be no resurrection to life."

CATECHESIS

RESPONSORIAL PSALM
Ps 17:1, 5-6, 8, 15

R℣. (15b) Lord, when your glory appears,
my joy will be full.

Hear, O LORD, a just suit;
    attend to my outcry;
        hearken to my prayer from lips without
            deceit.

R℣. Lord, when your glory appears, my joy
will be full.

My steps have been steadfast in your
        paths,
    my feet have not faltered.
I call upon you, for you will answer me,
        O God;
    incline your ear to me; hear my word.

R℣. Lord, when your glory appears, my joy
will be full.

Keep me as the apple of your eye,
    hide me in the shadow of your wings.
But I in justice shall behold your face;
    on waking I shall be content in your
        presence.

R℣. Lord, when your glory appears, my joy
will be full.

SECOND READING
2 Thess 2:16–3:5

Brothers and sisters:
May our Lord Jesus Christ himself and
        God our Father,
    who has loved us and given us
        everlasting encouragement
    and good hope through his grace,
    encourage your hearts and strengthen
        them in every good deed and word.

Finally, brothers and sisters, pray for us,
    so that the word of the Lord may speed
        forward and be glorified,
    as it did among you,
    and that we may be delivered from
        perverse and wicked people,
    for not all have faith.
But the Lord is faithful;
    he will strengthen you and guard you
        from the evil one.
We are confident of you in the Lord that
        what we instruct you,
    you are doing and will continue to do.
May the Lord direct your hearts to the love
        of God
    and to the endurance of Christ.

About Liturgy
Early communities' expectation of the end times: Note that the second reading for both last Sunday and this one has been from the Second Letter to the Thessalonians. The first and second letters to this Christian community are considered the earliest of Paul's writings (and the earliest in the Christian Scriptures). At this time the Christian community was still expecting Jesus' imminent return and no doubt this directly shaped their attitudes and behavior as Christians—novel and daring behavior, indeed—for example, their radical, shared community life and willingness to die rather than denounce their belief in Jesus. They were to be prepared, because the end was near.

During Ordinary Time the second reading does not usually accord with the first reading and gospel. But on these last Sundays of the liturgical year there is a consistent parousia (a technical term referring to Christ's Second Coming) motif. Therefore, the second reading can be a lens through which the gospel and first reading are interpreted.

About Liturgical Music
Cantor preparation: This responsorial psalm is a statement of personal conviction. Only if you believe God's promise of future life can you live God's teachings now. Do you believe God's promise of resurrection? What effect does this belief have on the way you live now?

Music suggestions: "In the Day of the Lord" [BB, JS2; SATB arrangement in *Choral Praise Comprehensive,* 2nd edition, OCP #11450] is an energetic song in anticipation of the Second Coming and the final resurrection. Since the text follows a verse-refrain rather than a hymn structure, verses can be omitted to fit ritual needs without doing damage to the meaning of the song as a whole. The style and tempo would fit the entrance procession, the presentation of the gifts, or the recessional. Another song celebrating the Second Coming and the resurrection is "Death Will Be No More" [BB]. More meditative in tone and style, this song would be suitable for Communion. "Soon and Very Soon" [found in most hymn resources] would make a fitting recessional song.

SPIRITUALITY

Gospel
Luke 21:5-19; L159C

While some people were speaking about
  how the temple was adorned
    with costly stones and
      votive offerings,
  Jesus said, "All that you see
    here—
  the days will come when there
    will not be left
  a stone upon another stone that
    will not be thrown down."

Then they asked him,
  "Teacher, when will this
    happen?
And what sign will there be when
  all these things are about to
    happen?"
He answered,
  "See that you not be deceived,
    for many will come in my name,
      saying,
    'I am he,' and 'The time has come.'
  Do not follow them!
  When you hear of wars and
    insurrections,
    do not be terrified; for such things
      must happen first,
    but it will not immediately be the
      end."
Then he said to them,
  "Nation will rise against nation, and
    kingdom against kingdom.
  There will be powerful earthquakes,
    famines, and plagues
    from place to place;
  and awesome sights and mighty signs
    will come from the sky.

Continued in Appendix A, p. 307.

Reflecting on the Gospel

"Do not be terrified." Such comforting and encouraging words of Jesus! For a number of weeks now we have been reading gospels which lead us to reflect on and prepare for the Second Coming. With the gospel of this Sunday we finally get a picture of the parousia events from every perspective: *cosmic* ("earthquakes," "awesome sights and mighty signs will come from the sky"); *social* ("wars and insurrections," "famines, and plagues"); *religious* ("temple . . . there will not be left another stone that will not be thrown down"); and *personal* ("seize you and persecute you"). In the midst of catastrophic events, Jesus instructs his disciples, "do not be terrified." Why? These events would seem to destroy us. Yet, Jesus tells us otherwise, because he will give us the wisdom we need to see like he does.

Jesus does not see what others see. The crowd looks upon the beauty of the Temple; Jesus sees when it will be a pile of rubble. The crowd sees wars, earthquakes, famines, etc. as terrifying; Jesus sees them as the beginning of the end. Jesus sees the end of time not as the end of life, but as the time when we will secure our lives. In every case, Jesus sees the immediate happenings in the context of God's eternal plan—a vision which calls us to hope and courage. We are always tempted at this time of the liturgical year to move too quickly to focus on the *signs* of the end times; this gospel calls us to focus on the *promise* of the end times.

To be sure, our hope does not lie in a future which is devoid of such frightening events—these catastrophic events will happen. But our hope lies in a future where, for those who "fear [Jesus'] name," "there will arise the sun of justice with its healing rays" (first reading). The first reading describes the day when evil will be destroyed and those who fear God will walk in the light of God's justice. This is the source of our hope.

The readings for this Sunday are filled with hope, not doom or fear. Along with all these terrifying things, good things happen: these things do not signal an immediate end so we have time to prepare; these things give all of us an opportunity to testify to Jesus' name and his reign; Jesus himself will give each of us the wisdom we need to speak boldly; and, most importantly, Jesus assures us that he will be the victor ("all your adversaries will be powerless to resist or refute"). Some will die, yes. Some will be hated, yes. All we need do is persevere—that is, be faithful to our call to follow Jesus—and we "will secure [our] lives." Why should we not be terrified? Because Jesus has promised us that if we persevere, we will live. And we know that Jesus always makes good on his promises!

Living the Paschal Mystery

Times of adversity, whether now or in the future, are opportunities in which the wisdom of Jesus and his teachings embolden his followers to testify to him and strengthen them to persevere. The trials and tribulations we face now in our lives are preparation for the end times. As we grow in our readiness to be faithful to the Gospel in this life, we are already choosing our final destiny.

Before new life, there must be dying to the old self. We know that Christ is the victor, and those who persevere in their faithfulness will share in the glory of that victory. But the full victory is not yet revealed. We await. We hope.

Focusing the Gospel

Key words and phrases: All that you see here, See that you not be deceived, death, secure your lives

To the point: Jesus does not see what others see. The crowd looks upon the beauty of the Temple; Jesus sees when it will be a pile of rubble. The crowd sees wars, earthquakes, famines, etc. as terrifying; Jesus sees them as the beginning of the end. Jesus sees the end of time not as the end of life, but as the time when we will secure our lives. In every case, Jesus sees the immediate happenings in the context of God's eternal plan—a vision which calls us to hope and courage.

Connecting the Gospel

to the first reading: The first reading describes the day when evil will be destroyed and those who fear God will walk in the light of God's justice. This is the source of our hope.

to experience: Masterpieces of art always invite us to see reality in new ways. Similarly, Jesus, in this gospel, is inviting us to see our own everyday experiences in a totally different way: with an appreciation of God's overall plan for us.

Understanding Scripture

End times: As Jesus nears the end of his earthly ministry, his thoughts turn to the end of time in what scholars call his "apocalyptic discourse." His use of the phrase, "the days will come," like Malachi's "the day is coming," is shorthand for "the day of the Lord." In the prophetic traditions of the Old Testament, it seems that the Day of the Lord was originally used to describe the Lord's coming against Israel's enemies to destroy them and to deliver God's people. It was a day of destruction and deliverance simultaneously. Some prophets transformed that tradition by making it a day of God's coming against sinful Israel to punish and purify. Some generalized it as a time of punishment for the wicked and of deliverance for the righteous, which is what we find in Malachi: "the proud and all evildoers will be stubble," consumed by the fire of God's wrath; but for those "who fear my name" it will be a time of justice and of healing.

The difference between prophetic and apocalyptic use of this theme is this: for most of the prophets, God's visitation would be realized in history; in apocalyptic thought, the "day" signals the end of the "present age" and the advent of "the world to come."

It was typically expected that the "end" would be accompanied by signs. While Jesus answers this question about what signs to expect with stock elements found in much apocalyptic literature, he deflects attention from the signs to the time before these final signs. The time before the end is for witnessing, or "giving testimony." This is the time of Luke's community and it is our time, too. Rather than calculating the time, cataloguing signs, chasing after those who claim, "I am he," or tracking world events, Jesus prepares his disciples for the sometimes arduous task of bearing witness to him and his way of life. Fidelity to him will cause persecutions, family division, and legal actions against believers. This is the lot of the disciple in any age, both in the present and in the end times.

Model Act of Penitence

Presider: In the day of Christ's coming, wrong will be righted, suffering will end, death will yield to eternal life. Let us prepare to meet Christ who comes to us in this Eucharist . . . [pause]

    Lord Jesus, you are the source of our hope: Lord . . .

    Christ Jesus, you rule the earth with justice: Christ . . .

    Lord Jesus, you will come with salvation for your people: Lord . . .

Appreciating the Responsorial Psalm

In the context of this Sunday's first reading and gospel, Psalm 98 is a statement of absolute certainty that the power of Christ will prevail over the forces of evil. We need not lose heart when wars, insurrections, earthquakes, famines arise. We need not be surprised when fidelity to discipleship brings persecution. Even amidst the direst evil, the vision we maintain is of Christ's final coming and victory. And so we sing, blow trumpets, clap hands, and shout for joy, for we know the Lord is coming to rule with justice.

Model General Intercessions

Presider: Let us pray for the grace to persevere and be ready when Christ comes.

Response:

Cantor:

That the Church may faithfully proclaim Christ's vision of hope and new life . . . [pause]

That all peoples of the world may work diligently to overcome war, famine, and disease . . . [pause]

That those suffering from fear, despair, or hopelessness may receive courage and strength . . . [pause]

That each of us may live faithfully every day, secure in the promise of eternal life . . . [pause]

Presider: O God, you are always faithful to your word: may your promise of eternal life inspire us to a life of faithful service, truthful testimony, and patient endurance. We ask this through Christ our Lord. **Amen.**

ALTERNATIVE OPENING PRAYER
Let us pray

Pause for silent prayer

Father in heaven,
ever-living source of all that is good,
from the beginning of time you promised
    man salvation
through the future coming of your Son,
    our Lord Jesus Christ.
Help us to drink of his truth
and expand our hearts with the joy of his
    promises,
so that we may serve you in faith and in
    love
and know for ever the joy of your
    presence.
We ask this through Christ our Lord.
Amen.

FIRST READING
Mal 3:19-20a

Lo, the day is coming, blazing like an oven,
    when all the proud and all evildoers will
      be stubble,
and the day that is coming will set them
    on fire,
    leaving them neither root nor branch,
    says the LORD of hosts.
But for you who fear my name, there will
    arise
    the sun of justice with its healing rays.

CATECHESIS

RESPONSORIAL PSALM
Ps 98:5-6, 7-8, 9

R⁈. (cf. 9) The Lord comes to rule the earth with justice.

Sing praise to the LORD with the harp,
     with the harp and melodious song.
With trumpets and the sound of the horn
     sing joyfully before the King, the LORD.

R⁈. The Lord comes to rule the earth with justice.

Let the sea and what fills it resound,
     the world and those who dwell in it;
let the rivers clap their hands,
     the mountains shout with them for joy.

R⁈. The Lord comes to rule the earth with justice.

Before the LORD, for he comes,
     for he comes to rule the earth;
he will rule the world with justice
     and the peoples with equity.

R⁈. The Lord comes to rule the earth with justice.

SECOND READING
2 Thess 3:7-12

Brothers and sisters:
You know how one must imitate us.
For we did not act in a disorderly way
          among you,
     nor did we eat food received free from
          anyone.
On the contrary, in toil and drudgery,
          night and day
     we worked, so as not to burden any of
          you.
Not that we do not have the right.
Rather, we wanted to present ourselves as
          a model for you,
     so that you might imitate us.
In fact, when we were with you,
     we instructed you that if anyone was
          unwilling to work,
     neither should that one eat.
We hear that some are conducting
          themselves among you in a disorderly
          way,
     by not keeping busy but minding the
          business of others.
Such people we instruct and urge in the
          Lord Jesus Christ to work quietly
     and to eat their own food.

About Liturgy
Eucharist and eschatology, part 2: The Catechesis about Liturgy for the Twenty-fifth Sunday in Ordinary Time addressed the eschatological thrust of liturgy, specifically mentioning the Eucharistic acclamations and the connection of the earthly liturgy with the heavenly liturgy. It would be a good exercise for the parish liturgy committee and liturgical ministers to take the Sacramentary and go through the Eucharistic rite to detect other areas where there is an eschatological thrust.

Although this time of the year this motif is prominent, in fact every liturgy has an eschatological thread running through it. Moreover, the Eucharistic liturgy itself is already a share in the messianic banquet. It is for this reason that the lines for the Communion procession need to process toward the altar, the place of the eschatological banquet. This helps make the connection between our receiving Communion now and our share in the eschatological banquet in the future.

About Liturgical Music
Cantor preparation: When you sing these verses from Psalm 98, you stand before the assembly as one who sees Christ coming in victory. Do you see him? Are you looking?

Music suggestions: Any of the songs suggested for last Sunday bear repeating this week.

A word to the music director: In this Sunday's gospel, Jesus speaks of the sufferings and persecutions which will mark the end times. The final victory of Christ can only come about through dissolution of the forces which oppose his kingdom. Jesus' words are meant to give you courage when, because of fidelity to discipleship, you face struggle and opposition in your ministry. Every time you confront cliques in the choir, jealousies between cantors, resistance to liturgical vision in the parish, egotism in yourself, etc., you are experiencing exactly what Jesus is talking about. And he has promised to give you the wisdom to know what to say and do in these situations. The saying and doing will not be easy—they will require death to self. But your perseverance in discipleship will secure not only your own life, but the coming of the kingdom.

SPIRITUALITY

Gospel

Luke 17:11-19; L947.6

As Jesus continued his journey to
    Jerusalem,
  he traveled through Samaria and
    Galilee.
As he was entering a village, ten
    lepers met him.
They stood at a distance from him
    and raised their voices, saying,
  "Jesus, Master! Have pity on us!"
And when he saw them, he said,
  "Go show yourselves to the
    priests."
As they were going they were
    cleansed.
And one of them, realizing he had
    been healed,
  returned, glorifying God in a loud
    voice;
  and he fell at the feet of Jesus and
    thanked him.
He was a Samaritan.
Jesus said in reply,
  "Ten were cleansed, were they not?
Where are the other nine?
Has none but this foreigner returned to
    give thanks to God?"
Then he said to him, "Stand up and go;
  your faith has saved you."

See Appendix A, p. 307, for the other readings.

FIRST READING
Sir 50:22-24; L943.2

RESPONSORIAL PSALM
Ps 67:2-3, 5, 6, 8; L919.1

SECOND READING
1 Cor 1:3-9; L944.1

*or any readings from the Mass "In Thanksgiving
to God"*

Reflecting on the Gospel

Whenever we say thank you, we do so because we have been given something. Sometimes the thank you springs from reflexive behavior in response, say, to something so minor as someone holding a door open for us. At other times a thank you may be something as thought-through as taking the time to write a formal thank you note for a wonderful social dinner at a friend's house. Parents sit down with their small children and help them "write" a thank you to the grandparents for a birthday present, or remind their older children to send a note for a graduation gift. Saying thank you becomes a learned behavior when we practice doing it. The more we say thank you, the more natural it becomes for us to utter these simple words at appropriate times.

On days like this one, Thanksgiving Day, we take time to say thanks to God for gifts which might not be on our minds all the time. As a country we are grateful for the abundant resources we have, for the democracy which enables us to live free lives, for the food on our tables. We would hardly think to write to Congress to say thank you! So Thanksgiving Day is our country's collective thank you for all the good we share as a nation.

It is not insignificant that Thanksgiving Day usually finds a special Mass being celebrated in our parish communities. We come to give God thanks not only for the blessings of our country, but also for all the spiritual gifts God has given us.

The gospel for this day about the ten lepers reminds us to take time to give God thanks for the most important gift we have been given beyond our life and Christian faith: salvation.

Ten lepers are healed. Only one, however, is pronounced "saved" by Jesus—the Samaritan who returns to offer thanks and praise. It is not enough to cry to God for help; it is not even enough to experience God's healing power. We must offer thanks and worship to the One who saves. We Christians, however, know that we do not offer God thanks and worship only on this one day a year set aside for this purpose. We offer God thanks and worship each Sunday. In this way do grateful hearts become a habit for us, a way to remember that all we have and all we are comes from God. But even this is not enough.

Our Sunday thanks and worship must become a *daily* habit, so that everything we do each day is really offered in thanks and praise of God. Like all giving thanks, this becomes an ingrained habit by the very doing. Salvation is surely not unrelated to thanksgiving. The more of a habit we develop of giving thanks to God, the deeper and more familiar is our relationship with God. Salvation is nothing less than this relationship with God as we faithfully live the gospel now, becoming a habit of ever-deepening relationship with the Divine.

Living the Paschal Mystery

It is something of a scandal that we live in a country with so much abundance, and yet so many people lack even the necessities of life. Our own thanksgiving must spill over into practical acts to alleviate the sufferings of so many who have so little. Indeed, giving to others less fortunate than we is in itself an acknowledgment of our own giftedness and gratitude for our abundance. Gratitude includes sharing our gifts with others.

Focusing the Gospel

Key words and phrases: ten, one, glorifying God, thanked him, saved

To the point: Ten lepers are healed. Only one, however, is pronounced "saved" by Jesus—the Samaritan who returns to offer thanks and praise. It is not enough to cry to God for help; it is not even enough to experience God's healing power. We must offer thanks and worship to the One who saves.

Model Act of Penitence

Presider: We gather today to give thanks to the God who fills us with good things. Let us prepare to celebrate this liturgy well . . .

Lord Jesus, you bring healing and salvation: Lord . . .

Christ Jesus, you do wondrous things for your people: Christ . . .

Lord Jesus, you are worthy of all glory and thanks: Lord . . .

Model General Intercessions

Presider: Our generous God gives us all good things. And so we bring our prayers in confidence.

Response:

Cantor:

That the Church offer God thanks and praise always and everywhere . . . [pause]

That our nation may cherish and safeguard the natural resources God has bestowed on us . . . [pause]

That the poor and hungry may share in the earth's abundance . . . [pause]

That each of us be ever grateful for the many gifts with which God has blessed us. . . [pause]

Presider: O God, you give us all good things: hear these our prayers that one day we might share in the fullness of your goodness at the heavenly banquet. We ask this through Christ our Lord and King. **Amen.**

OPENING PRAYER

Let us pray

Pause for silent prayer

Father all-powerful,
your gifts of love are countless
and your goodness is infinite.
On Thanksgiving Day we come before you
with gratitude for your kindness:
open our hearts to concern for our fellow
    men and women,
so that we may share your gifts in loving
    service.
We ask this through our Lord Jesus Christ,
    your Son,
who lives and reigns with you and the Holy
    Spirit,
one God for ever and ever. **Amen.**

FOR REFLECTION

- The earthly gifts for which I am thankful are . . .

- The extent to which the gift of salvation is important to me is . . .

- Some ways I could lead my family to giving thanks to God during this holiday are . . .

- For this year, the most significant reason I need to return to Jesus (like the Samaritan) and give thanks is . . .

SPIRITUALITY

Gospel

Luke 23:35-43; L162C

The rulers sneered at
   Jesus and said,
"He saved others,
   let him save
   himself
if he is the chosen
   one, the Christ
   of God."
Even the soldiers
   jeered at him.
As they approached
   to offer him wine
   they called out,
"If you are King of
   the Jews, save yourself."
Above him there was an inscription
   that read,
"This is the King of the Jews."

Now one of the criminals hanging there
   reviled Jesus, saying,
"Are you not the Christ?
Save yourself and us."
The other, however, rebuking him, said
   in reply,
"Have you no fear of God,
for you are subject to the same
   condemnation?
And indeed, we have been condemned
   justly,
for the sentence we received
   corresponds to our crimes,
but this man has done nothing
   criminal."
Then he said,
"Jesus, remember me when you come
   into your kingdom."
He replied to him,
"Amen, I say to you,
   today you will be with me in
   Paradise."

Reflecting on the Gospel

We end our liturgical year with a festive solemnity—that of Our Lord Jesus Christ the King. Yet the readings do not permit a one-sided approach to this day by only celebrating Christ's everlasting glory. Paul's exalted vision of Christ as ruling over all powers and all creation (see second reading) is tempered by the sober presentation of Jesus as a crucified "King of the Jews" (gospel). The tension between the two readings (and an inherent tension in this solemnity) is that we can never celebrate an exalted Christ without also acknowledging the suffering Jesus.

Yes, even a jubilant celebration of Christ our King includes the reality of our King as savior—one who suffered and died for us. This is the pattern of our own lives: we suffer, die to self, and only by joining ourselves to the suffering Christ will we share in the glory of the victorious Christ. How is Christ a king? Not by sitting on a throne; he hangs on a cross. Not by amassing territory; he establishes a kingdom of mercy and forgiveness. Not by wielding power; he does not save himself. What makes Christ our King is that he gave himself for the salvation of others.

Although Jesus, in fact, has the power to "save himself," he chooses, rather, to save a condemned criminal. The extent and reach of his kingship is revealed in saving mercy. In this gospel, one criminal acknowledges that "we have been condemned justly." Yet, when the same criminal asks, "Jesus, remember me," Jesus responds, "today you will be with me in Paradise." In this short exchange Jesus reveals the kind of King he is—one who is full of mercy and uses his power to save others. When we, like the criminal, confess our own sinfulness and seek divine mercy, then Jesus can be for us our merciful King. As the Good Thief had the insight of faith to recognize who Jesus was, so do we share in the same faith and the same glory, as we recognize who Jesus is for us. We can never celebrate the sovereignty of God revealed in Jesus without first acknowledging the suffering Christ.

Living the Paschal Mystery

Many of us have a hard time connecting with the idea of king and kingdom. What we are celebrating this solemnity is not a style of government but the sovereignty of God. Jesus is hung on a cross. This hardly fits our expectation of a "king." Yet, this is the ultimate meaning: Christ attains glory through the cross and, thereby, establishes forever his reign. So do we take up our own cross, and by doing so we attain our glory. Just as in the first reading David shepherds his people Israel, so does Jesus shepherd us. True, it is a strange kind of protection and shepherding which leads us to the same fate as he suffered! If we have no eyes to see, this is all there is: a cross.

With the second criminal we, too, ask, "Jesus, remember me when you come into your kingdom." The response to us, as to the second criminal, is "you will be with me in Paradise." Jesus promises. He always makes good on his promises. This is why we are faithful along the way. This is why we persevere in following Jesus. This is why we are willing to empty ourselves for the sake of others . . . because by dying we rise. By giving of ourselves we enter with Jesus into Paradise. Our journey ends at the cross. The cross is the door to Paradise.

Focusing the Gospel

Key words and phrases: King, condemned, remember me, today you will be with me in Paradise

To the point: In this gospel, one criminal acknowledges that "we have been condemned justly." Yet, when the same criminal asks, "Jesus, remember me," Jesus responds, "today you will be with me in Paradise." In this short exchange Jesus reveals the kind of king he is—one who is full of mercy and uses his power to save others. When we, like the criminal, confess our own sinfulness and seek divine mercy, then Jesus can be for us our merciful King.

Connecting the Gospel

to the second reading: Paul's exalted vision of Christ as ruling over all powers and all creation (see second reading) is tempered by the sober presentation of Jesus as a crucified "King of the Jews" (gospel). The tension between the two readings (and an inherent tension in this solemnity) is that we can never celebrate an exalted Christ without also acknowledging the suffering Jesus.

to culture: Many of us have a hard time connecting with the idea of king and kingdom. What we are celebrating is not a style of government but the sovereignty of God revealed in Jesus.

Understanding Scripture

The kingship of Jesus: The kind of king Jesus is finds its clearest expression on the cross. In Luke's gospel the cross does not appear unexpectedly. Luke has been preparing for this moment throughout his gospel and he presents the crucifixion in such a way as to allude to earlier episodes in the gospel.

At the outset of his public ministry, the question of Jesus' identity framed the temptations: in the first and last temptations, the devil taunts, "If you are the Son of God," do such and such (4:3, 9). On the cross, the identity of Christ is questioned three times: "if he is the chosen one, the Christ of God" (v. 35), "if you are the King of the Jews" (v. 37), and "are you not the Christ?" (v. 39). In both episodes, the nature of Jesus' identity is not what others think.

In the temptations, Jesus would not use his power to feed himself (4:3-4), though later he would feed the 5,000 (9:12-17). Although Jesus used his power to save others (7:50; 8:36, 48, 50; 18:42; 19:10), he would not use it to save himself. Jesus does not use power in the way others might expect.

The rulers sneer and wonder whether Jesus is "the chosen one"; this recalls the transfiguration in which God announces that Jesus is "my chosen son" (9:35). Being "chosen" by God is not about privilege as others might expect.

The crowd had welcomed Jesus to Jerusalem with palms and with shouts of "blessed is the king" (19:38); at the trial, they had accused him of being a king (23:2), and the charge on the cross identifies him as such (23:38). While the language is accurate, the concept is wrong. The kingship of Christ is not about power, certainly not the political or juridical power to "save yourself and us" from the ignominy of crucifixion. But, ironically, his power to save is revealed as he tells the criminal, "today you will be with me in Paradise." The cross reveals his identity, the meaning of power, the cost of being "chosen," and the nature of kingship.

ASSEMBLY & FAITH-SHARING GROUPS

- It makes sense to celebrate this solemnity by proclaiming a Gospel of Jesus' suffering on the cross because . . .
- When I witnessed the extent of Jesus' mercy (as he shared with the one criminal), for me it was . . .
- I help establish or extend Christ's reign by . . .

PRESIDERS

In the midst of sneers and jeers, Jesus forgives and saves; where I need to embody this kind of shepherding is . . .

DEACONS

I have incarnated the kingship of Christ in my workplace throughout this liturgical year by . . .

HOSPITALITY MINISTERS

My care and concern helps the assembly realize they are already "in Paradise" whenever I . . .

MUSIC MINISTERS

What I hope Jesus remembers about me and my manner of doing music ministry this past year is . . .

ALTAR MINISTERS

The kind of service which signifies to others that they "share in the inheritance of the holy ones" (second reading) is like . . .

LECTORS

My pondering and proclaiming of the word this past liturgical year has made me an "image of the invisible God" (second reading) in that . . .

EXTRAORDINARY MINISTERS OF HOLY COMMUNION

I distribute Christ the King at Eucharist; I "distribute" Christ's reign whenever . . .

Model Act of Penitence

Presider: We come together to honor Christ our King. As we prepare for this liturgy, let us acknowledge our need for his mercy . . . [pause]

Lord Jesus, you are the image of the invisible God: Lord . . .

Christ Jesus, in you we have redemption and forgiveness of our sins: Christ . . .

Lord Jesus, you make peace by the blood of your cross: Lord . . .

Appreciating the Responsorial Psalm

Israelites arriving at the gates of Jerusalem for annual worship sang Psalm 122. It was a song of great joy, for entering Jerusalem meant encountering God. It meant celebrating membership in God's people. It meant reaffirming who they were and who God was for them. On this solemnity we, too, celebrate who we are and who God is for us. We are the people forgiven by Christ's redeeming death (second reading). We are the very "bone and flesh" (first reading) of Christ who shepherds us through death to resurrection. We are the ones remembered by Christ and called to his kingdom (gospel). Let us enter with rejoicing!

Model General Intercessions

Presider: God raised Jesus to life and made him King of all creation. Let us pray that we might one day share in the glory of Paradise.

Response:

Lord, hear our prayer.

Cantor:

we pray to the Lord,

That the Church may faithfully reveal the glory of Christ's kingship through mercy and forgiveness . . . [pause]

That leaders of the world rule with compassion, truth, and integrity . . . [pause]

That those imprisoned and condemned may enter into Paradise through the mercy of Christ the King . . . [pause]

That all of us here one day enjoy fully the blessings of Christ's kingship . . . [pause]

Presider: O God, you make us worthy members of your kingdom: hear these our prayers that one day we may be with you forever in Paradise. We ask this through Christ our Lord and King. **Amen.**

Let us pray

Pause for silent prayer

Father all-powerful, God of love,
you have raised our Lord Jesus Christ from
    death to life,
resplendent in glory as King of creation.
Open our hearts,
free all the world to rejoice in his peace,
to glory in his justice, to live in his love.
Bring all mankind together in Jesus Christ
    your Son,
whose kingdom is with you and the Holy
    Spirit,
one God, for ever and ever. **Amen.**

FIRST READING
2 Sam 5:1-3

In those days, all the tribes of Israel came
        to David in Hebron and said:
    "Here we are, your bone and your flesh.
In days past, when Saul was our king,
    it was you who led the Israelites out and
        brought them back.
And the LORD said to you,
    'You shall shepherd my people Israel
    and shall be commander of Israel.'"
When all the elders of Israel came to
        David in Hebron,
    King David made an agreement with
        them there before the LORD,
    and they anointed him king of Israel.

RESPONSORIAL PSALM
Ps 122:1-2, 3-4, 4-5

℟. (cf. 1) Let us go rejoicing to the house
of the Lord.

I rejoiced because they said to me,
    "We will go up to the house of the
        LORD."
And now we have set foot
    within your gates, O Jerusalem.

℟. Let us go rejoicing to the house of the
Lord.

Jerusalem, built as a city
  with compact unity.
To it the tribes go up,
  the tribes of the LORD.

R̸. Let us go rejoicing to the house of the Lord.

According to the decree for Israel,
  to give thanks to the name of the LORD.
In it are set up judgment seats,
  seats for the house of David.

R̸. Let us go rejoicing to the house of the Lord.

SECOND READING
Col 1:12-20

Brothers and sisters:
Let us give thanks to the Father,
  who has made you fit to share
  in the inheritance of the holy ones in
    light.
He delivered us from the power of
  darkness
  and transferred us to the kingdom of
    his beloved Son,
  in whom we have redemption, the
    forgiveness of sins.

  He is the image of the invisible God,
    the firstborn of all creation.
  For in him were created all things in
    heaven and on earth,
    the visible and the invisible,
    whether thrones or dominions or
      principalities or powers;
    all things were created through
      him and for him.
  He is before all things,
    and in him all things hold together.
  He is the head of the body, the
    church.
  He is the beginning, the firstborn
    from the dead,
    that in all things he himself might
      be preeminent.
  For in him all the fullness was
    pleased to dwell,
    and through him to reconcile all
      things for him,
    making peace by the blood of his
      cross
    through him, whether those on
      earth or those in heaven.

About Liturgy

End/beginning of the liturgical year: The liturgical year concludes at the end of this Thirty-fourth Week in Ordinary Time. The motif of Christ's Second Coming which we have been focusing on especially these last weeks of the liturgical year comes to a climax as we celebrate Christ's victory and coming to glory on this solemnity of Our Lord Jesus Christ the King. But celebrating the victorious Christ does not end with this liturgical year nor with this solemnity. An eschatological motif continues into the first part of Advent which begins, not with looking to Christ's first coming, but with looking to Christ's Second Coming. In this way the liturgical year presents to us a seamless rhythm of passion and victory, death and new life.

About Liturgical Music

Cantor preparation: As you sing this responsorial psalm, you invite the people forward to enter the kingdom of God. They have journeyed through all of Ordinary Time. They have struggled and they have been faithful. Bring them in with joy.

A word to the music director: The past two Sundays and your reflections on them have set you up perfectly for the gospel to be proclaimed on this solemnity. Christ is king, but one who hangs on a cross. Your coming into glory with Christ is through the same passage—through death. And it is this paschal mystery which you strive week in and week out to invite the assembly to enter through the liturgy and its music. No easy task, for this mystery is not passing entertainment. For the many ways you have been faithful to your ministry this past liturgical year, make your prayer, "Jesus, remember me." For the ways you have been unfaithful, ask Jesus' forgiveness. Then listen for his response, "I do remember; you are with me."

Readings *(continued)*

The Immaculate Conception of the Blessed Virgin Mary, *December 8, 2006*

FIRST READING
Gen 3:9-15, 20

After the man, Adam, had eaten of the tree,
the LORD God called to the man and asked
him, "Where are you?"
He answered, "I heard you in the garden;
but I was afraid, because I was naked,
so I hid myself."
Then he asked, "Who told you that you were
naked?
You have eaten, then,
from the tree of which I had forbidden you
to eat!"
The man replied, "The woman whom you put
here with me—
she gave me fruit from the tree, and so I
ate it."
The LORD God then asked the woman,
"Why did you do such a thing?"
The woman answered, "The serpent tricked
me into it, so I ate it."

Then the LORD God said to the serpent:
"Because you have done this, you shall be
banned
from all the animals
and from all the wild creatures;
on your belly shall you crawl,
and dirt shall you eat
all the days of your life.
I will put enmity between you and the
woman,
and between your offspring and hers;
he will strike at your head,
while you strike at his heel."

The man called his wife Eve,
because she became the mother of all the
living.

RESPONSORIAL PSALM
Ps 98:1, 2-3, 3-4

℟. (1a) Sing to the Lord a new song, for he
has done marvelous deeds.

Sing to the LORD a new song,
for he has done wondrous deeds;
his right hand has won victory for him,
his holy arm.

℟. Sing to the Lord a new song, for he has
done marvelous deeds.

The LORD has made his salvation known:
in the sight of the nations he has revealed
his justice.
He has remembered his kindness and his
faithfulness
toward the house of Israel.

℟. Sing to the Lord a new song, for he has
done marvelous deeds.

All the ends of the earth have seen
the salvation by our God.
Sing joyfully to the LORD, all you lands;
break into song; sing praise.

℟. Sing to the Lord a new song, for he has
done marvelous deeds.

SECOND READING
Eph 1:3-6, 11-12

Brothers and sisters:
Blessed be the God and Father of our Lord
Jesus Christ,
who has blessed us in Christ
with every spiritual blessing in the
heavens,
as he chose us in him, before the foundation
of the world,
to be holy and without blemish before him.
In love he destined us for adoption to himself
through Jesus Christ,
in accord with the favor of his will,
for the praise of the glory of his grace
that he granted us in the beloved.

In him we were also chosen,
destined in accord with the purpose of the
One
who accomplishes all things according to
the intention of his will,
so that we might exist for the praise of his
glory,
we who first hoped in Christ.

Gospel (cont.)

Matt 1:1-25; L13ABC

David became the father of Solomon,
  whose mother had been the wife of Uriah.
Solomon became the father of Rehoboam,
  Rehoboam the father of Abijah,
  Abijah the father of Asaph.
Asaph became the father of Jehoshaphat,
  Jehoshaphat the father of Joram,
  Joram the father of Uzziah.
Uzziah became the father of Jotham,
  Jotham the father of Ahaz,
  Ahaz the father of Hezekiah.
Hezekiah became the father of Manasseh,
  Manasseh the father of Amos,
  Amos the father of Josiah.
Josiah became the father of Jechoniah and his brothers
  at the time of the Babylonian exile.

After the Babylonian exile,
  Jechoniah became the father of Shealtiel,
  Shealtiel the father of Zerubbabel,
  Zerubbabel the father of Abiud.
Abiud became the father of Eliakim,
  Eliakim the father of Azor,
  Azor the father of Zadok.
Zadok became the father of Achim,
  Achim the father of Eliud,
  Eliud the father of Eleazar.
Eleazar became the father of Matthan,
  Matthan the father of Jacob,
  Jacob the father of Joseph, the husband of Mary.
Of her was born Jesus who is called the Christ.

Thus the total number of generations
  from Abraham to David
  is fourteen generations;
  from David to the Babylonian exile,
  fourteen generations;
  from the Babylonian exile to the Christ,
  fourteen generations.

Now this is how the birth of Jesus Christ came about.
When his mother Mary was betrothed to Joseph,
  but before they lived together,
  she was found with child through the Holy Spirit.
Joseph her husband, since he was a righteous man,
  yet unwilling to expose her to shame,
  decided to divorce her quietly.

Such was his intention when, behold,
  the angel of the Lord appeared to him in a dream and said,
  "Joseph, son of David,
  do not be afraid to take Mary your wife into your home.
For it is through the Holy Spirit
  that this child has been conceived in her.
She will bear a son and you are to name him Jesus,
  because he will save his people from their sins."
All this took place to fulfill
  what the Lord had said through the prophet:
    Behold, the virgin shall conceive and bear a son,
      and they shall name him Emmanuel,
    which means "God is with us."
When Joseph awoke,
  he did as the angel of the Lord had commanded him
  and took his wife into his home.
He had no relations with her until she bore a son,
  and he named him Jesus.

or Matt 1:18-25

This is how the birth of Jesus Christ came about.
When his mother Mary was betrothed to Joseph,
  but before they lived together,
  she was found with child through the Holy Spirit.
Joseph her husband, since he was a righteous man,
  yet unwilling to expose her to shame,
  decided to divorce her quietly.
Such was his intention when, behold,
  the angel of the Lord appeared to him in a dream and said,
  "Joseph, son of David,
  do not be afraid to take Mary your wife into your home.
For it is through the Holy Spirit
  that this child has been conceived in her.
She will bear a son and you are to name him Jesus,
  because he will save his people from their sins."
All this took place to fulfill
  what the Lord had said through the prophet:
    Behold, the virgin shall conceive and bear a son,
      and they shall name him Emmanuel,
    which means "God is with us."
When Joseph awoke,
  he did as the angel of the Lord had commanded him
  and took his wife into his home.
He had no relations with her until she bore a son,
  and he named him Jesus.

The Nativity of the Lord, *December 25, 2006 (Vigil Mass)*

FIRST READING
Isa 62:1-5

For Zion's sake I will not be silent,
    for Jerusalem's sake I will not be quiet,
until her vindication shines forth like the dawn
    and her victory like a burning torch.

Nations shall behold your vindication,
    and all the kings your glory;
you shall be called by a new name
    pronounced by the mouth of the LORD.
You shall be a glorious crown in the hand of
    the LORD,
    a royal diadem held by your God.
No more shall people call you "Forsaken,"
    or your land "Desolate,"
but you shall be called "My Delight,"
    and your land "Espoused."
For the LORD delights in you
    and makes your land his spouse.
As a young man marries a virgin,
    your Builder shall marry you;
and as a bridegroom rejoices in his bride
    so shall your God rejoice in you.

RESPONSORIAL PSALM
Ps 89:4-5, 16-17, 27, 29

R̸. (2a) Forever I will sing the goodness of the Lord.

I have made a covenant with my chosen one,
    I have sworn to David my servant:
forever will I confirm your posterity
    and establish your throne for all
    generations.

R̸. Forever I will sing the goodness of the Lord.

Blessed the people who know the joyful shout;
    in the light of your countenance, O LORD,
    they walk.
At your name they rejoice all the day,
    and through your justice they are exalted.

R̸. Forever I will sing the goodness of the Lord.

He shall say of me, "You are my father,
    my God, the rock, my savior."
Forever I will maintain my kindness toward
    him,
    and my covenant with him stands firm.

R̸. Forever I will sing the goodness of the Lord.

SECOND READING
Acts 13:16-17, 22-25

When Paul reached Antioch in Pisidia and
    entered the synagogue,
    he stood up, motioned with his hand, and
    said,
    "Fellow Israelites and you others who are
    God-fearing, listen.
The God of this people Israel chose our
    ancestors
    and exalted the people during their sojourn
    in the land of Egypt.
With uplifted arm he led them out of it.
Then he removed Saul and raised up David
    as king;
    of him he testified,
    'I have found David, son of Jesse, a man
    after my own heart;
    he will carry out my every wish.'
From this man's descendants God, according
    to his promise,
    has brought to Israel a savior, Jesus.
John heralded his coming by proclaiming a
    baptism of repentance
    to all the people of Israel;
    and as John was completing his course, he
    would say,
    'What do you suppose that I am? I am not he.
Behold, one is coming after me;
    I am not worthy to unfasten the sandals of
    his feet.'"

The Nativity of the Lord, *December 25, 2006 (Mass at Midnight)*

Gospel (cont.)
Luke 2:1-14; L14ABC

The angel said to them,
    "Do not be afraid;
    for behold, I proclaim to you good news of great joy
    that will be for all the people.
For today in the city of David
    a savior has been born for you who is Christ and Lord.
And this will be a sign for you:
    you will find an infant wrapped in swaddling clothes
    and lying in a manger."
And suddenly there was a multitude of the heavenly host with the
    angel,
    praising God and saying:
        "Glory to God in the highest
            and on earth peace to those on whom his favor rests."

The Nativity of the Lord, *December 25, 2006 (Mass at Midnight)*

FIRST READING
Isa 9:1-6

The people who walked in darkness
    have seen a great light;
upon those who dwelt in the land of gloom
    a light has shone.
You have brought them abundant joy
    and great rejoicing,
as they rejoice before you as at the harvest,
    as people make merry when dividing
        spoils.
For the yoke that burdened them,
    the pole on their shoulder,
and the rod of their taskmaster
    you have smashed, as on the day of Midian.
For every boot that tramped in battle,
    every cloak rolled in blood,
    will be burned as fuel for flames.
For a child is born to us, a son is given us;
    upon his shoulder dominion rests.
They name him Wonder-Counselor, God-Hero,
    Father-Forever, Prince of Peace.
His dominion is vast
    and forever peaceful,
from David's throne, and over his kingdom,
    which he confirms and sustains
by judgment and justice,
    both now and forever.
The zeal of the LORD of hosts will do this!

RESPONSORIAL PSALM
Ps 96:1-2, 2-3, 11-12, 13

R⁄. (Luke 2:11) Today is born our Savior,
Christ the Lord.

Sing to the LORD a new song;
    sing to the LORD, all you lands.
Sing to the LORD; bless his name.

R⁄. Today is born our Savior, Christ the Lord.

Announce his salvation, day after day.
    Tell his glory among the nations;
    among all peoples, his wondrous deeds.

R⁄. Today is born our Savior, Christ the Lord.

Let the heavens be glad and the earth rejoice;
    let the sea and what fills it resound;
    let the plains be joyful and all that is in
        them!
Then shall all the trees of the forest exult.

R⁄. Today is born our Savior, Christ the Lord.

They shall exult before the LORD, for he
        comes;
    for he comes to rule the earth.
He shall rule the world with justice
    and the peoples with his constancy.

R⁄. Today is born our Savior, Christ the Lord.

SECOND READING
Titus 2:11-14

Beloved:
The grace of God has appeared, saving all
    and training us to reject godless ways and
        worldly desires
    and to live temperately, justly, and devoutly
        in this age,
    as we await the blessed hope,
    the appearance of the glory of our great
        God
    and savior Jesus Christ,
    who gave himself for us to deliver us from
        all lawlessness
    and to cleanse for himself a people as his
        own,
    eager to do what is good.

The Nativity of the Lord, *December 25, 2006 (Mass at Dawn)*

FIRST READING
Isa 62:11-12

See, the LORD proclaims
    to the ends of the earth:
say to daughter Zion,
    your savior comes!
Here is his reward with him,
    his recompense before him.
They shall be called the holy people,
    the redeemed of the LORD,
and you shall be called "Frequented,"
    a city that is not forsaken.

RESPONSORIAL PSALM
Ps 97:1, 6, 11-12

R⁄. A light will shine on us this day: the Lord
is born for us.

The LORD is king; let the earth rejoice;
    let the many isles be glad.
The heavens proclaim his justice,
    and all peoples see his glory.

R⁄. A light will shine on us this day: the Lord
is born for us.

Light dawns for the just;
    and gladness, for the upright of heart.
Be glad in the LORD, you just,
    and give thanks to his holy name.

R⁄. A light will shine on us this day: the Lord
is born for us.

SECOND READING
Titus 3:4-7

Beloved:
When the kindness and generous love
    of God our savior appeared,
not because of any righteous deeds we had
        done
    but because of his mercy,
he saved us through the bath of rebirth
    and renewal by the Holy Spirit,
whom he richly poured out on us
    through Jesus Christ our savior,
so that we might be justified by his grace
    and become heirs in hope of eternal life.

Gospel (cont.)
John 1:1-18; L16ABC

But to those who did accept him
    he gave power to become children of God,
    to those who believe in his name,
    who were born not by natural generation
    nor by human choice nor by a man's decision
    but of God.
        And the Word became flesh
        and made his dwelling among us,
        and we saw his glory,
        the glory as of the Father's only Son,
        full of grace and truth.
John testified to him and cried out, saying,
    "This was he of whom I said,
    'The one who is coming after me ranks ahead of me
    because he existed before me.'"
From his fullness we have all received,
    grace in place of grace,
    because while the law was given through Moses,
    grace and truth came through Jesus Christ.
No one has ever seen God.
The only Son, God, who is at the Father's side,
    has revealed him.

or John 1:1-5, 9-14

In the beginning was the Word,
    and the Word was with God,
    and the Word was God.
He was in the beginning with God.
All things came to be through him,
    and without him nothing came to be.
What came to be through him was life,
    and this life was the light of the human race;
    the light shines in the darkness,
    and the darkness has not overcome it.
The true light, which enlightens everyone,
    was coming into the world.
He was in the world,
    and the world came to be through him,
    but the world did not know him.
He came to what was his own,
    but his own people did not accept him.

But to those who did accept him
    he gave power to become children of God,
    to those who believe in his name,
    who were born not by natural generation
    nor by human choice nor by a man's decision
    but of God.
        And the Word became flesh
        and made his dwelling among us,
        and we saw his glory,
        the glory as of the Father's only Son,
        full of grace and truth.

FIRST READING
Isa 52:7-10

How beautiful upon the mountains
    are the feet of him who brings glad tidings,
announcing peace, bearing good news,
    announcing salvation, and saying to Zion,
    "Your God is King!"

Hark! Your sentinels raise a cry,
    together they shout for joy,
for they see directly, before their eyes,
    the LORD restoring Zion.
Break out together in song,
    O ruins of Jerusalem!
For the LORD comforts his people,
    he redeems Jerusalem.
The LORD has bared his holy arm
    in the sight of all the nations;
all the ends of the earth will behold
    the salvation of our God.

RESPONSORIAL PSALM
Ps 98:1, 2-3, 3-4, 5-6

℞. (3c) All the ends of the earth have seen the saving power of God.

Sing to the LORD a new song,
    for he has done wondrous deeds;
his right hand has won victory for him,
    his holy arm.

℞. All the ends of the earth have seen the saving power of God.

The LORD has made his salvation known:
    in the sight of the nations he has revealed
        his justice.
He has remembered his kindness and his
    faithfulness
    toward the house of Israel.

℞. All the ends of the earth have seen the saving power of God.

All the ends of the earth have seen
    the salvation by our God.
Sing joyfully to the LORD, all you lands;
    break into song; sing praise.

℞. All the ends of the earth have seen the saving power of God.

Sing praise to the LORD with the harp,
    with the harp and melodious song.
With trumpets and the sound of the horn
    sing joyfully before the King, the LORD.

℞. All the ends of the earth have seen the saving power of God.

The Nativity of the Lord, *December 25, 2006 (Mass During the Day)*

SECOND READING
Heb 1:1-6

Brothers and sisters:
In times past, God spoke in partial and
    various ways
  to our ancestors through the prophets;
  in these last days, he has spoken to us
    through the Son,
  whom he made heir of all things
  and through whom he created the universe,
  who is the refulgence of his glory, the very
    imprint of his being,
    and who sustains all things by his
      mighty word.
  When he had accomplished purification
    from sins,

he took his seat at the right hand of the
  Majesty on high,
  as far superior to the angels
    as the name he has inherited is more
      excellent than theirs.

For to which of the angels did God ever say:
  *You are my son; this day I have begotten
    you?*
Or again:
  *I will be a father to him, and he shall be a
    son to me?*
And again, when he leads the firstborn into
  the world, he says:
  Let all the angels of God worship him.

The Holy Family of Jesus, Mary, and Joseph, *December 31, 2006*

FIRST READING
Sir 3:2-6, 12-14

God sets a father in honor over his children;
  a mother's authority he confirms over her
    sons.
Whoever honors his father atones for sins,
  and preserves himself from them.
When he prays, he is heard;
  he stores up riches who reveres his mother.
Whoever honors his father is gladdened by
    children,
  and, when he prays, is heard.
Whoever reveres his father will live a long life;
  he who obeys his father brings comfort to
    his mother.

My son, take care of your father when he is old;
  grieve him not as long as he lives.
Even if his mind fail, be considerate of him;
  revile him not all the days of his life;
kindness to a father will not be forgotten,
  firmly planted against the debt of your sins
  —a house raised in justice to you.

RESPONSORIAL PSALM
Ps 128:1-2, 3, 4-5

R̸. (cf. 1) Blessed are those who fear the Lord
and walk in his ways.

Blessed is everyone who fears the LORD,
  who walks in his ways!
For you shall eat the fruit of your handiwork;
  blessed shall you be, and favored.

R̸. Blessed are those who fear the Lord and
walk in his ways.

Your wife shall be like a fruitful vine
  in the recesses of your home;
your children like olive plants

around your table.

R̸. Blessed are those who fear the Lord and
walk in his ways.

Behold, thus is the man blessed
  who fears the LORD.
The LORD bless you from Zion:
  may you see the prosperity of Jerusalem
  all the days of your life.

R̸. Blessed are those who fear the Lord and
walk in his ways.

SECOND READING
Col 3:12-21

Brothers and sisters:
Put on, as God's chosen ones, holy and beloved,
  heartfelt compassion, kindness, humility,
    gentleness, and patience,
  bearing with one another and forgiving one
    another,
  if one has a grievance against another;
  as the Lord has forgiven you, so must you
    also do.
And over all these put on love,
  that is, the bond of perfection.
And let the peace of Christ control your hearts,
  the peace into which you were also called in
    one body.
And be thankful.
Let the word of Christ dwell in you richly,
  as in all wisdom you teach and admonish
    one another,
  singing psalms, hymns, and spiritual songs
  with gratitude in your hearts to God.
And whatever you do, in word or in deed,
  do everything in the name of the Lord Jesus,
  giving thanks to God the Father through him.

Wives, be subordinate to your husbands,
  as is proper in the Lord.
Husbands, love your wives,
  and avoid any bitterness toward them.
Children, obey your parents in everything,
  for this is pleasing to the Lord.
Fathers, do not provoke your children,
  so they may not become discouraged.

or

Col 3:12-17

Brothers and sisters:
Put on, as God's chosen ones, holy and beloved,
  heartfelt compassion, kindness, humility,
    gentleness, and patience,
  bearing with one another and forgiving one
    another,
  if one has a grievance against another;
  as the Lord has forgiven you, so must you
    also do.
And over all these put on love,
  that is, the bond of perfection.
And let the peace of Christ control your hearts,
  the peace into which you were also called in
    one body.
And be thankful.
Let the word of Christ dwell in you richly,
  as in all wisdom you teach and admonish
    one another,
  singing psalms, hymns, and spiritual songs
  with gratitude in your hearts to God.
And whatever you do, in word or in deed,
  do everything in the name of the Lord Jesus,
  giving thanks to God the Father through him.

Solemnity of the Blessed Virgin Mary, Mother of God, *January 1, 2007*

FIRST READING
Num 6:22-27

The LORD said to Moses:
"Speak to Aaron and his sons and tell them:
This is how you shall bless the Israelites.
Say to them:
The LORD bless you and keep you!
The LORD let his face shine upon
you, and be gracious to you!
The LORD look upon you kindly and
give you peace!
So shall they invoke my name upon the
Israelites,
and I will bless them."

RESPONSORIAL PSALM
Ps 67:2-3, 5, 6, 8

R̞. (2a) May God bless us in his mercy.

May God have pity on us and bless us;
may he let his face shine upon us.
So may your way be known upon earth;
among all nations, your salvation.

R̞. May God bless us in his mercy.

May the nations be glad and exult
because you rule the peoples in equity;
the nations on the earth you guide.

R̞. May God bless us in his mercy.

May the peoples praise you, O God;
may all the peoples praise you!
May God bless us,
and may all the ends of the earth fear him!

R̞. May God bless us in his mercy.

SECOND READING
Gal 4:4-7

Brothers and sisters:
When the fullness of time had come, God sent
his Son,
born of a woman, born under the law,
to ransom those under the law,
so that we might receive adoption as sons.
As proof that you are sons,
God sent the Spirit of his Son into our
hearts,
crying out, "Abba, Father!"
So you are no longer a slave but a son,
and if a son then also an heir, through God.

Third Sunday in Ordinary Time, *January 21, 2007*

SECOND READING (cont.)
1 Cor 12:12-30

Now the body is not a single part, but many.
If a foot should say,
"Because I am not a hand I do not belong to
the body,"
it does not for this reason belong any less
to the body.
Or if an ear should say,
"Because I am not an eye I do not belong to
the body,"
it does not for this reason belong any less
to the body.
If the whole body were an eye, where would
the hearing be?
If the whole body were hearing, where would
the sense of smell be?
But as it is, God placed the parts,
each one of them, in the body as he
intended.
If they were all one part, where would the
body be?
But as it is, there are many parts, yet one
body.
The eye cannot say to the hand, "I do not need
you,"
nor again the head to the feet, "I do not
need you."
Indeed, the parts of the body that seem to be
weaker
are all the more necessary,
and those parts of the body that we
consider less honorable

we surround with greater honor,
and our less presentable parts are treated
with greater
propriety,
whereas our more presentable parts do not
need this.
But God has so constructed the body
as to give greater honor to a part that is
without it,
so that there may be no division in the
body,
but that the parts may have the same
concern for one another.
If one part suffers, all the parts suffer with it;
if one part is honored, all the parts share
its joy.

Now you are Christ's body, and individually
parts of it.
Some people God has designated in the
church
to be, first, apostles; second, prophets;
third, teachers;
then, mighty deeds;
then gifts of healing, assistance,
administration,
and varieties of tongues.
Are all apostles? Are all prophets? Are all
teachers?
Do all work mighty deeds? Do all have gifts
of healing?
Do all speak in tongues? Do all interpret?

or 1 Cor 12:12-14, 27

Brothers and sisters:
As a body is one though it has many parts,
and all the parts of the body, though many,
are one body,
so also Christ.
For in one Spirit we were all baptized into one
body,
whether Jews or Greeks, slaves or free
persons,
and we were all given to drink of one
Spirit.
Now the body is not a single part, but many.
You are Christ's body, and individually parts
of it.

Fourth Sunday in Ordinary Time, *January 28, 2007*

SECOND READING (cont.)
1 Cor 12:31–13:13

For we know partially and we prophesy
    partially,
    but when the perfect comes, the partial will
        pass away.
When I was a child, I used to talk as a child,
    think as a child, reason as a child;
    when I became a man, I put aside childish
        things.
At present we see indistinctly, as in a mirror,
    but then face to face.
At present I know partially;
    then I shall know fully, as I am fully known.
So faith, hope, love remain, these three;
    but the greatest of these is love.

or 1 Cor 13:4-13

Brothers and sisters:
Love is patient, love is kind.
It is not jealous, it is not pompous,
    it is not inflated, it is not rude,
    it does not seek its own interests,
    it is not quick-tempered, it does not brood
        over injury,
    it does not rejoice over wrongdoing but
        rejoices with the truth.
It bears all things, believes all things,
    hopes all things, endures all things.

Love never fails.
If there are prophecies, they will be brought
    to nothing;
    if tongues, they will cease;
    if knowledge, it will be brought to nothing.

For we know partially and we prophesy
    partially,
    but when the perfect comes, the partial will
        pass away.
When I was a child, I used to talk as a child,
    think as a child, reason as a child;
    when I became a man, I put aside childish
        things.
At present we see indistinctly, as in a mirror,
    but then face to face.
At present I know partially;
    then I shall know fully, as I am fully known.
So faith, hope, love remain, these three;
    but the greatest of these is love.

Fifth Sunday in Ordinary Time, *February 4, 2007*

SECOND READING (cont.)
1 Cor 15:1-11

After that, he appeared to more
        than five hundred brothers at once,
    most of whom are still living,
    though some have fallen asleep.
After that he appeared to James,
    then to all the apostles.
Last of all, as to one born abnormally,
    he appeared to me.
For I am the least of the apostles,
    not fit to be called an apostle,
    because I persecuted the church of God.
But by the grace of God I am what I am,
    and his grace to me has not been
        ineffective.
Indeed, I have toiled harder than all of them;
    not I, however, but the grace of God that is
        with me.
Therefore, whether it be I or they,
    so we preach and so you believed.

or 1 Cor 15:3-8, 11

Brothers and sisters,
    I handed on to you as of first importance
        what I also received:
    that Christ died for our sins
    in accordance with the Scriptures;
    that he was buried;
    that he was raised on the third day
    in accordance with the Scriptures;
    that he appeared to Cephas, then to the
        Twelve.
After that, he appeared to more
    than five hundred brothers at once,
    most of whom are still living,
    though some have fallen asleep.
After that he appeared to James,
    then to all the apostles.
Last of all, as to one abnormally born,
    he appeared to me.
Therefore, whether it be I or they,
    so we preach and so you believed.

Ash Wednesday, *February 21, 2007*

FIRST READING
Joel 2:12-18

Even now, says the LORD,
　　return to me with your whole heart,
　　with fasting, and weeping, and mourning;
Rend your hearts, not your garments,
　　and return to the LORD, your God.
For gracious and merciful is he,
　　slow to anger, rich in kindness,
　　and relenting in punishment.
Perhaps he will again relent
　　and leave behind him a blessing,
Offerings and libations
　　for the LORD, your God.

Blow the trumpet in Zion!
　　proclaim a fast,
　　call an assembly;
Gather the people,
　　notify the congregation;
Assemble the elders,
　　gather the children
　　and the infants at the breast;
Let the bridegroom quit his room
　　and the bride her chamber.
Between the porch and the altar
　　let the priests, the ministers of the LORD,
　　　　weep,
And say, "Spare, O LORD, your people,
　　and make not your heritage a reproach,
　　with the nations ruling over them!
Why should they say among the peoples,
　　'Where is their God?'"

Then the LORD was stirred to concern for his
　　　　land
　　and took pity on his people.

RESPONSORIAL PSALM
Ps 51:3-4, 5-6ab, 12-13, 14, and 17

R̂. (see 3a) Be merciful, O Lord, for we have
sinned.

Have mercy on me, O God, in your goodness;
　　in the greatness of your compassion wipe
　　　　out my offense.
Thoroughly wash me from my guilt
　　and of my sin cleanse me.

R̂. Be merciful, O Lord, for we have sinned.

For I acknowledge my offense,
　　and my sin is before me always:
"Against you only have I sinned,
　　and done what is evil in your sight."

R̂. Be merciful, O Lord, for we have sinned.

A clean heart create for me, O God,
　　and a steadfast spirit renew within me.
Cast me not out from your presence,
　　and your Holy Spirit take not from me.

R̂. Be merciful, O Lord, for we have sinned.

Give me back the joy of your salvation,
　　and a willing spirit sustain in me.
O Lord, open my lips,
　　and my mouth shall proclaim your praise.

R̂. Be merciful, O Lord, for we have sinned.

SECOND READING
2 Cor 5:20–6:2

Brothers and sisters:
We are ambassadors for Christ,
　　as if God were appealing through us.
We implore you on behalf of Christ,
　　be reconciled to God.
For our sake he made him to be sin who did
　　　　not know sin,
　　so that we might become the righteousness
　　　　of God in him.

Working together, then,
　　we appeal to you not to receive the grace of
　　　　God in vain.
For he says:

*In an acceptable time I heard you,
　　and on the day of salvation I helped you.*

Behold, now is a very acceptable time;
　　behold, now is the day of salvation.

First Sunday of Lent, *February 25, 2007*

SECOND READING
Rom 10:8-13

Brothers and sisters:
What does Scripture say?
　　*The word is near you,
　in your mouth and in your heart*
　　—that is, the word of faith that we preach—,
　　for, if you confess with your mouth that Jesus is Lord
　　and believe in your heart that God raised him from the dead,
　　you will be saved.
For one believes with the heart and so is justified,
　　and one confesses with the mouth and so is saved.
For the Scripture says,
　　No one who believes in him will be put to shame.
For there is no distinction between Jew and Greek;
　　the same Lord is Lord of all,
　　enriching all who call upon him.
For "everyone who calls on the name of the Lord will be saved."

Second Sunday of Lent, *March 4, 2007*

SECOND READING
Phil 3:20–4:1

Brothers and sisters:
Our citizenship is in heaven,
　　and from it we also await a savior, the Lord Jesus Christ.
He will change our lowly body
　　to conform with his glorified body
　　by the power that enables him also
　　to bring all things into subjection to himself.

Therefore, my brothers and sisters,
　　whom I love and long for, my joy and crown,
　　in this way stand firm in the Lord, beloved.

SECOND READING
1 Cor 10:1-6, 10-12

I do not want you to be unaware, brothers and
   sisters,
   that our ancestors were all under the cloud
   and all passed through the sea,
   and all of them were baptized into Moses
   in the cloud and in the sea.
All ate the same spiritual food,
   and all drank the same spiritual drink,
   for they drank from a spiritual rock that
      followed them,
   and the rock was the Christ.
Yet God was not pleased with most of them,
   for they were struck down in the desert.

These things happened as examples for us,
   so that we might not desire evil things, as
      they did.
Do not grumble as some of them did,
   and suffered death by the destroyer.
These things happened to them as an
      example,
   and they have been written down as a
      warning to us,
   upon whom the end of the ages has come.
Therefore, whoever thinks he is standing
      secure
   should take care not to fall.

Gospel
John 4:5-15, 19b-26, 39a, 40-42; L28A

Jesus came to a town of Samaria called Sychar,
   near the plot of land that Jacob had given to his son Joseph.
Jacob's well was there.
Jesus, tired from his journey, sat down there at the well.
It was about noon.

A woman of Samaria came to draw water.
Jesus said to her,
   "Give me a drink."
His disciples had gone into the town to buy food.
The Samaritan woman said to him,
   "How can you, a Jew, ask me, a Samaritan woman, for a drink?"
—For Jews use nothing in common with Samaritans.—
Jesus answered and said to her,
   "If you knew the gift of God
   and who is saying to you, 'Give me a drink,'
   you would have asked him
   and he would have given you living water."
The woman said to him,
   "Sir, you do not even have a bucket and the cistern is deep;
   where then can you get this living water?
Are you greater than our father Jacob,
   who gave us this cistern and drank from it himself
   with his children and his flocks?"
Jesus answered and said to her,
   "Everyone who drinks this water will be thirsty again;
   but whoever drinks the water I shall give will never thirst;
   the water I shall give will become in him
   a spring of water welling up to eternal life."
The woman said to him,
   "Sir, give me this water, so that I may not be thirsty
   or have to keep coming here to draw water."

"I can see that you are a prophet.
Our ancestors worshiped on this mountain;
   but you people say that the place to worship is in Jerusalem."
Jesus said to her,
   "Believe me, woman, the hour is coming
   when you will worship the Father
   neither on this mountain nor in Jerusalem.
You people worship what you do not understand;
   we worship what we understand,
   because salvation is from the Jews.
But the hour is coming, and is now here,
   when true worshipers will worship the Father in Spirit and truth;
   and indeed the Father seeks such people to worship him.
God is Spirit, and those who worship him
   must worship in Spirit and truth."
The woman said to him,
   "I know that the Messiah is coming, the one called the Christ;
   when he comes, he will tell us everything."
Jesus said to her,
   "I am he, the one speaking with you."

Many of the Samaritans of that town began to believe in him.
When the Samaritans came to him,
   they invited him to stay with them;
   and he stayed there two days.
Many more began to believe in him because of his word,
   and they said to the woman,
   "We no longer believe because of your word;
   for we have heard for ourselves,
   and we know that this is truly the savior of the world."

Gospel
John 4:5-42; L28A

Jesus came to a town of Samaria called Sychar,
  near the plot of land that Jacob had given to his son Joseph.
Jacob's well was there.
Jesus, tired from his journey, sat down there at the well.
It was about noon.

A woman of Samaria came to draw water.
Jesus said to her,
  "Give me a drink."
His disciples had gone into the town to buy food.
The Samaritan woman said to him,
  "How can you, a Jew, ask me, a Samaritan woman, for a drink?"
—For Jews use nothing in common with Samaritans.—
Jesus answered and said to her,
  "If you knew the gift of God
  and who is saying to you, 'Give me a drink,'
  you would have asked him
  and he would have given you living water."
The woman said to him,
  "Sir, you do not even have a bucket and the cistern is deep;
  where then can you get this living water?
Are you greater than our father Jacob,
  who gave us this cistern and drank from it himself
  with his children and his flocks?"
Jesus answered and said to her,
  "Everyone who drinks this water will be thirsty again;
  but whoever drinks the water I shall give will never thirst;
  the water I shall give will become in him
  a spring of water welling up to eternal life."
The woman said to him,
  "Sir, give me this water, so that I may not be thirsty
  or have to keep coming here to draw water."

Jesus said to her,
  "Go call your husband and come back."
The woman answered and said to him,
  "I do not have a husband."
Jesus answered her,
  "You are right in saying, 'I do not have a husband.'
For you have had five husbands,
  and the one you have now is not your husband.
What you have said is true."
The woman said to him,
  "Sir, I can see that you are a prophet.
Our ancestors worshiped on this mountain;
  but you people say that the place to worship is in Jerusalem."
Jesus said to her,
  "Believe me, woman, the hour is coming
  when you will worship the Father
  neither on this mountain nor in Jerusalem.
You people worship what you do not understand;
  we worship what we understand,
  because salvation is from the Jews.

But the hour is coming, and is now here,
  when true worshipers will worship the Father in Spirit and truth;
  and indeed the Father seeks such people to worship him.
God is Spirit, and those who worship him
  must worship in Spirit and truth."
The woman said to him,
  "I know that the Messiah is coming, the one called the Christ;
  when he comes, he will tell us everything."
Jesus said to her,
  "I am he, the one speaking with you."

At that moment his disciples returned,
  and were amazed that he was talking with a woman,
  but still no one said, "What are you looking for?"
  or "Why are you talking with her?"
The woman left her water jar
  and went into the town and said to the people,
  "Come see a man who told me everything I have done.
Could he possibly be the Christ?"
They went out of the town and came to him.
Meanwhile, the disciples urged him, "Rabbi, eat."
But he said to them,
  "I have food to eat of which you do not know."
So the disciples said to one another,
  "Could someone have brought him something to eat?"
Jesus said to them,
  "My food is to do the will of the one who sent me
  and to finish his work.
Do you not say, 'In four months the harvest will be here'?
I tell you, look up and see the fields ripe for the harvest.
The reaper is already receiving payment
  and gathering crops for eternal life,
  so that the sower and reaper can rejoice together.
For here the saying is verified that 'One sows and another reaps.'
I sent you to reap what you have not worked for;
  others have done the work,
  and you are sharing the fruits of their work."

Many of the Samaritans of that town began to believe in him
  because of the word of the woman who testified,
  "He told me everything I have done."
When the Samaritans came to him,
  they invited him to stay with them;
  and he stayed there two days.
Many more began to believe in him because of his word,
  and they said to the woman,
  "We no longer believe because of your word;
  for we have heard for ourselves,
  and we know that this is truly the savior of the world."

Third Sunday of Lent, *March 11, 2007*

FIRST READING
Exod 17:3-7

In those days, in their thirst for water,
the people grumbled against Moses,
saying, "Why did you ever make us leave
Egypt?
Was it just to have us die here of thirst
with our children and our livestock?"
So Moses cried out to the LORD,
"What shall I do with this people?
A little more and they will stone me!"
The LORD answered Moses,
"Go over there in front of the people,
along with some of the elders of Israel,
holding in your hand, as you go,
the staff with which you struck the river.
I will be standing there in front of you on the
rock in Horeb.
Strike the rock, and the water will flow from it
for the people to drink."
This Moses did, in the presence of the elders
of Israel.
The place was called Massah and Meribah,
because the Israelites quarreled there
and tested the LORD, saying,
"Is the LORD in our midst or not?"

RESPONSORIAL PSALM
Ps 95:1-2, 6-7, 8-9

℟. (8) If today you hear his voice, harden not
your hearts.

Come, let us sing joyfully to the LORD;
let us acclaim the Rock of our salvation.
Let us come into his presence with
thanksgiving;
let us joyfully sing psalms to him.

℟. If today you hear his voice, harden not
your hearts.

Come, let us bow down in worship;
let us kneel before the LORD who made us.
For he is our God,
and we are the people he shepherds, the
flock he guides.

℟. If today you hear his voice, harden not
your hearts.

Oh, that today you would hear his voice:
"Harden not your hearts as at Meribah,
as in the day of Massah in the desert,
where your fathers tempted me;
they tested me though they had seen my
works."

℟. If today you hear his voice, harden not
your hearts.

SECOND READING
Rom 5:1-2, 5-8

Brothers and sisters:
Since we have been justified by faith,
we have peace with God through our Lord
Jesus Christ,
through whom we have gained access by
faith
to this grace in which we stand,
and we boast in hope of the glory of God.

And hope does not disappoint,
because the love of God has been poured
out into our hearts
through the Holy Spirit who has been given
to us.
For Christ, while we were still helpless,
died at the appointed time for the ungodly.
Indeed, only with difficulty does one die for a
just person,
though perhaps for a good person one
might even find courage to die.
But God proves his love for us
in that while we were still sinners Christ
died for us.

Fourth Sunday of Lent, *March 18, 2007*

Gospel (cont.)
Luke 15:1-3, 11-32; L33C

I no longer deserve to be called your son;
treat me as you would treat one of your hired workers.""
So he got up and went back to his father.
While he was still a long way off,
his father caught sight of him, and was filled with compassion.
He ran to his son, embraced him and kissed him.
His son said to him,
'Father, I have sinned against heaven and against you;
I no longer deserve to be called your son.'
But his father ordered his servants,
'Quickly bring the finest robe and put it on him;
put a ring on his finger and sandals on his feet.
Take the fattened calf and slaughter it.
Then let us celebrate with a feast,
because this son of mine was dead, and has come to life again;
he was lost, and has been found.'
Then the celebration began.
Now the older son had been out in the field
and, on his way back, as he neared the house,
he heard the sound of music and dancing.
He called one of the servants and asked what this might mean.

The servant said to him,
'Your brother has returned
and your father has slaughtered the fattened calf
because he has him back safe and sound.'
He became angry,
and when he refused to enter the house,
his father came out and pleaded with him.
He said to his father in reply,
'Look, all these years I served you
and not once did I disobey your orders;
yet you never gave me even a young goat to feast on with my friends.
But when your son returns
who swallowed up your property with prostitutes,
for him you slaughter the fattened calf.'
He said to him,
'My son, you are here with me always;
everything I have is yours.
But now we must celebrate and rejoice,
because your brother was dead and has come to life again;
he was lost and has been found.'"

Gospel
John 9:1-41; L31A

As Jesus passed by he saw a man blind from birth.
His disciples asked him,
    "Rabbi, who sinned, this man or his parents,
    that he was born blind?"
Jesus answered,
    "Neither he nor his parents sinned;
    it is so that the works of God might be made visible through him.
We have to do the works of the one who sent me while it is day.
Night is coming when no one can work.
While I am in the world, I am the light of the world."
When he had said this, he spat on the ground
    and made clay with the saliva,
    and smeared the clay on his eyes, and said to him,
    "Go wash in the Pool of Siloam"—which means Sent—.
So he went and washed, and came back able to see.

His neighbors and those who had seen him earlier as a beggar said,
    "Isn't this the one who used to sit and beg?"
Some said, "It is,"
    but others said, "No, he just looks like him."
He said, "I am."
So they said to him, "How were your eyes opened?"
He replied,
    "The man called Jesus made clay and anointed my eyes
    and told me, 'Go to Siloam and wash.'
So I went there and washed and was able to see."
And they said to him, "Where is he?"
He said, "I don't know."

They brought the one who was once blind to the Pharisees.
Now Jesus had made clay and opened his eyes on a sabbath.
So then the Pharisees also asked him how he was able to see.
He said to them,
    "He put clay on my eyes, and I washed, and now I can see."
So some of the Pharisees said,
    "This man is not from God,
    because he does not keep the sabbath."
But others said,
    "How can a sinful man do such signs?"
And there was a division among them.
So they said to the blind man again,
    "What do you have to say about him,
    since he opened your eyes?"
He said, "He is a prophet."

Now the Jews did not believe
    that he had been blind and gained his sight
    until they summoned the parents of the one who had gained his
        sight.
They asked them,
    "Is this your son, who you say was born blind?
How does he now see?"
His parents answered and said,
    "We know that this is our son and that he was born blind.
We do not know how he sees now,
    nor do we know who opened his eyes.
Ask him, he is of age;
    he can speak for himself."

His parents said this because they were afraid
    of the Jews, for the Jews had already agreed
    that if anyone acknowledged him as the Christ,
    he would be expelled from the synagogue.
For this reason his parents said,
    "He is of age; question him."

So a second time they called the man who had been blind
    and said to him, "Give God the praise!
We know that this man is a sinner."
He replied,
    "If he is a sinner, I do not know.
One thing I do know is that I was blind and now I see."
So they said to him,
    "What did he do to you?
    How did he open your eyes?"
He answered them,
    "I told you already and you did not listen.
Why do you want to hear it again?
Do you want to become his disciples, too?"
They ridiculed him and said,
    "You are that man's disciple;
    we are disciples of Moses!
We know that God spoke to Moses,
    but we do not know where this one is from."
The man answered and said to them,
    "This is what is so amazing,
    that you do not know where he is from, yet he opened my eyes.
We know that God does not listen to sinners,
    but if one is devout and does his will, he listens to him.
It is unheard of that anyone ever opened the eyes of a person born
        blind.
If this man were not from God,
    he would not be able to do anything."
They answered and said to him,
    "You were born totally in sin,
    and are you trying to teach us?"
Then they threw him out.

When Jesus heard that they had thrown him out,
    he found him and said, "Do you believe in the Son of Man?"
He answered and said,
    "Who is he, sir, that I may believe in him?"
Jesus said to him,
    "You have seen him,
    and the one speaking with you is he."
He said,
    "I do believe, Lord," and he worshiped him.
Then Jesus said,
    "I came into this world for judgment,
    so that those who do not see might see,
    and those who do see might become blind."

Some of the Pharisees who were with him heard this
    and said to him, "Surely we are not also blind, are we?"
Jesus said to them,
    "If you were blind, you would have no sin;
    but now you are saying, 'We see,' so your sin remains."

Gospel

John 9:1, 6-9, 13-17, 34-38; L31A

As Jesus passed by he saw a man blind from birth.
He spat on the ground and made clay with the saliva,
    and smeared the clay on his eyes, and said to him,
    "Go wash in the Pool of Siloam"—which means Sent—.
So he went and washed, and came back able to see.

His neighbors and those who had seen him earlier as a beggar said,
    "Isn't this the one who used to sit and beg?"
Some said, "It is,"
    but others said, "No, he just looks like him."
He said, "I am."

They brought the one who was once blind to the Pharisees.
Now Jesus had made clay and opened his eyes on a sabbath.
So then the Pharisees also asked him how he was able to see.
He said to them,
    "He put clay on my eyes, and I washed, and now I can see."
So some of the Pharisees said,
    "This man is not from God,
    because he does not keep the sabbath."
But others said,
    "How can a sinful man do such signs?"

And there was a division among them.
So they said to the blind man again,
    "What do you have to say about him,
    since he opened your eyes?"
He said, "He is a prophet."

They answered and said to him,
    "You were born totally in sin,
    and are you trying to teach us?"
Then they threw him out.

When Jesus heard that they had thrown him out,
    he found him and said, "Do you believe in the Son of Man?"
He answered and said,
    "Who is he, sir, that I may believe in him?"
Jesus said to him,
    "You have seen him,
    and the one speaking with you is he."
He said,
    "I do believe, Lord," and he worshiped him.

FIRST READING   1 Sam 16:1b, 6-7, 10-13a

The LORD said to Samuel:
    "Fill your horn with oil, and be on your way.
I am sending you to Jesse of Bethlehem,
    for I have chosen my king from among his
        sons."

As Jesse and his sons came to the sacrifice,
    Samuel looked at Eliab and thought,
    "Surely the LORD's anointed is here before
        him."
But the LORD said to Samuel:
    "Do not judge from his appearance or from
        his lofty stature,
    because I have rejected him.
Not as man sees does God see,
    because man sees the appearance
    but the LORD looks into the heart."
In the same way Jesse presented seven sons
        before Samuel,
    but Samuel said to Jesse,
    "The LORD has not chosen any one of these."
Then Samuel asked Jesse,
    "Are these all the sons you have?"
Jesse replied,
    "There is still the youngest, who is tending
        the sheep."
Samuel said to Jesse,
    "Send for him;
    we will not begin the sacrificial banquet
        until he arrives here."
Jesse sent and had the young man brought to
        them.
He was ruddy, a youth handsome to behold
    and making a splendid appearance.

The LORD said,
    "There—anoint him, for this is the one!"
Then Samuel, with the horn of oil in hand,
    anointed David in the presence of his
        brothers;
    and from that day on, the spirit of the LORD
        rushed upon David.

RESPONSORIAL PSALM   Ps 23:1-3a, 3b-4, 5, 6

℞. (1) The Lord is my shepherd; there is nothing I shall want.

The LORD is my shepherd; I shall not want.
    In verdant pastures he gives me repose;
beside restful waters he leads me;
    he refreshes my soul.

℞. The Lord is my shepherd; there is nothing
I shall want.

He guides me in right paths
    for his name's sake.
Even though I walk in the dark valley
    I fear no evil; for you are at my side
with your rod and your staff
    that give me courage.

℞. The Lord is my shepherd; there is nothing
I shall want.

You spread the table before me
    in the sight of my foes;
you anoint my head with oil;
    my cup overflows.

℞. The Lord is my shepherd; there is nothing
I shall want.

Only goodness and kindness follow me
    all the days of my life;
and I shall dwell in the house of the LORD
    for years to come.

℞. The Lord is my shepherd; there is nothing
I shall want.

SECOND READING
Eph 5:8-14

Brothers and sisters:
You were once darkness,
    but now you are light in the Lord.
Live as children of light,
    for light produces every kind of goodness
    and righteousness and truth.
Try to learn what is pleasing to the Lord.
Take no part in the fruitless works of
        darkness;
    rather expose them, for it is shameful even
        to mention
    the things done by them in secret;
    but everything exposed by the light
        becomes visible,
    for everything that becomes visible is light.
Therefore, it says:
    "Awake, O sleeper,
    and arise from the dead,
    and Christ will give you light."

Gospel
Matt 1:16, 18-21, 24a; L543

Jacob was the father of Joseph, the husband of Mary.
Of her was born Jesus who is called the Christ.

Now this is how the birth of Jesus Christ came about.
When his mother Mary was betrothed to Joseph,
   but before they lived together,
   she was found with child through the Holy Spirit.
Joseph her husband, since he was a righteous man,
   yet unwilling to expose her to shame,
   decided to divorce her quietly.
Such was his intention when, behold,
   the angel of the Lord appeared to him in a dream and said,
   "Joseph, son of David,
   do not be afraid to take Mary your wife into your home.
For it is through the Holy Spirit
   that this child has been conceived in her.
She will bear a son and you are to name him Jesus,
   because he will save his people from their sins."
When Joseph awoke,
   he did as the angel of the Lord had commanded him
   and took his wife into his home.

FIRST READING
2 Sam 7:4-5a, 12-14a, 16

The LORD spoke to Nathan and said:
"Go, tell my servant David,
  'When your time comes and you rest with
     your ancestors,
  I will raise up your heir after you, sprung
     from your loins,
  and I will make his kingdom firm.
It is he who shall build a house for my name.
And I will make his royal throne firm forever.
I will be a father to him,
  and he shall be a son to me.
Your house and your kingdom shall endure
    forever before me;
  your throne shall stand firm forever.'"

RESPONSORIAL PSALM
Ps 89:2-3, 4-5, 27, and 29

℟. (37) The son of David will live forever.

The promises of the LORD I will sing forever,
  through all generations my mouth will
     proclaim your faithfulness,
For you have said, "My kindness is
  established forever";
  in heaven you have confirmed your
    faithfulness.

℟. The son of David will live forever.

"I have made a covenant with my chosen one;
  I have sworn to David my servant:
Forever will I confirm your posterity
  and establish your throne for all
    generations."

℟. The son of David will live forever.

"He shall say of me, 'You are my father,
  my God, the Rock my savior!'
Forever I will maintain my kindness toward
  him,
  my covenant with him stands firm."

℟. The son of David will live forever.

SECOND READING
Rom 4:13, 16-18, 22

Brothers and sisters:
It was not through the law
  that the promise was made to Abraham
    and his descendants
  that he would inherit the world,
  but through the righteousness that comes
    from faith.
For this reason, it depends on faith,
  so that it may be a gift,
  and the promise may be guaranteed to all
    his descendants,
  not to those who only adhere to the law
  but to those who follow the faith of Abraham,
  who is the father of all of us, as it is written,
  I have made you father of many nations.
He is our father in the sight of God,
  in whom he believed, who gives life to the
    dead
  and calls into being what does not exist.
He believed, hoping against hope,
  that he would become *the father of many
    nations,*
  according to what was said, *Thus shall
    your descendants be.*
That is why *it was credited to him as
  righteousness.*

Gospel

John 11:1-45; L34A

Now a man was ill, Lazarus from Bethany,
  the village of Mary and her sister Martha.
Mary was the one who had anointed the Lord with perfumed oil
  and dried his feet with her hair;
  it was her brother Lazarus who was ill.
So the sisters sent word to Jesus saying,
  "Master, the one you love is ill."
When Jesus heard this he said,
  "This illness is not to end in death,
  but is for the glory of God,
  that the Son of God may be glorified through it."
Now Jesus loved Martha and her sister and Lazarus.
So when he heard that he was ill,
  he remained for two days in the place where he was.
Then after this he said to his disciples,
  "Let us go back to Judea."
The disciples said to him,
  "Rabbi, the Jews were just trying to stone you,
  and you want to go back there?"
Jesus answered,
  "Are there not twelve hours in a day?
If one walks during the day, he does not stumble,
  because he sees the light of this world.
But if one walks at night, he stumbles,
  because the light is not in him."
He said this, and then told them,
  "Our friend Lazarus is asleep,
  but I am going to awaken him."
So the disciples said to him,
  "Master, if he is asleep, he will be saved."
But Jesus was talking about his death,
  while they thought that he meant ordinary sleep.
So then Jesus said to them clearly,
  "Lazarus has died.
And I am glad for you that I was not there,
  that you may believe.
Let us go to him."
So Thomas, called Didymus, said to his fellow disciples,
  "Let us also go to die with him."

When Jesus arrived, he found that Lazarus
  had already been in the tomb for four days.
Now Bethany was near Jerusalem, only about two miles away.
And many of the Jews had come to Martha and Mary
  to comfort them about their brother.
When Martha heard that Jesus was coming,
  she went to meet him;
  but Mary sat at home.
Martha said to Jesus,
  "Lord, if you had been here,
  my brother would not have died.
But even now I know that whatever you ask of God,
  God will give you."
Jesus said to her,
  "Your brother will rise."
Martha said to him,
  "I know he will rise,
  in the resurrection on the last day."
Jesus told her,

"I am the resurrection and the life;
  whoever believes in me, even if he dies, will live,
  and everyone who lives and believes in me will never die.
Do you believe this?"
She said to him, "Yes, Lord.
I have come to believe that you are the Christ, the Son of God,
  the one who is coming into the world."

When she had said this,
  she went and called her sister Mary secretly, saying,
  "The teacher is here and is asking for you."
As soon as she heard this,
  she rose quickly and went to him.
For Jesus had not yet come into the village,
  but was still where Martha had met him.
So when the Jews who were with her in the house comforting her
  saw Mary get up quickly and go out,
  they followed her,
  presuming that she was going to the tomb to weep there.
When Mary came to where Jesus was and saw him,
  she fell at his feet and said to him,
  "Lord, if you had been here,
  my brother would not have died."
When Jesus saw her weeping and the Jews who had come with her
    weeping,
  he became perturbed and deeply troubled, and said,
  "Where have you laid him?"
They said to him, "Sir, come and see."
And Jesus wept.
So the Jews said, "See how he loved him."
But some of them said,
  "Could not the one who opened the eyes of the blind man
  have done something so that this man would not have died?"

So Jesus, perturbed again, came to the tomb.
It was a cave, and a stone lay across it.
Jesus said, "Take away the stone."
Martha, the dead man's sister, said to him,
  "Lord, by now there will be a stench;
  he has been dead for four days."
Jesus said to her,
  "Did I not tell you that if you believe
  you will see the glory of God?"
So they took away the stone.
And Jesus raised his eyes and said,
  "Father, I thank you for hearing me.
I know that you always hear me;
  but because of the crowd here I have said this,
  that they may believe that you sent me."
And when he had said this,
  he cried out in a loud voice,
  "Lazarus, come out!"
The dead man came out,
  tied hand and foot with burial bands,
  and his face was wrapped in a cloth.
So Jesus said to them,
  "Untie him and let him go."

Now many of the Jews who had come to Mary
  and seen what he had done began to believe in him.

Gospel
John 11:3-7, 17, 20-27, 33b-45; L34A

The sisters of Lazarus sent word to Jesus saying,
"Master, the one you love is ill."
When Jesus heard this he said,
"This illness is not to end in death,
but is for the glory of God,
that the Son of God may be glorified through it."
Now Jesus loved Martha and her sister and Lazarus.
So when he heard that he was ill,
he remained for two days in the place where he was.
Then after this he said to his disciples,
"Let us go back to Judea."

When Jesus arrived, he found that Lazarus
had already been in the tomb for four days.
When Martha heard that Jesus was coming,
she went to meet him;
but Mary sat at home.
Martha said to Jesus,
"Lord, if you had been here,
my brother would not have died.
But even now I know that whatever you ask of God,
God will give you."
Jesus said to her,
"Your brother will rise."
Martha said,
"I know he will rise,
in the resurrection on the last day."
Jesus told her,
"I am the resurrection and the life;
whoever believes in me, even if he dies, will live,
and everyone who lives and believes in me will never die.
Do you believe this?"
She said to him, "Yes, Lord.
I have come to believe that you are the Christ, the Son of God,
the one who is coming into the world."

He became perturbed and deeply troubled, and said,
"Where have you laid him?"
They said to him, "Sir, come and see."
And Jesus wept.
So the Jews said, "See how he loved him."
But some of them said,
"Could not the one who opened the eyes of the blind man
have done something so that this man would not have died?"

So Jesus, perturbed again, came to the tomb.
It was a cave, and a stone lay across it.
Jesus said, "Take away the stone."
Martha, the dead man's sister, said to him,
"Lord, by now there will be a stench;
he has been dead for four days."
Jesus said to her,
"Did I not tell you that if you believe
you will see the glory of God?"
So they took away the stone.
And Jesus raised his eyes and said,
"Father, I thank you for hearing me.
I know that you always hear me;
but because of the crowd here I have said this,
that they may believe that you sent me."
And when he had said this,
he cried out in a loud voice,
"Lazarus, come out!"
The dead man came out,
tied hand and foot with burial bands,
and his face was wrapped in a cloth.
So Jesus said to them,
"Untie him and let him go."

Now many of the Jews who had come to Mary
and seen what he had done began to believe in him.

Fifth Sunday of Lent, *March 25, 2007*

FIRST READING
Ezek 37:12-14

Thus says the Lord GOD:
    O my people, I will open your graves
        and have you rise from them,
        and bring you back to the land of Israel.
Then you shall know that I am the LORD,
        when I open your graves and have you rise
            from them,
    O my people!
I will put my spirit in you that you may live,
    and I will settle you upon your land;
    thus you shall know that I am the LORD.
I have promised, and I will do it, says the
    LORD.

RESPONSORIAL PSALM
Ps 130:1-2, 3-4, 5-6, 7-8

R̂. (7) With the Lord there is mercy and fullness of redemption.

Out of the depths I cry to you, O LORD;
    LORD, hear my voice!
Let your ears be attentive
    to my voice in supplication.

R̂. With the Lord there is mercy and fullness of redemption.

If you, O LORD, mark iniquities,
    LORD, who can stand?
But with you is forgiveness,
    that you may be revered.

R̂. With the Lord there is mercy and fullness of redemption.

I trust in the LORD;
    my soul trusts in his word.
More than sentinels wait for the dawn,
    let Israel wait for the LORD.

R̂. With the Lord there is mercy and fullness of redemption.

For with the LORD is kindness
    and with him is plenteous redemption;
and he will redeem Israel
    from all their iniquities.

R̂. With the Lord there is mercy and fullness of redemption.

SECOND READING
Rom 8:8-11

Brothers and sisters:
Those who are in the flesh cannot please God.
But you are not in the flesh;
    on the contrary, you are in the spirit,
    if only the Spirit of God dwells in you.
Whoever does not have the Spirit of Christ
    does not belong to him.
But if Christ is in you,
    although the body is dead because of sin,
    the spirit is alive because of righteousness.
If the Spirit of the One who raised Jesus from
    the dead dwells in you,
    the One who raised Christ from the dead
    will give life to your mortal bodies also,
    through his Spirit dwelling in you.

The Annunication of the Lord, *March 26, 2007*

FIRST READING
Isa 7:10-14; 8:10

The LORD spoke to Ahaz, saying:
Ask for a sign from the LORD, your God;
    let it be deep as the netherworld, or high as
        the sky!
But Ahaz answered,
    "I will not ask! I will not tempt the LORD!"
Then Isaiah said:
    Listen, O house of David!
Is it not enough for you to weary people,
    must you also weary my God?
Therefore the Lord himself will give you this
    sign:
    the virgin shall conceive, and bear a son,
    and shall name him Emmanuel,
    which means "God is with us!"

RESPONSORIAL PSALM
Ps 40:7-8a, 8b-9, 10, 11

R̂. (8a and 9a) Here am I, Lord; I come to do your will.

Sacrifice or offering you wished not,
    but ears open to obedience you gave me.
Holocausts and sin-offerings you sought not;
    then said I, "Behold, I come";

R̂. Here am I, Lord; I come to do your will.

"In the written scroll it is prescribed for me.
To do your will, O God, is my delight,
    and your law is within my heart!"

R̂. Here am I, Lord; I come to do your will.

I announced your justice in the vast assembly;
    I did not restrain my lips, as you, O LORD,
        know.

R̂. Here am I, Lord; I come to do your will.

Your justice I kept not hid within my heart;
    your faithfulness and your salvation I have
        spoken of;
I have made no secret of your kindness and
    your truth
    in the vast assembly.

R̂. Here am I, Lord; I come to do your will.

SECOND READING
Heb 10:4-10

Brothers and sisters:
It is impossible that the blood of bulls and
    goats
    takes away sins.
For this reason, when Christ came into the
    world, he said:
    "Sacrifice and offering you did not desire,
    but a body you prepared for me;
    in holocausts and sin offerings you took no
        delight.
    Then I said, 'As is written of me in the scroll,
    behold, I come to do your will, O God.'"

First Christ says, "Sacrifices and offerings,
    holocausts and sin offerings,
    you neither desired nor delighted in."
These are offered according to the law.
Then he says, "Behold, I come to do your will."
He takes away the first to establish the
    second.
By this "will," we have been consecrated
    through the offering of the Body of Jesus
        Christ once for all.

Gospel at Mass
Luke 22:14–23:56; L38C

When the hour came,
    Jesus took his place at table with the apostles.
He said to them,
    "I have eagerly desired to eat this Passover with you before I suffer,
    for, I tell you, I shall not eat it again
    until there is fulfillment in the kingdom of God."
Then he took a cup, gave thanks, and said,
    "Take this and share it among yourselves;
    for I tell you that from this time on
    I shall not drink of the fruit of the vine
    until the kingdom of God comes."
Then he took the bread, said the blessing,
    broke it, and gave it to them, saying,
    "This is my body, which will be given for you;
    do this in memory of me."
And likewise the cup after they had eaten, saying,
    "This cup is the new covenant in my blood,
    which will be shed for you.

"And yet behold, the hand of the one who is to betray me
    is with me on the table;
    for the Son of Man indeed goes as it has been determined;
    but woe to that man by whom he is betrayed."
And they began to debate among themselves
    who among them would do such a deed.

Then an argument broke out among them
    about which of them should be regarded as the greatest.
He said to them,
    "The kings of the Gentiles lord it over them
    and those in authority over them are addressed as 'Benefactors';
    but among you it shall not be so.
Rather, let the greatest among you be as the youngest,
    and the leader as the servant.
For who is greater:
    the one seated at table or the one who serves?
Is it not the one seated at table?
I am among you as the one who serves.
It is you who have stood by me in my trials;
    and I confer a kingdom on you,
    just as my Father has conferred one on me,
    that you may eat and drink at my table in my kingdom;
    and you will sit on thrones
    judging the twelve tribes of Israel.

"Simon, Simon, behold Satan has demanded
    to sift all of you like wheat,
    but I have prayed that your own faith may not fail;
    and once you have turned back,
    you must strengthen your brothers."
He said to him,
    "Lord, I am prepared to go to prison and to die with you."
But he replied,
    "I tell you, Peter, before the cock crows this day,
    you will deny three times that you know me."

He said to them,
    "When I sent you forth without a money bag or a sack or sandals,
    were you in need of anything?"
"No, nothing," they replied.

He said to them,
    "But now one who has a money bag should take it,
    and likewise a sack,
    and one who does not have a sword
    should sell his cloak and buy one.
For I tell you that this Scripture must be fulfilled in me,
    namely, *He was counted among the wicked;*
    and indeed what is written about me is coming to fulfillment."
Then they said,
    "Lord, look, there are two swords here."
But he replied, "It is enough!"

Then going out, he went, as was his custom, to the Mount of Olives,
    and the disciples followed him.
When he arrived at the place he said to them,
    "Pray that you may not undergo the test."
After withdrawing about a stone's throw from them and kneeling,
    he prayed, saying, "Father, if you are willing,
    take this cup away from me;
    still, not my will but yours be done."
And to strengthen him an angel from heaven appeared to him.
He was in such agony and he prayed so fervently
    that his sweat became like drops of blood
    falling on the ground.
When he rose from prayer and returned to his disciples,
    he found them sleeping from grief.
He said to them, "Why are you sleeping?
Get up and pray that you may not undergo the test."

While he was still speaking, a crowd approached
    and in front was one of the Twelve, a man named Judas.
He went up to Jesus to kiss him.
Jesus said to him,
    "Judas, are you betraying the Son of Man with a kiss?"
His disciples realized what was about to happen, and they asked,
    "Lord, shall we strike with a sword?"
And one of them struck the high priest's servant
    and cut off his right ear.
But Jesus said in reply,
    "Stop, no more of this!"
Then he touched the servant's ear and healed him.
And Jesus said to the chief priests and temple guards
    and elders who had come for him,
    "Have you come out as against a robber, with swords and clubs?
Day after day I was with you in the temple area,
    and you did not seize me;
    but this is your hour, the time for the power of darkness."

After arresting him they led him away
    and took him into the house of the high priest;
    Peter was following at a distance.
They lit a fire in the middle of the courtyard and sat around it,
    and Peter sat down with them.
When a maid saw him seated in the light,
    she looked intently at him and said,
    "This man too was with him."
But he denied it saying,
    "Woman, I do not know him."
A short while later someone else saw him and said,
    "You too are one of them";
    but Peter answered, "My friend, I am not."

About an hour later, still another insisted,
"Assuredly, this man too was with him,
for he also is a Galilean."
But Peter said,
"My friend, I do not know what you are talking about."
Just as he was saying this, the cock crowed,
and the Lord turned and looked at Peter;
and Peter remembered the word of the Lord,
how he had said to him,
"Before the cock crows today, you will deny me three times."
He went out and began to weep bitterly.
The men who held Jesus in custody were ridiculing and beating him.
They blindfolded him and questioned him, saying,
"Prophesy! Who is it that struck you?"
And they reviled him in saying many other things against him.

When day came the council of elders of the people met,
both chief priests and scribes,
and they brought him before their Sanhedrin.
They said, "If you are the Christ, tell us,"
but he replied to them, "If I tell you, you will not believe,
and if I question, you will not respond.
But from this time on the Son of Man will be seated
at the right hand of the power of God."
They all asked, "Are you then the Son of God?"
He replied to them, "You say that I am."
Then they said, "What further need have we for testimony?
We have heard it from his own mouth."

Then the whole assembly of them arose and brought him before Pilate.
They brought charges against him, saying,
"We found this man misleading our people;
he opposes the payment of taxes to Caesar
and maintains that he is the Christ, a king."
Pilate asked him, "Are you the king of the Jews?"
He said to him in reply, "You say so."
Pilate then addressed the chief priests and the crowds,
"I find this man not guilty."
But they were adamant and said,
"He is inciting the people with his teaching
throughout all Judea,
from Galilee where he began even to here."

On hearing this Pilate asked if the man was a Galilean;
and upon learning that he was under Herod's jurisdiction,
he sent him to Herod who was in Jerusalem at that time.
Herod was very glad to see Jesus;
he had been wanting to see him for a long time,
for he had heard about him
and had been hoping to see him perform some sign.
He questioned him at length,
but he gave him no answer.
The chief priests and scribes, meanwhile,
stood by accusing him harshly.
Herod and his soldiers treated him contemptuously and mocked him,
and after clothing him in resplendent garb,
he sent him back to Pilate.
Herod and Pilate became friends that very day,
even though they had been enemies formerly.
Pilate then summoned the chief priests, the rulers, and the people
and said to them, "You brought this man to me
and accused him of inciting the people to revolt.

I have conducted my investigation in your presence
and have not found this man guilty
of the charges you have brought against him,
nor did Herod, for he sent him back to us.
So no capital crime has been committed by him.
Therefore I shall have him flogged and then release him."

But all together they shouted out,
"Away with this man!
Release Barabbas to us."
—Now Barabbas had been imprisoned for a rebellion
that had taken place in the city and for murder.—
Again Pilate addressed them, still wishing to release Jesus,
but they continued their shouting,
"Crucify him! Crucify him!"
Pilate addressed them a third time,
"What evil has this man done?
I found him guilty of no capital crime.
Therefore I shall have him flogged and then release him."
With loud shouts, however,
they persisted in calling for his crucifixion,
and their voices prevailed.
The verdict of Pilate was that their demand should be granted.
So he released the man who had been imprisoned
for rebellion and murder, for whom they asked,
and he handed Jesus over to them to deal with as they wished.

As they led him away
they took hold of a certain Simon, a Cyrenian,
who was coming in from the country;
and after laying the cross on him,
they made him carry it behind Jesus.
A large crowd of people followed Jesus,
including many women who mourned and lamented him.
Jesus turned to them and said,
"Daughters of Jerusalem, do not weep for me;
weep instead for yourselves and for your children
for indeed, the days are coming when people will say,
'Blessed are the barren,
the wombs that never bore
and the breasts that never nursed.'
At that time people will say to the mountains,
'Fall upon us!'
and to the hills, 'Cover us!'
for if these things are done when the wood is green
what will happen when it is dry?"
Now two others, both criminals,
were led away with him to be executed.

When they came to the place called the Skull,
they crucified him and the criminals there,
one on his right, the other on his left.
Then Jesus said,
"Father, forgive them, they know not what they do."
They divided his garments by casting lots.
The people stood by and watched;
the rulers, meanwhile, sneered at him and said,
"He saved others, let him save himself
if he is the chosen one, the Christ of God."
Even the soldiers jeered at him.
As they approached to offer him wine they called out,
"If you are King of the Jews, save yourself."

Above him there was an inscription that read,
  "This is the King of the Jews."

Now one of the criminals hanging there reviled Jesus, saying,
  "Are you not the Christ?
  Save yourself and us."
The other, however, rebuking him, said in reply,
  "Have you no fear of God,
    for you are subject to the same condemnation?
And indeed, we have been condemned justly,
    for the sentence we received corresponds to our crimes,
    but this man has done nothing criminal."
Then he said,
  "Jesus, remember me when you come into your kingdom."
He replied to him,
  "Amen, I say to you,
    today you will be with me in Paradise."

It was now about noon and darkness came over the whole land
    until three in the afternoon
    because of an eclipse of the sun.
Then the veil of the temple was torn down the middle.
Jesus cried out in a loud voice,
  "Father, into your hands I commend my spirit";
    and when he had said this he breathed his last.

Here all kneel and pause for a short time.

The centurion who witnessed what had happened glorified God and said,
  "This man was innocent beyond doubt."
When all the people who had gathered for this spectacle
      saw what had happened,
    they returned home beating their breasts;
    but all his acquaintances stood at a distance,
    including the women who had followed him from Galilee
    and saw these events.

Now there was a virtuous and righteous man named Joseph who,
    though he was a member of the council,
    had not consented to their plan of action.
He came from the Jewish town of Arimathea
    and was awaiting the kingdom of God.
He went to Pilate and asked for the body of Jesus.
After he had taken the body down,
    he wrapped it in a linen cloth
    and laid him in a rock-hewn tomb
    in which no one had yet been buried.
It was the day of preparation,
    and the sabbath was about to begin.
The women who had come from Galilee with him followed behind,
    and when they had seen the tomb
    and the way in which his body was laid in it,
    they returned and prepared spices and perfumed oils.
Then they rested on the sabbath according to the commandment.

Gospel (cont.)
John 13:1-15; L39ABC

So when he had washed their feet
and put his garments back on and reclined at table again,
he said to them, "Do you realize what I have done for you?
You call me 'teacher' and 'master,' and rightly so, for indeed I am.
If I, therefore, the master and teacher, have washed your feet,
you ought to wash one another's feet.
I have given you a model to follow,
so that as I have done for you, you should also do."

FIRST READING
Exod 12:1-8, 11-14

The LORD said to Moses and Aaron in the
land of Egypt,
"This month shall stand at the head of
your calendar;
you shall reckon it the first month of the
year.
Tell the whole community of Israel:
On the tenth of this month every one of
your families
must procure for itself a lamb, one apiece
for each household.
If a family is too small for a whole lamb,
it shall join the nearest household in
procuring one
and shall share in the lamb
in proportion to the number of persons
who partake of it.
The lamb must be a year-old male and
without blemish.
You may take it from either the sheep or the
goats.
You shall keep it until the fourteenth day of
this month,
and then, with the whole assembly of Israel
present,
it shall be slaughtered during the evening
twilight.
They shall take some of its blood
and apply it to the two doorposts and the
lintel
of every house in which they partake of
the lamb.
That same night they shall eat its roasted
flesh
with unleavened bread and bitter herbs.

"This is how you are to eat it:
with your loins girt, sandals on your feet
and your staff in hand,
you shall eat like those who are in flight.

It is the Passover of the LORD.
For on this same night I will go through Egypt,
striking down every firstborn of the land,
both man and beast,
and executing judgment on all the gods of
Egypt—I, the LORD!
But the blood will mark the houses where you
are.
Seeing the blood, I will pass over you;
thus, when I strike the land of Egypt,
no destructive blow will come upon you.

"This day shall be a memorial feast for you,
which all your generations shall celebrate
with pilgrimage to the LORD, as a perpetual
institution."

RESPONSORIAL PSALM
Ps 116:12-13, 15-16bc, 17-18

R/. (cf. 1 Cor 10:16) Our blessing-cup is a communion with the Blood of Christ.

How shall I make a return to the LORD
for all the good he has done for me?
The cup of salvation I will take up,
and I will call upon the name of the LORD.

R/. Our blessing-cup is a communion with the Blood of Christ.

Precious in the eyes of the LORD
is the death of his faithful ones.
I am your servant, the son of your handmaid;
you have loosed my bonds.

R/. Our blessing-cup is a communion with the Blood of Christ.

To you will I offer sacrifice of thanksgiving,
and I will call upon the name of the LORD.
My vows to the LORD I will pay
in the presence of all his people.

R/. Our blessing-cup is a communion with the Blood of Christ.

SECOND READING
1 Cor 11:23-26

Brothers and sisters:
I received from the Lord what I also handed
on to you,
that the Lord Jesus, on the night he was
handed over,
took bread, and, after he had given thanks,
broke it and said, "This is my body that is
for you.
Do this in remembrance of me."
In the same way also the cup, after supper,
saying,
"This cup is the new covenant in my blood.
Do this, as often as you drink it, in
remembrance of me."
For as often as you eat this bread and drink
the cup,
you proclaim the death of the Lord until he
comes.

Gospel (cont.)
John 18:1–19:42; L40ABC

So the band of soldiers, the tribune, and the Jewish guards seized Jesus,
     bound him, and brought him to Annas first.
He was the father-in-law of Caiaphas,
     who was high priest that year.
It was Caiaphas who had counseled the Jews
     that it was better that one man should die rather than the people.

Simon Peter and another disciple followed Jesus.
Now the other disciple was known to the high priest,
     and he entered the courtyard of the high priest with Jesus.
But Peter stood at the gate outside.
So the other disciple, the acquaintance of the high priest,
     went out and spoke to the gatekeeper and brought Peter in.
Then the maid who was the gatekeeper said to Peter,
     "You are not one of this man's disciples, are you?"
He said, "I am not."
Now the slaves and the guards were standing around a charcoal fire
     that they had made, because it was cold,
     and were warming themselves.
Peter was also standing there keeping warm.

The high priest questioned Jesus
     about his disciples and about his doctrine.
Jesus answered him,
     "I have spoken publicly to the world.
I have always taught in a synagogue
     or in the temple area where all the Jews gather,
     and in secret I have said nothing. Why ask me?
Ask those who heard me what I said to them.
They know what I said."
When he had said this,
     one of the temple guards standing there struck Jesus and said,
     "Is this the way you answer the high priest?"
Jesus answered him,
     "If I have spoken wrongly, testify to the wrong;
     but if I have spoken rightly, why do you strike me?"
Then Annas sent him bound to Caiaphas the high priest.

Now Simon Peter was standing there keeping warm.
And they said to him,
     "You are not one of his disciples, are you?"
He denied it and said,
     "I am not."
One of the slaves of the high priest,
     a relative of the one whose ear Peter had cut off, said,
     "Didn't I see you in the garden with him?"
Again Peter denied it.
And immediately the cock crowed.

Then they brought Jesus from Caiaphas to the praetorium.
It was morning.
And they themselves did not enter the praetorium,
     in order not to be defiled so that they could eat the Passover.
So Pilate came out to them and said,
     "What charge do you bring against this man?"
They answered and said to him,
     "If he were not a criminal,
     we would not have handed him over to you."
At this, Pilate said to them,
     "Take him yourselves, and judge him according to your law."

The Jews answered him,
     "We do not have the right to execute anyone,"
     in order that the word of Jesus might be fulfilled
     that he said indicating the kind of death he would die.
So Pilate went back into the praetorium
     and summoned Jesus and said to him,
     "Are you the King of the Jews?"
Jesus answered,
     "Do you say this on your own
     or have others told you about me?"
Pilate answered,
     "I am not a Jew, am I?
Your own nation and the chief priests handed you over to me.
What have you done?"
Jesus answered,
     "My kingdom does not belong to this world.
If my kingdom did belong to this world,
     my attendants would be fighting
     to keep me from being handed over to the Jews.
But as it is, my kingdom is not here."
So Pilate said to him,
     "Then you are a king?"
Jesus answered,
     "You say I am a king.
For this I was born and for this I came into the world,
     to testify to the truth.
Everyone who belongs to the truth listens to my voice."
Pilate said to him, "What is truth?"

When he had said this,
     he again went out to the Jews and said to them,
     "I find no guilt in him.
But you have a custom that I release one prisoner to you at Passover.
Do you want me to release to you the King of the Jews?"
They cried out again,
     "Not this one but Barabbas!"
Now Barabbas was a revolutionary.

Then Pilate took Jesus and had him scourged.
And the soldiers wove a crown out of thorns and placed it on his head,
     and clothed him in a purple cloak,
     and they came to him and said,
     "Hail, King of the Jews!"
And they struck him repeatedly.
Once more Pilate went out and said to them,
     "Look, I am bringing him out to you,
     so that you may know that I find no guilt in him."
So Jesus came out,
     wearing the crown of thorns and the purple cloak.
And he said to them, "Behold, the man!"
When the chief priests and the guards saw him they cried out,
     "Crucify him, crucify him!"
Pilate said to them,
     "Take him yourselves and crucify him.
I find no guilt in him."
The Jews answered,
     "We have a law, and according to that law he ought to die,
     because he made himself the Son of God."

Now when Pilate heard this statement,
   he became even more afraid,
     and went back into the praetorium and said to Jesus,
     "Where are you from?"
Jesus did not answer him.
So Pilate said to him,
   "Do you not speak to me?
Do you not know that I have power to release you
   and I have power to crucify you?"
Jesus answered him,
   "You would have no power over me
   if it had not been given to you from above.
For this reason the one who handed me over to you
   has the greater sin."
Consequently, Pilate tried to release him; but the Jews cried out,
   "If you release him, you are not a Friend of Caesar.
Everyone who makes himself a king opposes Caesar."

When Pilate heard these words he brought Jesus out
   and seated him on the judge's bench
   in the place called Stone Pavement, in Hebrew, Gabbatha.
It was preparation day for Passover, and it was about noon.
And he said to the Jews,
   "Behold, your king!"
They cried out,
   "Take him away, take him away! Crucify him!"
Pilate said to them,
   "Shall I crucify your king?"
The chief priests answered,
   "We have no king but Caesar."
Then he handed him over to them to be crucified.
So they took Jesus, and, carrying the cross himself,
   he went out to what is called the Place of the Skull,
   in Hebrew, Golgotha.
There they crucified him, and with him two others,
   one on either side, with Jesus in the middle.
Pilate also had an inscription written and put on the cross.
It read,
   "Jesus the Nazorean, the King of the Jews."
Now many of the Jews read this inscription,
   because the place where Jesus was crucified was near the city;
   and it was written in Hebrew, Latin, and Greek.
So the chief priests of the Jews said to Pilate,
   "Do not write 'The King of the Jews,'
   but that he said, 'I am the King of the Jews.'"
Pilate answered,
   "What I have written, I have written."

When the soldiers had crucified Jesus,
   they took his clothes and divided them into four shares,
   a share for each soldier.
They also took his tunic, but the tunic was seamless,
   woven in one piece from the top down.
So they said to one another,
   "Let's not tear it, but cast lots for it to see whose it will be,"
   in order that the passage of Scripture might be fulfilled that says:
     They divided my garments among them,
     and for my vesture they cast lots.

This is what the soldiers did.
Standing by the cross of Jesus were his mother
   and his mother's sister, Mary the wife of Clopas,
   and Mary of Magdala.
When Jesus saw his mother and the disciple there whom he loved
   he said to his mother, "Woman, behold, your son."
Then he said to the disciple,
   "Behold, your mother."
And from that hour the disciple took her into his home.

After this, aware that everything was now finished,
   in order that the Scripture might be fulfilled,
   Jesus said, "I thirst."
There was a vessel filled with common wine.
So they put a sponge soaked in wine on a sprig of hyssop
   and put it up to his mouth.
When Jesus had taken the wine, he said,
   "It is finished."
And bowing his head, he handed over the spirit.

Here all kneel and pause for a short time.

Now since it was preparation day,
   in order that the bodies might not remain
     on the cross on the sabbath,
   for the sabbath day of that week was a solemn one,
   the Jews asked Pilate that their legs be broken
   and that they be taken down.
So the soldiers came and broke the legs of the first
   and then of the other one who was crucified with Jesus.
But when they came to Jesus and saw that he was already dead,
   they did not break his legs,
   but one soldier thrust his lance into his side,
   and immediately blood and water flowed out.
An eyewitness has testified, and his testimony is true;
   he knows that he is speaking the truth,
   so that you also may come to believe.
For this happened so that the Scripture passage might be fulfilled:
   Not a bone of it will be broken.
And again another passage says:
   They will look upon him whom they have pierced.

After this, Joseph of Arimathea,
   secretly a disciple of Jesus for fear of the Jews,
   asked Pilate if he could remove the body of Jesus.
And Pilate permitted it.
So he came and took his body.
Nicodemus, the one who had first come to him at night,
   also came bringing a mixture of myrrh and aloes
   weighing about one hundred pounds.
They took the body of Jesus
   and bound it with burial cloths along with the spices,
   according to the Jewish burial custom.
Now in the place where he had been crucified there was a garden,
   and in the garden a new tomb, in which no one had yet been
     buried.
So they laid Jesus there because of the Jewish preparation day;
   for the tomb was close by.

FIRST READING

Isa 52:13–53:12

See, my servant shall prosper,
  he shall be raised high and greatly exalted.
Even as many were amazed at him—
  so marred was his look beyond human
    semblance
  and his appearance beyond that of the sons
    of man—
so shall he startle many nations,
  because of him kings shall stand speechless;
for those who have not been told shall see,
  those who have not heard shall ponder it.

Who would believe what we have heard?
  To whom has the arm of the LORD been
    revealed?
He grew up like a sapling before him,
  like a shoot from the parched earth;
there was in him no stately bearing to make
    us look at him,
  nor appearance that would attract us to him.
He was spurned and avoided by people,
  a man of suffering, accustomed to infirmity,
one of those from whom people hide their faces,
  spurned, and we held him in no esteem.

Yet it was our infirmities that he bore,
  our sufferings that he endured,
while we thought of him as stricken,
  as one smitten by God and afflicted.
But he was pierced for our offenses,
  crushed for our sins;
upon him was the chastisement that makes
    us whole,
  by his stripes we were healed.
We had all gone astray like sheep,
  each following his own way;
but the LORD laid upon him
  the guilt of us all.

Though he was harshly treated, he submitted
  and opened not his mouth;
like a lamb led to the slaughter
  or a sheep before the shearers,
  he was silent and opened not his mouth.
Oppressed and condemned, he was taken away,
  and who would have thought any more of
    his destiny?
When he was cut off from the land of the living,
  and smitten for the sin of his people,
a grave was assigned him among the wicked
  and a burial place with evildoers,
though he had done no wrong
  nor spoken any falsehood.
But the LORD was pleased
  to crush him in infirmity.

If he gives his life as an offering for sin,
  he shall see his descendants in a long life,
  and the will of the LORD shall be
    accomplished through him.

Because of his affliction
  he shall see the light
    in fullness of days;
through his suffering, my servant shall justify
    many,
  and their guilt he shall bear.
Therefore I will give him his portion among
    the great,
  and he shall divide the spoils with the
    mighty,
because he surrendered himself to death
  and was counted among the wicked;
and he shall take away the sins of many,
  and win pardon for their offenses.

RESPONSORIAL PSALM

Ps 31:2, 6, 12-13, 15-16, 17, 25

R̂. (Luke 23:46) Father, into your hands I
commend my spirit.

In you, O LORD, I take refuge;
  let me never be put to shame.
In your justice rescue me.
Into your hands I commend my spirit;
  you will redeem me, O LORD, O faithful God.

R̂. Father, into your hands I commend my
spirit.

For all my foes I am an object of reproach,
  a laughingstock to my neighbors, and a
    dread to my friends;
  they who see me abroad flee from me.
I am forgotten like the unremembered dead;
  I am like a dish that is broken.

R̂. Father, into your hands I commend my
spirit.

But my trust is in you, O LORD;
  I say, "You are my God.
In your hands is my destiny; rescue me
  from the clutches of my enemies and my
    persecutors."

R̂. Father, into your hands I commend my
spirit.

Let your face shine upon your servant;
  save me in your kindness.
Take courage and be stouthearted,
  all you who hope in the LORD.

R̂. Father, into your hands I commend my
spirit.

SECOND READING

Heb 4:14-16; 5:7-9

Brothers and sisters:
Since we have a great high priest who has
    passed through the heavens,
  Jesus, the Son of God,
  let us hold fast to our confession.
For we do not have a high priest
  who is unable to sympathize with our
    weaknesses,
  but one who has similarly been tested in
    every way,
  yet without sin.
So let us confidently approach the throne of
    grace
  to receive mercy and to find grace for
    timely help.

In the days when Christ was in the flesh,
  he offered prayers and supplications with
    loud cries and tears
  to the one who was able to save him from
    death,
  and he was heard because of his reverence.
Son though he was, he learned obedience
  from what he suffered;
  and when he was made perfect,
  he became the source of eternal salvation
    for all who obey him.

FIRST READING
Gen 1:1–2:2

In the beginning, when God created the
  heavens and the earth,
    the earth was a formless wasteland, and
      darkness covered the abyss,
    while a mighty wind swept over the waters.

Then God said,
  "Let there be light," and there was light.
God saw how good the light was.
God then separated the light from the darkness.
God called the light "day," and the darkness
  he called "night."
Thus evening came, and morning followed—
  the first day.

Then God said,
  "Let there be a dome in the middle of the
    waters,
  to separate one body of water from the
    other."
And so it happened:
  God made the dome,
  and it separated the water above the dome
    from the water below it.
God called the dome "the sky."
Evening came, and morning followed—the
  second day.

Then God said,
  "Let the water under the sky be gathered
    into a single basin,
  so that the dry land may appear."
And so it happened:
  the water under the sky was gathered into
    its basin,
  and the dry land appeared.
God called the dry land "the earth,"
  and the basin of the water he called "the
    sea."
God saw how good it was.
Then God said,
  "Let the earth bring forth vegetation:
  every kind of plant that bears seed
  and every kind of fruit tree on earth
    that bears fruit with its seed in it."
And so it happened:
  the earth brought forth every kind of plant
    that bears seed
  and every kind of fruit tree on earth
    that bears fruit with its seed in it.
God saw how good it was.
Evening came, and morning followed—the
  third day.

Then God said:
  "Let there be lights in the dome of the sky,
    to separate day from night.
  Let them mark the fixed times, the days and
    the years,

and serve as luminaries in the dome of the
  sky,
  to shed light upon the earth."
And so it happened:
  God made the two great lights,
  the greater one to govern the day,
  and the lesser one to govern the night;
  and he made the stars.
God set them in the dome of the sky,
  to shed light upon the earth,
  to govern the day and the night,
  and to separate the light from the darkness.
God saw how good it was.
Evening came, and morning followed—the
  fourth day.

Then God said,
  "Let the water teem with an abundance of
    living creatures,
  and on the earth let birds fly beneath the
    dome of the sky."
And so it happened:
  God created the great sea monsters
  and all kinds of swimming creatures with
    which the water teems,
  and all kinds of winged birds.
God saw how good it was, and God blessed
  them, saying,
  "Be fertile, multiply, and fill the water of
    the seas;
  and let the birds multiply on the earth."
Evening came, and morning followed—the
  fifth day.

Then God said,
  "Let the earth bring forth all kinds of
    living creatures:
  cattle, creeping things, and wild animals of
    all kinds."
And so it happened:
  God made all kinds of wild animals, all
    kinds of cattle,
  and all kinds of creeping things of the earth.
God saw how good it was.
Then God said:
  "Let us make man in our image, after our
    likeness.
Let them have dominion over the fish of the sea,
  the birds of the air, and the cattle,
  and over all the wild animals
  and all the creatures that crawl on the
    ground."
God created man in his image;
    in the image of God he created him;
    male and female he created them.
God blessed them, saying:
  "Be fertile and multiply;
  fill the earth and subdue it.
Have dominion over the fish of the sea, the
  birds of the air,

and all the living things that move on the
  earth."
God also said:
  "See, I give you every seed-bearing plant all
    over the earth
  and every tree that has seed-bearing fruit
    on it to be your food;
  and to all the animals of the land, all the
    birds of the air,
  and all the living creatures that crawl on
    the ground,
  I give all the green plants for food."
And so it happened.
God looked at everything he had made, and
  he found it very good.
Evening came, and morning followed—the
  sixth day.

Thus the heavens and the earth and all their
  array were completed.
Since on the seventh day God was finished
  with the work he had been doing,
  he rested on the seventh day from all the
    work he had undertaken.

or

Gen 1:1, 26-31a

In the beginning, when God created the
  heavens and the earth,
  God said: "Let us make man in our image,
    after our likeness.
Let them have dominion over the fish of the sea,
  the birds of the air, and the cattle,
  and over all the wild animals
  and all the creatures that crawl on the
    ground.
God created man in his image;
    in the image of God he created him;
    male and female he created them.
God blessed them, saying:
  "Be fertile and multiply;
  fill the earth and subdue it.
Have dominion over the fish of the sea, the
  birds of the air,
  and all the living things that move on the
    earth."
God also said:
  "See, I give you every seed-bearing plant all
    over the earth
  and every tree that has seed-bearing fruit
    on it to be your food;
  and to all the animals of the land, all the
    birds of the air,
  and all the living creatures that crawl on
    the ground,
  I give all the green plants for food."
And so it happened.
God looked at everything he had made, and
  found it very good.

RESPONSORIAL PSALM

Ps 104:1-2, 5-6, 10, 12, 13-14, 24, 35

R̸. (30) Lord, send out your Spirit, and renew the face of the earth.

Bless the LORD, O my soul!
  O LORD, my God, you are great indeed!
You are clothed with majesty and glory,
  robed in light as with a cloak.

R̸. Lord, send out your Spirit, and renew the face of the earth.

You fixed the earth upon its foundation,
  not to be moved forever;
with the ocean, as with a garment, you
    covered it;
  above the mountains the waters stood.

R̸. Lord, send out your Spirit, and renew the face of the earth.

You send forth springs into the watercourses
  that wind among the mountains.
Beside them the birds of heaven dwell;
  from among the branches they send forth
    their song.

R̸. Lord, send out your Spirit, and renew the face of the earth.

You water the mountains from your palace;
  the earth is replete with the fruit of your
    works.
You raise grass for the cattle,
  and vegetation for man's use,
producing bread from the earth.

R̸. Lord, send out your Spirit, and renew the face of the earth.

How manifold are your works, O LORD!
  In wisdom you have wrought them all—
the earth is full of your creatures.
  Bless the LORD, O my soul!

R̸. Lord, send out your Spirit, and renew the face of the earth.

or

Ps 33:4-5, 6-7, 12-13, 20 and 22

R̸. (5b) The earth is full of the goodness of the Lord.

Upright is the word of the LORD,
  and all his works are trustworthy.
He loves justice and right;
  of the kindness of the LORD the earth is full.

R̸. The earth is full of the goodness of the Lord.

By the word of the LORD the heavens were
    made;
  by the breath of his mouth all their host.
He gathers the waters of the sea as in a
    flask;
  in cellars he confines the deep.

R̸. The earth is full of the goodness of the Lord.

Blessed the nation whose God is the LORD,
  the people he has chosen for his own
    inheritance.
From heaven the LORD looks down;
  he sees all mankind.

R̸. The earth is full of the goodness of the Lord.

Our soul waits for the LORD,
  who is our help and our shield.
May your kindness, O LORD, be upon us
  who have put our hope in you.

R̸. The earth is full of the goodness of the Lord.

SECOND READING

Gen 22:1-18

God put Abraham to the test.
He called to him, "Abraham!"
"Here I am," he replied.
Then God said:
  "Take your son Isaac, your only one, whom
    you love,
  and go to the land of Moriah.
There you shall offer him up as a holocaust
  on a height that I will point out to you."
Early the next morning Abraham saddled his
    donkey,
  took with him his son Isaac and two of his
    servants as well,
  and with the wood that he had cut for the
    holocaust,
  set out for the place of which God had told
    him.

On the third day Abraham got sight of the
    place from afar.
Then he said to his servants:
  "Both of you stay here with the donkey,
  while the boy and I go on over yonder.
We will worship and then come back to you."
Thereupon Abraham took the wood for the
    holocaust
  and laid it on his son Isaac's shoulders,
  while he himself carried the fire and the
    knife.
As the two walked on together, Isaac spoke to
    his father Abraham:
  "Father!" Isaac said.
"Yes, son," he replied.
Isaac continued, "Here are the fire and the
    wood,
  but where is the sheep for the holocaust?"
"Son," Abraham answered,
  "God himself will provide the sheep for the
    holocaust."
Then the two continued going forward.

When they came to the place of which God
    had told him,

Abraham built an altar there and arranged
    the wood on it.
Next he tied up his son Isaac,
  and put him on top of the wood on the altar.
Then he reached out and took the knife to
    slaughter his son.
But the LORD's messenger called to him from
    heaven,
  "Abraham, Abraham!"
"Here I am," he answered.
"Do not lay your hand on the boy," said the
    messenger.
"Do not do the least thing to him.
I know now how devoted you are to God,
  since you did not withhold from me your
    own beloved son."
As Abraham looked about,
  he spied a ram caught by its horns in the
    thicket.
So he went and took the ram
  and offered it up as a holocaust in place of
    his son.
Abraham named the site Yahweh-yireh;
  hence people now say, "On the mountain
    the LORD will see."

Again the LORD's messenger called to
    Abraham from heaven and said:
  "I swear by myself, declares the LORD,
  that because you acted as you did
  in not withholding from me your beloved
    son,
  I will bless you abundantly
  and make your descendants as countless
  as the stars of the sky and the sands of the
    seashore;
  your descendants shall take possession
  of the gates of their enemies,
  and in your descendants all the nations of
    the earth
    shall find blessing—
  all this because you obeyed my
    command."

or

Gen 22:1-2, 9a, 10-13, 15-18

God put Abraham to the test.
He called to him, "Abraham!"
"Here I am," he replied.
Then God said:
  "Take your son Isaac, your only one, whom
    you love,
  and go to the land of Moriah.
There you shall offer him up as a holocaust
  on a height that I will point out to you."

When they came to the place of which God
    had told him,
  Abraham built an altar there and arranged
    the wood on it.

Then he reached out and took the knife to
   slaughter his son.
But the LORD's messenger called to him from
   heaven,
   "Abraham, Abraham!"
"Here I am," he answered.
"Do not lay your hand on the boy," said the
   messenger.
"Do not do the least thing to him.
I know now how devoted you are to God,
   since you did not withhold from me your
   own beloved son."
As Abraham looked about,
   he spied a ram caught by its horns in the
   thicket.
So he went and took the ram
   and offered it up as a holocaust in place of
   his son.

Again the LORD's messenger called to
   Abraham from heaven and said:
   "I swear by myself, declares the LORD,
   that because you acted as you did
   in not withholding from me your beloved son,
   I will bless you abundantly
   and make your descendants as countless
   as the stars of the sky and the sands of the
   seashore;
   your descendants shall take possession
   of the gates of their enemies,
   and in your descendants all the nations of
   the earth
   shall find blessing—
   all this because you obeyed my command."

RESPONSORIAL PSALM
Ps 16:5, 8, 9-10, 11

R̘. (1) You are my inheritance, O Lord.

O LORD, my allotted portion and my cup,
   you it is who hold fast my lot.
I set the LORD ever before me;
   with him at my right hand I shall not be
   disturbed.

R̘. You are my inheritance, O Lord.

Therefore my heart is glad and my soul rejoices,
   my body, too, abides in confidence;
because you will not abandon my soul to the
   netherworld,
   nor will you suffer your faithful one to
   undergo corruption.

R̘. You are my inheritance, O Lord.

You will show me the path to life,
   fullness of joys in your presence,
   the delights at your right hand forever.

R̘. You are my inheritance, O Lord.

THIRD READING
Exod 14:15–15:1

The LORD said to Moses, "Why are you crying
   out to me?
Tell the Israelites to go forward.
And you, lift up your staff and, with hand
   outstretched over the sea,
   split the sea in two,
   that the Israelites may pass through it on
   dry land.
But I will make the Egyptians so obstinate
   that they will go in after them.
Then I will receive glory through Pharaoh
   and all his army,
   his chariots and charioteers.
The Egyptians shall know that I am the LORD,
   when I receive glory through Pharaoh
   and his chariots and charioteers."

The angel of God, who had been leading
   Israel's camp,
   now moved and went around behind them.
The column of cloud also, leaving the front,
   took up its place behind them,
   so that it came between the camp of the
   Egyptians
   and that of Israel.
But the cloud now became dark, and thus the
   night passed
   without the rival camps coming any closer
   together all night long.
Then Moses stretched out his hand over the
   sea,
   and the LORD swept the sea
   with a strong east wind throughout the night
   and so turned it into dry land.
When the water was thus divided,
   the Israelites marched into the midst of the
   sea on dry land,
   with the water like a wall to their right and
   to their left.

The Egyptians followed in pursuit;
   all Pharaoh's horses and chariots and
   charioteers went after them
   right into the midst of the sea.
In the night watch just before dawn
   the LORD cast through the column of the
   fiery cloud
   upon the Egyptian force a glance that
   threw it into a panic;
   and he so clogged their chariot wheels
   that they could hardly drive.
With that the Egyptians sounded the retreat
   before Israel,
   because the LORD was fighting for them
   against the Egyptians.

Then the LORD told Moses, "Stretch out your
   hand over the sea,
   that the water may flow back upon the
   Egyptians,
   upon their chariots and their charioteers."
So Moses stretched out his hand over the sea,
   and at dawn the sea flowed back to its
   normal depth.
The Egyptians were fleeing head on toward
   the sea,
   when the LORD hurled them into its midst.
As the water flowed back,
   it covered the chariots and the charioteers
   of Pharaoh's whole army
   which had followed the Israelites into the sea.
Not a single one of them escaped.
But the Israelites had marched on dry land
   through the midst of the sea,
   with the water like a wall to their right and
   to their left.
Thus the LORD saved Israel on that day
   from the power of the Egyptians.
When Israel saw the Egyptians lying dead on
   the seashore
   and beheld the great power that the LORD
   had shown against the Egyptians,
   they feared the LORD and believed in him
   and in his servant Moses.

Then Moses and the Israelites sang this song
   to the LORD:
   I will sing to the LORD, for he is gloriously
   triumphant;
   horse and chariot he has cast into the sea.

RESPONSORIAL PSALM
Exod 15:1-2, 3-4, 5-6, 17-18

R̘. (1b) Let us sing to the Lord; he has covered
himself in glory.

I will sing to the LORD, for he is gloriously
   triumphant;
   horse and chariot he has cast into the sea.
My strength and my courage is the LORD,
   and he has been my savior.
He is my God, I praise him;
   the God of my father, I extol him.

R̘. Let us sing to the Lord; he has covered
himself in glory.

The LORD is a warrior,
   LORD is his name!
Pharaoh's chariots and army he hurled into
   the sea;
   the elite of his officers were submerged in
   the Red Sea.

R̘. Let us sing to the Lord; he has covered
himself in glory.

The flood waters covered them,
　　they sank into the depths like a stone.
Your right hand, O LORD, magnificent in
　　　power,
　　your right hand, O LORD, has shattered the
　　　enemy.
R̸. Let us sing to the Lord; he has covered
himself in glory.

You brought in the people you redeemed
　　and planted them on the mountain of your
　　　inheritance—
the place where you made your seat, O LORD,
　　the sanctuary, LORD, which your hands
　　　established.
The LORD shall reign forever and ever.
R̸. Let us sing to the Lord; he has covered
himself in glory.

FOURTH READING
Isa 54:5-14

The One who has become your husband is
　　　your Maker;
　　his name is the LORD of hosts;
your redeemer is the Holy One of Israel,
　　called God of all the earth.
The LORD calls you back,
　　like a wife forsaken and grieved in spirit,
　　a wife married in youth and then cast off,
　　says your God.
For a brief moment I abandoned you,
　　but with great tenderness I will take you
　　　back.
In an outburst of wrath, for a moment
　　I hid my face from you;
but with enduring love I take pity on you,
　　says the LORD, your redeemer.
This is for me like the days of Noah,
　　when I swore that the waters of Noah
　　should never again deluge the earth;
so I have sworn not to be angry with you,
　　or to rebuke you.
Though the mountains leave their place
　　and the hills be shaken,
my love shall never leave you
　　nor my covenant of peace be shaken,
　　says the LORD, who has mercy on you.
O afflicted one, storm-battered and unconsoled,
　　I lay your pavements in carnelians,
　　and your foundations in sapphires;
I will make your battlements of rubies,
　　your gates of carbuncles,
　　and all your walls of precious stones.
All your children shall be taught by the LORD,
　　and great shall be the peace of your children.

In justice shall you be established,
　　far from the fear of oppression,
　　where destruction cannot come near you.

RESPONSORIAL PSALM
Ps 30:2, 4, 5-6, 11-12, 13

R̸. (2a) I will praise you, Lord, for you have
rescued me.

I will extol you, O LORD, for you drew me clear
　　and did not let my enemies rejoice over me.
O LORD, you brought me up from the
　　netherworld;
　　you preserved me from among those going
　　　down into the pit.
R̸. I will praise you, Lord, for you have
rescued me.

Sing praise to the LORD, you his faithful ones,
　　and give thanks to his holy name.
For his anger lasts but a moment;
　　a lifetime, his good will.
At nightfall, weeping enters in,
　　but with the dawn, rejoicing.
R̸. I will praise you, Lord, for you have
rescued me.

Hear, O LORD, and have pity on me;
　　O LORD, be my helper.
You changed my mourning into dancing;
　　O LORD, my God, forever will I give you
　　　thanks.
R̸. I will praise you, Lord, for you have
rescued me.

FIFTH READING
Isa 55:1-11

Thus says the LORD:
All you who are thirsty,
　　come to the water!
You who have no money,
　　come, receive grain and eat;
come, without paying and without cost,
　　drink wine and milk!
Why spend your money for what is not bread,
　　your wages for what fails to satisfy?
Heed me, and you shall eat well,
　　you shall delight in rich fare.
Come to me heedfully,
　　listen, that you may have life.
I will renew with you the everlasting
　　covenant,
　　the benefits assured to David.
As I made him a witness to the peoples,
　　a leader and commander of nations,
so shall you summon a nation you knew not,

and nations that knew you not shall run
　　to you,
because of the LORD, your God,
　　the Holy One of Israel, who has glorified you.

Seek the LORD while he may be found,
　　call him while he is near.
Let the scoundrel forsake his way,
　　and the wicked man his thoughts;
let him turn to the LORD for mercy;
　　to our God, who is generous in forgiving.
For my thoughts are not your thoughts,
　　nor are your ways my ways, says the LORD.
As high as the heavens are above the earth,
　　so high are my ways above your ways
　　and my thoughts above your thoughts.

For just as from the heavens
　　the rain and snow come down
and do not return there
　　till they have watered the earth,
　　making it fertile and fruitful,
giving seed to the one who sows
　　and bread to the one who eats,
so shall my word be
　　that goes forth from my mouth;
my word shall not return to me void,
　　but shall do my will,
　　achieving the end for which I sent it.

RESPONSORIAL PSALM
Isa 12:2-3, 4, 5-6

R̸. (3) You will draw water joyfully from the
springs of salvation.

God indeed is my savior;
　　I am confident and unafraid.
My strength and my courage is the LORD,
　　and he has been my savior.
With joy you will draw water
　　at the fountain of salvation.
R̸. You will draw water joyfully from the
springs of salvation.

Give thanks to the LORD, acclaim his name;
　　among the nations make known his deeds,
　　proclaim how exalted is his name.
R̸. You will draw water joyfully from the
springs of salvation.

Sing praise to the LORD for his glorious
　　achievement;
　　let this be known throughout all the earth.
Shout with exultation, O city of Zion,
　　for great in your midst
　　is the Holy One of Israel!
R̸. You will draw water joyfully from the
springs of salvation.

289

SIXTH READING
Bar 3:9-15, 32–4:4

Hear, O Israel, the commandments of life:
   listen, and know prudence!
How is it, Israel,
   that you are in the land of your foes,
   grown old in a foreign land,
defiled with the dead,
   accounted with those destined for the
      netherworld?
You have forsaken the fountain of wisdom!
   Had you walked in the way of God,
   you would have dwelt in enduring peace.
Learn where prudence is,
   where strength, where understanding;
that you may know also
   where are length of days, and life,
   where light of the eyes, and peace.
Who has found the place of wisdom,
   who has entered into her treasuries?

The One who knows all things knows her;
   he has probed her by his knowledge—
the One who established the earth for all
    time,
   and filled it with four-footed beasts;
he who dismisses the light, and it departs,
   calls it, and it obeys him trembling;
before whom the stars at their posts
   shine and rejoice;
when he calls them, they answer, "Here we
    are!"
   shining with joy for their Maker.
Such is our God;
   no other is to be compared to him:
he has traced out the whole way of
    understanding,
   and has given her to Jacob, his servant,
   to Israel, his beloved son.

Since then she has appeared on earth,
   and moved among people.
She is the book of the precepts of God,
   the law that endures forever;
all who cling to her will live,
   but those will die who forsake her.
Turn, O Jacob, and receive her:
   walk by her light toward splendor.
Give not your glory to another,
   your privileges to an alien race.
Blessed are we, O Israel;
   for what pleases God is known to us!

RESPONSORIAL PSALM
Ps 19:8, 9, 10, 11

℟. (John 6:68c) Lord, you have the words of
everlasting life.

The law of the LORD is perfect,
   refreshing the soul;
the decree of the LORD is trustworthy,
   giving wisdom to the simple.

℟. Lord, you have the words of everlasting life.

The precepts of the LORD are right,
   rejoicing the heart;
the command of the LORD is clear,
   enlightening the eye.

℟. Lord, you have the words of everlasting life.

The fear of the LORD is pure,
   enduring forever;
the ordinances of the LORD are true,
   all of them just.

℟. Lord, you have the words of everlasting life.

They are more precious than gold,
   than a heap of purest gold;
sweeter also than syrup
   or honey from the comb.

℟. Lord, you have the words of everlasting life.

SEVENTH READING
Ezek 36:16-17a, 18-28

The word of the LORD came to me, saying:
   Son of man, when the house of Israel lived
    in their land,
   they defiled it by their conduct and deeds.
Therefore I poured out my fury upon them
   because of the blood that they poured out
    on the ground,
   and because they defiled it with idols.
I scattered them among the nations,
   dispersing them over foreign lands;
   according to their conduct and deeds I
    judged them.
But when they came among the nations
    wherever they came,
   they served to profane my holy name,
   because it was said of them: "These are the
    people of the LORD,
   yet they had to leave their land."
So I have relented because of my holy name
   which the house of Israel profaned
   among the nations where they came.
Therefore say to the house of Israel: Thus
   says the Lord GOD:
   Not for your sakes do I act, house of Israel,
   but for the sake of my holy name,
   which you profaned among the nations to
    which you came.
I will prove the holiness of my great name,
   profaned among the nations,
   in whose midst you have profaned it.
Thus the nations shall know that I am the
   LORD, says the Lord GOD,
   when in their sight I prove my holiness
    through you.
For I will take you away from among the
   nations,

gather you from all the foreign lands,
   and bring you back to your own land.
I will sprinkle clean water upon you
   to cleanse you from all your impurities,
   and from all your idols I will cleanse you.
I will give you a new heart and place a new
    spirit within you,
   taking from your bodies your stony hearts
   and giving you natural hearts.
I will put my spirit within you and make you
    live by my statutes,
   careful to observe my decrees.
You shall live in the land I gave your fathers;
   you shall be my people, and I will be your
    God.

RESPONSORIAL PSALM
Ps 42:3, 5; 43:3, 4

℟. (42:2) Like a deer that longs for running
streams, my soul longs for you, my God.

Athirst is my soul for God, the living God.
   When shall I go and behold the face of God?

℟. Like a deer that longs for running streams,
my soul longs for you, my God.

I went with the throng
   and led them in procession to the house of
    God,
amid loud cries of joy and thanksgiving,
   with the multitude keeping festival.

℟. Like a deer that longs for running streams,
my soul longs for you, my God.

Send forth your light and your fidelity;
   they shall lead me on
and bring me to your holy mountain,
   to your dwelling-place.

℟. Like a deer that longs for running streams,
my soul longs for you, my God.

Then will I go in to the altar of God,
   the God of my gladness and joy;
then will I give you thanks upon the harp,
   O God, my God!

℟. Like a deer that longs for running streams,
my soul longs for you, my God.

or

Isa 12:2-3, 4bcd, 5-6

℟. (3) You will draw water joyfully from the
springs of salvation.

God indeed is my savior;
   I am confident and unafraid.
My strength and my courage is the LORD,
   and he has been my savior.
With joy you will draw water
   at the fountain of salvation.

℟. You will draw water joyfully from the
springs of salvation.

Give thanks to the LORD, acclaim his name;
   among the nations make known his deeds,
   proclaim how exalted is his name.

R℘. You will draw water joyfully from the
springs of salvation.

Sing praise to the LORD for his glorious
   achievement;
   let this be known throughout all the earth.
Shout with exultation, O city of Zion,
   for great in your midst
   is the Holy One of Israel!

R℘. You will draw water joyfully from the
springs of salvation.

or

Ps 51:12-13, 14-15, 18-19

R℘. (12a) Create a clean heart in me, O God.

A clean heart create for me, O God,
   and a steadfast spirit renew within me.
Cast me not out from your presence,
   and your Holy Spirit take not from me.

R℘. Create a clean heart in me, O God.

Give me back the joy of your salvation,
   and a willing spirit sustain in me.
I will teach transgressors your ways,
   and sinners shall return to you.

R℘. Create a clean heart in me, O God.

For you are not pleased with sacrifices;
   should I offer a holocaust, you would not
     accept it.
My sacrifice, O God, is a contrite spirit;
   a heart contrite and humbled, O God, you
     will not spurn.

R℘. Create a clean heart in me, O God.

EPISTLE
Rom 6:3-11

Brothers and sisters:
Are you unaware that we who were baptized
   into Christ Jesus
   were baptized into his death?
We were indeed buried with him through
   baptism into death,
   so that, just as Christ was raised from the
     dead
   by the glory of the Father,
   we too might live in newness of life.

For if we have grown into union with him
   through a death like his,
   we shall also be united with him in the
     resurrection.
We know that our old self was crucified with
   him,
   so that our sinful body might be done away
     with,
   that we might no longer be in slavery to sin.
For a dead person has been absolved from
   sin.
If, then, we have died with Christ,
   we believe that we shall also live with
     him.
We know that Christ, raised from the dead,
   dies no more;
   death no longer has power over him.
As to his death, he died to sin once and for
   all;
   as to his life, he lives for God.
Consequently, you too must think of
   yourselves as being dead to sin
   and living for God in Christ Jesus.

RESPONSORIAL PSALM
Ps 118:1-2, 16-17, 22-23

R℘. Alleluia, alleluia, alleluia.

Give thanks to the LORD, for he is good,
   for his mercy endures forever.
Let the house of Israel say,
   "His mercy endures forever."

R℘. Alleluia, alleluia, alleluia.

The right hand of the LORD has struck with
   power;
   the right hand of the LORD is exalted.
I shall not die, but live,
   and declare the works of the LORD.

R℘. Alleluia, alleluia, alleluia.

The stone which the builders rejected
   has become the cornerstone.
By the LORD has this been done;
   it is wonderful in our eyes.

R℘. Alleluia, alleluia, alleluia.

Gospel
Luke 24:1-12; L41ABC

At daybreak on the first day of the week
   the women who had come from Galilee with Jesus
   took the spices they had prepared
   and went to the tomb.
They found the stone rolled away from the tomb;
   but when they entered,
   they did not find the body of the Lord Jesus.
While they were puzzling over this, behold,
   two men in dazzling garments appeared to them.
They were terrified and bowed their faces to the ground.
They said to them,
   "Why do you seek the living one among the dead?
He is not here, but he has been raised.
Remember what he said to you while he was still in Galilee,

that the Son of Man must be handed over to sinners
   and be crucified, and rise on the third day."
And they remembered his words.
Then they returned from the tomb
   and announced all these things to the eleven
   and to all the others.
The women were Mary Magdalene, Joanna, and Mary the mother of
     James;
   the others who accompanied them also told this to the apostles,
   but their story seemed like nonsense
   and they did not believe them.
But Peter got up and ran to the tomb,
   bent down, and saw the burial cloths alone;
   then he went home amazed at what had happened.

or, at an afternoon or evening Mass

Gospel
Luke 24:13-35; L46

That very day, the first day of the week,
   two of Jesus' disciples were going
   to a village seven miles from Jerusalem called Emmaus,
   and they were conversing about all the things that had occurred.
And it happened that while they were conversing and debating,
   Jesus himself drew near and walked with them,
   but their eyes were prevented from recognizing him.
He asked them,
   "What are you discussing as you walk along?"
They stopped, looking downcast.
One of them, named Cleopas, said to him in reply,
   "Are you the only visitor to Jerusalem
   who does not know of the things
   that have taken place there in these days?"
And he replied to them, "What sort of things?"
They said to him,
   "The things that happened to Jesus the Nazarene,
   who was a prophet mighty in deed and word
   before God and all the people,
   how our chief priests and rulers both handed him over
   to a sentence of death and crucified him.
But we were hoping that he would be the one to redeem Israel;
   and besides all this,
   it is now the third day since this took place.
Some women from our group, however, have astounded us:
   they were at the tomb early in the morning
   and did not find his body;
   they came back and reported
   that they had indeed seen a vision of angels
   who announced that he was alive.
Then some of those with us went to the tomb
   and found things just as the women had described,
   but him they did not see."

And he said to them, "Oh, how foolish you are!
How slow of heart to believe all that the prophets spoke!
Was it not necessary that the Christ should suffer these things
   and enter into his glory?"
Then beginning with Moses and all the prophets,
   he interpreted to them what referred to him
   in all the Scriptures.
As they approached the village to which they were going,
   he gave the impression that he was going on farther.
But they urged him, "Stay with us,
   for it is nearly evening and the day is almost over."
So he went in to stay with them.
And it happened that, while he was with them at table,
   he took bread, said the blessing,
   broke it, and gave it to them.
With that their eyes were opened and they recognized him,
   but he vanished from their sight.
Then they said to each other,
   "Were not our hearts burning within us
   while he spoke to us on the way and opened the Scriptures to us?"
So they set out at once and returned to Jerusalem
   where they found gathered together
   the eleven and those with them who were saying,
   "The Lord has truly been raised and has appeared to Simon!"
Then the two recounted
   what had taken place on the way
   and how he was made known to them in the breaking of bread.

Easter Sunday, *April 8, 2007*

FIRST READING
Acts 10:34a, 37-43

Peter proceeded to speak and said:
   "You know what has happened all over
      Judea,
   beginning in Galilee after the baptism
    that John preached,
   how God anointed Jesus of Nazareth
    with the Holy Spirit and power.
He went about doing good
   and healing all those oppressed by the devil,
   for God was with him.
We are witnesses of all that he did
   both in the country of the Jews and in
    Jerusalem.
They put him to death by hanging him on a
    tree.
This man God raised on the third day and
    granted that he be visible,
   not to all the people, but to us,
   the witnesses chosen by God in advance,
   who ate and drank with him after he rose
    from the dead.
He commissioned us to preach to the people
   and testify that he is the one appointed by
    God
   as judge of the living and the dead.
To him all the prophets bear witness,
   that everyone who believes in him
   will receive forgiveness of sins through his
    name."

RESPONSORIAL PSALM
Ps 118:1-2, 16-17, 22-23

R̂. (24) This is the day the Lord has made; let
us rejoice and be glad.
   or:
R̂. Alleluia.

Give thanks to the LORD, for he is good,
   for his mercy endures forever.
Let the house of Israel say,
   "His mercy endures forever."

R̂. This is the day the Lord has made; let us
rejoice and be glad.
   or:
R̂. Alleluia.

"The right hand of the LORD has struck with
   power;
   the right hand of the LORD is exalted.
I shall not die, but live,
   and declare the works of the LORD."

R̂. This is the day the Lord has made; let us
rejoice and be glad.
   or:
R̂. Alleluia.

The stone which the builders rejected
   has become the cornerstone.
By the LORD has this been done;
   it is wonderful in our eyes.

R̂. This is the day the Lord has made; let us
rejoice and be glad.
   or:
R̂. Alleluia.

SECOND READING Col 3:1-4

Brothers and sisters:
If then you were raised with Christ, seek what
   is above,
   where Christ is seated at the right hand of
    God.
Think of what is above, not of what is on earth.
For you have died, and your life is hidden
    with Christ in God.
When Christ your life appears,
   then you too will appear with him in glory.

or

1 Cor 5:6b-8

Brothers and sisters:
Do you not know that a little yeast leavens all
   the dough?
Clear out the old yeast,
   so that you may become a fresh batch of
    dough,
   inasmuch as you are unleavened.
For our paschal lamb, Christ, has been
    sacrificed.
Therefore, let us celebrate the feast,
   not with the old yeast, the yeast of malice
    and wickedness,
   but with the unleavened bread of sincerity
    and truth.

SEQUENCE *Victimae paschali laudes*

Christians, to the Paschal Victim
   Offer your thankful praises!
A Lamb the sheep redeems;
   Christ, who only is sinless,
   Reconciles sinners to the Father.
Death and life have contended in that combat
    stupendous:
   The Prince of life, who died, reigns
    immortal.
Speak, Mary, declaring
   What you saw, wayfaring.
"The tomb of Christ, who is living,
   The glory of Jesus' resurrection;
Bright angels attesting,
   The shroud and napkin resting.
Yes, Christ my hope is arisen;
   To Galilee he goes before you."
Christ indeed from death is risen, our new life
    obtaining.
   Have mercy, victor King, ever reigning!
   Amen. Alleluia.

Second Sunday of Easter (or Divine Mercy Sunday), *April 15, 2007*

Gospel (cont.)
John 20:19-31; L44B

Then he said to Thomas, "Put your finger here and see my hands,
   and bring your hand and put it into my side,
   and do not be unbelieving, but believe."
Thomas answered and said to him, "My Lord and my God!"
Jesus said to him, "Have you come to believe because you have seen
    me?
Blessed are those who have not seen and have believed."

Now Jesus did many other signs in the presence of his disciples
   that are not written in this book.
But these are written that you may come to believe
   that Jesus is the Christ, the Son of God,
   and that through this belief you may have life in his name.

Third Sunday of Easter, *April 22, 2007*

Gospel
John 21:1-14; L48C

At that time, Jesus revealed himself again to his disciples at the Sea of
    Tiberias.
He revealed himself in this way.
Together were Simon Peter, Thomas called Didymus,
    Nathanael from Cana in Galilee,
    Zebedee's sons, and two others of his disciples.
Simon Peter said to them, "I am going fishing."
They said to him, "We also will come with you."
So they went out and got into the boat,
    but that night they caught nothing.
When it was already dawn, Jesus was standing on the shore;
    but the disciples did not realize that it was Jesus.
Jesus said to them, "Children, have you caught anything to eat?"
They answered him, "No."
So he said to them, "Cast the net over the right side of the boat
    and you will find something."
So they cast it, and were not able to pull it in
    because of the number of fish.
So the disciple whom Jesus loved said to Peter, "It is the Lord."

When Simon Peter heard that it was the Lord,
    he tucked in his garment, for he was lightly clad,
    and jumped into the sea.
The other disciples came in the boat,
    for they were not far from shore, only about a hundred yards,
    dragging the net with the fish.
When they climbed out on shore,
    they saw a charcoal fire with fish on it and bread.
Jesus said to them, "Bring some of the fish you just caught."
So Simon Peter went over and dragged the net ashore
    full of one hundred fifty-three large fish.
Even though there were so many, the net was not torn.
Jesus said to them, "Come, have breakfast."
And none of the disciples dared to ask him, "Who are you?"
    because they realized it was the Lord.
Jesus came over and took the bread and gave it to them,
    and in like manner the fish.
This was now the third time Jesus was revealed to his disciples
    after being raised from the dead.

Fourth Sunday of Easter, *April 29, 2007*

SECOND READING
Rev 7:9, 14b-17

I, John, had a vision of a great multitude,
    which no one could count,
        from every nation, race, people, and
            tongue.
They stood before the throne and before the
    Lamb,
        wearing white robes and holding palm
            branches in their hands.

Then one of the elders said to me,
    "These are the ones who have survived the
        time of great distress;
    they have washed their robes
    and made them white in the blood of the
        Lamb.

        "For this reason they stand before God's
            throne
            and worship him day and night in his
               temple.
        The one who sits on the throne will
            shelter them.
        They will not hunger or thirst anymore,
            nor will the sun or any heat strike
               them.
        For the Lamb who is in the center of the
            throne
             will shepherd them
            and lead them to springs of life-
               giving water,
        and God will wipe away every tear
            from their eyes."

Sixth Sunday of Easter, *May 13, 2007*

SECOND READING
Rev 21:10-14, 22-23

The angel took me in spirit to a great, high
    mountain
    and showed me the holy city Jerusalem
    coming down out of heaven from God.
It gleamed with the splendor of God.
Its radiance was like that of a precious stone,
    like jasper, clear as crystal.
It had a massive, high wall,
    with twelve gates where twelve angels
        were stationed
    and on which names were inscribed,
    the names of the twelve tribes of the
        Israelites.
There were three gates facing east,
    three north, three south, and three west.
The wall of the city had twelve courses of
        stones as its foundation,
    on which were inscribed the twelve names
    of the twelve apostles of the Lamb.

I saw no temple in the city
    for its temple is the Lord God almighty and
        the Lamb.
The city had no need of sun or moon to shine
        on it,
    for the glory of God gave it light,
    and its lamp was the Lamb.

The Ascension of the Lord, *May 17, 2007 (Thursday) or May 20, 2007*

Brothers and sisters:
May the God of our Lord Jesus Christ, the
    Father of glory,
  give you a Spirit of wisdom and revelation
  resulting in knowledge of him.
May the eyes of your hearts be enlightened,
  that you may know what is the hope that
      belongs to his call,
  what are the riches of glory
  in his inheritance among the holy ones,
  and what is the surpassing greatness of
      his power
  for us who believe,
  in accord with the exercise of his great
      might,
  which he worked in Christ,
  raising him from the dead
  and seating him at his right hand in the
      heavens,
  far above every principality, authority,
      power, and dominion,
  and every name that is named
  not only in this age but also in the one to
      come.

And he put all things beneath his feet
  and gave him as head over all things to the
      church,
  which is his body,
  the fullness of the one who fills all things
      in every way.

or

Heb 9:24-28; 10:19-23

Christ did not enter into a sanctuary made by
    hands,
  a copy of the true one, but heaven itself,
  that he might now appear before God on
      our behalf.
Not that he might offer himself repeatedly,
  as the high priest enters each year into the
      sanctuary
  with blood that is not his own;
  if that were so, he would have had to suffer
      repeatedly
  from the foundation of the world.
But now once for all he has appeared at the
    end of the ages
  to take away sin by his sacrifice.
Just as it is appointed that men and women
    die once,

and after this the judgment, so also Christ,
  offered once to take away the sins of many,
  will appear a second time, not to take away
      sin
  but to bring salvation to those who eagerly
      await him.

Therefore, brothers and sisters, since through
    the blood of Jesus
  we have confidence of entrance into the
      sanctuary
  by the new and living way he opened for us
      through the veil,
  that is, his flesh,
  and since we have "a great priest over the
      house of God,"
  let us approach with a sincere heart and in
      absolute trust,
  with our hearts sprinkled clean from an
      evil conscience
  and our bodies washed in pure water.
Let us hold unwaveringly to our confession
    that gives us hope,
  for he who made the promise is
      trustworthy.

Pentecost Sunday Mass During the Day, *May 27, 2007*

Brothers and sisters:
Those who are in the flesh cannot please God.
But you are not in the flesh;
  on the contrary, you are in the spirit,
  if only the Spirit of God dwells in you.
Whoever does not have the Spirit of Christ
    does not belong to him.
But if Christ is in you,
  although the body is dead because of sin,
  the spirit is alive because of righteousness.
If the Spirit of the one who raised Jesus from
    the dead dwells in you,
  the one who raised Christ from the dead
  will give life to your mortal bodies also,
  through his Spirit that dwells in you.
Consequently, brothers and sisters,
  we are not debtors to the flesh,
  to live according to the flesh.
For if you live according to the flesh, you will
    die,
  but if by the Spirit you put to death the
      deeds of the body,
  you will live.

For those who are led by the Spirit of God are
    sons of God.
For you did not receive a spirit of slavery to
    fall back into fear,
  but you received a Spirit of adoption,
  through whom we cry, "Abba, Father!"
The Spirit himself bears witness with our
    spirit
  that we are children of God,
  and if children, then heirs,
  heirs of God and joint heirs with Christ,
  if only we suffer with him
  so that we may also be glorified with him.

SEQUENCE
Veni, Sancte Spiritus

Come, Holy Spirit, come!
And from your celestial home
    Shed a ray of light divine!
Come, Father of the poor!
Come, source of all our store!
    Come, within our bosoms shine.
You, of comforters the best;
You, the soul's most welcome guest;
    Sweet refreshment here below;

In our labor, rest most sweet;
Grateful coolness in the heat;
    Solace in the midst of woe.
O most blessed Light divine,
Shine within these hearts of yours,
    And our inmost being fill!
Where you are not, we have naught,
Nothing good in deed or thought,
    Nothing free from taint of ill.
Heal our wounds, our strength renew;
On our dryness pour your dew;
    Wash the stains of guilt away:
Bend the stubborn heart and will;
Melt the frozen, warm the chill;
    Guide the steps that go astray.
On the faithful, who adore
And confess you, evermore
    In your sevenfold gift descend;
Give them virtue's sure reward;
Give them your salvation, Lord;
    Give them joys that never end. Amen.
    Alleluia.

OPTIONAL SEQUENCE

Lauda Sion

Laud, O Zion, your salvation,
Laud with hymns of exultation,
   Christ, your king and shepherd true:

Bring him all the praise you know,
He is more than you bestow.
   Never can you reach his due.

Special theme for glad thanksgiving
Is the quick'ning and the living
   Bread today before you set:

From his hands of old partaken,
As we know, by faith unshaken,
   Where the Twelve at supper met.

Full and clear ring out your chanting,
Joy nor sweetest grace be wanting,
   From your heart let praises burst:

For today the feast is holden,
When the institution olden
   Of that supper was rehearsed.

Here the new law's new oblation,
By the new king's revelation,
   Ends the form of ancient rite:

Now the new the old effaces,
Truth away the shadow chases,
   Light dispels the gloom of night.

What he did at supper seated,
Christ ordained to be repeated,
   His memorial ne'er to cease:

And his rule for guidance taking,
Bread and wine we hallow, making
   Thus our sacrifice of peace.

This the truth each Christian learns,
Bread into his flesh he turns,
   To his precious blood the wine:

Sight has fail'd, nor thought conceives,
But a dauntless faith believes,
   Resting on a pow'r divine.

Here beneath these signs are hidden
Priceless things to sense forbidden;
   Signs, not things are all we see:

Blood is poured and flesh is broken,
Yet in either wondrous token
   Christ entire we know to be.

Whoso of this food partakes,
Does not rend the Lord nor breaks;
   Christ is whole to all that taste:

Thousands are, as one, receivers,
One, as thousands of believers,
   Eats of him who cannot waste.

Bad and good the feast are sharing,
Of what divers dooms preparing,
   Endless death, or endless life.

Life to these, to those damnation,
See how like participation
   Is with unlike issues rife.

When the sacrament is broken,
Doubt not, but believe 'tis spoken,

That each sever'd outward token
   doth the very whole contain.

Nought the precious gift divides,
Breaking but the sign betides
   Jesus still the same abides,
      still unbroken does remain.

The shorter form of the sequence begins here.

Lo! the angel's food is given
To the pilgrim who has striven;
   See the children's bread from heaven,
      which on dogs may not be spent.

Truth the ancient types fulfilling,
Isaac bound, a victim willing,
   Paschal lamb, its lifeblood spilling,
      manna to the fathers sent.

Very bread, good shepherd, tend us,
Jesu, of your love befriend us,
   You refresh us, you defend us,
   Your eternal goodness send us
In the land of life to see.

You who all things can and know,
Who on earth such food bestow,
   Grant us with your saints, though lowest,
   Where the heav'nly feast you show,
Fellow heirs and guests to be. Amen. Alleluia.

FIRST READING
Ezek 34:11-16

Thus says the Lord GOD:
  I myself will look after and tend my sheep.
As a shepherd tends his flock
    when he finds himself among his scattered
      sheep,
    so will I tend my sheep.
I will rescue them from every place where
      they were scattered
    when it was cloudy and dark.
I will lead them out from among the peoples
    and gather them from the foreign lands;
    I will bring them back to their own country
    and pasture them upon the mountains of
      Israel
    in the land's ravines and all its inhabited
      places.
In good pastures will I pasture them,
    and on the mountain heights of Israel
    shall be their grazing ground.
There they shall lie down on good grazing
      ground,
    and in rich pastures shall they be pastured
    on the mountains of Israel.
I myself will pasture my sheep;
    I myself will give them rest, says the Lord
      GOD.
The lost I will seek out,
    the strayed I will bring back,
    the injured I will bind up,
    the sick I will heal,
    but the sleek and the strong I will destroy,
    shepherding them rightly.

RESPONSORIAL PSALM
Ps 23:1-3a, 3b-4, 5, 6

R̸. (1) The Lord is my shepherd; there is nothing I shall want.

The LORD is my shepherd; I shall not want.
    In verdant pastures he gives me repose;
beside restful waters he leads me;
    he refreshes my soul.

R̸. The Lord is my shepherd; there is nothing
I shall want.

He guides me in right paths
    for his name's sake.
Even though I walk in the dark valley
    I fear no evil; for you are at my side
with your rod and your staff
    that give me courage.

R̸. The Lord is my shepherd; there is nothing
I shall want.

You spread the table before me
    in the sight of my foes;
you anoint my head with oil;
    my cup overflows.

R̸. The Lord is my shepherd; there is nothing
I shall want.

Only goodness and kindness follow me
    all the days of my life;
and I shall dwell in the house of the LORD
    for years to come.

R̸. The Lord is my shepherd; there is nothing
I shall want.

SECOND READING
Rom 5:5b-11

Brothers and sisters:
The love of God has been poured out into our
      hearts
    through the Holy Spirit that has been given
      to us.
For Christ, while we were still helpless,
    died at the appointed time for the ungodly.
Indeed, only with difficulty does one die for a
      just person,
    though perhaps for a good person
    one might even find courage to die.
But God proves his love for us
    in that while we were still sinners Christ
      died for us.
How much more then, since we are now
      justified by his blood,
    will we be saved through him from the
      wrath.
Indeed, if, while we were enemies,
    we were reconciled to God through the
      death of his Son,
    how much more, once reconciled,
    will we be saved by his life.
Not only that,
    but we also boast of God through our Lord
      Jesus Christ,
    through whom we have now received
      reconciliation.

Gospel (cont.)

Luke 7:36–8:3; L93C

Then he turned to the woman and said to Simon,
  "Do you see this woman?
When I entered your house, you did not give me water for my feet,
    but she has bathed them with her tears
    and wiped them with her hair.
You did not give me a kiss,
    but she has not ceased kissing my feet since the time I entered.
You did not anoint my head with oil,
    but she anointed my feet with ointment.
So I tell you, her many sins have been forgiven
    because she has shown great love.
But the one to whom little is forgiven, loves little."
He said to her, "Your sins are forgiven."
The others at table said to themselves,
  "Who is this who even forgives sins?"
But he said to the woman,
  "Your faith has saved you; go in peace."

Afterward he journeyed from one town and village to another,
  preaching and proclaiming the good news of the kingdom of God.
Accompanying him were the Twelve
    and some women who had been cured of evil spirits and infirmities,
    Mary, called Magdalene, from whom seven demons had gone out,
    Joanna, the wife of Herod's steward Chuza,
    Susanna, and many others who provided for them out of their
      resources.

or Luke 7:36-50

A Pharisee invited Jesus to dine with him,
  and he entered the Pharisee's house and reclined at table.
Now there was a sinful woman in the city
  who learned that he was at table in the house of the Pharisee.
Bringing an alabaster flask of ointment,
    she stood behind him at his feet weeping
    and began to bathe his feet with her tears.
Then she wiped them with her hair,
    kissed them, and anointed them with the ointment.
When the Pharisee who had invited him saw this he said to himself,
  "If this man were a prophet,
    he would know who and what sort of woman this is who is
        touching him,
    that she is a sinner."
Jesus said to him in reply,
  "Simon, I have something to say to you."
"Tell me, teacher," he said.
"Two people were in debt to a certain creditor;
    one owed five hundred day's wages and the other owed fifty.
Since they were unable to repay the debt, he forgave it for both.
Which of them will love him more?"
Simon said in reply,
  "The one, I suppose, whose larger debt was forgiven."
He said to him, "You have judged rightly."
Then he turned to the woman and said to Simon,
  "Do you see this woman?
When I entered your house, you did not give me water for my feet,
    but she has bathed them with her tears
    and wiped them with her hair.
You did not give me a kiss,
    but she has not ceased kissing my feet since the time I entered.
You did not anoint my head with oil,
    but she anointed my feet with ointment.
So I tell you, her many sins have been forgiven
    because she has shown great love.
But the one to whom little is forgiven, loves little."
He said to her, "Your sins are forgiven."
The others at table said to themselves,
  "Who is this who even forgives sins?"
But he said to the woman,
  "Your faith has saved you; go in peace."

SS. Peter and Paul, Apostles, *June 29, 2007*

FIRST READING
Acts 12:1-11

In those days, King Herod laid hands upon
      some members of the church to harm
      them.
He had James, the brother of John, killed by
      the sword,
   and when he saw that this was pleasing to
      the Jews
   he proceeded to arrest Peter also.
—It was the feast of Unleavened Bread.—
He had him taken into custody and put in
      prison
   under the guard of four squads of four
      soldiers each.
He intended to bring him before the people
      after Passover.
Peter thus was being kept in prison,
   but prayer by the church was fervently
      being made
   to God on his behalf.

On the very night before Herod was to bring
      him to trial,
   Peter, secured by double chains,
   was sleeping between two soldiers,
   while outside the door guards kept watch
      on the prison.
Suddenly the angel of the Lord stood by him
   and a light shone in the cell.
He tapped Peter on the side and awakened
      him, saying,
   "Get up quickly."
The chains fell from his wrists.
The angel said to him, "Put on your belt and
      your sandals."
He did so.
Then he said to him, "Put on your cloak and
      follow me."

So he followed him out,
   not realizing that what was happening
      through the angel was real;
   he thought he was seeing a vision.
They passed the first guard, then the second,
   and came to the iron gate leading out to
      the city,
   which opened for them by itself.
They emerged and made their way down an
      alley,
   and suddenly the angel left him.
Then Peter recovered his senses and said,
   "Now I know for certain
      that the Lord sent his angel
   and rescued me from the hand of Herod
   and from all that the Jewish people had
      been expecting."

RESPONSORIAL PSALM
Ps 34:2-3, 4-5, 6-7, 8-9

R̗. (8) The angel of the Lord will rescue those
who fear him.

I will bless the LORD at all times;
   his praise shall be ever in my mouth.
Let my soul glory in the LORD;
   the lowly will hear me and be glad.

R̗. The angel of the Lord will rescue those
who fear him.

Glorify the LORD with me,
   let us together extol his name.
I sought the LORD, and he answered me
   and delivered me from all my fears.

R̗. The angel of the Lord will rescue those
who fear him.

Look to him that you may be radiant with joy,
   and your faces may not blush with shame.

When the poor one called out, the LORD heard,
   and from all his distress he saved him.

R̗. The angel of the Lord will rescue those
who fear him.

The angel of the LORD encamps
   around those who fear him, and delivers
      them.
Taste and see how good the LORD is;
   blessed the man who takes refuge in him.

R̗. The angel of the Lord will rescue those
who fear him.

SECOND READING
2 Tim 4:6-8, 17-18

I, Paul, am already being poured out like a
      libation,
   and the time of my departure is at hand.
I have competed well; I have finished the race;
   I have kept the faith.
From now on the crown of righteousness
      awaits me,
   which the Lord, the just judge,
   will award to me on that day, and not only
      to me,
   but to all who have longed for his
      appearance.

The Lord stood by me and gave me strength,
   so that through me the proclamation might
      be completed
   and all the Gentiles might hear it.
And I was rescued from the lion's mouth.
The Lord will rescue me from every evil
      threat
   and will bring me safe to his heavenly
      kingdom.
To him be glory forever and ever. Amen.

Fourteenth Sunday in Ordinary Time, *July 8, 2007*

Gospel (cont.)
Luke 10:1-12, 17-20; L102C

The seventy-two returned rejoicing, and said,
   "Lord, even the demons are subject to us because of your name."
Jesus said, "I have observed Satan fall like lightning from the sky.
Behold, I have given you the power to 'tread upon serpents' and
      scorpions
   and upon the full force of the enemy and nothing will harm you.
Nevertheless, do not rejoice because the spirits are subject to you,
   but rejoice because your names are written in heaven."

or Luke 10:1-9

At that time the Lord appointed seventy-two others
   whom he sent ahead of him in pairs
   to every town and place he intended to visit.
He said to them,
   "The harvest is abundant but the laborers are few;

   so ask the master of the harvest
   to send out laborers for his harvest.
Go on your way;
   behold, I am sending you like lambs among wolves.
Carry no money bag, no sack, no sandals;
   and greet no one along the way.
Into whatever house you enter, first say,
   'Peace to this household.'
If a peaceful person lives there,
   your peace will rest on him;
   but if not, it will return to you.
Stay in the same house and eat and drink what is offered to you,
   for the laborer deserves his payment.
Do not move about from one house to another.
Whatever town you enter and they welcome you,
   eat what is set before you,
   cure the sick in it and say to them,
   'The kingdom of God is at hand for you.'

Gospel (cont.)
Luke 10:25-37; L105C

He approached the victim,
    poured oil and wine over his wounds and bandaged them.
    Then he lifted him up on his own animal,
    took him to an inn, and cared for him.
The next day he took out two silver coins
    and gave them to the innkeeper with the instruction,
    'Take care of him.
If you spend more than what I have given you,
    I shall repay you on my way back.'
Which of these three, in your opinion,
    was neighbor to the robbers' victim?"
He answered, "The one who treated him with mercy."
Jesus said to him, "Go and do likewise."

RESPONSORIAL PSALM
Ps 19:8, 9, 10, 11

℟. (9a) Your words, Lord, are Spirit and life.

The law of the Lord is perfect,
    refreshing the soul;
the decree of the Lord is trustworthy,
    giving wisdom to the simple.

℟. Your words, Lord, are Spirit and life.

The precepts of the Lord are right,
    rejoicing the heart;
the command of the Lord is clear,
    enlightening the eye.

℟. Your words, Lord, are Spirit and life.

The fear of the Lord is pure,
    enduring forever;
the ordinances of the Lord are true,
    all of them just.

℟. Your words, Lord, are Spirit and life.

They are more precious than gold,
    than a heap of purest gold;
sweeter also than syrup
    or honey from the comb.

℟. Your words, Lord, are Spirit and life.

Seventeenth Sunday in Ordinary Time, July 29, 207

Gospel (cont.)
Luke 11:1-13; L111C

"And I tell you, ask and you will receive;
    seek and you will find;
    knock and the door will be opened to you.
For everyone who asks, receives;
    and the one who seeks, finds;
    and to the one who knocks, the door will be opened.
What father among you would hand his son a snake
    when he asks for a fish?
Or hand him a scorpion when he asks for an egg?
If you then, who are wicked,
    know how to give good gifts to your children,
    how much more will the Father in heaven
    give the Holy Spirit to those who ask him?"

SECOND READING
Col 2:12-14

Brothers and sisters:
You were buried with him in baptism,
    in which you were also raised with him
    through faith in the power of God,
    who raised him from the dead.
And even when you were dead
    in transgressions and the uncircumcision of your flesh,
    he brought you to life along with him,
    having forgiven us all our transgressions;
obliterating the bond against us, with its legal claims,
    which was opposed to us,
    he also removed it from our midst, nailing it to the cross.

Gospel (cont.)
Luke 12:32-48; L117C

Then Peter said,
"Lord, is this parable meant for us or for everyone?"
And the Lord replied,
"Who, then, is the faithful and prudent steward
whom the master will put in charge of his servants
to distribute the food allowance at the proper time?
Blessed is that servant whom his master on arrival finds doing so.
Truly, I say to you, the master will put the servant
in charge of all his property.
But if that servant says to himself,
'My master is delayed in coming,'
and begins to beat the menservants and the maidservants,
to eat and drink and get drunk,
then that servant's master will come
on an unexpected day and at an unknown hour
and will punish the servant severely
and assign him a place with the unfaithful.
That servant who knew his master's will
but did not make preparations nor act in accord with his will
shall be beaten severely;
and the servant who was ignorant of his master's will
but acted in a way deserving of a severe beating
shall be beaten only lightly.
Much will be required of the person entrusted with much,
and still more will be demanded of the person entrusted with more."

or Luke 12:35-40

Jesus said to his disciples:
"Gird your loins and light your lamps
and be like servants who await their master's return from a
wedding,
ready to open immediately when he comes and knocks.
Blessed are those servants
whom the master finds vigilant on his arrival.
Amen, I say to you, he will gird himself,
have them recline at table, and proceed to wait on them.
And should he come in the second or third watch
and find them prepared in this way,
blessed are those servants.
Be sure of this:
if the master of the house had known the hour
when the thief was coming,
he would not have let his house be broken into.
You also must be prepared, for at an hour you do not expect,
the Son of Man will come."

SECOND READING
Heb 11:1-2, 8-19 *(cont.)*

So it was that there came forth from one man,
himself as good as dead,
descendants as numerous as the stars in
the sky
and as countless as the sands on the
seashore.

All these died in faith.
They did not receive what had been promised
but saw it and greeted it from afar
and acknowledged themselves to be
strangers and aliens on earth,
for those who speak thus show that they
are seeking a homeland.
If they had been thinking of the land from
which they had come,
they would have had opportunity to return.
But now they desire a better homeland, a
heavenly one.
Therefore, God is not ashamed to be called
their God,
for he has prepared a city for them.

By faith Abraham, when put to the test,
offered up Isaac,
and he who had received the promises was
ready to offer his only son,
of whom it was said,

"Through Isaac descendants shall bear
your name."
He reasoned that God was able to raise even
from the dead,
and he received Isaac back as a symbol.

or Heb 11:1-2, 8-12

Brothers and sisters:
Faith is the realization of what is hoped for
and evidence of things not seen.
Because of it the ancients were well attested.

By faith Abraham obeyed when he was called
to go out to a place
that he was to receive as an inheritance;
he went out, not knowing where he was to
go.
By faith he sojourned in the promised land as
in a foreign country,
dwelling in tents with Isaac and Jacob,
heirs of the same promise;
for he was looking forward to the city with
foundations,
whose architect and maker is God.
By faith he received power to generate,
even though he was past the normal age
—and Sarah herself was sterile—
for he thought that the one who had made
the promise was trustworthy.

So it was that there came forth from one man,
himself as good as dead,
descendants as numerous as the stars in
the sky
and as countless as the sands on the
seashore.

Gospel (cont.)
Luke 1:39-56; L622

He has cast down the mighty from their thrones,
  and has lifted up the lowly.
He has filled the hungry with good things,
  and the rich he has sent away empty.
He has come to the help of his servant Israel
  for he has remembered his promise of mercy,
  the promise he made to our fathers,
  to Abraham and his children forever."

Mary remained with her about three months
  and then returned to her home.

FIRST READING
Rev 11:19a; 12:1-6a, 10ab

God's temple in heaven was opened,
  and the ark of his covenant could be seen
    in the temple.

A great sign appeared in the sky, a woman
    clothed with the sun,
  with the moon beneath her feet,
  and on her head a crown of twelve stars.
She was with child and wailed aloud in pain
    as she labored to give birth.
Then another sign appeared in the sky;
  it was a huge red dragon, with seven heads
    and ten horns,
  and on its heads were seven diadems.
Its tail swept away a third of the stars in the
    sky
  and hurled them down to the earth.
Then the dragon stood before the woman
    about to give birth,
  to devour her child when she gave birth.
She gave birth to a son, a male child,
  destined to rule all the nations with an iron
    rod.
Her child was caught up to God and his
    throne.
The woman herself fled into the desert
  where she had a place prepared by God.

Then I heard a loud voice in heaven say:
  "Now have salvation and power come,
    and the Kingdom of our God
    and the authority of his Anointed One."

RESPONSORIAL PSALM
Ps 45:10, 11, 12, 16

R̂. (10bc) The queen stands at your right
hand, arrayed in gold.

The queen takes her place at your right hand
  in gold of Ophir.

R̂. The queen stands at your right hand,
arrayed in gold.

Hear, O daughter, and see; turn your ear,
  forget your people and your father's house.

R̂. The queen stands at your right hand,
arrayed in gold.

So shall the king desire your beauty;
  for he is your lord.

R̂. The queen stands at your right hand,
arrayed in gold.

They are borne in with gladness and joy;
  they enter the palace of the king.

R̂. The queen stands at your right hand,
arrayed in gold.

SECOND READING
1 Cor 15:20-27

Brothers and sisters:
Christ has been raised from the dead,
  the firstfruits of those who have fallen
    asleep.
For since death came through man,
  the resurrection of the dead came also
    through man.
For just as in Adam all die,
  so too in Christ shall all be brought to life,
  but each one in proper order:
  Christ the firstfruits;
  then, at his coming, those who belong to
    Christ;
  then comes the end,
  when he hands over the Kingdom to his
    God and Father,
  when he has destroyed every sovereignty
  and every authority and power.
For he must reign until he has put all his
    enemies under his feet.
The last enemy to be destroyed is death,
  for "he subjected everything under his feet."

Gospel (cont.)

Luke 15:1-32; L132C

Then he said,
  "A man had two sons, and the younger son said to his father,
  'Father give me the share of your estate that should come to me.'
So the father divided the property between them.
After a few days, the younger son collected all his belongings
  and set off to a distant country
  where he squandered his inheritance on a life of dissipation.
When he had freely spent everything,
  a severe famine struck that country,
  and he found himself in dire need.
So he hired himself out to one of the local citizens
  who sent him to his farm to tend the swine.
And he longed to eat his fill of the pods on which the swine fed,
  but nobody gave him any.
Coming to his senses he thought,
  'How many of my father's hired workers
  have more than enough food to eat,
  but here am I, dying from hunger.
I shall get up and go to my father and I shall say to him,
  "Father, I have sinned against heaven and against you.
I no longer deserve to be called your son;
  treat me as you would treat one of your hired workers."'
So he got up and went back to his father.
While he was still a long way off,
  his father caught sight of him,
  and was filled with compassion.
He ran to his son, embraced him and kissed him.
His son said to him,
  'Father, I have sinned against heaven and against you;
  I no longer deserve to be called your son.'
But his father ordered his servants,
  'Quickly bring the finest robe and put it on him;
  put a ring on his finger and sandals on his feet.
Take the fattened calf and slaughter it.
Then let us celebrate with a feast,
  because this son of mine was dead, and has come to life again;
  he was lost, and has been found.'
Then the celebration began.
Now the older son had been out in the field
  and, on his way back, as he neared the house,
  he heard the sound of music and dancing.
He called one of the servants and asked what this might mean.
The servant said to him,
  'Your brother has returned
  and your father has slaughtered the fattened calf
  because he has him back safe and sound.'

He became angry,
  and when he refused to enter the house,
  his father came out and pleaded with him.
He said to his father in reply,
  'Look, all these years I served you
  and not once did I disobey your orders;
  yet you never gave me even a young goat to feast on with my
      friends. But when your son returns,
  who swallowed up your property with prostitutes,
  for him you slaughter the fattened calf.'
He said to him,
  'My son, you are here with me always;
  everything I have is yours.
But now we must celebrate and rejoice,
  because your brother was dead and has come to life again;
  he was lost and has been found.'"

or Luke 15:1-10

Tax collectors and sinners were all drawing near to listen to Jesus,
  but the Pharisees and scribes began to complain, saying,
  "This man welcomes sinners and eats with them."
So to them he addressed this parable.
"What man among you having a hundred sheep and losing one of
      them
  would not leave the ninety-nine in the desert
  and go after the lost one until he finds it?
And when he does find it,
  he sets it on his shoulders with great joy
  and, upon his arrival home,
  he calls together his friends and neighbors and says to them,
  'Rejoice with me because I have found my lost sheep.'
I tell you, in just the same way
  there will be more joy in heaven over one sinner who repents
  than over ninety-nine righteous people
  who have no need of repentance.

"Or what woman having ten coins and losing one
  would not light a lamp and sweep the house,
  searching carefully until she finds it?
And when she does find it,
  she calls together her friends and neighbors
  and says to them,
  'Rejoice with me because I have found the coin that I lost.'
In just the same way, I tell you,
  there will be rejoicing among the angels of God
  over one sinner who repents."

Twenty-Fifth Sunday in Ordinary Time, *September 23, 2007*

Gospel (cont.)
Luke 16:1-13; L135C

"For the children of this world
   are more prudent in dealing with their own generation
   than are the children of light.
I tell you, make friends for yourselves with dishonest wealth,
   so that when it fails, you will be welcomed into eternal dwellings.
The person who is trustworthy in very small matters
   is also trustworthy in great ones;
   and the person who is dishonest in very small matters
   is also dishonest in great ones.
If, therefore, you are not trustworthy with dishonest wealth,
   who will trust you with true wealth?
If you are not trustworthy with what belongs to another,
   who will give you what is yours?
No servant can serve two masters.
He will either hate one and love the other,
   or be devoted to one and despise the other.
You cannot serve both God and mammon."

or Luke 16:10-13

Jesus said to his disciples,
   "The person who is trustworthy in very small matters
   is also trustworthy in great ones;
   and the person who is dishonest in very small matters
   is also dishonest in great ones.
If, therefore, you are not trustworthy with dishonest wealth,
   who will trust you with true wealth?
If you are not trustworthy with what belongs to another,
   who will give you what is yours?
No servant can serve two masters.
He will either hate one and love the other,
   or be devoted to one and despise the other.
You cannot serve both God and mammon."

Twenty-Sixth Sunday in Ordinary Time, *September 30, 2007*

Gospel (cont.)
Luke 16:19-31; L138C

He said, 'Then I beg you, father,
   send him to my father's house, for I have five brothers,
   so that he may warn them,
   lest they too come to this place of torment.'
But Abraham replied, 'They have Moses and the prophets.
Let them listen to them.'
He said, 'Oh no, father Abraham,
   but if someone from the dead goes to them, they will repent.'
Then Abraham said, 'If they will not listen to Moses and the prophets,
   neither will they be persuaded if someone should rise from the dead.'"

All Saints, *November 1, 2007*

FIRST READING
Rev 7:2-4, 9-14

I, John, saw another angel come up from the
East,
holding the seal of the living God.
He cried out in a loud voice to the four angels
who were given power to damage the land
and the sea,
"Do not damage the land or the sea or the
trees
until we put the seal on the foreheads of
the servants of our God."
I heard the number of those who had been
marked with the seal,
one hundred and forty-four thousand
marked
from every tribe of the children of Israel.

After this I had a vision of a great multitude,
which no one could count,
from every nation, race, people, and tongue.
They stood before the throne and before the
Lamb,
wearing white robes and holding palm
branches in their hands.
They cried out in a loud voice:

"Salvation comes from our God,
who is seated on the throne,
and from the Lamb."
All the angels stood around the throne
and around the elders and the four living
creatures.
They prostrated themselves before the throne,
worshiped God, and exclaimed:

"Amen. Blessing and glory, wisdom and
thanksgiving,
honor, power, and might
be to our God forever and ever. Amen."

Then one of the elders spoke up and said to
me,
"Who are these wearing white robes, and
where did they come from?"
I said to him, "My lord, you are the one who
knows."
He said to me,
"These are the ones who have survived the
time of great distress;
they have washed their robes
and made them white in the Blood of the
Lamb."

RESPONSORIAL PSALM
Ps 24:1-2, 3-4, 5-6

R̶. (cf. 6) Lord, this is the people that longs to
see your face.

The LORD's are the earth and its fullness;
the world and those who dwell in it.
For he founded it upon the seas
and established it upon the rivers.

R̶. Lord, this is the people that longs to see
your face.

Who can ascend the mountain of the LORD?
or who may stand in his holy place?
One whose hands are sinless, whose heart is
clean,
who desires not what is vain.

R̶. Lord, this is the people that longs to see
your face.

He shall receive a blessing from the LORD,
a reward from God his savior.
Such is the race that seeks for him,
that seeks the face of the God of Jacob.

R̶. Lord, this is the people that longs to see
your face.

SECOND READING
1 John 3:1-3

Beloved:
See what love the Father has bestowed on us
that we may be called the children of God.
Yet so we are.
The reason the world does not know us
is that it did not know him.
Beloved, we are God's children now;
what we shall be has not yet been revealed.
We do know that when it is revealed we shall
be like him,
for we shall see him as he is.
Everyone who has this hope based on him
makes himself pure,
as he is pure.

All Souls, *November 2, 2007*

(Other options can be found in the Lectionary for Mass, L668.)

FIRST READING
Wis 3:1-9

The souls of the just are in the hand of God,
    and no torment shall touch them.
They seemed, in the view of the foolish, to be
        dead;
    and their passing away was thought an
        affliction
    and their going forth from us, utter
        destruction.
But they are in peace.
For if before men, indeed they be punished,
    yet is their hope full of immortality;
chastised a little, they shall be greatly
        blessed,
    because God tried them
    and found them worthy of himself.
As gold in the furnace, he proved them,
    and as sacrificial offerings he took them to
        himself.
In the time of their visitation they shall shine,
    and shall dart about as sparks through
        stubble;
they shall judge nations and rule over
        peoples,
    and the LORD shall be their King forever.
Those who trust in him shall understand
        truth,
    and the faithful shall abide with him in
        love:
because grace and mercy are with his holy
        ones,
    and his care is with his elect.

RESPONSORIAL PSALM
Ps 23:1-3a, 3b-4, 5, 6

R̶̸. (1) The Lord is my shepherd; there is
nothing I shall want.
    or:
R̶̸. (4ab) Though I walk in the valley of
darkness, I fear no evil, for you are with me.

The LORD is my shepherd; I shall not want.
    In verdant pastures he gives me repose;
beside restful waters he leads me;
    he refreshes my soul.

R̶̸. The Lord is my shepherd; there is nothing
I shall want.
    or:
R̶̸. Though I walk in the valley of darkness, I
fear no evil, for you are with me.

He guides me in right paths
    for his name's sake.
Even though I walk in the dark valley
    I fear no evil; for you are at my side
with your rod and your staff
    that give me courage.

R̶̸. The Lord is my shepherd; there is nothing
I shall want.
    or:
R̶̸. Though I walk in the valley of darkness, I
fear no evil, for you are with me.

You spread the table before me
    in the sight of my foes;
you anoint my head with oil;
    my cup overflows.

R̶̸. The Lord is my shepherd; there is nothing
I shall want.
    or:
R̶̸. Though I walk in the valley of darkness, I
fear no evil, for you are with me.

Only goodness and kindness follow me
    all the days of my life;
and I shall dwell in the house of the LORD
    for years to come.

R̶̸. The Lord is my shepherd; there is nothing
I shall want.
    or:
R̶̸. Though I walk in the valley of darkness, I
fear no evil, for you are with me.

SECOND READING
Rom 6:3-9; L1014.3

Brothers and sisters:
Are you unaware that we who were baptized
        into Christ Jesus
    were baptized into his death?
We were indeed buried with him through
        baptism into death,
    so that, just as Christ was raised from the
        dead
    by the glory of the Father,
    we too might live in newness of life.

For if we have grown into union with him
        through a death like his,
    we shall also be united with him in the
        resurrection.
We know that our old self was crucified with
        him,
    so that our sinful body might be done away
        with,
    that we might no longer be in slavery to sin.
For a dead person has been absolved from sin.
If, then, we have died with Christ,
    we believe that we shall also live with him.
We know that Christ, raised from the dead,
        dies no more;
    death no longer has power over him.

Thirty-Second Sunday in Ordinary Time, *November 11, 2007*

Gospel
Luke 20:27, 34-38; L156C

Some Sadducees, those who deny that there is a resurrection,
    came forward.

Jesus said to them,
    "The children of this age marry and remarry;
    but those who are deemed worthy to attain to the coming age
    and to the resurrection of the dead
    neither marry nor are given in marriage.
They can no longer die,
    for they are like angels;

and they are the children of God
    because they are the ones who will rise.
That the dead will rise
    even Moses made known in the passage about the bush,
    when he called out 'Lord,'
    the God of Abraham, the God of Isaac, and the God of Jacob;
    and he is not God of the dead, but of the living,
    for to him all are alive."

Gospel (cont.)
Luke 21:5-19; L159C

"Before all this happens, however,
 they will seize and persecute you,
 they will hand you over to the synagogues and to prisons,
 and they will have you led before kings and governors
 because of my name.
It will lead to your giving testimony.
Remember, you are not to prepare your defense beforehand,
 for I myself shall give you a wisdom in speaking
 that all your adversaries will be powerless to resist or refute.
You will even be handed over by parents, brothers, relatives, and
  friends,
 and they will put some of you to death.
You will be hated by all because of my name,
 but not a hair on your head will be destroyed.
By your perseverance you will secure your lives."

Thanksgiving Day, *November 22, 2007*
(Other options can be found in the Lectionary for Mass, L943.)

FIRST READING
Sir 50:22-24; L943.2

And now, bless the God of all,
 who has done wondrous things on earth;
Who fosters people's growth from their
  mother's womb,
 and fashions them according to his will!
May he grant you joy of heart
 and may peace abide among you;
May his goodness toward us endure in Israel
 to deliver us in our days.

SECOND READING
1 Cor 1:3-9; L944.1

Brothers and sisters:
Grace to you and peace from God our Father
 and the Lord Jesus Christ.

I give thanks to my God always on your
  account
 for the grace of God bestowed on you in
   Christ Jesus,
 that in him you were enriched in every way,
 with all discourse and all knowledge,
 as the testimony to Christ was confirmed
   among you,
 so that you are not lacking in any spiritual
   gift
 as you wait for the revelation of our Lord
   Jesus Christ.
He will keep you firm to the end,
 irreproachable on the day of our Lord Jesus
   Christ.
God is faithful,
 and by him you were called to fellowship
   with his Son, Jesus Christ our Lord.

APPENDIX B

Choral Settings for the General Intercessions

Purchasers of this volume may reproduce these choral arrangements for use in their parish or community. The music must be reproduced as given below, with composer's name and copyright line.

ADVENT

Cantor:

we pray to the Lord,

SATB Response:
Descant

Lord,———— hear our prayer.

Lord,———— hear our prayer.

Lord, hear our prayer.

Music: Kathleen Harmon, SNDdeN, ©1999, Institute for Liturgical Ministry, 4960 Salem Avenue, Dayton OH 45416. All rights reserved.

CHRISTMAS and EASTER

Cantor:

we pray to the Lord,

SATB Response:
Descant

Lord, hear our prayer.

Lord, hear———— our prayer.

Music: Kathleen Harmon, SNDdeN, ©1999, Institute for Liturgical Ministry, 4960 Salem Avenue, Dayton OH 45416. All rights reserved.

LENT

Cantor:

we pray to the Lord,

SATB Response:

Lord, hear our prayer.

Music: Kathleen Harmon, SNDdeN, ©1999, Institute for Liturgical Ministry, 4960 Salem Avenue, Dayton OH 45416. All rights reserved.

SOLEMNITIES

Cantor:

we pray to the Lord,

SATB Response:
Descant

Lord, hear our prayer.

Lord, hear our prayer.

Music: Kathleen Harmon, SNDdeN, ©1999, Institute for Liturgical Ministry, 4960 Salem Avenue, Dayton OH 45416. All rights reserved.

308

ORDINARY TIME, WEEKS 2-7

ORDINARY TIME, WEEKS 11-20

ORDINARY TIME, WEEKS 21-33

APPENDIX C

Lectionary Pronunciation Guide

Lectionary Word	Pronunciation
Aaron	EHR-uhn
Abana	AB-uh-nuh
Abednego	uh-BEHD-nee-go
Abel-Keramin	AY-b'l-KEHR-uh-mihn
Abel-meholah	AY-b'l-mee-HO-lah
Abiathar	uh-BAI-uh-ther
Abiel	AY-bee-ehl
Abiezrite	ay-bai-EHZ-rait
Abijah	uh-BAI-dzhuh
Abilene	ab-uh-LEE-neh
Abishai	uh-BIHSH-ay-ai
Abiud	uh-BAI-uhd
Abner	AHB-ner
Abraham	AY-bruh-ham
Abram	AY-br'm
Achaia	uh-KAY-yuh
Achim	AY-kihm
Aeneas	uh-NEE-uhs
Aenon	AY-nuhn
Agrippa	uh-GRIH-puh
Ahaz	AY-haz
Ahijah	uh-HAI-dzhuh
Ai	AY-ee
Alexandria	al-ehg-ZAN-dree-uh
Alexandrian	al-ehg-ZAN-dree-uhn
Alpha	AHL-fuh
Alphaeus	AL-fee-uhs
Amalek	AM-uh-lehk
Amaziah	am-uh-ZAI-uh
Amminadab	ah-MIHN-uh-dab
Ammonites	AM-uh-naitz
Amorites	AM-uh-raits
Amos	AY-muhs
Amoz	AY-muhz
Ampliatus	am-plee-AY-tuhs
Ananias	an-uh-NAI-uhs
Andronicus	an-draw-NAI-kuhs
Annas	AN-uhs
Antioch	AN-tih-ahk
Antiochus	an-TAI-uh-kuhs
Aphiah	uh-FAI-uh
Apollos	uh-PAH-luhs
Appius	AP-ee-uhs
Aquila	uh-KWIHL-uh
Arabah	EHR-uh-buh
Aram	AY-ram
Arameans	ehr-uh-MEE-uhnz
Areopagus	ehr-ee-AH-puh-guhs
Arimathea	ehr-uh-muh-THEE-uh
Aroer	uh-RO-er

Lectionary Word	Pronunciation
Asaph	AY-saf
Asher	ASH-er
Ashpenaz	ASH-pee-naz
Assyria	a-SIHR-ee-uh
Astarte	as-TAHR-tee
Attalia	at-TAH-lee-uh
Augustus	uh-GUHS-tuhs
Azariah	az-uh-RAI-uh
Azor	AY-sawr
Azotus	uh-ZO-tus
Baal-shalishah	BAY-uhl-shuh-LAI-shuh
Baal-Zephon	BAY-uhl-ZEE-fuhn
Babel	BAY-bl
Babylon	BAB-ih-luhn
Babylonian	bab-ih-LO-nih-uhn
Balaam	BAY-lm
Barabbas	beh-REH-buhs
Barak	BEHR-ak
Barnabas	BAHR-nuh-buhs
Barsabbas	BAHR-suh-buhs
Bartholomew	bar-THAHL-uh-myoo
Bartimaeus	bar-tih-MEE-uhs
Baruch	BEHR-ook
Bashan	BAY-shan
Becorath	bee-KO-rath
Beelzebul	bee-EHL-zee-buhl
Beer-sheba	BEE-er-SHEE-buh
Belshazzar	behl-SHAZ-er
Benjamin	BEHN-dzhuh-mihn
Beor	BEE-awr
Bethany	BEHTH-uh-nee
Bethel	BETH-el
Bethesda	beh-THEHZ-duh
Bethlehem	BEHTH-leh-hehm
Bethphage	BEHTH-fuh-dzhee
Bethsaida	behth-SAY-ih-duh
Beth-zur	behth-ZER
Bildad	BIHL-dad
Bithynia	bih-THIHN-ih-uh
Boanerges	bo-uh-NER-dzheez
Boaz	BO-az
Caesar	SEE-zer
Caesarea	zeh-suh-REE-uh
Caiaphas	KAY-uh-fuhs
Cain	kayn
Cana	KAY-nuh
Canaan	KAY-nuhn
Canaanite	KAY-nuh-nait
Canaanites	KAY-nuh-naits

Lectionary Word	Pronunciation
Candace	kan-DAY-see
Capernaum	kuh-PERR-nay-uhm
Cappadocia	kap-ih-DO-shee-u
Carmel	KAHR-muhl
carnelians	kahr-NEEL-yuhnz
Cenchreae	SEHN-kree-ay
Cephas	SEE-fuhs
Chaldeans	kal-DEE-uhnz
Chemosh	KEE-mahsh
Cherubim	TSHEHR-oo-bihm
Chislev	KIHS-lehv
Chloe	KLO-ee
Chorazin	kor-AY-sihn
Cilicia	sih-LIHSH-ee-uh
Cleopas	KLEE-o-pas
Clopas	KLO-pas
Corinth	KAWR-ihnth
Corinthians	kawr-IHN-thee-uhnz
Cornelius	kawr-NEE-lee-uhs
Crete	kreet
Crispus	KRIHS-puhs
Cushite	CUHSH-ait
Cypriot	SIH-pree-at
Cyrene	sai-REE-nee
Cyreneans	sai-REE-nih-uhnz
Cyrenian	sai-REE-nih-uhn
Cyrenians	sai-REE-nih-uhnz
Cyrus	SAI-ruhs
Damaris	DAM-uh-rihs
Damascus	duh-MAS-kuhs
Danites	DAN-aits
Decapolis	duh-KAP-o-lis
Derbe	DER-bee
Deuteronomy	dyoo-ter-AH-num-mee
Didymus	DID-I-mus
Dionysius	dai-o-NIHSH-ih-uhs
Dioscuri	dai-O-sky-ri
Dorcas	DAWR-kuhs
Dothan	DO-thuhn
dromedaries	DRAH-muh-dher-eez
Ebed-melech	EE-behd-MEE-lehk
Eden	EE-dn
Edom	EE-duhm
Elamites	EE-luh-maitz
Eldad	EHL-dad
Eleazar	ehl-ee-AY-zer
Eli	EE-lai
Eli Eli Lema Sabachthani	AY-lee AY-lee luh-MAH sah-BAHK-tah-nee

310

Lectionary Word	Pronunciation	Lectionary Word	Pronunciation	Lectionary Word	Pronunciation
Eliab	ee-LAI-ab	Gilead	GIHL-ee-uhd	Joppa	DZHAH-puh
Eliakim	ee-LAI-uh-kihm	Gilgal	GIHL-gal	Joram	DZHO-ram
Eliezer	ehl-ih-EE-zer	Golgotha	GAHL-guh-thuh	Jordan	DZHAWR-dn
Elihu	ee-LAI-hyoo	Gomorrah	guh-MAWR-uh	Joseph	DZHO-zf
Elijah	ee-LAI-dzhuh	Goshen	GO-shuhn	Joses	DZHO-seez
Elim	EE-lihm	Habakkuk	huh-BAK-uhk	Joshua	DZHAH-shou-ah
Elimelech	ee-LIHM-eh-lehk	Hadadrimmon	hay-dad-RIHM-uhn	Josiah	dzho-SAI-uh
Elisha	ee-LAI-shuh	Hades	HAY-deez	Jotham	DZHO-thuhm
Eliud	ee-LAI-uhd	Hagar	HAH-gar	Judah	DZHOU-duh
Elizabeth	ee-LIHZ-uh-bth	Hananiah	han-uh-NAI-uh	Judas	DZHOU-duhs
Elkanah	el-KAY-nuh	Hannah	HAN-uh	Judea	dzhou-DEE-uh
Eloi Eloi Lama	AY-lo-ee AY-lo-ee	Haran	HAY-ruhn	Judean	dzhou-DEE-uhn
Sabechthani	LAH-mah sah-	Hebron	HEE-bruhn	Junia	dzhou-nih-uh
	BAHK-tah-nee	Hermes	HER-meez	Justus	DZHUHS-tuhs
Elymais	ehl-ih-MAY-ihs	Herod	HEHR-uhd	Kephas	KEF-uhs
Emmanuel	eh-MAN-yoo-ehl	Herodians	hehr-O-dee-uhnz	Kidron	KIHD-ruhn
Emmaus	eh-MAY-uhs	Herodias	hehr-O-dee-uhs	Kiriatharba	kihr-ee-ath-AHR-buh
Epaenetus	ee-PEE-nee-tuhs	Hezekiah	heh-zeh-KAI-uh	Kish	kihsh
Epaphras	EH-puh-fras	Hezron	HEHZ-ruhn	Laodicea	lay-o-dih-SEE-uh
ephah	EE-fuh	Hilkiah	hihl-KAI-uh	Lateran	LAT-er-uhn
Ephah	EE-fuh	Hittite	HIH-tait	Lazarus	LAZ-er-uhs
Ephesians	eh-FEE-zhuhnz	Hivites	HAI-vaitz	Leah	LEE-uh
Ephesus	EH-fuh-suhs	Hophni	HAHF-nai	Lebanon	LEH-buh-nuhn
Ephphatha	EHF-uh-thuh	Hor	HAWR	Levi	LEE-vai
Ephraim	EE-fray-ihm	Horeb	HAWR-ehb	Levite	LEE-vait
Ephrathah	EHF-ruh-thuh	Hosea	ho-ZEE-uh	Levites	LEE-vaits
Ephron	EE-frawn	Hur	her	Leviticus	leh-VIH-tih-kous
Epiphanes	eh-PIHF-uh-neez	hyssop	HIH-suhp	Lucius	LOO-shih-uhs
Erastus	ee-RAS-tuhs	Iconium	ai-KO-nih-uhm	Lud	luhd
Esau	EE-saw	Isaac	AI-zuhk	Luke	look
Esther	EHS-ter	Isaiah	ai-ZAY-uh	Luz	luhz
Ethanim	EHTH-uh-nihm	Iscariot	ihs-KEHR-ee-uht	Lycaonian	lihk-ay-O-nih-uhn
Ethiopian	ee-thee-O-pee-uhn	Ishmael	ISH-may-ehl	Lydda	LIH-duh
Euphrates	yoo-FRAY-teez	Ishmaelites	ISH-mayehl-aits	Lydia	LIH-dih-uh
Exodus	EHK-so-duhs	Israel	IHZ-ray-ehl	Lysanias	lai-SAY-nih-uhs
Ezekiel	eh-ZEE-kee-uhl	Ituraea	ih-TSHOOR-ree-uh	Lystra	LIHS-truh
Ezra	EHZ-ruh	Jaar	DZHAY-ahr	Maccabees	MAK-uh-beez
frankincense	FRANGK-ihn-sehns	Jabbok	DZHAB-uhk	Macedonia	mas-eh-DO-nih-uh
Gabbatha	GAB-uh-thuh	Jacob	DZHAY-kuhb	Macedonian	mas-eh-DO-nih-uhn
Gabriel	GAY-bree-ul	Jairus	DZH-hr-uhs	Machir	MAY-kih
Gadarenes	GAD-uh-reenz	Javan	DZHAY-van	Machpelah	mak-PEE-luh
Galatian	guh-LAY-shih-uhn	Jebusites	DZHEHB-oo-zaits	Magdala	MAG-duh-luh
Galatians	guh-LAY-shih-uhnz	Jechoniah	dzhehk-o-NAI-uh	Magdalene	MAG-duh-lehn
Galilee	GAL-ih-lee	Jehoiakim	dzhee-HOI-uh-kihm	magi	MAY-dzhai
Gallio	GAL-ih-o	Jehoshaphat	dzhee-HAHSH-uh-fat	Malachi	MAL-uh-kai
Gamaliel	guh-MAY-lih-ehl	Jephthah	DZHEHF-thuh	Malchiah	mal-KAI-uh
Gaza	GAH-zuh	Jeremiah	dzhehr-eh-MAI-uh	Malchus	MAL-kuhz
Gehazi	gee-HAY-zai	Jericho	DZHEHR-ih-ko	Mamre	MAM-ree
Gehenna	geh-HEHN-uh	Jeroham	dzhehr-RO-ham	Manaen	MAN-uh-ehn
Genesis	DZHEHN-uh-sihs	Jerusalem	dzheh-ROU-suh-lehm	Manasseh	man-AS-eh
Gennesaret	gehn-NEHS-uh-reht	Jesse	DZHEH-see	Manoah	muh-NO-uh
Gentiles	DZHEHN-tailz	Jethro	DZHEHTH-ro	Mark	mahrk
Gerasenes	DZHEHR-uh-seenz	Joakim	DZHO-uh-kihm	Mary	MEHR-ee
Gethsemane	gehth-SEHM-uh-ne	Job	DZHOB	Massah	MAH-suh
Gideon	GIHD-ee-uhn	Jonah	DZHO-nuh	Mattathias	mat-uh-THAI-uhs

Lectionary Word	Pronunciation	Lectionary Word	Pronunciation	Lectionary Word	Pronunciation
Matthan	MAT-than	Parmenas	PAHR-mee-nas	Sabbath	SAB-uhth
Matthew	MATH-yoo	Parthians	PAHR-thee-uhnz	Sadducees	SAD-dzhoo-seez
Matthias	muh-THAI-uhs	Patmos	PAT-mos	Salem	SAY-lehm
Medad	MEE-dad	Peninnah	pee-NIHN-uh	Salim	SAY-lim
Mede	meed	Pentecost	PEHN-tee-kawst	Salmon	SAL-muhn
Medes	meedz	Penuel	pee-NYOO-ehl	Salome	suh-LO-mee
Megiddo	mee-GIH-do	Perez	PEE-rehz	Salu	SAYL-yoo
Melchizedek	mehl-KIHZ-eh-dehk	Perga	PER-guh	Samaria	suh-MEHR-ih-uh
Mene	MEE-nee	Perizzites	PEHR-ih-zaits	Samaritan	suh-MEHR-ih-tuhn
Meribah	MEHR-ih-bah	Persia	PER-zhuh	Samothrace	SAM-o-thrays
Meshach	MEE-shak	Peter	PEE-ter	Samson	SAM-s'n
Mespotamia	mehs-o-po-TAY-mih-uh	Phanuel	FAN-yoo-ehl	Samuel	SAM-yoo-uhl
		Pharaoh	FEHR-o	Sanhedrin	san-HEE-drihn
Micah	MAI-kuh	Pharisees	FEHR-ih-seez	Sarah	SEHR-uh
Midian	MIH-dih-uhn	Pharpar	FAHR-pahr	Sarai	SAY-rai
Milcom	MIHL-kahm	Philemon	fih-LEE-muhn	saraph	SAY-raf
Miletus	mai-LEE-tuhs	Philippi	fil-LIH-pai	Sardis	SAHR-dihs
Minnith	MIHN-ihth	Philippians	fih-LIHP-ih-uhnz	Saul	sawl
Mishael	MIHSH-ay-ehl	Philistines	fih-LIHS-tihnz	Scythian	SIH-thee-uihn
Mizpah	MIHZ-puh	Phinehas	FEHN-ee-uhs	Seba	SEE-buh
Moreh	MO-reh	Phoenicia	fee-NIHSH-ih-uh	Seth	sehth
Moriah	maw-RAI-uh	Phrygia	FRIH-dzhih-uh	Shaalim	SHAY-uh-lihm
Mosoch	MAH-sahk	Phrygian	FRIH-dzhih-uhn	Shadrach	SHAY-drak
myrrh	mer	phylacteries	fih-LAK-ter-eez	Shalishah	shuh-LEE-shuh
Mysia	MIH-shih-uh	Pi-Hahiroth	pai-huh-HAI-rahth	Shaphat	Shay-fat
Naaman	NAY-uh-muhn	Pilate	PAI-luht	Sharon	SHEHR-uhn
Nahshon	NAY-shuhn	Pisidia	pih-SIH-dih-uh	Shealtiel	shee-AL-tih-ehl
Naomi	NAY-o-mai	Pithom	PAI-thahm	Sheba	SHEE-buh
Naphtali	NAF-tuh-lai	Pontius	PAHN-shus	Shebna	SHEB-nuh
Nathan	NAY-thuhn	Pontus	PAHN-tus	Shechem	SHEE-kehm
Nathanael	nuh-THAN-ay-ehl	Praetorium	pray-TAWR-ih-uhm	shekel	SHEHK-uhl
Nazarene	NAZ-awr-een	Priscilla	PRIHS-kill-uh	Shiloh	SHAI-lo
Nazareth	NAZ-uh-rehth	Prochorus	PRAH-kaw-ruhs	Shinar	SHAI-nahr
nazirite	NAZ-uh-rait	Psalm	Sahm	Shittim	sheh-TEEM
Nazorean	naz-aw-REE-uhn	Put	puht	Shuhite	SHOO-ait
Neapolis	nee-AP-o-lihs	Puteoli	pyoo-TEE-o-lai	Shunammite	SHOO-nam-ait
Nebuchadnezzar	neh-byoo-kuhd-NEHZ-er	Qoheleth	ko-HEHL-ehth	Shunem	SHOO-nehm
		qorban	KAWR-bahn	Sidon	SAI-duhn
Negeb	NEH-gehb	Quartus	KWAR-tuhs	Silas	SAI-luhs
Nehemiah	nee-hee-MAI-uh	Quirinius	kwai-RIHN-ih-uhs	Siloam	sih-LO-uhm
Ner	ner	Raamses	ray-AM-seez	Silvanus	sihl-VAY-nuhs
Nicanor	nai-KAY-nawr	Rabbi	RAB-ai	Simeon	SIHM-ee-uhn
Nicodemus	nih-ko-DEE-muhs	Rabbouni	ra-BO-nai	Simon	SAI-muhn
Niger	NAI-dzher	Rahab	RAY-hab	Sin (desert)	sihn
Nineveh	NIHN-eh-veh	Ram	ram	Sinai	SAI-nai
Noah	NO-uh	Ramah	RAY-muh	Sirach	SAI-rak
Nun	nuhn	Ramathaim	ray-muh-THAY-ihm	Sodom	SAH-duhm
Obed	O-behd	Raqa	RA-kuh	Solomon	SAH-lo-muhn
Olivet	AH-lih-veht	Rebekah	ree-BEHK-uh	Sosthenes	SAHS-thee-neez
Omega	o-MEE-guh	Rehoboam	ree-ho-BO-am	Stachys	STAY-kihs
Onesimus	o-NEH-sih-muhs	Rephidim	REHF-ih-dihm	Succoth	SUHK-ahth
Ophir	O-fer	Reuben	ROO-b'n	Sychar	SI-kar
Orpah	AWR-puh	Revelation	reh-veh-LAY-shuhn	Syene	sai-EE-nee
Pamphylia	pam-FIHL-ih-uh	Rhegium	REE-dzhee-uhm	Symeon	SIHM-ee-uhn
Paphos	PAY-fuhs	Rufus	ROO-fuhs	synagogues	SIHN-uh-gahgz

Lectionary Word	Pronunciation	Lectionary Word	Pronunciation	Lectionary Word	Pronunciation
Syrophoenician	SIHR-o fee-NIHSH-ih-uhn	Timon	TAI-muhn	Zebedee	ZEH-beh-dee
Tabitha	TAB-ih-thuh	Titus	TAI-tuhs	Zebulun	ZEH-byoo-luhn
Talitha koum	TAL-ih-thuh-KOOM	Tohu	TO-hyoo	Zechariah	zeh-kuh-RAI-uh
Tamar	TAY-mer	Trachonitis	trak-o-NAI-tis	Zedekiah	zeh-duh-KAI-uh
Tarshish	TAHR-shihsh	Troas	TRO-ahs	Zephaniah	zeh-fuh-NAI-uh
Tarsus	TAHR-suhs	Tubal	TYOO-b'l	Zerah	ZEE-ruh
Tekel	TEH-keel	Tyre	TAI-er	Zeror	ZEE-rawr
Terebinth	TEHR-ee-bihnth	Ur	er	Zerubbabel	zeh-RUH-buh-behl
Thaddeus	THAD-dee-uhs	Urbanus	er-BAY-nuhs	Zeus	zyoos
Theophilus	thee-AH-fih-luhs	Uriah	you-RAI-uh	Zimri	ZIHM-rai
Thessalonians	theh-suh-LO-nih-uhnz	Uzziah	yoo-ZAI-uh	Zion	ZAI-uhn
Theudas	THU-duhs	Wadi	WAH-dee	Ziph	zihf
Thyatira	thai-uh-TAI-ruh	Yahweh-yireh	YAH-weh-yer-AY	Zoar	ZO-er
Tiberias	tai-BIHR-ih-uhs	Zacchaeus	zak-KEE-uhs	Zorah	ZAWR-uh
Timaeus	tai-MEE-uhs	Zadok	ZAY-dahk	Zuphite	ZUHR-ait
		Zarephath	ZEHR-ee-fath		

Living Liturgy™
for Extraordinary Ministers of Holy Communion

Joyce Ann Zimmerman, C.PP.S., Thomas A. Greisen,
Kathleen Harmon, S.N.D. de N., and Thomas L. Leclerc, M.S.

Living Liturgy™ for Extraordinary Ministers of Holy Communion is a new resource that provides a way for Eucharistic Ministers to prepare for the coming Sunday. Besides being a guide for administering Communion of the Sick, this little book offers encouragement for Eucharistic Ministers and for those to whom they minister.

The content for each Sunday is shown using two-color text and images throughout. It includes Communion of the Sick for Sundays and particular Feast Days including Ash Wednesday, Holy Thursday, and All Souls Day.

The first edition of *Living Liturgy™ for Extraordinary Ministers of Holy Communion* begins with the First Sunday of Advent 2006 and includes the following:

- Page for inscription of minister's name and church
- "How to" guide for using this book
- A brief theology of the ministry
- Commissioning rite
- Sunday by Sunday content
- Personal reflections for Extraordinary Ministers
- Communion of the Sick and Homebound for each Sunday
- External Use Guide to administer Communion of the Sick
- Short form for use with people having special needs
- Adaptations for exceptional circumstances where pastorally appropriate

FE0-8146-3171-1/FE978-0-8146-3171-3
Paper, 176 pp., 5 ¼ x 8 ½, 1-5 copies $6.95; 6 or more copies $4.95* net
(Asterisk indicates discount price available only on "no-returns"

Available September 2006

Available September 2006
1-800-858-5450 or 320-363-2213

INTRODUCTORY RITES

 Greeting

Grace and peace to you from our loving God. I bring you greetings from your brothers and sisters in Christ from [name] parish.

*Penitential Rite*

As we begin this season of Advent, Christ, who promised to return in glory, is present as we gather in his name. Aware of his holy presence, let us ask for his mercy . . . [pause]

Lord Jesus, you will come in great glory:
Lord have mercy.

Christ Jesus, you will come to bring redemption: **Christ have mercy.**

Lord Jesus, you strengthen us on our journey toward everlasting life: **Lord have mercy.**

May almighty God have mercy on us, forgive us our sins, and bring us to life everlasting. **Amen.**

C *Opening Prayer*

O redeeming God, you are with us even as we await your coming. Strengthen and heal us, and give us patience. We ask this through our Savior, Jesus Christ our Lord. **Amen.**

A.	Greeting
B.	Penitential Rite
C.	Opening Prayer

1

Available September 2006
www.litpress.org

LITURGY OF THE WORD

D *Reading of the Gospel (Luke 21:25-28, 34-36)*

Jesus said to his disciples: "There will be signs in the sun, the moon, and the stars, and on earth nations will be in dismay, perplexed by the roaring of the sea and the waves. People will die of fright in anticipation of what is coming upon the world, for the powers of the heavens will be shaken. And then they will see the Son of Man coming in a cloud with power and great glory. But when these signs begin to happen, stand erect and raise your heads because your redemption is at hand.

"Beware that your hearts do not become drowsy from carousing and drunkenness and the anxieties of daily life, and that day catch you by surprise like a trap. For that day will assault everyone who lives on the face of the earth. Be vigilant at all times and pray that you have the strength to escape the tribulations that are imminent and to stand before the Son of Man."

Brief Silence

E *Reflecting on the Gospel*

If the followers of Christ allow themselves to get caught up in "carousing and drunkenness and the anxieties of daily life" (gospel), they will become "drowsy" and complacent with Christ's coming and be caught "by surprise like a trap." On the other hand, if the followers of Christ are vigilant and have lives "blameless in holiness," then when Christ comes they can "stand erect" without fear but with joyful anticipation of their redemption.

God is faithful: the promise of the Messiah is fulfilled in Jesus who also makes a promise—he will return in glory with redemption. We ca[n]   because God is faithful. We tend to thi[nk]   are faithful, *then* God will be faithful t[o]   the opposite is true: *because* God is fai[thful]   be faithful. God is the One who is just and always fa[ithful]   tice" here means "righteousness," that is, being in rig[ht]   ship. We are in right relationship with God and each   we align ourselves (by right living) with the "Son of Man" (Christ).

D. Reading of the Gospel
E. Reflecting on the Gospel
(The shaded area indicates text that can be used for personal reflection to help Ministers prepare to distribute the Eucharist within and outside of the parish.)

2

Available September 2006
1-800-858-5450 or 320-363-2213

Faithful living, then, presupposes right relationship with God expressed by patterning our life after that of the divine Son.

F *Communion Minister's Private Reflection*

✦ My visits with the elderly and infirmed embody God's faithfulness to his promises made to his people in that . . .

G LITURGY OF HOLY COMMUNION

The Lord's Prayer

Casting aside the anxieties of daily life, we pray with confidence in the words Jesus taught us.
Our Father . . .

H *Communion*

This is the Lamb of God
who takes away the sins of the world.
Happy are those who are called to his supper.

All: Lord, I am not worthy to receive you,
   but only say the word and I shall be healed.

The body of Christ. **Amen**.

Silent Prayer

I *Prayer After Communion*

Gracious God, you have fed us with the Body of your only Son. Be with us as we go our separate ways, and help us to look forward to your coming and to remain faithful to your presence. We ask this through that same Son, Jesus Christ our Lord. **Amen.**

CONCLUDING RITE

J *Blessing*

May the almighty and merciful God bless and protect us,
the Father, and the Son, ✠ and the Holy Spirit. A

K *Sign of Peace*

Share parish bulletin, announcements, activities

F. Reflection for the Eucharist Minister
G. The Lord's Prayer
H. Communion
I. Prayer After Communion
J. Blessing
K. Sign of Peace

3

INTRODUCTORY RITES

Greeting

Grace and peace to you from our loving God. I bring you greetings from your brothers and sisters in Christ from [name] parish.

Penitential Rite

Today's gospel is about the wedding feast at Cana at which Jesus reveals his glory. As we stand before the glory of God, let us prepare ourselves to celebrate Holy Communion . . . [pause]

Lord Jesus, you reveal your glory to us: **Lord have mercy.**

Christ Jesus, you are attentive to the needs of others:

Christ have mercy.

Lord Jesus, you are the One in whom we believe:

Lord have mercy.

May almighty God have mercy on us,

forgive us our sins,

and bring us to life everlasting. **Amen.**

Opening Prayer

Glorious God, you are ever attentive to our needs. May we be open to your presence and drink deeply of the wine of your love and compassion. We ask this through Christ our Lord. **Amen.**

LITURGY OF THE WORD

Reading of the Gospel (John 2:1-11)

There was a wedding at Cana in Galilee, and the mother of Jesus was there. Jesus and his disciples were also invited to the wedding. When the wine ran short, the mother of Jesus said to him, "They have no wine." And Jesus said to her, "Woman, how does your concern affect me? My hour has not yet come." His mother said to the servers, "Do whatever he tells you." Now there were six stone water jars there for Jewish ceremonial washings, each holding twenty to thirty gallons. Jesus told them, "Fill the jars with water." So they filled them to the brim. Then he told them, "Draw some out now and take it to the headwaiter." So they took it. And when the headwaiter tasted the water that had become wine, without knowing where it came from—although the servers who had drawn the water knew—, the headwaiter called the bridegroom and said to him, "Everyone serves good wine first, and then when people have drunk freely, an inferior one; but you have kept the good wine until now." Jesus did this as the beginning of his signs at Cana in Galilee and so revealed his glory, and his disciples began to believe in him.

Brief Silence

Reflecting on the Gospel

The critical line in the gospel comes in the very last sentence: "Jesus did this as the beginning of his signs at Cana in Galilee and so revealed his glory, and his disciples began to believe in him." This sign of the beginning of Jesus' public ministry also contains a preview of the end: the abundance and worth of the water made into wine announce the age of the Messiah when mes-

sianic abundance will be evident. This abundance reveals the glory of God, leads us to believe in Jesus, and invites us to become his disciples.

This sign Jesus performed at the wedding feast at Cana inaugurates Jesus' public ministry, but not the life the miracle might lead us to expect. Jesus' life was an entire life spent meeting the needs of other people. This is his true glory and his whole ministry: not only turning water into wine but giving himself for others. His total attentiveness and response to others is the model for our own self-giving and is the promise of our own glory.

Communion Minister's Private Reflection

✦ The abundance of wine Christ offered at the wedding inspires my own self-giving for others when . . .

LITURGY OF HOLY COMMUNION

The Lord's Prayer

We prepare for Communion by turning to our compassionate God
in prayer, using the words Jesus taught us.
Our Father . . .

Communion

This is the Lamb of God
who takes away the sins of the world.
Happy are those who are called to his supper.

All: Lord, I am not worthy to receive you,
but only say the word and I shall be healed.

The body of Christ. **Amen.**

Silent Prayer

Prayer After Communion

Gracious God, you give your Son to us in this Communion which
we share. May we live this week mindful that we are the Body of
Christ bringing your risen Son's presence to all those we meet. We
ask this through Christ our Lord. **Amen.**

CONCLUDING RITE

Blessing

May the almighty and merciful God bless and protect us,
the Father, and the Son, ✠ and the Holy Spirit. **Amen.**

Sign of Peace

Share parish bulletin, announcements, activities